INDIVIDUAL IN SOCIETY

A TEXTBOOK OF SOCIAL PSYCHOLOGY

BY DAVID KRECH
RICHARD S. CRUTCHFIELD
AND EGERTON L. BALLACHEY

UNIVERSITY OF CALIFORNIA, BERKELEY

1962

McGraw-Hill Book Company, Inc.   NEW YORK SAN FRANCISCO TORONTO LONDON

INDIVIDUAL IN SOCIETY

To the memory of EDWARD CHACE TOLMAN

PREFACE

IN THIS BOOK WE HAVE ATTEMPTED TO WRITE A COMPREHENSIVE *and coherent introduction to social psychology. We have found it most meaningful and fruitful to work with the interpersonal behavior event as our unit of analysis. As social psychologists, our major concern is with what goes on within the skin of the individual. He and his ever-to-be-cherished individuality are the objects of our inquiry. But as social psychologists our data insistently force us to look at man in his social habitat. This has led us to search in the domains of the two other major behavioral sciences—social anthropology and sociology—for concepts and findings which would help us to round out our story of the individual in society.*

Perhaps one of the most heartening theoretical developments in American psychology in the last decade or so has been the increased acceptance of cognitive theory among psychologists—among even the most respectable and the most scientific of the tribe. This has been especially true in social psychology where we have seen various attempts to apply cognitive theory toward the understanding of this or that aspect of social behavior. We have incorporated and developed some of these theoretical contributions in this book.

Beginning with World War II, social psychology, along with the other behavioral social sciences has burgeoned on many fronts. There have been stress on empirical data collection as well as on theory, use of laboratory experimentation as well as field observation methods, concern with a wide variety of concrete social problems. It is our hope that this book—in the number and variety of empirical studies cited, in the hypotheses and theories espoused, in the range of social problems commented upon—fully reflects this burgeoning scientific activity.

We, like all writers, are beholden to many people for their help— to too many to name. But at the very least we must express a general, nonetheless profound, gratitude to the many behavioral social scientists—anthropologists, sociologists, and social psychologists— in this country and abroad, whose theoretical writings and experimental studies we have appropriated and have woven into the fabric of this work.

David Krech
Richard S. Crutchfield
Egerton L. Ballachey

CONTENTS

Trait interaction. *Interpersonal response traits and history of want satisfaction (Guide 12).* Effect of want fulfillment. Frustration. Frustration and interpersonal response traits. The self and interpersonal response traits. *The interaction of cognitions, wants, and interpersonal response traits.* An illustration: psychological factors in occupational choice.

PART TWO: SOCIAL ATTITUDES

PART THREE: THE SOCIAL AND CULTURAL HABITAT

INDIVIDUAL IN SOCIETY

A REVOLUTIONARY IDEA IS AFFECTING MAN'S THINKING ABOUT *social problems. He is hopefully pursuing the notion that the sciences of man will soon be effective in preventing the hateful turning of man upon man in racial prejudice, the bitter conflicts among peoples of different economic and political ideologies, and the awful obscenity of war. And the urgency of this hope grows as he contemplates the even greater evils now made possible by the science of things.*

The social scientists encourage this hope as they engage in a bewildering variety of activities. They can be observed studying the effectiveness of polar exploration teams and PTA conference committees. They sit with management and labor at the bargaining table to discover the sources of misunderstanding and conflict. They climb stairs, push doorbells, and interview the citizenry as they seek to measure public opinion. They experiment on groups in the laboratory. Nor do they limit themselves to observing and measuring and experimenting. Many of them engage in action designed to achieve a tolerant world, a peaceful world, a better world.

Among the sciences of man, social psychology is a significant and leading discipline. And it is the facts and theories and problems of social psychology to which this book introduces us.

1: THE DOMAIN OF SOCIAL PSYCHOLOGY

TODAY, THE SCIENCES OF MAN NO LESS THAN the sciences of things are receiving unprecedented public support. Men of affairs, government administrators, heads of labor and industry, cultural and religious leaders, military leaders, and foundation heads are ready, in increasing numbers, to seek out the help of the social psychologist in an attempt to deal with problems of human relations, group effectiveness, conflicts among people. But this attitude toward the social psychologist and his discipline is not at all universal. There still remain many leaders of our society— many government administrators, businessmen, labor leaders, university trustees, and others—who are skeptical about the possibilities inherent in a social psychology or even about the need for a "science" of social psychology. This skeptical attitude is partly responsible for the fact that the money spent by the government on social-psychological research is a minuscule sum compared with the money spent on "hardware" research—on the development and testing of weapons of war.

Many people believe that they already know the essential facts and principles of social behavior—facts and principles which they have learned as a result of *practical* experience in dealing with people. They feel that they do not need any "theoretical" or "so-called scientific" knowledge. Unquestionably these men of affairs have accumulated a great deal of practical information about how people behave. And in a pragmatic sense, their knowledge of human nature may be adequate to handle many of their daily problems of business, administration, and normal social intercourse. But it is just as obviously true that these men of affairs do not have the knowledge needed to deal with some of the most significant social problems of our day. For example, despite the vast reservoir of good will found among men the world over, these men of affairs often lack the knowledge of how to convert this vast reservoir of good will into international understanding and permanent peace. Industrial unrest, racial prejudice, crime, and delinquency continue to be major problems in most of the countries of the world.

Practical vs. scientific knowledge

There is an important difference between practical and scientific knowledge about social behavior. The major objective of science is not primarily to control and predict, but to *understand*. Effective control is a reward of understanding, and accuracy in prediction is a check on understanding. The African savage who tips his spear with poison and succeeds in killing his game or his enemy demonstrates some practical knowledge about the pharmacology of some toxic substances. However, no one would think of calling the savage a pharmacologist. He can control with some efficiency, and he can predict with some degree of accuracy, but he does not understand what he is doing or why his prediction is correct when it happens to be so. Similarly, the huckster, the propagandist, or the politician who has a "practical" knowledge about social psychology can sometimes control and predict the behavior of men. Yet as far as understanding is concerned, he is no more a social psychologist than is the savage a pharmacologist.

Of course, the African savage and the common-sense social psychologist may assert that they *do* understand. The savage may aver that his poisoned spear kills because it was tipped in the food of an evil god—a food that is fatal to the enemies of that particular god. The huckster, the propagandist, or the politician can also ascribe reasons for his successful control and prediction. His "explanatory" generalizations, like the savage's, are taken from the lore and superstitions of his culture (see Box 1.1); his "understanding," like the savage's, fails to meet the requirements of science.

The failure to differentiate between the scientific understanding of behavior and practical know-how about behavior has unfortunate consequences. It inhibits the careful study of the facts of social psychology because of a belief that we already know enough. It discourages an attempt to create a *theory* to encompass the facts we do know because theories "have no practical value." And yet, as Kurt Lewin insisted, there is nothing so practical as sound theory—theory which provides understanding. Recent world history has well demonstrated the danger of depending upon an inadequate understanding of social behav-

BOX 1.1: *"Psychological" generalizations*

If these don't work . . .	*Try these*
Repeat a lie frequently enough and people will believe it.	The truth will always prevail.
Clothes make the man.	You can't make a silk purse out of a sow's ear.
Never too old to learn.	You can't teach an old dog new tricks.
Absence makes the heart grow fonder.	Out of sight, out of mind.
East is east and west is west and never the twain shall meet.	Brothers under the skin.

ior. When man turns his attention to new and difficult social problems, the complete and tragic inadequacy of his practical knowledge, his rule-of-thumb reasoning, and his tradition-based explanations may be revealed in all of their disastrous consequences (see Box 1.2).

THE NEED FOR SCIENTIFIC PRINCIPLES OF SOCIAL BEHAVIOR

We have only the beginnings of a science of social psychology. As Box 1.3 reveals, social psychology has a long past in prescientific philosophical inquiries about the problems of man in society, but only a short history as a scientific discipline. The recent boom in social psychology has resulted in the amassing of an impressive array of useful facts in many different areas of the field. It has not, however, resulted in correspondingly important advances in the development of a *systematic theory* of social behavior. To be sure, there have been many significant theoretical insights and reformulations concerning limited aspects of specific problems; but more comprehensive theories have not been forthcoming.

The lack of an adequate coherent theoretical structure has limited the advance of social psychology at three points. (1) It has made it difficult for the social psychologist to ask fundamentally important questions about social behavior. Without a guiding theory, it is easy to mistake trivial questions about prac-

tical problems for the basically important and enduring questions about social behavior. (2) It has limited the value of the social psychologist's practical research by making possible only a rather narrow understanding (sometimes a wrong understanding) of the meaning of his data. (3) It has tended to repel the more theoretical-minded psychologists from concerning themselves with problems of social psychology. Social psychology has lacked status among the more "scientific" psychologists.

Whether we are interested in social psychology as a basic science or as an applied science, a set of scientific principles is essential.

Social psychology as a basic science

Among the sciences of society it is only social psychology that deals primarily with the behavior of the *individual*. Economics, political science, sociology, anthropology, and the other social disciplines mainly study the behavior of larger groupings and classifications of people and analyze various behavioral indices (buying and selling, voting, churchgoing, etc.) which describe regularities in the specific activities of specific classifications of people. Moreover, when these social disciplines do deal with the individual they tend to be concerned only with special *segments* of his behavior—with "economic man," "political man," etc. Social psychology, on the other hand, is concerned with *every aspect* of the social behavior of man—with "social man." Social psychology may therefore be broadly viewed as the science of the behavior of the individual in society.

THE INTERPERSONAL BEHAVIOR EVENT

As in any other science, deciding upon the proper unit of analysis is one of the first problems we must deal with in the study of social psychology. The unit of analysis we choose not only must be a convenient and manageable one, but must preserve the two major characteristics of human action. First, human action is motivated, or goal-directed; second, human action is integrated—that is, the individual's wants, emotions, and cognitions operate in concert to influence his actions. The unit of analysis which best meets these criteria is the *interpersonal behavior event*.

AN EXAMPLE. Before attempting a formal definition of the interpersonal behavior event, let us point to an example. In their record of "One Boy's Day," R. G. Barker and H. F. Wright [1951] report the following incident, involving Raymond, Susan, and Roy. Raymond and Susan had been playing together in the sand pile in the schoolyard for some time before Roy joined them.

> Vehemently Roy said, "This is no road here." He stamped up and down violently, making a perfect wreck of one of Raymond's roads.
>
> Raymond said in an irritated fashion, definitely reprimanding Roy, and emphasizing each word, "It is, too!"
>
> At once Roy stopped stamping and shoving his feet around, seemingly in direct subservience to Raymond's authoritative manner. He didn't feel he dared go further with out-and-out destructive activity.
>
> Raymond paused in his play and looked up indignantly to see whether Roy would quit bothering him or not. Raymond then scraped and smoothed off a space a foot square.

> "Here is the pasture," he said in a pleasant, positive way. The pasture was another addition to the construction on which he and Susan were working.

PROCESS OF INTERACTION. This example reveals the essential features of the interpersonal behavior event. As a first approximation, it may be thought of as a process of interaction between two or more individuals, in which the action of one person, e.g., Roy, is a *response* to the second person, e.g., Raymond, and, at one and the same time, is a *stimulus* for the second person. In responding to Raymond, Roy's actions are guided by his interpretation of Raymond's actions; in turn, Raymond's responses are guided by his interpretation of Roy's actions. For example, Raymond's speech has a certain sound which Roy interprets as "anger." His reaction, ceasing to stamp and shove his feet around, is determined by his *interpretation* of Raymond's feelings. In turn, Raymond "looked up indignantly to see whether Roy would quit bothering him or not," that is, to perceive the effect of his behavior upon Roy. His perception of Roy's reaction then guides or determines his behavior toward Roy. Thus we see that the actions of each are *in reference to the other*. The actions of each are at once a *result* of and a *cause* of the actions of the other.

The actions of the participants in an interpersonal behavior event may be bodily movements. In the case of the lower animals, interaction consists largely of a series of such bodily movements. In the case of human beings, however, "body language" has given way to verbal language. Man interacts primarily by using words.

The interpersonal behavior event is a complex unit of behavior whose psychological properties we shall explore throughout this book. Here it is sufficient to point out that it constitutes the basic object of our inquiry. In so far as any science can be specifically defined in terms of its basic unit or object of inquiry, social psychology can be defined as *the science of interpersonal behavior events.* The goal of social psychology is to derive the laws of the development, change, and nature of interpersonal behavior events.

THE INTERPERSONAL BEHAVIOR EVENT AS AN INTEGRATED, INSTRUMENTAL ACT. As we have said, human action is characterized by its integration and goal-directedness. Each interpersonal behavior event must retain these characteristics. It is for this reason that we think of an interpersonal behavior event as beginning with the arousal of wants in the participants. Each phase of the event succeeds

BOX 1.2: *Practical knowledge among the policy makers*

Under the auspices of the Center for International Studies of the Massachusetts Institute of Technology, Harold R. Isaacs, a reporter with a special interest in China, studied the attitudes of a selected sample of Americans toward the peoples of China and India.

Isaacs collected a panel of 32 nationally prominent Americans, 77 professionally prominent persons in government service and in the academic world, and 72 persons who held important mass-media positions. Each person on the panel was chosen *because of his potential importance in influencing the ideas of the American people about Asia and especially about China and India.* They were all opinion leaders and policy determiners. Of the 181 panel members, 49 had a primary interest in Asian affairs, 59 a secondary involvement, and 73 only an incidental involvement.

Each panel member was intensively interviewed to uncover his feelings and attitudes toward the peoples of China and of India and the sources of his attitudes. The interviews lasted from two to four hours.

The first question in the interview was, "When you think of Asia, what comes to your mind?" For 80 of the respondents an "image of an undifferentiated crush of humanity was summoned up instantly . . . and for many this is the 'Asia' that carries with it a dread blur of mystery and fearfulness, associated with vast numbers, with barbarism, and with disease." One hundred and twenty-nine of the members of the panel said that Asia has become a source of future danger to the United States.

When asked about the Chinese people, a majority—70 per cent—of the panel expressed predominantly positive attitudes (but this does not, of course, represent the attitudes of the sample toward the *government* of China). Thirty-one members of the panel (17 per cent) held negative attitudes. Whether positive or negative, the attitudes of the panelists tended to be sweeping generalizations. Whether positive or negative, they were generally based upon "limited notions, scanty, even wispy, yet sufficient to establish some kind of attitude or bias, sometimes a vague sort of feeling. . . ."

The attitudes of the majority of the panel toward the people of India were generally unfavorable; 54 per cent expressed more or less strongly negative views. This antipathy reflected the image of the "very benighted heathen Hindu . . . evoked from distant memory or from last week's issue of *Time* . . . out of remembered things that people somewhere said or wrote, or the sharp recall of things and people seen or pictured in India itself." Isaacs concludes:

The images of Asia and of Asian-Western relationships persisting in the minds of men educated and conditioned primarily to an Atlantic-Western-white view of the world certainly have a major place in the slowness and pain with which major American policy makers have reacted to the new realities in Asia since 1945.

Isaacs, H. R. Scratches on our minds. New York: John Day, 1958.

BOX 1.3: *A capsule account of milestones in social psychology*

THE ANCIENTS LOOK AT MAN IN SOCIETY
Plato, *The Republic*
Aristotle, *Politics*

PHILOSOPHERS SEARCH FOR THE SOURCES OF SOCIAL CONDUCT
Men Seek Power
1651: Thomas Hobbes, *Leviathan*
Men Seek Self-interest
1776: Adam Smith, *Wealth of Nations*
Men Seek Pleasure
1789: Jeremy Bentham, *An Introduction to the Principles of Morals and Legislation*

SOCIAL PSYCHOLOGY IS ENVISAGED
1854: Auguste Comte, in his *Système de Politique Positive*, states his intention to publish *Le Système de Morale Positive*, which is the term he preferred for a social psychology. Comte died before he could carry out this project.
1862: The first volume of Wilhelm Wundt's *Völkerpsychologie* was originally outlined by the "father of psychology" in *Beiträge zur Theorie der Sinneswahrnehmung.*

SOCIAL SCIENTISTS SEEK THE DETERMINANTS OF SOCIAL BEHAVIOR
Habit
1890: William James, *Principles of Psychology*

Imitation
1890: Gabriel Tarde, *The Laws of Imitation*

Suggestion
1895: Gustave Le Bon, *The Crowd*

Instinct
1908: William McDougall, *Introduction to Social Psychology*

Attitude
1918–1920: W. I. Thomas and F. Znaniecki, *The Polish Peasant in Europe and America*

---

the preceding phase in a consistent manner, as action in the event tends in the direction of goal achievement. It is for this reason that the interpersonal behavior event can be characterized as a social *instrumental act.*

Often an interpersonal behavior event may seem unmotivated because we have failed to identify correctly the goals involved, or because we have artificially abstracted a part of the individual's behavior from its context. An illustration may make this clear.

Churchgoing by a person who demonstrates no religious motives may seem, on superficial analysis, to be a habitual, unmotivated act,

carried over from childhood. Analysis of this behavior will reveal it to be, on the contrary, a meaningful, motivated action, fulfilling *present* goals of gregariousness, social approval, wealth display, rest, or something else.

The interpersonal behavior event is an integrated act. It reflects the integrated influence of the individual's wants and goals upon his emotions, thoughts, perceptions, memories. Two persons, hurrying to meet a friend at the race track, *talk* about their selections for the first race, *worry* about the possibility of losing more money than they can afford to lose, *fantasy* winning the daily double, *anticipate*

THE DOMAIN OF SOCIAL PSYCHOLOGY

THE FIRST TEXTBOOKS APPEAR
> 1908: William McDougall, *Introduction to Social Psychology*
> 1908: Edward A. Ross, *Social Psychology*

THE FIRST JOURNAL IS FOUNDED
> 1921: Morton Prince's journal, *The Journal of Abnormal Psychology,* becomes *The Journal of Abnormal Psychology and Social Psychology* (later shortened to *Journal of Abnormal and Social Psychology*)

SOCIAL PSYCHOLOGY ENTERS THE LABORATORY
> 1897: N. Triplett, *The Dynamogenic Factors in Pacemaking and Competition*

SOCIAL PSYCHOLOGY GOES INTO THE FIELD
> 1899: E. D. Starbuck, *The Psychology of Religion*

SOCIAL PSYCHOLOGY IS APPLIED
> 1900: H. Gale, *On the Psychology of Advertising, in Psychological Studies*

GROUP INFLUENCES ARE EXPERIMENTALLY STUDIED
> 1924: V. M. Bechterew and M. de Lange, *Die Ergebnisse des Experiments auf dem Gebiete der kollectiven Reflexologie*

ATTITUDES ARE MEASURED
> 1927–1928: L. L. Thurstone, *Attitudes Can Be Measured*
> 1936: George Gallup makes the measurement of public opinion "Big Business"
> 1940: Rensis Likert develops the open-end survey technique

SOCIAL PSYCHOLOGISTS ESPOUSE ACTION RESEARCH
> 1936: The Society for the Psychological Study of Social Issues is founded

EXPERIMENTAL GROUP DYNAMICS BEGINS
> 1938: Kurt Lewin and Ronald Lippitt, *An Experimental Approach to the Study of Autocracy and Democracy: A Preliminary Note*

with pleasure joining a friend in the clubhouse bar for a drink before the meeting, and *remember* their last visit to the track as they *walk* quickly along. All of their activities are integrated and organized by the goal of getting to the track.

SOCIAL PSYCHOLOGY AND GENERAL PSYCHOLOGY

We have, in the preceding discussion, made use of many terms drawn from general psychology: motivation, cognition, goals, fantasy, etc. It might, therefore, be fruitful, at this point, to consider the relation between social psychology and psychology in general. Let us begin by saying that the isolated individual is a fiction. Whether we are studying the behavior of a man in a laboratory, in a clinic, or in a crowd; whether we are studying his ability to memorize, his performance on an intelligence test, or his churchgoing, we are studying the behavior of a man as a participant in interpersonal behavior events. The effects of a man's past, present, and anticipated interpersonal behavior events influence each of his activities, no matter how simple or apparently remote. As a consequence, every man lives in a social world, and no psychol-

BOX 1.4: *Social psychology and the common cold*

(*Reproduced with permission of* Scientific American.)

The influence of social interaction is pervasive and omnipresent. Even the experimental virologist, in his animal laboratory, encounters its effects and must deal with its consequences to understand his experimental data.

Christopher H. Andrewes, a virologist who directs the Common Cold Research Unit in Salisbury, England, infected some day-old chicks with a particularly virulent strain of Newcastle disease (a respiratory ailment). The infection spread very quickly to the other chicks in the same cage.

When uninfected chicks were separated from infected chicks by a wire barrier, the uninfected chicks, driven toward social interaction with their infected neighbors, still picked up the infection. However, when an uninfected group was given a choice between interacting with an uninfected or an infected group the spread of infection was stopped. ". . . they [the uninfected group] lost interest in the sick birds and collected against the partition separating them from the other normals. As a result the healthy chicks, thus sandwiched between the sick and the well, failed to pick up infection." (See illustrations.)

This experiment may explain why colds are so much more prevalent in winter than in summer. Earlier work at the Common Cold Research Unit had scotched a number of old wives' tales about the causes of common colds. For example, when volunteer subjects took hot baths and then stood in a cold, drafty passage in wet bathing suits for half an hour, no colds were produced. Andrewes suggests that cold weather produces colds not because of chills and drafts, but because cold weather changes the *social behavior* of people. In winter, people huddle together in their homes and in various public places; they become much more "sociable" and are thus thrown into close contact with infected persons.

It is not the winter rains and winds—it is "winter social psychology" which is responsible for the common, or better still, the social cold.

Andrewes, C. H. The viruses of the common cold. Sci. Amer., 1960, 203, 88–102.

ogist can study the behavior of an asocial man. Consider Mr. Arbuthnot, in the privacy of his bedroom, dressing for the day. If he selects his tie to please his secretary, he is behaving with reference to another person and hence is displaying social behavior. En route to his office, hurrying to keep an early appointment, he comes upon a stop sign at a deserted intersection. If he darts through the intersection after estimating the probability of arrest and after anticipating the consequences, he is behaving with reference to other persons and is, therefore, displaying social behavior. Interpersonal behavior events are ubiquitous (see Box 1.4).

THE LAWS OF GENERAL PSYCHOLOGY. Much of the work in psychology has been concerned with the study of the functional relations between easily manipulable objects and conditions in the external environment and the experience and action of individuals. For example, in the field of perception, experimental psychologists have sought to determine how changes in the physical stimulus (e.g., light waves) correspond to changes in how we perceive colors; in the field of learning, they have tried to discover whether spacing or massing trials will be more efficient in memorizing a series of words. This work of what we may call general psychology has sought to provide us with a body of experimental data and with a set of scientific principles about the basic psychological processes of perception, motivation, thinking, learning, and remembering.

In this work, the experimental psychologist has often chosen to ignore the effects of social factors on these basic processes. It is not that he denies the influence of social factors on the experience and action of his experimental subjects; he accepts the proposition that he is necessarily studying a social man. It is rather that in his experimental study of perception, learning, motivation, etc., he prefers to deal only with the factors that are readily manipulable and to control out as experimental error the less easily handled social factors. It should be clear, however, that a truly human psychology, adequate to comprehend all the diverse psychological experiences and actions of man, must incorporate the findings and principles not only of general psychology, as traditionally defined, but also of social psychology.

SOCIAL PSYCHOLOGY BUILDS UPON GENERAL PSYCHOLOGY. In its attempts to develop a science of social behavior, social psychology builds upon the findings of general psychology. To understand the actions of man in relation to man, to understand interpersonal behavior events, we need to know the wants and goals of man and how man perceives, thinks, learns. The principles of motivation, perception, and cognition formulated by general psychology will assist us in understanding how the individual develops his social goals, how he perceives persons and groups, how he learns social behaviors.

BY WAY OF CAUTION. In applying general psychological principles to the understanding of social behavior, it is necessary to make direct checks upon the applicability of these principles to social behavior. They have been formulated on the basis of experimental data gathered in the relatively simple laboratory situation. In a more complex situation, critical psychological features may be involved which were not included or observed in the laboratory situation. The basic psychological principles of the laboratory may, therefore, have to be modified before they can be applied to the understanding and prediction of social behavior.

Social psychology as an applied science

To understand the task of the *applied* social psychologist one must be clear about the nature of the "social problems" with which one is concerned. Social problems—crime, divorce, intergroup conflict, prejudice, etc.—are not to be thought of as separate cases of "aberrant" social conduct which can be isolated from other aspects of the totally functioning society, and treated solely by the officially designated "watchmen of society"—legislators, policemen, probation officers, judges, and jailers. Rather, we must recognize that social problems and social "misbehavior" are inseparable from normal social processes and normal social behavior, and thus the research and theories of social scientists must also be brought to bear on the solution of social problems. As Nisbet [Merton and Nisbet, 1961] puts it:

> Too often the popular view of social problems likens them to cancers: for most citizens, the image of society and its problems is that of an essentially healthy organism invaded by alien substances. The legislator, or policeman, is thought of as a kind of physician, bound to remove the cyst, destroy the virus, but without altering the character of the organism itself. . . . Such an analogy seriously distorts social reality . . . social problems, even the worst of them, often have a functional relationship to the institutions and values by which we live.

Nisbet then goes on to point out that such "deviant" behavior as stealing, suicide, divorce, and prostitution are perhaps best described as normal consequences of normal social institutions. Thus, for example, much of crime can be traced to the goals and status wants which characterize our society; our high rate of divorce cannot be isolated from the values we place upon individualism and romance; and "even prostitution exists only as a reflection, so to speak, of the value we place on the monogamous family and the sanctity of marriage." As we shall see later in this book, in no instance is this general thesis more clearly demonstrated than in the racial, ethnic, and religious prejudice and discrimination which are so widespread in this country. Such practices, opposed as they are to our professed national ideals, nevertheless stem directly from certain social practices which are equally firmly rooted in our society. Racial, ethnic,

and religious discrimination helps many of us to satisfy many wants and achieve many goals which the American culture teaches us are good.

It is because social behavior and "misbehavior" are so closely interrelated that the "applied" social psychologist not only must be expert in the details of the practical problem but also must be thoroughly grounded in "pure" social psychology. Despite this essential interdependence of the pure and the applied aspects of the science, there are significant differences in the roles and research objectives of the social psychologist when he functions as a diagnostician and therapist of society's ills and when he functions as a "pure" scientist.

THE ROLE OF THE APPLIED SOCIAL PSYCHOLOGIST

Exactly what can the social psychologist contribute to man's problems? It is not his unique function to *solve* social problems, to be the "master fixer." He may contribute to such solutions, but the solution of complex social problems requires authority, techniques, and resources that fall far outside the province of the social psychologist. His proper task in dealing with a social problem is to analyze and diagnose and advise with respect to only *one* feature of the whole problem—the behavior of the people who are involved in it. The solution of any social problem requires the integrated efforts of many different persons in society—government administrators, legislators, lay leaders, other social scientists, and Mr. Arbuthnot.

Take the problem of racial prejudice. The task of the social psychologist is to ascertain why people are prejudiced, how and why prejudice forms and changes, what effects prejudice has on the behavior and personality of the individual who holds the prejudice, what effects prejudice has on the attitudes, personality, and behavior of the victim, by what changes in the social situation prejudice can be reduced.

THE DOMAIN OF SOCIAL PSYCHOLOGY

It is not the job of the social psychologist alone to bring about the changes in social circumstances necessary to remedy prejudice, or to examine the broader political, economic, and social consequences of a program. That is the function of the social planner, the administrator, and of social action groups. Successful change is dependent upon the diverse political, economic, social, and educational activities of large segments of society.

Social psychology is no cure-all. It can provide indispensable understanding, prediction, evaluation, and advice; but even if at some future time the social psychologist could indeed know all that it is necessary to know about the psychological bases of, say, racial prejudice, the possibility of actually solving the problem would depend entirely upon the wishes and actions of most of the members of society. Even today in the present relatively undeveloped state of social psychology, enough is probably known to enable society to solve many of the critical aspects of the problem of racial prejudice. The use which is made of this body of knowledge will depend upon the decisions of the various groups in society which are concerned with the problems of governing men.

THE RESEARCH OF THE APPLIED SOCIAL PSYCHOLOGIST

We have emphasized the importance of a basic science of social psychology and the contribution of its principles to the understanding of social problems. However, in dealing with such acute problems as international tensions, economic conflicts, and racial discrimination, general principles and sound theory are not enough. The social psychologist, as an applied scientist, must study each specific social problem in its own right, uncovering the relevant factors, determining the relative potency of these factors and how they interrelate. He must take into account the facts about the *particular* people who are involved in the problem and the *specific* social context in which the problem occurs. Only with this knowledge about the concrete details of the problem in his possession can he bring to bear basic psychological principles in understanding the problem and in recommending remedial action (see Box 1.5). Obtaining these concrete details requires painstaking research, the carefully planned accumulation of data, and ingenuity and skill in the same degree as are required in "pure" research. In addition, it often requires the adaptation of standard research methods or the development of new techniques.

The concrete problems to which the applied social psychologist addresses himself are almost always determined for him by the particular interpersonal and intergroup problems that are of special concern to society. These problems change from time to time and in this sense the subject matter of applied social psychology is constantly changing.

The plan of the book

Our plan for this book is to develop the principles of the interpersonal behavior event by proceeding from a relatively "molecular" analysis to a more "molar" analysis—that is, by moving from the study of the wants and thoughts of the individual as he interacts with other people to the study of the functioning of groups and organizations. In Part One we discuss in some detail the three *basic psychological factors*—cognition, motivation, and interpersonal response traits—which shape and, in turn, reflect the influence of interpersonal behavior events. In Part Two we consider the manner in which beliefs, feelings, and reaction tendencies become organized into *attitudes*—enduring systems which play a continuing and crucial role in man's social behavior. In discussing attitudes we shall seek to clarify their nature, the methods employed in their detection and measurement, the process of their formation, and the manner wherein they can be changed. In Part Three, in preparation for the study of the behavior of groups and organizations, we describe the *social and cultural habitat of man*—selecting for special attention the nature and uses of language, the effects of social class, status-strivings, social mobility, cultural norms, values, and beliefs. With Part Four we end our study of social psychology by focusing our attention on the *group*—how it is organized, the nature of group leadership, what makes a group effective and what limits its effectiveness, its beneficial as well as baleful influence on the expression of the individuality of man.

In recognition of the close interdependence between theory and problems, between the pure and the applied science, we have interlarded the contributions of these two "kinds" of social psychologists throughout the book. Thus, for example, the research data accumulated on the problem of racial, ethnic, and religious discrimination are integrated with our discussion of motivation, cognition, interpersonal response traits, attitudes—and any other topic where such data can be helpful. In this way it is hoped that the social psychologist whose major interest is in racial discrimination as a "social problem" will find this problem illumined by the theoretical discussions in those sections, and the "pure" social

BOX 1.5: *The demography of desegregation*

Much of the anti-Negro discrimination in the Southern United States would appear to be due primarily to strong and pervasive pressures to conform to Southern norms of white supremacy. It is important, for those who would seek to eliminate discrimination, to pinpoint the *source* of these pressures to conform.

Thomas F. Pettigrew and M. Richard Cramer have attempted to do just this—to locate the strongholds of diehard prejudice—through the use of demographic data reported by the U.S. Bureau of the Census. The speed with which school desegregation has taken place in the counties of the six states of Texas, Oklahoma, Missouri, Kentucky, West Virginia, and Maryland was studied as a function of three predictive variables: the percentage of urban dwellers, the percentage of Negroes, and the percentage of employed white women. (This last was taken to measure Southern traditionalism, on the assumption that an area with few employed white women is conforming to the historical Southern taboo against white women entering the labor force.)

Scores on these three variables were secured for each county with 100 or more Negroes in the 1950 census in each of the six states. Multiple correlations were then computed between the three variables taken together and speed of school desegregation. Speed was measured as follows: counties that desegregated at least one school during the state's first year of desegregation were given a score of 1, during the second year, a score of 2, and so on.

The multiple correlation coefficients were found to be positive for every state and ranged from .45 to .72.

These results suggest that opposition to educational integration in the South flourishes especially in (1) *rural areas* with (2) *a high percentage of Negroes* in which (3) *the traditional Southern culture is still strong*. In planning their strategy to achieve desegregation, the government and the citizen must consider these facts about the areas where resistance to integration is highly concentrated.

Pettigrew, T. F., and Cramer, M. R. The demography of desegregation. J. soc. Issues, 1959, 15, 61–71.

psychologist will find an opportunity to check out his laboratory data and theory against data collected in the maelstrom of social life. Problems cannot be separated in any meaningful sense into theoretical and applied. The problem of attitude change, for example, is the very same problem whether we approach it as a student of propaganda, as a student of education, or as a "pure" student of social behavior. Thus, we will find in Part Two a discussion of the measurement techniques of the public-opinion pollster inextricably bound up with a discussion of the nature of attitudes—and a discussion of the processes of attitude change closely tied in with a discussion of the processes of attitude formation. Much the same is true for such problems as what makes for an effective group or effective leadership.

What the plan of this book reflects is the nature of the discipline which is social psychology, and the nature of this discipline is such that the student of social psychology must truly be a student of the theory and the problems of social behavior.

GUIDES FOR THE READER

The form and content of this book have been determined by the two major objectives we have sought to achieve. As we have seen, the sciences of man in society—frequently referred to as the "social sciences"—have enjoyed an extended boom in recent years. Many social scientists, coming from many different backgrounds of education and training, working with many different techniques and skills, seeking many different objectives, have produced an imposing mass of observations, facts, theories, and speculations about the behavior of man in society. Our first objective in writing this book was to organize what man has learned about man—from general psychology, personality psychology, social psychology, anthropology, sociology—to make manifest the harmony which appeared to us to inhere in these accumulated facts, observa-

tions, and speculations. In other words, we have sought to present a science of social psychology as an organic whole—in so far as this is currently possible in this complex and fast-changing field without doing violence to the available facts. The critical reader will, we hope, find in these pages a synthesis of the behavioral social sciences which will merit his attention.

In addition to presenting what we believe to be a useful systematization of the behavioral social sciences, we have sought to create an effective teaching instrument. This book is addressed both to the social scientist and to the student who seeks to become a social scientist. In the furtherance of the needs of the student, we have made use of several pedagogic devices. Among these are the "Guides," the periodic sections labeled "To Recapitulate," the "Chapter Glossaries," and the "Boxes."

The discussion of the four main areas of study in this book (basic psychological factors, attitudes, social and cultural habitat of man, and group and organizational behavior) is organized around sets of guides. These guides are intended to help summarize the available facts and theories relevant to the particular topic under scrutiny. They are not, of course, to be regarded as statements of formal principles. They are simply pedagogic devices with the dual function of providing the reader with a highly condensed capsule summary of a lengthy discussion and, quite literally, with a *guide* to that discussion. These guides will always be found preceding the detailed discussion of a subject, and will provide the reader with a frame of reference for the material which he will find under the guide. He should thereby be enabled to see more clearly, as he reads on in the section, how the various findings fit together into a coherent story. These same guides are repeated in a list at the close of each chapter, thus serving as an aid in reviewing the material of the chapter.

In addition to the guides we have provided two other kinds of summary devices. First, we have, in each chapter, several part-summaries under the heading "To Recapitulate." As their title implies, these part-summaries are intended as résumés of some of the principles and facts which merit repetition and emphasis, before the student goes on to further sections of the chapter. Second, the chapter glossaries, printed at the end of each chapter, provide the student with another valuable aid for summary and review. To a considerable degree the information and concepts of any science are embodied in its technical language, its definitions of technical terms. The student who reviews the glossary terms at the end of each chapter will thereby be reviewing much of the content of the chapter. With this function in mind, many of the terms in the glossary have been elucidated in considerable detail—more than is found in a usual "dictionary definition."

Finally, the many boxes distributed throughout the book may be of particular interest—not only to the student but to the general reader. The boxes contain materials of various kinds. Most of them—and this is their major function—present samples of the research material upon which the discussion in the text is based, and from which generalizations and "conclusions" are derived.

We regard these boxes as of first importance in the reading of this book. No science is sounder than its research, and if the reader is to acquire an appreciation of the nature of the discipline of social psychology he must develop some feel for its research work. Reading a smooth-flowing exposition is not enough. The reading should be interrupted, every now and then, by at least a brief glimpse at the working-papers on the basis of which the exposition was written. The boxes are intended to provide the reader with such a glimpse, enabling him to develop at least a nodding acquaintance with the nature of research in social psychology—with its tactics and strategies, its difficulties, its limitations, its successes, and its failures. Each box also contains the relevant references so that the reader may go to the original sources should any attract his special interest.

It is our hope that the guides, the various summaries and glossaries, and the boxes, together with our attempt to write a systematic social psychology, will make this book a contribution to social scientists and their students.

Part One: BASIC PSYCHOLOGICAL FACTORS

MAN ACTS UPON HIS IDEAS. HIS IRRATIONAL ACTS NO LESS THAN *his rational acts are guided by what he thinks, what he believes, what he anticipates. However bizarre the behavior of men, tribes, or nations may appear to an outsider, to the men, to the tribes, to the nations their behavior makes sense in terms of their own world views. Every man, through "cognitive work," attempts to construct for himself his own meaningful world, and he classifies and orders within it a multitude of objects, among which the most significant are other people. As Sir Frederick Bartlett has suggested, "It is fitting to speak of every human cognitive reaction—perceiving, imagining, thinking, and reasoning—as an effort after meaning."*

If we understand how man comes by the ideas about things and people which make up his world image, if we understand the principles which govern the growth and development and interaction of these ideas, we will have taken the first step toward understanding man's behavior in this world of his own making. Our purpose in this chapter is to examine the formation and change of man's cognitions.

2: COGNITION

THE RESPONSES OF THE INDIVIDUAL TO PERSONS and things are shaped by the way they look to him—his *cognitive world*. And the image, or "map," of the world of every person is an individual one. No two persons live in the same cognitive world.

This truism is often difficult for us to accept in our dealings with people. Like Piaget's young children (see Box 2.1), we often think that *our* perspective of the world is the only possible one, that other people must and do see the world in the same way that we do. This egocentric assumption hinders our attempts to understand the behavior of others. The social behavior of a person is shaped by the view of the world he has from his particular vantage point. And unless we have some understanding of his world, his behavior may seem queer, incomprehensible, perverse.

Each person has an individualized image of the world because his image is the product of the following determinants: (1) *his physical* and social environments, (2) *his* physiological structure, (3) *his* wants and goals, (4) *his* past experiences.

How an individual conceives the world is dependent, first of all, upon the nature of the *physical and social environments* in which he is immersed. The world images of the Park Avenue "pueblo dweller" and the Tennessee mountaineer are different because their physical and social environments differ. And the world images of different members of the same family—Park Avenue or Tennessee mountain—will differ because of subtle differences in the nature of their social environments: different members of the same family will receive varying treatment from their associates depending upon their age, sex, position in the family, etc. They will seek out different environments of persons, books, and other cultural things in trying to satisfy their wants. But this is not all.

What a person sees among the things that are "out there" to be seen and how he sees them are in part determined by his *physiological structure*. Individual differences in sensory capacity and in intellectual abilities reflect physiological differences. The cognitions of the dull person are less complex and less inte-

grated than the cognitions of the bright person. But this is not all.

For reasons we shall discuss in Chapter 3, each person develops a set of *wants and goals* that is characteristic of him and different from the wants and goals of other persons. And as we shall see later in the present chapter, an individual's conception of the world is partly determined by his wants and goals. But this is not all.

The psychological history of an individual is a record of *past experiences* unique to him. And we know that the content and organization of a person's image of the world are shaped by his past experience.

Although no two persons have precisely the same conception of the world, there are many common features in the world images of all people. This is true because all men have similar nervous systems, because all men share certain wants, and because all men must cope with certain common problems. The cognitive worlds of the members of a particular culture group are similar to an even greater degree because of greater similarities in their wants and goals, in the physical and social environments to which they are exposed, and in their learning experiences.

BOX 2.1: *The egocentric world of the little ones*

In a series of books, Jean Piaget, the famous Swiss child psychologist, has demonstrated and documented what he has called the "egocentric" nature of perception and thinking in young children.

He asks, "What will happen when it is a question of imagining distant objects, and of coordinating the perspective of different observers?" He answers, "The child is placed opposite a small model of three mountains, and given a certain number of colored pictures of these mountains; he is then asked which of the pictures show the mountains from the [different] positions occupied successively by a doll on the mountains in the model. The function of age in this development of these reactions is very clear. The littler ones do not understand that the observer sees the same mountains quite differently from different points of view, and hence they consider their own perspective absolute. But the older ones discover the relativity necessary to objectivity. . . ."

Piaget, J. Principal factors determining intellectual evolution from childhood to adult life. In Factors determining human behavior. *Cambridge, Mass.: Harvard Univer. Press, 1937.*

BASIC PSYCHOLOGICAL FACTORS

BOX 2.2: *Many perspectives on Old City*

Alison Davis, B. B. Gardner, and M. R. Gardner, who were associated with W. Lloyd Warner, a cultural anthropologist at the University of Chicago, in his studies of the social structure of American communities, examined the caste and class systems of Old City, a town of about 10,000 in the southern United States. They did not assume that their sociological description of the class system of Old City would be identical with the way different people in the community themselves perceived the class system. Hence, they went on to investigate how members of the different class groups themselves apprehended their social environment.

Davis and the Gardners distinguished six social classes in the white society of Old City: the "upper-upper" (UU), the "lower-upper" (LU), the "upper-middle" (UM), the "lower-middle" (LM), the "upper-lower" (UL), and the "lower-lower" (LL). People in any one class, however, perceived the community's class system differently from the anthropological "outsiders" and differently from people in other classes. As the following table indicates, members of the upper-upper class recognize five class divisions in the white society. They do not differentiate between the two lower classes, perceiving only "po' whites" at the bottom of the class hierarchy. The class perspective of the lower-lower group sharply contrasts with that of the upper-upper group. All persons above the lower-middle class are lumped together as "Society" or the "folks with money." The lower-middle class, known to the upper-upper as "good people, but nobody," are "way-high-ups" for the lower-lower class person.

The upper-class perspective	The social scientist's perspective	The lower-class perspective
"Old aristocracy"	UU ⎱	
"Aristocracy but not old"	LU ⎰	"Society" or the "folks with money"
"Nice, respectable people"	UM ⎰	
"Good people, but nobody"	LM	"Way-high-ups" but not "Society"
"Po' whites"	⎰ UL	"Snobs trying to push up"
	⎱ LL	"People just as good as anybody"

The bases of class distinction are also variously defined by the different social classes. The upper-uppers think of class position largely in terms of time—an individual has a particular class position because his family has "always had" that position. The lower-lowers view the whole class system as a hierarchy of wealth. All persons above them on the social ladder are increasingly wealthy, and their own inferior status is due to lack of money.

Davis, A., Gardner, B. B., Gardner, M. R. Deep south: a social anthropological study of caste and class. Chicago: Univer. of Chicago Press, 1941.

PROBLEMS IN DESCRIBING COGNITIVE WORLDS. There are two major sources of error which plague the student of social behavior when he attempts to describe the cognitive worlds of people. The first of these is the tendency to describe the world of the individual as it is seen by the scientist rather than by the person himself. For example, the church or political party that may influence an individual's behavior is frequently described, not as it is apprehended by the individual whose behavior we are trying to understand, but as it is apprehended by a social scientist. (See Box 2.2 for the different ways in which a community may be apprehended by the social scientist and by the community members.)

The second type of error involves reading one's own logical deductions into the cognitive world of the individual we are observing. For example, it has been found [Hovland and Sears, 1940] that over a period of years the number of lynchings of Negroes tended to increase with each decrease in the price of cotton. From this correlation, we might argue that a worsening economic situation is an important condition for an increase in anti-Negro actions. But we cannot legitimately conclude that the Southern white necessarily *sees* the Negro as an economic competitor. To learn how the Southern white sees the Negro it is necessary to examine the Southerner's cognitions directly.

Little has been done by psychologists and other social scientists in describing the world images of different people. Almost the entire task still remains to be done. For the student interested in obtaining insight into the social behavior of people, this whole area offers an exciting and rewarding field of research.

GUIDE 1: *The cognitions of the individual are selectively organized*

Cognition is selectively organized, and to say that is to say three things. First, the individual sees organized objects—he sees landscapes and buildings and people. Retinally, an object can be described only as a mosaic of discrete pinpoints of light of varying wavelengths. But the perceiver does not see a mere conglomeration of colored sensations merging into one another, without form and without defined boundaries. He sees an object which has color, form, and solidity. And he recognizes it as a meaningful object—as a landscape or a building or a person. And all of this occurs immediately and without conscious effort. Second, among all the objects in the individual's physical environment, only certain ones enter into his cognitions of the external world. Other objects either are not

included at all or play a minor role. Third, among all the possible characteristics of an object, only certain ones are perceived. And even these characteristics may be molded or altered to fit the requirements of the individual. The cognitive map of the individual is not, then, a photographic representation of the physical world; it is, rather, a partial, personal construction in which certain objects, selected out by the individual for a major role, are perceived in an individual manner. Every perceiver is, as it were, to some degree a non-representational artist, painting a picture of the world that expresses his individual view of reality.

Every cognitive organization has two main kinds of determinants: *stimulus factors* and *personal factors*. By stimulus factors are meant those factors which derive from the nature of the external stimulus object. By personal factors are meant those factors which derive from the characteristics of the perceiving individual.

COGNITIVE SELECTIVITY AND STIMULUS FACTORS

The familiar figure-on-background experiment of the perception laboratory illustrates one stimulus factor affecting cognitive selectivity. A single red dot, among many black dots, will *stand out* in perception. A single Negro in a crowd of white people is highly visible. Other stimulus factors determining selection include: *frequency*—the slogan most frequently repeated is more likely to come to the attention of the individual than the infrequently mentioned one; *intensity*—a shout is more attention-demanding than the normal speaking voice; *movement and change*—the animated neon sign attracts attention; *number*—the more objects there are, the greater the selectivity.

The stimulus factors involved in the creation and presentation of propaganda and educational materials are quite important in determining what cognitions the audience will experience. In attempting to tailor propaganda or educational materials for a particular audience, we must constantly be on guard against neglecting these stimulus factors because of an overconcern with the personal factors which characterize our audience.

COGNITIVE SELECTIVITY AND PERSONAL FACTORS

Experimental studies support three conclusions regarding the operation of personal factors in cognition: (1) Personal factors limit the number of objects that can be perceived at any one moment—the span of apprehension; (2) personal factors selectively sensitize the perceptual mechanism of the individual and lower his threshold for recognizing and attending to relevant stimulus objects and aspects of objects; (3) personal factors may distort cognitions of relevant objects so that they "fit" the requirements of the individual.

SPAN OF APPREHENSION. Experimental studies of the span of apprehension are among the oldest experiments in psychology. Woodworth [1938] gives us the following quotation from the lectures on metaphysics which Sir William Hamilton gave at the University of Edinburgh between 1836 and 1856:

> How many objects can the mind simultaneously survey, not with vivacity, but without absolute confusion? I find this problem stated and differently answered by different philosophers. . . . You can easily make the experiment for yourselves. . . . If you throw a handful of marbles on the floor, you will find it difficult to view at once more than six, or seven at the most, without confusion. . . .

Later and better-controlled experiments have established that when the requirement is that the exact number of objects shall be correctly apprehended and when the objects are black dots scattered irregularly over a white card, the average span of apprehension for "keen adults" is about 8. It may be that Sir William's different philosophers gave different answers because there are wide individual differences in average spans. The range in span of apprehension is found to be from 6 to 11. Furthermore, the span varies in the same person from moment to moment. It is partly because of individual differences in span of apprehension that two witnesses of the same set of events may give conflicting testimony.

SELECTIVE SENSITIZATION. The role of such personal factors as *mental set* in selectively sensitizing the perceptual mechanism has been studied by Postman and Brown [1952]. They studied the effect of success and failure upon the recognition threshold of words exposed briefly in a tachistoscope. Before taking the threshold test, some subjects were caused to succeed and some to fail on an experimental task. The "success subjects" had a lower threshold for success words (e.g., excellent, perfection, winner) than subjects who were caused to fail. The "failure subjects," on the other hand, were more sensitive to failure words (e.g., unable, obstacle, defeat) than the success group. This finding suggests that individual differences in experiences may arouse different momentary sets which in turn differentially sensitize the individual to certain objects in his world. And this fact is important for the understanding of the interpersonal behavior event. What occurs in an interpersonal behavior event arouses momentary sets which selectively influence the cognitions of the participants and help to govern the further course of the interpersonal action.

What we select out to recognize and attend to is also a function of enduring sets. A popular singer and a fire inspector view the auditorium from behind the asbestos curtain. In his first glance, the singer notes the large number of teenage girls in the audience; the fire inspector, in his first glance, notes that there are only three exit doors.

On a more complex level, mental sets may also influence which of the many alternative meanings of an object will be salient. Thus Foley and MacMillan [1943] asked five groups of subjects (first-year law students, second-year law, first-year medical, second-year medical, and a control group of non-

BOX 2.3: *Executives look at a company*

DeWitt C. Dearborn and Herbert A. Simon, social scientists at the Carnegie Institute of Technology, give the following instance of the selective organization of the cognitions of industrial executives.

A group of 23 executives, enrolled in an executive training program, were the subjects of the study. The departmental affiliations of the executives were as follows: sales (6); production (5); accounting (4); miscellaneous (8).

The executives were asked to read a standard textbook case, the "Castengo Steel Company," which gives a great deal of factual detail about the organization and activities of the Castengo Steel Company. Interpretation and evaluation are deliberately avoided in the case presentation.

Before discussion of the case the executives were asked to indicate in a brief written statement "what they considered to be the most important problem facing the Castengo Steel Company— the problem a new company president should deal with first." The findings are given in the following table.

| DEPARTMENT AFFILIATION | N | Sales | NUMBER WHO GAVE AS MOST IMPORTANT PROBLEM | |
			Clarify organization	*Human relations*
Sales	6	5	1	0
Production	5	1	4	0
Accounting	4	3	0	0
Miscellaneous	8	1	3	3
Total	23	10	8	3

Note that 5 of the 6 sales executives (83%) mentioned sales as the most important problem facing the company. In contrast, only 5 of the remaining 17 executives (29%) mentioned sales. Moreover, of the 5 nonsales executives who mentioned sales, three were in the accounting department in positions that involved the analysis of product profitability.

Organization problems were mentioned by 4 of the 5 production executives (80%) and by only 4 of the remaining 18 executives (22%). Only 3 executives mentioned human-relations problems; these were executives in the public relations, industrial relations, and medical departments of their companies.

Industrial executives looking at exactly the same information select for emphasis those aspects of a complex problem which relate to the activities and goals of their particular departments. The selective organization of cognition shapes organizational planning and policy.

Dearborn, DeWitt C., and Simon, H. A. Selective perception: a note on the departmental identification of executives. Sociometry, 1958, 21, 140–144.

professional students) to write down associations to a list of 40 stimulus words. Each of 20 of the stimulus words (e.g., administer, complaint, cell) could be interpreted in legal, or medical, or nonprofessional senses. Significant differences among the groups in the number of appropriate professional interpretations were secured. For example, law students more frequently responded to the stimulus word *administer* with such words as *gov-*

ern, business, estate; medical students more frequently gave such associations as *dosage, anesthetic, drugs.* It was also observed that the consistency of professional interpretation increased with amount of professional training. Thus, mental sets through selective sensitization may cause the same objects to have different meanings for different perceivers (see Box 2.3).

SELECTIVE DISTORTION. An individual's emotions and wants may act so as to select certain aspects of a stimulus object, and from these aspects a cognition of the object develops which may deviate markedly from a veridical cognition. This distorted cognition will tend to be congruent with the emotions and wants of the individual.

The role of emotions in influencing the "look of things" has long been known. Over two thousand years ago, Aristotle, in his *Parva Naturalia,* had this to say:

> Under the influence of strong feeling we are easily deceived regarding our sensations, different persons in different ways, as e.g., the coward under the influence of fear and the lover under that of love have such illusions that the former owing to a trifling resemblance thinks he sees an enemy and the latter his beloved. And the more impressionable the person is, the less is the resemblance required. Similarly, everybody is easily deceived when in anger or influenced by any strong desire, and the more subject one is to these feelings the more one is deceived. This is the reason why men sick of a fever sometimes think they see animals on the walls owing to some slight resemblance in the figures drawn there. And this tendency to illusion at times keeps pace with the intensity of emotional experience, so that in cases where the patient is not very sick, he is still conscious of the deception, but where his condition is more aggravated, he even rushes upon these animals.

For contemporary experimental studies of how wants and aversions can distort the perception of persons, see Boxes 2.4 and 2.5.

SOME SOCIAL IMPLICATIONS

The failure to understand the implications of Guide 1, that cognition is selectively organized, has led to much misguided effort and heartbreaking disappointment on the part of teachers, parents, religious missionaries, and leaders of causes. Take a child on a slumming trip to teach him the facts of social life, and show him how haggard, lean, scrawny, and undernourished the children are, and what does he see? He may perceive only the interesting alleys and inviting fire escapes where these children play as contrasted to the clean, sterile, and uninteresting playrooms provided for him.

On the occasion of the 1946 reprinting of Upton Sinclair's *The Jungle,* R. L. Duffus, reviewing the book in the *New York Times* of October 13, 1946, gave an interesting illustration of how the selective organization of cognition can subvert the best intentions of the social reformer. Duffus wrote:

> After this book appeared, four decades ago, quite a number of Americans temporarily stopped eating meat. . . . They just didn't care for meat after they had read young Mr. Sinclair's fictionalized account of how meat was handled in the Chicago stockyards. This was not Mr. Sinclair's intention. He was a socialist and an ardent friend of the underpaid and overworked. He did not foresee that the American people, after reading of the misfortunes of his Lithuanian hero, would clamor, not for a cooperative commonwealth, but a pure food law. . . . Young Mr. Sinclair admired the strong peasant stock that was pouring into this country so hopefully at the turn of the century. He hated to see it abused, as it was. He hated the cruelty which ground the lives out of men. He hated child labor. He hated the growling tyranny that fired and blacklisted when men formed unions to better their lot. He hated the cheating and the foul corruption that battened on the innocent. So he spent some seven weeks observing how people lived "back of the yards" and then wrote

this book. . . . He . . . threw into it his burning indignation, lighted it with his ingenuous hopes of a world redeemed by socialism, and got it into print. . . . it became a best seller, it has been translated into twenty-seven languages, it led to reforms in the handling of meat.

Upton Sinclair was a socialist, and the facts he perceived demonstrated, to him, the need for socialism. So he saw them, and so he wrote them down. However, the vast majority of his readers were not socialists; but they were meat eaters, and they perceived his facts in their own way and read therefrom their own lesson. They selected out for major attention, not the stories about the little Stanislovs who were forced to work in the packing houses or the men like Jurgis who averaged a weekly salary of $6.65, but the other stories—about the workmen and the stockyard rats that had fallen into lard vats and had gone out to the world as "pure leaf lard." Accordingly, his readers did not conclude from Sinclair's facts that the world must be redeemed by socialism but, through the process of selective organization of cognition, concluded that a new pure food act was required.

There are no impartial facts. Data do not have a logic of their own that results in the same cognitions for all people.

BOX 2.4: *Wants distort cognition . . .*

Albert Pepitone, a social psychologist, studied the distorting influence of wants and goals upon our perception of other persons. In one part of his experiment he used high school boys with a strong interest in basketball, who were given an opportunity to apply to a three-man board (working with the experimenter) for a free ticket to an important basketball game.

In their meetings with the boys, the members of the board played the following different roles:

Mr. Friendly (exhibited an approving attitude toward the boy)

Mr. Neutral (exhibited a nonevaluative attitude toward the boy)

Mr. Negative (exhibited a disapproving attitude toward the boy)

In playing their roles the three members attempted to exhibit an equal amount of power in determining the final decision of the board. That they succeeded is shown by the fact that adult observers rated each man as showing an equal amount of power behavior.

After each boy had met with the board, he was given an interview to secure a measure of his perception of the power of each member of the board. Degree of power was rated on a scale that ranged from 8 (the board member had everything to say about it) to 1 (he had nothing to say about it).

The results are shown in the following table. Despite the fact that all three members actually exhibited equal amounts of power, the boys perceived Mr. Friendly as considerably higher in power than Mr. Neutral, and Mr. Negative as somewhat lower in power than Mr. Neutral. There was considerable distortion in the direction of goal achievement.

	Observers' rating of power	Boys' rating of power
Mr. Friendly	4–5	6.60
Mr. Neutral	4–5	4.20
Mr. Negative	4–5	3.90

Pepitone, A. Motivational effects in social perception. Hum. Relat., 1950, 3, 57–76.

The cognitions of the individual—his ideas about persons and things—are selectively organized. Only certain objects, among all the objects that are "out there," enter into his conception of the external world. And the characteristics of these objects may be "distorted" to fit his psychological requirements. The selective organization of cognition is determined by two interacting sets of factors: stimulus factors and personal factors. By stimulus factors are meant those which derive from the nature of the stimulus object, e.g., frequency and intensity. Personal factors are those which derive from the characteristics of the perceiving individual, e.g., his wants, emotions, and mental sets, as he strives to construct a meaningful world.

GUIDE 2: *Cognitions develop into systems in accordance with the principles of learning and stimulus organization*

The separate cognitions of the individual about objects and persons in his world develop

. . . Fear infuses cognition: BOX 2.5

Seymour Feshbach and Robert D. Singer, psychologists at the University of Pennsylvania, studied how fear affects the way individuals form cognitions about another person.

Two experimental groups and one control group were used. All subjects (college students) were told that the experiment was a study of the effect of distraction upon the accuracy of one's judgment of other people, and that after seeing a film showing a young man performing a variety of mechanical assembly tasks they would be asked to judge his personality.

The subjects in the two experimental groups were given eight painful electric shocks while watching the film. The control subjects were not shocked.

After the showing of the film, two measures of the subjects' evaluation of the stimulus person in the film were secured: (1) General Fear Judgment score—a measure of the degree to which the stimulus person was judged by the college students to be generally fearful or anxious; (2) Specific Fear Judgment score—a measure of the degree to which the stimulus person was judged to be fearful or anxious in the specific situation portrayed in the film.

The results are shown in the following table. Note that both of the experimental groups judged the stimulus person to be more generally fearful than did the control group. The judgments of amount of specific fear in the film situation were in the same direction but were less striking.

Scale	Control group	Experimental group I	Experimental group II
General fear (24 items)	55.9	68.9	74.2
Specific fear (4 items)	8.5	9.7	11.2

The investigators conclude: "The results, when considered as a whole, lend substantial support to the hypothesis that the arousal of fear results in a tendency to perceive another person as fearful and anxious. . . ."

Feshbach, S., and Singer, R. D. The effects of fear arousal and suppression of fear upon social perception. J. abnorm. soc. Psychol., *1957, 55, 283–288.*

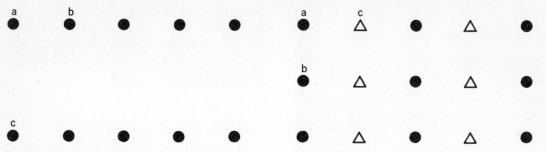

FIGURE 2.1

FIGURE 2.2

into *systems* of cognitions. It is these systems that direct the social actions of the individual.

If we are to know how systems of cognitions develop, we must first understand why an individual will organize his cognitions in such a way that object A is grouped with object B into one common cognitive structure rather than with object C. Why, for example, do some people have a cognitive system in which socialism and Christianity are organized together, while other people have a cognitive system in which socialism and atheism are found together?

One approach to an understanding of the development of cognitive systems emphasizes the stimulus determinants of grouping. Another approach emphasizes the role of experience in grouping.

STIMULUS FACTORS AND GROUPING

Experimental studies of visual perception have demonstrated that proximity (nearness in space or time) and similarity are important organizing factors. Figure 2.1 illustrates that in simple perception those objects which are close to each other in space tend to be organized together in perception. Dot *a* is perceived as belonging with dot *b* rather than with dot *c* simply because *a* is closer to *b* than it is to *c*. Figure 2.2 illustrates the principle of similarity. Here, dot *a* will be organized with dot *b* rather than with dot *c* because *a* is more similar to *b* than it is to *c*. Proximity in time also works in very much the same way. The birth of a two-headed calf

occurring at the same time as a calamitous flood can be organized together as an indication of the work of the Devil. An increase in the divorce rate of a country, occurring about the same time as a turning of artists to pure abstractionism, may be joined together by some moralists as a sign of a deteriorating society.

LEARNING AND GROUPING

The way in which we group objects to form larger cognitive systems is also determined by our experiences. Thus, for example, a zoologist, because of his professional training, might select out in perception, when viewing a new species of animal, the presence or absence of mammaries. All animals having this anatomical feature will be perceived by him as similar, and so horses, human beings, and whales will be organized into a common cognitive system—"mammals." Other people may emphasize the differences among these instances of land animals, human beings, and "fish" and therefore will not group them into a single cognitive system.

CULTURE AND GROUPING. The specific cues to which we pay major attention and which therefore determine our cognitive systems are largely determined by our culture. Thus, if our culture emphasizes signs of wealth, we will perceive these cues most readily and will group people according to similarity of "wealth signs"—the kind of houses they live in (e.g., the "used-brick set"), the automobiles they ride in (e.g., the "station-wagon set"), the schools they send their children to (e.g., the "prep school set"). If a culture emphasizes skin color, we will tend to group people into Negroes and whites; if a culture emphasizes the importance of tattoo marks, people who have similar tattoo marks will be seen as belonging together.

The concepts which the individual has learned determine the groupings which he imposes on the objects in his world. Bousfield and Cohen [1955] have demonstrated the role of concepts in grouping, or, as they term it, "associative clustering." In their experiments, names of objects belonging to different categories were presented in random order, e.g., bayonet, ferret, mandolin, cow, carbine, piano. The subjects were then tested for retention after an interval of time. It was found that there was a tendency to recall the words in a sequence that was organized into related categories, e.g., bayonet, carbine; ferret, cow; mandolin, piano.

CAUSE AND EFFECT

Perhaps one of the most important kinds of cognitive system is the *causal* system, that is, our perception of two objects or events in a cause-and-effect relation. Parents may be perceived as the "cause" of juvenile delinquency; the big oil companies, as the "cause" of international discord; the current political administration, as the "cause" of every national difficulty and calamity. What determines which cause will be organized together with which effect? This is an extremely important question because so much of our social action is shaped by the way we perceive cause and effect.

PROXIMITY AND CAUSAL SYSTEMS. In a new situation or in an ambiguous one, our immediate perception of cause and effect is largely determined by the temporal coincidence of two events. Duncker [1945], in his analysis of the thinking process, gives some compelling illustrations of how proximity may determine our perception of causation:

Someone comes home of an evening. A gust of wind slams the door behind him. At the same moment at the other end of the corridor, the light goes on in a room whose door is ajar. Although one knew ever so well that no causal connection exists between the door's blowing shut, and the light's going on, that rather someone in that room has turned on the light, by chance at exactly the same moment—still he would be unable to escape the compelling impression of causal relations . . . *the time and place of cause coincide phenomenally with the time and place of the effect.*

SIMILARITY AND CAUSAL SYSTEM. For an illustration of the factor of similarity in the development of a causal system, we can again quote from Duncker:

At least as important for man's dealing with causation as those spatial and temporal correspondences of *position* are certain correspondences of *form* between cause and effect. . . . An example of temporal correspondence of form: the rhythm of the sounds of knocking corresponds to the rhythm of the motions of knocking . . . heavy things make "heavy" noises, dainty things move daintily.

On a more complicated level, as in the perception of "human causation," Heider [1944] in his very helpful analysis of the perception of causality points out that the perception of responsibility (e.g., the attribution of a crime to a person) can be due to several types of similarity:

A crime can be blamed on a person because of a physical similarity; "he looks as if he could have committed this crime." Or he can be held responsible for it because of "spiritual" similarity, that is, a similarity between a crime as a moral event and the natural disposition of the "responsible". . . .

In his discussion, Heider refers to an early experiment by Zillig [1928] to illustrate this point. In that experiment two groups of children performed calisthenic exercises before an audience of their classmates. One of the performing groups was composed of children who

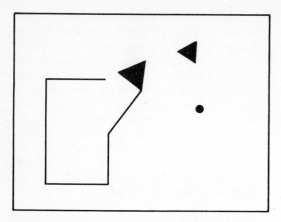

FIGURE 2.3: A still from an animated cartoon used in a study of the perception of causality. The two triangles and the disk move around and in and out of the rectangle through the opening in its upper right-hand corner. [Heider and Simmel, 1944.]

were almost uniformly disliked by their classmates, and the other group, of children who were liked. The experimenter had trained the liked group to make mistakes deliberately and the disliked group to perform the calisthenics letter-perfect. At the end of the two performances the experimenter discovered that the audience had "seen" the disliked group as having made the mistakes. A mistake, it appears, is much more likely to be organized together with disliked people than with liked people. As Heider says, "A bad act is easily connected with a bad person." The organization of a cause-and-effect system is influenced by our value judgments and our emotional reactions.

COMPLEX STIMULUS PATTERNS AND CAUSAL SYSTEMS. Heider and Simmel [1944] have experimentally shown that the movements of discrete, inanimate objects are spontaneously organized into cause-and-effect systems. They showed an animated cartoon in which three geometric figures—a large triangle, a smaller triangle, and a disk—moved around and in and out of a large rectangle (see Figure 2.3). When subjects were asked to report what they saw, their responses revealed two conspicuous

tendencies. First, they did not simply report the objective movements of the figures; they interpreted the movements of the figures in causal terms. The objects were seen as fighting, chasing, attacking, fleeing, etc. Second, their descriptions were overwhelmingly animistic. The figures were described as human beings engaged in interpersonal behavior events, e.g., two men in rivalry for a girl, or family conflict between parents and child. In the drama of the figures, the large triangle was seen by a majority as aggressive, mean and bullying, while the smaller triangle appeared as heroic and defiant. The circle was predominantly viewed as fearful, timid, and female. The use of animistic language in describing the movements of the figures clearly suggests the role of learning in the perceptions of the subjects.

(For an experimental attempt to specify the particular stimulus conditions which determine whether or not causal action will be perceived, see Box 2.6.)

SOME SOCIAL IMPLICATIONS. The politician, among others, seems to be aware of the role of such factors as proximity and similarity in the perception of causality. In a critical political or economic situation, the politician may refuse a leading position in the government because he knows that the coincidental facts of his being in power and the national calamity will tend to be seen by many people as causally related—no matter how conclusively he tries to demonstrate that he was not at fault.

This tendency to group objects or events on the basis of proximity or similarity is a universal one. It is not something that only the unsophisticated do. This does not mean that we can never change our perceptions of causality and integrate into a common system objects and events not originally perceived as linked. Nor does it mean that we cannot come to perceive proximal and similar events as causally unrelated. But it does mean that initially and prior to any corrections, our cognitions of cause and effect tend to be organ-

BOX 2.6: *Cause and effect—the inevitable experience*

The Belgian psychologist Albert Michotte has carried out a large number of laboratory studies of the stimulus conditions for the perception of causality. In one study, he showed subjects two small rectangles moving toward or away from each other under varying conditions of speed, direction, and distance. Certain sequences of movement consistently resulted in the perception of cause and effect; others did not.

Sequence 1. Object A moves toward and reaches B, which remains stationary. When A moves rapidly, the subject perceives it as "striking" B; when A moves slowly, it is perceived as "gently joining," "touching," or "uniting" with B.

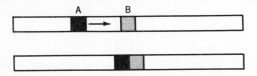

Sequence 2. Object A reaches B and stops; B begins to move. If A's rate of approach is faster than the subsequent motion of B, the moving away of B is seen as caused by A and is sometimes interpreted as anger toward A. However, if A's rate of approach is slower than B's subsequent motion, B's movement is seen as autonomous flight, which is sometimes interpreted as fear of A. This is the impression produced when the duration of contact between A and B is short. When the contact is of longer duration "the impression produced is often interpreted in the sense of a momentary agreement between two accomplices who meet, but which gives place to a disagreement, followed by separation."

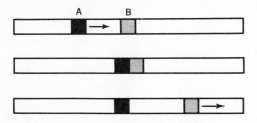

Sequence 3. Object B begins to move after being touched by A, and the two continue to move together at the same speed and in a common direction. If a short pause occurs after contact, the sequence of movement is perceived as a friendly "getting together." If there is no pause, and A approaches B slowly with a marked increase in rate of movement after the period of contact, A is seen as "carrying B off by brute force."

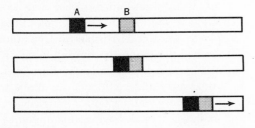

(Continued)

Michotte's findings have important implications for the perception of cause and effect in social actions. We see that the tendency to perceive cause and effect is basic to man's cognitive processes. If this is true of the perception of moving rectangles, how much truer it must be of the perception of social events which involve the actions of human beings. To ask people to refrain from assigning blame, responsibility, or credit for events until "all the facts are in" is to ask them to do a very difficult thing. Our cognitive organizing processes *force* us to jump to conclusions about causes. No matter how cogently the logician may argue against the concept of cause, our *perception* will pay him no heed.

Michotte, A. La perception de la causalité. (*2nd ed.*) *Louvain: Publications Universitaires de Louvain, 1954.*

ized in terms of objects or events which are perceived as similar or in proximity.

TO RECAPITULATE

The separate cognitions of the individual about objects and persons in his world develop into systems of cognitions. The particular grouping of separate cognitions to form such systems is determined both by stimulus factors and by personal factors, e.g., individual interests and experiences. In so far as such individual experiences are culturally shaped, members of a culture will tend to form similar cognitive systems. One of the socially most significant kinds of cognitive system is the grouping of objects or events into cause-and-effect relations. These causal groupings can be understood partly in terms of factors of proximity and similarity, and partly in terms of more complex features of the stimulus pattern.

GUIDE 3: *The properties of a cognition are influenced by the system of which it is a part*

When several cognitions are grouped to form a system, the properties of each cognition undergo change. A suggestion about a possible way that a cognitive system influences

its component cognitions is found in the part-whole relation in simple visual perception.

We usually perceive the drawing in Figure 2.4 as a simple, two-dimensional figure of three lines meeting at a center point *o*. Each angle made by any two adjacent lines, say angle *aoc,* can be described as a part of the whole figure. This angle is usually perceived as an obtuse angle (i.e., as larger than a right angle)—a veridical perception. What would happen to our perception of angle *aoc* if we added a few lines, thus changing the *whole* figure without in any way changing the lines that make up angle *aoc?* The answer is immediately clear if we look at Figure 2.5. Now we perceive angle *aoc* as a right angle. Although we have not done anything physically to angle *aoc,* it "looks" different. It looks different because the *whole* figure of which angle *aoc* is a part is now seen as tridimensional, as a cube.

Suppose you were told that your neighbor insisted that he perceived angle *aoc* of Figure 2.5 as an obtuse angle rather than as a right angle. Would not his perception appear completely incomprehensible to you until you learned that he was permitted to see only *part* of Figure 2.5 (i.e., only the lines making up angle *aoc*) and could not see the whole figure? The generalization is simple, but, as we shall see, it may have many profound implications in social psychology. We cannot understand an individual's perception unless we know the properties of the system in which the perception exists for *him*.

The influence of the whole on its parts is also seen in *assimilation* and *contrast* experiments in visual perception. The perceived similarity among parts of a whole will tend to be exaggerated when the physical differences are relatively small—assimilation. The perceived *dissimilarity* among parts of a whole will tend to be exaggerated when the physical differences are relatively large—contrast. Thus, a series of black dots, in a single row, will all appear equally black despite the existence of minor differences in physical intensity among them. Each dot, as a part of the row of dots, is assimilated, and the actual differences in physical intensity are not usually perceived. What would happen if the physical intensity of one dot in the series were made appreciably greater than that of the others? Through contrast, the dot would be perceived as even brighter than called for by its actual physical intensity. Again we see that the perception of a single object is determined by the relations which exist between that single object and the other objects which go into making up an organized system of perceptions. And again we can draw the same generalization: To understand what a person sees when he looks at one object it is frequently essential to know the perceptual properties of the system of which this object is a single member.

What is true for the relatively simple instances of visual perception just discussed may be equally true for the more complex cognitions which guide and control our social actions. Our mental world is typically made up of systems of cognitions; it is rare indeed to find a single cognition "living a life of its own." And, therefore, we can rarely understand a man's cognition with respect to any object in his social world unless we also know something about the properties of the system in which the cognition exists for *him*. This generalization, if valid, may go a long way in

formulating a basic description of many psychological processes important in social behavior. Among other things it can be helpful in aiding us to understand why we are frequently "biased" or "unjust" in our judgments of people, social practices, institutions, foreign cultures, etc.

We can take, for an example, the cognitions many Americans have about their fellow Americans who belong to the so-called minority groups or foreign peoples. Because so many Americans ascribe a *stereotyped* set of personality traits to such groups as Jews, Negroes, Catholics, or Russians, judgments of individual members of these groups often show typical and stereotyped biases.

Thus, many Americans, through the operation of the assimilation phenomenon, tend to overestimate the shrewdness of a particular Jew, or the inscrutability of a somewhat reticent Russian—because they believe Jews to be shrewd and Russians to be inscrutable. Through contrast, they tend to overestimate the intelligence of an intelligent Negro and to overestimate the liberalism of a Catholic who is liberal in some of his religious views. Again, the reason appears to be due to the stereotyped notion that Negroes are stupid and that Catholics hold extremely conservative religious beliefs.

The critical point to remember is that this bias in perceiving people is not a fault found

FIGURE 2.4

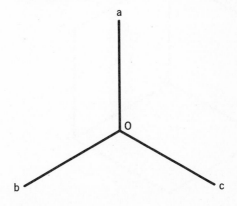

only among the prejudiced many. It is found in all men and is due to the very nature of our perceptual processes. Our perception of angle *aoc* as a right angle, our judgment of the shrewdness of a particular Jew, our estimate of a particular Russian's inscrutability, and our appraisal of a Negro's intelligence are but special instances of the general principle that the properties of an object are determined in large measure by the properties of the system of which it is a part (see Box 2.7).

FRAME OF REFERENCE

The term *frame of reference* denotes the larger contextual system with respect to which an object is viewed or judged. Illustrations of the influence of frame of reference upon the perception of objects can be found in simple psychophysical experiments and in more complex social judgments. Thus, for example, Wever and Zener [1928] have shown that when subjects are required to judge the weights of a series of objects in categories "light," "heavy," etc., the judgment of each weight is a function of the total series of weights which serves as a frame of reference. If the series is changed from a generally light one to a generally heavy one, the same weight

FIGURE 2.5

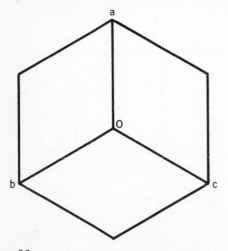

that was formerly judged "heavy" will now be judged "light." The judged weight of an object is determined by the company it keeps.

Similar findings are obtained when the judgments to be made are of a much more complicated sort and have social content. Thus, McGarvey [1943] showed that the introduction of a high prestige occupation as a standard significantly lowered the judgments of the "social prestige" of a series of occupations. The higher the prestige value of the occupation given as the standard, the greater the downward shift in the ratings.

It will be seen that the widely used concept of frame of reference is but another way of describing the influence of the whole on its parts as expressed in Guide 3.

ADAPTATION LEVEL

Still another approach to the part-whole principle of Guide 3 is Helson's [1959] theory of *adaptation level.* He first developed this theory in an attempt to understand and predict the "universality of shifts in scale-value with change in comparison-stimulus."

Briefly, Helson's formulation can be stated in the following way: The adaptation level is represented by the stimulus to which the individual either does not respond or responds in an indifferent or neutral manner. The adaptation level has been shown by Helson to be a weighted log mean of three classes of stimuli: (1) the stimulus which is being responded to and which is in the focus of attention; (2) all the immediately present stimuli which form the context or background for the focal stimulus; and (3) residuals from past experience with similar stimuli. Any given stimulus is judged in terms of the relevant adaptation level. For example, whether an object is judged "light" or "heavy" depends upon whether its actual weight is lower or higher than the weight represented by the adaptation level. Adaptation levels change as a function of such factors as the frequency of presentation of new stimuli, their intensity,

BOX 2.7: *Compatriot and foreigner*

Jerome S. Bruner of Harvard University and Howard V. Perlmutter of the Menninger Foundation in Kansas present some interesting data to support the generalization that our judgments of individuals are strongly influenced by our notions about the groups to which these individuals belong. The study is also of interest because of the international sample of subjects who participated in it.

University students from Boston, Paris, Dijon, Berlin, Hanover, and Cologne were given brief written sketches of fictitious persons (of a specified nationality) and were told that they would be asked to form impressions of the personalities of these fictitious persons. For example, one of the sketches they were given ran as follows:

He is a very typical American businessman (French businessman, German businessman). There is general agreement among those who know him that he is intelligent, energetic, and well-adjusted. Now 42 years old, he is married and lives in a large city in the United States (France, Germany).

The students were next instructed to choose from a list of 38 traits those which "best characterized the person described." Finally, they were asked to indicate why they chose each trait.

Some groups of students were presented with a single person (the "single-impression groups"), and others with three persons of three different nationalities (the "triple-impression groups"). The investigators assumed that when three persons were presented, alike in all respects except their nationality, the nationality of each would be noticed more clearly by the student judge than if only one person of a particular nationality were presented.

The following table shows the mean number of times that the students indicated that *nationality* was the reason they ascribed a particular trait to the fictitious person. Note that the triple-impression groups based their trait choices on nationality more often than did the single-impression groups. It seems clear that when nationality is salient in the mind of the judge, his stereotype of that nationality will influence his judgment of the person.

	AMERICAN STUDENTS		FRENCH STUDENTS		GERMAN STUDENTS	
	Foreign fictitious person	American fictitious person	Foreign fictitious person	French fictitious person	Foreign fictitious person	German fictitious person
Single-impression	3.3	1.3	4.6	2.8	3.9	1.4
Triple-impression	5.2	4.3	6.8	6.8	6.6	4.5

It is also interesting to note that when the students were judging compatriots (e.g., a French student judging the fictitious French businessman) they tended to rely less upon nationality as a reason for their judgments than when they were judging a foreigner. Apparently the more we know about a group the less we are apt to characterize individual members of that group by simplex group stereotypes. But again, it should be noted that even if we restrict our attention to the compatriot groups, the triple-impression groups still leaned more heavily upon nationality than did the single-impression groups. It appears that we cannot escape the effect of group stereotypes in our judgment of people.

Bruner, J. S., and Perlmutter, H. V. Compatriot and foreigner: a study of impression formation in three countries. J. abnorm. soc. Psychol., 1957, 55, 253–260.

size, nearness, emotional impact, and interest or excitement value for the individual.

Adaptation-level theory can aid our understanding of the effectiveness of certain propaganda techniques. For example, one might ask what would be the effect of publicizing *extreme* statements concerning any social issue? Let us choose disarmament, and let us assume that the publicly stated opinions about disarmament range from a strong militaristic position opposed to any kind of disarmament to a position which asserts the desirability of seeking an international ban on nuclear bombs. Presumably, the average person subjected to such differing opinions would soon achieve an adaptation level with respect to this issue somewhere between the two extreme statements given above. He will now judge any opinion in terms of this adaptation level. And the position of seeking an international ban on the nuclear bomb will be seen perhaps as a pacifistic one. Now let us assume that some public figure or organization bombards the public with statements proposing complete and immediate unilateral disarmament. The adaptation-level theory would suggest that if such a statement were publicized frequently, and with intensity and emotional impact, the average citizen's adaptation level would change, and he would now regard an international agreement to ban nuclear bombs as a middle-of-the-road position—neither militaristic nor pacifistic.

TO RECAPITULATE

Cognitions do not exist in isolation, but in larger cognitive systems. The properties of a given cognition depend in part upon the particular nature of the inclusive system; the "same" cognition embedded in different systems will have different properties. This part-whole relation is manifested in simple perception as well as in more complex cognitions. That the whole influences the part is shown, for example, in the phenomena of assimilation and contrast, in which the perceived characteristics of an object may be exaggerated in one direction or another, depending upon its relation to the whole. The concepts of frame of reference and adaptation level may be seen as ways of describing the dependence of a part upon the whole.

GUIDE 4: *Cognitive change is typically initiated by changes in the individual's information and wants*

It is a commonplace that as new information becomes available to a person, changes in his thinking may occur. But to the psychologist this observation is just the beginning of an understanding of cognitive change. In the first place, the same bit of new information can cause quite different changes in similar cognitions. The problem of how new information is incorporated within cognitive systems, how, for example, different people handle new or contradictory information, is an important one, which we will discuss under the next guide. In the second place, just as it is a commonplace that as new information becomes available to a person, changes in his thinking may occur, so is it a commonplace that new information does not *always* bring about cognitive change and that sometimes cognitive change—or the drive toward cognitive change—seems to be initiated by other events than new information. Frequently cognitive change is initiated by changes in the individual's *wants* rather than in his information.

Changes in the wants of the individual and changes in his information are, in most cases, interdependent. As people acquire new wants, they are led to seek out new information, to learn more. As they learn more about a subject, new wants may be induced, thus impelling them to learn still more. It is also possible, of course, that changes in wants may inhibit the seeking of more information.

In any event, it is clear that the problem of wants and cognitive change is a complicated one, and it is to this problem that we now turn.

CHANGES IN WANTS

In this section, we are anticipating the detailed discussion of the influences of wants and goals upon behavior which will be found in Chapter 3 and the discussion of the effects of the blocking of want satisfaction in Chapter 4. However, the relations among wants, goals, obstructions, and cognitive change are so intimate and important that it is essential to begin any systematic formulation of the process of cognitive change with a statement of these relations.

As we shall see in Chapter 4, the wants and goals of the individual continuously develop and change. If the individual encounters blockage to the satisfaction of a want, cognitive change will tend to take place. Blocks to a goal may be of many different kinds, simple or complex. The block may be a physical barrier, it may be a long waiting period, it may be an unsatisfactory personal relationship which prevents the achievement of a particular goal.

The nature of the cognitive change that will enable the individual to remove the block and achieve his goal may also vary from the very simple to the very complex. The nature of the change may even involve the differentiation of a major system into component parts. Apprehending all members of the Democratic party, for example, as constituting one major undifferentiated group may be adequate for a person who wishes to elect his party to power. However, for the attainment of certain other goals, such as the election of Congressmen friendly to desegregation, so undifferentiated a cognitive system may be inadequate, and the change that is required may involve breaking up the system, Democratic party, into subsystems: Northern liberal Democrats, Southern Democrats, etc.

WANTS, BLOCKS, AND DISTORTED COGNITIVE ORGANIZATIONS. While the existence of a goal and a block to that goal typically initiate cognitive change, it must not be assumed that the resulting cognitive change will be adaptive in every case. Frequently the effect of frustration upon cognitive change can be distorting, in the sense that the resulting cognitive change diverges radically from reality. Thus, as we shall see in Chapter 4, the frustration of wants can lead to fantasies and bizarre thinking which do not aid the individual in coping with the situation.

Whether a blocked goal will lead to a distorted cognitive system or to an adequate and useful one seems to depend upon a number of factors, among which are the strength of the want and the nature of the individual's perception of the block to the goal.

STRENGTH OF THE WANT. Two experiments, one with the problem-solving behavior of the chimpanzee and the other with human subjects, give some illuminating illustrations of the relation between the strength of wants and the adequacy of the cognitive reorganization that takes place in response to those wants.

Birch [1945] studied the effects of different degrees of food deprivation on the problem-solving ability of six young chimpanzees. The problems given to the animals were the familiar string pattern and stick problems used in experimental work with these animals. In these problems, the solution requires the perception of the relations between crossed strings and food objects attached to some of the strings; it requires the ability to perceive roundabout paths, the use of sticks far removed from the goal objects as tools to rake in the food, etc. The animals were deprived of food for 2, 6, 12, 24, 36, or 48 hours.

The results of this experiment clearly indicated that with a very long period of food deprivation the problem-solving efficiency of the animals was reduced considerably. Birch interprets this finding as follows:

BOX 2.8: *Wanting and thinking*

David C. McClelland, a psychologist at Harvard University, has reviewed experimental and clinical studies of the effect of varying levels of want strength upon thinking and imagining.

The sequence of cognitive events as wants increase in intensity has been hypothetically schematized in the following figure adapted from McClelland.

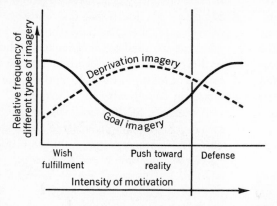

At very low levels of motivation, the individual experiences simple wish-fulfilling desires—his imagery is of goal objects. With an increase in strength of motivation, there is a "push to reality." The person becomes increasingly aware of the want and of the block and thinks of various ways of coping with the block to satisfy his want. His thinking comes to be dominated by experiences of deprivation. If the want becomes still more intense, the concern of the individual with his deprivation arouses painful anxiety which leads to defensive imagery. Goal-directed behavior is abandoned. Bizarre imagery appears. McClelland gives this example:

> Let us suppose that a man is driving through a desert when his car breaks down miles from the nearest water. In the beginning he may not be particularly thirsty and he imagines that he will be picked up by some passing motorist. As the hours under the hot sun go by, his thirst increases and he begins to imagine delicious cool drinks, thick milk shakes or ice cubes tinkling in a glass. As more hours pass, his thirst becomes more acute and the unrealistic images give way to an intense preoccupation with how thirsty he is and the absence of any sign of water in the desert. He may now begin to think up various schemes for getting water out of his car or to search in the surrounding territory for a spring, but he no longer spends much time in idle dreams of cooling drinks. Instead, he is active, anxious, and very conscious of his thirst. If we assume that many hours pass by, his thirst increasing in intensity all the time, his anxiety may become so acute and so painful that the bounds of reality begin to break down and he may begin to have hallucinations or see mirages of water in the distance or think that he actually hears the tinkle of ice cubes in a glass. Eventually, he may, as it were, lose consciousness of his thirst altogether and become delirious, existing in a fantasy world in which his needs are being gratified. . . . It is as if increasing awareness were at first useful in preparing the organism to satisfy the need in question, and then beyond a certain point of intensity it becomes so painful that there is a need for defense and repression.

McClelland, D. C. Personality. New York: Holt, Rinehart, and Winston, Inc., 1951.

When motivation is very low, the animals are easily diverted from the problem by extraneous factors. . . . Under conditions of very intense motivation, the animals concentrated upon the goal to the relative exclusion of other features of the situation which were essential to the solution of the problem. Also, the frequent occurrence of frustration responses, such as tantrums and screaming . . . hindered the animals in their problem-solving efforts. Those animals . . . under the intermediate conditions of motivational intensity behaved in a manner which indicated that, although the food acted as a central factor in determining the direction in which they organized new patterns of response, they were not so dominated by . . . the food that they were incapable of responding to other relevant features of the problem situation.

In the classic experiment of Dembo [Lewin and Dembo, 1931], University of Berlin students were given the task of reaching for a flower, which was four feet away from a marked square on the floor in which the subject stood and out of which he was not allowed to move. Although there were only two possible ways of reaching the flower, the subjects were told that there were three ways. After using the two available methods, the subjects found themselves in a frustrating situation. As time went on and their frustration became more severe, all sorts of bizarre cognitions were reported by the subjects. One subject, for example, "saw" the room as filled with water and the flower floating to her. Rings, which had been placed near the square, were picked up again and again in a futile attempt to solve the problem. (See Box 2.8, which throws further light on the relation between intensity of wants and cognition.)

PERCEIVING THE BLOCK. The correct perception of the block frequently offers difficulties. Sometimes the individual *does not perceive the block at all*—he does not know, for example, why he cannot apply himself to his work. In such a case there will be no change

in his thinking about the block; only his thoughts about himself will change. More frequently, however, the *wrong* object is perceived as the block. Thus, a man may think he has been refused a promotion because his boss has religious prejudice, whereas, in fact, his failure to advance is due to his own lack of competence. His cognitions of his boss will change, but there will be no change in his beliefs about himself.

SOME SOCIAL IMPLICATIONS. The significance for social behavior of the relations among wants, blocks, and cognitive change cannot be overemphasized. We must constantly remember that *cognition is not a cold affair but is intimately related to wants and goals.* Wants not only initiate, but also determine the resultants of learning and thinking.

It is difficult to teach an individual to adopt a new belief concerning national sovereignty, for example, unless we can first produce a situation in which his old concept of national sovereignty is no longer adequate for the achievement of his goals. On the other hand, if people are too highly motivated, it is dangerous to assume that they will achieve an adequate reorganization of their social concepts. The angry man is not the best social planner. New and workable economic and political systems cannot be expected of people on a chronic starvation diet. The brave new world cannot be built by the deprived people of the old world. Such people can become violent, like Birch's 48-hour starved chimpanzee; they can engage in fantasy and achieve distorted cognitive changes, like Dembo's students; but they will probably not achieve a workable and efficient solution of major social problems. The maxim, "Necessity is the mother of invention," is true only if the necessity is not too great.

TO RECAPITULATE

One main factor that initiates cognitive change is the blockage of want satisfaction.

Whether the resultant cognitive change is or is not adaptive depends upon the strength of the want, and the accuracy with which the block to the goal is perceived.

Another main factor initiating cognitive change is change in the individual's information. But mere *exposure* to new information does not guarantee that the individual will pay attention to or accept the new information. Despite new information, his feelings, emotions, and wants may prevent cognitive change.

GUIDE 5: *Cognitive change is in part governed by the characteristics of pre-existing cognitive systems*

The degree and manner in which changes in wants and information produce changes in cognition depend upon the characteristics of the pre-existing cognitive system. Three main systemic characteristics are *multiplexity, consonance*, and *interconnectedness*.

MULTIPLEXITY

Some individuals may have a simple, undifferentiated cognitive system relating to, say, religious objects and events. All religions are seen as alike; all religious people are grouped together without any differentiation. Other individuals may have highly complex and differentiated cognitive systems relating to religion. They may differentiate between "good" and "bad" religions, between Catholics, Protestants, Jews, Moslems, etc. They may differentiate the organized church from the spiritual creed of any religion; the rank-and-file members from the official clergy. These differences in the number and variety of cognitions incorporated in one cognitive system define the dimension of *multiplexity* of the system. There is evidence that this dimension has some degree of generality for the individual (see Boxes 2.9 and 2.10).

CONSONANCE

The various cognitive elements that make up a whole system are necessarily interrelated with one another; it is for just this reason that it is appropriate to describe them as forming a system. The specific nature of such interrelations varies. Elements may be in close agreement with one another, being congruous, harmonious, "fitting." Or they may be to some degree in disagreement, being incongruous or contradictory. Some cognitive systems are characterized by a high over-all degree of such internal harmony. Thus, some individuals may have a well-knit set of beliefs about religion, in which each religious cognition "fits" with all the others. To use our previous illustration, the person with a multiplex religious cognitive system may believe that the hierarchy of the church, the official religious dogma of the church, and the clergy of the church are all harmoniously interrelated around the goal of bringing peace on earth and good will toward men. Other individuals may have less harmonious sets of religious beliefs—systems in which the religious dogma and the clergy, for example, are designed to bring peace on earth and good will toward men, but in which the hierarchy is seen as primarily interested in gaining temporal power—at the expense of universal good will and even, perhaps, at the risk of provoking conflict and war.

These differences in degree of congruity or incongruity of interrelated cognitions define the degree of *cognitive consonance*.

Other things being equal, simplex systems tend to be higher in consonance than multiplex systems. This follows from the fact that a greater number of elements provides a greater probability for disagreement among them, and from the fact that multiplex systems can accommodate more dissonance than can simplex systems. The larger a system, the more "distant" the contradictory elements can be from one another. Indeed, multiplex sys-

BOX 2.9: *Multiplex mind*

James Bieri and Edward Blacker, while at Harvard University, reported an experiment which suggests that degree of multiplexity is relatively consistent over different cognitive systems.

Cognitive multiplexity in the perception of persons was measured by means of the Repertory Test (Rep Test) devised by George Kelly. In this test, the subject is given the names of three persons known to him and asked to sort the three in such a manner that two are seen as alike or similar in some important personal quality and different from the third. The subject is then asked to state the similarity between the two sorted together and to give the opposite of this characteristic. A second set of three persons is next presented and the subject is asked to sort them in the same way.

In this study six persons were used in the Rep Test. These six persons were sorted by the subjects (40 male university undergraduates) in all possible combinations of three, so that no three names appeared together in a sort more than once. A total of 20 sorts was thus obtained. The multiplexity of the subject's perceptions of these persons was measured by counting the number of different perceptions (NDP) he gave in the 20 sorts.

Cognitive multiplexity in the perception of nonhuman objects was measured by means of a modified Rorschach ink-blot procedure which yielded two general measures of multiplexity: determinant multiplexity and content multiplexity. Determinant multiplexity was scored in four ways by counting: (1) the total number of different determinants used (e.g., form, movement, shading); (2) the total number of cards on which the same determinant was used at least twice; (3) the total number of cards on which the same determinant was used at least three times; (4) the total number of cards on which three different determinants were used. Note that *high* scores on 1 and 4 reflect greater multiplexity; *low* scores on 2 and 3 reflect greater multiplexity.

Content multiplexity was scored in two ways by counting (1) the total number of responses to the same card which were repeated; (2) the total number of cards on which a response was repeated. Note that low scores on both of these measures reflect greater multiplexity.

The correlations between the Rorschach multiplexity scores and multiplexity scores in the perception of people (NDP) were as follows:

Rorschach determinant measures	*NDP*
1. Number of determinants used	+.27
2. Number of cards with two determinants repeated	−.40
3. Number of cards with three determinants repeated	−.39
4. Number of cards with three different determinants	+.42

Rorschach content measures	
1. Number of responses repeated	−.44
2. Number of cards on which a response was repeated	−.50

All the intercorrelations between Rorschach multiplexity scores and multiplexity in the perception of persons are significant and in a direction consonant with the hypothesis that multiplexity is a *general* characteristic of the individual's cognitive systems. Verbal fluency, as measured by a vocabulary test, was found not to be responsible for the intercorrelations.

Bieri, J., and Blacker, E. The generality of cognitive complexity in the perception of people and ink blots. J. abnorm. soc. Psychol., 1956, 53, 112–117.

Kelly, G. A. The psychology of personal constructs. New York: Norton, 1955.

tems tend to be made up of various subsystems, and the contradictions that exist between elements in *different* subsystems produce less dissonance in the total system than do contradictions that occur within the *same*

subsystems. For example, our man with the multiplex religious cognitive system may believe that the Catholic Church provides a truer insight into Divine Purpose than does the Jewish religion. Yet he may also believe

BOX 2.10: *The wide and multiplex mind*

Thomas F. Pettigrew, a psychologist at Harvard University, has developed a measure of a cognitive variable discovered by Bruner and Rodrigues. Using such standard laboratory equipment as color-mixing wheels and audio-oscillators, the latter investigators asked their subjects to select the darkest and lightest or the highest and lowest of a wide variety of categories, such as the brightness of an overcast sky and the pitch of a female singing voice. They found that their subjects tended to be consistently broad, medium, or narrow in their category widths.

Stimulated by this finding, Pettigrew developed an objectively scored paper-and-pencil test (the C-W scale) which requires subjects to estimate the extremes of 20 diverse categories from the length of whales to annual rainfall in Washington, D.C. The scale was found to have substantial validity. The rank-order correlation between scale scores and rankings of category width determined by laboratory procedures similar to those used by Bruner and Rodrigues was .57.

Scores on the C-W scale correlate significantly with two different measures of cognitive multiplexity: Rokeach's "narrow-mindedness" task and a "self-concept span" instrument. In the Rokeach "narrow-mindedness" task, subjects are presented with 10 terms (Buddhism, Capitalism, Catholicism, Christianity, Communism, Democracy, Fascism, Judaism, Protestantism, and Socialism). After defining the terms, the subject is asked to write a paragraph indicating how the terms might be interrelated.

Rokeach has delineated three types of categorizers on this task—comprehensive, narrow, and isolated. Comprehensive categorizers organize all ten terms under one concept; narrow categorizers use more than one concept; and isolated categorizers use no integrating concepts. Comprehensive categorizers (or persons capable of organizing multiplex cognitive systems) were found to have significantly broader category widths (as measured by the C-W scale) than narrow and isolated categorizers (or persons who organize more simplex systems).

The "self-concept span" of a sample of 106 male students who had previously taken the C-W scale was determined by counting the number of adjectives on an adjective check list checked as descriptive of the self. As predicted, the self-concept span was related positively to category width.

Category width is a consistent characteristic of individuals—they are consistently broad, medium, or narrow in their category widths relative to other persons. And this cognitive variable is related to the multiplexity of their cognitive systems.

Striking sex differences in category width were found, men having a broader category width than women. This difference manifests itself in early childhood.

Pettigrew, T. F. *The measurement and correlates of category width as a cognitive variable.* J. Pers., *1958*, **26**, *532–544.*

Bruner, J. S., Goodnow, J. J., and Austin, G. A. A study of thinking. *New York: Wiley, 1956.*

Rokeach, M. *A method for studying individual differences in "narrow-mindedness."* J. Pers., *1951*, **20**, *219–233.*

that some Jews are spiritually superior to some Catholics. This discrepancy between elements in the two subsystems, Catholics and Jews, can be accommodated quite easily without disturbing the consonance of the whole religious system. However, a discrepancy within the same subsystem (e.g., the Church hierarchy and the religious dogma of Catholicism being seen to be in conflict, as in our previous example) can have much wider effects, and may call for more radical restructuring of the whole system.

Not only is there variance in degree of consonance among elements of a system, but there is also variance in degree of consonance between that system and other systems with which it is more or less interconnected. Thus, some people's religious beliefs may be harmonious with their economic and political beliefs. A man may believe that his religion, his business practices, and his political behavior are all guided by a set of principles designed to bring peace on earth. Another may show no such consonance. In his religious beliefs, he worships the Prince of Peace; in business, he manufactures armaments; in politics, he believes in the principles of the "war party."

It may appear paradoxical that systems ever have anything less than perfect consonance, for it might be expected that contradictory elements would simply not come together to form a common system. But this view overlooks the fact that cognitive systems are formed in many ways other than by sheer "logic," and that reality itself (which cognition mirrors with varying degrees of veridicality) is contradictory. We know enough about perceptual organization, and such simple learning processes as conditioning, association formation, etc., to know that objects which are contiguous in time and space (with little else in common) may frequently be organized together, or associated to form a single molar unit—whether in perception or in cognition (see page 26).

BALANCE THEORY. One current approach to the study of cognitive consonance which has led to active research is *balance theory*. Stated generally, this theory defines a state of balance as existing in a cognitive system to the extent that the elements of the system form units which have noncontradictory relationships. A noncontradictory relationship is one in which each element "fits" with, is compatible with, is harmonious with, the other elements. What is meant can easily be seen when we consider a lack of simple "logical" relations among elements. For example: "I favor free speech for everyone; this man preaches against civil liberties; I favor muzzling him."

Balance theory asserts that unbalanced cognitive systems tend to shift toward a state of balance. This shift may occur in various ways. Thus, in the above example, the individual may come to approve free speech only for people who espouse democratic principles; or he may come to extend free speech to the man who preaches against civil liberties.

For social psychology, the most significant application of balance theory is concerned with the individual's *affective cognitions* pertaining to people and social objects; that is, the person's own positive or negative evaluations of people and objects, and his cognition of the positive or negative evaluative relations that exist among these people and objects. Heider [1958] has made this use of balance theory in presenting a detailed account of the phenomenology of interpersonal relationships. As he points out, in a cognitive system made up of three elements (the triadic system)— the person himself (P) and his perceptions of another person (O), and an object, e.g., the Democratic party (X)—there is *balance* if P likes O, O is perceived as liking X, and P likes X (i.e., all three signs are positive). In common-sense terms: "I like him and he shares my liking for the Democratic party." The system is also balanced, but in quite a different way, if P likes O, O is perceived as disliking X, and P dislikes X (i.e., one positive and two negative signs). "I like him and he shares my dislike for the Democratic party." Finally, the system is balanced in still a third way if P dislikes O, P dislikes X, and O is perceived as liking X (again, one positive and two negative signs). "I dislike him and I'm not surprised that he likes the Democratic party, which I despise."

The triadic system is *unbalanced* if there are two positive relations and one negative one; for example, P likes O, O is perceived as liking X, P dislikes X. Here in common-sense terms we can see the locus of the individual's cognitive imbalance: "How can it be that he, whom I like, can like the Democratic party, which I despise?" The system can obviously be unbalanced in other ways also. Thus, P may like both O and X, but O is perceived as disliking X. "How can it be that he, whom I like, doesn't like the Democratic party, as I do?" Finally, there is a special case of imbalance in which all three relations are negative—P dislikes O and X, O is perceived as disliking X.

To generalize, a system is balanced if there are *no* negative relations or if there is an *even* number of negatives; it is unbalanced if there is only *one* or any other *odd* number of negatives.

Other formulations of balance theory have been offered by Osgood and Tannenbaum [1955], Cartwright and Harary [1956], Festinger [1957], and Newcomb [1959].

As we have seen, balance theory suggests that the cognitive process persistently strives toward cognitive balance; that is, an unbalanced cognitive structure will tend to become a balanced structure. To use our previous example, if I dislike the Democratic party but admire and like my friend who is a fervid Democrat, then, as we have seen, my cognitive system is in a state of imbalance. I can achieve cognitive balance by coming around to the belief that the Democratic party is not as venal as I've always thought it to be, or I can achieve the same end result through an

"agonizing reappraisal" of my friend which leads me to conclude that he is not quite as bright, or honorable, or patriotic as I had always believed him to be.

It is obvious that this process of "balancing" an unbalanced cognitive structure is of immediate importance and concern to the social psychologist, and considerable research on this problem has already been reported. As such research accumulates, it is becoming clear that the process of achieving cognitive balance is far from a simple one. Indeed, balance is often not achieved. This seems to be especially true when cognitive balance can be achieved only by harboring "unpleasant" cognitive systems (see Box 2.11).

INTERCONNECTEDNESS

A cognitive system may exist in isolation from other systems, or it may be interrelated with other systems. For example, in some individuals the cognitive system pertaining to religion may be relatively isolated from their cognitive systems relating to all other matters. In other individuals, the religious system may be part of a larger cluster of cognitive systems—economic, political, philosophical, philanthropic, historical, etc. These differences in degree of such isolation or interrelation define the dimension of *interconnectedness* of the system. When there is a high degree of such interconnectedness, we often speak of the existence of an "ideology."

COGNITIVE SYSTEMS AND COGNITIVE CHANGE

We have pointed out in our discussion of Guide 4 that the same bit of information may have quite different effects as far as cognitive change is concerned. We can now be somewhat more specific on this matter. Whether any new bit of information will bring about cognitive change, and what the nature of the change will be, depend, in large measure, on the degree of multiplexity, consonance, and interconnectedness of the cognitive system

BOX 2.11: *Pleasantness and consistency*

Robert P. Abelson and Milton J. Rosenberg, social psychologists at Yale University, studied the way in which a person, starting with an unbalanced set of cognitions, "thinks" his way through to cognitive balance—or fails to do so—when he is presented with new information.

First, they "implanted" cognitive dilemmas in their subjects. Two groups of subjects were asked to play the role of the owner of a large department store who placed great value on keeping sales at the highest possible volume. The subjects in group I were also instructed to feel positively toward modern art and toward Fenwick, the manager of the rug department. In group II the subjects were instructed to feel negatively toward both modern art and Fenwick. All subjects were then given "facts" to support the following beliefs: Displays of modern art in a department store reduce sales volume; Fenwick plans to mount such a display; Fenwick has a good past record of increasing the volume of sales. Thus the two groups were presented with these dilemmas:

> *Group I:* High volume of sales is desirable; Fenwick is a fine fellow; Fenwick has a past record of increasing sales volume; modern art is very fine; Fenwick is going to display modern art; BUT modern art displays will decrease sales.

> *Group II:* High volume of sales is desirable; Fenwick is not much of a man; modern art is of little value; modern art displays decrease sales; Fenwick plans a modern art display; BUT Fenwick has a past record of increasing sales volume.

The subjects who could successfully play these roles (as tested by various techniques) then read three communications (presumably from three different store officers): the Art-Sales communication that modern art displays *increase* sales volume; the Fenwick-Art communication that Fenwick does *not* plan a modern art display; the Fenwick-Sales communication that Fenwick has *failed*, in the past, to maintain sales volume.

Group I members by accepting the Art-Sales communication could resolve their dilemma without requiring changes in their other beliefs and attitudes (e.g., toward Fenwick, modern art, etc.). But by adopting the Fenwick-Sales communication, they would be required to change their evaluation of Fenwick, of his past record, and of modern art. For group II the communication which could most efficiently resolve the dilemma was the Fenwick-Sales.

It should be clear that when the subjects of the first group accept the belief that modern art is good for sales, the person ends up with a *consistent and pleasant* set of beliefs that good old Fenwick is about to display that good modern art which will increase sales volume! For group II, on the other hand, the acceptance of the Fenwick-Sales communication would lead efficiently and swiftly to a balanced cognitive system, *but one which was unpleasant,* that is, that so-and-so Fenwick, who is planning to do something unpleasant that will hurt sales, actually has injured sales in the past. All the beliefs and attitudes are consistent, but how unpleasant for a store owner!

The results showed quite clearly that most of the members of group I did indeed adopt the simplest solution of their dilemma. They accepted the Art-Sales communication and achieved balance. But the members of group II not only accepted the communication making Fenwick completely negative (the Fenwick-Sales communication) but also tended to accept the one which said that he was *not* going to mount the modern art display (the Fenwick-Art communication). Accepting these two communications, of course, did not lead to balance; actually only 4 of the 18 subjects in this group achieved balance. Apparently, it is better to entertain cognitive *imbalance* than to entertain a consistently *unpleasant* cognitive structure. *(Continued)*

As the experimenters commented, "In resolving cognitive discrepancies, subjects seek not only the attainment of balance and consistency, but also the solution that maximizes potential gain and minimizes potential loss." The satisfaction of wants plays a crucial role in the process of cognitive balance.

Rosenberg, M. J., and Abelson, R. P. An analysis of cognitive balancing. In M. J. Rosenberg et al., Attitude organization and change. *New Haven, Conn.: Yale Univer. Press, 1960.*

which must accommodate to this new bit of information. The relations, however, between the effectiveness of information in bringing about cognitive change and the multiplexity, consonance, and interconnectedness of the pre-existing cognitive system appear to be highly complicated. Further, relatively little research on these relations has been undertaken by cognitive theorists and experimentalists in psychology. For these reasons we cannot state any precise generalizations defining these relations. The best we can do is to point to some rather simple illustrations of possible relations. The student should not regard the following discussion as the conclusions of science, but as some hunches of some scientists about an insufficiently explored field.

CONTRADICTORY FACTS AND RESISTANCE TO COGNITIVE CHANGE. Often we are forced to pay attention to new facts, facts that seem not to fit in with our existing cognitions or that even contradict them. At times, this results in a fairly radical change of the whole system— a formerly consonant system may be thrown into disharmony and a widespread readjustment may result. At other times, however, despite such contradictory facts, a relatively slight cognitive change seems to accommodate the new facts within the old system. We continue stubbornly to hold on to our major beliefs in the face of contradiction after contradiction. This ubiquitous cognitive phenomenon is, of course, of profound importance for social psychology. Suppose your perception of Russia's foreign policy is one of imperialism and aggression. And suppose you read that her foreign minister has appealed for international good will and peace. Will you change your beliefs about Russia's foreign policy? Probably not. You will interpret the foreign minister's statement as a "lie" or as "diplomatic double talk." Or suppose that a Frenchman who firmly believes that all Germans are cruel and untrustworthy meets a German who acts kindly and honorably. Will that change the Frenchman's concept of Germans in general? Again, probably not. He may ascribe some ulterior motive to this particular German, who will then be perceived as a "make-believe honest German." This will result in no change in his cognitive system about the nature of Germans.

Often the cognitive system resists major change through the creation of new parts. Thus, for example, in the above illustration, the Frenchman may perceive this German as an "exception." In such an event we can see that some reorganization has occurred in that a new part has been differentiated ("exceptional cases"), but his major system, "Germans in general," remains intact. (For an experimental illustration of various ways in which cognitive consonance is maintained in the face of contradictory facts, see Box 2.12.)

It should be noted, however, that in the above illustrations—as well as in all available experimental studies—the accommodation of discrepant facts without a change in the major system is more apparent than real: facts must be "reinterpreted," the multiplexity of a cognitive system must be increased (e.g., new categories such as "exceptions" are created), and, in general, a new consonant system must be achieved.

Finally, we should point out that it is fortunate indeed that our more complex cognitive systems tend to maintain their major character despite apparently contradictory facts and experiences. If this were not true, there would be little stability in our cognitive life.

VULNERABILITY TO COGNITIVE CHANGE. Some cognitive systems seem to be more vulnerable to cognitive change than do others. To illustrate: A single new item of information could have a relatively decisive effect on a major system that was simplex and undifferentiated, but it might have a relatively minor effect on a multiplex system. Thus, a man who believes that "religion is good" and does not differentiate further might be persuaded that everything about religion is "bad" by a single, strongly unhappy religious experience. On the other hand, a man who has a highly differentiated religious cognitive system could more easily assimilate an unpleasant experience without changing his major religious system. It might, for example, affect one of his religious cognitions ("church officials" or "religious ceremonies") but permit his major system to remain relatively intact.

Or, another example: An economic argument or event, for the person with a relatively isolated religious system, cannot result in a noticeable change in his religious system simply because his economic and religious systems are not interconnected. For the man whose religious system is interconnected with other systems, the matter is more complex. On the one hand, there are, as it were, more avenues of approach or avenues by which to attack his religious cognitions. Economic, political, social, scientific, or other kinds of facts may have repercussions on his religious beliefs. For him the price of beans *may* affect his beliefs about the Prince of Peace. In that sense, the man

with a highly interconnected religious system is more vulnerable to change than is the person with a relatively isolated religious system. On the other hand, these very interconnections also provide—to continue our metaphor—more routes for "defense forces" to be brought up when his religious system is attacked by one or another fact or argument. His religious system, being connected with diverse kinds of beliefs, will tend to make these interconnected cognitions *salient* when his religious system is attacked. The net effect of any one antireligious argument for the man with an interconnected religious system may be the reverse of what was intended. The attack, by reviving the nascent *supporting* social or economic beliefs, may strengthen his original religious beliefs.

TO RECAPITULATE

The degree and manner in which changes in wants and information produce changes in cognition depend upon the multiplexity, interconnectedness, and consonance of the pre-existing cognitive systems. The relations between vulnerability to cognitive change and the dimensions of multiplexity and interconnectedness are complex and little understood. Cognitive systems of high multiplexity are more immune to radical change than those of low multiplexity. No such general relation can be stated for interconnectedness. But no matter how much the cognitive change, the direction of change seems to be such as to approach a more consonant structure. This is true even in those instances where a major system of beliefs seems to be immune to contradictory facts.

Balance theory is an approach to the study of cognitive consonance which is especially concerned with the individual's "affective cognitions" of people and social objects. Balance theory assumes that the cognitive process persistently strives toward balance or consonance.

However, balance is often not achieved. This is especially true when cognitive balance would lead to an unpleasant state of affairs for the individual.

GUIDE 6: *Cognitive change is in part governed by personality factors*

Not only is cognitive change a function of the nature of the pre-existing cognitive system; it is also a function of the characteristics of the person within whom the cognitive system resides—his intellectual ability, his ability to tolerate cognitive ambiguity and dissonance, his "open-mindedness" or "closed-mindedness," his typical manner of coping with blocks to want satisfaction.

INTELLECTUAL ABILITY

It is a truism that ease of cognitive change partly reflects the level of intellectual ability of the person. On the one hand, the more intelligent person is capable of more "cognitive work"—is better able to *reorganize* his cognitive systems, to incorporate new information, to achieve insightful restructuring. On the other hand, less intelligent persons may uncritically accept the simply stated "word facts" of the propagandist, changing their opinions and beliefs with easy gullibility.

The important point is that this personality variable—intellectual ability—determines the quality of the restructurings achieved by the individual. And intellectual ability reflects in large measure genetically determined differences in the structure of the nervous system. Not all men are created equal. No amount of education can completely eliminate these biological differences in intellectual ability. In every society there will aways be people who are ahead of others in their ability to conceive new and insightful solutions to society's problems, to create new systems of thought. An adequate social psychology must deal with this fact of social life.

INTOLERANCE OF COGNITIVE AMBIGUITY AND DISSONANCE

Frenkel-Brunswik [1949] proposed that some people find it difficult to tolerate or manage cognitive ambiguities, inconsistencies, and surprises. Such people tend to display a generalized tendency to dichotomize the world. Things and people are seen as all good or all bad; the world is black or white. When they are faced with an ambiguous situation, they will quickly fix on one concrete interpretation. This way of managing ambiguous situations is said to characterize much of their behavior—their cognitions of persons and objects, their interpersonal relations, their ways of coping with problems.

Support for the concept of *intolerance of ambiguity* is provided by a factor analysis of personality inventory scores. Guilford et al. [1959] have discovered a factor whose two defining scores are Black-White Thinking (e.g., feels there are just two ways to attack any problem—the right way and the wrong way) and Need for Definiteness (e.g., does not like things to be indefinite and uncertain). They found this factor to be correlated somewhat negatively with scores on various tests of thinking abilities. This suggests that people who cannot manage ambiguity may be less intelligent and less creative than those who are better able to cope with ambiguous situations.

People who are intolerant of ambiguity are relatively "closed" to new information which would increase the multiplexity of a cognitive system. Their cognitive palette contains only blacks and whites. Simplified good-evil solutions to complex social, political, and economic issues—"devil theories"—will be sought by those who cannot tolerate ambiguity.

CLOSED-MINDEDNESS

Rokeach [1960] has suggested that *closed-mindedness* is a general personality trait which is related to the ability to form new cognitive systems of various kinds—perceptual, conceptual, aesthetic. To measure this variable, he has developed a Dogmatism Scale. Two sample items from this scale follow:

It is only natural that a person would have a much better acquaintance with ideas he believes in than with ideas he opposes.

When it comes to differences of opinion in religion we must be careful not to compromise with those who believe differently from the way we do.

Agreement with these two items is scored as closed-mindedness.

The Dogmatism Scale may be thought of

BOX 2.12: *College students see a factory worker*

The strategies which individuals adopt to maintain their ideas in the face of contradictory information are nicely revealed in a study by Mason Haire and Willa Grunes of the University of California, Berkeley. They presented two groups of college students with the following description of a "certain working man."

To group I: "Works in a factory, reads a newspaper, goes to movies, average height, cracks jokes, intelligent, strong, active."

To group II: "Works in a factory, reads a newspaper, goes to movies, average height, cracks jokes, strong, active."

The two descriptions were identical except that for group I the man was characterized as intelligent.

The subjects were asked to describe in a paragraph what sort of person they thought the worker was.

The typical description given by group II was summarized by the investigators as follows:

Virtually every description would fit into the pattern of a typical American Joe: likable and well liked, mildly sociable, healthy, happy, uncomplicated and well-adjusted, in a sort of earthy way, not very intelligent, but trying to keep abreast of current trends, interested in sports and finding his pleasures in simple, undistinguished activities.

The introduction of the term "intelligent" created difficulties for group I. This was, for many of the students in this group, inconsistent with their set of beliefs about factory workers. Most of them, however, managed to overcome this "nonbelonging" quality by engaging in what has been termed "cognitive work." Following are some of the ways they protected their original systems of cognitions regarding factory workers:

Denial of the quality: "He is intelligent, but not too much so, since he works in a factory."

Modification of the quality (thus rendering it harmless to the original system): "He is intelligent, but doesn't possess initiative to rise above his group."

Denial of the group membership of the person: Some students denied the man was a worker by promoting him to a foreman.

Recognizing the incongruity, but maintaining the original cognition: "The traits seem to be conflicting . . . most factory workers I have heard about aren't too intelligent."

Haire, M., and Grunes, W. F. Perceptual defenses: processes protecting an original perception of another personality. Hum. Relat., *1950, 3, 403–412.*

as a measure of "general authoritarianism." But Rokeach considers it "first and foremost a measure of the extent to which the total mind is an open mind or a closed one."

Closed-mindedness is said to be characterized by a high magnitude of rejection of opposing beliefs, a relatively low degree of interconnectedness among belief systems, a markedly greater multiplexity of cognitions about objects which are positively evaluated as compared with cognitions about objects which are negatively evaluated. The more closed the mind, the more cognitions are said to depend upon irrelevant wants and external authority.

In two separate studies, scores on the Dogmatism Scale were found to correlate only .02 and −.01 with intelligence as measured by standard group tests. These zero correlations strongly suggest that open-mindedness and intelligence represent quite different aspects of an individual's personality.

NOTE: BEFORE READING FURTHER, READ BOX 2.13; FOLLOW THE INSTRUCTIONS GIVEN THERE AND WHEN YOU HAVE FINISHED, CONTINUE READING HERE.

The validity of the Dogmatism Scale as a measure of closed-mindedness is suggested by a study carried out by Rokeach and Vidulich [1960]. In this study, the 30 college sophomores who, on the Dogmatism Scale, scored the highest (the Closed-minded group) and the 30 who scored the lowest (the Open-minded group) were selected from a pool of 249 students. Each of these subjects was tested individually on the Doodlebug problem. This problem, as the reader may have discovered, is a difficult one because to solve it three commonly held beliefs must be overcome and replaced with three new beliefs. These new beliefs must then be synthesized into a new cognitive system.

The three beliefs which must be overcome to solve the Doodlebug problem are:

1. The "facing belief." In everyday life we have to face the food we are about to eat. But Joe does not have to face the food in order to eat it. He can land on top of it.

2. The "direction belief." In everyday life we can change direction of movement. But Joe is not able to do so because he is forever trapped facing north. Thus, the only way Joe can change direction is by jumping sideways and backwards.

3. The "movement belief." In everyday life we can change direction of movement at any moment. But Joe's freedom of movement is restricted by the fact that once he moves in a particular direction—north, south, east, or west—he has to continue four steps before he can change direction.

As predicted, the Open-minded group was significantly superior to the Closed-minded group in mean time required to solve the problem. The superiority of the Open-minded group was *not* due to greater analytic ability as measured by time required to overcome the three commonly held beliefs. From the questions and comments of the subjects during the course of the experiment, it was relatively easy to tell how long it took them to overcome each of the three beliefs. (The subjects were encouraged to think out loud.)

The superiority of the Open-minded group *was* related to their greater ability to synthesize the new beliefs into a new cognitive system. Table 2.1 shows the mean time required to solve the problem after the first, second, and third beliefs had been overcome.

The greater ability of persons with open minds to integrate the new beliefs into a new cognitive system seems to be related to a greater capacity to remember the beliefs, as measured by postexperimental recall tests. This capacity, in turn, appears to reflect the greater willingness of the open-minded to entertain novel and strange problems. Emotional rejection of the problem was found more frequently among the persons with closed minds. Illustrative rejecting comments

BOX 2.13: *Joe Doodlebug*

Milton Rokeach, a psychologist at Michigan State University, has used the following problem in studying the effect of closed-mindedness upon the ability to form new cognitive systems. This problem was first developed by M. Ray Denny, a colleague of Rokeach at the University.

Presented below is the problem. See if you can solve it.

THE CONDITIONS

Joe Doodlebug is a strange sort of imaginary bug. He can and cannot do the following things:

1. He can jump in only four different directions, north, south, east, and west. He cannot jump diagonally (e.g., southeast, northwest, etc.).

2. Once he starts in any direction, that is, north, south, east, or west, he must jump four times in that same direction before he can switch to another direction.

3. He can only jump, not crawl, fly, or walk.

4. He can jump very large distances or very small distances, but not less than one inch per jump.

5. Joe cannot turn around.

THE SITUATION

Joe has been jumping all over the place getting some exercise when his master places a pile of food three feet directly west of him. Joe notices that the pile of food is a little larger than he. As soon as Joe sees all this food he stops dead in his tracks facing north. After all his exercise Joe is very hungry and wants to get the food as quickly as he possibly can. Joe examines the situation and then says, "Darn it, I'll have to jump four times to get the food."

THE PROBLEM

Joe Doodlebug was a smart bug and he was dead right in his conclusions. Why do you suppose Joe Doodlebug had to take four jumps, no more and no less, to reach the food? Now you try to solve the problem.

If you have not solved the problem at the end of 10 minutes, read hint 1 below; if you have not solved the problem at the end of 15 minutes, read hint 2 below; if you have not solved the problem at the end of 20 minutes, read hint 3 below.

Hint 1: Joe does not have to face the food in order to eat it.

Hint 2: Joe can jump sideways and backward as well as forward.

Hint 3: Read the problem again. Joe was moving east when the food was presented.

Now return to the problem *before reading further.*

The solution to the problem is as follows: At the moment Joe's master placed the food down, Joe had already jumped once to the east. He therefore has to jump sideways three times more to the east, and once sideways back to the west, landing on top of the food. He can now eat.

Try this problem on your dogmatic friends! Now return to page 48 of the text.

Rokeach, M. The open and closed mind. New York: Basic Books, 1960.

TABLE 2.1: MEAN TIME (IN MINUTES) TO SOLUTION AFTER OVERCOMING THE FIRST, SECOND, AND THIRD BELIEFS [After Rokeach and Vidulich, 1960]

Group	After first belief overcome	After second belief overcome	After third belief overcome
Closed-minded	19.1	14.3	9.4
Open-minded	12.9	8.4	3.6

were: "He can starve for all I care." "Jeez, what a screwball of an outfit."

The above interpretation is supported by two experimental findings. First, there is no relation between intelligence and performance on the Doodlebug problem. Second, in a study by Rokeach, Swanson, and Denny [1960] it was found that when the Doodlebug problem was transformed into a chess-like game, closed-minded chess players were not inferior to open-minded chess players. The strange world of Joe Doodlebug had been transformed into the familiar world of chess, in which closed-minded chess players could function effectively. In contrast, closed-minded non-chess players *were* inferior to open-minded non-chess players. For the closed-minded non-chess player, the world of chess is as strange as the world of Joe Doodlebug, and he cannot accept it.

CHARACTERISTIC WAYS OF RESPONDING TO BLOCKING

In Chapter 4 we will suggest that as a result of the individual's biological constitution and past history he develops a distinctive pattern of responses to blocking. For example, he may come to react in an "aggressive" manner, or in a "withdrawing" manner, or in a "regressive" manner, etc. Each one of these ways of reacting will help determine the nature of his cognitive change.

Two men, both of whom have fairly simplex notions about the nature of their country's economy, the "ideal" state, and the "destiny of man," lose their jobs in a period of severe economic depression. Let us assume

that the first of these men typically reacts to obstacles in an aggressive manner; the other, by withdrawal. The first man—an aggressor—may adopt with relative ease a whole new set of cognitions about economics and politics that demand violent revolutionary social change. The second man—a withdrawer—may be immune to such concepts. His beliefs may change, but they may change in the direction of minimizing the importance of economic security, of maximizing man's "spiritual" destiny. The same economic depression, working through two men with different characteristic ways of responding to blocks, has produced a revolutionary, materialistic social ideology on the one hand, and an escapist, spiritual ethos on the other.

TO RECAPITULATE—AND A FINAL WORD

The ease and rapidity of cognitive change is not, of course, determined only by the intellectual capacity of the individual—although intellectual capacity is important. The ability to alter our concepts and beliefs is also determined by our ability to manage ambiguous situations full of inconsistencies and surprises, by our open-mindedness, and by the techniques we have developed to cope with obstacles.

One consistent theme has appeared throughout the six guides we have studied in this chapter on cognition. Again and again we have found that the study of cognition, which on the face of it would seem to be limited to the study of the intellectual life of man, involves pretty much the whole man—his wants and goals, his experiences, and his reactions to difficulties. Although, for purposes of exposition, we have discussed each of the many determinants of cognitive development and change separately, in actuality, of course, *all* these factors operate simultaneously and in complex interactive ways to produce our beliefs, or to immunize us against new beliefs; to organize our beliefs into interconnected systems, or to isolate our beliefs from one another; to change our beliefs, or to guard them against change.

Perceiving and judging people

In this section, we will apply what we have learned about cognition in general to the cognitive process of greatest importance to the social psychologist: how people perceive and judge one another and how they perceive and judge public figures—the power elite in the societies of the world.

FORMING AND CHANGING
IMPRESSIONS OF PERSONS

The first step in responding to another person is to form an impression of him. This impression steers our reaction to him and thus influences the course of the interpersonal behavior event. In forming an impression of another, we observe his actions, we notice his voice and expressive movements, we follow what he says and what he does as he responds to us and to other objects. This information we then use to make judgments about his characteristics. We make inferences about his cognitions, his wants, his feelings and emotions, his goals, his attitudes, his personality traits. And our actions toward him are guided by these judgments. In turn, the other person makes judgments about us and thus guides his actions with respect to us. If our judgment and the judgments of the other are correct, genuine communication is established and effective joint social action is made possible.

If our judgments or the judgments of the other are incorrect, adjustive action is hindered and difficulties may develop which will tend toward precarious interpersonal relations.

SELECTIVE ORGANIZATION. In an experiment by Asch [1946] an attempt was made to determine how people form impressions of personality. The experimenter read to his subjects (college students) a number of discrete characteristics which were said to belong to an unknown person. One such list, for example, was: "energetic, assured, talkative, cold, ironical, inquisitive, persuasive." The list was read with an interval of approximately five seconds between the terms. Then the reading was repeated. Asch then instructed his subjects to write a brief description of the impression they had gained of this unknown person. Below are reproduced two typical sketches obtained from the subjects:

> He is the type of person you meet all too often: sure of himself, talks too much, always trying to bring you around to his way of thinking, and with not much feeling for the other fellow.
>
> He impresses people as being more capable than he really is. He is popular and never ill at ease. Easily becomes the center of attraction at any gathering. He is likely to be a jack-of-all-trades. Although his interests are varied, he is not necessarily well versed in any of them. He possesses a sense of humor. His presence stimulates enthusiasm and very often he does arrive at a position of importance.

Note how the discrete terms of the list have been organized into a meaningful and even colorful personality. Not only have the individual terms energetic, assured, talkative, etc., been perceived in an organized way, but the resulting organization of the terms has permitted the subject to perceive characteristics that were not even mentioned ("He possesses a sense of humor"). Asch summarizes the results of his experiment as follows:

> When a task of this kind is given, a normal adult is capable of responding to the instruc-

In a study of the process of forming impressions of a person, E. S. Gollin, a psychologist now at Queens College, New York, showed 79 college students a motion picture that portrayed a young woman in a series of five different scenes. These scenes were intended to portray contradictory aspects in her personality. In two scenes, sexually promiscuous behavior was suggested. (In one scene she was shown being "picked up" in front of a shabby hotel; in the second she was shown entering a bar and emerging shortly thereafter with a man other than the one who had "picked her up" in the first scene.) In two other scenes the young woman was shown behaving in a kindly and considerate manner. (First, she was shown giving aid to a woman who had fallen on a public stairway, and then she was shown giving money to a beggar.) The fifth scene was a neutral one in which the young woman was shown walking along and talking with another woman.

After the subjects had seen the film, they were asked to write a sketch describing the woman's personality. The sketches were classified into three categories by judges:

Unified: Impressions which retained and attempted to integrate both major character qualities (sexual promiscuity and kindliness)—23 per cent.

Simplified: Impressions which retained only one of the major character qualities—48 per cent.

Aggregated: Impressions which retained both major character qualities but without attempt to unify them—29 per cent.

We see that only one-fourth of the students were able to achieve an organized impression that integrated the two sets of contradictory information.

Gollin, E. S. Forming impressions of personality. J. Pers., *1954, 23, 65–76.*

tion by forming a unified impression. Though he hears a sequence of discrete terms, his resulting impression is not discrete. All subjects . . . of whom there were over 1,000 fulfilled the task in the manner described. . . . Starting from the bare terms, the final account is completed and rounded.

We find in Asch's study an instance of the selective organizing of cognitions discussed in Guide 1, page 20. Sometimes, however, the complexities and contradictions that inhere in every person are sufficiently obtrusive to make the task of organization difficult and some perceivers may fail to achieve a unified impression (see Box 2.14).

HALO EFFECT. In our perception of persons we often come to exaggerate the homogeneity of the personality of an individual. If you have a generally favorable impression of another person this impression will tend to spread to your judgment of specific traits, leading you to judge him too high on desirable traits and too low on undesirable traits. Conversely, if you have a generally unfavorable impression of him, you will judge him too low on desirable traits and too high on undesirable traits. This tendency has been called the *halo effect.* The halo effect can be seen as a special instance of the kind of cognitive process described by Guide 3, page 30; the properties of a cognition are influenced by the system of which it is a part.

IMPLICIT PERSONALITY THEORY. Another way in which the part-whole principle governs our perception of persons can be seen in connection with what has been called "implicit personality theory." How an individual perceives other persons is importantly influenced by his beliefs about how personality is organized—what traits go with what other traits. In this sense, each one of us has his own implicit personality theory. To illustrate, if you judge a person to be *aggressive,* will you tend to judge him high or low in *energy?* If you judge a person to be *kind,* will you tend also to judge him as *honest?*

Kelley [1950] has provided us with experimental data which can be interpreted as demonstrating the influence of implicit personality theory upon the perception of a person. Students in a college class were given brief written descriptions of a guest lecturer prior to his appearance. The descriptions were of two kinds—identical except for one item, which in one case described him as a "rather cold" person and in the other case as a "very warm" person. Some students received the "warm" and some the "cold" description. The students did not know that two different descriptions had been distributed.

After hearing his lecture the students who had received the "warm" description rated the lecturer as more considerate of others, more informed, more sociable, more popular, better natured, more humorous, and more humane than did the students who had received the "cold" description. These results were not due to a general halo effect. For example, *both* groups of students rated the lecturer "intelligent." Rather, the findings stem from the implicit beliefs among the subjects as to what traits go with warmth and what traits go with coldness.

Kelley also found a tendency for the warm-cold variable to affect the amount of interaction of the students with the guest lecturer. Fifty-six per cent of the students who received the "warm" description participated in class discussion with the lecturer; in contrast, only thirty-two per cent of the subjects who received the "cold" description did so. This was true even though the students were sitting in the same room hearing the same lecture. Thus do our impressions of people steer our reactions to them and influence the course of interpersonal behavior.

Wishner [1960], in a follow-up of Asch's [1946] original study on the warm-cold effect, has secured experimental data that support the above interpretation of the effect. Asch presented each of two groups of subjects with a short list of traits said to describe a fictitious person. The lists were identical except that one included the term "warm" and the other the term "cold." The resulting impressions of the two groups were significantly different with respect to 53 other traits. Wishner had a group of college students rate their instructors on each of the 53 traits and on the warm-cold dimension. All the intercorrelations between these traits and the warm-cold dimension were then computed. The highest correlations proved to be with just those traits which most sharply differentiated the warm and cold groups in the Asch study. Thus in his study Wishner has directly measured certain of the underlying trait-linkages in the implicit personality theories of his subjects.

STEREOTYPES. The influence of *stereotypes* in forming impressions of people is another instance of the part-whole principle. As we have already pointed out (pages 30 to 32), this tendency to attribute to an individual traits which we assume characterize his group is pervasive and socially significant. Stereotypes are relatively simplex cognitions of social groups which blind the individual to the manifold differences among the members of any group—racial, ethnic, age, sex, social class—and tend to freeze his judgments.

One important way in which stereotyping occurs in all societies is through the grouping of people into status classes and ascribing to the individual characteristics which are believed to pertain generally to his status class. In an experiment by Thibaut and Riecken [1955], 20 undergraduate students were given the task of attempting to persuade an audience of two persons to donate blood for a Red Cross drive. The two-person audience was made up of confederates of the experimenters, one of whom played the role of a "high-status

Abraham S. Luchins, a social psychologist, conducted a number of studies of the relative importance of primacy and recency upon the formation of impressions of persons. In one of his studies, four groups of subjects were used. Group E was given the following paragraph describing a person named Jim as rather friendly and extroverted:

> Jim left the house to get some stationery. He walked out into the sun-filled street with two of his friends, basking in the sun as he walked. Jim entered the stationery store, which was full of people. Jim talked with an acquaintance while he waited for the clerk to catch his eye. On his way out, he stopped to chat with a school friend who was just coming into the store. Leaving the store, he walked toward school. On his way out he met the girl to whom he had been introduced the night before. They talked for a short while, and then Jim left for school.

Group I was given the following paragraph which described Jim as behaving in a more introverted manner:

> After school Jim left the classroom alone. Leaving the school, he started on his long walk home. The street was brilliantly filled with sunshine. Jim walked down the street on the shady side. Coming down the street toward him, he saw the pretty girl whom he had met on the previous evening. Jim crossed the street and entered a candy store. The store was crowded with students, and he noticed a few familiar faces. Jim waited quietly until the counterman caught his eye and then gave his order. Taking a drink, he sat down at a side table. When he had finished the drink he went home.

Group EI was given a combined description in which the E description preceded the I description. Group IE was given a combined description in which the I description preceded the E description.

person" (a neatly dressed young instructor) and the other a "low-status person" (a sloppily dressed undergraduate). The confederates alternated in these roles. As each undergraduate finished his persuasive argument both members of the audience indicated that they had been persuaded and would contribute blood. The successful undergraduate "persuaders" were then privately interviewed by the experimenter. Among the questions asked was, "Suppose you had to decide that one of the members of the audience said 'yes' because you had forced him to and the other said 'yes' because he just naturally wanted to anyway. Which one would you say you had forced and which one just wanted to anyway?" Of the 19 subjects who were able to make this distinction, 18 reported that the high-status person was the one who "just naturally wanted to anyway," and that the low-status fellow was the one who had been "forced" by the speaker's persuasive arguments. Here, then, were two people responding in the same way to the same persuasive argument, yet the *cause* of their response was seen quite differently by the persuader. Apparently in our culture to perceive a man as belonging to a high-status group is to perceive his behavior as being internally determined, as showing "free will" and self-determination, whereas to perceive a man as belonging to a low-status group is to perceive him as more easily pushed around by external pressures.

CHANGING OF IMPRESSIONS. Our impres-

The subjects were then asked to write a paragraph giving their impressions of Jim and to predict his behavior in a variety of social situations. The descriptions were coded for frequency of mention of extroverted and introverted characteristics.

The order of presentation of the E and I descriptions was found to be significant in determining the subjects' impression of Jim. As the following table shows, the EI group tended to give predominantly extroverted descriptions, though not as markedly as the E group. The IE group tended to give predominantly introverted descriptions, though not as markedly as the I group.

| | PERCENTAGES OF GROUPS | | | |
CHARACTERISTICS	*E*	*EI*	*IE*	*I*
Extroverted	79	52	34	16
Introverted	14	36	56	73

The first block of information about Jim was more influential than the second block in determining the subjects' impressions of him.

The EI group typically characterized Jim as sociable, friendly, outgoing, popular, likable, and happy; the IE group typically described him as shy, reserved, quiet, lonely, unpopular, and unfriendly. The EI group tended to predict that he would display outgoing social behavior; he would accept an invitation to a party; he would stop and talk with acquaintances. The IE group tended to predict Jim would be withdrawn in these situations.

The old adage about the importance of first impressions seems to have some basis in experimental fact.

Luchins, A. S. Primary-recency in impression formation. In C. I. Hovland (Ed.), The order of presentation in persuasion, vol. I. New Haven, Conn.: Yale Univer. Press, 1957.

sions of a person may change as we get more information about him. However, as we have seen, stereotypes tend to freeze our judgments. Moreover, first impressions resist change (see Box 2.15).

The study reported in Box 2.15 should not be interpreted as meaning that the individual need be the passive victim of primacy in his impressions of other persons. In another experiment by Luchins [1957], different ways of overcoming the effect of primacy in impression formation were studied. Luchins found that warning his subjects about the fallacy of "first impressions" effectively eliminated the disproportionate influence of the first-presented information about the personality of a stranger. In fact, warning subjects about possible first-impression fallacies resulted in a tendency for the information presented second to have a greater influence than the first information—a "recency effect."

We have stressed that cognitive systems tend to change in the direction of increased consonance (see especially pages 41 to 45). This is true also of our impressions of persons. People adopt various cognitive strategies in reorganizing their judgments of an individual to accommodate new and incongruent information (see Box 2.12, page 47).

TO RECAPITULATE

The cognition of persons, no less than the cognition of objects, is selectively organized.

Our cognitions of the personalities of people tend to be unified.

Three cognitive systems in the perceiver influence his perceptions and judgments of persons: the halo effect, implicit personality theory, and stereotypes.

Our first impressions of persons tend to resist change. This "primacy effect" can be eliminated by a warning about the fallacy of first impressions.

Our cognitions of other persons, like our cognitions of objects, tend to change in the direction of increased consonance. New information tends to be accommodated in such a manner as to maintain the consonance of our pre-existing cognitions.

ACCURACY OF INTERPERSONAL PERCEPTION

In day-by-day transactions with people, most persons, most of the time, make reasonably accurate judgments of others. If our understanding of others were not reasonably accurate we could not live and work together as members of groups, organizations, and societies. But individuals vary in the accuracy of their interpersonal judgments and the same individual varies in accuracy from time to time. Six factors that influence accuracy of interpersonal perception have been studied by psychologists: the nature of the interpersonal behavior event, the ability of the judge, the characteristics of the other, the amount of information available to the judge, the order of the information, and the nature of the attribute judged.

NATURE OF THE INTERPERSONAL BEHAVIOR EVENT. The nature of the interaction between judge and the other has been found to influence accuracy of judgment. Kelley [1948] found that when judges assume different roles vis-à-vis the other, such as leader or follower, the judges tend to concern themselves with different aspects of the other.

How the nature of the interpersonal behavior event affects the manner in which one person perceives another may be clarified by an example. Suppose the interpersonal behavior event involves a physician (the judge) examining a patient (the other). The physician will be concerned with those aspects of the patient that are relevant to his purposes. He will form an impression of the patient's reliability in reporting his medical history, his attitudes toward his body, his state of anxiety. Other aspects of the patient, such as his political or religious attitudes, may go unnoticed. Further, the doctor-patient relationship will lead the patient to act like a patient and thus supply the doctor with the very behavioral cues which the doctor needs to make accurate judgments. If the patient and his doctor should meet each other at a cocktail party, different patterns of behavior would be called out in the patient, and the doctor would not have available the necessary behavioral cues to make accurate judgments about the patient's attitudes toward his body, or his state of anxiety.

The nature of the interpersonal behavior event thus influences accuracy of interpersonal perception by tending to call out relevant behavior in the other, and by tending to focus the attention of the judge on these relevant characteristics.

ABILITY OF THE JUDGE. Here we are concerned with two issues: (1) Is accuracy of interpersonal perception consistent over *people?* Is a person who is a good judge of a particular characteristic in one person or class of persons a good judge of that same characteristic in most other persons or classes of persons? (2) Is accuracy of interpersonal perception consistent over *characteristics?* Is a person who is a good judge of one characteristic in a group of individuals, a good judge of other characteristics in those same individuals?

Studies of these two issues have produced evidence which is both extensive and controversial. (For two recent studies which seem to lead to opposing conclusions, see Boxes 2.16 and 2.17. In the accounts of these two studies, information is presented which may enable the reader to suggest a reconciliation of the seemingly contradictory findings.)

It would seem that the assumption of a general trait of ability to judge others is questionable. Writing in 1959, Guilford stated:

> The most appropriate conclusion to draw at present is that if there is a generalized ability to judge people, it is a poorly organized trait in most individuals. It appears for the most part that abilities of this kind are specific, depending upon many circumstances, such as the combination of rater and ratee [here he denies generality over persons], the kind of judgment required [here he denies generality over characteristics] and the information available.

The assumption of a rather general trait of ability to perceive others accurately has led many investigators to look for the personality characteristics which make a person a "good judge" of others. The contradictory findings one discovers in reading these studies may be due to the rather specific nature of the ability to judge others. The characteristics which make one individual a good judge of one class of persons may be different from those which make another individual a good judge of another class of persons. And, similarly, accuracy in judging one trait in people may be related to a pattern of characteristics in the judge which is different from the characteristics associated with accuracy in estimating other traits in people.

It is of interest to ask whether general psychological training will enhance a judge's ability to make accurate interpersonal perceptions. For one study relevant to this question, see Box 2.18.

CHARACTERISTICS OF THE OTHER. It seems that some persons are easier to judge accurately than others. This problem was examined in an early study by Norsworthy [1910] in which seven college girls rated ten members of a sorority. Norsworthy concludes that ". . . it would seem that among ten girls

who know each other well there may be twice as much difference of opinion about some one member of the group as about some other." Estes [1938] found that the "openness" of the "other" was a critical factor affecting accuracy of judgment. Tagiuri, Kogan, and Bruner [1955] found that the personal likes and dislikes of some people are easier to predict than are those of others. Some people are "transparent"—they wear their hearts on their sleeves.

AMOUNT OF INFORMATION. How much information does a judge need to perceive a person accurately? Studies of the recognition of emotions throw some light on this question. The expression of any given emotion varies greatly among individuals. Knowledge of the context in which these ambiguous "expressions" are displayed will help the judge correctly identify the emotion. This finding is in accordance with Guide 3, page 30.

In studies of the reliability and validity of ratings of various personality traits, length of acquaintance has been used as a measure of amount of information available to the judge. Symonds [1931] summarizes the early literature by noting: "It seems probable that degree of acquaintance or friendship after passing a certain threshold does not affect the reliability of ratings." A study by Hollander [1956] corroborates Symonds's conclusion. Hollander found that peer ratings obtained from students in an officer candidate school after five days of acquaintance had about the same predictive utility as those obtained later. The information required to make accurate judgments is acquired early in the acquaintanceship. Other studies have shown that, with longer acquaintance, systematic errors creep in to lower accuracy. The judge tends to become lenient or to show favoritism toward old acquaintances.

ORDER OF INFORMATION. The order in which information about a person is presented is another factor of importance in determining the impression of the judge. There seems to be some evidence that *primacy* is more important in shaping the impression than *recency*. Information presented first, in other words, outweighs later information. (We have already discussed one study which supports this primacy principle; again see Box 2.15.) It is therefore difficult to correct an erroneous first impression.

ATTRIBUTE JUDGED. Early studies of the accuracy of interpersonal perception were concerned with the extent to which emotions are recognizable from facial expression alone. Many of the early investigators concluded that accuracy of recognition is no greater than chance. Woodworth [1938] pointed out, however, that the size of errors of recognition was not taken into account in many of these early studies. He constructed a scale which consisted of the following steps: (1) love, happiness, and mirth; (2) surprise; (3) fear and suffering; (4) anger and determination; (5) disgust; (6) contempt. Using this scale, Woodworth found that judgments of emotion seldom missed by more than one step. When we consider that what the judges saw were posed photographs, this conclusion becomes

BOX 2.16: *Is ability to judge others general . . .*

An investigation by Victor B. Cline and J. M. Richards, Jr., two psychologists at the University of Utah, led them to conclude that there is a general ability to judge others. Brief sidewalk interviews with 25 persons were filmed in sound and color. After the filming, these 25 persons were interviewed in their homes by the investigators and given a variety of paper-and-pencil personality tests. In addition, five close associates of each subject were asked to rate him on a personality trait scale. Ten of the films, chosen because of their technical excellence, significance of content, and "on the basis of the extent to which the films discriminated good judges from poor judges," were shown to a group of fifty judges (university summer school students). These judges then attempted to guess how the film subjects had performed on various measures of personality.

The method of scoring resulted in accuracy scores that reflected two different abilities: a measure of the judge's ability to predict the behavior of people *in general* ("stereotype accuracy") and a measure of ability to predict the *differences between the responses of different individuals* ("differential accuracy"). The accuracy scores were a composite of these two different measures.

The accuracy scores obtained by the judges on the first five subjects were correlated with the scores of the judges on the second five subjects. This was done separately for each of the five major predictions which the judges had attempted. These correlations ranged from .66 to .79. Thus it appears that the ability to judge others is general over *persons*. A good judge of one person, on the characteristics sampled in this study, tends to be a good judge of other persons; a poor judge of one person tends to be a poor judge of others.

The accuracy scores on each test were correlated with the accuracy scores on each of the other tests. The intercorrelations ranged from .30 to .65. All but one of these intercorrelations were statistically significant. Thus it appears that the ability to judge others is general over the different *characteristics* sampled in this study. A good judge of one characteristic tends to be a good judge of other characteristics; a poor judge of one characteristic tends to be a poor judge of others.

These investigators conclude that their findings are clear evidence that the ability to judge others is a highly general trait.

*Cline, V. B., and Richards, J. M., Jr. Accuracy of interpersonal perception—a general trait? J. abnorm. soc. Psychol., 1960, **60**, 1–7.*

even more significant. In real life, an emotional state is expressed by a temporal pattern of facial movements. In posed photographs, the judge is limited to a single static moment.

Studies of the reliability of ratings have indicated clearly that certain traits can be rated more reliably than others. In a reanalysis of data collected earlier by Cattell and Norsworthy, Hollingworth [1922] sorted the traits rated in these two investigations into three classes: (1) those which showed close agreement among raters—termed class A traits; (2) those which showed fair agreement—class B

traits; (3) those which showed poor agreement—class C traits. He differentiated between the A and C traits as follows:

The A traits we may designate as "objective" in the sense that they represent reactions to objects and impersonal situations and tasks, and are likely to result in objective products such as inventions, factories, books, bank accounts, salaries, positions, records, etc. The C traits, on the other hand, represent reactions to the presence and character of other persons. They are personal, social, moral, they do not so definitely produce objective products open

. . . or is it specific? **BOX 2.17**

An investigation by W. J. Crow and K. R. Hammond, psychologists at the University of Colorado, led them to question the assumption of a general ability to judge others. Senior medical students ($N = 65$) were used as judges. Three different tests of accuracy in judging others were used.

The Movie Test Case consisted of sound motion pictures of a physician interviewing patients. The patients were also given the vocabulary section of an intelligence test, the Minnesota Multiphasic Personality Inventory (MMPI), a "reticence" test, and a self-rating scale for a number of characteristics that roughly resembled MMPI scales. Ten of these films, randomly selected from 36 available films, were shown to the judges, who were then required to predict the patients' responses to the above measures.

A sociometric test was used to determine the ability of the judges to predict three sociometric measures: (1) how each member of a small group, of which the judge was one member, would be ranked by others in the group on leadership, cooperation, and likability; (2) how the judge himself would be ranked by the other members of the group on these three traits; (3) how each of the members had ranked himself.

An Estimates of Group Opinion Test was used to measure ability to estimate the attitudes of others. The judges answered a questionnaire to measure attitudes toward medical education and were then asked to estimate the percentage of their classmates who answered each question affirmatively.

These three tests were scored to yield a total of 15 different measures of accuracy in the judgment of others. Each of these measures presumably measured the ability of the judge to predict how various others would respond in the various tests (differential accuracy).

Intercorrelating the 15 measures yielded a total of 105 correlations. Only eight of these were statistically significant and two of the eight were negative. These authors conclude that the assumption of a general ability to judge different traits is thrown into question by these findings.

Crow, W. J., and Hammond, K. R. The generality of accuracy and response sets in interpersonal perception. J. abnorm. soc. Psychol., 1957, 54, 384–390.

BOX 2.18: *People and psychology*

Johan Kremers, a psychologist at the University of Nijmegen in the Netherlands, undertook to investigate the question of whether the study of scientific psychology improves the ability of the student to judge another individual's personality traits.

The person to be judged (the object person) was first selected from among six volunteers by a special test consisting of such questions as the following:

1. You are attending a lecture; the audience consists of more than 30 people. You do not agree with the speaker:
    a. Do you stand up and tell him so?
    b. Do you remain silent during the lecture and communicate your objections to your neighbors afterward?
2. Which do you prefer:
    a. Thrilling films (e.g., with crime interest)?
    b. Romantic films (e.g., with love interest)?

The test was administered several times, at one-month intervals. The individual who showed most consistency in his replies was chosen as the object person. Then very close acquaintances of his were also asked how this person would react to the same real life situations. The responses of the object person and his acquaintances were identical for 25 of the situations. And these situations made up the final test.

Six groups of undergraduate and graduate students majoring in psychology, classics, and the natural sciences were used as judges. These judges predicted how the object person would act in the 25 situations after observing the object person expound his views in a ten-minute speech on "the place of labor in life." An accuracy score was computed for each student judge by counting the number of his predictions which agreed with the "true" responses (a "true" response being the one which the object person and his close acquaintances had made).

As the following table of results shows, no differences were found between the accuracy scores of undergraduate and graduate students, or psychology, classics, and science majors.

	Majors	*Average number of correct predictions*
Undergraduate students	Psychology	14.7
	Classics	13.3
	Natural science	14.7
Graduate students	Psychology	15.7
	Classics	14.6
	Natural science	14.1

The results of this experiment are congruent with the findings of somewhat similar experiments carried out in the United States. In science, the ability to make accurate predictions of concrete events is possible only where the crucial variables have been isolated and understood. Social psychology has not yet succeeded in doing this for the process of interpersonal perception.

Kremers, J. Scientific psychology and naive psychology. Nijmegen: Drukkerij Gebr. Janssen N.V., 1960.

to general inspection. Instead, they lead mainly to personal and emotional reactions on the part of others; hence we may designate them "subjective" traits.

A study of a class C trait is found in an investigation by Tagiuri, Bruner, and Blake [1958]. They studied the accuracy of perception of the feelings of others toward oneself— a "subjective" trait of central importance in social conduct. Three voluntary discussion groups, each made up of 10 adults, were used. After each of a series of 12 meetings, the subjects were asked to indicate those persons in the group they "liked best," those they "liked least," and to *guess* which persons liked them best and least. After several meetings, it was found that accuracy of perceiving the feelings of others exceeded chance level. Further analysis showed that the subjects perceived liking or acceptance more accurately than disliking or rejection. The authors advance three possible hypotheses in an attempt to explain this difference. First, people in the American culture learn to mask hostility by politeness; second, cues of rejection or dislike may be denied by the individual to maintain his self-esteem; third, individuals may lack adequate opportunity to recognize cues of disliking or rejection, because dislike leads to separation, with little chance to learn about its behavioral manifestations.

PROBLEMS IN THE MEASUREMENT OF ABILITY TO JUDGE OTHERS

The procedure for securing a measure of the *accuracy score* of a judge in predicting the responses of another is simple and straightforward. The judge's predictions are compared with the actual responses of the other. If the predictions of the judge agree closely with the responses of the other, the judge receives a high accuracy score. But as we shall see, this score cannot be taken as a pure measure of the *ability* to judge accurately. Measures of the accuracy of social perception are difficult to interpret because accuracy scores may be the

resultant of a number of different processes. We shall consider three processes which complicate the measurement of the ability to perceive and judge others accurately: the implicit personality theory of the judge, generalizing from the self, and general evaluative sets.

IMPLICIT PERSONALITY THEORY. We have seen that the implicit personality theory of an individual is a cognitive system that influences our perception of persons (see page 52). The particular implicit personality theory held by a judge may so influence his accuracy score as to invalidate it as a measure of ability. For example, if a judge believes that traits x and y are associated in *all* people, he will tend to infer y when he observes x in a *particular* other. The judge will thus be credited with "accuracy" when traits x and y *happen* to occur together in the particular other, and with "inaccuracy" when they do not. But in neither case has the ability of the judge to perceive trait y been measured. Judges may differ in their beliefs about the closeness and direction of correlations among traits. These differences influence the weight of the judges' implicit personality theories in determining accuracy scores.

When the judge is required to predict how the other sees himself (i.e., the other's self-description), accuracy scores may reflect the fact that the judge and the other have similar notions about the way personality is organized. If they entertain common implicit personality theories, the judge seeing that the other is high on trait x will also judge him high on trait y, and the other who knows himself to be high on x will also describe himself as high on y. But the accuracy score of the judge reflects, in part, the fact that both the judge and the other *happen* to hold similar implicit personality theories.

GENERALIZING FROM THE SELF. Bender and Hastorf [1953] have indicated that a high accuracy score may be partly a function of attributing to others what the judge sees in himself. In those cases where the judge and the other *happen* to be similar, the judge who generalizes to others what he sees in himself "earns" a high accuracy score. Bender and Hastorf in their refined empathy score have proposed a method for eliminating this factor. In effect, they exclude all items in which there is *real* similarity between the judge and the other from entering into the refined empathy score. As they recognize, however, this may result in an overcorrection. Thus, on some of these "real similarity items," a judge may be predicting accurately; on others, he may merely be generalizing from himself.

GENERAL EVALUATIVE SETS. Gage and Cronbach [1955] report that judges seem to differ significantly in their general tendencies to respond favorably or unfavorably to others. Dubin, Burke, Neel, and Chesler [1954] have found that raters tend rather consistently to be "soft" or "hard." If a judge is generally favorable or lenient toward an other, and he is given the task of predicting how the other sees himself, he will predict socially desirable self-descriptions by the other. Since the other generally describes himself in socially desirable terms, the judge will "earn" a high accuracy score. But the judge's high accuracy score reflects the fact that his *general evaluative set* is positive and this score therefore is not truly a measure of his ability to judge people. Conversely, if his general evaluative set is negative, his accuracy score in predicting how others see themselves will tend to be rather low.

A study by Edwards [1953] reveals the extent to which persons do describe themselves in socially desirable terms in responding to personality inventories. In the first part of his study, 152 subjects rated the social desirability of each of 140 personality-trait items. Scale values for the items were then determined which showed the relative positive or negative social value attributed to each trait. The items were next used to construct a personality inventory. This inventory was administered to a group of students with instructions to respond "Yes" to each item that characterized them and "No" to each item that did not characterize them. Edwards found a correlation of .87 between the judged social desirability of items and the proportion of people who endorsed the items as characterizing themselves.

PERCEIVING PUBLIC FIGURES

Frequently interpersonal perception takes place in other than face-to-face encounters. Now for the first time, millions of people are able to see and hear national and international figures through the radio, television, and motion pictures. This kind of massive one-way interpersonal perception is a new phenomenon in society and deserves our special attention. When we perceive a public figure through mass media, we do not have available to us the rich variety of behavioral cues evoked by interaction. Instead, we are forced to depend upon such data as the person's voice, gestures, and facial expressions—all of which are one-way cues under the control of the public figure.

In all of their appearances—on the radio, television, motion pictures—our public figures wear a mask. A political leader makes a speech to the nation over television. A professional actor may coach him in his delivery of the speech; the timing and setting of the speech are carefully arranged. The attempt is made to manipulate both expressive cues (voice, facial expression, etc.) and situational cues to produce a calculated impression of the personality of the political leader in the members of the audience. The art of politics and the art of the theater have been joined. This is the time of the mask. Judge John D. Voelker [1960] may have had this in mind when he said, "If democracy depends upon choice and choice upon accuracy of data, then I suspect our country may be in a hell of a fix. For it seems that today the more we hear about our public figures the less we really know them."

FACIAL FEATURES AND PERSONALITY JUDG-
MENTS. Many of the inferences we make
about the personalities of public figures are
based on facial cues. Secord [1958] has summarized his research and that of his associates
on impressions of personality from facial cues.
One finding, repeatedly confirmed in their
work, is that people agree in attributing certain personality traits to faces which have
particular characteristics. The amount of
agreement on a particular photograph has
usually been measured by splitting the group
of judges into halves, and computing the
mean ratings on each trait for the two subgroups. These two sets of mean ratings are
then correlated. In one study of 24 male
photographs, a median correlation coefficient
of .65 was obtained, with a range from .54 to
.78 for the different traits rated. In a study of
24 female photographs, the median correlation
coefficient was .59, with a range from .36
to .87.

Secord attributes this rather high degree of
agreement in the personality traits associated
with facial cues to cultural stereotyping. For
example, he finds that cultural standards concerning the use of cosmetics and other groom-
ing aids are important in judging women.
The general physiognomic variable well-
groomed leads to an impression of social ac-
ceptability and of sexuality. More specific
facial characteristics also play a role in shaping impressions of women. The amount of
lipstick worn is related positively to sexuality;
bowed lips result in an impression of being
conceited, demanding, immoral, and receptive
to the attentions of men. In another study,
it was found that people tend to see older-
aged men as more distinguished, responsible,
refined, and conscientious.

Another type of cue that helps to account
for the consensus among subjects in the personality traits attributed to particular photographs is facial expression. Thus, in one
study, two expressive characteristics, mouth
curvature and facial tension, appeared to

account for the greatest proportion of the
association between facial characteristics and
personality attributes. Some of the traits associated with mouth curvature were: friendly,
sense of humor, easygoing. Facial tension was
also found to correlate in a predictable manner with impressions of personality.

These various findings indicate clearly that
in forming impressions of the personality of
others, we make inferences from facial cues.
The members of a given culture learn a common set of beliefs about the meaning of various physiognomic cues.

The relationship between physiognomic
characteristics and inferred personality traits
seems to work both ways. Just as we have
seen that personality traits are inferred from
facial features, it also appears that facial features can be inferred from personality traits
(see Box 2.19).

VOICE PATTERNS AND PERSONALITY JUDG-
MENTS. There is good evidence that listeners
tend to judge a speaker's personality by his
speech pattern. To quote Ben Jonson, "Language most showeth a man: speak that I may
see thee." Among the many experiments
that have attempted to determine whether
listeners judge a speaker's personality by his
individual speech pattern and how adequately
they make such judgments is that of Allport
and Cantril [1934]. These experimenters had
their speakers read uniform material from
typewritten texts, thus eliminating differences
in vocabulary and grammatical accuracy.
Eighteen male speakers and over six hundred
judges took part in the experiment. The subjects who served as judges did not know or
see the speakers but merely listened to their
voices as they were broadcast. They were then
asked to match certain personality data about
the speakers (which were provided them)
with the voices of the speakers. Thus, for example, the subjects were given a list of several
vocations, political preferences, ascendance-
submission scores, photographs, extroversion-
introversion scores, etc., belonging to the vari-

BOX 2.19: *An impression launches a face*

In an undergraduate honors thesis, Linda Johnson, a student of Paul F. Secord's, of the University of Nevada, reversed the usual procedure of judging personality from faces. She gave 21 college freshmen two brief descriptions of fictitious persons:

A. This man is warmhearted and honest. He has a good sense of humor and is intelligent and unbiased in his opinion. He is responsible and self-confident with an air of refinement.

B. This man is ruthless and brutal. He is extremely hostile, quick-tempered, and overbearing. He is well-known for his boorish and vulgar manner and is a very domineering and unsympathetic person.

The subjects were then asked to imagine what these two men looked like and to rate 32 facial features on a seven-point scale. They had no difficulty in doing so and produced widely different physiognomic ratings for the two descriptions. Twenty-five of the facial features were rated in a significantly different manner for the two fictitious persons. The following table lists six of these.

Feature	Person A	Person B
Directness of gaze	Direct gaze	Averted gaze
Upward-downward gaze	Upward gaze	Downward gaze
Widened-narrowed eyes	Widened eyes	Narrowed eyes
Knitted-relaxed brow	Smooth brow	Knitted brow
Nostrils	Relaxed	Distended
Mouth curvature	Corners up	Corners down

Secord, P. F. Facial features and inference processes in interpersonal perception. In R. Tagiuri and L. Petrullo (Eds.), Person perception and interpersonal behavior. Stanford: Stanford Univer. Press, 1958.

ous speakers and were required to match the personality score or vocation or photograph with the voice. In one experiment the judges were provided with a brief thumbnail sketch of each speaker, and then attempted to match the proper thumbnail sketch with the proper voice. On the basis of the data obtained, the investigators drew certain conclusions which are summarized as follows:

1. Voice alone conveys some correct information concerning such outer characteristics as age, and such inner characteristics as ascendance-submission. The majority of the judges' matchings were better than chance, and 47 per cent of them were better by large margins.

2. The more significant personality traits are judged more consistently and more cor-

rectly than the specific "outer" characteristics. Thus, for example, the ascendance-submission scores tended to be matched more correctly than the individuals' photographs. In addition, the matchings between voice and the thumbnail sketches were better than the matchings with single personality features.

3. Judgments of personality based on voice alone, even when the judgments are erroneous, do not represent mere guesses. A voice seems to arouse a more or less uniform impression or stereotype among the different members of a group of listeners even when the impression is incorrect.

4. If the voice of a speaker arouses a stereotype in the perception of the listener, it is likely that several features of personality will be subsumed under that stereotype. (This

"totalizing" effect again illustrates the operation of Guide 3; that is, the properties of a cognition are influenced by the system of which it is a part.)

EXPRESSIVE MOVEMENTS AND PERSONALITY JUDGMENTS. In addition to his voice, the expressive movements of a public figure—his gestures and postures—help to determine how he is perceived. And these cues, too, can be manipulated and controlled in the mass-media appearances of the public figure.

Although it is clear from experimental studies of expressive movements [Allport and Vernon, 1933] that they possess a high degree of reliability and consistency, studies which have correlated judgments or measurements of expressive movements with other measures of personality have commonly found positive but low correlations. In many instances expressive movements reflect the cultural background of the person rather than his personality. Whether a person shrugs his shoulders with every sentence or flings out his hands or whether he delivers his speech with a "dead pan" may be only an expression of cultural learning or of stage directions; yet the listener and viewer may react to his expressive movements as though they reflected his personality. The social-stimulus value of an individual is, in fact, largely determined in public encounters by his expressive behavior. The man who gestures forcefully is perceived as "forceful"; the immobile speaker, as "cold, controlled."

TO RECAPITULATE

Studies of the determinants of accuracy of interpersonal perception lead to the following conclusions: (1) the nature of the interpersonal behavior event may influence accuracy by tending to call out the relevant behavior in the person being judged and to focus the attention of the judge on these relevant characteristics; (2) there is no clear evidence for a generalized ability to judge others; (3) some individuals are easier to judge than are others; (4) a brief acquaintance or an extended acquaintance with the person may reduce accuracy; (5) the effect of information about a person upon accuracy of judgment is conditioned by the order in which it is acquired; (6) some attributes can be judged more accurately than others.

The measurement of accuracy of interpersonal perception is complicated by the operation in the judge of his implicit personality theory, of generalizing from the self, and of general evaluative sets.

In the socially important process of perceiving public figures, the voice patterns, expressive movements, and facial features of the speaker markedly influence the personality characteristics inferred. Such cues may be manipulated by the public figure to produce a calculated effect.

CHAPTER GUIDES AND GLOSSARY

GUIDE 1: *The cognitions of the individual are selectively organized*

GUIDE 2: *Cognitions develop into systems in accordance with the principles of learning and stimulus organization*

GUIDE 3: *The properties of a cognition are influenced by the system of which it is a part*

GUIDE 4: *Cognitive change is typically initiated by changes in the individual's information and wants*

GUIDE 5: *Cognitive change is in part governed by the characteristics of pre-existing cognitive systems*

GUIDE 6: *Cognitive change is in part governed by personality factors*

adaptation level. A concept proposed by Helson to account for various phenomena of relativity in perception and judgment. Defined as the stimulus value (e.g., brightness, loudness) which is indifferent or neutral and with respect to which stimuli above or below it are relatively judged. The adaptation level is a joint product of the stimuli being judged, background stimuli, and residuals of past experience with similar stimuli.

assimilation. The tendency in perception for the highly similar parts of a whole to look as much alike as possible, i.e., to assimilate. Assimilation occurs when the stimulus differences among the parts are sufficiently small; if the differences are sufficiently large, the opposite phenomenon of *contrast* will tend to occur.

balance theory. A theory of cognitive consonance primarily associated with the name of Heider. This theory asserts that unbalanced cognitive systems tend to shift toward a state of balance. Heider's major development of this theory is seen in his analysis of the triadic cognitive system—one made up of three elements. In this analysis a detailed account of the phenomenology of interpersonal relations is presented.

causal system. A cognitive system involving the perception of two or more objects or events in a cause-and-effect relation. This cognitive system is found universally among people, and is determined by the factors of similarity and proximity and by other features of the stimulus pattern. Events which appear similar or in close spatial or temporal proximity frequently tend to be organized into cause-and-effect relations.

cognitive consonance. The characteristic of a cognitive system which refers to the internal harmony existing among the component cognitions in the system. A cognitive system is said to be high in consonance when its component cognitions are congruent; low in consonance when they are incongruent or contradictory. Other things being equal, *simplex* systems tend to be higher in consonance than *multiplex* systems.

cognitive interconnectedness. The characteristic of a cognitive system which refers to the degree to which it is interrelated with other systems. When there is a high degree of interconnectedness among many cognitive systems we speak of the existence of an ideology; when there is a low degree of interconnectedness among the individual's cognitive systems we speak of the compartment-tight mind.

cognitive multiplexity. The characteristic of a cognitive system which refers to the number and variety of the separate cognitions incorporated within the system. A cognitive system which has a large number and variety of cognitions is referred to as a *multiplex* system; one with relatively few or highly similar cognitions, as a *simplex* system.

cognitive selectivity. The tendency of the individual to select out certain objects in his physical and social environment to incorporate into his cognitions. Only certain characteristics of these selected objects are perceived, and these characteristics may be distorted to fit the wants, emotions, and sets of the individual. Cognitive selectivity is determined by both the characteristics of the stimulus object (stimulus factors) and the characteristics of the perceiving individual (personal factors).

cognitive system. An interrelated complex of separate cognitions about objects and persons. The determinants of which cognitions become organized into a single system seem to be of two kinds: stimulus determinants and experience. As illustrations of the first, one would point to the factors of similarity and proximity. Thus two cognitions which are similar or which occur in close spatial or temporal proximity might be grouped into one cognitive system. As illustrations of the experience factor, one might point to the observation that the individual can be *taught* to organize into one cognitive system such apparently disparate objects as whales, human beings, and mice. Cognitive systems differ in *multiplexity, consonance,* and *interconnectedness.*

cognitive world. The social and physical environments as apprehended by the individual. Because the individual's cognitions reflect his own environment, his physiological structure, his wants and goals, and his experiences, no two persons have precisely the same conception of the world. Nevertheless, there are many common features in the cognitive worlds of all people. This is true because all people have similar nervous systems, share common wants, and cope with common problems.

contrast. The tendency in perception for the somewhat dissimilar parts of a whole to look as different as possible. Contrast occurs when the stimulus differences among the parts are sufficiently large; if the differences are sufficiently small, the opposite phenomenon of *assimilation* will occur.

frame of reference. The standard or framework which serves as a reference against which the properties of a particular object are judged. For example, the perception of the weight of a single object in a series of objects is partly determined by the weights of all the objects making up the series. This series serves as a frame of reference. Frame of reference can be seen as a way of referring to the influence of a cognitive system upon its component cognitions.

general evaluative set. The general disposition of an individual to be "soft" or "hard" in his judgments of other persons. This set complicates and makes ambiguous the interpretation of scores of the individual's ability to judge others.

halo effect. The tendency in forming an impression or judgment of a particular characteristic of an individual to be influenced by one's general impression of him. If the general impression is favorable, he will be overrated on desirable traits; if the general impression is unfavorable, the opposite effect will occur. Halo results in spuriously high intercorrelations among trait ratings.

implicit personality theory. The beliefs of an individual about the way in which traits are generally interrelated in people, i.e., the belief that when you find trait x in a person, he will also have trait y. The trait-linkages which make up the implicit personality theory of the individual form a cognitive system which influences the accuracy of his perceptions and judgments of persons. The implicit personality theories of members of the same culture tend to be similar.

intolerance of ambiguity. A general personality disposition, proposed by Frenkel-Brunswik, according to which people consistently differ in their capacity to tolerate or cope with ambiguous or unstructured objects and events. A person who is high in intolerance of ambiguity will tend to engage in black-and-white thinking and to form simplex, clearly organized cognitive systems.

mental set. A readiness of the individual to organize his perceptions and cognitions in a particular way. Mental sets may be transient or persistent. They reflect the emotions, physiological states, and experiences of the individual.

span of apprehension. The maximum number of objects which can be simultaneously apprehended correctly. There is no single span of apprehension since not only does the span vary from person to person, but it varies within the same person from moment to moment. The range in the span of apprehension in the visual mode is from 6 to 11.

stereotype. A relatively simplex cognition, especially of a social group (e.g., "All Orientals look alike"). Stereotypes tend to be widely shared by members of a given society. Stereotypes may be seen as an instance of the part-whole principle in cognition, in that our judgment of any particular individual member of a group is influenced by our stereotypes of the group to which he belongs.

MAN'S ACTIONS ARE GUIDED BY HIS COGNITIONS—BY WHAT HE *thinks, believes, and anticipates. But when we ask why he acts at all, we are asking the question of motivation. And the motivational answer is given in terms of active, driving forces represented by such words as "wanting" and "fearing": the individual wants power, he wants status, he fears social ostracism, he fears threats to his self-esteem. In addition, a motivational analysis specifies a goal for the achievement of which man spends his energies. Wanting power, he commits his effort, time, and substance to become governor of his state; wanting status, he tries to buy his way into the "proper" country club; fearing social ostracism, he shies away from acquaintances and friends who would engage him in the support of an unpopular social cause; fearing threats to self-esteem, he avoids situations in which his intellectual competence might be challenged.*

With the study of motivation in this chapter, we add to our picture of Cognitive Man—the subject of our previous chapter— the driving dynamic of purpose. And as we do so, we will be taking the second major step toward understanding the individual's behavior in a society of thinking, striving, achieving—and failing—men.

3: MOTIVATION

AN ACCOUNT OF THE ACTIONS OF INDIVIDUALS in interpersonal behavior events involves two different questions of "why." First, we ask why individuals choose one action and reject alternative actions. Why does Mr. Arbuthnot go to church? And why this church rather than that church? Why did his brother refuse a political appointment in order to remain a judge? Why did his son accept a bid to join a fraternity? Why has his cousin chosen to join the Democratic party? Questions such as these have to do with the *direction* of action.

Second, we ask why people persist in a chosen action, often over a long time, and often in the face of difficulties and obstacles. Why does Dr. Albert Schweitzer endure hardship and privation to provide medical care for the people of Lambarene, Gabon, in Africa? Why do men work long hours in the United Nations in an attempt to establish a permanent peace? Why do men risk death to convert others to their religious ways? Questions such as these have to do with the *persistence* of action.

The study of the direction and persistence of action is the study of motivation. But as we have already seen in Chapter 2 motivation is also implicated in the determination of cognitive processes. We therefore start our present chapter with a brief discussion of the role of wants in the determination and control of action *and* thoughts.

The motives of man form an organized and unified system. It is because of this that we will discuss not only the growth and change of man's wants and goals, but also the nature and the development of the self—around which man's wants and goals are organized, and in the defense of which much of his energy is expended. Finally, having examined the sources of want arousal, we will review the major methods of measuring wants and briefly describe some of the major social wants that drive Western man.

WANTS AND GOALS DEFINED

As we have already indicated, in any account of motivation we start our description with reference to some kind of driving force in the individual. One can distinguish two types of such forces, *positive* and *negative*. Thus such terms as "wants," "desires," "needs" are usually seen as positive forces which *impel* a person *toward* certain objects or conditions, whereas such terms as "fears" and "aversions" are usually seen as negative forces which *repel* a person *away from* certain objects or conditions. There are many differences between these positive forces and these negative forces: they may have quite different emotional accompaniments, and the behavior they initiate may, on the face of it, appear quite different. Yet both types of forces have a similar—or perhaps identical—meaning: they both are seen as the *initiating and sustaining forces of behavior*. It is for this reason that in many different motivational theories both positive and negative forces are subsumed under a single term, e.g., motive, need, want. We shall follow this precedent. Throughout our discussion we will sometimes use the word *want* to cover both the positive driving forces of man (desires, needs, etc.) and the negative driving forces (fears, aversions, etc.).

In addition to wants we must also specify the objects toward which these wants are directed or away from which they are directed. The former are sometimes referred to as "approach objects"; the latter, as "avoidance objects." But again, as in the case of positive and negative wants, in considering approach and avoidance objects, we will be guided more by their basic similarities than by their apparent differences.

When a man desires an attractive object, he does so in order to do something to it, or with it; the aim of the hungry man is *eating* bread and cheese. And when a man fears a dangerous object, his aim is *escaping* from it to safety. We will refer to the sought-after terminal actions with respect to both approach and avoidance objects as *goals*. Just as the one term "want" will sometimes be used to refer to both positive and negative driving forces, so will the one term "goal" be used to refer to both appetitive actions toward approach objects and aversive actions toward avoidance objects.

Wants and goals are interdependent—the one does not exist without the other. It is doubtful, for example, whether one can really speak of a "power want"—as though people experienced or were driven by some sort of free-floating, unattached drive toward power. Usually the man to whom we ascribe a power want is aware only that he seeks such and such a goal. As far as *his* experiences are concerned, as far as *his* cognitive systems are involved, the want-goal complex is an indissoluble single unit. For purposes of scientific analysis, however, we will distinguish between wants and goals and sometimes speak as though a want, for example, can undergo change independently of the goal.

GUIDE 7: *The thought and action of the individual reflect his wants and goals*

As we have pointed out on page 37, ". . . *cognition is not a cold affair but is intimately related to wants and goals.*" Ascribing to wants and goals a directive influence in both thought and action is to assign to them a very important role indeed. In essence what we are now saying is that the wants of the individual integrate and organize *all* of his psychological activities in directing and sustaining action

BOX 3.1: *God is food*

"To the millions who have to go without two meals a day the only acceptable form in which God dare appear is food." Thus spoke Gandhi.

During World War II, a group of conscientious objectors volunteered to serve as subjects in a study of the physiological and psychological effects of semistarvation. The study was directed by the physiologist Ancel Keys of the University of Minnesota.

The volunteers were subjected to semistarvation for six months, during which period their daily food intake was limited to 1,500 calories, approximately 1,000 calories below the necessary minimum. At the end of this six-month period, the men had dropped from an average weight of approximately 155 pounds to less than 120 pounds.

The effect of chronic hunger upon the cognitions, feelings, and attitudes of the men as well as their behavior is vividly revealed in the following account of psychologists H. S. Guetzkow and P. H. Bowman, who collaborated in the study.

> *Cognitions.* The intensive preoccupation with food made it difficult for the men to concentrate upon the tasks they had intellectually decided they would work on. If a man tried to study, he soon found himself daydreaming about food . . . he would muse about opportunities he had missed to eat a certain food when he was at this or that place. Often he would daydream by the hour about the next meal. . . .

> *Feelings.* There was a dulling of the emotional response of the individual with concomitant depression. Humor was gone. The men did not sing or whistle of their own accord. Music did not bring its former warmth. The dejection was exhibited in the lack of conversation at mealtimes.

> Petty defects became very important and were the source of much irritation. . . . The men "blew up" at each other on occasion. Mannerisms which formerly went unnoticed now became sources of friction.

> *Attitudes.* One of the more profound changes which took place was the decreased sociability of the men . . . even the men who managed to continue their social contacts often felt animosity toward strangers, merely because they were strangers. . . . They were especially alienated by the individual who supposed he knew what it was like to be hungry because he had gone without food for a couple of days.

> *Behavior.* "It wasn't what the boys did with their food that I didn't like but it was their method. They would cuddle it like a baby or handle it and look over it as they would some gold."

Keys, A., Brozek, J., Henschel, A., Mickelsen, O., and Taylor, H. L. The biology of human starvation. *Minneapolis: Univer. of Minnesota Press, 1950.*

Guetzkow, H. S., and Bowman, P. H. Men and hunger: a psychological manual for relief workers. *Elgin, Ill.: Brethren Press, 1946.*

toward a goal. What he perceives, what he thinks about, what he feels, what old habits are activated, what new habits are formed— all of these activities are influenced by the wants which impel the individual and the goals which he strives to secure. (For a dramatic illustration of this kind of pervasive influence of a strong want upon behavior, see Box 3.1.)

Guide 7, in asserting that all of the behavior of the individual—his thoughts as well as his actions—reflects his wants and goals, does not imply, of course, that the relation between a particular want and a particular action or cognition is a simple and direct one. It is almost an understatement to say that the relations among wants, goals, and behavior are extremely complex and difficult to uncover. There are a number of barriers to uncovering these relations, some of which we shall examine later in this chapter when we discuss methods of measuring wants. Here we can point out two simple and complementary generalizations which will immediately indicate the complexity of the relations among wants, goals, and actions.

On the one hand, *similar* actions may be related to *different* wants. Why do men join the Young Republicans? To satisfy a desire to affiliate with other people? Yes. Because of the fear of being dubbed "radical" or "queer" by their neighbors? Yes. To seek political power and advancement? Yes. Because they want to secure material gain? Yes.

On the other hand, *different* actions may reflect *similar* wants. Three sons may want to assert their independence of their father. They may all want to repudiate his conventional, middle-class, business values. But in seeking to do this, they may adopt three quite different patterns of rebellion. One may become a labor organizer; the second, a paleographer; the third, a Bohemian dilettante.

We end this discussion of Guide 7, therefore, with the caution that although behavior may reflect wants and goals, it is not determined by them alone. Behavior is multi-determined—by situational conditions, cognitions, social habits and attitudes, as well as by the wants of the individual. (For a simple illustration of the multidetermination of behavior, see Box 3.2.)

GUIDE 8: *The wants and goals of the individual continuously develop and change*

Wants are as varied as the individuals who possess them. They are the products of the individual's physiological state and his interactions with objects and persons; old wants disappear and new wants appear with changes in his physiological state and his experience.

WANTS AND PHYSIOLOGY

Man's wants and goals emerge, in part, as a result of his physiological organization. Thus the normal development of the sex want depends upon the production of gonadal hormones. Food and water wants are related to the direct biochemical effects of deprivation of these substances. This does not mean, however, that these so-called physiological wants are determined only by the levels of the sex hormones, water, and nutritive substances in the body. Modern research in the physiology of motivation has amply demonstrated that the central nervous system is also intimately involved. The brain, no less than the viscera, is involved in the sex want, the food want, the thirst want. Changes in almost any part of the complexly interrelated series of structures we call man's physiological constitution (including changes caused by learning) may cause old physiological wants to disappear and new wants to appear. Manifestly, the body's biochemical state is an important factor in determining wants. The role of biochemical aberrations in developing specific wants (without any apparent influence of learning) is vividly illustrated in the development of specific appetites. (For one such illustration see Box 3.3.)

BOX 3.2: *The closest or the "farest"*

A study by Irvin L. Child, a developmental psychologist at Yale University, illustrates two important motivational principles: (1) action is determined by both cognition and wants; (2) the same action may reflect different wants and different actions may reflect the same want.

Child was interested in how age affects preferences for easy versus difficult goals. Some 600 grade school children were tested individually. In a "table barrier" condition, the child was asked to stand in front of one end of a library table. A piece of candy was before him within his immediate reach; a second, identical piece was at the opposite end of the table so that to get it the child had to walk halfway around the table. In a "ladder barrier" condition, the child faced a set of shelves in front of which was a library ladder. One piece of candy was on a low shelf within the child's immediate reach; a second, identical piece was on a high shelf so that to get it the child had to climb up the ladder.

The experimenter said, "Do you see those two pieces of candy? You could get that one by walking around the table (by climbing up the ladder). You could get this one by reaching right over there. Well, you may take either one you want."

On another day, the child returned to the experimental room and was again offered a choice between a piece of candy within his immediate reach and a more distant piece. After the child had made his choice, the experimenter asked him, "How did you happen to take this (or that) piece instead of that (or this) one?"

In the lowest grades, the percentage of children choosing the more distant piece of candy was about 20. The percentage increased with age to a maximum of about 50 around grades 3 to 5.

Illustrative reasons the children gave for choosing the more distant piece are classified below into the two categories of cognitions and wants.

Cognitions

"I thought the hard one would be bigger." Why? "I figured the hard one would always be better."

"I thought there might be a trick, that you wouldn't think anyone would want to climb up the ladder, so I thought I'd take that one."

EXPERIENCE AND WANTS

As a result of learning, man acquires a host of specific wants. A hungry infant fed warm milk will develop a want for warm milk; fed rice water, it will develop a want for rice water. The young white child of Tennessee, as Horowitz and Horowitz [1938] have shown, at first plays freely with Negro children. He shows no dislike or fear. He must be taught this aversion. According to these investigators the white child is often whipped when found playing with a Negro child, and is given to understand that as long as he persists in playing with Negro children he will continue to be whipped. His racial prejudice is learned in fear of the whip.

As the individual's experiences become more complex and varied, his old wants may change and new wants may arise. To take a simple example, dear to the heart of the cynic: a man of great wealth finds that his ruthless business practices have made him an object of hatred and scorn in his country. He grows old, and begins to worry about his place in history and his fate in the hereafter. He wants social approval, and he wants it desperately. On the advice of friends he hires an eminent public-relations expert, who advises him to become a great philanthropist—to give

Wants

"I like to take fartherest things. It's more fun to go around after something than to just take the thing that's nearest you."

"I'm going to take the high one, because I like to climb. My father's a steeplejack."

"I like to work for something I get—I don't like to be lazy and take the nearest thing."

Illustrative reasons for taking the nearer piece are given below.

Cognitions

"Because they're both the same and if they're just the same, I might as well take the nearest and not use up energy."

"It isn't sensible to go a long way when it isn't necessary. My brother would go a round-about way probably but I wouldn't. . . . When you grow up, you know better and you'd take the nearest one."

Wants

"Because my mother always taught me to be polite and take the nearest one to you."

"I was afraid I couldn't reach the other one."

"Because like if there was a person over there, they would take that piece and get away before I could get it. So I take the closest and don't try to take the farest."

The reasons quoted above show that the child's understanding of the situation and his expectations about the two pieces of candy influence his decision. Note also that desire for social approval may sometimes result in a choice of the nearer piece and sometimes in a choice of the more distant piece, depending on how the child interprets the situation.

Child, I. L. Children's preference for goals easy or difficult to obtain. Psychol. Monogr. 1946, 60, no. 4.

large sums of money to churches, universities, research foundations, hospitals, libraries, etc. This he does, and gradually the name that was anathema to the public becomes highly respected. But the billionaire continues to give money to the support and expansion of these many institutions. Why?

One answer is that he is still buying social approval; another, that he may still dread retribution in the hereafter—and is trying to buy his way out of the fires of hell. These may be the correct answers. Guide 8, however, suggests the possibility of another answer: his behavior may now express *new* wants. Our billionaire, in giving money to public institutions, has met theologians, scientists, philosophers, writers, doctors—people he had not known intimately before. He has been exposed to new ideas; he has talked with men of strange enthusiasms. These new experiences may have altered his values and his range of appreciations, and thus led to the establishment of new wants. Philanthropic behavior, initially a means of satisfying the want for social approval, now satisfies his altruistic want to extend human knowledge.

FUSION OF WANTS. Psychiatric observations suggest that wants may assume new forms as a result of the *fusion* of originally distinct wants. In some individuals, the food want may be fused with the want for love and affiliation (see Box 3.4); in others, it may be integrated with a state of anxiety. Sexual behavior may reflect a fusion of many wants and fears: the want for affiliation, the want to dominate, the fear of loss of virility.

COMMON WANTS. The fact that the wants of the individual reflect his particular learning experiences and are constantly changing does not rule out the possibility of certain common wants and fears. Because man, as a biological organism, has certain invariant physiological mechanisms, we would expect all men to display a food want, a water want, a sex want, a fear of pain, etc.

And it is highly probable that there are common wants because of invariants in the cultural arrangements which men face in all societies. In most cultures, men are taught to want to become a "good man," a "successful man." Thus we should expect to find some universal *social* wants.

SATISFACTION, FRUSTRATION, AND WANTS

The development and change of the wants of the individual reflect his experiences of want fulfillment and frustration. If he is experiencing only meager satisfaction of most of his wants, the constant fulfillment of one particular want may result in a fixation on it. His threshold for the arousal of the want becomes lower and lower and he will insistently tend to seek gratification of the want in his relations with things and people. For example, a man whose affiliation, prestige, and achievement wants are frustrated, but who

BOX 3.3: *The wisdom of the body*

The spontaneous emergence of a specific want due to a physiological requirement is illustrated by the case of a boy who showed a great craving for salt throughout his short life of three and one-half years.

When he was about a year old, he began to lick the salt off soda crackers. He would chew the crackers until he got the salt off them, then spit them out and ask for more. At the age of 18 months, he learned to say a few words. "Salt" was among the first words he spoke. Almost all of the foods he liked were salty: crackers, pretzels, potato chips, salt mackerel. In addition, he ate about a teaspoonful of salt every day.

When he was three and one-half years old, he was placed in a children's hospital for medical treatment. There he was restricted to the routine diet. Seven days after admission, he was dead. A post-mortem examination revealed deficient tissue in the cortex of the adrenal glands.

The significance of this post-mortem finding is shown in the results of studies of the effects of adrenalectomy (surgical removal of the adrenal glands) in animals. After adrenalectomy, rats that are fed a standard diet will die within 10 to 15 days. Death occurs largely because of the excessive loss of salt from the body through the urine.

It is known that when adrenalectomized rats are given salt in a container separate from the food container, they will eat large amounts of salt and thus keep themselves alive.

The boy had literally kept himself alive for three and one-half years by eating great quantities of salt to balance the excessive loss of salt through the urine due to his corticoadrenal insufficiency. In the hospital, the medical authorities, unaware of this corticoadrenal insufficiency, fed him a diet containing only the regular amount of salt. He died.

Wilkens, L., and Richter, C. P. A great craving for salt by a child with corticoadrenal insufficiency. J. Amer. Med. Ass., *1940,* **114,** *866–868.*

BASIC PSYCHOLOGICAL FACTORS

BOX 3.4: *Food is love*

"Imprisoned in every fat man, a thin one is wildly signaling to be let out."—Cyril Connolly.

Some cases of obesity are due to malfunctioning of the body's metabolism or to pathological conditions in the hypothalamus. Some cases may be due to personality difficulties in which the food want becomes peculiarly fused with other wants.

Dr. Hilde Bruch, a psychoanalyst, has studied such cases of obese people having personality problems. Her findings are summarized in the following statements:

Eating and exercise, physiologically represented as calories in the energy balance, are at the same time very important aspects of a person's behavior. A systematic inquiry into the living habits of many obese people has revealed that these functions are endowed in the obese with an emotional meaning different from the normal. Food has an exaggerated positive value for the obese person. It stands for love, security, and satisfaction. Muscular activity and social contacts, on the other hand, are associated with the concept of danger, threat, and insecurity. The simultaneous occurrence of love of food and avoidance of activity becomes thus comprehensible. . . .

The obese adult, like the fat child, is emotionally immature, passively dependent and helpless in meeting the exigencies of life. He seeks comfort in overeating in the face of failure and of frustrating experiences.

A woman of thirty described this misuse of food in periods of emotional stress as follows: "Sometimes I think I'm not hungry at all. It is that I am just unhappy in certain things—things I cannot get. Food is the easiest thing to get that makes me feel nice and comfortable. I try to reason with myself and tell myself that these problems cannot be solved by eating." She was one of the many fat people who succeeded in showing a fairly complacent attitude towards the world during the daytime but who became tense and anxious when alone at night. As she describes it, "I think then that I am ravenously hungry and I do my utmost not to eat. My body becomes stiff in my effort to control my hunger. If I want to have my rest at all—I've got to get up and eat. Then I go to sleep like a newborn baby."

Bruch, Hilde. Psychological aspects of obesity. Bull. N.Y. Acad. of Med., 1948, 24, 73–86.

finds that his want for material gain is readily satisfied, may tend to seek material gain as his one major goal in life.

On the other hand, if an individual is living a life of motivational abundance—achieving satisfaction of most of his wants—the fulfillment of any one want is likely to be less important to him. This decline in the prepotency of any single want will make possible the emergence of new and "higher order" wants.

The chronic failure of "higher order" want satisfaction will tend to result in a reduction of the goals of the individual to "lower order" goals. For example, Chinoy [1952] states that "by and large they [automobile workers] confine their aims to those limited alternatives which seem possible for men with their skills and resources." The assembly-line worker in an American automobile plant does not dream the American Dream. Only eight of Chinoy's 62 subjects felt they had a promising future outside the factory; only five felt they had any real hope of becoming foremen within the factory; only three felt it might become possible to become skilled workers. The remaining workers felt they had little opportunity to advance and therefore reduced their goals.

The effect of chronic want frustration is also illustrated in the following two observations.

Guetzkow and Bowman [1946], who collaborated in the study of the physiological and psychological effects of semistarvation upon men (summarized briefly in Box 3.1, page 70), state in their account:

> It was the rare individual who continued courtship at the end of the starvation. Budding romances collapsed, and some men wondered how they could have been so interested in *that* girl. One fellow's girl friend visited him from a distant city during the low days of starvation, and she found his ostensible affection disappointingly shallow. His reservoir of affectional responses was drying up.

Holmberg [1950] has made a field study of the Siriono society, a seminomadic Bolivian Indian group. Among the Siriono, the food want is constantly frustrated. The tropical climate in which they live makes difficult the preservation and storage of food. Exhausting hunts for food must be made daily and about a fourth of the hunts are not successful. Holmberg noted that art forms, folk tales, and mythology are only sparsely developed in the culture of the Siriono. Men who must grub for food cannot want and seek beauty and intellectual understanding.

A THEORY OF SEQUENTIAL DEVELOPMENT. Maslow [1943] has proposed a theory of the specific order of the development of wants in terms of the individual's history of want satisfaction. He has proposed that the wants of man develop in the following sequential order from "lower" wants to "higher" wants. (Maslow uses the term "need" to refer to what we call want.)

1. Physiological needs, e.g., hunger, thirst.
2. Safety needs, e.g., security, order.
3. Belongingness and love needs, e.g., affection, identification.
4. Esteem needs, e.g., prestige, success, self-respect.
5. Need for self-actualization, i.e., the desire for self-fulfillment.

Maslow argues that a "lower" need must be adequately satisfied before the next "higher" need can emerge in the development of the individual. "It is quite true that man lives by bread alone—when there is no bread. But what happens to man's desires when there *is* plenty of bread, and when his belly is chronically filled? *At once other (and 'higher') needs* emerge, and these rather than physiological hungers, dominate the organism. And when these in turn are satisfied new (and still 'higher') needs emerge, and so on."

Once a person has moved from a lower level of wants, because of their adequate satisfaction, to a higher level, the lower-level wants assume a less important role in his total system of wants. They may, of course, become temporarily dominant again as a result of deprivation. After a person has passed through the various levels of psychological growth, he possesses a personality structure in which the various wants form a hierarchical system. The lower wants in the hierarchy are no longer insistently imperious; the individual is freed to realize his higher desires and potentialities—to think new thoughts, to dream new dreams. With this increased richness of his cognitive life, his "catalogue" of wants and goals increases in number and variety as he ascends the ladder of wants from belly to brain (see Figure 3.1). His private universe of wants and goals comes to extend the limits of his physical universe. (In this connection see also the discussion in Chapter 2 of the relation of strength of wants to creative thinking and problem solving—especially pages 35 to 37.)

THE NATURE OF GOALS

The goals for which men strive in seeking satisfaction of their wants are multitudinous. For any given want there may be many dif-

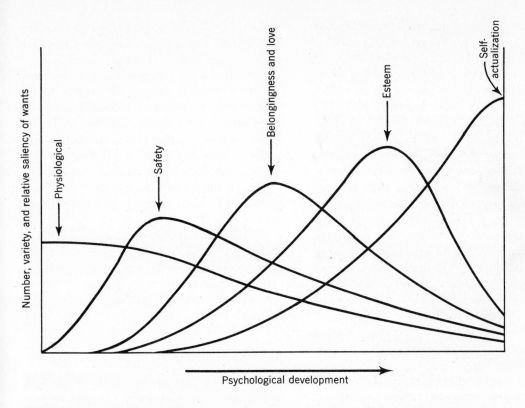

FIGURE 3.1: Schematic portrayal of the progressive changes in relative saliency, number, and variety of wants as described by Maslow. Note that the peak of an earlier main class of wants must be passed before the next "higher" want can begin to assume a dominant role. Note also that as psychological development takes place the number and variety of wants increase.

ferent appropriate goals. For example, the power want may, in different individuals, be satisfied by such diverse goals as becoming dean of a college, president of a PTA, leader of a criminal gang, or the "power behind the throne." Which particular goal is selected by an individual depends upon a number of factors:

1. Cultural norms and values—in the slum areas of Metropoli an approved way of achieving power may be gang leadership; across the tracks on Egghead Hill, an approved way may be through an administrative post in education.

2. Biological capacity—the strong, tough youngster in the slum may seek to satisfy his power want through direct physical domina-

tion of others; his bright but frail companion may seek to become the "power behind the throne" of his tough friend.

3. Personal experience—the mother who has learned to speak in public and to organize groups is more prone to seek satisfaction of her power want through becoming president of the PTA than the mother who has not had those personal experiences.

4. Accessibility in the physical and social environment—the lower-class person who grows up in a highly stratified society will not be as likely to seek political advancement as a means of satisfying his power want as will the man who grows up in a more open society.

SUBSTITUTE GOALS. In the absence of goals

which are fully appropriate to the satisfaction of a want, the individual may come to develop *substitute goals*. Becoming a good wife and mother is a primary goal for many girls, in the fulfillment of their wants for affiliation, security, prestige, and self-actualization. If a girl cannot become a mother because of physiological disabilities, for example, she has available a number of socially approved substitute goals. She may seek to become a teacher or to adopt children. Such substitute goals will not, however, have exactly the same properties or the same power to satisfy the relevant wants as will the goals for which they substitute. Through experience with the distinctive properties of these substitute goals, the individual may gradually come to develop new wants pertaining to them. Thus the girl may come to value and desire teaching "in its own right" rather than as a means of achieving vicarious motherhood. The substitute goal has now become a primary goal.

INTERMEDIATE GOALS. Many of the goals for which man strives are remote in time and require a long series of interlocking accomplishments for their realization. One of the most conspicuous features of human action is persistence in the pursuit of such remote goals. What sustains such persistent action?

For one thing, man is sustained by the symbolic representations of the remote goal which he continuously carries in his mind. For another thing, he sets up *intermediate goals* that he must reach en route to his final goal. For example, the young lawyer who aspires ultimately to become governor of his state may first seek the intermediate goal of membership on the executive committee of the political club of his precinct, and this is but the first of a long series of steps which he envisages on the road to the governorship. The successive achieving of these intermediate goals sustains a long-range action because the reaching of them is perceived as signs of progress toward the ultimate goal.

As laboratory and clinical studies have shown, even small steps toward the remote goal can thus reinforce and sustain action. To maintain the morale of people, whether in a dictatorship or in a democracy, it is essential to signal progress toward the main national objectives by a continuous series of successes— even though the successes are illusory. It was partly in this way that Hitler, through a long series of repudiations of the Treaty of Versailles and aggressions against neighboring countries, maintained the morale of the Nazi partisans in their striving for world domination.

Whenever an individual can see or believes he can see evidences of advance toward the goal, motivation is likely to be strengthened. The converse is also true. Just as "Nothing succeeds like success," so "Nothing fails like failure."

TO RECAPITULATE

The thought and action of the individual reflect his wants and goals. The relation is a complex one: similar actions may reflect different wants, and different actions may reflect the same want.

Wants and goals continuously develop and change as a result of changes in the physiological states of the individual and his experiences as he interacts with objects and persons. Wants may assume new forms through the fusion of originally distinct wants. The degree to which wants are regularly satisfied or chronically frustrated helps determine the strength and primacy of these wants and the readiness with which other wants may emerge in an orderly developmental sequence.

For any given want there may be many different appropriate goals. Which particular goal develops for a given individual depends upon cultural values, biological capacity, personal experience, and availability in the environment. If fully appropriate goals are lacking, the individual may develop substitute goals, which may, in time, become primary goals in their own right. Prolonged action toward remote goals is sustained by the achievement of intermediate goals.

GUIDE 9: *Wants and goals become organized around the self*

The human being responds not only to objects and persons in the outer environment but to his own body, his own thoughts, his own feelings. In so doing he develops cognitions about the *self* as a central and valued object. Important wants and goals emerge which have to do with the enhancement and defense of the self. And the self becomes a nucleus around which the many diverse wants and goals of the individual become organized.

The understanding of motivation requires that we take account of the crucial role of the self, and in understanding these relations of the self to motivation, we must first clarify the nature of the self.

THE NATURE AND DEVELOPMENT OF THE SELF

The self is a product of social interaction. The infant does not distinguish between the self and the not-self. Only as he interacts with objects and persons in interpersonal behavior events does he come to perceive himself as an object separate and distinct from other objects and other persons.

Mead [1934], in his description of the processes involved in the development of the self, writes:

> The self arises in conduct, when the individual becomes a social object in experience to himself. This takes place when the individual assumes the attitude or uses the gesture which another individual would use and responds to it himself or tends to so respond. . . . The child gradually becomes a social being in his own experience, and he acts toward himself in a manner analogous to that in which he acts toward others.

This description may be made clear by a simple example. The child plays being mother or father, for instance. In his play, he talks to himself as his mother and father have talked to him, and he responds to this imaginary talk of his mother and father. The end result of speaking to himself as others have spoken to him is that he comes to perceive himself as a social object to which other people respond. And he learns to conceive of himself as having characteristics which are perceived by others: "I am heavy," "I am bright," "I am lazy," "I am shy."

THE SELF AND GROUP MEMBERSHIP. A study by Kuhn and McPartland [1954] suggests that the conception of the self as a member of groups and classes takes priority over other self-conceptions. A group of 288 college students was asked to write 20 answers to the question, "Who am I?" The responses were classified into two categories: (1) those which refer to groups and social classes, e.g., girl, student, husband, Baptist, premedical student, daughter; (2) those which are evaluative, e.g., happy, bored, pretty good student, too heavy. One of the principal findings was that when subjects are limited to 20 responses they tend to describe themselves as members of groups and classes before they describe themselves in evaluative terms. In other words, a student described himself as a husband, Baptist, or premedical student before he described himself as a good husband, happy, or too heavy. If we accept the assumption of the investigators that this ordering of responses is a valid reflection of the individual's self-concept, it appears that the self-concept is heavily infused with group membership.

SELF-EVALUATION

In seeking to understand the process of self-evaluation, we face three related questions: (1) What determines the values which the individual aspires to realize? (2) What defines for him a successful degree of realization of these values? (3) What social cues does he use in assessing his achievement?

DETERMINANTS OF VALUES. Let us approach the question of how the individual determines the relative importance of different self-characteristics by listening to an old Navaho, Mr. Moustache, as he told his life story to the anthropologist Kluckhohn [1945].

My father always told me to tell the truth. It's all wrong to lie. My father said not to lie or steal. Don't touch anybody else's rope or anything. Try not to think about stealing. Behave. Don't try to catch girls. I never did. Don't gamble or you'll forget other things. Don't drink, my father said, or you'll spend all your money. Even if I had lots of sheep, it wouldn't last long if I drank. My father said, "Take care of yourself. Have good horses, bridle, saddle blankets so I could go anywhere to a sing without being ashamed." Without good clothes you couldn't go anywhere where there were lots of people. Might get ashamed where they had good times.

I minded my father and mother. I believed what they said was true. And so I got along all right. I never got poor. I could go any place. Well, that was right. That is why I don't try to touch bad things. I never think about bad business. I don't like it. I know now that my father was right.

Mr. Moustache is here telling us that the important self-characteristics for him are those characteristics which are highly *valued* by his primary reference group—his family. And his father, who was a chief of the Navaho, expresses in large measure values shared by the Navaho people. And so it is with people everywhere. People are influenced by and tend to accept as their wants and goals the values shared by members of their reference groups and, less directly, the values of their larger society. The "desirables" tend to become the "desired." The self-esteem of most men is based on the achievement of goals which reflect group values. And of these goals the most important are those which represent the dominant values of their groups.

But the values of a society do change, and they change because of the actions of individuals. Men are not mere carbon copies of their groups. Because of his particular life experiences, an individual may acquire new values and goals which dominate his life. And the accomplishment of these goals may result in a major social change. In a complex society, individuals are members of many different groups and the values of these different groups may conflict. In resolving this conflict, a synthesis of the conflicting values may be arrived at, resulting in a new value. This new value may then become accepted by the other members of the society. When this happens, a whole new complex of socially valued self-characteristics has been set up. For example, the early merchants who waxed rich synthesized their conflicting spiritual and temporal values by achieving an ethic which combined the virtues of the shrewd businessman and the pious churchgoer. Now the "good" man was one who walked in fear of poverty as well as of God. The "godly" man was the rich man.

LEVEL OF REALIZATION. We have seen that the individual tends to accept the values of his reference groups as his goals and that he judges himself in terms of his success in accomplishing these group-defined goals. What level of achievement defines for him whether he is a "success" or a "failure," a "good" man or a "bad" man?

There are at least four sets of important factors which determine the acceptable level of achievement of these goals. In the first place the individual's *understanding of his capacities and limitations* helps set these levels. The man who sets as his goal success as a scholar, but who thinks of himself as possessing only a "fair" intellect, will not seek to become the top scholar in his field. He will feel that he has realized his goal when he is accepted as merely another scholar among the vast company of scholars.

A second factor is the *awareness of what*

BASIC PSYCHOLOGICAL FACTORS

levels of achievement are possible. Thus the rustic who values wealth, and believes that no man ever has amassed more than a house, a pig or two, and forty acres of farming land, will accept a much lower level of achievement as "success" than will the cosmopolite who knows that others have amassed millions and billions of dollars in wealth.

The third factor is an experiential one— *the individual's own history of success and failure.* The chronically successful man will demand of himself higher and higher levels of achievement before he will consider himself "successful"; the chronically failing man will progressively reduce his level in order to defend himself against further failures.

Finally, we have the social factor—*the status of the individual in his group.* An evaluation of the self, like any other evaluation, requires a comparison with something else. In the judgment of the self, the "something else" consists of comparative reference individuals and reference groups. In Hyman's [1942] pioneering study of subjective status (the individual's conception of his own position relative to other individuals) 31 adult subjects were asked whether they had ever thought their standing was higher or lower than that of other individuals and in what different ways they had thought of their status, e.g., economic, intellectual, looks, etc. For each of the different status dimensions which the subjects reported, they were then asked with what group or individual they compared themselves. Hyman found that the individual's evaluation of himself is primarily determined by his perception of his relative position or standing in two different kinds of reference groups: (1) membership groups, i.e., those groups to which he actually belongs, and (2) groups of which he is not a member but in which he aspires to membership. A premedical student may, for example, sometimes evaluate his intelligence by comparing himself with his fellow college students (a membership group); at other times

he may evaluate his intelligence by comparing himself with "great physicians," a group to which he aspires to belong.

One particular way in which status in the group helps govern self-evaluation has been studied by Harvey [1953]. Ten three-person groups were used, each group consisting of the leader, a middle-ranking member, and the lowest-ranking member of junior high school clique groups. Each subject performed on a dart-throwing test with his two clique mates present. After ten practice trials, the subject, before each trial, called aloud the score he actually expected to make on the next trial. His two clique mates wrote down their estimates of his performance before the subject called his estimate aloud. The results of this study are conclusive. The higher an individual's status in his group, the more he will overestimate his future performance; the lower his status, the less he will tend to overestimate. Indeed, three of the ten lowest-ranking subjects *under*estimated their future performance. None of the leaders or middle-ranking members gave underestimates. Harvey also found that the higher-status members not only set higher goals for themselves but were *expected* by their clique mates to perform at a higher level. The performance of the lowest-status members was, on the average, underestimated by both the leaders and the middle-ranking members. The lowest-status members were expected to perform more poorly than they actually did.

An observation by Whyte [1943] suggests a further consequence of the underestimation of performance observed in low-status persons. Among the Nortons (one of the clique groups he studied) bowling was a favorite sport. Alec, a low-ranking member of the group, was a skilled bowler in individual matches. But when he bowled with the entire group, his performance deteriorated. He was *expected* to do poorly, and he did poorly. He had several opportunities to prove himself, but each time he had an "off" night and failed.

SOCIAL CUES FOR SELF-EVALUATION. We now turn to the third question we face in seeking to understand the process of self-evaluation: what social cues does the individual use in evaluating himself as successful or unsuccessful? What cues does he receive from the reactions of others in interpersonal behavior events?

Let us listen again to Mr. Moustache.

When a boy gets married, he has to build up his house and stay there and try to make his field bigger—five or six acres—ten or fifteen. Try to plant all what he wants—pumpkins, beans, wheat. Then make some place to put it up for winter. That way never get hungry. *If you do that people would say "Good man, good worker, not lazy man."*

You have to think about things for home—dishes and so on. Try to get all kinds of dishes so they can eat with them. Then other people think: *"Good man. He is getting along all right. Just as well as anyone else."* If you do that, they call you a good man. [Italics ours.]

Mr. Moustache is here revealing, simply and clearly, that his evaluation of himself is determined by the way he thinks other people judge him.

It is safe to assume that Mr. Moustache had never heard of Cooley, a pioneer American sociologist. But note that Cooley [1902] in his concept of "the looking-glass self" says much the same thing we have just heard from Mr. Moustache.

In a very large and interesting class of cases the social reference takes the form of a somewhat definite imagination of how one's self . . . appears in a particular mind, and the kind of self-feeling one has is determined by the attitude toward this attributed to that other mind. A social self of this sort might be called the reflected or looking-glass self.

"Each to each a looking glass
Reflects the other that doth pass."

The self that is most important is a reflection, largely, from the minds of others. . . . We live on, cheerful, self-confident . . . until in some rude hour we learn that we do not stand as well as we thought we did, that the image of us is tarnished. Perhaps we do something, quite naturally, that we find the social order is set against, or perhaps it is the ordi-

BOX 3.5: *Status breeds status*

A study of Muzafer Sherif, B. J. White, and O. J. Harvey, of the University of Oklahoma, suggests the nature of the interaction between the established status of a person in his group and the reinforcing cues he gets from others who judge him. The behavior of two groups of boys was observed. The boys were given the task of throwing a handball at a target. The task was introduced as a practice exercise just before a softball game. The performance of each boy was watched by the other boys. To make the practice "more fun," the experimenter asked the boys to estimate the performance of each other. To maximize the role of personal factors in their judgments, the target was covered with a cloth to make it difficult to determine precisely the point of impact of the ball.

In both groups, the judgment of a boy's performance was significantly related to his status rank in the group. (The correlations between judgments of performance and status were .74 and .68 in the two groups.) The performance of high-status members was overestimated by the members of the group; the performance of low-status members was underestimated. The judgments of the performance made by the boys were *not* significantly related to objective measures of performance made by the experimenter.

Sherif, M., White, B. J., and Harvey, O. J. Status in experimentally produced groups. Amer. J. Sociol., 1955, 60, 370–379.

nary course of our life that is not so well regarded as we supposed. At any rate, we find with a chill of terror that the world is cold and strange, and our self-esteem, self-confidence, and hope, being chiefly founded upon the opinions attributed to others, go down in the crash. . . .

The looking-glass self, in other words, is the person's self-image which is formed on the basis of perceiving how others react toward him.

As the study in Box 3.5 indicates, high-status persons tend to get cues from others that further enhance their high status; low-status persons tend to get cues from others that further depress their low status. The self of a high-status person is reflected from a magnifying looking glass, that of a low-status person from a reducing looking glass.

> Each to each a looking glass
> Reflects the other that doth pass—
> But in terms of social class!

We see here, in the process of self-appraisal by the individual, the importance of his accurate perception and interpretation of the reactions of other persons to him (see pages 56 to 61).

WANTS, GOALS, AND SELF-CONCEPTION

We can now see more clearly the ways in which the specific characteristics of the individual's self-conception and self-evaluation help account for the particular wants and goals he develops. For one thing, there are important wants and goals which have directly to do with achieving and maintaining feelings of self-esteem. For another thing, there is a selection of and emphasis on certain wants and goals in terms of their relevance for a particular self-picture of the individual.

SELF-ESTEEM AND IDEAL SELF. The child is early told by his parents and other adults what he should and should not be like. He is told what are desirable, or "good," personal characteristics and what are undesirable, or "bad," characteristics. As a result of these teachings in the values of his culture, the child comes to develop a conception of what he ought to be—the *ideal self.*

For most persons it becomes a major goal to achieve an "actual" self which is as similar as possible to the ideal self. To the extent that the gap between actual-self and ideal-self pictures is small, the individual feels a sense of enhancement of self-esteem. (There is, however, clinical evidence to suggest that an *extremely close* correspondence between self and ideal self is really indicative of a precarious self-esteem, being based as it is on a blanket denial by the person of all shortcomings.) To the extent that his actual self falls far short of his ideal self, he experiences a diminished self-esteem. A great deal of the action and thought of the individual is driven by the want to enhance self-esteem and to remove threats to self-esteem. As we shall see in Chapter 4, the various ways of responding to frustration of wants may be seen as *mechanisms* to defend the self-picture.

SELF-SELECTION OF WANTS. The individual's conception of himself serves to render dominant certain specific wants. For the Don Juan the sexual want becomes dominant, since the successful pursuit of many women enables him to maintain his image of himself as a Great Lover (and possibly to defend himself against latent homosexual wants). The Southern Belle, to maintain her picture of herself as a feminine person, needs to cling, softly and sweetly, to a man. The Career Woman highly values independence and professional competence.

The specific goals selected by the individual in satisfying his dominant wants are also importantly determined by his conception of himself. The very foods that an individual chooses to eat must not only satisfy his hunger but also be congruent with his conception of himself as a certain kind of person. Thus the less nutritious white bread came to be preferred to the more nutritious dark bread because the dark bread was reminiscent of the

European peasant's black bread. The color of the bread had become a status symbol and, therefore, a determinant of how well it would assuage the status seeker's hunger (see Box 3.6). The houses people live in, the cars they drive, the women (or men) they marry, the groups they join—these varied goal objects may both satisfy specific wants and enhance self-esteem.

The self plays a crucial role in motivation—organizing the wants and goals of the individual, and being the object of important wants and goals that have to do with self-enhancement and self-defense. The self is a product of social interaction and tends to be defined in terms of group membership.

Self-evaluation consists mainly of comparisons of self with reference groups, groups to which the person belongs and those to which he aspires to belong. Self-evaluation depends heavily upon achievement of goals which reflect group values. The standards of performance on which self-evaluation is based are determined in part by the relative status of the individual—higher status leads to higher levels of aspiration, lower status to lower levels of aspiration. Moreover, the high-status individual is more likely to receive cues from other people that serve further to reinforce his high self-evaluation.

The individual's self-conception helps to render dominant certain specific wants and goals, especially those having to do with self-esteem.

GUIDE 10: *The arousal of any particular set of wants depends upon the momentary physiological state, situation, and cognitions of the individual*

Most of the many wants of the individual are inactive or latent; only a particular set of wants is active in directing and sustaining behavior in any one interpersonal behavior event. The arousal of a particular set of wants in the individual depends upon his physio-

BOX 3.6: *The white bread of London Town*

The adulteration of the good honest dark bread of the peasant into the soft, unappetizing, tasteless white, white, white bread of America was a borrowed innovation designed to gratify the American's middle-class urge to escape from the lower class and all of its symbols.

Tobias Smollett, the eighteenth-century English novelist, observed in his last novel, *Humphrey Clinker,* published in 1771, that the good people of London Town ate white bread in preference to the darker bread of the countryman.

The bread I eat in London, is a deleterious paste, mixed up with chalk, alum, and bone-ashes; insipid to the taste, and destructive to the constitution. The good people are not ignorant of this adulteration, but they prefer it to wholesome bread, because it is whiter than the meal of corn: thus they sacrifice their taste and their health, and the lives of their tender infants, to a most absurd gratification . . . and the miller, or the baker, is obliged to poison them and their families, in order to live by his profession.

Smollett, T. Humphrey Clinker, 1771.

logical state, the environmental situation, and his thoughts.

PHYSIOLOGICAL STATES IN WANT AROUSAL

One source of want arousal is found in complex sets of interacting physiological events. Thus, for example, the physiological factors involved in the arousal of the food want seem to include taste sensitivity, stomach contractions, blood-sugar level, hormonal state, and neural activity originating in the hypothalamus.

The more recent experimental data concerning the physiological instigation and control of wants give the brain an important role. This can be illustrated by reference to another physiological want—sex. The arousal of the sex want in the male and female is at least partially related to the rate of secretion of the sex hormones. But this is less true of man than of the lower animals. Thus, for example, in postpubertal men, castration (which in the rat, for example, eliminates copulation and sex play) may sometimes have little or no effect on man's sexual activity—this despite the fact that castration does, of course, drastically reduce secretion of sex hormones. This finding suggests that in man, mechanisms other than hormones control sexual arousal and activity. The physiological control of the sexual want, at least in man, seems to be vested in the integrating mechanisms of the cerebrospinal nervous system, the autonomic nervous system, and the hormonal system.

However, for the majority of man's wants we have not yet been able to isolate their physiological bases, as has been done for the hunger and sex wants. Why then do the facts concerning physiological factors have a relevant place in an account of social psychology?

There are several points to be made. First, there are crucially important effects on the individual's social behavior of those few but vital wants whose physiological bases have been studied (hunger, sex, "abnormal" drives such as alcoholism, drug addiction). Second, some physiological states which we can now define and describe can have important effects on the arousal or nonarousal of other kinds of wants in the individual (e.g., apathy through malnutrition, usurpation of higher wants by a pressing biological want; see page 76). Third, individual differences in the potency of various wants are based partly on physiological factors. Finally, it may well be that there are important *general* effects of the brain on want arousal, as seen, for instance, in the alerting functions of the reticular formation.

For all these reasons a complete social psychology cannot safely neglect the study of physiological factors.

SITUATIONAL CUES IN WANT AROUSAL

The particular set of wants which is activated at any one moment is also determined by specific cues in the environmental situation. Such situational cues may instigate a latent want; they may also serve to strengthen a want already active.

The situational cues which are most powerful in arousing and intensifying wants are the *goal objects* actually present in the situation. Both genetic factors and learning are responsible for the want-arousing power of goal objects. A man's hunger for food may be aroused if he smells the odor of broiled steak emanating from his neighbor's barbecue; his sexual want may be aroused if he sees his neighbor's comely wife; his acquisitive want may be aroused if he catches a glimpse of his neighbor driving up in a new Mercedes Benz 300 SL.

The situational cues may also take the form of *symbols* and other indirect cues pertaining to the goal and its achievement. The man's hunger may be activated by hearing the noon whistle; his acquisitive want by opening the pages of the *Wall Street Journal*.

COMPLEXITY OF SITUATION. The number and variety of the wants aroused are a function of the complexity of the situation. There is little opportunity, for example, for any want to remain latent in a rich, varied, complex environment.

The correct assessment of the want-arousing potential of a situation is of great importance for social psychology. Errors in evaluating this potential have been costly in industry as well as in other social organizations. For example, what wants are aroused when a man enters his place of work? The Economic Man might answer, "The acquisitive want—the want for money." How then explain the finding that men will work harder when their work conditions permit them to establish friendly relations with fellow workers? The failure to see that the work situation may arouse the affiliation want, and management's corresponding failure to provide for the satisfaction of that want, may contribute to decreased productivity and impaired labor-management relations. Or, to continue with our example of the work situation, how can we explain the fact that men will sometimes give up high-salaried positions in business to enter government service? Clearly the work a man does may arouse not only the acquisitive want but also the prestige want, the power want, the curiosity want. The work situation is complex and the man's office, or shop, or factory may activate many different wants.

Just as we have seen that the number and variety of the wants a man *develops* are congruent with the complexity of his environment, so also are the opportunities for their *arousal*—and, to a fair degree, the opportunities for their fulfillment.

If the environment is an impoverished one, with very few goal objects available, fewer wants will be triggered off. In a country without universities, libraries, and laboratories, few men will strive to become scholars and scientists; in a country with very few material objects, the acquisitive want may be only infrequently aroused; in a community without the poor and the suffering, the altruistic want may remain latent.

There is, however, a limit to the effects of the simplicity of the environment on the motivational life of man. This may best be seen, perhaps, in the case of the man who has developed many wants and has then been transplanted, by the fortunes of fate, into a relatively impoverished environment. This is a common occurrence: the cultured refugee from a European capital who finds asylum on a remote ranch in South America; the college graduate who returns to his rural home town; the politician who, after political defeat, must leave Washington to return to selling automobiles. Such an individual will carry with him many wants for which his new environment will not provide the necessary "arousal objects." But he will not be completely at the mercy of his impoverished environment as far as the arousal of his wants is concerned. At least during the first period of his "exile," his wants may be aroused through his thoughts. Just as we must not underestimate the want-arousing potential of complex situations, so must we not underestimate the want-arousing potential of self-generated cognitive processes in the individual.

COGNITIONS IN WANT AROUSAL

The product of thinking is, frequently, want arousal. This is particularly the case with the kind of autistic thinking found in fantasy and daydreaming. Sometimes fantasy results from the absence of immediate gratifications in the real world; the individual may imagine himself in all sorts of situations which come to arouse and intensify in him various wants—wants which may get sufficiently intense that he feels obliged to do something realistic about them (recall McClelland's thirsty man, Box 2.8, page 36), or which may get autistic "satisfaction" in his fantasy world.

Sometimes fantasy results from sheer boredom and lack of external stimulation. This is well illustrated in a study by Bexton, Heron, and Scott [1954], who subjected college students to severely reduced environmental stimulation. Each student, for twenty-four hours a day, was required to lie on a bed in a small, soundproof cubicle, with ears plugged, hands insulated from external contact, etc. Hebb [1955], who was associated with the study, has given us some information on the reactions of the subjects. For doing nothing, these students were paid $20 a day plus board and cubicle. After four to eight hours in the cubicle, many of the subjects became more and more unhappy. They displayed a strong want for stimulation. Some subjects had available a pamphlet for six-year-old children on the dangers of alcohol. Some of these adult subjects asked for this bit of childish propaganda 15 to 20 times in the course of a 30-hour period. Other subjects were offered and repeatedly requested a recording of an old stock-market report.

Temporary sensory deprivation may lead, then, to a heightened level of want arousal. The individual, through a constant stream of ideas and images, represents to himself the rich variety of goal objects in the larger environment. This autonomous activity in the brain may be independent of immediate stimulus inputs. Wants may suddenly emerge, apparently "uncaused." They are, of course, "caused" by the never-ending activity of the nervous system.

The effect of *protracted* existence in an environment which is unstimulating and poor in goal objects may be altogether different. Constantly frustrated because of the impossibility of achieving certain goals, the individual may "forget" the related wants. His *active* wants may become "cut down to size" to fit the impoverished want-arousing potential of his environment. The man who for too long is fed only childish tracts may come to want only such puerile pap in his literature and entertainment.

Methods and problems in the measurement of wants

We will here examine briefly the problem of the ascertaining and measurement of the many and varied social wants and goals whose development and arousal we have been discussing. As we shall see, this problem presents many difficulties.

The methods by which any want or goal can be ascertained and measured fall into three types: (1) those making inferences from actions, (2) those utilizing subjective reports, and (3) those employing various kinds of projective techniques. These three methods are complementary, and all are likely to be used in any investigation of human motivation.

INFERENCES FROM ACTION

In the first method, characteristics of the individual's actions are made the basis for inferences about the effective wants that are driving him. Various action characteristics are used, including perceptual and emotional behavior. Among the indices of wants are: the search for, selection of, and attention to a specific object or class of objects; persistence in a consistent course of action until a specific object is reached or a specific activity is engaged in, at which point the action seems to terminate; the manifestation of satisfaction with the achievement of a specific goal or the manifestation of dissatisfaction when there is failure to achieve a specific goal. The consistent *avoidance* of an object—as when the youngster crosses the street to avoid the neighborhood bully—may also lead to an inference about motivation.

Obviously no one index, taken by itself, can be expected to yield an infallible indication of underlying wants, but several indices taken together will often prove to be diagnostic. Thus, for example, the person who turns first to the financial pages of the newspaper before reading the more general news; who seeks out the company of the wealthy; who works long and hard in his place of business, preferring to spend an extra half-hour there rather than at the cocktail bar or at home; and who is obviously put into very poor humor when his ledgers show a drop in profits—such a person, we can infer, is motivated by the acquisitive want.

But how safely can we make that inference? Often, the apparent consistency of a number of behavioral indices of a particular want can lead to a fallible inference. For example, suppose it is desired to ascertain the major active wants of a man at a party. Observation of his behavior yields the following facts: He moves restlessly about the room, never stopping to talk to anyone, never standing in a single place, until finally he buttonholes another guest—a celebrity—and talks at length to him. He follows the celebrity about the room, breaking into conversation in which the celebrity is engaged; he refuses to be drawn off into conversation or other activity in which the celebrity is not involved; he appears pleased and happy when the celebrity turns attention upon him and unhappy when the celebrity turns away. These indices—his searching, his persistence, his manifestation of satisfaction or displeasure—are all consistent with the inference that the man is seeking social prestige through identification with the celebrity. But this inference may be quite wrong. As we have seen in our discussion of Guide 8, quite different wants may manifest themselves in actions that look alike. Thus the actual fact may be that our man at the party is not at all interested in social prestige. All he wants is to sell the celebrity an insurance policy. The cocktail party has provided him with good opportunity to satisfy his acquisitive want—to get on intimate terms with his intended victim, to prepare him for the "kill."

In order to avoid such errors in inference, a motivational analysis based on behavioral criteria should be supplemented wherever possible by other methods, among which is the subjective report.

SUBJECTIVE REPORT

A great deal about the wants of an individual can be revealed simply by *asking* him what he wants. In many cases, the individual can report directly on his wants as he experiences them, on the goals toward which he is striving, on his fears and aversions, on his feelings of success and failure. Such reports can, of course, yield quantifiable data for which we can assign a score indicating the "strength" of the want. For example, Schachter [1959] used the following self-rating scale to secure a quantitative measure of the strength of individuals' affiliation want.

_____ I very much prefer being alone	(-3)
_____ I prefer being alone	(-2)
_____ I slightly prefer being alone	(-1)
_____ I slightly prefer being together with others	(1)
_____ I prefer being together with others	(2)
_____ I very much prefer being together with others	(3)

However, as we shall see in our discussion of rationalization and repression in Chapter 4, an individual's subjective report may not reveal the truth, the whole truth, and nothing but the truth about his motivations. Frequently the individual will deliberately conceal or fake his subjective reports about his goals, his fears, his aversions, and his aspirations. He will do so for many reasons—because he wishes to make a good impression, because he wishes to please his interviewer, because he wishes to avoid social sanctions. But even when the individual is trying to be completely honest in his subjective reports—in his interviews or in his self-ratings—we still cannot take such material at face value.

For example, the member of a self-appointed censorship group who asserts that she reads pornographic literature through a sense of duty, because she wants to keep such material from corrupting the innocent, may actually be motivated by sexual wants of which she may be only very vaguely aware—or not at all aware.

It is because of these and other considerations that psychologists, in their attempt to determine the wants of the individual, have recourse to still another technique—one designed to "break through" the barriers of concealment or lack of awareness. This is the *projective technique.*

PROJECTIVE TECHNIQUES

The projective technique involves asking the subject to react to ambiguous stimuli (untitled pictures, ink-blot designs, etc.). This technique assumes that the subject's wants will influence the way he perceives these ambiguous stimuli—that he will "project" his private idiosyncratic meanings upon the stimuli. And presumably it matters not whether the wants be conscious or unconscious, for one of the assumptions underlying the projective method is that the individual remains unaware of what his responses reveal. (For an illustration of an attempt to develop a method for measuring the strength of a want through the use of a projective device, see Box 3.7.)

All of the above suggests that a proper description of the wants impelling social behavior requires the insights, concepts, and techniques of the clinician no less than those of the social psychologist. Taken together, the behavioral approach, as exemplified in the many experimental researches; the subjective approach, as embodied in rating forms, interviews, etc.; and the approach by projective techniques constitute the main avenues available to us at present for the exploration of human motivation.

Some major social wants common to Western Man

Man has more wants than any other animal, largely because of his more highly differentiated nervous system. As Tolman [1932] put it, man "reeks with purpose." In this section we will examine some of the major social wants that influence the social behavior of Western Man: affiliation, acquisitiveness, prestige, power, altruism, curiosity.

THE AFFILIATION WANT

People everywhere seem to derive a considerable amount of satisfaction from associating with, or just being near, other persons. We have all experienced, on many occasions, a demanding need for the company of our fellows. Indeed, the *affiliation want,* by drawing men together, makes society possible—and provides social psychology with its object of study! Groups, crowds, organizations, societies—all of these testify to the universality of the affiliation want.

This does not mean, of course, that the existence of groups, societies, and organizations reflects simply the outcome of a "togetherness" want—to be with fellow human beings. The affiliation want, as is true of many wants, is often fused with other wants, and the associations found among men satisfy such fused wants. In seeking fraternal fellowship some men also seek to achieve prestige. The social climber tries to identify himself with elite groups. The power-driven person joins groups so that he can have someone over whom to exercise his power. The salesman combines his fraternal fellowship with a search for customers.

In Chapter 11 we shall examine in some detail the motivations that lead people to join groups and the goals that are satisfied by group membership. The want to belong is an

BOX 3.7: *Fantasies of achievement*

While at Wesleyan University, David C. McClelland and his associates adapted Murray's Thematic Apperception Test in order to measure the strength of the achievement motive.

In this method, stories written in response to untitled pictures showing people in simple situations are scored for "achievement imagery." Achievement imagery is scored when one of the following criteria of concern with some standard of excellence is met: (1) One of the characters in the story expresses concern with winning or doing as well as or better than others. (2) One of the characters is involved in an extraordinary accomplishment that will result in his personal success. (3) One of the characters is involved in reaching a long-term achievement goal, such as becoming a doctor or a lawyer.

Judges tabulate the number of instances of achievement imagery in the stories of a subject. A total score for each individual is secured by summing the number of instances of achievement imagery in his stories. With proper training of judges, this method is quite reliable as measured by interjudge agreement. Interjudge reliability coefficients of .90 or higher for total scores have been reported.

One of the pictures used shows a college youth seated at a table with open books before him. His head is supported by his left hand, as he stares into space. A story told to this picture is reproduced below. Achievement imagery is indicated by italics.

The boy is taking an hour written. He and the others are high school students. The test is about two-thirds over and *he is doing his best to think it through.*

He was supposed to study for the test and did so. But because it is factual there were some items he saw but did not learn.

He knows he has studied the answers he can't remember and *is trying to summon up the images and related ideas to remind him of them.*

He may remember one or two but he will miss most of the items he can't remember. *He will try hard until five minutes is left, then give up, go back over his paper, and be disgusted for reading but not learning the answers.*

McClelland, D. C., Atkinson, J. W., Clark, R. A., and Lowell, E. L. The achievement motive. *New York: Appleton-Century-Crofts, 1953.*

---

imperious want that profoundly influences the social actions of man. It can lead him to aspire to lofty human purposes; it can lead him to treason and murder.

The interpretation of the affiliation want has a long history. For Trotter [1920] it was one of the four instincts which play the most important role in the life of man (the other three were self-preservation, nutrition, and sex). Sumner and Keller [1927] denied the instinctive nature of the affiliative want. They argued that the affiliation want has become characteristic of human beings because of its high survival value. In the group, functions can be carried on (trade and exchange of goods, defense against enemies, ritual ceremonies, division of labor, etc.) which the individual alone cannot accomplish. Also, group life is generally easier and more secure. Thus, according to Sumner and Keller, group life, originally a means to an end, gradually develops—for some people—into a goal sought for itself alone.

Whatever the origin of group life, it is clear

that the expression of the affiliation want inevitably leads to the development of some form of group life. It is for this reason that some social scientists have suggested that the number of groups to which an individual belongs can be taken as a measure of his affiliation want. Indeed, it has been suggested that the number of formal groups—hiking clubs, fraternal orders, charitable organizations, card clubs, etc.—found in a society is a measure of that society's emphasis on "togetherness," or the affiliation want (see Box 3.8).

Sometimes the affiliation want becomes overpowering—the all-important want of the individual. One can almost speak of a pathological affiliation want. Schachter [1959] has pointed out that a strong affiliation want may be related to anxiety. His research indicates that persons who are rendered highly anxious have a stronger desire to be with others than do persons who are less anxious. Here we have a nice illustration of an interaction between a fear (anxiety) and a want (affiliation). The greater intensity of the affiliation want in anxious persons, however, is not a generalized want for the company of others; the highly anxious person wants only to be with those who are in a similar plight (see Box 3.9).

According to Schachter, being with others serves two major functions for the anxious individual. First, the company of others in a similar plight is anxiety-reducing. The simple physical presence of others is comforting. Second, being with others may provide the individual with social cues which will help him to interpret strange and anxiety-evoking situations.

Schachter has reported an additional fact. Persons who were first-born and only children, when they are made highly anxious, strongly prefer the company of others, whereas persons who were later-born children do not (see Table 3.1). This finding, by itself, is ambiguous because it may be specific to situations where anxiety is aroused or it may simply indicate that first-born and only children are more gregarious than later-born children. The table shows that in *low*-anxiety conditions first-born and only children do *not* show a stronger tendency to desire the company of others than do later-born. In fact, the trend is somewhat reversed, for 31 per cent (14 out of 45) of first-born and only children choose to be with others as compared with 41 per cent (23 out of 56) of later-born children. The greater affiliative tendency of first-born and only children is clearly specific to situations where anxiety is aroused.

Further analysis of his data led Schachter to conclude that the stronger affiliation want of first-born and only children when exposed to a fear stimulus is due to two factors: (1) first-born and only children are more *susceptible* to arousal of anxiety by fear-producing conditions; (2) with degree of induced anxiety held constant, first-born and only children are considerably more prone to want to be with others than later-born children.

The above findings may suggest some of

TABLE 3.1: BIRTH ORDER, LEVEL OF ANXIETY, AND NUMBER OF AFFILIATIVE CHOICES [After Schachter, 1959]

Group	HIGH ANXIETY		LOW ANXIETY	
	Affiliation choices	Nonaffiliation choices	Affiliation choices	Nonaffiliation choices
First-born and only children	32	16	14	31
Later-born children	21	39	23	33

BOX 3.8: *America, land of the joiner?*

Folklore has it that the American people are inveterate and insatiable joiners. To check the validity of this common notion, C. R. Wright and H. H. Hyman analyzed data derived from two national surveys conducted by the National Opinion Research Center of the University of Chicago. The first survey in 1953 sampled 2,809 men and women; the second in 1955, 2,379. The results are given in the following table:

<table>
<tr><td align="center">1955 SURVEY</td><td align="center">1953 SURVEY</td></tr>
<tr><td>Question: "Does anyone in the family belong to any sort of club, lodge, fraternal order, or union with ten or more members in it?"</td><td>Question: "Do you happen to belong to any groups or organizations in the community here?" (Union membership is *not* included in this survey.)</td></tr>
</table>

Number of voluntary associations	Percentage of families whose members belong to organizations	Percentage of adults who were themselves members of organizations
None	47	64
One	31	20
Two	12	9
Three	5	4
Four or more	4	3
Unknown	1	0
	100	100

The results clearly indicate that membership in voluntary associations is not characteristic of the majority of Americans. When union membership is not counted, almost two-thirds of Americans belong to no organization. The affiliation want of Americans is thus not mainly met by membership in formal groups in the community.

Wright and Hyman also investigated the relation between socioeconomic status and frequency of membership in organizations. The data are summarized in the following table.

	PERCENTAGES BELONGING TO ORGANIZATIONS	
Socioeconomic indices	No organizations	Two or more organizations
Income level:		
Under $2,000	76	7
$7,500 or over	48	30
Education:		
0 to 6 years	83	5
4 years' college or more	39	36
Level of living (interviewers' rating):		
Very low	92	1
Very high	18	64

Wright, C. R., and Hyman, H. H. Voluntary association memberships of American adults: evidence from national sample surveys. Amer. sociol. Rev., 1958, 23, 284–294.

the developmental factors that determine the intensity of the affiliation want under anxiety-producing conditions.

THE ACQUISITIVE WANT

The want for material gain has been said to be central in the cultures of the countries of the Western world. It would appear, however, that people from other cultures also quickly develop or express this *acquisitive want* when given an opportunity to do so.

This has been particularly true of travelers and students from the underdeveloped nations as they become familiar with the West and its wealth.

For many people material objects become identified with the self, and the acquisition of wealth is self-enhancing. William James [1890] saw this plainly in his discussion of the "extended self":

> It is clear that between what a man calls *me* and what he simply calls *mine* the line is

BOX 3.9: *Misery loves misery*

In his studies of the sources of the affiliation want, Stanley Schachter, a social psychologist at Columbia University, has investigated whether the affiliation want of anxious people is a desire to be with people in general or a desire to be with people who are faced with the same anxiety-evoking situation.

The subjects were undergraduate women, randomly assigned to two experimental conditions, in both of which they were tested individually. On entering the experimental room, the subjects were met by a ". . . gentleman of serious mien, horn-rimmed glasses, dressed in a white laboratory coat, stethoscope dribbling out of his pocket, behind him an array of formidable electrical junk."

After a few preliminaries, the experimenter began: "Allow me to introduce myself. I am Dr. Gregor Zilstein of the Medical School Department of Neurology and Psychiatry. I have asked you to come today to serve as a subject in an experiment concerned with effects of electrical shock." "Dr. Zilstein" paused ominously and then went on to discuss the importance of research upon electroshock therapy. In his concluding remarks, he twice said the shocks the subject was to receive would be quite painful, but would do no permanent damage.

The two experimental conditions differed in only one respect. In the "Same State" condition, the subject was told there would be a ten-minute period of waiting and that the subject could choose to wait alone in the room or could choose to wait with some other girls who were also subjects in the experiment—persons who were in the "same boat." In the "Different State" condition, the subject was given a choice between waiting alone or joining other girls who were waiting to talk with their professors and advisers.

The results of the study were clear. In the "Same State" condition, six of the ten subjects chose to wait with other girls. In the "Different State" condition, *not a single subject* chose to wait with other girls.

In another study, Schachter found that only 33 per cent of subjects with a low level of anxiety chose to wait with other persons in a similar situation.

Under conditions of high anxiety the affiliation want tends to be directed toward the goal of being with other persons who face the same anxiety-evoking situation. "Misery doesn't love just any kind of company, it loves only miserable company . . . it would seem that . . . the satisfaction of [the wants aroused by anxiety] demands the presence of others in a similar situation."

Schachter, S. The psychology of affiliation. Stanford, Calif.: Stanford Univer. Press, 1959.

difficult to draw. . . . In the widest possible sense . . . a man's self is the sum total of all that he can call his, not only his body, and his psychic powers, but his clothes and his house, his wife and his children, his ancestors and friends, his reputation and works, his land and horses and yacht and bank account. All these things give him the same emotions. If they wax and prosper, he feels triumphant, if they dwindle and die away, he feels cast down—not necessarily in the same degree for each thing, but in much the same way for all.

The sociological study of "Middletown" by the Lynds [1929] reveals the pervasive effect of the dominance of the acquisitive want in the American culture. Middletown is a Midwestern town (Muncie, Indiana) with a population, at the time of the study, of about 40,000. The six main activities of the people in this community were: earning a living; making a home; training the young; leisure, play, and art; religious activities; and participation in community affairs. Of these, earning a living was the dominant problem for the people in Middletown, and the amount of money earned served as a standard of one's achievement. Earning a living was a source of great concern from childhood on. Old age was feared because it meant loss of earning power. Education was highly valued as a means of training the young to make a good livelihood. The Lynds comment at length on the "dominance of the dollar" among the people in Middletown and observe that they were "running for dear life to make the money they earn keep pace with the rapid growth of their subjective wants."

The acquisitive want seems to be almost entirely lacking in the members of certain of the simpler societies of the world. The economic system of such societies has been described as a kind of partial or complete "communism." Powdermaker [1933] has reported that among the people of Lesu, a Melanesian group, there is no private ownership of land or of fishing or hunting rights. There is a certain amount of private ownership of ornaments, work implements, and ceremonial currency. The private property that does exist among the people of Lesu is used by the men to perform ancestral rites and thus gain prestige. (For a study which suggests that the acquisitive want must be *un*learned in such "communistic" societies, see Box 3.10.)

It should, however, be pointed out that the acquisition of wealth is often essential for the psychological development of the individual and the building of a culture. It is the accumulation of excess wealth—goods in excess of the immediate requirements of a people—which releases man from an unceasing, day-by-day concern with the problems of securing food, clothing, and shelter. The accumulation of wealth may help provide, in other words, the necessary condition for the unfolding of the "higher" wants (see page 76). The acquisitive want, like so many other wants, can result in good or in evil. Money is the root of all things.

THE PRESTIGE WANT

If the defense and enhancement of the self are as basic as we have said (pages 83 to 84), we should expect to find all men everywhere competing for status and struggling to avoid social failure. And this is what we do find when we look at Mr. Everyman. As we shall see in Chapter 9 it is the *prestige want* that is mainly responsible for the marked social mobility characteristic of Western society.

The expression of the prestige want takes different forms in different societies. Thus, in the "acquisitive societies" of the Western world, prestige is often reckoned by counting the number and value of the material goods accumulated by the individual. Here there is fusion of the prestige and acquisitive wants.

In some societies prestige is accorded the indigent mystic. And in some societies the prestige want seems to take the paradoxical form of deliberate self-effacement. This may

BOX 3.10: *The sabras of Kiryat Yedidim*

Melford E. Spiro, an anthropologist, and his wife, Audrey G. Spiro, spent a year (1951–1952) as participant observers of Kiryat Yedidim, one of the more than 300 *kibbutzim* (communal-operated farms) which dot the Israeli landscape.

In Kiryat Yedidim all work is performed by work crews under an elected foreman. All capital goods are owned by the Kibbutz and money has been abolished as a medium of exchange. Individuals possess only a few personal effects. Distribution of goods is determined at the biweekly Town Meeting according to the principle "from each according to his ability, to each according to his needs." Presumably the acquisitive want does not—or cannot—operate here.

The structure of the family and the rearing and education of the young have undergone a revolutionary transformation in the Kibbutz. The Kibbutz grants a combined bedroom–sitting room to married couples. This room is their home. Meals are cooked in the communal kitchen and eaten in the communal dining room. The children live in communal nurseries where they are reared by "nurses" and teachers. Both parents work a full nine-hour day and see their children only during the period between their return from work and the children's bedtime.

What impact has this Kibbutz culture had upon personality development? The Spiros studied 11 sabras (persons born and raised in the Kibbutz) intensively through observation of their behavior, interviews, and personality tests. We will here describe only the findings concerning the acquisitive want.

There was abundant evidence of strong concern with private property among the preschool and grammar school children. Among the adult sabras, on the other hand, there was little or no concern with private property. The following interview excerpts are illustrative of the attitudes the sabras expressed when queried about personal possessions.

"I've never felt any desire for personal property. But if someone offered me a million dollars, I'd take it."

"Sometimes I would like to dress better, to have a nicer room. But the lack of these things does not ruin my life, and I really feel that I lack nothing. I have satisfactions from living here, and I have never felt that I was not working for myself."

The interview findings are supported by the results of the Stewart Emotional Response Test, a personality inventory. The acquisition of personal belongings was never given as a condition for happiness; only 6 per cent of the responses gave the acquisition of personal possessions as the "best thing" that could happen to one. Conversely, the lack of possessions made up only 4 per cent of their responses concerning the causes of anger, 0 per cent concerning the causes of sadness, and 0 per cent concerning the worst thing that could happen to them. Spiro interprets these findings by noting:

The sabra attitude toward private property would suggest that the Kibbutz value of collective ownership has been successfully transmitted from the founding to the second generation. And this, as our data on early childhood indicate, is no easy task. For these data suggest . . . that the child's early motivations are strongly directed toward private ownership, an orientation from which he is only gradually weaned by effective cultural techniques.

Spiro, M. E. Children of the Kibbutz. *Cambridge, Mass.: Harvard Univer. Press, 1958.*

be true, for example, of the Hopi and Zuñi Indians of the American Southwest.

The early students of the Zuñi and Hopi cultures were wont to point to them as the prime example of peoples who have no prestige wants. It was pointed out by these anthropologists, for example, that Hopi children were loath to engage in competitive games and, when they did so, were careful not to best their companions. However, later field observations and more careful analyses of the data indicate that these people merely have a method of expressing their prestige want which is quite foreign (and therefore not easily recognizable) to the Western anthropologist. For them the "good man" is the person one never hears anything about—but each man strives to become "anonymous" so that he will stand out as the "good man." Moreover, while Asch [1937] confirmed the observation that Hopi children are reluctant to compete with one another in games, he also found that they were pathetically eager for any sort of recognition they could get and resorted to "fishing" for compliments. And Goldman [1937] has pointed out that among the Zuñi there is much backbiting and recrimination. A person may not compete openly but he can and does depreciate others—and thereby gains in status.

Careful analysis of the Zuñi and Hopi, then, suggests that they are not altogether lacking in the prestige drive. The struggle to preserve or enhance feelings of self-worth or prestige marks all men who live above a bare subsistence level.

This pervasive want may lead men to accomplish good works or it may lead them into destructive, antisocial behavior. In a scientist, the prestige want may provide much of the force behind his work and may eventually lead to a discovery of tremendous importance for the advancement of scientific understanding and the welfare of people everywhere. In a Napoleon Bonaparte it may lead to endless wars, bloodshed, and misery—for the glorification and prestige of the Emperor.

THE POWER WANT

The *power want*—the desire to control other persons or objects, to obtain their obedience, to compel their actions, to determine their fate—has enormous significance for the workings of a society. It is this want with which effective leaders must be liberally endowed—and it is the society with effective leaders which survives periods of crises. It is also this want which can bring a society to destruction. Indeed, the formal norms (constitutions, laws, etc.) of many of the Western societies make specific provision for the regulation and control of this want in their leaders.

Just as the acquisition and prestige wants are frequently fused together in many cultures, so also are the prestige and power wants. This fusion can be seen very frequently in the behavior of leaders of various groups and organizations—labor leaders, religious leaders, political leaders, and business executives. Thus, in an early study, Houser [1927] interviewed a large number of top business executives in an effort to uncover the wants that were influencing their business actions. The following quotations reveal the importance of the power want.

> Frequently the craving of the executive for the exercise of power was actually greater than the desire for financial returns.
>
> The desire for self-expression [in executives] is closely related to the desire to obtain and exercise power over others. . . . Power is very often the definite form of expression desired. . . . Their trampling upon other personalities, their hunger for self-expression and their keen joy in using their power constantly produce in workers a bitter resentment.

The power want may have its origin in self-defense and self-enhancement. The objects which are incorporated into the extended self have been said by several writers to be those over which the individual can exercise power or control. Thus, Rogers [1948] has stated that perhaps the basis for incorporating an event into the self is the person's awareness

BASIC PSYCHOLOGICAL FACTORS

"of a feeling of control over some aspect of his world experience." Power over objects and persons may lead the individual to make them part of his self-picture. With an extension of the self to include objects and persons comes a feeling of increased self-potency.

The power want does not necessarily lead to antisocial actions. In a Franklin D. Roosevelt it may be harnessed to socially desirable ends; in a Hitler, to death, destruction, and terror.

THE ALTRUISTIC WANT

Man's behavior is both self-oriented and other-oriented. He works both to advance himself and to help others. The desire to help others, or the *altruistic want,* appears early in childhood. For some observations of "sympathetic" behavior in nursery school children, see Box 3.11.

These illustrations from the nursery school playground may seem far removed from the affairs of society. But it is from such simple beginnings in childhood that the altruistic want is elaborated into the ameliorative and philanthropic works of man. The promotion of man's welfare is a major preoccupation of many people in many parts of the world and seems to be highly valued in most societies. It is therefore curious indeed that so little re-

BOX 3.11: *Altruism on the playground*

In an exploratory study, Lois B. Murphy, a child psychologist, observed several different categories of sympathetic responses of nursery school children to the distress of others. These systematically recorded observations, which could be multiplied many times by informal everyday accounts, indicate that the altruistic want appears early in childhood.

1. Sympathetic responses sometimes took the form of comforting the crying child.

   Mary fell and cried. Douglas and Evan were near; they looked, and went off. Winifred approached, looked, then put her arm around Mary and kissed her.

2. Sometimes the sympathetic responses took the form of verbal assistance.

   Winifred was on top of the sliding board. She cried, "Miss S., I can't get down, I can't get down." Evan runs up, "Why can't you?" Winifred, "I can't!" Evan, "Yes you can. Go down like this with your feet." Winifred climbed on the sliding board from the box and slid down.

3. Direct attempts to help one another were sometimes observed.

   Mary bounced a ball. It rolled away. Douglas ran to the ball and said, "I'll get it for you, Mary." He gave her the ball.

4. Occasionally, the children did "thoughtful" things.

   Nancy's mother came to the roof. Kirk looked at her, went to the cupboard, took out a folding chair, opened it, and said, "Here," to Nancy's mother. She said, "Thank you." Kirk smiled.

5. Sympathetic responses frequently took the form of punishing or reproving a child who had attacked another or who had taken property from another.

   Peter pushed Evan as they got into a large box. Evan cried. Douglas approached and spanked Peter.

   Murphy, Lois B. Social behavior and child personality. *New York: Columbia Univer. Press, 1937.*

BOX 3.12: *The playful ape*

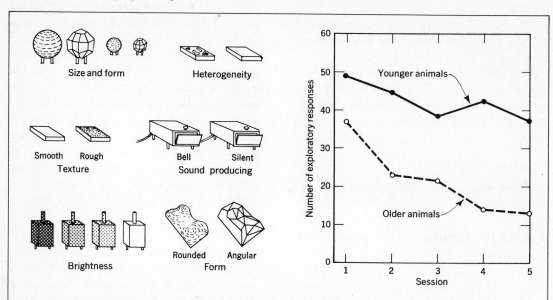

In a study carried out at the Yerkes Primate Laboratory, W. I. Welker observed play and exploration in three young chimpanzees (3–4 years of age) and three older chimpanzees (7–8 years) when presented with various "playthings."

The animals were presented with 13 successive objects, some of which are pictured in the above figure. The sets of objects were so designed as to vary in different dimensions, e.g., size, movability, texture.

Each set of objects was presented to each animal for sessions of six minutes, or until his exploration of and play with the object ceased. As measures of play and exploration the experimenter recorded (during five-second observation periods) the occurrence of manipulation of the object, e.g., mouthing, smelling, scratching, slapping, groping, and head orientation directed toward the object. The major findings of the study were:

1. Exploratory responses decreased with the repeated presentation of the same set of objects over the course of several successive sessions. Thus, with familiarity, the objects gradually lost their novelty and curiosity-arousing capacity for the animal. *Familiarity breeds boredom.*

2. As the graph shows, the rate of the satiation of manipulation responses toward the familiar objects was faster for the older animals. *The old bore easily.*

3. The three younger animals were significantly more responsive to all objects during the 112 observation sessions than were the older animals. This age difference was due to the slower rate of satiation found in the younger chimpanzees. *The young stay curious.*

4. When a novel set of objects was introduced, it elicited a renewed burst of exploratory activity significantly higher in amount than had occurred with the previous familiar objects. Even such a slight stimulus novelty as changing the color of the tray on which the objects were presented (from gray to red) evoked increased exploratory action. *The curious are grateful for any novelty.*

*Welker, W. I. Some determinants of play and exploration in chimpanzees. J. comp. physiol. Psychol., 1956, **49**, 84–89.*

search by psychologists and sociologists has been done on this most "social" want. In recent years only one sociologist [Sorokin, 1950] has written extensively on it.

THE CURIOSITY WANT

Man is a curious animal. He displays an almost insatiable interest in exploring his world and in manipulating the objects in it. That the *curiosity want* is a biologically deep-rooted one is indicated by the fact that even the lower animals display a strong exploratory or manipulative drive (see Box 3.12).

The play behavior of the child has been interpreted by many writers as a means of gaining an understanding and mastery of the environment. Thus, White [1959] writes:

> The child appears to be occupied with the agreeable task of developing an effective familiarity with his environment. This involves discovering the effects he can have on the environment and the effects the environment can have on him. To the extent that these results are preserved by learning, they build up increased competence in dealing with the environment.

The curiosity want is closely related to man's insistent search for knowledge. It is true that a great deal of man's search for knowledge is motivated by the need to solve practical problems. A want is aroused, and knowledge is needed to satisfy it.

But this is not the whole story. Man frequently engages in thinking simply to find an explanation for something that perplexes him. The strange and puzzling arouse his curiosity and he seeks an explanation that will make the strange familiar, and the puzzling meaningful and understandable. As William James put it, "The philosophic brain responds to an inconsistency or a gap in its knowledge, just as the musical brain responds to a discord in what it hears." The inconsistent demands to be made consistent; the gap demands to be filled in. The curious man delights in knowl-edge for its own sweet sake. Indeed, when there is no puzzle facing man, he will frequently search out—or even create—puzzles which he will then work to solve.

The curiosity want, like the other social wants we have discussed, varies markedly in strength among individuals. In his factor analyses of human motives, Cattell [1957] has repeatedly found a want he calls exploration, which shows marked individual differences. In Cattell's tests, exploration or curiosity was manifested in the desire to read books, newspapers, and magazines, to listen to music, to know more about science, to satisfy curiosity about neighborhood affairs, to study paintings and sculpture, to learn more about mechanical and electrical gadgets, to see films and plays.

The arousal of the curiosity want, of course, depends in part upon the environment in which the individual lives. The rich and complex environment will evoke more wonder and more search for an "explanation" of the wonder than will the impoverished environment. Some studies have been made in an attempt to determine which particular properties of stimuli are most effective in eliciting curiosity responses (see Box 3.13).

However, quite apart from external sources of curiosity arousal, there appears to be a compelling "self-generated" need for ever-varied stimulation. As Bexton, Heron, and Scott have shown, when the individual is deprived of his "normal" amount of stimulation, he makes strong efforts to increase the complexity of his surroundings (see page 87).

A FINAL WORD. The want for affiliation; the want to accumulate wealth; the want to surpass all others; the want to control one's fellows, obtain their obedience, and compel their action; the want to come to their succor when they are in need; and the deep-rooted driving want to *know*—it is the expression of these wants, often contradictory in their effects and conflicting in their demands on the self, which we will trace as we continue our study of the behavior of man in society.

BOX 3.13: *The curious world—incongruous, complex, surprising, and irregular*

INCONGRUITY

"Animals" series
1 2 3 4 5 6 7

"Birds" series
1 2 3 4 5 6 7

COMPLEXITY

"Bear" series
1 2 3 4 5 6

"Clown" series
1 2 3 4 5 6

D. E. Berlyne, an experimental psychologist, has carried out a number of studies on the stimuli which arouse the curiosity want.

In one series of experiments, the subject was seated in a darkened room before a tachistoscope. By pressing a lever, he could expose a figure in the tachistoscope for 0.14 second. The instructions emphasized that the purpose of the experiments was to determine how "interesting" certain figures were, and that no questions about the figures would be asked at any time. The subject could look at any particular figure as often as he liked. When he had seen enough of one figure, he was to say "Yes" and the figure would be replaced by a new one.

Each subject took part in four experiments. The stimulus variables studied are shown in the figures.

The results showed that these four properties of stimulus figures arouse the looking or curiosity response:

1. *Incongruity.* In Experiment 1 it was found that such incongruous pictures as animals 2 and 4 and birds 3 and 5 elicited more looking than pictures of normal animals and birds.

2. *Complexity.* The two series of six figures used in Experiment 2 progressively increase in complexity from 1 to 6. The mean number of curiosity responses per card increased with the

CHAPTER GUIDES AND GLOSSARY

GUIDE 7: *The thought and action of the individual reflect his wants and goals*
GUIDE 8: *The wants and goals of the individual continuously develop and change*
GUIDE 9: *Wants and goals become organized around the self*
GUIDE 10: *The arousal of any particular set of wants depends upon the momentary physiological state, situation, and cognitions of the individual*

acquisitive want. The desire to possess or to hoard material possessions, e.g., money, sea shells, clothing, stamps, houses, wampum. The objects of the acquisitive want are often those objects esteemed by the individual's society. The objects may become part of the "extended self" and thus serve to increase self-esteem.

affiliation want. The desire to be associated with

or to be in the presence of another person or persons. This want seems to be universal.

altruistic want. The desire to help others. It expresses itself in many ways—through sympathy, philanthropy, etc. The person with a strong altruistic want has affection and concern for other people and is usually contrasted with the "selfish" person.

curiosity want. The impelling force to explore

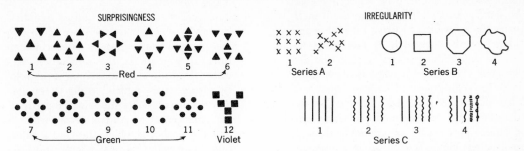

increased degree of complexity, whether a series was presented in numerical order from 1 to 6 or in a random order.

3. *Surprisingness.* The twelve cards of Experiment 3 contained geometric figures of colored spots. Numbers 1 to 6 were made up of red triangles, 7 to 11 of green circles, and 12 of violet squares. Surprisingness may be attributed to 7 and 12, since they both differ sharply in color and form from at least five immediately preceding figures. These surprising figures elicited more curiosity responses than did 2 to 6 and 8 to 11.

4. *Irregularity.* In Experiment 4, three series of figures were used which increased progressively in irregularity. In all cases, the more irregular figures attracted more curiosity responses.

Experiment 1 and slightly modified versions of Experiments 2 and 3 were also tried on five-year-old children. On the average, the children responded 12.1 times per figure, as compared with a mean response of only 2.3 times per figure for advanced college students. The young do not bore easily; their eyes see freshness and wonderment in all things. This resistance of children to the satiation of curiosity responses is similar to that we have seen in the young chimpanzees studied by Welker (see Box 3.12).

Berlyne, D. E. Conflict, arousal, and curiosity. *New York: McGraw-Hill, 1960.*

and investigate one's environment, to seek novel stimulation, to strive after knowledge. While curiosity behavior frequently occurs in the service of other wants, it is assumed that the curiosity want is an autonomous one.

goal. The objects and activities with respect to those objects which fulfill or satisfy the relevant want; the end result, immediate or remote, which the individual seeks. Goals may involve either "approach objects" or "avoidance objects." The former are associated with positive wants; the latter, with negative wants.

ideal self. The person's conception of what he *ought* to be like, how he *ought* to act; the set of *values* which he holds for himself. The ideal self provides a standard against which his behavior and achievements are evaluated. The ideal self is significantly influenced by social factors, and the person's conception of the ideal self tends to reflect the values of his reference groups.

intermediate goals. Subgoals which the individual must successively achieve en route to his final goal. Intermediate goals are set up by the individual when the final goal is remote in time. The setting up of such successive intermediate goals which are capable of achievement in a relatively short time may help to maintain the morale and sustain the long-term effort of the individual in striving for a remote goal.

power want. The desire to control other persons or objects, to obtain their obedience, to compel their actions, to determine their fate.

The power want is often fused with the prestige want.

prestige want. The desire to be highly regarded by one's associates. The prestige want motivates the individual to strive for higher and higher status, inasmuch as prestige is accorded high-status persons in class-stratified societies. The prestige want is often fused with the acquisitive and power wants.

projective technique. A method intended for the detection and measurement of wants and attitudes not readily ascertainable through more direct methods. Consists in the presentation of ambiguous materials (e.g., ink blots, untitled pictures, etc.), in the interpretation of which the viewer is said to "project" tendencies which he may be unaware or wish to conceal. The Thematic Apperception Test is one instance of a projective test.

reference group. Any group with which an individual identifies himself such that he tends to use the group as a standard for self-evaluation and as a source of his personal values and goals. The reference groups of the individual may include both membership groups and groups to which he aspires to belong.

self. The individual as he sees himself. According to Mead and other social psychologists, the self is a product of social interaction and develops gradually. The nature of the self helps to determine the organization of the individual's wants and goals, and the defense of the self may become one of his major concerns.

substitute goal. A sought-after object, condition, or activity which takes the place of an original goal. In the absence of goals which are fully appropriate to the satisfaction of a want, the individual may come to develop substitute goals which, while acceptable, will not have exactly the same properties or the same power to satisfy relevant wants as will the goals for which they are a substitute. Through experience with substitute goals, the individual's wants may be so changed that a substitute goal becomes primary.

values. Beliefs about what is a desirable or a "good" (e.g., free speech) and what is an undesirable or a "bad" (e.g., dishonesty). Values reflect the culture of a society and are widely shared by the members of the culture. If the individual accepts a value for himself, it may become a goal for him.

wants. The initiating and sustaining forces of behavior. Wants may be either positive or negative. A positive want (e.g., a desire) is an assumed force which impels a person toward the achievement of a goal. A negative want (e.g., anxiety) is a force which repels a person away from certain objects or conditions. Common synonyms for positive wants are *drives, needs;* for negative wants, *fears, aversions.*

WE ARE NOW READY TO ADD THE THIRD DIMENSION TO OUR
*picture of man as a thinking, wanting, and acting being. And with
this psychological factor, as with the two previous ones, our main
concern is its functioning in the social context. That is, in our
analysis of man's actions we are primarily interested in his
interactions—in how he interacts with his fellows.*

*Each one of us, through the vagaries of chance and the determining
influence of heredity and personal experience, develops a distinctive
set of enduring dispositions to respond to other people in
characteristic ways. Thus one man will eye all of his neighbors as
potential enemies and will be wary and suspicious in his dealings
with them; another will see himself surrounded only by well-wishing
friends and will be free and open in his social intercourse. These
dispositions—here called* interpersonal response traits—*play the
same kind of central explanatory role for the social psychologist that
psychodynamic personality traits play for the personologist and
clinical psychologist. Interpersonal response traits help us to describe
social man, to understand his behavior, and to predict his actions.*

*With the examination of the origins, development, and structure of
interpersonal response traits in this chapter, we complete Part One
of the book.*

4: INTERPERSONAL RESPONSE TRAITS

TO COMPREHEND FULLY THE SIGNIFICANCE OF
cognition and motivation in the governance
of social behavior we must consider in some
detail what happens to the individual as he
reacts to his world and to his wants. In the
course of the history of man's wants—the frequency and circumstances of their arousal,
their satisfaction, and their frustration—various residual and lasting effects are, as it were,
laid down in him. It is perhaps fair to say that
every time a man reacts to his environment he
becomes a permanently changed man—be it

ever so slightly. Of particular importance to the social psychologist are those residual effects which become embodied in characteristic ways of reacting to other persons.

With this last chapter of Part One we will have come full circle. In Chapter 2 we started with a discussion of cognition—of how man learns about his world. We then proceeded in Chapter 3 to examine the wants of man. Now we turn our attention to a study of how the cognitions and wants of man help determine his interpersonal response traits. And in our study of the genesis and formation of interpersonal response traits, we will find that we are, perforce, studying the social techniques whereby man learns about his world and develops and fulfills his wants.

GUIDE 11: *The social behavior of the individual is channeled by his interpersonal response traits— relatively consistent and stable dispositions to respond in distinctive ways to other persons*

Within any given society, each person develops a distinctive pattern of *interpersonal response traits* that characterizes his social conduct. These traits are consistent and stable response dispositions that channel the behavior of the individual in a variety of social situations (see Box 4.1).

As we shall presently see, the pattern of such traits characteristic of an individual is the resultant of constitutional factors, the growth of the individual within the confines of a given social environment, and the past history of his experiences of success and failure with various means of want satisfaction.

To refer to such an interpersonal disposition, e.g., aggressiveness, as a "trait" is to emphasize that it describes something distinctive about the *individual*. Obviously, the occurrence of an aggressive act depends partly on the nature of the particular situation. Some situations tend to be especially aggression-evoking and every individual will display some degree of aggressiveness in them. But the important point is that some individuals show more aggressiveness in a particular situation than do others and may *regularly show more in a wide variety of situations*. We are led to infer that such characteristic behavior is the expression of a "trait" of aggressiveness in the individual.

A trait is not, of course, something that exists on an all-or-none basis. It exists in different amounts in different persons. Every individual possesses some degree of aggressiveness and, indeed, of every other interpersonal response trait.

The number of possible interpersonal traits is extremely large. There are endless different nuances in styles of reacting to, dealing with, and handling other persons. Some of these forms of behavior are, however, of lesser social significance than others. Ruesch [1953], using the term "social techniques" which Tolman [1942] had invented to cover what we call interpersonal response traits, has distinguished between long-term social techniques—what we may think of as interpersonal strategies—and short-term techniques—interpersonal tactics.

Under long-term techniques, one might mention social climbing or prestige seeking, maintenance of superiority and dominance, nurturance (mothering or fathering), conformance, cooperation, competition, rivalry, dependence, social decline, self-abasive, avoidant, isolating, aggressive-destructive techniques, and acquisition or use of others. Among the short-term techniques one might mention testing out, unthawing, startling, joking, teasing, flattering, offending, seducing, threatening, bribing, and pitying.

It should not be assumed that these various techniques are deliberately selected and employed by the individual. Though it is sometimes true that he is fully aware of what he is doing in his social tactics and strategies, more

BOX 4.1: *Moving toward, against, and away from people*

Karen Horney was one of the leaders in the neo-Freudian movement which asserted that neurotic difficulties must be seen as disturbances in interpersonal relations. At one point in her theoretical work she found it convenient to classify her patients into three types according to their predominant interpersonal response trait: (1) moving *toward* people, (2) moving *against* people, and (3) moving *away from* people.

A person whose predominant interpersonal trait is one of moving toward people

> . . . shows a marked need for affection and approval and an especial need for a "partner"— that is, a friend, lover, husband or wife who is to fulfill all expectations of life and take responsibility for good and evil. . . . [He] needs to be liked, wanted, desired, loved; to feel accepted, welcome, approved of, appreciated; to be needed, to be of importance to others, especially to one particular person; to be helped, protected, taken care of, guided.

A person whose predominant interpersonal response trait is one of moving against people perceives

> . . . that the world is an arena where, in the Darwinian sense, only the fittest survive and the strong annihilate the weak. . . . a callous pursuit of self-interest is the paramount law. . . . He needs to excel, to achieve success, prestige or recognition in any form. . . . A strong need to exploit others, to outsmart them, to make them of use to himself, is part of the picture. Any situation or relationship is looked at from the standpoint of "What can I get out of it?"

For the person whose interpersonal response trait is moving away from people:

> The underlying principle . . . is never to become so attached to anybody or anything that he or it becomes indispensable. . . . Another pronounced need is for privacy. He is like a person in a hotel room who rarely removes the "Do Not Disturb" sign from his door. . . . Self-sufficiency and privacy both serve his outstanding need, the need for utter independence. . . . His independence, like the whole phenomenon of detachment of which it is a part, has a negative orientation; it is aimed at *not* being influenced, coerced, tied, obligated. . . . To conform with accepted rules of behavior or traditional sets of values is repellent to him. He will conform outwardly in order to avoid friction, but in his own mind he stubbornly rejects all conventional rules and standards.

Horney summarizes the three types as follows:

> Where the compliant type looks at his fellow men with the silent question, "Will he like me?"—and the aggressive type wants to know, "How strong an adversary is he?" or "Can he be useful to me?"—the detached person's concern is, "Will he interfere with me? Will he want to influence me or leave me alone?"

While Horney's tripartite typology serves to illustrate the concept of interpersonal response trait, we should point out that it is, of course, an oversimplification of the multifarious interpersonal response traits which help to govern behavior.

Horney, Karen. Our inner conflicts. *New York: Norton, 1945.*

often he is unaware of the distinctive interpersonal response traits that he exhibits.

It is with the socially more relevant long-term techniques that we will here be mainly concerned. And among these we will concentrate on that limited number of primary traits which seem to be of major importance in governing action in the interpersonal behavior event.

SOME PRIMARY INTERPERSONAL RESPONSE TRAITS

Table 4.1 presents 12 primary interpersonal response traits. This list is fairly representative of the traits that have been enumerated and discussed by various investigators. (See, for example, Guilford's 1959 review.)

We have classified the traits into three arbitrary categories: Role Dispositions, Sociometric Dispositions, and Expressive Dispositions. For each trait, a number of behavioral indicators is given to define its nature.

ROLE DISPOSITIONS. Under this rubric, we have placed ascendance, dominance, social initiative, and independence. These four dispositions are assumed to be most concerned with determining the manner in which the individual performs his roles in interpersonal behavior events.

Ascendance is to be interpreted as "social

TABLE 4.1: **SOME PRIMARY INTERPERSONAL RESPONSE TRAITS** (Only one pole of each of these response traits is described here. The other pole is given in parentheses.)

ROLE DISPOSITIONS

Ascendance (social timidity). Defends his rights; does not mind being conspicuous; not self-reticent; self-assured; forcefully puts self forward

Dominance (submissiveness). Assertive; self-confident; power-oriented; tough; strong-willed; order-giving or directive leader

Social initiative (social passivity). Organizes groups; does not stay in background; makes suggestions at meetings; takes over leadership

Independence (dependence). Prefers to do own planning, to work things out in own way; does not seek support or advice; emotionally self-sufficient

SOCIOMETRIC DISPOSITIONS

Accepting of others (rejecting of others). Nonjudgmental in attitude toward others; permissive; believing and trustful; overlooks weaknesses and sees best in others

Sociability (unsociability). Participates in social affairs; likes to be with people; outgoing

Friendliness (unfriendliness). Genial, warm; open and approachable; approaches other persons easily; forms many social relationships

Sympathetic (unsympathetic). Concerned with the feelings and wants of others; displays kindly, generous behavior; defends underdog

EXPRESSIVE DISPOSITIONS

Competitiveness (noncompetitiveness). Sees every relationship as a contest—others are rivals to be defeated; self-aggrandizing; noncooperative

Aggressiveness (nonaggressiveness). Attacks others directly or indirectly; shows defiant resentment of authority; quarrelsome; negativistic

Self-consciousness (social poise). Embarrassed when entering a room after others are seated; suffers excessively from stage fright; hesitates to volunteer in group discussions; bothered by people watching him at work; feels uncomfortable if different from others

Exhibitionistic (self-effacing). Is given to excess and ostentation in behavior and dress; seeks recognition and applause; shows off and behaves queerly to attract attention

BASIC PSYCHOLOGICAL FACTORS

boldness" or "self-assurance." It is not the same as dominance, although there is a high correlation between the two traits. The ascendant person does not necessarily act so as to dominate others. The opposite pole of ascendance is social timidity, or fear of strangers; the opposite pole of dominance is submissiveness.

Dominance is a trait observed in many animals, including man. Thus, the well-known pecking order in chickens is a dominance hierarchy. For studies illustrating the effects of constitutional factors and "cultural training" upon the development of dominance, see Boxes 4.2 and 4.3.

A person with a high score on social initiative is the social "organizer"—the person who seizes the initiative in group meetings and aspires to leadership.

Independence, the fourth of the role dispositions, has sometimes been termed "self-sufficiency." Horney's two types, "moving away from others" and "moving toward others" (again see Box 4.1), appear to be related to the polar extremes of this trait.

SOCIOMETRIC DISPOSITIONS. In this category are placed those interpersonal response traits which primarily pertain to the sociometric relations of the individual with others—his liking for others, his concern for and trust in others, etc. Persons with high scores on these four sociometric dispositions tend to become easily involved with other persons, to identify with them, and, usually, to be skilled in managing human relations.

EXPRESSIVE DISPOSITIONS. In the third category fall those four dispositions which pertain to the *style* of interpersonal functioning, i.e., to the particular fashion in which the individual expresses himself in responding to others. These traits, in extreme form, may reflect themselves in virtually everything an individual does in a social situation. One person may compete incessantly; another may find endless targets for his aggressiveness; another may "show off" at every conceivable

opportunity; another may suffer the "torments of the damned" whenever he is exposed to the merciless view of other people.

ASCERTAINING INTERPERSONAL RESPONSE TRAITS

The principal source of data for ascertaining and measuring interpersonal response traits has been *self-descriptions* secured through personality inventories or clinical interviews. From the mass of information on such personality inventories, "primary" interpersonal response traits have been extracted by a statistical procedure known as *factor analysis*. This procedure was developed to determine the smallest number of factors or clusters which it is necessary to assume to account for all the intercorrelations between a set of tests.

A factor analysis begins with the intercorrelations among the tests. Those tests which intercorrelate highly and which are relatively independent of other tests are said to form a factor or cluster. The next step is to examine the content of the tests which make up the factor to determine what is common among them. The factor is then described and named.

A concrete example may be useful. Guilford [1959] has provided us with a simple illustration which we have adapted for our use. Table 4.2 shows the intercorrelations among scores on the following four personality inventories:

1. Liking for social affairs (Sample item: Do you like to have many social engagements?)

2. Gregariousness (Sample item: Do you prefer to work with others rather than to work alone?)

3. Self-defense (Sample item: Are you rather good at bluffing when you find yourself in difficulty?)

4. Maintaining one's rights (Sample item: Do you ever protest to a waiter or clerk when you think that you have been overcharged?)

Note that tests 1 and 2 correlate highly (.56) and both are virtually independent of

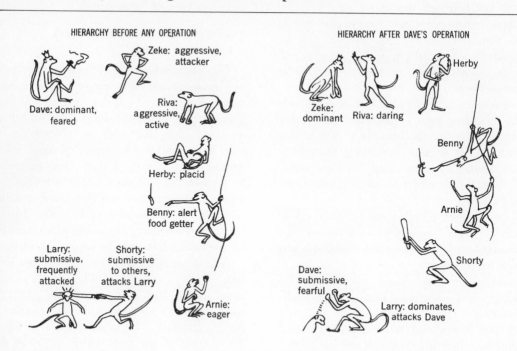

HIERARCHY BEFORE ANY OPERATION

Zeke: aggressive, attacker

Dave: dominant, feared

Riva: aggressive, active

Herby: placid

Benny: alert food getter

Larry: submissive, frequently attacked

Shorty: submissive to others, attacks Larry

Arnie: eager

HIERARCHY AFTER DAVE'S OPERATION

Herby

Zeke: dominant   Riva: daring

Benny

Arnie

Dave: submissive, fearful

Shorty

Larry: dominates, attacks Dave

H. Enger Rosvold, Allan F. Mirsky, and Karl H. Pribram studied at Yale University the modification of the social dominance hierarchy in a group of monkeys produced by cortical lesions.

Observations of dominance in food getting and aggressive chasing, biting, and threatening gestures among eight young male rhesus monkeys revealed a firmly established dominance hierarchy in the group. (In the figure the "interpersonal response traits" ascribed to these monkeys are taken from the original descriptions provided by Rosvold, Mirsky, and Pribram.)

When the dominance hierarchy had been reliably determined, Dave, the most dominant monkey, was operated upon and an extensive, bilateral lesion was produced in the temporal lobes. After recovery, Dave was returned to the group. He became submissive to all the monkeys and Zeke now became the most dominant.

Zeke was next subjected to the brain operation. He maintained his top position for four days after being returned to the group, but then became submissive to all but Larry and Dave. Riva now dominated the group.

Finally, Riva was subjected to the cortical operation. Riva continued to maintain his No. 1 position and *at no time during a two-month postoperative observation period did he show a drop in dominance.*

The results of this experiment indicate two things: (1) Interference with the normal functioning of the nervous system produces marked changes in the social behavior of the monkeys. (2) These changes are in large measure limited and modulated by the normal "interpersonal response traits" of the monkeys. Dave, after his operation, was faced with aggressive and active

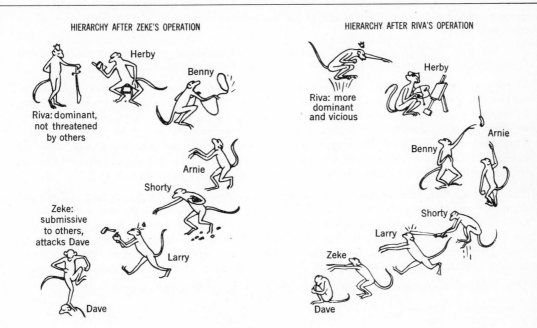

HIERARCHY AFTER ZEKE'S OPERATION

Herby

Benny

Riva: dominant, not threatened by others

Arnie

Shorty

Zeke: submissive to others, attacks Dave

Larry

Dave

HIERARCHY AFTER RIVA'S OPERATION

Herby

Riva: more dominant and vicious

Arnie

Benny

Shorty

Larry

Zeke

Dave

Zeke. Dave fell in the dominance hierarchy. Zeke, after surgery, was confronted by an aggressive Riva. Zeke dropped in dominance. Riva, after surgery, was returned to the colony to face Herby, a placid, nonaggressive animal who was not interested in challenging Riva. Riva remained dominant.

Dominance was also related to the length of time that the operated animal had been dominant. Dave, whose dominance dropped immediately, had been dominant only six weeks; Zeke, who maintained his top position in the hierarchy for four days after surgery, had been dominant for ten weeks; Riva, who did not change in dominance, had been No. 1 in the hierarchy for 16 weeks.

The investigators conclude:

> This study, then, suggests that the pattern of social interaction within the group to which [the animal] is returned after surgery and the length of preoperative time the relationship had existed may be as important a consideration as the locus and extent of a lesion in determining the effects of a brain operation on the social behavior of a monkey.

In other words, a complete description of the *physiological* control of social behavior must include specification of the *social setting* of the event and the normal *interpersonal response traits* of the participants.

> *Rosvold, H. E., Mirsky, A. F., and Pribram, K. H. Influence of amygdalectomy on social behavior in monkeys. J. comp. physiol. Psychol., 1954, 47, 173–178.*

BOX 4.3: *Training and dominance patterns*

R. E. Miller, J. V. Murphy, and I. A. Mirsky, of the University of Pittsburgh, have reported a study in which they successfully modified the social-dominance hierarchy in a group of monkeys through training.

As a first step, the social-dominance hierarchy in the experimental group of eight male and two female monkeys was observed over a period of 20 months. It was found to be quite stable.

Monkey 53, who was consistently low in the hierarchy, was chosen as the special experimental subject. Each of the other monkeys in the group was, one at a time, given avoidance training to monkey 53. This was done by placing monkey 53 in a compartment visible to the "trainee" monkey. As soon as monkey 53 became visible, the trainee monkey was given an electric shock. The shock continued until the trainee pressed a lever which, by dropping a door, removed monkey 53 from view and immediately terminated the shock. The training continued until the trainee monkey learned to press the lever as soon as monkey 53 came into view.

The experimenters were interested to see how this learned avoidance to monkey 53 affected dominance relations in the normal group situation. As training went on, the dominance of monkey 53 increased markedly. Moreover, the monkeys who, early in the training period, had not yet been conditioned to monkey 53 also displayed changes in their dominance relations with him. Thus, as the following figure shows, monkey 61, who was not conditioned to avoid monkey 53 during the first three sessions, dropped markedly in rank in the dominance hierarchy.

(The monkeys conditioned to avoid monkey 53 are indicated by stippled circles.)

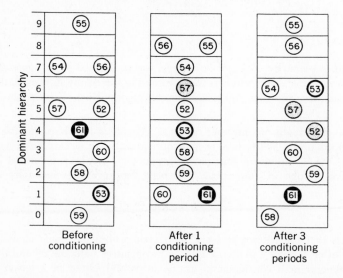

Miller, R. E., Murphy, J. V., and Mirsky, I. A. The modification of social dominance in a group of monkeys by interanimal conditioning. J. comp. physiol. Psychol., *1955, 48, 392–396.*

tests 3 and 4. Tests 1 and 2 thus can be taken to reflect a "factor." Similarly, tests 3 and 4 correlate highly (.49) and are independent of tests 1 and 2. The operation of two fac-

tors is assumed to account, then, for the six intercorrelations among the four tests. The psychological dimension common to tests 1 and 2 is clearly the trait of sociability or gre-

TABLE 4.2: INTERCORRELATIONS OF SCORES ON FOUR PERSONALITY INVENTORIES [Adapted from Guilford, 1959]

	TEST MEASURES			
	1	2	3	4
1	...	.56	.11	−.19
2		...	−.07	.06
3			...	.49
4				...

gariousness. The factor is, therefore, named sociability. The second factor, from the information available in our illustration, seems to be concerned with defense of the self. In the larger study from which this illustration was taken, tests which were highly correlated with this factor indicated that it is best interpreted as ascendance.

But the fact that personality inventory items tend to cluster does not necessarily reflect the existence of an underlying interpersonal response trait. Rather, the clusters that emerge may merely reflect the individual's need to be self-consistent, answering different items in a way which fits his "implicit personality theory" (see page 52). For example, an individual who sees himself as making friends easily may report, in answering a personality inventory, that he does not stay in the background, that he is easy to talk to, that he is asked to plan parties, etc., because these various behaviors are, for him, internally consistent, that is, they hang together in his "implicit personality theory." If we had records of his actual behavior in a sample of interpersonal behavior events, we might find less consistency than he indicates in responding to an inventory. Thus we may get a spuriously high consistency as an artifact of our method of measurement. We need to check the results of analyses of personality inventory and interview data with analyses of good behavioral data based on observations of action in a representative sample of interpersonal behavior events.

Unfortunately, relatively few attempts have been made to record and measure the *actions* of individuals in a wide sampling of interpersonal behavior events. The reason for this neglect of behavior data is the cost and difficulty of collecting such information. Cattell [1955] is one of the few investigators who has made extensive use of "miniature-situational" behavior tests in his studies of the basic personality traits of the individual.

CHARACTERISTICS OF INTERPERSONAL RESPONSE TRAITS

To know what a person's interpersonal response traits are is to know a good deal, since it helps us to predict much of his behavior vis-à-vis other people and even some of his nonsocial activities (see Box 4.4). However, a mere listing of an individual's interpersonal response traits is not enough, since these traits differ along a number of dimensions. That is, the same trait, e.g., sociability, may have quite different characteristics in two persons. Among such characteristics are *stability, pervasiveness, consistency,* and *patterning.*

STABILITY. Only scanty data are available on the question of the stability of interpersonal response traits over time. In preparation for a longitudinal study of marriage, Kelly [1955], during the years 1935–1938, collected a large amount of information on 300 engaged couples. Almost two decades later, in 1954, retest data were secured from 446 of the subjects. The degree of stability of two interpersonal response traits, self-confidence and sociability, that were measured and remeasured by a personality inventory is shown in Fig. 4.1. For comparative purposes the short-term stability of the two traits is also given. These results, although admittedly only suggestive, indicate that interpersonal response traits may be relatively stable over time.

Stott [1957] studied the stability of the interpersonal response trait of ascendance over a period of approximately twelve years. Children were first observed and rated while

BOX 4.4: *The strong, tough, hard, dominant female*

A. H. Maslow, a psychologist at Brandeis University, has brought together a number of studies by him and others which suggest that the interpersonal response trait of dominance governs a wide spectrum of behavior.

Maslow reports that high-dominance women (as measured by Maslow's Social Personality Inventory) differ from low-dominance women in their tastes in food and in music, in their language, in their sexual conduct, and in their ability to withstand stress.

1. The high-dominance woman typically prefers

> . . . foods that are saltier, sourer, and more bitter, more sharp and of stronger taste, e.g., strong cheeses rather than milder ones; foods that taste good even though ugly and unattractive, e.g., shellfish; foods that are novel and unfamiliar, e.g., fried squirrel, snails. They are less finicky, less easily nauseated, less fussy about unattractive or sloppily prepared food. And yet they are more sensuous and hearty and lusty about good food than are the low-dominance women.

2. The high-dominance women are more ". . . open to strange, wild, unfamiliar music, to cacophony, and to lack of melody, to the powerful rather than the sweet."

3. ". . . these same qualities [in the high-dominance women] show themselves in other areas, e.g., their language is tougher, stronger, harder. . . ."

4. The sexual conduct of high-dominance women is sharply different from that of low-dominance women. The high-dominance woman ". . . is much more apt to be pagan, permissive, and accepting in all sexual realms. . . . In other words, here too she is apt to be more forward, less inhibited, tougher, harder, stronger."

5. The low-dominance subjects, when put under stress, show greater deterioration in their intellectual performance than do high-dominance subjects.

From Maslow's observations dominance appears to be a widely pervasive, indeed an almost ubiquitous, trait.

Maslow, A. H. Motivation and personality. *New York: Harper, 1954.*

in nursery school and later in the recreational clubs which they attended. A rather marked degree of stability was observed, 82 per cent of the children showing only minor systematic changes in direction on the scale. The changes which did occur were temporary in most cases, with a later return to the earlier pattern of behavior.

Morris et al. [1954] studied the behavior of 54 adults who had been referred to a child guidance clinic 16 to 27 years earlier. As children they were diagnosed as Internal Reactors, defined as "Those showing predominantly shy, withdrawn, fearful or anxious behavior, those who are tending to develop neuroses, or those who are bothering themselves rather than others." These persons, as adults, continued to be "quiet and retiring." In their choice of work, they tended to choose jobs in which "security on the job is greatly emphasized over increasing opportunities and competitiveness."

PERVASIVENESS. The pervasiveness of an interpersonal response trait refers to the extent to which it is manifested in the behavior of an individual. Some traits can be expressed in

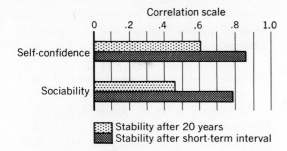

Correlation scale

Self-confidence

Sociability

Stability after 20 years
Stability after short-term interval

FIGURE 4.1: Stability over almost two decades of the interpersonal response traits of self-confidence and sociability. For comparative purposes, the short-term stability of the two traits is also shown. [Adapted from Kelly, 1955.]

almost all the social actions of an individual, whereas others can be exhibited only in a restricted number of interpersonal behavior events.

Interpersonal response traits range in degree of pervasiveness from such broadly pervasive traits as competitiveness, which can be manifested in nearly all of the interpersonal relations of the individual, to traits of much lower pervasiveness, such as social poise, which can be expressed only in situations where an individual is confronted by an audience of strangers.

A second source of restriction of pervasiveness is that imposed by the individual himself. Thus, for example, an individual may not have a highly pervasive trait of sociability because he discriminates sharply between different classes of persons and social situations. The most sociable of aristocrats might think it inappropriate to be sociable in the presence of the lower classes. Clearly, the more generally pervasive a trait, the more potent the trait in the determination of behavior.

CONSISTENCY. Interpersonal response traits vary greatly in degree of consistency. The level of consistency of a trait is measured by the average intercorrelation among trait scores in a variety of pertinent situations. If the average intercorrelation is low, the trait is rela-

tively inconsistent. For example, Dudycha's study [1936] of the relations among punctuality in four different situations—returning library books, turning in class assignments, returning course change slips to the registrar's office, and meeting appointments—showed very low intercorrelations, the average r being .19.

On the other hand, if the average intercorrelation is relatively high, the trait is relatively consistent. For example, Guilford [1959] reports that the intercorrelations among the three following personality inventory items averaged .44: liking friends and acquaintances, being gregarious, liking social affairs.

If the following four items are added, the average level of intercorrelation remains almost as high (.42): leading on social occasions, having social poise, liking to be in the limelight, not being shy or bashful.

Highly consistent interpersonal response traits better enable us to predict behavior than do traits of low consistency. If a trait is found to have low consistency, situational factors are more potent in determining action than the disposition which the individual brings to the interpersonal behavior event.

PATTERNING. The score of an individual on, say, the trait of sociability is determined by summing his scores on items, such as the above, which are the behavioral indicators of the trait. Two persons with the same total score would very infrequently have the same pattern of scores on the seven items. One person's sociability score may reflect a high score on liking social affairs and a low score on liking friends and acquaintances; a second person's sociability score may reflect the opposite pattern.

The problem of patterning is not an artifact created by our testing techniques. For the man in the street, no less than for the personality tester, "sociability" consists of quite different patterns of dispositions in individuals who may be judged equally sociable.

TRAIT INTERACTION

Each of the interpersonal response traits we have listed (and others) is important in governing action in the interpersonal behavior event. But action is determined by the *combination* of the traits of the individual and not by single traits acting separately.

Gough [1957] has speculated about how the interaction of traits taken two at a time operates to produce differential effects upon behavior. The interaction between measured dominance and sociability is of some interest for understanding and predicting action. Gough's predictions of the influence upon behavior of the interaction of these two traits are given in Figure 4.2. It is clear that high dominance means one thing when it is associated with low sociability and something quite different when it is associated with high sociability. The person who has high dominance and low sociability tends to analyze, criticize, disapprove, judge, and resist. The person who is high in both dominance and sociability tends to show a very different set of responses: he advises, coordinates, directs, leads, and initiates. Thus the "high dominance–low sociability" syndrome characterizes the disapproving, judging critic—the "thinker." The "high dominance–high sociability" syndrome characterizes the activist—the "doer."

FIGURE 4.2: Interaction between two interpersonal response traits. [After Gough, 1957.]

DOMINANCE (HIGH)

SOCIABILITY (LOW)	Analyzes Criticizes Disapproves Judges Resists	Advises Coordinates Directs Leads Initiates	SOCIABILITY (HIGH)
	Evades Concedes Relinquishes Retreats Withdraws	Acquiesces Agrees Assists Cooperates Obliges	

DOMINANCE (LOW)

When we consider the interactions between three or more traits, we face difficult problems of profile analysis and interpretation. Various methods, both intuitive and statistical, have been applied to these problems. These methods consider such properties of a profile as its level, its variability, its form or shape.

Although it is widely assumed that the individual's social behavior is determined by complex interactions among his various traits, profile interpretation is still an art of undetermined validity. The quantitative methods that have been proposed have proved cumbersome, and relatively little has been done with them.

TO RECAPITULATE

The actions of the individual in interpersonal behavior events are guided by his system of interpersonal response traits—dispositions to respond in characteristic ways to other persons.

The primary interpersonal traits are classified into three categories: Role Dispositions (ascendance, dominance, social initiative, and independence); Sociometric Dispositions (accepting of others, sociability, friendliness, and sympathetic); Expressive Dispositions (competitiveness, aggressiveness, self-consciousness, and exhibitionistic).

The major technique used to isolate and identify interpersonal response traits has been factor analysis. This technique has been applied for the most part to self-descriptions secured through personality inventories and clinical interviews. The use of self-report data raises the possibility that the traits identified may reflect the implicit personality theories which are commonly held by people.

Interpersonal response traits tend to be relatively stable over time. They differ in other major characteristics: degree of pervasiveness, consistency, and patterning or internal structure.

The behavior of the individual is governed by the pattern of his interpersonal response traits. Trait interaction modifies the influence of interpersonal response traits upon behavior.

GUIDE 12: *The interpersonal response traits of the individual are the end products of his characteristic experiences in satisfying his most frequently and most intensely aroused wants*

In the previous chapter we have seen some of the conditions that govern the arousal of wants. And we have seen that individuals differ in their most important and their most frequently aroused wants. What, now, can we say about the outcome of wants once aroused, and about the different possible consequences of these outcomes on the genesis of interpersonal response traits?

An aroused want has many possible fates. One fate is for the want to be immediately and effortlessly satisfied, with few demands upon the cognitions and coping behavior of the individual. A second possible fate is for the want to remain unfulfilled over a considerable period of time, and thus provide the driving force for the solution of many problems, for learning, for creative thinking, and for sustained action ending in goal achievement. Third, an aroused want may end in a truncated "want episode," in that midway through a goal-directed action a sharp change in the individual's situation shunts aside the original want and permits a more urgent want to take over the direction of behavior. A fourth possible fate is for the want to result in complete frustration—the individual cannot satisfy the want, feels thwarted, disappointed, defeated, and certain important "frustration effects" may ensue.

All people experience all of these outcomes. But because of differences in ability, temperament, and circumstance people differ widely in the relative frequencies with which they experience fulfillment and frustration. They differ, too, in how they fulfill their wants and in how they cope with frustration. We turn now to a consideration of how these varying experiences leave residual effects in the form of interpersonal response traits.

EFFECT OF WANT FULFILLMENT

It is perhaps fortunate for the well-being of most people that the great proportion of aroused wants lead smoothly and directly to the achievement of the primary goal. A man experiences hunger for food and affiliation: he invites a colleague to join him for lunch; they walk leisurely to a restaurant where they enjoy good food and good talk. His wants are satisfied and they disappear. This pattern of want arousal and immediate satisfaction is so common in the life of man that little attention has been paid to it by either the wanting and fulfilling individual or the observing psychologist. As one psychology textbook has put it: "That a hungry man bites food, is not 'news,' and it does not seem to make 'interesting psychology.'" Yet even in the course of uncomplicated want fulfillment, the individual can use quite different techniques and both adaptive and maladaptive effects may result which become generalized into interpersonal response traits.

The principal and most obvious *immediate* effect of the fulfillment of an aroused want is the loss of its sovereign power over the cognitions and actions of the individual. The individual is thus liberated to pay attention to other aspects of his environment, to pursue other goals. The more *enduring* effect of want satisfaction has already been dealt with in some detail in the preceding chapter. As we have pointed out (page 76) the normal fulfillment of certain wants sets the stage for the emergence of "higher" wants. The psychological development of the individual—including the development of such interpersonal response traits as social initiative, independence, sociability, and friendliness—progresses at a faster pace if his "lower" wants are easily, smoothly, and habitually satisfied. The social effects of this—both in terms of the individual's action in interpersonal behavior events and in terms of the accomplishments of the members of society as a whole—are fairly obvious.

Furthermore, want satisfaction may have important and lasting effects on the individual's self-evaluation and self-esteem. He may become more confident in his approach to the problems facing him; his level of aspiration may progressively rise (see Box 4.5). And his interpersonal response traits will reflect this enhanced self-esteem. He may come to display greater ascendance, dominance, social poise, etc.

THE COST OF "EASY" FULFILLMENT. On the other hand, chronically *easy* fulfillment of wants may have maladaptive individual and social effects.

Although it is true that easy want fulfillment may make the relevant action sequence habitual and thus free the individual to cope with other problems, he may not take advantage of that opportunity. The habituation of his action pattern, far from freeing him, may "freeze" him. Should the situation change

BOX 4.5: *Success, failure, and aspiration*

Irvin L. Child, a psychologist at Yale University, and John W. M. Whiting, an anthropologist at Harvard University, collaborated on a study of the effect of success and failure upon the level of aspiration. Each student in an undergraduate psychology course was required to write a description of three incidents in his life: one of complete frustration in which the goal was never attained, one of frustration followed by goal attainment, and one of direct, unhindered goal attainment. Illustrative incidents are given below.

Complete frustration. My family moved to X five years ago, and it didn't take me long to find out that a terrific girl lived around the corner. It was an old case of "love at first sight." . . . The only trouble was that someone else was there first and I immediately assumed the well-known "second fiddle" role in the triangle which developed. My love for her (and I do believe it was that) grew as time went by. . . . But all my heartache, time, and money eventually proved to be of no avail, for she finally married my rival a little over a year ago.

Frustration followed by goal attainment. I had made a date for a hockey game desiring feminine companionship and . . . necking and petting. A week before the hockey game my ex-girl friend and I decided to "break up." . . . However, the night of the game I decided I would like to go, and called a friend of mine who I thought might have an extra ticket. He had two tickets and also a cousin (female) who was visiting him; he gave me the tickets and "fixed me up" with his cousin. In the course of the evening I found my goal completely attained.

Simple goal attainment. Recently I talked with a good friend of mine who said he was going to Bermuda for spring vacation . . . and I set my heart on going to Bermuda for the vacation. But it would cost quite a lot, and I knew things had been a little rough with my father recently. Also, he had mentioned previously wanting me to stay home and do some concentrated study over the holidays. But I determined to make a try at it, anyway. . . . It took quite a lot of nerve to ask the old man, but finally [I] put the proposition to him. Much to my surprise, he thought it was wonderful and gave his immediate sanction to the trip—parental and monetary. My big obstacle had proved to be not so big. . . .

and he be confronted with a new problem for which his habitual mode of response is inadequate, he may be at a loss. The individual who over a long period of time has had no problems to solve because all, or most, of his wants have been so easily satisfied, may forgo the opportunity to learn to learn. He sees no problems, hears no problems, speaks no problems. His repertory of interpersonal response traits as social techniques for the solution of interpersonal problems fails to develop.

Finally, chronically easy want satisfaction may result in the individual's overestimation of his capacities. He may become overconfi-dent; his level of aspiration may be placed at too high and unrealistic a point—all of which may result in an agonizing and shattering reappraisal when reality finally catches up with him. And in the process of reappraisal, his set of interpersonal response traits may undergo radical changes which reflect his changed self-concept.

FRUSTRATION

When progress toward a goal is blocked and the want remains unsatisfied, we speak of *frustration.* Such blocking of goal-directed behavior is a common occurrence in the lives of

---

After the descriptions of the incidents had been written, the students answered a questionnaire which included a question designed to determine the effect of each incident on the level of aspiration. The question was phrased as follows:

The level of desirability of the chosen goal is often referred to as a person's level of aspiration. Now consider the effect that this incident had or is likely to have on the next occasion on which you were or might be starting to strive for a goal of essentially the same kind. What was the effect of the incident on your level of aspiration?
  (1) Raised it considerably   (3) Lowered it slightly
  (2) Raised it slightly   (4) Lowered it considerably

The results are summarized in the following table. The evidence suggests that goal attainment, whether or not it is preceded by frustration, produces a rise in level of aspiration. The tendency for complete frustration to depress the level of aspiration is not so marked.

Further analysis of the data showed that the more marked the success, the greater the probability of a rise in the level of aspiration; the more complete the failure, the greater the probability of a lowering.

	FREQUENCY OF EACH TYPE OF SHIFT IN LEVEL OF ASPIRATION		
TYPE OF INCIDENT	*Lowering*	*None*	*Rise*
Complete frustration	66	36	38
Frustration: goal attainment	15	15	95
Direct goal attainment	3	17	112

We must point to an obvious caution. The students' accounts of shifts in level of aspiration may very well reflect only what they felt *should* happen—according to their readings in psychology.

Child, I. L., and Whiting, J. W. M. Determinants of level of aspiration: evidence from everyday life. J. abnorm. soc. Psychol., 1949, 44, 303–314.

all men. Its consequences take many forms, both good and bad. It may lead the individual to creative changes in cognition, to new and better ways of satisfying wants; it may result in severe emotional upset, to maladaptive behavior, to deteriorative changes in the individual's personality. On the level of social life, the prolonged motive blocking of large masses

BOX 4.6: *Drives toward war*

During World War II, Edward C. Tolman, the noted psychologist at the University of California, Berkeley, published a speculative account of how "neurotically motivated" warlike behavior in the individual might be interpreted as a particular *social technique* (i.e., interpersonal response trait) developed as a consequence of the frustration of basic human wants.

Tolman asserted that when the primary biological drives—which he postulated as the basic source of all motivational energy—are frustrated, individuals tend in general to learn and fixate either "self-assertive techniques" or "collective techniques." When these, in turn, are frustrated, individuals develop social techniques of identification with parents, of identification with the group, or of self-abasement with repressed hostility. Identification with parents tends to lead to various forms of socially approved behavior. Identification with the group may ultimately lead to defense of the group against outside attack and action directed at federation into larger groups.

On the other hand, as the following schema of Tolman's shows, self-abasement plus repressed hostility has the potentiality of leading to the development of any one of a variety of socially undesirable techniques, including aggression against outsiders, for example, in war.

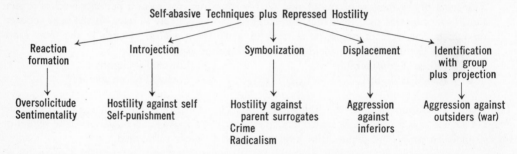

This attempt of Tolman's represents a provocative and—within its context—a valuable way of systematizing the multifarious social consequences of want frustration. There are, however, two limitations of this analysis to which we would like to point. In the first place, from our point of view, Tolman's account is too heavily dependent upon a relatively few so-called "basic biological drives" as sources of human wants. In the second place, the analysis of the motivational source of *wars* may be valid for tribal warfare and perhaps even for what we used to call the "World Wars," but it is probably inadequate for THE war of the future—if such a war ever comes. Compared with previous wars, not only will nuclear war be physically unique, but the whole sociology of such a war will be radically different. Most of the people who will be slaughtered in such a war will, in a genuine psychological sense, be "innocent bystanders." The issues will not derive from their wants or frustrations and neither will the decisions to aggress against the enemy. Indeed, there may be very little aggression involved in such a holocaust. The carefully calculated and coordinated decisions of a very, very few people will suffice to destroy entire cities, vast provinces, and, perhaps, even continents.

Tolman, E. C. Drives toward war. New York: Appleton-Century-Crofts, 1942.

BASIC PSYCHOLOGICAL FACTORS

of people has sometimes led to the invention of new social processes and organizations, or to such signs of social pathology as group conflict, crime and delinquency, and war (see Box 4.6).

What are the obstacles that block man's goal achievement? The specific ones are, of course, innumerable, but they can all be traced to four main sources: (1) the physical environment, (2) biological limitations, (3) the complexity of psychological make-up, (4) the social environment.

FRUSTRATION AND THE PHYSICAL ENVIRONMENT. It is obvious that many of the individual's motive blocks lie in restrictions imposed by the external environment. Moreover, an entire society can have basic wants blocked by the characteristics of the physical environment. As we noted in Chapter 3 (see page 76), the Siriono society, a seminomadic Bolivian group, is subject to the constant blockage of the food want because the tropical climate in which these people live makes difficult the preservation and storage of food.

FRUSTRATION AND BIOLOGICAL STRUCTURE. Often the blocking agents lie within the individual himself—in his motor and mental incapacities. A man may simply not have the physique to achieve the fame as an athlete which he desires; or he may lack the necessary intelligence to graduate from medical school and achieve his goal of becoming a doctor. Adler [1925] made such biological deficiencies the basis of an entire theory of personality development, with emphasis upon the concept of the "inferiority complex."

FRUSTRATION AND PSYCHOLOGICAL COMPLEXITY. Man is remarkably complex with his many simultaneously active wants. These wants often conflict, and the satisfaction of one may necessarily mean the blockage of others. A man may desire to win a political election to satisfy his power want but may not be willing to take orders from the local political boss because to do so would damage his self-esteem. Such conflicts are perhaps the most important source of motive blocking for the individual and present particularly difficult problems of adjustment.

FRUSTRATION AND THE SOCIAL ENVIRONMENT. Society sets up norms and social barriers which may serve to block the satisfaction of the individual's wants. Indeed, a society may set goals whose attainment is blocked by the very culture patterns and institutionalized ways characteristic of that society. For instance, the American society, through its democratic philosophy of mass education, instills in many Negroes the goal of a college education and then, through another of its culture patterns—racial discrimination—makes it difficult for them to secure that goal. Also, it may, through its democratic social philosophy, instill the goal of individual professional attainment and then through discriminations based on family background, wealth, religion, or race prevent certain individuals from achieving this goal. Another way a society may present obstacles to want satisfaction is by holding up opposing values and by making contradictory demands of its members. (Box 4.7 lists a few such contradictions as they are expressed in popular American ideology.)

FRUSTRATION AND INTERPERSONAL RESPONSE TRAITS

When an individual suffers severe or prolonged frustration, his inability to achieve his goal may give rise to feelings of personal failure and anxiety. His goal-directed problem-solving behavior may then be supplanted by behavior aimed at defending his self-conception and warding off threats to self-esteem. In the course of such defensive behavior he may develop or reinforce interpersonal response traits of aggressiveness, unsociability, competitiveness, rejection of others, etc.

Among the defensive reactions to frustration that are of greatest importance to an understanding of social behavior are (1) aggression, (2) regression, (3) withdrawal, (4) repression, (5) reaction formation, (6) ration-

Many Americans hold that:	*But many others hold that:*
Individual initiative is the basis of American greatness.	The good American is a good team player.
Hard work and thrift are the way to get ahead.	Nobody gets rich by pinching nickels; know the right people.
Honesty is the best policy.	Business is business.
No man should live for himself alone.	A man has to look out for himself.
All men are created free and equal.	Some people are more equal than others; the Negro should know his place.
Education is the means for solving the problems of society.	Brain trusters and eggheads are impractical visionaries.

alization, (7) projection, (8) autism, (9) identification.

AGGRESSION. The accumulated tension arising out of persistent frustration often finds expression in aggressive acts which seem to allay, at least temporarily, the frustrated state. Aggressiveness may take the form of feelings and actions of anger and rage, of actual physical violence against objects and people, of verbal attacks (denunciations and slander), of fantasies of violence and attack.

The targets of aggression are not necessarily related logically to the frustrating situation. Often they are completely unconnected with the thwarting agent. A man frustrated by failure to get ahead in his job may be a likely recruit for an aggressive hate group. Under some circumstances the aggression may even be turned inward against the self. Mowrer [1939] has reported the following instance of aggression against the self.

A small boy in an institution displayed unusually strong aggression toward adults. This took the form of biting, pinching, and hair pulling. Under the severe discipline of the institution, this overt aggression was soon inhibited by expectation of punishment. Then the child began running after other children, biting them, pinching them, and pulling their hair. These manifestations of aggression were in turn eliminated, in fact so thoroughly that the child ceased biting altogether, even refusing to bite into solid food. Then the child began to pinch himself, bang his head, and to pull out his own hair. These actions were so injurious that he created bad sores on his body and two large bald spots on his head, and he finally had to be sent to another institution for treatment. Therapy consisted of removing frustrations, particularly those centering around toilet training and eating, and of attempting, by complete absence of threats, to remove the anticipations of punishment which were inhibiting direct aggression against adults. Under this treatment the child first expressed more aggression against adults and less against himself. Then, as the frustrations which seemed to have been the root of his trouble were lessened, his manifestations of aggressions against adults began to weaken.

For a study which throws some light on the factors that predispose children to display the interpersonal response trait of aggressiveness, see Box 4.8.

REGRESSION. Barker, Dembo, and Lewin [1941] have studied the phenomenon of *regression* as a consequence of frustration. They observed that in certain frustrating situations, the behavior of the child undergoes a kind of primitivization. His actions become less mature, more childish; the sensitivity of his discriminations and judgments diminishes; his feelings and emotions become more poorly differentiated and controlled, like those of a younger child. Such interpersonal response traits as dependence or aggressiveness may be strengthened.

In their experiment, for example, the play behavior of children who were deprived of highly desired playthings deteriorated from a more advanced level of constructive play (in which blocks were used to build things) to a more immature level of play (in which blocks were used merely as things to bang about). On a more significant level, the same phenomenon may be observed in the field of international relations. A diplomat may be seeking to achieve international agreement on certain complex issues. He behaves on a mature level, searching for some advanced and sophisticated *modus vivendi* by which common understanding can be achieved, being constantly sensitive to the refinements and subtleties of the problem, and not permitting his feelings and emotions to color his perspective on the whole issue. Then, at some point in the negotiations, he is severely thwarted in his purpose by irreconcilable points of controversy, by the apparent bullheadedness of his confreres. He may, as a consequence of his frustration, regress to a less mature level of behavior: desk pounding, recriminations, and threats of aggression.

WITHDRAWAL. Frustration may often be resolved by withdrawal from the frustrating situation. The failing college student may quit college for a job. While this may be an adap-

BOX 4.8: *Seeds of aggression*

Charlene T. Meyer has studied the relation between the behavior of parents and aggressiveness in children.

In her study, nursery school children were rated for the amount of domination and cooperation they displayed. An index of aggressiveness was obtained by dividing the child's score on domination by his score on cooperation. Thus, a high index would indicate that a child was highly dominant but very uncooperative, i.e., aggressive. Information on the child-rearing behavior of the parents of the children was secured through home visits.

The following table shows some of the correlations between various measures of parental behavior and amount of aggressiveness displayed by the children.

Parent behavior	Correlation with child's aggressiveness score
Friction over discipline of child	+.57
Discord in the home	+.41
Closeness of relationship to child	−.61
Understanding of child's problems	−.59
Quickness of approving or disapproving of child's conduct	−.56
Democracy of child-rearing policy	−.52

The findings of this study suggest that the interpersonal response trait of aggressiveness is, at least in part, an outgrowth of the pattern of parent-child relations.

Meyer, Charlene T. The assertive behavior of children as related to parent behavior. J. Home Econ., *1947*, **39**, *77–80.*

tive response for the student who does not have the capacity to do college work, it is maladaptive for the capable student and he may develop such interpersonal response traits as noncompetitiveness, submissiveness, etc.

In other situations the individual may be unable to leave the scene of his frustration; instead, he erects psychological fences that cut him off from contact with the situation. The "tired liberal," frustrated in his attempts at political reform, loses all interests in politics and refuses to participate actively in political affairs. Here, society loses by this individual's frustration response, and the individual may develop the interpersonal response trait of social passivity, and unfriendliness or social timidity. Withdrawal may become generalized into the interpersonal response trait of unfriendliness in an aggressive person; in the trait of social timidity in a nonaggressive person. Here we have an instance of interaction among mechanisms in the formation of interpersonal response traits.

REPRESSION. Another way that the individual avoids the disturbances arising out of frustration is through the mechanism of *repression,* one of Freud's basic concepts. Frustrated wants and the anxieties they engender are sometimes subjected to forces that render them inaccessible to consciousness; the individual "forgets" or "represses" the unsatisfied want. It is especially those wants (e.g., sex, aggression, power) whose expression conflicts with social values and taboos as incorporated in the ideal self of the person that are, according to Freud, the most susceptible to repression. A son of the church, taught to revere humility, may never become fully conscious of his strong power want—it is repressed and is manifested indirectly in a socially acceptable form. For instance, in his pastoral duties he comes to exercise power over the fate of his dependent parishioners. A puritanical person who has repressed his sex desires may become an ardent community reformer; a man who has repressed his hostile feelings toward his father may become a revolutionary hero, fighting entrenched authority.

The relevance of repression to the development of interpersonal response traits is clear. The highly repressed individual may, for example, display traits of excessive and handicapping social submissiveness and lack of aggression because of his fear of his own hostile impulses. A person who is unable to acknowledge his basic wants for love and emotional support, because he perceives them as signs of "weakness," may typically display traits of unfriendliness and excessive, tough self-sufficiency.

REACTION FORMATION. As a consequence of the repression of basically frustrated and anxiety-arousing wants, an individual may display behavior that is the direct opposite of that to which the want would be expected to lead. This is known as *reaction formation.* For example, a vigorous crusader against racial discrimination may be reacting against his own "sinful" racial prejudice.

A person who has a great deal of basic hostility may, through reaction formation, display interpersonal response traits of excessive "friendliness" and "sympathy." A person with deep-seated anxieties about his abilities may react by developing exhibitionistic traits.

RATIONALIZATION. Since frustration is due to goal blockage as perceived by the individual, it is evident that an important form of defense can occur through some form of cognitive redefinition of the frustrating situation. Some of these cognitive redefinitions are called *rationalizations.* They take the form of the concoction of plausible "reasons" to account for and justify the failure of goal achievement. Thus, a political candidate who loses an election may come to see the office which he lost as a thankless burden, or the electorate as uninformed, or his supporters as lackadaisical. Rationalizations are not deliberate "lies"; the individual is not fully aware of the cognitive distortions produced by the frustration.

BASIC PSYCHOLOGICAL FACTORS

The person who rationalizes extensively is enabled thereby to develop in excessive degree such interpersonal response traits as competitiveness and aggressiveness. Through rationalization he justifies to himself and others his socially undesirable behavior.

PROJECTION. Another form of redefinition of the situation is found in the mechanism of *projection*. In projection the individual attributes to others disvalued characteristics that pertain to him. He assigns blame for his own failures and frustrations to other objects and persons; he "projects" the blame. The tennis player muffs a stroke and looks at his racket for the offending "hole." The incompetent who fails to get ahead in his job blames those who are "against him." The man who feels moral guilt about his own conduct projects it on others and finds sin in them.

Obviously such interpersonal response traits as rejection of others and unfriendliness may readily come to characterize a person who has learned to project extensively.

AUTISM. Closely related to rationalization and projection is another form of cognitive distortion produced by frustration which is known as *autism,* or autistic thinking. This refers to thinking that is almost completely dominated by wants and emotions, wherein no attempt is made to "check" the content of the thinking against reality. The individual who cuts himself off from communication with another person or group and then proceeds to "think" about that person or group without bothering to check his thinking with the facts of the case is engaging in autistic thinking. Newcomb [1947] has stressed the importance of autism in the development of the interpersonal response traits of aggressiveness, rejecting of others, unsociability, etc. As he puts it:

Hostile impulses commonly arise . . . when status-relationship is so perceived that another is viewed as threat. Such a perception arises through interaction, and it is likely to persist until modified by further interaction. If, as a result of a hostile attitude emerging from the newly perceived status-relationship, communication with the other person is avoided, the conditions necessary for eliminating the hostile attitude are not likely to occur.

Therefore, he concludes:

The likelihood that a persistently hostile attitude will develop varies with the degree to which the perceived interpersonal relationship remains autistic. . . .

Autism, in Newcomb's example, is seen as a consequence of withdrawal from a dangerous or frustrating situation. Other autisms can be seen as operating more directly to satisfy wants. Daydreaming and other fantasies are such autisms. By such means there is imaginary gratification of unfulfilled wants and overcoming of barriers to goal achievement. Socially, this kind of behavior may be very "expensive." The individual who is motivated to see social justice done but gratifies it by fantasy or daydreaming thereby dissipates his energy in socially useless autism, even though he himself may, by this means, get transient satisfaction of his wants.

IDENTIFICATION. A highly effective avenue for the resolution of some types of frustration is through a process of *identification* in which the person comes to incorporate traits of another person or group of persons. The political or military achievements of the national hero may become the conquests of the frustrated and chronically failing "little man."

The significance of identification for the development of interpersonal response traits is obvious. In identifying with a dominant model, or an exhibitionistic model, or a highly gregarious model, the individual may himself take on the traits of dominance, exhibitionism, sociability.

The process of identification is singularly important in understanding group formation and leadership and will be discussed in detail in Chapter 11. Identification, like autism, may be "expensive" and maladaptive if it is used as a substitute for achievement or if it is used to condone antisocial conduct in the person with whom the individual identifies. Identification with the leader of a socially useful organization which motivates the individual to work in its support may have beneficial effects both for the individual and for society.

INDIVIDUAL PATTERN OF DEFENSIVE REACTIONS. This listing of general "mechanisms" does not encompass all of what seem to be a virtually limitless number of specific ways of coping with frustration. (For a concrete illustration of some of the manifold responses persons may display in attempting to satisfy a strong frustrated want, see Box 4.9.) These

BOX 4.9: *Varieties of motherhood*

The following "case example" (a composite of the case histories of many patients) has been adapted from one provided by Jules H. Masserman, an experimental psychiatrist at the University of Chicago. This case example illustrates the bewildering variety of responses an individual may make in attempting to satisfy a strong frustrated want. The responses to frustration may range all the way from rational, direct attempts to overcome the frustration, through the discovery and acceptance of personally satisfying and socially useful goals, to bizarre and fantastic symbolic satisfactions. Note also that the denial of the want may lead to the emergence of other and new wants:

A married woman with a strong maternal want finds herself physiologically incapable of bearing children. To begin with, she may seek medical treatment. If this proves fruitless, she has a wide variety of goals available to her from which she may, more or less consciously, select any combination that most nearly satisfies her maternal want.

Accepting her sterility as inevitable she may attempt to satisfy her maternal longings through substitute goals, e.g., adopting a child, or becoming a kindergarten teacher and thus being entrusted with the part-time care of many children. If these goals are unavailable, because of external circumstances or inner conflicts involving jealousies, her goals may become ". . . more deviously substitutive and symbolic: She may keep cats or parrots, or found a pet hospital, or join an antivivisection society—in all of which activities her behavior could range from 'normal' to the borderlines of what most observers would characterize as fanatic."

If she finds such remote gratifications inadequate, she may abandon all attempts to satisfy her maternal wants and instead seek satisfactions for narcissistic, erotic, or other nonmaternal wants

. . . in regressive dependency, sexual promiscuity, multiple marriages, social or economic aggressivity, or various other displacements and deviant consummations. . . . Finally, however, if these diversions alone should prove inadequate while the unconscious maternal drives continue strong and undeniable, their satisfactions by more abstractly symbolic, fantastic . . . devices might be attempted, in which case her behavior will become "neurotic" or "psychotic." For example, the woman, still driven by her unconscious desires to be pregnant, may express them "psychosomatically" by developing functional amenorrhea, morning nausea or even pseudo-cyetic abdominal enlargement. If, on the other hand, her wishful fantasies harden into delusions, she may insist that she is pregnant despite all external evidences to the contrary, and invest her belief with various grandiose, persecutory, religious or other ideational content, e.g., that she had been "drugged and raped," or that she is destined "to give birth to a new Messiah."

Masserman, J. H. Principles of dynamic psychiatry. Philadelphia: Saunders, 1946.

BASIC PSYCHOLOGICAL FACTORS

manifold responses provide a rich "breeding ground" for the emergence of almost every conceivable interpersonal response trait.

No one person uses equally all the ways of coping with frustration which have been described. Each individual comes to display a *pattern* of adjustive tendencies which is more or less characteristic of him, and this distinctive pattern seems to appear fairly early in life. The origin and development of such individual patterns is but little understood. It must be assumed that both constitutional and experiential factors are involved, especially the experiences of the individual in satisfying his wants. (For two complementary studies which suggest the role of wants and of training in determining the mode of reaction to frustration, see Boxes 4.10 and 4.11.)

DEFENSIVE VS. GOAL-ORIENTED TRAITS. It will not have escaped the reader that some of the very "same" interpersonal response traits which we have discussed as stemming from and reinforced by defensive reactions to frustration also can be seen as deriving from adaptive, goal-directed behavior. For example, "friendliness" can be the result of repeated satisfaction of the individual's wants as he interacts with other persons; but "friendliness" can also, as we have seen, represent a reaction formation against a deep-seated hostility of the individual toward other people.

The important point to stress is that however similar these two kinds of "friendliness" may appear on the surface, they have different implications for action in the interpersonal behavior event. "Satisfied friendliness" will tend to be appropriate and selective; "dissatisfied friendliness" will tend to be excessive and promiscuous. To take another example, the interpersonal response trait of ascendance, when it arises as the generalized embodiment of defensive maneuvers, may appear, superficially, to be the same as the trait of ascendance formed in the process of want fulfillment. Basically, however, we would expect goal-oriented and defensive-oriented ascendance to be quite different. For one thing, we might expect the ascendant behavior of the defensive person to be more fragile, yielding easily to social timidity when strongly challenged. Goal-oriented ascendance we would expect to be a stronger trait—rooted, as it is, in successful achievement; incorporated, as it is, in a self that is held to be worthy.

For another thing, we might expect defensive ascendance to have about it a quality of compulsiveness. The person *must* act in this ascendant way with respect to other people whether it be appropriate to the social situation or not. The person who has learned to be ascendant in the course of successful goal achievement does not feel this compulsion; he is able to use the trait, as it were, as an adaptive means of want fulfillment, displaying ascendant behavior when it is seen as instrumental to the attainment of his goals, but modulating the trait when it is seen as an inappropriate means.

INTERPERSONAL RESPONSE TRAITS VS. WANTS. The last point suggests that under some circumstances a particular form of interpersonal behavior becomes for the individual an end in itself rather than merely a means. That is, the behavior no longer represents just an habitual form of social response, but represents the gratification of a *want*. Thus one man may exhibit a characteristically aggressive style of social behavior; another may *need* to be aggressive. One man typically acts in a friendly fashion; another may actively seek out and strive for friendship relations.

THE SELF AND INTERPERSONAL RESPONSE TRAITS

That the self plays a crucial role in the development of interpersonal response traits has already been made clear in our discussion of how enhanced self-esteem may lead to social initiative, ascendancy, etc., and how threatened self-esteem under frustration may lead to aggressiveness, unfriendliness, etc. It should also now be noted that the way interpersonal response traits develop and change often reflects the fact that an individual's view of himself is inseparably related to his view of others.

For one thing, the self-concept is shaped by how one thinks he is evaluated by others. To an important degree the self is—as we have earlier noted—the "looking-glass" self (page 82). Hence, the way other people treat one may, through modifying one's self-image, come to modify one's interpersonal response traits (for an example, see Box 4.12).

BOX 4.10: *Wants and frustration behavior*

A study by Nancy Barker Otis and Boyd McCandless, psychologists at the Child Welfare Research Station of the State University of Iowa, suggests that even very young children have characteristic modes of responding to frustration and that these characteristic response modes are related to the relative strength of the wants served.

In this study, the investigators subjected 63 nursery school children to a series of mild and repeated frustrations by interfering with their play. The frequency and intensity of dominant-aggressive (Ag) and compliant-submissive (Su) responses to frustration were scored by five independent observers. The correlation between total Ag responses and total Su responses was found to be −.65.

Nursery school teachers familiar with the children rated them for strength of the power-dominance want (PD/w) and love-affection want (LA/w). The relations between the strength of the power-dominance want and frustration behavior were as follows:

PD/w vs. total Ag	+.49
PD/w vs. Ag increase	+.45
PD/w vs. total Su	−.33

Note that children high in power-dominance wants tend to respond more aggressively to frustration than children low in power-dominance wants, and also show an increase in aggressive behavior from the first half to the second half of the frustration series. The children high in power-dominance also show less compliant-submissive behavior than children low in power-dominance.

As the following table shows, children high in love-affection wants show less dominant-aggressive frustration behavior and a smaller increase in the amount of this behavior in the second half of the frustration series than children low in love-affection wants. They also have higher total compliant-submissive scores.

LA/w vs. total Ag	−.33
LA/w vs. Ag increase	−.38
LA/w vs. total Su	+.33

A word of caution is in order. As the investigators remark, the teacher ratings of the strength of the power-dominance and love-affection wants may have been influenced by their observations of the children's frustration behavior in the nursery school situation, thus inflating the obtained correlations.

Otis, Nancy B., and McCandless, B. Responses to repeated frustrations of young children differentiated according to need area. J. abnorm. soc. Psychol., 1955, 50, 349–353.

BOX 4.11: *Twigs are bent*

In an experiment by Joel R. Davitz of Teachers College, Columbia University, the effects of specific training upon the pattern of reaction to a frustrating situation were studied.

Forty children between the ages of seven and nine were divided into five pairs of four-person groups, each pair matched for age and sex.

First, the ten groups were allowed to play freely with any of the materials in an experimental playroom for a period of 18 minutes. Motion pictures were taken of their play behavior. Five of the ten groups were then trained to be *aggressive*. This was done by teaching the children to play three rough, body-contact games in two of which the object of the game was to damage the property of others. These games were played for seven sessions of ten minutes each. Throughout the play sessions, aggressive behavior was praised and encouraged.

One of the three games used to teach aggressiveness was called "Spot." In this game, a cross was marked in the center of a mat. The winner was the child who was standing on the cross at the end of the game. To win, a child had to shove, push, and wrestle the other children off the spot and resist being shoved and pushed off himself.

The other five groups were given *constructive* training, defined as that which encouraged the use of materials in building objects (e.g., jigsaw puzzles). During the seven constructive training sessions, aggressive behavior was discouraged and constructiveness was praised and encouraged. At the end of the training sessions, the children in all ten groups were subjected to a frustrating situation. A movie they were watching was interrupted at the climactic moment, and candy which they had been given was taken away. The children were then ushered into the experimental playroom by the experimenter. As he locked the door of the room he said, "You cannot have any more candy or see any more films but you can play with anything in the room." The free play behavior of the children was then filmed for a period of 18 minutes.

The records of the pre- and post-frustration behavior of the 40 children were ranked in order of aggressiveness independently by four judges; and by a second set of five judges in order of constructiveness. The judges were not, of course, permitted to learn which children had been trained aggressively and which constructively.

Analysis of the differences between the pre- and post-frustration behavior of the aggressively and constructively trained children showed that those who had been aggressively trained behaved more aggressively after frustration than did the constructively trained children. Conversely, the constructively trained children behaved more constructively after frustration than did the aggressively trained children.

This study suggests that reaction to frustration may be importantly influenced, at least temporarily, by past training. However, a word of caution is in order. Before we can safely talk about the influence of training upon responses to frustration, it is necessary to determine whether the aggressiveness of the aggressively trained children will generalize to *other* situations. It may be that the children in Davitz's study learned it was safe to behave aggressively in the specific situation of the experimental playground and that little or no generalization to other situations may have been produced by the training.

Davitz, J. R. *The effects of previous training on post-frustration behavior.* J. abnorm. soc. Psychol., *1952, 47, 309–315.*

For another thing, the way the person perceives others is influenced by the way he perceives himself. Every person, to a greater or lesser extent, sees others in his own image, through attributing his traits to others (see Box 4.13).

The self-concept thus importantly influences the way the individual judges and evaluates other persons. And action in the interpersonal behavior event is guided by cognitions of the other. If an insecure person sees the other as threatening, he will tend to respond with one or another of the many defensively based interpersonal response traits which he has acquired, e.g., aggressiveness or unfriendliness. These traits may then be reinforced. And thus our interpersonal response traits may often, paradoxically, reflect what we see in ourselves.

TO RECAPITULATE

An aroused want may have diverse destinies: it may be immediately and effortlessly satisfied; it may be fulfilled only after much coping with blocks to immediate goal achievement; it may remain frustrated because the block to goal achievement cannot be overcome. In seeking to reduce his frustration, the individual may adopt one or another of the various defense mechanisms. The ways in which an individual proceeds to fulfill his wants and the ways he reduces the frustration of his wants may have either adaptive or maladaptive generalizable consequences for his later behavior. These generalizable consequences are the more or less stable and consistent dispositions of the individual to respond in distinctive and characteristic ways to other persons—his interpersonal response traits. Superficially similar traits formed in the process of want fulfillment and traits formed in the process of coping with frustration may have quite different implications for behavior.

The self-concept of the individual influences the formation and change of interpersonal response traits in the individual. His interpersonal response traits often reflect his cognition of himself.

BOX 4.12: *A campus Galatea*

The following case, cited by E. R. Guthrie, psychologist at the University of Washington, serves to illustrate how the treatment an individual receives from others may modify his self-concept and re-form his interpersonal response traits.

A small group of college men . . . agreed to cooperate in establishing a shy and inept girl as a social favorite. They saw to it . . . that she was invited to college affairs that were considered important and that she always had dancing partners. They treated her by agreement as though she were the reigning college favorite. Before the year was over she had developed an easy manner and a confident assumption that she was popular. These habits continued her social success after the experiment was completed and the men involved had ceased to make efforts in her behalf. They themselves had accepted her as a success. What her college career would have been if the experiment had not been made is impossible to say, of course, but it is fairly certain that she would have resigned all social ambitions and would have found interests compatible with her social ineptitude.

Guthrie, E. R. The psychology of human conflict. New York: Harper, 1938.

BASIC PSYCHOLOGICAL FACTORS

BOX 4.13: *The self and the other*

Harry Stack Sullivan was one of the leaders of the neo-Freudian movement in American psychiatry which, in challenging the instinctivist doctrines of Freud, insisted upon the prime role of the interpersonal relations of the individual in personality development and functioning. For Sullivan, indeed, psychiatry *was* the study of interpersonal relations.

Sullivan was much influenced in his thinking by Cooley, Mead, and Sapir, among other social scientists. For Sullivan, like Cooley and Mead, the individual's self-concept develops in the course of interaction with "significant others"—the persons who most intimately provide the rewards and punishments in his life.

> The self may be said to be made up of reflected appraisals. If these were chiefly derogatory . . . then the self dynamism will itself be chiefly derogatory. It will facilitate hostile, disparaging appraisals of other people and it will entertain disparaging and hostile appraisals of itself.

> As I have said, the peculiarity exists that one can find in others only that which is in the self.

Psychologist Emanuel M. Berger attempted to test the alleged "peculiarity . . . that one can find in others only that which is in the self." Guided by certain theoretical conceptions of the self-accepting person and the person who is accepting of others, Berger selected and constructed a large number of statements about the self and about others. Preliminary scales were subjected to item analysis. For the final form of the self-acceptance scale, 36 items were selected; for the acceptance-of-others scale, 28 items were used.

The final scales were administered to five markedly different kinds of groups. The subjects were instructed to respond to each item by marking one of five different alternatives ranging from "not at all true of myself (others)" to "true of myself (others)." Item scores ranged from 1 (low acceptance of self or others) to 5 (high acceptance of self or others). An individual's total score on each scale was the sum of his item scores.

The correlations between acceptance of self and acceptance of others for the five groups are shown in the following table.

Group	N	r
Day students	183	.36
Evening students	33	.65
Prisoners	33	.56
Stutterers	38	.70
YMCA class	18	.45

The correlations, it will be seen, are consistently positive. The "peculiarity" that Sullivan spoke about seems to be a general human peculiarity. Perhaps these positive correlations between acceptance of self and acceptance of others found by Berger partly reflect the operation of such processes as general evaluative sets and generalizing from the self (see page 61).

Sullivan, H. S. Conceptions of modern psychiatry. New York: Norton, 1953.

Berger, E. M. *The relation between expressed acceptance of self and expressed acceptance of others.* J. abnorm. soc. Psychol., *1952,* **47,** *778–782.*

The interaction of cognitions, wants, and interpersonal response traits

We have pointed out in the introduction to this chapter that the cognitions and wants of man help determine his interpersonal response traits, and that, in turn, his interpersonal response traits help determine his cognitions about his world and how he seeks to fulfill his wants. This fundamental kind of interaction among the three psychological factors which we have examined in Part One permeates the social behavior of man. We can give a single vivid illustration of such interaction by looking at how the individual copes with the basic social problem of occupational choice.

AN ILLUSTRATION: PSYCHOLOGICAL FACTORS IN OCCUPATIONAL CHOICE

One of the critical choice-points which occur in the lives of most men is the choice of a job, position, career—or whatever term it is fashionable to apply to a man's pattern of work activity. To be sure, for many men this choice is stringently limited among very few possibilities, but some degree of choice is always present. And whether a man's possible occupational choices are few or many, his final choice will help determine the kind of person he becomes. For, through his work or his profession, through the manner in which he uses most of his waking hours, his cognitions and his wants and his interpersonal response traits are heavily molded (see page 501). His business of the hour determines his experiences and the arousal of his wants, how he will satisfy his wants, with whom he is required to interact.

But—and this is the important point for us here—the individual's choice of occupation is itself determined by those very psychological factors which it affects. Perhaps the most complete documentation of this point is found in a study by Rosenberg [1957]. He has made an extensive study of the part which the psychological factors of values, wants, and interpersonal response traits play in the choice of jobs of college men and women. His findings were based on the responses to a set of questionnaires obtained from three samples: a 1950 sample of 2,758 Cornell University students, a 1952 sample of 1,571 Cornell students, and a 1952 nationwide sample of 4,585 students (including Cornell).

COGNITIONS. Although Rosenberg did not attempt an intensive study of the cognitions of his college students about jobs, it is clear that a person's choice of a career reflects his knowledge about the world of work: his ideas of the nature of various occupations—their educational and training requirements, the abilities and skills required, their demands and rewards, their prestige. And in making his choice, he is also guided by his cognitions concerning himself—he assesses his own capacities. He, as it were, holds up his self-concept and looks at it in relation to his job-concepts.

VALUES AND WANTS. To gain an understanding of the relative importance of wants and values in determining occupational choice, the subjects in the 1952 nationwide sample were given a list of wants and values and were asked to "consider to what extent a job or career would have to satisfy each of these requirements before you could consider it IDEAL." The data obtained are summarized in Table 4.3.

As Table 4.3 shows, self-fulfillment, interpersonal satisfactions, and security were ranked as more important than earning a good deal of money.

To determine the major "value orientations" in people which determine their choice of jobs, Rosenberg calculated the coefficient of association (Q) between every pair of the wants and values in the list. Three major clusters were identified:

1. "Opportunity to work with people rather

TABLE 4.3: RATINGS OF IMPORTANCE OF REQUIREMENTS FOR IDEAL JOB OR CAREER [After Rosenberg, 1957]

Want or value	High importance, per cent	Medium importance, per cent	Little or no importance, per cent
Uses my special abilities or aptitudes	78	20	2
Gives chance to earn a good deal of money	39	48	13
Permits creativity and originality	48	39	13
Has social status and prestige	26	53	21
Gives opportunity to work with people rather than things	44	36	20
Provides a stable, secure future	61	31	8
Is relatively free of supervision by others	38	48	14
Gives chance to exercise leadership	32	53	15
Provides adventure	16	40	44
Permits being helpful to others	43	44	13

than things" and "Being helpful to others" correlated .58. This can be termed a "people-oriented" value cluster.

2. "Chance to earn a good deal of money" and "Has social status and prestige" correlated .59. This cluster may be referred to as the "extrinsic reward-oriented" want complex.

3. "Permits creativity and originality" and "Uses my special abilities or aptitudes" correlated .47. This may be called the "self-expression-oriented" cognitive cluster.

Because a job means work with people, Rosenberg attempted to discover how attitudes toward other persons influence choice of jobs. A five-item Guttman scale (see page 154) was developed to measure "faith in people . . . the individual's degree of confidence in the trustworthiness, honesty, goodness, generosity, and brotherliness of the mass of men."

Table 4.4 presents the students' occupational choices and the percentage of students—for each occupational choice—who had high faith in people. Such occupations as social work, personnel work, and teaching attract people with high faith in people; advertising and public relations, business and finance, and sales promotion attract misanthropic persons.

INTERPERSONAL RESPONSE TRAITS. The part interpersonal response traits play in occupational choice was also studied. Rosenberg used Horney's tripartite typology of interpersonal response traits (see Box 4.1, page 105), clas-

TABLE 4.4: FAITH IN PEOPLE OF STUDENTS WITH DIFFERENT OCCUPATIONAL CHOICES [After Rosenberg, 1957]

Occupational choice	High faith, per cent
Social work	62
Personnel	59
Teaching	56
Science	51
Government	50
Farming	45
Art	43
Hotel	41
Medicine	40
Journalism, drama	39
Architecture	39
Law	39
Engineering	36
Advertising, public relations	36
Business, finance	34
Sales promotion	22

TABLE 4.5: COMPLIANT TYPE AND OCCUPATIONAL VALUES [After Rosenberg, 1957]

Occupational value	Compliant type, per cent	All others, per cent
"Opportunity to work with people":		
Ranked high	53	33
Ranked low	14	28
"Opportunity to be helpful":		
Ranked high	45	31
Ranked low	14	21
Either "people" or "helpful":		
Ranked high	74	48
Ranked low	22	38

TABLE 4.6: AGGRESSIVE TYPE AND OCCUPATIONAL VALUES [After Rosenberg, 1957]

Occupational value	Aggressive type, per cent	All others, per cent
"Earn a good deal of money":		
Ranked high	61	31
Ranked low	2	14
"Give me social status and prestige":		
Ranked high	44	20
Ranked low	9	22
Either "money" or "status":		
Ranked high	73	39
Ranked low	10	30

TABLE 4.7: DETACHED TYPE AND OCCUPATIONAL VALUES [After Rosenberg, 1957]

Occupational value	Detached type, per cent	All others, per cent
"Leave me free of supervision":		
Ranked high	66	36
Ranked low	7	14
"Permit me to be creative and original":		
Ranked high	68	46
Ranked low	8	13
Either "freedom" or "creative":		
Ranked high	84	63
Ranked low	14	24

TABLE 4.8: INTERPERSONAL RESPONSE TRAITS AND CHOICE OF OCCUPATIONAL AREA [After Rosenberg, 1957]

Occupational choice	Interpersonal response trait	
Social work, medicine, teaching, social science, and personnel	Compliant, 43%	All others, 24%
Real estate, hotel, sales, law, advertising, and business	Aggressive, 32%	All others, 20%
Art, architecture, journalism, drama, and natural science	Detached, 30%	All others, 14%

sifying his subjects, on the basis of questionnaire responses, into those who seek to "move toward people"—the "compliant type"; those who seek to "move against people"—the "aggressive type"; and those who seek to "move away from people"—the "detached type."

Students were classified into the "compliant type" if they said they were anxious to be well-liked, were not bothered by getting orders but were bothered at giving them, and expressed a positive view of human nature.

Students were classified into the "aggressive type" if they were chiefly concerned with becoming successful (rather than independent or well-liked), if they were not bothered by giving orders, and if they said that "if you don't watch yourself, people will take advantage of you."

Rosenberg characterized students as "detached" if they were concerned with being independent (rather than successful or well-liked), said they were bothered by receiving orders from others, considered being well-liked relatively unimportant, and said that, when in a group, they preferred to make decisions themselves rather than have others make the decisions.

As expected, the compliant type places a high value upon "opportunity to be helpful to others" and "opportunity to work with people" in his conception of an ideal job (see Table 4.5).

The aggressive type is concerned with earning a "good deal of money" and with gaining social status and prestige—two important means of gaining power (see Table 4.6).

The detached type, as expected, wants, in a job, to be "free of supervision" and to be creative and original (see Table 4.7).

It would seem that the interpersonal response traits of the individual importantly influence what he values in work. How do these response dispositions influence occupational choice? It might be expected that the students would tend to choose occupations which they believe will enable them to realize the values they cherish. Thus, compliant persons should prefer such "people-oriented occupations" as social work, teaching, and personnel work; aggressive persons should prefer the "misanthropic occupations" of sales promotion, business, and advertising; detached persons should select "autonomous occupations," such as art, architecture, and natural science, in which independence and creativity and originality can be realized. The data of Table 4.8 confirm these predictions.

A FINAL WORD. And thus we end Part One of this book. Action in the interpersonal behavior event reflects man's perceptions and cognitions, his wants and aversions, his interpersonal response traits. But these factors do not operate separately in the governance of behavior. Rather, they become organized into complex systems. And we now turn to an examination of the nature of these complex systems as we begin our study of social attitudes in Part Two.

CHAPTER GUIDES AND GLOSSARY

GUIDE 11: *The social behavior of the individual is channeled by his interpersonal response traits—relatively consistent and stable dispositions to respond in distinctive ways to other persons*

GUIDE 12: *The interpersonal response traits of the individual are the end products of his characteristic experiences in satisfying his most frequently and most intensely aroused wants*

aggression. Attack upon an obstacle or barrier to want satisfaction, or upon an object or person to which the aggression is displaced.

autism. A tendency for the thinking of the individual to be regulated by personal wants and emotions at the expense of regulation by objective reality. Autism is a common reaction to want frustration.

consistency, trait. The degree to which the ranks of individuals on a trait remain the same in a sample of different applicable situations. Trait consistency is measured by the average intercorrelation among trait scores in the sample of different applicable situations. If the average intercorrelation is high, the trait is relatively consistent.

frustration. The motivational and emotional state which results from persistent blockage of goal-directed behavior.

identification. The process of modeling oneself after another individual or group. Through identification the individual comes to incorporate the attributes of the other individual or group, and to display similar behavior.

interpersonal response trait. A more or less stable and consistent disposition of the individual to respond to other persons in a characteristic way.

patterning, trait. The profile or pattern of the scores of an individual on the specific indicators of a trait. Two persons with the same total trait score may have two quite different profiles or patterns of scores.

pervasiveness, trait. The degree to which a trait is manifested in the behavior of an individual. Traits which are highly pervasive are manifested in a wide variety of situations; traits of low pervasiveness, in only a restricted number of situations.

projection. The process of ascribing to other persons one's own disvalued attributes, e.g., unacknowledged and unacceptable wants and faults.

rationalization. The process of justifying one's wants, beliefs, and behavior when they are challenged by oneself or others. The justification takes the form of inventing reasons which the individual believes are the real reasons.

reaction formation. The establishment of an interpersonal response trait that is directly opposed to a strong unconscious trend. The development of the trait of sympathy to deny hostility is an example.

regression. A manifestation of earlier and less mature behavior after having learned more mature forms, as a consequence of frustration.

repression. The exclusion of specific wants and psychological activities or content from conscious awareness through a process of which the individual is not aware. The repressed material conflicts with social values and taboos as incorporated in the individual's ideal self-concept.

stability, trait. The degree of constancy of the trait scores of individuals over time. Stability is measured by determining the correlation between trait scores on two different occasions.

withdrawal. A response to frustration in which a person removes himself from the frustrating obstacle and obtains want satisfaction in ways such as daydreaming, sleeping, alcoholism, drug addiction, or escape into work.

Part Two: SOCIAL
ATTITUDES

AS MAN IN HIS FINITE WORLD IS REPEATEDLY FORCED TO COPE
with the same object, the repeatedly evoked cognitions, feelings, and
response dispositions become organized into a unified and enduring
system—for man is an organizing and conserving animal. This
entire "package" of particular beliefs, feelings, and response
tendencies is henceforth always there, on the ready, whenever
the individual is confronted by the appropriate object. In other
words, he now has an attitude *toward the object.*

And as the individual acquires more and more attitudes—as he
"assimilates" more and more objects in his world—his improvisations
toward these objects and his fresh examinations and interpretations
of them decrease. His actions become stereotyped, predictable, and
consistent—and social life becomes possible. For where there are
no enduring beliefs, evaluations, and action tendencies which can
be shared by a company of men, social life as we know it would
be impossible.

Whatever the costs and values of attitude formation may be, it is
clear that the understanding of attitudes is one of the central
problems of social psychology. With this chapter we start our study
of these ruling systems of man's behavior.

5: THE NATURE AND MEASUREMENT OF ATTITUDES

IN CHAPTER 1 WE DESCRIBED THE INTERPER-
sonal behavior event as a process of communication. In all interpersonal behavior events,
the participants may be observed to be communicating with one another about some referent. This may be anything that exists in
their psychological worlds. It may be a concrete thing, an internal state, an event, an abstraction; it may be "real," it may be fictitious.

In Box 5.1 we observe a man talking with
another man about Jews. Note that he has a
number of *beliefs* about Jews:

"They're richer than the rest of us . . . and
they have less principle and easier conscience.

BOX 5.1: *A Christian talks about Jews*

In 1942, Angus Campbell, then with the Program Surveys Division, U. S. Department of Agriculture, conducted a nationwide survey to study factors associated with attitudes toward Jews. In the course of the survey, special interviews were also secured from 34 former subscribers to certain "hate" magazines which the government had suppressed in the interest of national defense during World War II.

The following excerpt is taken from one of these interviews. The respondent was a mailman, unmarried, 32 years old, a college graduate, faced with the imminent prospect of being drafted.

Q. Do you think the Jewish people are doing their share [in the war effort]?

A. They're trying to get out of it, but so are all of us. They're richer than the rest of us and probably succeed a little better—and they have less principle and easier conscience. What great art has the Jew given the world except that of making money? I'm not anti-Jewish—I can't be because I'm Roman Catholic. They're hated by all alike—must be something wrong with them.

Q. Why do you think people feel that way?

A. If I could answer that I would become a great man. A lot of it's just instinct—like a dog that whirls around three times before he lies down. He had to do it in the brush to mash down a bed for himself, but he still does it in the city—just instinct. We dislike Jews because that's the way we grow up to feel toward them.

Q. Do you have much contact with Jewish people from day to day?

A. I work with a few and they're regular fellows—they never make themselves superior and never sneer—but others are not like that. Most of them think they have superior intellects. How come 90 per cent of the communist parades are made up of Jews?

Q. Now we've been talking about how other people feel; how do you yourself feel about the Jews?

A. Oh, I think they are clannish and very shrewd. I wouldn't say always dishonest, but plenty scheming. They never become assimilated—never become part of a country they live in. From an artistic standpoint they have lowered the standard of the drama since they got control of the theatre business.

Q. Do you think Jews should be treated differently from other people?

A. No, but they should be made to act as other people. Why should I be browbeaten by a guy holding Stalin's picture? Who's ruling this country—the Reds? I've never been able to understand why Jews want to force their way into restricted places anyway. I sure wouldn't want to go where I'm not wanted.

Q. When did you begin to feel about Jews the way you do now?

A. I've always felt the same way. We used to do home work together in school sometimes, but I've never liked to be around them.

Q. What things made you feel the way you do now about the Jewish people?

A. Just instinct.

Campbell, A. A. Factors associated with attitudes toward Jews. In T. M. Newcomb and E. L. Hartley (Eds.), Readings in social psychology. *New York: Holt, 1947.*

. . . Oh, I think they are clannish and very shrewd. I wouldn't say always dishonest, but plenty scheming."

His beliefs about Jews are related to his *feelings* toward them:

"We dislike Jews . . . ."

His beliefs and feelings about Jews are, in turn, related to his *action tendencies* with respect to them:

". . . they should be made to act as other people . . . ." "I've never liked to be around them."

The way this man treats Jews is determined by his beliefs about them, his feelings toward them, and his dispositions to respond to them. These cognitions, feelings, and action tendencies are interrelated to form a system. This particular system we call his *attitude* toward Jews. Man's social actions—whether the actions involve religious behavior, ways of earning a living, political activity, or buying and selling goods—are directed by his attitudes.

It is not surprising, therefore, that the measurement of attitudes has become a major American industry. Every American can now buy information on "attitudes." For the price of a daily newspaper he can avail himself of the results of public-opinion studies conducted regularly by local and national polling agencies. For the price of a slick-paper magazine, he can get more specialized attitude studies. And if he wishes to spend a great deal of money, he can buy the services of a commercial agency which will carry out a custom-built attitude survey to meet his own business or political needs.

The basis of this demand for information about people's attitudes is not hard to find. By knowing the attitudes of people it is possible to do something about the prediction and control of their behavior. And for many persons in our society, the prediction and control of the behavior of others are important desiderata.

If a political party knows the attitudes of the American people toward political issues, it is better able to predict the behavior of people at the polls and to devise a platform with the greatest appeal. If the Department of State knows the attitudes of people in the area of foreign affairs, it can estimate the support or resistance that will appear among the people toward proposed foreign policies. If the members of a minority group know the attitudes of the rest of the community toward them, they are better able to foresee and perhaps to forestall aggressive acts. If public health officials know the details of people's attitudes toward cancer, they can institute an intelligent educational campaign. If the manufacturer of a car wants to increase his sales, it is useful for him to arrange a price, design, and promotion plan in terms of what he can find out about people's attitudes toward automobiles.

This chapter is concerned with a discussion of the nature of attitudes and with the general issues involved in methods for measuring them.

GUIDE 13: *The social actions of the individual reflect his attitudes— enduring systems of positive or negative evaluations, emotional feelings, and pro or con action tendencies with respect to social objects*

As the individual develops, his cognitions, feelings, and action tendencies with respect to the various objects in his world become organized into enduring *systems* called attitudes.

In defining attitudes as systems, we are emphasizing the interrelatedness of the three attitude components. When incorporated in a system, these components become mutually interdependent. The cognitions of an individual about an object are influenced by his feelings and action tendencies toward that object. And a change in his cognitions about the object will tend to produce changes in his feelings and action tendencies toward it.

THE OBJECTS OF ATTITUDES

The object of an attitude may be anything that exists for the individual. Thus an individual has a vast array of attitudes toward objects in the physical world that surrounds him. He has perhaps an even more imposing array of attitudes toward objects in the social world in which he lives. He has attitudes toward other people and groups of people, toward social organizations, and toward political and economic events. He has a variety of attitudes toward art, philosophy, God, and the hereafter. And he has many attitudes toward himself.

However, the number of any individual's attitudes is finite. He can have attitudes only with respect to those objects which exist in *his* psychological world. In so far as his psychological world is limited, the kinds of attitudes he has will be limited. Not every American, for example, has attitudes toward strontium 90; not every American has attitudes toward Communist China or the segregation of Negroes. Yet this simple fact is sometimes forgotten by attitude testers and public-opinion pollsters. We cannot assume that simply because we have an attitude-measuring device, we can therefore measure the attitudes of all men with respect to any given object. The failure to recognize this fact has often led to misinterpretations of the results of attitude tests. People can respond, in one way or another, to any test, but this may not mean that they have the attitude in which the investigator is interested. Before the attitude of an individual can meaningfully be measured, the investigator must first determine that the individual *has* an attitude toward the given object. As we shall see, this presents a difficult problem in attitude measurement. That an object exists is a necessary, but not a *sufficient,* condition for a person to hold an attitude.

THE COMPONENTS OF ATTITUDES

The *cognitive* component of an attitude consists of the beliefs of the individual about the object. For example, your attitude toward Communism may include your understanding of Marxist theory, your knowledge of the history of the USSR and Communist China, your beliefs about the way the Communist parties in Russia and China administer internal affairs, your conception of their foreign policies, and so on. The most critical cognitions incorporated in the attitude system are *evaluative* beliefs which involve the attribution of favorable or unfavorable, desirable or undesirable, "good" or "bad" qualities to the object: The Communist system makes people free; Russia is plotting war. The cognitive component may also include the beliefs of the individual about appropriate and inappropriate ways of responding to the object: Communists in America should be imprisoned; Red China should be admitted to the UN. Thus the cognitive and the action tendency components may be closely related.

The *feeling* component of an attitude refers to the emotions connected with the object. The object is felt to be pleasing or displeasing; it is liked or it is disliked. It is this emotional loading which gives attitudes their insistent, stirred-up, motivating character. If you are an Anglophile, you feel friendly toward Englishmen; you like their ways of speaking and acting; you admire British craftsmanship; you love the Royal Family and follow its activities with intense interest. (That the feeling component of an attitude has physiological manifestations which can be experimentally measured is shown in Box 5.2.)

The *action tendency* component of an attitude includes all the behavioral readinesses associated with the attitude. If an individual holds a positive attitude toward a given object, he will be disposed to help or reward or support the object; if he holds a negative attitude, he will be disposed to harm or punish or destroy the object. Thus if you have a favor-

Joseph B. Cooper, a psychologist at San Jose State College, has experimentally demonstrated that even when attitudes are aroused in an "artificial" laboratory setting, they are accompanied by relatively strong emotion.

In one of his studies, 20 college students who had displayed in previous testing either extremely favorable or unfavorable attitudes toward 20 ethnic groups were used as subjects in individual laboratory sessions.

Four evaluative statements were prepared. Two of the statements were used to derogate any given group; two were used to compliment any given group. One of the derogatory statements was: "People can be divided into two groups: The good and the bad. Close to the bottom of the list are the ————. They certainly can be said to have caused more trouble for humanity than they are worth." One of the complimentary statements was: "The world over, no single group of people has done as much for us, for our civilization, as the ————. The world will undoubtedly come to recognize them as honest, wise and completely unselfish."

For a particular subject, the name of his most liked group was inserted into one of the derogatory statements and the name of his most disliked group into one of the complimentary statements. The names of the groups toward which the subject was relatively neutral were inserted into the two other statements—one derogatory and one complimentary.

The subject was attached to an apparatus for measuring the galvanic skin response; this response is commonly taken to be a measure of a physiological correlate of emotionality. The statements were then read aloud to the subject by the experimenter and the galvanic skin response to each statement was measured.

The galvanic skin responses of 14 of the 20 subjects were greater to derogatory statements about their most liked groups than to statements about relatively neutral groups. And for 19 of the 20 subjects, galvanic skin responses were greater to complimentary statements about their most disliked groups than to statements about neutral groups.

Here we have physiological evidence from the laboratory that the feeling component is evoked when an attitude is tapped.

*Cooper, J. B. Emotion in prejudice. Science, 1959, **130**, 314–318.*

able attitude toward Jews, you may have a tendency to seek them out, to accept them as friends, to aid them, to treat them as equals; if you are anti-Semitic, you may have a tendency to avoid Jews, to reject them as friends, to withhold help, to treat them as inferior persons.

GUIDE 14: *Attitudes differ in their effects on social action according to their primary characteristics*

Not all attitudes are alike in their systemic structure. They differ from one another in a number of basic characteristics. How an attitude governs action is in part determined by its particular pattern of characteristics. Some of these basic characteristics pertain to the nature of the *components* of an attitude system. Some pertain to the nature of the *system* itself. And some pertain to the nature of the total *constellation* of attitudes of an individual.

CHARACTERISTICS OF THE COMPONENTS

Each of the three components of an attitude may vary in *valence* and in degree of *multiplexity*.

VALENCE. As we have seen, an attitude may always be described as either favorable or unfavorable, for or against the object. But it is usually not enough to describe merely this *direction,* or sign, of an individual's attitude toward a given object. It is often necessary to derive a quantitative measure of valence—to specify the *degree* of favorability or unfavorability.

Valence is a characteristic that applies to each of the three components of an attitude system. The cognitive component of an individual's attitude may be highly favorable—he may think of the object as a supreme good. On the other hand, the cognitive component may be highly unfavorable—he may believe that the object is an unmixed evil. The feeling component can similarly vary from extreme positive valence to extreme negative valence—from unconditional love to unconditional hate. And the action tendency component can vary from tendencies to help or support or protect the object in all possible ways to extreme tendencies to attack and destroy the object.

As we shall see when we turn to the measurement of the characteristics of attitudes, the assessment of valence has been the major interest of persons concerned with the problem of measurement. A number of different methods for securing quantitative measures of valence have developed. The aim of these measurement methods is to order individuals on a linear continuum which runs from extreme unfavorableness, through zero (i.e., absence of attitude), to extreme favorableness.

MULTIPLEXITY. Each of the components of an attitude also may vary with respect to degree of multiplexity. This refers to the number and variety of the elements or parts making up a component (see page 38). The cognitive component can vary from that minimal knowledge about an object necessary to recognize it and to distinguish it from other objects to an exhaustive set of beliefs about the object. Thus the cognitive component of a man's attitude toward "science" may be multiplex, involving a differentiation between the physical and social sciences, between applied and pure science, between science and scientist, between the theories of science and the data of science. On the other hand, his beliefs about religion may be simplex; he may not differentiate between the church as an organization and religion as a "way of life," between one religious sect and another, one dogma and another. The cognitive component of every attitude can, in short, be placed on a continuum of degree of multiplexity.

The feeling component of an attitude similarly may vary from the extreme of undifferentiated positive or negative affectivity about the object to a highly multiplex set of emotions about it. A man may experience feelings of love, tenderness, friendship, respect, and passion for one woman and simple liking for another woman.

The action tendency associated with an attitude may vary in degree of multiplexity from a single disposition to attack the object (or to aid it) to a highly elaborated family of dispositions toward the object. A person who holds a favorable attitude toward the Democratic party may, in his attitude, incorporate such multiplex action tendencies as to campaign in his precinct, to contribute money to the party, to "get out the vote" on election day; or he may incorporate in his attitude only a simplex tendency to vote for the party's candidates on election day.

CONSISTENCY CHARACTERISTICS OF THE ATTITUDE SYSTEM

The conception of attitude as a system having three components raises the question of the degree to which these components are consistently related to one another. Is the valence of an individual's cognitions about an object similar to the valence of his feelings toward the object and the valence of his action tendencies? Is the degree of multiplexity similar for the three components? In other words, what are the intercorrelations among the three components in valence and in multiplexity? This is the question of *consistency*.

The evidence suggests that there is a general trend toward consistency in valence among attitudinal components. The correlations between the valence scores of the different components are generally found to be moderately high. (For one study of this problem see Box 5.3.)

In their study of "The Authoritarian Personality," Adorno et al. [1950] developed an anti-Semitism scale that was made up of a number of subscales. Some subscales tapped the valence of the cognitive component of attitudes toward the Jew. (Typical items: "A major fault of the Jews is their conceit, over-bearing pride, and their idea that they are a chosen race." "The Jew's first loyalty is to Jewry rather than to his country.") Another subscale measured the valence of the action tendency component. (Typical items: "In order to maintain a nice residential neighborhood it is best to prevent Jews from living in it." "It is wrong for Jews and Gentiles to intermarry.") The investigators found that correlations between these two sets of subscales ranged from .74 to .84, indicating a high de-

BOX 5.3: *Attitude systems: consistent or inconsistent?*

While at the University of California, Berkeley, Donald T. Campbell, a social psychologist, undertook the study of the interrelations among five "subtopics" which are involved in attitudes toward minority groups in the United States. These are: (1) *social distance,* the tendency to deny intimacy to minority group members and to demand segregation from them; (2) beliefs regarding the *blame* of a minority group for social problems; (3) beliefs regarding the *capability* or intelligence of a minority group; (4) beliefs regarding the *morality* of a minority group; and (5) *affection,* the feeling of like or dislike for a minority group.

It will be seen that social distance is a measure of what we have called the action tendency component of attitude; blame, capability, and morality are measures of the cognitive component; affection is a measure of the feeling component.

Scales were constructed to measure each of these attitudinal subtopics. The referents were five minority groups: the Negro, Japanese, Jew, Mexican, and English. The scales (each consisting of five items) were administered to a sample of 170 college students and 239 high school students, all of whom were non-minority-group persons.

The degree of consistency in attitudes toward minority groups was measured by computing, for each group, the average intercorrelations among the five scales. The values obtained are shown in the following table:

	College sample	High school sample
Negro	.65	.58
Japanese	.54	.58
Jewish	.50	.56
Mexican	.58	.62
English	.34	.57

These values suggest that, except perhaps for the atypical English group, there is a rather substantial degree of consistency among the components of attitudes toward minority groups.

Campbell, D. T. *The generality of a social attitude. Unpublished doctoral dissertation,* Univer. of California, Berkeley, 1947.

gree of consistency between the valence of beliefs about Jews and the valence of action orientations toward them.

These correlations, however, are probably inflated by the fact that the same item-form was used to measure the two components; further, all the statements were worded in terms extremely unfavorable to Jews. Cronbach [1946] has shown that when subjects respond to questionnaires composed of items of the same form, "response sets" are induced which lead subjects to respond in a more consistent manner than they would if the questionnaire were made up of items of differing forms.

In a study by MacKenzie [1948], items of *different* forms were used to measure the action tendency and cognitive components of attitude toward the Negro. Five multiple-choice items dealing with characteristics of Negroes as workers tapped the cognitive component of individuals' attitudes toward Negroes. A "social distance scale" of six items was used to measure the action tendency component. Such a scale requires that the subject indicate the degree of social intimacy to which he would accept a social group. (For a discussion of this scale, see page 153). The action tendency items—willingness to "ride with," "eat with," and "live near"—correlated .48, .52, and .46, respectively, with the scores on the five multiple-choice items dealing with the characteristics of Negroes as workers. On the other hand, willingness to work with Negroes and to have them upgraded on the job was found to have lower relations with beliefs about their characteristics as workers ($r = .30$ and $.18$, respectively). This study suggests that the degree of consistency of ethnic attitudes may be somewhat lower than the previous studies indicate.

We might expect to find greater consistency among attitude components at the *extremes* of the valence continuum. And this is what Bettelheim and Janowitz [1950] did find in their study of prejudice toward Negroes and

Jews, based upon intensive interviews with 150 World War II veterans living in Chicago. In two extreme types of anti-Semitic attitude (the "intensely anti-Semitic" and the "outspoken anti-Semitic") the cognitive, emotional, and action tendency components were found to be highly consistent. Veterans holding violent or outspoken anti-Semitic attitudes perceived the Jew in a highly unfavorable light, disliked him intensely, and were in favor of taking strong repressive measures against him.

Concerning the question of the tendency toward consistency among the three attitude components in their degree of *multiplexity*, there appears to be little in the way of empirical evidence. (For some speculation on this issue, see Box 5.4.)

INTERCONNECTEDNESS IN THE ATTITUDE CONSTELLATION

The total set of attitudes of an individual makes up his attitude constellation. In this section, we inquire into the interconnectedness among the various attitudes in the individual's constellation.

Just as we have seen that cognitions may differ in degree of isolation from or interrelation with other cognitions (see page 42), so may attitudes. For example, a man may have a strong aversive attitude toward the personal income tax but this attitude may not be connected in any close fashion with other economic attitudes that he has, for example, attitudes toward private enterprise or inflation. It stands virtually alone, cut off from his other attitudes. In contrast, another of the same individual's attitudes may be closely interconnected with a whole body of attitudes, influencing them and being influenced by them. Thus his attitudes toward the Roman Catholic Church may be connected with a large number of related attitudes about, for example, political systems, science, poetry, art, family relationships. His attitudes toward these things will tend to be organized and

BOX 5.4: *An attitude typology*

Some aspects of the question of intercomponent consistency in attitudes have been explored by Daniel Katz and Ezra Stotland, social psychologists at the University of Michigan. These writers distinguish five basic attitude types, four of which are of interest to us here.

Affective associations have minimal cognitive content and little or no action orientation. This type of attitude is not related to other cognitive systems. It is an evaluative response based heavily upon emotional feeling evoked by the object. Because it has little or no action orientation, it is not possible to make predictions about the actions of an individual from a knowledge of his affective associations.

Intellectualized attitudes have a heavy cognitive component, in addition to a feeling component, but lack action orientation. Like affective associations, they cannot be used to make accurate predictions of behavior.

Action-oriented attitudes represent action tendencies toward evaluated objects with a minimum of cognitive content.

Balanced attitudes are fully developed with elaborate cognitive and action-orientation components, to supplement the rich feeling component. This type of multiplex attitude tends to be related to other attitude systems in the individual's attitude constellation.

Of these four types, only the last would seem to be characterized by high consistency in the degree of multiplexity among the three components.

> Katz, D., and Stotland, E. A preliminary statement to a theory of attitude structure and change. In S. Koch (Ed.), Psychology: a study of a science, vol. 3. New York: McGraw-Hill, 1959.

structured in a way highly interconnected with his attitude toward the Catholic Church.

Few attitudes can be thought of as existing in a complete state of isolation. Most of them form *clusters* with other attitudes. The degree to which all the attitudes of a person form a comprehensive and orderly pattern may be taken as one indication of the degree of unity of his personality. Only rarely will an individual exhibit such a high degree of unity of attitudes that we are justified in saying he has a single ideology or life philosophy. More commonly, an individual's political, religious, artistic, and scientific ideologies are somewhat separable. But even this statement needs qualification. One should not assume that for every area of human life which we can label with a distinct name there necessarily exists for a given person a corresponding cluster of homogenous attitudes. It is more likely that for a given person any one cluster of attitudes will include heterogeneous attitudes, e.g., some religious, some political, and some scientific attitudes.

Ferguson's [1939] attempt to isolate the primary social attitudes illustrates the concept of attitude cluster. He administered 10 Thurstone attitude scales (see page 151 for discussion of the Thurstone attitude scaling technique) to a sample of 185 university students. The 10 scales were designed to measure attitudes toward war, the reality of God, patriotism, the treatment of criminals, capital punishment, censorship, evolution, birth control, law, and communism.

The intercorrelations among the 10 attitude scale scores were factor analyzed (see page 107) to determine the smallest number of primary attitude clusters that would account for the set of intercorrelations. Ferguson found that three different primary attitude clusters would serve. These primary clusters he named "religionism," "humanitarianism," and "nationalism." Religionism accounted for attitudes toward evolution, God, and birth control; humanitarianism accounted for attitudes toward capital punishment, treatment of criminals, and war; nationalism accounted for attitudes toward Communism, law, censorship, and patriotism.

CONSONANCE CHARACTERISTICS OF THE ATTITUDE CLUSTER

We have seen that the cognitive elements making up a system may be in close agreement with one another, being consonant, harmonious, "fitting," or they may, to varying degrees, be in disagreement, being incongruent or contradictory (see page 38). Similarly, attitude clusters may vary with respect to degree of consonance among the attitudes that make them up. Some attitude clusters may be characterized by a high degree of internal harmony; other attitude clusters may be characterized by lesser harmony.

Campbell, Converse, Miller, and Stokes [1960] examined the effect upon political behavior of the degree of consonance among the component attitudes in the political attitude cluster. Six attitude objects were identified that seemed most clearly to be objects of popular attitudes in the presidential election of 1956. These were the personal attributes of Stevenson, the Democratic candidate; the personal attributes of Eisenhower, the Republican candidate; the groups involved in politics and the questions of group interest affecting them; the issues of domestic policy; the issues of foreign policy; the comparative record of the Democratic and Republican parties in managing the affairs of government.

A sample of persons, designed to represent the national electorate, was interviewed after the election. Measures of the valence of the attitudes of each individual in the sample toward the six attitude objects listed above were secured. These measures reflected the partisan direction of an individual's attitude toward each of the six objects (pro-Republican, neutral, or pro-Democratic) and the intensity of partisan attitude (how strongly pro-Republican or pro-Democratic was the attitude of an individual toward each of the six objects). These valence measures made it easy to determine roughly the degree of consonance among the political attitudes of an individual. For example, a person holds consonant attitudes who likes Eisenhower and also likes the Republican position on foreign issues, as does a person who both dislikes Eisenhower and Republican foreign policies; but the person who likes Eisenhower and dislikes the Republican position or who dislikes Eisenhower but approves his party's position holds dissonant political attitudes.

The effects of attitudinal dissonance upon political behavior were found to be substantial and pervasive. The degree of attitude consonance affected the earliness of the individual's vote decision: the percentage of persons who decided late increased consistently with increase in degree of attitude dissonance. Further, the person whose political attitudes were in some degree of dissonance tended to cast his vote for President with much less enthusiasm, he was much more prone to split his ballot in voting for other candidates, and he was somewhat less likely to vote at all.

TO RECAPITULATE

The actions of the individual are governed to a large extent by his *attitudes*. An attitude can be defined as an enduring system of three components centering about a single object: the beliefs about the object—the *cognitive component;* the affect connected with the object—the *feeling component;* and the disposition to take action with respect to the object—the *action tendency component.*

The components of attitudes may differ in *valence* and *multiplexity*. Valence refers to the degree of favorability or unfavorability with respect to the object of the attitude.

Thus a given attitude may incorporate highly favorable beliefs about its object, mildly favorable feelings, and some slight tendencies to take favorable action with respect to that object. Multiplexity refers to the variation in the number and kind of the elements making up the components. Thus the cognitive component of an attitude may include an exhaustive set of beliefs about the object; the feeling component may be a relatively simple and undifferentiated love for the object; and the action tendency component may be multiplex in that the individual is prepared to take many and varied sorts of protective acts toward the object. The available evidence suggests that there is a general trend toward consistency among the components of attitudes in their valence and in their multiplexity.

An individual's various attitudes may differ in the degree to which they are isolated from one another or are *interconnected* with one another. Few attitudes exist in a state of complete isolation. Most of them form *clusters* with other attitudes, but only rarely will all the attitudes of an individual exhibit such a high degree of interconnectedness that we are justified in saying the individual has a single ideology. Attitude clusters vary with respect to degree of *consonance*.

Methods and problems in the measurement of attitudes

To use the concept of attitude in understanding and predicting action, we need reliable and valid measures. The measurement of attitudes, like the measurement of all psychological determinants, is necessarily indirect. Attitudes can be measured only on the basis of inferences drawn from the responses of the individual toward the object—his overt actions and his verbal statements of belief, feeling, and disposition to act with respect to the object.

ATTITUDE SCALES

Of all methods for the measurement of attitudes, by far the most widely used and the most carefully designed and tested is the so-called attitude scale. Actually, most attitude scales have been concerned only with the measurement of valence. Recently, however, some attempts to develop scales to measure the multiplexity of the cognitive component of an attitude have been reported (see Box 5.5).

An attitude scale consists of a set of statements or items to which the person responds. The pattern of his responses provides a way of inferring something about his attitude. Scales differ markedly in type and in method of construction, but in every case their objective is identical: to assign an individual a numerical position on a continuum, a position which indicates, for example, the valence of his attitude toward a particular object.

CRITERIA FOR THE SELECTION OF SCALE ITEMS. In determining which items shall be included in a scale, and how many items are required, the following four criteria are relevant.

1. *Discriminating function.* An item must actually discriminate: people of different attitude complexion must respond to the item in systematically different ways.

Sometimes the diagnostic relationship of an item to the characteristic of the attitude we are measuring can be clearly assured by making the manifest content of the item bear directly on the object of the attitude. For example, to ascertain attitudes toward Russia's foreign policies an item might be phrased as follows: "Russia is sincerely trying to make the United Nations work." The individual's assent or dissent to this proposition presumably reveals something about the valence of the cognitive component of his attitude toward Russian foreign policy.

Sometimes, however, the content of an item may not bear such obvious relationship to the object. Because of the wide interconnected-

BOX 5.5: *Scaling multiplexity*

Ulf Himmelstrand, a Swedish sociologist at the University of Upsala, has developed a scale to measure the degree of cognitive differentiation or multiplexity of an attitude.

In a test of attitude toward child-rearing practices, Himmelstrand inserted six purposely vague statements. For example, one of the statements read, "You cannot bring up children without loving them." After each of these statements the subjects were asked: "Is there anything in the *content* or form of the above statement which you spontaneously, as you read it, wish to comment upon? If so, write your comments here."

In a sample of 215 student teachers, 128 commented upon one or more of the six statements. Two judges classified the comments into the following three categories:

(*a*) Paraphrasing and asking rhetorical questions that repeat the content of the statement.

(*b*) Asking questions regarding the meaning of terms used in the statement; pointing out that several meanings may be attributed to the same word; restricting the reliability of the statement to make it fit one's own point of view more precisely; suggesting an argument in causal terms.

(*c*) Making a detailed description of a situation in which the statement might apply as a way of making the statement more precise; making detailed references to conditions under which the statement would or would not hold; rationalizing the statement *rather extensively* in causal terms.

Comments in category (*c*), regarded as indicating the highest degree of cognitive differentiation, were assigned an arbitrary weight of +3; comments in category (*b*) were weighted +2; the "empty" and undifferentiating comments in category (*a*) were weighted −1. (When a subject offered no comment upon a particular statement a score of zero was assigned.)

The weights were summed algebraically over the six statements to obtain an index of cognitive differentiation for each subject. Himmelstrand found that this index proved to be quite useful in his study of attitudes toward child-rearing practices.

Himmelstrand, U. Social pressures, attitudes, and democratic processes. *Stockholm: Almquist and Wiksell, 1960.*

ness of attitudes, any given attitude of the individual will tend to influence judgments of many things only indirectly related to the attitude object under measurement. Thus, for example, an item in a scale for the measurement of attitude toward Communism might take the following form: "Religious values are of the highest importance in a person's life." Assent or dissent to this proposition might have been discovered in preliminary testing to be highly related to people's attitudes toward Communism, and hence the item could be used as a discriminating item in the scale, even though its manifest reference is to religion rather than to Communism.

2. *Sharpness of discrimination.* Items should also discriminate as sharply as possible. Thus, all those persons assenting to a favorable proposition concerning the attitude object should lie farther toward the favorable end of the attitude scale than any of the dissenters to the proposition; ideally there should be no overlap. In selecting items for a scale, those are chosen which show the smallest overlap and which therefore are the sharpest discriminators.

3. *Discrimination along the entire scale.* Not only is it necessary to be able to separate the sheep from the goats, the friends from the foes, the pros from the antis; it is also desir-

able to be able to make much finer differentiations. We need to be able to separate the more extreme sheep from the less extreme sheep, the more extreme goats from the less extreme goats.

The degree of effective differentiation may vary at different places on an attitude scale. Thus attitude differences among people who fall toward the middle of the scale may be reliably measured, whereas attitude differences among people falling near the extremes may be obscured. Beyond a certain degree of unfavorability, for example, a scale may not distinguish among people; the rabid reactionary is not differentiated in a measurable way from the strong reactionary. The social implication of this shortcoming of attitude scales may, in some instances, be serious. It is often the most extreme, rabid, bitter-enders who play the critical role in social events, and it is these people whom scales need also to identify. That scales are often inadequate in this respect is probably accounted for by the technical difficulties involved in finding items which will truly discriminate at the very extremes of a scale.

4. *Minimal number of items for reliability.* The greater the number of items in a scale, the higher the reliability. This is because irrelevant "errors of measurement" tend to cancel out. Though an individual may ascribe unique meanings to various items in a way that distorts measurement, it is not likely that the distortions will always be in the same direction. The larger the number of items, the less the danger of a net distortion in one direction or the other. However, considerations of efficiency and practicality in testing sharply limit the total number of items that can be comfortably accommodated in attitude scales.

TYPES OF ITEMS. Two major types of items have been used in constructing attitude scales. The most widely used type is an evaluative statement about the object which taps the cognitive and feeling components.

The following evaluative items are taken from a Thurstone scale used to study attitudes toward natives in South Africa [MacCrone, 1937]. The scale value of each item is given in parentheses on the left. The scale value of an item is a numerical representation of its placement along an 11-point favorability-unfavorability continuum. (For a further discussion of the meaning of scale values, see Box 5.6.)

(10.2) The idea of contact with the black or dark skin of the native excites horror and disgust in me.

(8.4) To my mind the native is so childish and irresponsible that he cannot be expected to know what is in his best interest.

(3.1) It seems to me that the white man by placing restrictions such as the "Colour Bar" upon the native is really trying to exploit him economically.

The following evaluative items are taken from a Likert scale (the Internationalism Scale) used by Murphy and Likert [1938]. The number in parentheses below each alternative is the score value of the alternative. On a positive item, a score of 5 is assigned "Strongly approve," a score of 4 is assigned "Approve" and so on to a score of 1 for "Strongly disapprove." On negative items, the scoring system is reversed.

In the interest of permanent peace, we should be willing to arbitrate absolutely all differences with other nations which we cannot settle by diplomacy.

Strongly approve	Approve	Un-decided	Dis-approve	Strongly dis-approve
(5)	(4)	(3)	(2)	(1)

We must strive for loyalty to our country before we can afford to consider world brotherhood.

Strongly approve	Approve	Un-decided	Dis-approve	Strongly dis-approve
(1)	(2)	(3)	(4)	(5)

A second type of item, used in but a few scales, consists of a description of a specific action toward the object of the attitude in a particular situation. The subject is asked to indicate whether he would or would not take the action specified. The following "action items" are taken from a Thurstone scale developed by Rosander [1937] to measure attitude toward the Negro. The scale value of each item is given in parentheses on the left.

(1.2) You are bathing at a beach. Some Negroes approach and enter the water near you. You start a fight with them.

(6.2) In the community where you live a Negro marries a white girl. You do nothing about it.

(11.5) A Negro family moves into the residential district where you live. You invite them to your home.

SCALING METHODS

There are five principal scaling methods for the measurement of attitudes.

THE METHOD OF EQUAL-APPEARING INTERVALS. Early in the history of the development of attitude scales, Thurstone and his co-workers [Thurstone, 1929; Thurstone, 1931; Thurstone and Chave, 1929] originated a method of attitude-scale construction to which we have already referred. They published a number of specific scales for the measurement of attitudes toward war, the church, capital punishment, evolution, the Negro, birth control, censorship, the Chinese, etc. Thurstone scales can be developed to measure attitudes toward any object, and the method has been widely used by other investigators. Basic to this method is the use of judges to assign scale values to each item in the test. (The steps in the construction of a Thurstone scale are detailed in Box 5.6.)

One of the major criticisms of the method of equal-appearing intervals is that the attitudes of the judges may influence their judgments. For, as Thurstone and Chave put it, "If a scale is regarded as valid, the scale values of the statements should not be affected by the opinions of the people who help to construct it."

Early studies [Hinckley, 1932; Ferguson, 1935; Pintner and Forlano, 1937] all indicated that the attitudes of the judges do not influence the scale values of items. In the Hinckley study, 114 statements about the Negro were assigned scale values by a group of Southern white students who were prejudiced against the Negro and by a group of Northern white students who were favorable toward the Negro. The correlation between the scale values obtained from the two groups of judges was .98. The attitude of the judge seemingly had nothing to do with his judgment as to the proper placement of items on the favorability continuum.

This finding is in sharp conflict with the principle of the selectivity of cognition (see pages 20 to 25). Hovland and Sherif [1952] and Sherif and Hovland [1953] carried out studies which have resolved this contradiction. These investigators criticized the early studies for not using judges with extreme attitudes. They pointed out that Hinckley, in rejecting as careless those judges who sorted 30 or more statements in one category (a procedure recommended by Thurstone), may have eliminated those judges with the most extreme attitudes.

In their replication of Hinckley's study, Hovland and Sherif asked four groups of judges to sort the same 114 statements which had been used by Hinckley. The four groups of judges were (1) Negro graduate and undergraduate college students; (2) white students who were pro-Negro as indicated by their activities; (3) white students who were unselected for attitudes toward the Negro; (4) anti-Negro white students as indicated by scores on a Likert scale.

Hovland and Sherif found that if the criterion of eliminating judges who sorted 30 or more statements in a single category were applied to their data, over three-fourths of the Negro judges and two-thirds of the pro-Negro white judges would be eliminated. This finding confirms their guess that the use of this

BOX 5.6: *The fate of four Thurstone items*

L. L. Thurstone and E. J. Chave, while at the University of Chicago, used the method of equal-appearing intervals in constructing a scale to measure attitudes toward the church.

A set of 130 statements representing both favorable and unfavorable views of the church was collected from a wide variety of sources. The statements were then given to a large number of judges together with a set of 11 slips on which the letters A to K were printed. These slips were arranged alphabetically in front of the judges, who were instructed as follows:

On slip A, put those statements which you believe express the highest *appreciation* of the church. On slip F, put those expressing a neutral position. On slip K, put those which express the strongest *depreciation* of the church. On the rest of the slips arrange statements in accordance with the degree of appreciation or depreciation expressed in them.

To get a single value to represent the position of a statement on the 11-point scale, the median of the positions assigned to the statement by all the judges was determined. This median is the *scale value* of that statement. To obtain an objective measure of the degree of ambiguity of a statement, Thurstone and Chave calculated the interquartile range, or Q, of the distribution of judgments obtained for the statement. High agreement among the judges on the scale value of a statement produced a small Q value; relatively little agreement produced a large Q value.

After the scale value and Q of each of the statements were secured, the 130 statements were presented to a sample of 300 subjects with the instruction to check those statements that they agreed with. Their responses were then analyzed to study the internal consistency of the statements. If subjects who agreed with a particular statement were found to endorse other statements which had widely different scale values, the statement was rejected as irrelevant to the attitude being measured. If subjects who agreed with a particular statement checked only statements similar to it in scale values, the statement was judged to pass the criterion of relevance.

Let us now follow the fate of four of the 130 statements to illustrate how items were retained or eliminated in constructing the final scale:

Statement 23. "I am interested in a church that is beautiful and that emphasizes the aesthetic role of life." This statement (scale value 4.1) was discarded because it was found to be irrelevant. Both the most pious church member and the most outspoken atheist endorsed this statement. Both can enjoy beautiful buildings.

Statement 8. "I believe the church has a good influence on the lower and uneducated classes but has no value for the upper, educated classes." This statement (scale value 6.7) was discarded because it was found to be ambiguous. Its Q value of 3.6 was the largest Q value obtained. It is a double-barreled statement, and the judges could not agree on its scale position.

Statement 50. "I feel the church services give me inspiration and help me to live up to my best during the following week." This statement (scale value 1.7) was retained. It was relatively unambiguous (Q 1.4) and proved to be a relevant statement.

Statement 66. "I think the church is a place for religious instruction of young and old and is essential in every community." This statement (scale value 1.5) was not used because it was not needed. Although it was an unambiguous statement (Q 1.4) and met the criterion of relevance, it was too similar in scale value to statement 50.

Thurstone, L. L., and Chave, E. J. The measurement of attitudes. *Chicago: Univer. of Chicago Press, 1929.*

criterion tends to eliminate judges with extreme attitudes.

The scale values obtained from the Negro judges and the pro-Negro white judges were found to be significantly different from the scale values obtained from the unselected white judges. Judges with extreme attitudes toward the Negro bunched a disproportionately large number of the statements in the extreme categories. The direction of displacement was systematic. Judges with strong pro-Negro attitudes displaced items toward the *anti* end of the scale. Thus an item which a relatively "neutral" person would judge somewhat favorable was judged extremely unfavorable by judges with strongly pro-Negro attitudes. Judges with anti-Negro attitudes tended to displace mildly unfavorable statements toward the *pro* end of the scale. This tendency

can be seen as indicating a difference in the adaptation level of the extremely favorable and extremely unfavorable judges (see page 32).

The scale values of 11 statements, obtained from five different groups of judges, selected because they seemed to be equally appropriate for the Negro and white judges and because they were fairly evenly spaced over the scale, are shown in Fig. 5.1. Note that the scale values originally obtained by Hinckley and the scale values obtained by Hovland and Sherif, using Thurstone's criterion for the elimination of careless judges, are highly similar. The scale values assigned the items by the pro-Negro white judges and by the Negro judges are also very similar. But note that these latter two groups of judges displace items toward the unfavorable end of the scale

FIGURE 5.1: Scale values of 11 statements selected from a Thurstone scale of attitude toward the Negro obtained from 5 different groups of judges. [Adapted from Hovland and Sherif, 1952.]

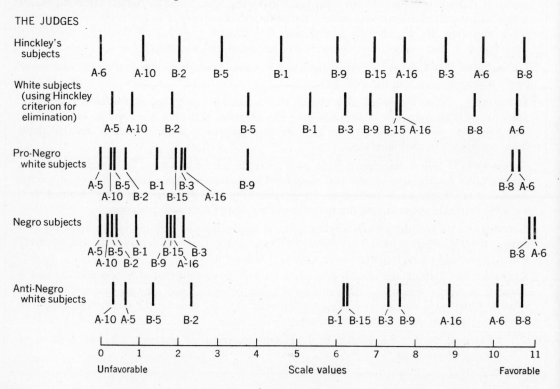

which were judged to be neutral or moderately favorable by the former two groups of judges. The anti-Negro judges show a tendency, although not marked, to displace neutral and moderately unfavorable items toward the favorable end of the scale.

It seems, then, that the attitude of the judge will bias his judgment of items. However, in most cases this effect will be small. Only judges with extreme attitudes will show substantial distortion.

Edwards [1957] has pointed out that the chief unsolved problem in the Thurstone scaling method is the problem of selecting the most discriminating items among those having approximately the same scale value. He notes that items of approximately the same scale value may vary markedly in discriminatory value. Thus, in one instance, items within a single interval correlated with total score on the scale from .24 to .78. In the Thurstone method there is no determination of such correlations and therefore there is no objective basis for choosing the most discriminating items. (For a method of overcoming this shortcoming, see page 155.)

THE METHOD OF SUMMATED RATINGS. A different approach to the scaling of attitudes was developed by Likert [1932] in his study of various attitudes—toward imperialism, toward internationalism, and toward the Negro. His procedure, which differs from the Thurstone technique in several important ways, involves the following steps: (1) the collection of a large number of statements considered by the experimenter to relate to the object in question; (2) the administering of these statements to a group of subjects who indicate for each statement whether they strongly approve, approve, are undecided, disapprove, or strongly disapprove; (3) the determination of a total score for each individual by summing his responses to all the items, scoring the above five categories 5, 4, 3, 2, and 1, respectively, for favorable items, and reversing the scoring for unfavorable items (see page 149); (4) the

carrying out of an item analysis to select the most discriminating items. This last step is done by computing for each item the correlation between scores on that item and the total scores on all the items. Then, those items with highest correlations, that is, those that hang together with or measure the same thing as the other items in the test, are retained for the final scale. It is the use of item analysis in the Likert method that most clearly distinguishes it from the Thurstone method.

In the Thurstone scaling method the necessity for agreement among judges as to the proper scale placement of an item requires that the manifest content of the item relate rather directly to the attitude being measured. In the Likert method there is no such necessity. Even if the manifest content of an item does not bear directly on the object in question, it can, by virtue of its correlation with the total score, be proved diagnostic and thus be included in the final scale.

The score yielded by a Likert scale can be interpreted only in terms of where the individual's score falls relative to the distribution of scores of other people; the score does not have *absolute* meaning. The interpretation of the minimum and maximum possible scores is usually clear: the minimum score indicates an unfavorable attitude; the maximum score, a favorable attitude. But scores falling between the minimum and maximum scores are more difficult to interpret because the score corresponding to the neutral point (see page 156) is not known. Clearly it is illegitimate to assume that the neutral region on a Likert scale corresponds to the mid-point of the possible range of scores. This is a weakness of the method when our interest is in determining whether an individual is favorable or unfavorable in his attitude toward an object.

THE SOCIAL-DISTANCE SCALE. Bogardus [1925] was one of the first to design a technique for the specific purpose of measuring and comparing attitudes toward different nationalities. His *social-distance scale* was made up of a number of statements which were selected, on an a priori basis, to elicit responses indicative of the subject's degree of acceptance of any nationality group.

The instructions for the scale read as follows: "According to my first feeling reactions, I would willingly admit members of each race (as a class, and not the best I have known, nor the worst members) to one or more of the classifications under which I have placed a cross." For each nationality to be measured, seven classifications are offered:

1. To close kinship by marriage
2. To my club as personal chums
3. To my street as neighbors
4. To employment in my occupation
5. To citizenship in my country
6. As visitors only in my country
7. Would exclude from my country

The classifications progress in an orderly way from one implying a willingness to accept a close degree of relationship with the nationality to one implying a willingness to accept only an extremely remote relationship or none at all. The valence of the individual's attitude toward the nationality is then taken to be the highest degree of intimacy he would accept. In practice, in applying the scale, it has been found that there are relatively few reversals, that is, instances in which a nationality is accepted by an individual for a closer relationship and rejected by him for a more remote relationship (e.g., accepting Turks to close kinship by marriage but rejecting them as neighbors on his street).

With the social-distance scale, it is possible to compare different people's attitudes toward the same nationality or to compare a single individual's attitudes toward various nationalities. The social-distance scale has been widely and successfully used for these purposes in social-psychological research. With appropriate modifications, this type of scale can be adapted to measure attitudes toward any category of persons. One adaptation of

the Bogardus technique has been made by Crespi [1945] in the form of a Social Rejection Thermometer for measurement of attitudes toward conscientious objectors. The scale statements are as follows:

1. I would treat a conscientious objector no differently than I would any other person, even so far as having him become a close relative by marriage.
2. I would accept conscientious objectors only so far as having them for friends.
3. I would accept conscientious objectors only so far as having them for speaking acquaintances.
4. I don't want anything to do with conscientious objectors.
5. I feel that conscientious objectors should be imprisoned.
6. I feel that conscientious objectors should be shot as traitors.

It is noteworthy that in building this scale Crespi found it necessary to include steps 5 and 6, which go beyond a mere statement of psychological "distance" from the group. This suggests that the social-distance scale is not an adequate attitudinal measure. The most extreme negative attitude requires something more than mere remoteness of the group; it also involves (as is implied in items 5 and 6) a desire for punishment or harm or destruction of the object of the attitude.

CUMULATIVE SCALING. Cumulative scaling is a method for evaluating sets of statements to determine whether they meet the requirements of a particular kind of scale—commonly called the Guttman scale. Such a scale is defined by Guttman [1950] as follows: "We shall call a set of items of common content a scale if a person with a higher rank than another person is just as high or higher on every item than the other person." An example of a perfect Guttman scale would be one concerning weight, in which the items read as follows: (1) I weigh more than 100 pounds; (2) I weigh more than 120 pounds; (3) I weigh more than 140 pounds, etc. In such a scale, a person who responds positively to item 3, will also have responded positively to items 1 and 2.

In the example above, we know that the scale was measuring only one physical dimension—weight. The purpose of the Guttman procedure is to determine whether or not a set of attitude statements is measuring only one attitude. If the statements form a Guttman scale, they are said to constitute a *unidimensional scale*, that is, they measure only one attitude. In a perfect Guttman scale, the total score of an individual would have a one-to-one relation with the pattern of his responses to the items making up the scale. Knowing the total score of an individual, it would be possible to *reproduce* perfectly his responses to each of the items. Suppose we scored our weight questionnaire by assigning a score of 1 to each "Yes" response and a score of zero to each "No" response. Then, knowing that the total score of a subject is 2, we know that he has responded "Yes" to items 1 and 2 and "No" to item 3; similarly, we know that a person with a total score of 3 has responded "Yes" to items 1, 2, and 3.

Perfect reproducibility is, of course, never realized in attitude scales. Some degree of irrelevancy is always found. Thus, a subject might endorse statement 50 (scale value 1.7) of Box 5.6 (page 151), fail to endorse statement 23 (scale value 4.1), and endorse statement 8 (scale value 6.7). Irrelevancy leads to imperfect reproducibility. Various techniques have been developed for estimating the *coefficient of reproducibility*. This is a proportion which is supposed to indicate the accuracy with which responses to the various statements in a set can be reproduced from the total scores. Guttman has suggested that the major necessary condition for determining whether a set of items constitutes a cumulative scale is that the coefficient of reproducibility be at least .90.

The Guttman scaling method has been criticized for its neglect of the problem of representativeness in selecting the initial set of statements. Guttman [1945] has asserted that the selection of a sample of statements is a matter of intuition and experience. The content validity of cumulative scales is thus impossible to estimate. In many cumulative scales, the set of items has a very narrow range of content.

THE SCALE-DISCRIMINATION TECHNIQUE. Edwards and Kilpatrick [1948] developed a method which they term the *scale-discrimination technique*. The steps in this technique are as follows. A large set of dichotomous items is first selected. Judges are then asked, as in the Thurstone method, to sort these items into categories according to degree of favorableness. Items which are not sorted consistently by the judges are rejected as ambiguous. The remaining items are then prepared in multiple-choice form with six response categories (strongly agree, agree, mildly agree, mildly disagree, disagree, strongly disagree). The statements in this form are administered to a new group of subjects who are instructed to respond to each item by choosing the alternative which best expresses their own agreement or disagreement with it. The responses of each subject are then scored to derive a total score for him. Each item is then subjected to item analysis, as in the Likert method, and nondiscriminating items are rejected. The remaining items are then dichotomized and subjected to cumulative scaling. As can readily be seen, the scale-discrimination technique is an attempt to synthesize the methods of scale construction developed by Thurstone, Likert, and Guttman. This approach, however, has not yet been sufficiently tested by various research workers to enable us to determine its strengths and weaknesses.

THE NEUTRAL REGION OF SCALES

We have pointed out that one attribute of an attitude is its valence. A person's attitude may always be characterized as pro or con, for or against the object. This means that attitude scales have a region where the sign changes. This is the *neutral region* of the scale. To one side of this region attitudes grow more positive; to the other side they grow more negative. A score falling within this region must indicate the absence of any attitude, since, as we have said, attitudes are always positive or negative in some degree.

The determination of the neutral region of scales is of considerable importance in the measurement of attitudes. It may often be important to know whether an individual's attitude falls just slightly to the left or slightly to the right of the neutral region. Thus, where there is polarization of attitudes induced by a crisis, we may predict that a person initially standing slightly to the left will, other things being equal, swing more strongly to the left than to the right, and vice versa.

INADEQUACY OF CURRENT SCALES. The types of scales we have reviewed do not satisfactorily define the neutral region. The Thurstone scale does, to be sure, make an attempt to do so. It will be recalled that in ascertaining the scale values of items, the original judges assigned the items to 11 piles, including a middle, or neutral, pile. It might be argued, therefore, that the middle score in the Thurstone-type scale is an approximation of the neutral region. There is, however, no guarantee that what appears as neutral to judges will actually *be* neutral for the subject.

In the Likert scale, as we have already indicated (page 153), the interpretation of a neutral point is highly ambiguous. The score of a given individual who falls at the middle point of the scoring range can be achieved in two quite different ways: by taking a neutral position on most or all of the items, or by taking a strongly favorable position on some items and a strongly unfavorable position on other items. These two ways of arriving at the same score have obviously different psychological meanings. A neutral score which is obtained by a nice balancing of pro and con

judgments may represent an artifact as far as the particular scale is concerned. It may mean that the total score is a combination of two scores, relating to two quite different attitudes; that is, the scale is not unidimensional.

On the other hand, an individual may receive a neutral score because the object of the attitude does not even exist for him. It is obviously meaningless to attempt to measure something that does not exist. Yet, as we have pointed out, this frequently happens in attitude measurement as a result of the indiscriminate application of all sorts of scales to all sorts of people without an adequate preliminary analysis.

We find, then, that the neutral regions of attitude dimensions cannot adequately be ascertained in a direct way from the scales themselves. For crude purposes, of course, it may be sufficient to know that individuals falling approximately in the middle of a scale are probably fairly close to the neutral region. But to arrive at a more precise and more logical determination of the neutral region, it is necessary to consider certain other related attributes of attitudes.

INTENSITY AND NEUTRAL REGION. A person holding an extreme attitudinal position (pro or con) is likely to feel more intense, more certain, and more emotional about the issue than someone who holds a less extreme position. If we were able to plot the scale scores on the horizontal axis and the corresponding intensity or certainty values on the vertical axis, a U curve would result, intensities being lowest in the middle and highest at the extremes. The bottom of the U curve is the region where the sign changes.

Guttman and Suchman [1947] have made this relationship between scale position and intensity the basis for a refined way to establish the neutral region of a scale. Their approach involves the scaling of items by the cumulative scaling method (see page 154) and the ascertaining of the average intensity or certainty with which each item is approved or rejected by the sample of people being measured. The average intensity or certainty is then plotted against the scale position of the items. The neutral region of the scale is taken by Guttman and Suchman as the region where the lowest part of the curve falls. This approach to the establishment of the neutral region of a scale is by far the most convincing that has yet been proposed. (See Box 5.7 for examples of intensity curves.)

THE RELIABILITY AND VALIDITY OF ATTITUDE SCALES

The ultimate consideration concerning any measurement technique is its *validity*, i.e., the extent to which it measures what it purports to measure. The validity of a technique is dependent in an intimate way upon its *reliability*, i.e., the extent to which it yields consistent measures. Obviously, a measurement technique cannot be more valid than it is reliable. Before we can turn to the critical question of validity, therefore, we must first consider the reliability of attitude scales.

RELIABILITY. Repeated measurements of an individual's attitude may give different results. Such variation may be indicative of the internal unreliability of the scale itself, or it may arise from two other, "external," sources of variation: (1) apparent variation in the attitude, which is caused by changes in the psychological conditions under which the measurements are made; (2) true variation in the attitude over time. It might be found that a soldier's score on a scale designed to measure attitudes toward military officers would differ when he was tested publicly and when he was tested anonymously (apparent variation). And it might be found that his scores on this scale would be different before and after experience with officers (true variation). Neither of these findings would necessarily impugn the reliability of the scale itself. In order to evaluate the reliability of the measuring instrument itself the influence of these two other types of variation must be eliminated.

The reliability of a scale may be ascertained in three different ways: (1) the *test-retest* method, in which the measurement with the given test is repeated, immediately or after a lapse of time, and the two measurements compared; (2) the *equivalent-forms* method, in which measurements on two comparable forms of the same test are compared; (3) the *split-half* method, in which scores on one half of the test are compared with those on the other half. The degree of reliability is customarily expressed as the coefficient of correlation between the two sets of measurements. While the split-half method does eliminate the two "external" sources of variation, it may result in spuriously high correlations owing to the action of response sets (see page 144). Reliability estimates obtained in these three different ways will not necessarily be equal, and the decision as to the most appropriate way to determine the reliability of a given test must depend mainly upon the specific nature of the test and the manner in which it is to be used.

RELIABILITY OF ATTITUDE-SCALE SCORES. Ferguson [1939] quotes Thurstone as reporting the reliabilities of equal-appearing-interval scales constructed under his direction as being "all over .8, most of them being over .9." In his own work, Ferguson obtained reliability coefficients ranging from .52 to .80 for 20-item forms, and from .68 to .89 for 40-item forms.

The reliabilities of Likert scales are generally higher than those reported for Thurstone scales. Murphy and Likert [1938] found their Internationalism scale of 24 items to have reliabilities ranging from .81 to .90. A 12-item Imperialism scale yielded reliability coefficients ranging from .80 to .92; a Negro scale of 14 items gave coefficients ranging from .79 to .91.

The Bogardus social-distance scale has shown itself to be a highly reliable measure of *general* social distance, as distinguished from distances expressed for *specific* groups. Split-half reliability coefficients of .90 and

Edward A. Suchman, while a member of the Research Branch of the Information and Education Division of the War Department which studied "The American Soldier" of World War II, analyzed the relation between scale position and intensity of attitudes.

The subjects were first given a Guttman scale, and then intensity scores for each subject were obtained by asking the following *intensity question* after each statement in the scale:

How strongly do you feel about this?

Not at all strongly   Not so strongly   Fairly strongly   Very strongly

Intensity scores were then converted into percentiles and were plotted against the corresponding scale position of the item. The resulting curve is called an *intensity curve*.

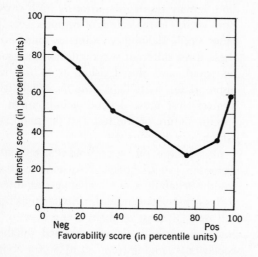

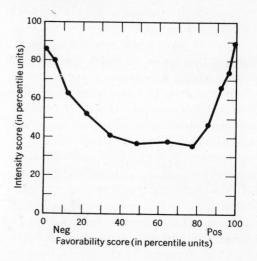

The illustration at the left, "Enlisted men's attitude toward the Women's Army Corps," is an example of a very sharp intensity curve. There is a sharply defined low region at the 75th-percentile value on the valence continuum. This low region is taken as the neutral region, the region where the sign changes. Soldiers scoring below this region (about 75 per cent of all soldiers tested) are thus defined as holding unfavorable attitudes toward the WAC. The remaining 25 per cent whose scores fall above the neutral region hold favorable attitudes.

The illustration at the right, "Satisfaction with one's Army job," is an example of an extremely flat-bottomed intensity curve. Note that there is a wide zone of neutrality that extends from the 34th-percentile value to the 77th-percentile value on the valence continuum. A very large group of soldiers were neither satisfied nor dissatisfied with their Army jobs; they just didn't care one way or the other.

Suchman, E. A. The intensity component in attitude and opinion research. In S. A. Stouffer et al., Measurement and prediction. *Princeton, N. J.: Princeton Univer. Press, 1950.*

higher have been secured by different investigators. This means that if we know an individual's social-distance score for a random half of a large number of different ethnic groups on which he has been tested, we can make a good prediction of his score for the other half of the groups.

Guttman scales have yielded reliabilities in the neighborhood of .85 and higher.

VALIDITY

Once the reliability of an attitude scale has been established as satisfactory, the remaining problem is to ascertain the validity of the scale. There are several approaches to the determination of validity: (1) the judgment by experts of the representativeness of the sample of items; (2) the measurement of "known" groups, or of types of people who on a priori grounds should differ in an expected way in their attitudes; (3) the study of the accuracy of prediction of behavior based upon the measurement of the attitude.

EXPERTS' JUDGMENTS OF CONTENT. If a scale measures a representative sample of all the beliefs, feelings, and action tendencies pertaining to the object, it may be said to be intrinsically valid, or to have *content validity*. Content representativeness can be estimated by getting the opinions of experts [see Gulliksen, 1950]. It will be remembered that both Thurstone and Likert, as the first step in constructing their scales, collected a very large and heterogeneous sample of items, presumably touching on all the main kinds of beliefs and feelings about the attitude object. These scaling methods, then, can be said to have content validity for the measurement of the belief and feeling components of an attitude. We have pointed out earlier that the cumulative-scaling method, on the other hand, suffers from a weakness in that it depends solely upon the scale constructor's intuition and skill in making the initial selection of items.

MEASUREMENT OF "KNOWN" GROUPS. There are often a priori grounds for assuming that if a scale is valid, it should differentiate certain defined types of people in a specified direction. We should probably have little confidence in a scale for measuring attitude toward war if typical members of peace organizations did not score toward the extreme anti-war position.

A Likert scale for measuring attitude toward the Tennessee Valley Authority, the first large-scale utility program owned and operated by the government, was validated by applying it to various groups of people who might be expected to show differential approval of a government utility program of this sort [Sims, 1938]. The groups scoring most extremely were as follows (a high score indicates disapproval):

N. Y. Edison Co. employees	75
Stockholders in private power companies	68
Merchants in the TVA region	34
Government employees in Washington, D.C.	23

This validation method has several shortcomings which limit its usefulness. One is that people who join organizations are likely to be different in many respects from people who are not joiners. The scale may be valid in differentiating organization members but may fail to differentiate other people who hold attitudes just as extreme. Another difficulty is that even though a scale may validly differentiate people of extreme attitudes, such as organization members, it may not be equally valid in distinguishing among people who hold more moderate attitudes. It is not likely that one can find all the needed different organizations, each of which ideologically represents a different scale position on an attitude continuum; organizations are almost always centered around fairly extreme positions. A third practical difficulty is that for some attitudes, one cannot find organizations that ideologically represent even the extremes.

ACCURACY OF PREDICTION OF ACTION. The ultimate practical test of the validity of attitude measurement may seem to lie in the usefulness of the measurements for the understanding and prediction of the individual's action with respect to attitude objects.

There are, on the whole, very few good examples of this type of validation. A pioneering study was that of Telford [1934] on a scale measuring attitude toward the church. He examined the average scores of people who reported different frequencies of church attendance and discovered the following clear-cut relationship between frequency of church attendance and attitude scores (a high score indicates an unfavorable attitude):

Frequency of church attendance	Average score on attitude scale
Regularly	1.91
Frequently	2.48
Occasionally	3.50
Seldom	4.95
Never	6.75

This would seem to constitute a reasonably sure validation of the attitude scale, but unfortunately church attendance was not ascertained independently; the investigator accepted the individual's own report.

A number of other investigations have found that verbal measures of attitude predict the social actions of the individual with variable accuracy. The reasons for discrepancies between the stated attitudes of people and their behavior are many. For one thing, actions are typically determined by all the psychological factors and by many attitudes. For another thing, actions are also situationally determined (see Boxes 5.8 and 5.9). Finally, we must also remember that the objects of attitude tests may not be the same as the objects of the "action" test. For example, the "Negro" on an attitude scale may be quite a different object for the person taking a paper-and-pencil test from the Negro in a face-to-face situation. Only to the extent that there is

psychological identity of the two objects can we expect that there will be congruence between attitude and action. And this relationship, it should again be emphasized, may be a very complex one.

With regard to overt behavior as a validation of attitude measurement, Murphy, Murphy, and Newcomb [1937] make the following observation:

Actions are no more inherently "valid," in the first place, than words. The following remarks seem to us patently true: "Actions are frequently designed to distort or conceal 'true' attitude quite as fully as verbal behavior. . . . All behavior is subject to modification in the process of execution from considerations of courtesy, expediency, or other social pressures." And it is furthermore apparent that when verbal behavior is used to distort or conceal the "true" attitudes, the distortion commonly conforms to everyday behavior. The reasons for concealing "true" attitudes are the same for both verbal and "overt" behavior. If conditions of secrecy, and preferably of anonymity, are observed, there is more reason to expect free and complete expression of attitudes through words, thus freed from social pressures, than from behaviors which are open to all beholders. . . . And, finally, it may be observed that a man's categorical agreement or disagreement with a strongly stated opinion about the Chinese, or Jews, or Rotarians, or Communists, is in everyday life regarded (if the man is sincere) as a *significant* part of his behavior.

TO RECAPITULATE

One of the most widely used methods for measuring attitudes is the so-called attitude scale, which typically consists of a set of statements or items of which the person indicates his approval or disapproval. His pattern of responses to the items provides a way for the psychologist to infer something about his attitudes. There are five principal scaling methods: the method of *equal-appearing intervals,* the method of *summated ratings,* the *social-*

distance scale, the *cumulative-scaling method,* the *scale-discrimination technique.*

The determination of the neutral region of scales (the region of no attitude) is of considerable importance in attitude measurement. None of the scaling methods can satisfactorily identify this region. The most satisfactory solution is one in which the neutral region is taken to be the lowest region of the curve when intensity or certainty scores are plotted against valence scores.

The *reliability* of attitude scales, which may be estimated by the test-retest, the split-half, or the equivalent-forms method, has generally been found to be satisfactory.

Content validity refers to the degree to which the items in a scale adequately sample the universe of beliefs, feelings, and action tendencies with reference to the object.

The validity of scales may also be estimated by comparing the attitudes of groups known to differ in their attitudes toward a particular object. Many of the scales are found to have useful validities determined in this way.

The *predictive validity* of a scale may be estimated by determining the correlation between scale scores and some measure of action toward the object.

SPECIAL TECHNIQUES

In recent years, a number of special techniques have been developed in an attempt to improve the validity of attitude measurement. We shall briefly review two approaches— measurement by disguised techniques and measurement by the semantic-differential rating instrument.

DISGUISED TECHNIQUES. It was pointed out earlier in this chapter that the measurement of attitudes is necessarily indirect. But there are degrees of "indirection." Some methods of measurement involve an explicit, frontal approach to the attitude, as in the scaling techniques, which require the individual to respond to statements that refer more or less directly to the object of the attitude. Other methods of measurement may be relatively indirect, involving a concealed or disguised approach to the attitude, through the measurement of cognitions and feelings which are more subtly connected with the object in question.

One principal advantage of disguised techniques is that under certain conditions they may have higher validity than direct measures. This advantage applies particularly to attitudes which violate group norms and hence are not readily revealed in public by an individual, and to attitudes which are unacceptable to the self-concept of the individual. A second principal advantage of disguised techniques is that they enable the experimenter to measure without producing an effect on the attitude itself; direct measurements may, as we shall see, produce changes in the attitude being measured (a not uncommon problem in the general science of measurement).

Among the disguised techniques used to measure attitudes are projective devices— originally designed to measure wants (see page 89) and other personality variables. For an example of the usefulness of a projective device in attitude measurement, see Box 5.10.

Another illustration of a disguised test of attitudes is the error-choice technique developed by Hammond [1948] to measure attitudes toward labor-management. Hammond forced subjects to choose between two alternative answers to questions, each of which was made equally wrong, but in opposite directions from the correct answer. Illustrative items from the labor-management test were: "Average weekly wage of the war worker in 1945 was (1) $37.00, (2) $57.00." "Financial reports show that out of every dollar (1) 16¢, (2) 3¢ is profit." Predominant choices of those wrong alternatives giving a more favorable picture of labor (or management) were assumed to reflect an underlying prolabor (or promanagement) attitude.

Bernard Kutner, then of the American Jewish Congress, worked with Carol Wilkins and Penny R. Yarrow in a study of the discriminatory behavior of restaurant managers toward Negroes in two different circumstances.

Their procedure was as follows. Three young women, two white and one Negro, entered 11 different restaurants in a fashionable Northeastern community. *In every restaurant visited, they were served in the same way as other patrons.*

Two weeks after each restaurant was visited, the following letter was sent to the manager:

Dear Sir:

A group of friends and I are planning a social affair to be held in Subtown in the near future. I should like to make reservations to have them for dinner at your restaurant. Since some of them are colored, I wondered whether you would object to their coming.

Could you let me know if the reservations may be made so that I may complete the arrangements as soon as possible?

Seventeen days after the letters were mailed, telephone calls were made to each restaurant requesting reservations for a group of persons including some Negroes. One day later, a control telephone call was made requesting reservations for a party of friends, with no mention of race. The table below summarizes some of the typical responses of the restaurant managers to the letter and to the phone call.

Restaurant	Response to letter	Response to telephone call	Response to control call
A	No reply	Didn't get any letter. We've got dancing after 6 P.M. (They actually don't.) Are you colored? (Yes.) I like everyone. My kitchen help are colored and they are wonderful people. But we have a certain clientele here. . . . This place is my bread and butter. Frankly, I'd rather you not come. Try in T_____ (next town).	Took reservation.
B	No reply	I didn't get your letter. We can't have you. It's against the law.	Took reservation.
C	No reply	I got the letter. How many? (Negroes) I don't mind but customers might. In fact some of my help are colored. I had trouble about this before. Frankly I prefer you don't come but if you can't find another place, we won't embarrass you here.	Took reservation.

Restaurant	Response to letter	Response to telephone call	Response to control call
D	No reply	We didn't get a letter. We don't take reservations. We take care of our regulars. A few Negroes come in just to eat. I would mind you coming.	Said they didn't take reservations but we should come in any time about them.
G	Reply received 19 mail days after the letter was mailed	A letter to you is in the mail. Reservations are available if you come in and make them.	Took reservation.
I	Reply sent as result of phone call	Didn't get letter. (Hostess:) We don't like that. Is it absolutely necessary to have them? (Manager:) If it's okay with you I guess it's okay with us.	Took reservation.
J	No reply	Didn't get letter. How many? (10) No reservations for more than 8 on week end. I will mail you our menu for the following week end. (Never received.) I'm too busy to look up reservation availability.	Took reservation.
K	No reply	Didn't get letter. I'd think you'd want to come in to discuss something like that. Mixed group? How many people? We can't turn anyone away but never take reservations. You can have a separate room if you come in about it.	Took reservation.

This study suggests that discriminatory treatment may be less likely to occur in a face-to-face situation. Indirect evidence of discriminatory behavior (subterfuges of various sorts) may appear in situations where there is no face-to-face confrontation.

This difference in behavior may be understood when we remember that action is determined, not by a single attitude, but by a number of attitudes, wants, and situational conditions, operating simultaneously. Thus the restaurant manager, although he may hold strong discriminatory attitudes, may serve a Negro customer on the spot in order to avoid a scene. Attitude test scores alone are usually not enough to predict behavior.

Kutner, B., Wilkins, Carol, and Yarrow, Penny R. Verbal attitudes and overt behavior involving racial prejudice. J. abnorm. soc. Psychol., 1952, 47, 649–652.

BOX 5.9: *Prejudice in action*

Melvin L. De Fleur and Frank R. Westie, sociologists at Indiana University, have studied the relation between attitudes and action. Twenty-three white college students scoring in the top quartile on a scale of attitude toward the Negro (the prejudiced group) and 23 white students scoring in the bottom quartile (the unprejudiced group) were used in the study. The groups were matched with respect to age, sex, marital status, religion, social class, residential history, and previous contact with Negroes. Each subject was given a projective test in which he was shown a number of photographic slides of pairs of Negro and white men and women. In some of the slides, a young Negro man was photographed seated by a young white woman; in others, a white man was photographed with a Negro woman. The scene was similar to a living room or dormitory lounge.

At the end of the projective testing session, the subject was told that another set of slides was needed for further research and was asked whether he would consent to pose with a Negro person of the opposite sex. He was given a form which he was told was a "standard photograph release agreement, which is necessary in any situation where a photograph of an individual is to be used in any manner." The form consisted of a graded series of situations in which the photograph would be used, ranging from laboratory experiments only (for which the subject received a low score on the "signed level of agreement" scale) to a nationwide publicity campaign for racial integration (for which he received a high score). The subject was asked to sign his name to each use he would authorize. The relation between amount of prejudice toward the Negro and level of signed agreement to be photographed with a Negro is shown in the following table.

Signed level of agreement	Prejudiced	Unprejudiced
Below mean	18	9
Above mean	5	14

The findings reveal a substantial degree of consistency between attitude and action toward the Negro. As the investigators note, "In American society the affixing of one's signature to a document is a particularly significant act. The signing of checks, contracts, agreements and the like is clearly understood to indicate a binding obligation on the signer to abide by the provisions of the document."

Note, however, that nine of the unprejudiced and five of the prejudiced (almost one-third of the total) show inconsistency between their attitudes and their action. The behavior of the individual in any situation reflects his cognitions, wants, and interpersonal response traits as well as his attitudes. A one-to-one correspondence between attitude and action should not, therefore, be expected.

De Fleur, M. L., and Westie, F. R. Verbal attitudes and overt acts: an experiment on the salience of attitudes. Amer. sociol. Rev., 1958, 23, 667–673.

The test was administered as an information test to a labor-union group and to a business group. Total scores on the 20 items of the test differentiated, with almost no overlap, the labor-union group from the business group with respect to attitudes toward labor-management. This test, in other words, met the "known" group validity criterion. Reliabilities for the two groups were estimated to be .78 and .87, respectively. (For another application of the error-choice technique, see Box 5.11.)

BOX 5.10: *A psychologist looks at housewives indirectly*

The usefulness of a disguised approach in uncovering attitudes governing buying behavior is revealed in a study by Mason Haire, an industrial psychologist at the University of California, Berkeley.

Haire set out to learn what factors determined the attitudes of housewives toward instant coffee. First he asked a sample of housewives these questions: "Do you use instant coffee?" (If "No") "What do you dislike about it?" Most of the reasons given for disliking instant coffee were dislike of the flavor. Haire suspected that this answer was a rationalization of the true reasons, and proceeded to use a disguised method to uncover them.

Two shopping lists were prepared which were identical except that one specified Nescafé Instant Coffee and the other Maxwell House Coffee (drip grind):

List I	*List II*
Pound and a half of hamburger	Pound and a half of hamburger
2 loaves Wonder bread	2 loaves Wonder bread
Bunch of carrots	Bunch of carrots
1 can Rumford's baking powder	1 can Rumford's baking powder
Nescafé instant coffee	1 pound Maxwell House coffee (drip grind)
2 cans Del Monte peaches	2 cans Del Monte peaches
5 pounds potatoes	5 pounds potatoes

The two lists were given to two different groups of housewives with the instructions: "Read the shopping list below. Try to project yourself into the situation as far as possible until you can more or less characterize the woman who bought the groceries. Then write a brief description of her personality and character. Wherever possible indicate what factors influenced your judgment."

The woman who bought Nescafé was described quite differently from the woman who bought Maxwell House coffee. The following table gives the percentage of subjects who ascribed the specified characteristics to the Nescafé and Maxwell House coffee purchasers.

Characteristic	*Nescafé purchaser, per cent*	*Maxwell House purchaser, per cent*
Lazy	48	4
Fails to plan buying	48	12
Thrifty	4	16
Good wife	4	16

It is clear that Nescafé and Maxwell House coffee users were seen differently by the housewives in this study. And it is a reasonable inference that these differences in perception reflected differences in attitudes toward instant coffee—attitudes not so easily detected through direct questioning.

Haire, M. Projective techniques in marketing research. J. Marketing, 1950, 14, 649–656.

Irving R. Weschler, an industrial psychologist at the University of California, Los Angeles, used the "error-choice" technique to develop a disguised test of attitudes toward labor-management relations.

The test, entitled The Labor Relations Information Inventory, Form A, consisted of 40 items, to each of which there were two alternative answers. Twenty-four of the items were straight information or factual items; the remaining sixteen were nonfactual, i.e., they dealt with controversial questions or presented two incorrect alternatives. The majority of the nonfactual questions were constructed so that the true answer lay midway between the two incorrect alternatives. Thus the wrong alternative selected by a subject was assumed to reflect the direction of his bias. Following is one of the nonfactual items:

> During April 7, 1948, the coal and meat strikes increased the number of work days lost through voluntary stoppage to (*a*) 10 million work days, (*b*) 6 million work days. (Correct answer: 8 million work days.)

The test was administered to a group of 186 advanced university students who were classified into prolabor and promanagement groups upon the basis of their reported sympathies. An item analysis revealed that 11 of the 16 nonfactual items significantly discriminated between the two groups. These 11 items were given weights determined by their discriminatory power.

In a second study, Weschler administered the attitude test to a sample of labor mediators—members of the Federal Mediation and Conciliation Service, persons in the New York and California state mediation services, and a few persons who were not full-time mediators but who accepted emergency assignments. Each mediator was asked to name those of his colleagues he would select for an assignment of importance and those he would pass over. A total evaluation score was secured and the mediators were sorted into "good," "poor," and "other" categories.

Of the 64 mediators who took the test, 21 had been judged "good"; 19, "poor"; and 24, "other." The scores of these three groups on the attitude test are shown in the following table.

| | NUMBER OF MEDIATORS | | |
EVALUATION CATEGORY	Promanagement zone	Neutral zone	Prolabor zone
"Good"	1	7	13
"Other"	4	1	19
"Poor"	5	0	14

As Weschler warns, these data cannot be taken as evidence that most labor mediators are actively biased toward labor in their work as mediators.

The data do show that one-third of "good" mediators made "neutral" scores, whereas none of the "poor" mediators scored in the neutral zone.

Weschler, I. R. An investigation of attitudes toward labor and management by means of the error-choice method. J. soc. Psychol., 1950, 32, 51–62.

Weschler, I. R. The personal factor in labor mediation. Personnel Psychol., 1950, 3, 113–132.

On a priori grounds, at least, it may be expected that through projective tests unconscious components of attitudes or socially disapproved attitudes can be measured more validly than by the conventional attitude scale. Systematic study, however, of the comparative validity of projective methods and direct methods has not yet been made.

A study by Seeman [1947] illustrates some of the problems in the use of disguised techniques to measure attitudes. In this study a disguised technique to measure attitude toward the Negro was developed. It consisted of a number of brief descriptions of relations between men and women which involved such problems as premarital and extramarital sexual intercourse, divorce, etc. The following is an illustrative item:

> Bob and Helen want to get married soon. They have been engaged for a year. So far as they can foresee, it will be impossible for the marriage to take place for another two years at least. Bob and Helen have already had complete sexual relations upon a number of occasions. Helen says she can see nothing wrong with this "as long as people marry eventually" and "do not feel guilty about it."
> *a*) Is this wrong for Helen?
>   Yes_____ No_____ Uncertain_____
> *b*) Is this wrong for Bob?
>   Yes_____ No_____ Uncertain_____
> Any remarks?

In one-half of the test forms, each item was accompanied by a picture of a white couple; in the other half, by a picture of a Negro couple.

One half of a sample of white college students was given the Negro form; the remaining half, the white form. As predicted, the subjects who received the white form more often judged unconventional sexual behavior as wrong. The subjects who received the Negro form gave more "No" and "Uncertain" responses.

Seeman had predicted that highly prejudiced subjects would tend to make different moral judgments for Negroes and for whites more frequently than less prejudiced subjects. To test this hypothesis, the subjects were divided into "more prejudiced" and "less prejudiced" subgroups on the basis of their scores on a Likert scale of attitude toward Negroes.

A comparison of the responses of the "less prejudiced" subjects who had received the Negro form with the responses of the "less prejudiced" subjects who had received the white form revealed significant differences, whereas the responses of the "more prejudiced" subjects to the two forms were much the same. This unexpected finding led Seeman to question what his disguised technique and the Likert scale were actually measuring, and which method was more valid for what purpose. He concluded by emphasizing the "need for extreme care in interpretation of projective and semiprojective techniques for the study of specific attitudes."

THE SEMANTIC DIFFERENTIAL. Osgood, Suci, and Tannenbaum [1957] have developed a technique, known as the semantic-differential rating instrument, to secure a measure of the meaning of concepts. The hypothesis underlying the technique is that the meaning of an object for an individual includes not only the more obvious denotative meaning which he can readily state, but also more subtle connotative meanings which he can less easily describe. To measure these important connotative meanings of a given object, an indirect approach is used, in which quantitative ratings of the object in respect to a number of bipolar adjectives are secured from the individual. The "meaning" of the object for the person is the pattern or profile of his ratings on the different adjective scales (see Box 5.12).

Through a factor-analytic study of the ratings of many different objects on such bipolar adjective scales, Osgood and Suci [1955] established three general factors of meaning. The first is an *evaluative* factor. It is most prominently identified by the following adjective scales: good-bad, beautiful-ugly, sweet-

Charles E. Osgood, George J. Suci, and Percy H. Tannenbaum, of the Institute of Communications Research of the University of Illinois, developed the semantic-differential technique to measure the connotative meaning of concepts. Briefly, the technique involves asking a subject to rate a concept on each of a number of bipolar adjective scales (e.g., fair-unfair, strong-weak). The meaning of the concept for a subject is his pattern or profile of ratings on the bipolar adjective scales.

The "semantic geography" of two groups of American voters in 1952—Eisenhower Republicans and Stevenson Democrats—is shown in the following figures, which portray the ratings assigned by the two groups to six concepts on three scales: fair-unfair, strong-weak, and active-passive.

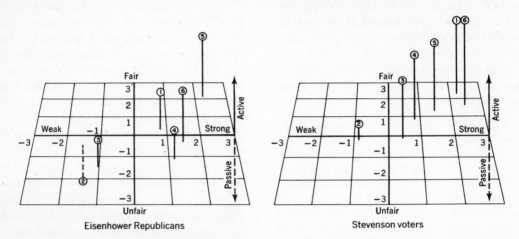

Eisenhower Republicans   Stevenson voters

Each of the six concepts is numbered according to the key below. The point at which the line for a given concept starts shows its ratings on the scales *fair-unfair* and *strong-weak*. The length of the line for a given concept shows the rating of the concept on the scale *active-passive*. A solid line indicates a rating toward the active end of the bipolar scale; a dashed line, a rating toward the passive end. (Key: 1. Stevenson, 2. Policy in China, 3. Federal spending, 4. Truman, 5. Eisenhower, 6. Roosevelt.)

Note the differences in the meaning of the concepts for the two groups of voters.

Osgood, C. E., Suci, G. J., and Tannenbaum, P. H. The measurement of meaning. Urbana: Univer. of Illinois Press, 1957.

sour, clean-dirty, tasty-distasteful, valuable-worthless, kind-cruel, pleasant-unpleasant, bitter-sweet. The second is the *potency* factor. It is most prominently identified by the following scales: strong-weak, large-small, heavy-light, thick-thin. The third is the *activity* factor. It is most prominent in the following scales: active-passive, fast-slow, hot-cold, sharp-dull.

Of the three factors, the evaluative factor is by far the most conspicuous. And it is this factor which corresponds to what we have called the valence of the attitude components. Thus, by averaging the rating scores of an individual on the most highly loaded scales for this evaluative factor, the valence of his attitude toward any given object can be measured. Evidence that the semantic differential measures the valence of the cognitive and feeling components of attitudes is cited by Osgood and his associates. Three objects (the Negro, the church, and capital punishment) were rated by a group of subjects on five bipolar scales: fair-unfair, valuable-worthless, pleasant-unpleasant, clean-dirty, and good-bad. In addition, the attitudes of the subjects toward the three objects were measured by Thurstone scales. The correlations between the evaluative-rating scores and the corresponding Thurstone scale scores ranged from .74 to .82, and in no case were they significantly lower than the reliability coefficients for the Thurstone scale.

A comparison of attitude scores toward crop rotation obtained by summing over three evaluative scales (good-bad, fair-unfair, and valuable-worthless) and Guttman scale scores toward crop rotation yielded a rank-order correlation of .78. It seems clear that the evaluative scales of the semantic differential and the Guttman scale are to a considerable extent measuring the same thing.

The reliability of the semantic differential as an attitude test is quite satisfactory. The test-retest reliabilities of attitude scores toward the Negro, the church, and capital punishment, obtained in the study cited above, were found to be .87, .83, and .91, respectively.

The validity of the semantic differential as an attitude test is suggested by the substantial correlations which have been found between evaluative-scale ratings and scores on Thurstone and Guttman scales. In addition, evaluative-scale ratings of ethnic objects differentiated between persons scoring high and low on the California F scale (see page 201).

Osgood, Suci, and Tannenbaum suggest that the predictive validity of evaluative-scale ratings may be increased by combining ratings on scales representing the potency and activity factors. In the Thurstone comparison study cited above, one subject rated the Negro as unfavorable, strong, and active; another subject rated the Negro as equally unfavor-

able, but as weak and passive. The experimenters conclude: "Although no behavioral criteria were available in this study, it seems likely that the former subject would behave differently in a real-life situation (e.g., with fear and avoidance) than the latter."

TO RECAPITULATE

Among special techniques that have been developed for the measurement of attitudes are disguised techniques and the semantic differential.

Among the disguised techniques are projective tests and the error-choice technique. The reliability and validity of disguised measures have not yet been adequately established. Many unresolved problems in the use of such techniques remain to be worked out.

The semantic-differential technique, originally developed to measure the connotative meaning of concepts, has been used to measure attitudes as well. The evaluative factor appears to measure the valence of the belief and feeling components.

THE SURVEY INTERVIEW

The use of attitude scales is, for rather obvious reasons, restricted to situations where the individuals being measured are readily available to the experimenter and are motivated to cooperate. Special types of persons, such as college students, institutionalized abnormal persons, soldiers, and others readily accessible for controlled measurement, have therefore been given disproportionate emphasis in the development and use of attitude-measurement techniques. Relatively few attitude studies using scales and special techniques have been based on representative samples of the whole population of a society. This suggests the possibility that some of the current theoretical principles of attitude formation and change may not be validly extensible to the entire population, reflecting, as they may, special factors to be found in the restricted samples upon which the research was conducted.

However, the development of the survey interview technique for measuring the distribution of attitudes in representative samples of the population is helping to overcome this limitation. (For an illustration of an international survey, see Box 5.13.)

TYPES OF SURVEY QUESTIONS

The two principal types of questions that are used in survey interviews are the *fixed-alternative* question and the *open-end* question. We shall examine each of these and compare them.

THE FIXED-ALTERNATIVE QUESTION. The fixed-alternative question offers the respondent a choice between two or more specified alternative answers. For example, a fixed-alternative question may ask, "Which party do you think would do a better job of running the government during the next few years—the Republicans or the Democrats?" The respondent's opinion is simply recorded as favoring the Republicans or as favoring the Democrats. In all such questions the respondent must choose among the stated alternatives. There is no provision for any other answer (except, of course, that the person may say that he has no opinion or can make no choice).

THE OPEN-END QUESTION. The open-end question permits a free response not restricted to predetermined categories. For example, an open-end question may be phrased as follows: "What do you think about the Republican party?" The interviewer, in so far as possible, makes a verbatim record of the respondent's reply. The unique feature of the open-end question is that the respondent is given no predetermined structure for his reply and hence is permitted to answer in whatever terms and whatever frame of reference he chooses.

The open-end question technique has endeavored to combine the advantages of a standard schedule of questions to be asked of all respondents with the advantages of a free clinical interview. In order that the answers from all respondents in the sample may be susceptible to classification and summary on a set of common dimensions, it is necessary to construct clusters of questions that follow smoothly and naturally from one to another, thus unobtrusively guiding the respondent to talk in the specific areas and in the specific contexts desired by the interviewer. The same open-end questions are asked (in the same order) of each respondent. The task of the interviewer is to get full answers by nondirective means, that is, by encouraging the person to talk without asking additional substantive questions not in the standard schedule. To stimulate the respondent to talk fully, the interviewer may use such nondirective probes as "Why?" or "Will you tell me more about that?"

CODING OF OPEN-END QUESTIONS. In the fixed-alternative question the responses are precoded, that is, the interviewer has simply to check the appropriate category for each question in accordance with the respondent's choice. Responses from all interviews are tabulated, and the percentages of answers in each category computed. In the use of open-end questions, on the other hand, each interview protocol consists of a detailed verbatim record of the respondent's answers. Before tabulation and analysis can proceed, it is necessary to "code" each response on each interview. In the process of coding, each response is classified into one of a small number of categories. For an illustration of the coding of open-end questions, see Figure 5.2.

Coding introduces a number of methodological problems and is a costly and time-consuming operation. As a short cut, the interviewer is sometimes provided in advance with the code categories, and codes the respondent's answers on the spot without making a verbatim record.

SUMMARY COMPARISON OF FIXED-ALTERNATIVE AND OPEN-END QUESTIONS. The open-end question is superior to the fixed-alternative question in ascertaining the respondent's interpretations, in being less dependent upon specific wordings that might induce bias, in determining the reasons for attitudes, and in providing fuller data for analysis. In the study of issues upon which attitudes are highly crystallized or in determining matters of fact,

BOX 5.13: *The Cold War*

An international survey was carried out in the early 1950s under the auspices of UNESCO to learn "How Nations See Each Other." A question in the survey read: "From the list of words on this card, which seems to you to describe the _____ people best? Select as many as you wish. . . . If you have no particular feelings one way or the other, just say so." The words listed were: hard-working, intelligent, practical, conceited, generous, cruel, backward, brave, self-controlled, domineering, progressive, peace-loving, impossible to characterize.

This question was asked of national samples in Australia, Britain, France, Germany, Italy, Holland, Norway, and the United States. The following table shows the three adjectives most frequently used by members of each country to describe Russian and American people. (Brackets indicate tie percentages.)

DESCRIPTION OF RUSSIANS BY:

Australians	*British*	*French*	*Germans*
Domineering	Hard-working	Backward	Cruel
Hard-working	Domineering	Hard-working	Backward
Cruel	Cruel	Domineering	{ Hard-working { Domineering

Italians	*Dutch*	*Norwegians*	*Americans*
Backward	Cruel	Hard-working	Cruel
Cruel	Domineering	Domineering	{ Hard-working { Domineering { Backward
Domineering	Backward	Backward	

DESCRIPTION OF AMERICANS BY:

Australians	*British*	*French*	*Germans*
Progressive	Progressive	Practical	Progressive
Practical	{ Conceited { Generous { Peace-loving	Progressive	Generous
Intelligent		Domineering	Practical

Italians	*Dutch*	*Norwegians*	*Americans*
Generous	Practical	Hard-working	Peace-loving
Practical	Progressive	Practical	Generous
Hard-working	Hard-working	Progressive	Intelligent

It must be emphasized that the sample of respondent countries was limited to Western, pro-American countries.

Buchanan, W., and Cantril, H. How nations see each other. Urbana: Univer. of Illinois Press, 1953.

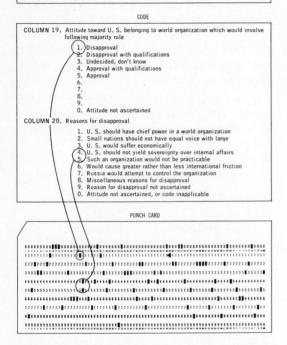

QUESTION

Q. 8: How would you feel about this country belonging to a world organization where we would have to follow the decisions of the majority of the nations?

ANSWER

"No, American people don't want laws from someone else. We want to make our own and live by them. We do pretty well by ourselves. It's fine to have an organization to settle fighting and war -- but leave America out of everything else. We've got it pretty good here, and we don't want to change. You said the majority of the nations. What if they gang up on us? Then we're liable to have to do pretty near anything. Look at how Europe followed Hitler -- he'd have had lots of votes. We don't want any messing with our government. Anyway, that kind of organization wouldn't work. You couldn't get the nations to follow what was decided. They'd walk out on what they didn't like, just the way Russia's been doing."

CODE

COLUMN 19. Attitude toward U. S. belonging to world organization which would involve following majority rule

  1. Disapproval
  2. Disapproval with qualifications
  3. Undecided, don't know
  4. Approval with qualifications
  5. Approval
  6.
  7.
  8.
  9.
  0. Attitude not ascertained

COLUMN 20. Reasons for disapproval

  1. U. S. should have chief power in a world organization
  2. Small nations should not have equal voice with large
  3. U. S. would suffer economically
  4. U. S. should not yield sovereignty over internal affairs
  5. Such an organization would not be practicable
  6. Would cause greater rather than less international friction
  7. Russia would attempt to control the organization
  8. Miscellaneous reasons for disapproval
  9. Reason for disapproval not ascertained
  0. Attitude not ascertained, or code inapplicable

PUNCH CARD

FIGURE 5.2: An illustration of the coding of open-end questions. Shown are a typical open-end question, a verbatim answer, the codes relating to the question, and the manner in which the appropriate columns in the punch cards are punched to indicate how the answer is coded. Column 20 is double-punched (4 and 5) because both of these reasons are found in the answer. [Krech and Crutchfield, 1948.]

the fixed-alternative question, because of its greater simplicity and economy, may be preferred. And, as we shall soon see, the fixed-alternative question seems to yield more reliable data than the open-end question. The two methods may be profitably used together, the open-end question to explore the dimensions of the problem and to establish the

context and reasons, and the fixed-alternative question to measure certain specific dimensions.

In his book *Interviewing in Social Research*, Hyman [1954] has reviewed a number of studies dealing with the relative reliability of interview data obtained in the field through the use of fixed-alternative and open-end questions. He finds few instances of significant disagreement in the case of trained interviewers using fixed-alternative questions. In contrast, several studies have demonstrated a high degree of disagreement in the answers to open-end questions when asked by different trained interviewers. The major sources of error are selective recording of responses and differences in probing on the part of interviewers.

The relative unreliability of the open-end question does not mean that this type of question should be abandoned in favor of the fixed-alternative question. For the reasons we have discussed, the open-end question may be required to accomplish the purposes of an investigation.

RELIABILITY AND VALIDITY OF THE SURVEY INTERVIEW

RELIABILITY. The reliability of interview data can be measured in two ways. First, it can be measured by determining the consistency in the answers of respondents interviewed on two different occasions; this is a "test-retest" method. Second, it can be measured by determining the amount of agreement among interviewers who interview independent but comparable samples of respondents; this is a "split-half" method. The reliability of the information given by *individual* respondents and the stability of means or frequency distributions for entire *samples* can both be estimated by the above two methods.

It is generally found that the reliability of sample scores (means and frequency distributions) is higher than the reliability of the information provided by individuals. For example, in a study by Withey [1952] the same sample of respondents was interviewed twice in a study of consumer finances. Table 5.1 shows that the two distributions of incomes secured in the two surveys were quite similar despite the fact that the incomes reported by individuals differed considerably in the two surveys. As can be seen, the reported incomes of less than two-thirds of the respondents were in the same bracket in the two surveys. (Among persons whose reports varied, upward and downward shifts nearly canceled out.)

The reliability of the frequency distributions of opinions obtained from independent but comparable samples of respondents is generally quite high. In a study of bond buying [Cartwright, 1949], carried out during World War II, respondents were asked why they thought the government was interested in selling war bonds. The reasons given occurred in highly similar proportions in successive surveys, as is shown in Table 5.2.

The reliability of the survey interview technique, in the hands of competent investigators, seems to be quite satisfactory.

VALIDITY. The appropriate measure of the validity of the survey interview depends in part on the purpose of the study. If the study is intended only to *describe* public opinion on an issue, it is valid to the extent that major sources of bias (sampling errors and errors due to the interviewer and the interview) have been controlled. If a survey interview study is carried out to forecast action, its

TABLE 5.1: REPORTED INCOMES IN TWO SUCCESSIVE SURVEYS
[Adapted from Withey, 1952]

1947 INCOME BEFORE TAXES	INCOME REPORTED, PER CENT Early 1948	INCOME REPORTED, PER CENT Early 1949	SAME BRACKET IN BOTH SURVEYS, PER CENT
Under $1,000	8	7	6
$1,000 to $1,999	14	14	10
$2,000 to $2,999	23	28	17
$3,000 to $3,999	22	18	12
$4,000 to $4,999	14	13	6
$5,000 to $7,499	12	13	7
Over $7,500	7	7	6
	100	100	64

TABLE 5.2: REASONS ATTRIBUTED TO GOVERNMENT FOR SELLING BONDS IN FOUR SUCCESSIVE SURVEYS [Adapted from Cartwright, 1949]

Reason	Jan. 1944, per cent	Jun. 1944, per cent	Nov. 1944, per cent	Jun. 1945, per cent
To finance the war, to win the war, to help soldiers	65	65	67	68
To prevent inflation	14	15	15	14
To get people to save	7	8	7	10
To provide postwar security	2	3	2	3
Other reasons	12	9	9	5
	100	100	100	100

validity is measured by its *predictive* accuracy. Box 5.14 shows that a well-executed sample survey can predict political participation and voting behavior with a high degree of accuracy.

THE PRESENT STATE OF THE ART

Attitude measurement is perhaps the outstanding technical achievement of the social psychologist. Scaling techniques have been developed which have proved their value in studies of attitude development and change (see Chapters 6 and 7); interview procedures have been developed which have demonstrated their usefulness in measuring the distribution of attitudes in large populations. Yet attitude measurement, as it exists today, has a number of limitations and misapplications.

MEASURING WHAT ISN'T THERE. As we have pointed out, attitude testers, both in the laboratory and in the field, too frequently "measure" attitudes that people do not hold. Hyman

BOX 5.14: *The vote is determined*

The American presidential election is a massive event. Every four years tens of millions of Americans enter voting booths on Election Day and tens of millions of eligible voters fail to vote.

Angus Campbell, Gerald Gurin, and Warren E. Miller, members of the staff of the Survey Research Center of the University of Michigan, have made an analysis of factors determining the political action and inaction of American voters. A representative nationwide sample of 1,614 people was interviewed in October, 1952, before the election, and in November, 1952, after the election. The interview schedule used in the study consisted primarily of open-end questions.

The investigators measured three indicators of political attitude which were assumed to determine the extent of participation of persons in the campaign and their choice of candidate. The three indicators, measured in the pre-election survey, were:

Party identification. This indicator was measured by asking a direct, categorical question: "Generally speaking, do you usually think of yourself as a Republican, a Democrat, an independent, or what?" Those respondents who said they were "independents" were asked: "Do you think of yourself closer to the Republican or Democratic party?" Most of the self-styled independents agreed they were closer to one party than the other. Those few who rejected the party labels were classified as Independents. The respondents were thus sorted into three groups with respect to party identification: Democrats (D), Republicans (R), and Independents (?).

Issue partisanship. This indicator was measured by combining a measure of knowledge of party differences on political issues and a measure of preference for party position on the issues, i.e., pro-Democratic (D), anti-Democratic (R), and neutral (?).

Candidate orientation. This indicator was measured by coding the spontaneous references of the respondents to the candidates, such as statements about personal characteristics (leadership, honesty, sincerity) and statements suggesting the respondent's personal attraction to a candidate ("I like him," "He's wonderful"). Respondents were sorted into three classes: pro-Stevenson (D), pro-Eisenhower (R), and indifferent (?).

All respondents were classified into indicator patterns based on the above three indicators. Thus a respondent whose party identification and issue partisanship were Democratic, but whose candidate orientation was Republican, was designated as having a DDR indicator pattern.

The following table shows the relation between indicator patterns and degree of political participation (as ascertained in the post-election follow-up survey).

SOCIAL ATTITUDES

and Sheatsley [1947], in a reanalysis of survey data, pointed out that there is a "hard core of chronic 'know-nothings'" in the American population. In a national survey conducted in May, 1946, the National Opinion Research Center asked five information questions on issues crucial at that time in the field of foreign affairs. The five topics covered by these questions were:

1. The report of the Anglo-American Committee on Palestine.

2. The Acheson-Lilienthal report on atomic energy.

3. The Paris meeting of the Big Four foreign ministers, then in progress.

4. The proposed loan to England, then being debated in Congress.

5. The political status of Palestine, then ruled by England.

Table 5.3 shows how the respondents in the sample were divided with respect to awareness of these five issues. Roughly one

POLITICAL PARTICIPATION	INDICATOR PATTERNS, PER CENT									
	DDD	DDR	DRR	RRR	DD?	D?R	RR?	D??	R??	???
High (voted and engaged in other political activity)	29	29	35	46	32	20	40	16	19	10
Medium (voted but did not engage in other activity)	54	52	50	50	41	49	47	44	49	38
Low (did not vote)	17	19	15	4	27	31	13	40	32	52

Indicator patterns seem to be excellent predictors of amount of political activity. Note, for example, that failure to vote varied from 52 per cent in the ??? pattern to only 4 per cent in the RRR pattern.

Can we also use indicator patterns to predict candidate choice? In the post-election survey, each respondent was asked for whom he had voted. (Nonvoters were asked for whom they would have voted.)

The relation of candidate choice to indicator pattern is shown in the following table.

CANDIDATE PREFERENCE	INDICATOR PATTERNS, PER CENT									
	DDD	DDR	DRR	RRR	DD?	D?R	RR?	D??	R??	???
Eisenhower	7	29	81	98	18	50	94	28	81	39
Stevenson	93	69	17	1	78	48	6	64	15	40
Other or none	0	2	2	1	4	2	0	8	4	21

The major dependent variable in this study was the vote as measured by the reports of the respondents. Before we can conclude that the indicator patterns are valid predictors of voting, it is necessary to examine the validity of self-report as a measure of voting behavior. A comparison of the division of the two-party vote as measured in the post-election survey and as recorded in election statistics showed no discrepancies larger than those that might be attributed to sampling errors.

The findings of this study are impressive evidence that a well-executed sample survey can validly predict political action.

Campbell, A., Gurin, G., and Miller, W. E. The voter decides. Evanston, Ill.: Row, Peterson, 1954.

TABLE 5.3: PERCENTAGE OF RESPONDENTS AWARE OF FIVE CRUCIAL ISSUES IN FOREIGN AFFAIRS. [After Hyman and Sheatsley, 1947.]

Issue	National sample, per cent (N = 1,292)
None of the issues	14
One issue	18
Two issues	20
Three issues	17
Four issues	19
All five issues	12
	100

person in seven had never heard of any of the issues; approximately one person in three had heard of no more than one of them. The hard core of chronic know-nothings is a large one. And clearly people cannot hold attitudes toward issues of which they have no awareness.

The standard practice of most survey organizations is first to ask information questions to screen out respondents who report no knowledge of an issue. These respondents are not asked attitude questions on this issue. However, even persons who do report knowledge may not hold a pre-existing attitude toward the issue in question. And to ask them attitude questions may lead them to generate an apparent attitude during the interview to please the interviewer.

ONE-SIDED MEASUREMENT. The attitude scale is a useful device for securing quantitative measures of the valence of the cognitive and feeling components of an attitude. Most attitude scales do not, however, measure the other primary characteristics of attitudes which were discussed on pages 142 to 146. Other techniques need to be developed which will yield reliable quantitative measures of these characteristics. The open-end interview can yield *qualitative* data on all the primary characteristics. The development of metrics for *quantifying* these data would represent a notable advance.

NEGLECT OF ACTION TENDENCY. Another major limitation of attitude-measurement techniques is that they do not adequately tap the action tendency component of attitudes. Scales consisting of items describing specific actions (see page 150) perhaps come closer to measuring action tendency than do scales using other types of items. But in responding to such items, the subject reports merely what he *thinks* he would do in a hypothetical situation; this may differ markedly from his real action tendency.

THE MEASUREMENT EFFECT. The influence of the process of measurement upon the object of measurement is a problem in every science. Certainly it plagues the attitude tester. The very process of asking an individual questions about an object may encourage the development of an attitude toward the object, strengthen an existing attitude, make it more salient, or in other ways change the status of the attitude. It is for this reason that leaders of some minority groups, guided by the "Let sleeping dogs lie" maxim, have objected to national surveys of attitudes toward their groups.

While disguised attitude tests (see page 161) have attempted to deal with the problem of the influence of measurement upon the attitude being measured, there still remain many difficulties. Among these is the problem of spurious consistency. We have seen that attitudes, as measured, tend to be internally consistent systems. This apparent consistency may, however, be an artifact of the method of measurement. In an attitude scale or survey interview, various aspects of the object—or rather, symbols of various aspects of the object—are presented in close succession to the subject, and thus may impose the necessity for some degree of consistency in his responses. In his daily life, on the other hand, the individual confronts the object in situations which are widely separated in time and space. And it is easier to be inconsistent when the inconsistent responses can be separated in time and space. Measures of attitudes based on behavior observations distributed in time and space would undoubtedly show much less consistency. In test and interview situations, the need to be consistent is allowed full play, and thus again, the very attempt to measure changes the attitude being measured.

UNIDIMENSIONAL SCALE VERSUS MULTIDIMENSIONAL MAN. The emphasis on unidimensionality in scale construction has led some investigators to overlook two points: (1) A unidimensional scale may not be the most valid instrument for measuring attitudes toward a complex object or for predicting action toward the object. (2) The attitude of one group of individuals toward a given object may have a unidimensional structure, whereas the same object may be the referent for a number of different attitudes in another group, that is, their attitudes may have a multidimensional structure.

To illustrate the first point, consider a man's attitudes toward the complex issue of disarmament. They may include attitudes toward national sovereignty, defense expenditures, peace, Russia, Communist China, diplomacy, nuclear testing, nuclear warfare, etc., etc. Suppose unidimensional scales have been developed to measure each of these component attitudes. No single one of these scales will adequately represent our man's attitude toward disarmament or provide a basis for predicting what action he will take with respect to disarmament proposals.

Our second point is that unidimensionality is a property of a group of individuals and not a property of the measuring instrument. For one group of persons, a set of items may be arranged unidimensionally in a given order. For another group they may not be so arranged. Coombs [1948] has made this point clearly:

> In a highly organized social order with standardized education, there will tend to be certain traits generated which will be common to the population subjected to the same pattern of forces. There is, however, at the same time, opposition, contradiction, and interaction of these forces on organisms that are not equally endowed in the first place—with the result that the structure of a psychological trait is less complete in some individuals than in others. . . . A psychological trait, in other words, may or may not be a functional unity and it may or may not be general, i.e., common to a large number of individuals.

If an investigator insists upon unidimensional scales, he eliminates the possibility of studying persons whose attitudes are not patterned unidimensionally. What is needed is the application of multidimensional scaling methods (see Torgerson, 1958) to the measurement of attitudes.

CHAPTER GUIDES AND GLOSSARY

GUIDE 13: *The social actions of the individual reflect his attitudes—enduring systems of positive or negative evaluations, emotional feelings, and pro or con action tendencies with respect to social objects*

GUIDE 14: *Attitudes differ in their effects on social action according to their primary characteristics*

action tendency component of attitude. The dispositions to take action, positive or negative, toward an object which are incorporated in an individual's attitude toward that object.

attitude. An enduring system of positive or negative evaluations, emotional feelings, and pro or con action tendencies with respect to a social object.

attitude cluster. A set of two or more attitudes which are relatively highly interrelated and relatively isolated from other attitude clusters.

attitude constellation. The total set of attitudes of an individual.

cognitive component of attitude. The beliefs about an object which are incorporated in an individual's attitude toward that object. Especially important are the *evaluative* beliefs.

consistency of attitude system. The tendency in any given attitude system for the three components—cognitions, feelings, and action tendencies—to be congruent in valence and in multiplexity.

consonance of attitude cluster. The degree of internal harmony existing among the component attitudes in the cluster. An attitude cluster is said to be high in consonance when the component attitudes are high in congruence, and lower in consonance when they are lower in congruence.

cumulative scaling method. An attitude scaling method developed by Guttman. In a cumulative scale the items can be so ordered that a subject who responds positively to any particular item also responds positively to all items of lower rank. A perfect cumulative scale has a *coefficient of reproducibility* of 1.0 and is a *unidimensional scale.*

equal-appearing-interval scaling method. A scaling method adapted by Thurstone for the measurement of attitudes. In this method judges sort a large and representative pool of evaluative statements about an object into groups separated by *equal steps or intervals.* The median of their judgments defines the *scale value* of a statement. Statements which are not judged consistently are discarded as ambiguous. The surviving statements are then given to subjects who are asked to check the ones with which they agree. If a statement is frequently checked by subjects who also check other statements differing widely in scale value, it is discarded as *irrelevant.*

feeling component of attitude. The feelings, positive or negative, toward an object which are incorporated in an individual's attitude toward that object.

fixed-alternative question. A survey interview question-form which offers the respondent a choice between two or more specified alternative answers.

interconnectedness, attitude. The characteristic of an attitude which refers to the degree to which it is interrelated with other attitudes. Attitudes may be relatively isolated from one another in the attitude *constellation* of the individual or they may be related with other attitudes to form attitude *clusters.*

item analysis. A way of determining the degree to which attitude items discriminate among individuals who differ in their attitudes toward an object. The discriminatory power of an item is measured by computing the correlation between item scores and total scores. Items which correlate most highly with the total score are retained as the most discriminating items.

multiplexity of attitude component. The number and variety of the separate elements which make up the cognitive, feeling, or action tendency components of an attitude. A component which has a large number and variety of elements is referred to as a multiplex component; one with relatively few or highly similar elements, as a simplex component.

neutral region. The region on the favorability continuum which lies between the zone of negativity and the zone of positivity of an attitude. The neutral region is the region of transition from negative to positive attitudes. If an individual's score on a unidimensional scale falls in the neutral region and therefore indicates neither a negative nor a positive evaluation of an object, the individual cannot be said to have an attitude toward the object.

open-end question. A survey interview question-form which permits the respondent to answer freely in his own words.

reproducibility, coefficient of. A statistic invented by Guttman to indicate the proportional accuracy with which responses to the individual statements in a set of statements can be reproduced from the total scores.

scale-discrimination technique. An attitude scaling technique developed by Edwards and Kilpatrick. It attempts to synthesize in one method the advantages of the methods of equal-appearing intervals, summated ratings, and the cumulative scale.

scale value. A measure of the degree of favorableness of a statement in a Thurstone equal-appearing-interval scale. The scale value of a statement is the median of the distribution of judgments of the item.

semantic-differential rating instrument. A technique developed by Osgood for measuring the connotative meaning of concepts by getting ratings on a number of bipolar adjective scales. The technique has also been applied to the measurement of attitudes.

social-distance scaling method. An attitude scaling method developed by Bogardus to measure attitudes toward social groups. Consists of a number of items which permit the subject to indicate the closest social intimacy he will accept between himself and a typical member of the social group in question.

summated-rating scaling method. A method of constructing attitude scales developed by Likert. Subjects are asked to indicate on a five-step scale the degree of their agreement or disagreement with each of a large and representative set of items. The total score of each subject is computed by summing his item scores. The items are then subjected to item analysis, and the most discriminating items are retained for inclusion in the final scale.

unidimensional scale. A scale which measures only one attitude dimension. In a unidimensional scale a person with a higher total score will have on every item a score equal to, or higher than, that of a person with a lower total score. The *cumulative scaling method* yields the closest approximation to unidimensional scales of any of the scaling methods.

valence of attitude component. The degree of positivity or negativity of the cognitive, feeling, or action tendency components of an attitude system. Valence may vary from extreme positivity, through a neutral valence region (corresponding to the absence of an attitude), to extreme negativity.

MAN'S ATTITUDES DEVELOP AS HE DEVELOPS. BUT NO MAN'S LIFE
*develops apart from the lives of his fellows. And just as each man's
life intersects the lives of others—but only at certain points—and
just as each man's life story is similar to—but not identical with—
the life stories of his neighbors, so are the attitudes which each man
develops similar to—yet different from—the attitudes of his family,
friends, neighbors, and compatriots. This, on the individual and
psychological level, is one of the sources of a stable culture—stable
but yet complex—with subcultures and status hierarchies,
conformists and deviates. It is because of this that the formation of
attitudes is of such great importance to the student of society, and of
such great concern to parents, educators, political leaders, and all
men who would teach or lead or control other men.*

*In this chapter we continue our study of attitudes by turning to an
examination of their formation and growth.*

6: THE FORMATION OF ATTITUDES

TO KNOW THE CHARACTERISTICS OF ATTITUDES
(our concern of the last chapter) is to know
a great deal. But it is not enough. If we are to
predict the behavior of people over extended
periods of time, and if we are to control their
actions, we must also know how attitudes
develop and how they change. These are matters of concern not only for the social scientist
as "pure" scientist, but also for all those who
would seek to influence social action. Educators, leaders of causes, reformers, politicians,
minority-group leaders, businessmen—all are
interested in knowing how to develop new
attitudes and how to strengthen or to weaken
existing ones. The National Association of

Manufacturers wants to *strengthen* traditional
attitudes against governmental control of private enterprise; the National Association for
the Advancement of Colored People wants to
eliminate traditional discriminatory attitudes;
the inventors of "teaching machines" want to
develop a whole new set of attitudes—favorable to a new concept of teaching.

In this chapter we shall examine the forces
which determine the development of attitudes, and the resulting pattern of attitudes
which we find among individuals and groups
of individuals. Among the determinants which
we shall examine are the individual's wants,
information, group affiliations, and personality.

An understanding of how attitudes are formed will set the stage for an examination in the next chapter of how attitudes, once formed, can be changed.

GUIDE 15: *Attitudes develop in the process of want satisfaction*

In coping with various problems in trying to satisfy his wants, the individual develops attitudes. He develops favorable attitudes toward objects and people that satisfy his wants: final goal objects will be favorably evaluated (being alive is good); means-goal objects will also be seen in a favorable light (the patient has positive attitudes toward his doctor). The individual will develop unfavorable attitudes toward objects and persons that block the achievement of his goals (see Box 6.1).

The individual's attitudes may come to have "surplus" instrumental value for him. He develops his attitudes in response to problem situations—in trying to satisfy specific wants. In so far as his attitudes are enduring

BOX 6.1: *Attitudes and goals*

Milton J. Rosenberg, a social psychologist at Yale University, has demonstrated that the sign and intensity of feelings toward the object of an attitude are associated with what the individual believes to be its *instrumental value* in facilitating or blocking the achievement of goals.

One hundred and twenty college students were given an attitude questionnaire that contained an item dealing with the issue of "whether members of the Communist Party should be allowed to address the public." Each student was required to check his choice among five alternative statements that ranged from extreme disapproval to extreme approval of allowing members of the Communist Party to address the public. This questionnaire thus yielded a measure of the sign and intensity of the subjects' feelings concerning the issue.

Three to five weeks after the administration of the attitude questionnaire, the students were given two tasks. In the first, each student was asked to indicate how much satisfaction he gets, or would get, from the attainment of each of 35 goals. Some of these were: "Being looked up to by others." "Change and variety; having new kinds of experience." "Having a steady income." "Being with other people; socializing." This test thus gave a measure of the importance of the goals as *sources of satisfaction* for the students.

In the second task, the students were required to judge and place each of the 35 goals in one of 11 categories. These categories ranged from a judgment that the goal "is completely attained by allowing admitted Communists to address the public" to the judgment that the goal "is completely blocked by allowing admitted Communists to address the public." This second test thus gave a measure for each goal of the *instrumental value* of allowing Communists to address the public.

Analysis of the data showed that the sign and intensity of feelings toward freedom of speech for the Communists were significantly related to beliefs about its instrumental value for achieving goals important to the individual.

This study suggests that attitude objects which are seen as means of goal achievement are evaluated favorably, whereas those which are seen as sources of frustration are evaluated unfavorably. The findings also support the principle of consistency: the components of an attitude system tend to be congruent in valence (see pages 142 to 144).

Rosenberg, M. J. Cognitive structure and attitudinal affect. J. abnorm. soc. Psychol., *1956*, **53**, *367–372.*

systems, they remain with him and may be used by him to solve a number of different problems—to satisfy a number of different wants. For example, a boy may acquire a favorable attitude toward politics merely to please his father who is a professional politician; as an adult, this attitude becomes involved in satisfying his want for power, or in achieving prestige, or in securing material gain, or in helping other people.

One study which shows how people use their attitudes to satisfy various wants is the study of attitudes toward Russia by Smith, Bruner, and White [1956]. In this study, 10 men, chosen because of their varying attitudes toward Russia, were subjected to 29 test procedures which furnished personality descriptions and diagnoses and detailed descriptions of their attitudes toward Russia. These attitudes of the men were found to play a major role in their life adjustments. Their attitudes were harnessed to their dominant wants, serving to satisfy major interests and aspirations. Their attitudes toward Russia were also involved in their relations with other persons. In some cases they were used to maintain the individual's relationship with a group which he valued; in other cases they were used by the individual to differentiate him from a group, to disrupt a group, or to dominate a group.

THE FUNCTIONAL CHARACTER OF RACIAL PREJUDICE

The role of wants in the development of attitudes is clearly revealed in the case of a socially important kind of attitude—racial prejudice. And we shall therefore examine this attitude in some detail.

The answers to the questions—What do attitudes of racial prejudice do for people? What wants do they serve?—can almost be described as an inventory of all the wants of man. Prejudice may serve the functions of justifying pathological hostility, rationalizing culturally unacceptable wants and behavior in the service of culturally acceptable aspirations,

managing repressed wants, enhancing feelings of self-regard, protecting the self against threats to self-esteem, helping a person to become wealthy, providing a "reasonable" explanation of why one remains poor. In the service of these varied functions, prejudice can be many things to many men.

In considering the various major categories of functions that are served by attitudes of prejudice, it is essential to keep the following caution in mind. Many prejudices cannot be assigned to any one category, and any one attitude of prejudice may serve several functions. In listing these categories we are admittedly abstracting and purifying for purposes of exposition and analysis.

RACIAL PREJUDICE AND PERSONALITY PATHOLOGY. Racial prejudice is often found among the mentally ill. It must be emphasized that not all mentally ill people develop racial prejudice, nor, of course, are all racially prejudiced people mentally ill. The point is, however, that the pathological individual can, and sometimes does, develop attitudes of racial prejudice that rationalize and support his deviant behavior.

In all societies there are persons who experience intense pathological hostility which is likely to spread into all aspects of their personalities and influence all of their behavior. The hostile impulses of these people are dissipated mainly through aggressive attacks upon others. And since characteristic modes of want satisfaction come to be learned and fixated by the individual, these people learn to manage their hostility through aggressive behavior against a specific racial group. The attitudes lying behind and rationalizing such directed aggression can be seen as racial prejudice in the service of pathological hostility.

The paranoid person—in or out of a mental hospital—lives in a world of dire suspicions. If and when he fixates these suspicions, or delusions, on members of a specific racial group, we have attitudes in the service of the peculiar wants of the paranoiac. These attitudes give meaning to his actions and justify his behavior.

Though perhaps insignificant in number, persons whose racial prejudices spring from mental pathology can occasionally come to exercise powerful social influence. Because of the high intensity and saliency of their attitudes, these people are often found among the leaders of antiracial mobs and organizations and sometimes among the ideological "theorists" of hate movements. Since their racial prejudices have very low thresholds, these are the people who seek out targets against which to aggress. They do not wait for an "incident" to occur; they create incidents. Through acting out their hostilities by inciting violence against minority groups, they may be able to escape commitment to a mental hospital. Thus the very act of racial aggression which endangers society gives the pathological hater a "license" to remain at large in a society which supports racial prejudice. These persons constitute the "lunatic fringe" of the racially prejudiced.

RACIAL PREJUDICE AND AGGRESSION INDUCED BY FRUSTRATION. The persistent frustration of almost *any* significant want often finds expression in aggressive acts which seem temporarily to allay the frustrated state (see page 120. The targets of such aggression are not necessarily related logically to the frustrating situation. When the target of aggression is a racial group, the condition is created for the development of an attitude of racial prejudice that will rationalize such aggression.

Attitudes of racial prejudice which serve to support aggressions induced by frustration can derive from economic, social, political, or sexual frustration. For some individuals, frustration may be a chronic state and may be seen as an almost inevitable reflection of their status in society. For others, the experience of significant frustration may be intermittent and may give rise to acute but temporary aggressive impulses. But the universality of some degree of frustration among people in our

culture suggests that the incidence of aggressive impulses deriving from such frustration is probably very great.

An illustrative study which suggests the role of displaced aggression in the formation of ethnic prejudice is the study by Campbell [1947] referred to earlier (see Box 5.1, page 138). In Campbell's study, a representative national sample of 316 white, non-Jewish Americans was interviewed to obtain information on factors in their personal situation which were associated with negative attitudes toward Jews. On the basis of his interview, each subject was rated for (1) attitude toward Jews; (2) degree of satisfaction with his own personal economic situation; (3) degree of satisfaction with the national political situation. The latter two ratings were made independently of the rating of attitude toward Jews.

It was found that persons who were rated as dissatisfied with their own economic situation expressed hostile attitudes toward Jews more frequently than those who were economically satisfied. Only 10 per cent of the economically satisfied subjects expressed hostility, in contrast to 38 per cent of the economically dissatisfied. It should be noted that prejudice was *not* consistently related to *level of income;* degree of dissatisfaction with one's income at whatever level was the significant factor.

Persons rated as dissatisfied with the current political situation in the country also exhibited a greater incidence of hostility toward Jews than persons rated as politically satisfied. Figure 6.1 shows the pronounced relation found between a combined rating of satisfaction-dissatisfaction with both economic and political matters, and attitude toward Jews.

RACIAL PREJUDICE AND SOCIALLY DISAPPROVED WANTS. Clinical studies have suggested that many people have strong impulses of cruelty, greed, or sexual aggression which society interdicts and which the individual is thus forced to control because of his fear of

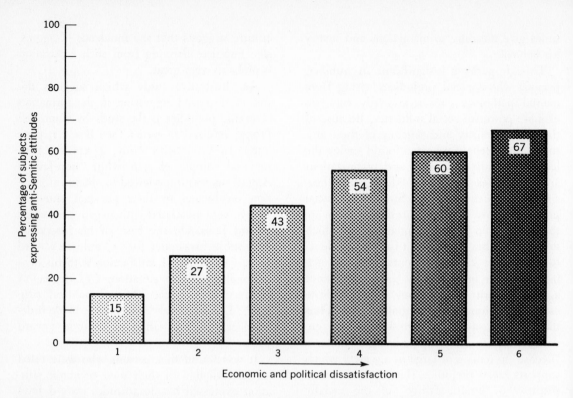

FIGURE 6.1: Economic and political dissatisfaction and attitudes toward Jews. The six bars represent the percentage of persons of varying degrees of economic and political dissatisfaction who express negative attitudes toward Jews. Bar 1 represents those *satisfied* in both economic and political matters; 2, those satisfied in one and intermediate in the other; 3, those intermediate in both; 4, those satisfied in one and dissatisfied in the other; 5, those dissatisfied in one and intermediate in the other; 6, those dissatisfied in both. It will be seen that the prevalence of anti-Semitic attitudes increases with degree of dissatisfaction. [Based on data from Campbell, 1947.]

social repercussions. The attempt to solve such conflicts can lead the individual to a rationalization (see page 122) in which the nature of the act that can satisfy these antisocial wants is reinterpreted to remove its "baseness." When such a reinterpretation involves certain discriminatory ways of regarding the members of a specific racial group, we have an instance of racial prejudice in support of culturally disapproved wants. As Redl [1946] points out:

These suppressed impulses must find an outlet, and frequently express themselves in ways for which there is presumptive alibi. A common way is for a person to say to himself,

"You couldn't do this to a 'white man' (a person of your own group), but when I do it to a person of another group it doesn't count (because he isn't really a person at all)"! For such suppressed impulses of greed, cruelty, and so forth, prejudice may serve as a good disguise.

RACIAL PREJUDICE AND SOCIALLY DISAPPROVED MEANS. Many Americans have strong wants for political eminence or for wealth. These wants are recognized by our society as good wants, as wants that all enterprising Americans should respect. When the individual, in trying to satisfy such socially *approved*

SOCIAL ATTITUDES

wants, engages in socially *disapproved* action he may rationalize this action in many ways. One way may be through the development of a racial prejudice. Thus, for example, a Southern politician who prevents Negroes from voting (through fear that the Negro vote may block his political aspirations) may allege that "the mental level of those people renders them incapable of suffrage"; he may thus be using racial prejudice to rationalize illegal behavior in the service of a socially approved want. Or a farmer who, in order to increase the profitability of his farm, cheats the Mexican laborer on the grounds that "Mexicans would only use the money to get drunk" may similarly be using prejudice in the service of what is basically a culturally approved want.

RACIAL PREJUDICE IN THE SERVICE OF RE-PRESSED WANTS. As we have seen, culturally disapproved wants may find expression through the building up of "presumptive alibis" for their expression, and this may result in attitudes of racial prejudice. But sometimes, culturally disapproved wants—especially those which conflict with the moral ideology of the person—are repressed. However, this does not mean that the repressed wants are rendered impotent or that the conflict is resolved. The further fate of such repressed wants may be seen in such mechanisms as projection. And projection can lead to racial prejudice.

A study by Frenkel-Brunswik and Sanford [1945] is suggestive of this functional pattern in prejudice. After administering a test of anti-Semitism to a group of university students, these investigators selected out for intensive clinical study those students who obtained extremely high or extremely low scores on the anti-Semitism scale. Among the techniques and devices they used were clinical interviews, the Thematic Apperception Test, and the Rorschach Ink Blot Test. On the basis of the resulting data, the investigators felt that they were able to get a fair picture of the wants (including the repressed wants) of their anti-Semitic subjects.

As one procedure they asked their subjects to interpret a picture of a boy and a girl dressed in obviously lower-class clothing. The extremely anti-Semitic college girls tended to see these "inferior" people as aggressive and sexually uninhibited. Examples of their responses were:

It is a young girl and her boy friend. They are lower class people, and don't know any better than to do this sort of thing. I have an aversion for the things such people do. . . .

I think they will marry young but will divorce before long. They allow their emotions to get too much in their way. . . .

I don't approve of them. She goes out to dances, etc. She is finally caught and brought into court. . . .

The girl is the typical type of jitterbug. . . . The couple has a nice time at the dance; that is, in that kind of way.

As Frenkel-Brunswik and Sanford comment:

These sentences express contempt and at the same time envy for the "lower class sexuality." An important tendency of the girls high on anti-Semitism is thus to keep one's basic impulses repressed, to keep oneself pure and reputable. Primitive needs are rendered ego-alien and projected onto an alien group.

The anti-Semitic girls in the group "declared without exception that they liked their parents" and tended to show, on the surface, an uncritical devotion to their parents. However, in the Thematic Apperception Test stories of these same girls *aggressive* themes against parents and other people were found to stand out. The writers give the following illustrations of the aggressive themes:

In story No. 1, of Case 6, a murder is being committed; in story No. 3, the husband has lost both legs, and the father is mentioned only to tell us that he has been killed; in story No. 4, a man is being foiled and captured; in story No. 5, a man has been killed; in story No. 6, the hero is being convicted and severely punished. Very similar are the stories of Case

4: in story No. 3, the father and son are both killed; in story No. 4, the man is a traitor; in story No. 5, he is sent to the concentration camp; in story No. 6, the hero is electrocuted; and in story No. 10, the hero is burned to death and the father killed in battle. . . . By way of contrast, in the stories of Case 1 and Case 13, both extremely low on anti-Semitism, nobody gets murdered or killed. On the whole, little aggression is manifested.

In general, the responses of the anti-Semitic girls on the Thematic Apperception Test indicated repressed hatred, jealousy, and suspicion of parental figures. Frenkel-Brunswik and Sanford suggest that these repressed tendencies find outlet in attitudes of antipathy toward various racial groups which serve as scapegoats.

The implications of this study, however, must be carefully evaluated. This description is not to be interpreted as a description of *the* personality of the anti-Semitic individual. Nor does the study demonstrate that the repressed wants were responsible for the development of prejudice. However, the data do suggest that the mechanisms which a person adopts to manage repressed wants—in the effort to reduce the conflict—may involve projecting onto minority groups certain "base" attributes or may involve the diverting of aggression from parental figures to these minority groups. *If and when* this happens, we have an instance of attitudes in the service of repressed wants.

RACIAL PREJUDICE AND SELF-REGARD. As we pointed out in Chapter 3, many of the most potent wants of the individual pertain to the enhancement and defense of the self. We know that in our culture, for example, the want for prestige—for superior status—is a strong and driving want in many individuals. Some individuals will attempt to gratify this want by finding other individuals to whom they can feel superior. Thus the individual who is on the lowest rung of the social ladder can feel superior by creating a still lower rung—by placing the Mexican or Negro or Jew at the very bottom. Attitudes of prejudice may in this way serve the want for a feeling of superiority in the social hierarchy.

Pride and prejudice often go hand in hand. For example, a man may be fired from his job. Unable to accept himself as "no good," and wishing to avoid this blow to his self-esteem, he will seek some other explanation—one that will not threaten his pride. In the course of such active seeking for a different explanation he may seize upon the belief that the unscrupulous actions of his Jewish fellow workers have resulted in his dismissal. This belief meets his wants. His pride has been saved; an anti-Semite has been created.

TO RECAPITULATE

One important factor in the formation of attitudes is want satisfaction. Not only do attitudes give meaning to the individual's world; they serve in his attempted achievement of various other goals. Any given attitude may serve various goals, and different wants can give rise to the same enduring attitude.

The functional character of attitudes is well demonstrated by the manner in which racially prejudiced attitudes reflect the individual's wants having to do with pathological hostility, aggression induced by frustration, socially disapproved goals and activities, repressed impulses, and defense of self.

GUIDE 16: *The attitudes of the individual are shaped by the information to which he is exposed*

Attitudes are not only developed in the service of wants; they are also shaped by the information to which the individual is exposed.

Illustrations of how gaining knowledge about an object can be important in bringing about the development of an attitude toward that object are numerous. For example, suppose that the people of a community know very little about chemical and biological warfare and have no attitudes concerning these matters. A newspaper publishes a series of factual articles describing the present "state of the art." Through reading these articles, many people learn about the massive disruptive and lethal effects of the new poisonous "nerve gases," germs, and viruses. As a result, a strong negative attitude toward chemical and biological warfare may develop; a strong positive attitude toward disarmament and the control of such weapons may be formed.

Information, however, is rarely a determinant of an attitude except in the context of other attitudes. New information is frequently used to form attitudes which are consonant with pre-existing related attitudes (see Box 6.2).

Attitudes, primarily because of their responsiveness to information, may therefore be "valid" in that the cognitive components of

BOX 6.2: *Balanced attitudes*

In a series of studies at the University of Michigan, Julian O. Morrissette has tested some of the consequences of the Cartwright and Harary extension of Heider's balance theory (see pages 41 to 42). Morrissette's research is one of the few studies of the applicability of balance theory to the formation of attitudes. In one experiment, college women were presented with the following paper-and-pencil test situation.

The setting. Three students, trying to cut living expenses, have been sharing an apartment for several months. As usual when two or more persons live together, they have run into problems, but they have successfully worked through many of these problems. During these several months it has become a common practice for them to do many things together—shopping, studying, "going out." Because of illness in the family, one of the students had to withdraw from school. The two remaining students advertised for another student to share the apartment with them.

Now assume this kind of living arrangement would be to your advantage also. Assume further that you have replied to the ad, and by mutual agreement the three of you have decided to share the apartment together.

The task. Try to predict as accurately as you can the relations that you believe you will establish between yourself and the other students. On meeting one of the students, Carol, you were favorably impressed. She seemed to you to be socially adaptable and fair-minded. From talking with her it was evident that she personally liked Helen. Predict as accurately as you can how *you believe you will feel toward Helen* after you have lived with her for *two weeks.*

Morrissette found that 91 per cent of his subjects predicted that they would *like* Helen (perhaps not too surprising a finding in view of the fact that the subjects had no other information about Helen to go on!). Liking Helen results in a balanced system in which all three relations are positive. This finding suggests people use information (i.e., Carol's attitude toward Helen) to form attitudes toward objects and persons that are harmonious wtih pre-existing, interrelated attitudes.

Cartwright, D., and Harary, F. Structural balance: A generalization of Heider's theory. Psychol. Rev., *1956, **63**, 277–293.*

Morrissette, J. O. An experimental study of the theory of structural balance. Hum. Relat., *1958, **11**, 239–254.*

attitudes may correspond to the facts about the objects of those attitudes. If this were not so, the individual could not cope effectively with the many problems he faces as a member of a complex society.

Not all attitudes correctly reflect the facts, however. Certain attitudes develop in men (such as superstitions, delusions, prejudices) which are characterized by their wide divergence from the facts. Because these attitudes frequently result in troublesome social actions, an analysis of the reasons for the discrepancy between facts and beliefs assumes a high priority. For example, many people who hold unfavorable attitudes toward the fluoridation of water believe that fluoridation of water is a communistic plot. This is a "fact" for them which supports a strong, negative attitude toward fluoridation. They campaign and vote against fluoridation, and a medically approved way to prevent dental caries in children is rejected by many communities because people hold incorrect beliefs (see Box 6.3).

Many of the attitudes held by people lack validity simply because they are not sufficiently well informed. The information they do possess is sadly inadequate to represent the essential facts. Even if the few facts that a person possesses are substantially correct, a lack of knowledge of related facts can distort the significance of his correct facts. Attitudes are compounded of many facts; and as we have seen (page 31), the meaning of a single fact is never independent of the other

facts with which it is associated. As long, then, as the repertory of facts possessed by the ill-informed fails to include certain of the essential facts about an object, his known facts may be distorted, and his beliefs wrong.

In this sense it might be said that "a few facts are a dangerous thing." Thus, for example, to know that, on the average, Southern Negroes score lower on intelligence tests than whites is to know a fact. However, one may not know some of the other essential facts, to wit: Southern Negroes receive very little schooling, whereas whites receive measurably more schooling; Negroes are not motivated to do well on tests, whereas whites are well-motivated. Lack of knowledge of such related facts can (and very frequently does) lead to a completely erroneous interpretation of the one fact known to the person. The misinterpretation may buttress his racial prejudice.

SOURCES OF FACTS

One of the major reasons why so many of us incorporate invalid and inadequate facts into our attitudes lies in the complexity of the world in which we live, in its rapidly changing nature, and in the nature of our sources for our facts. Of particular interest to the social psychologist, in this connection, are the functions of authorities in providing us with ready-made facts and beliefs, and our own proclivity to "create facts."

AUTHORITIES AS A SOURCE OF FACTS. It is inevitable that in the complex world in which

BOX 6.3: *Water on the brain*

Morris Davis studied the beliefs about fluoridation held by a sample of residents of Seattle, Washington. Interviews with these respondents revealed some of the "facts" that lead people to vote against this effective public health measure.

Some of the reasons for opposition to fluoridation were that it is mass medication, socialized medicine, rat poison, and Nazi; that it ruins batteries, radiators, and lawns; that it causes hardening of the arteries and veins, premature aging, loss of memory, and nymphomania; and that it weakens the will.

Davis, M. Community attitudes toward fluoridation. Publ. Opin. Quart., 1959, 23, 474–82.

we live no single individual can hope to ascertain, at first hand, the essential facts about most objects. He must necessarily depend upon what the "experts" tell him. For the young child, the experts are mainly his parents; for the student, they are his teachers and the writers of his books; for the religious person, they are his priests, ministers, rabbis; for the scientist, they are other specialists in his field. For all individuals, then, facts are frequently mediated by other people as authorities, and the amount of discrepancy between the facts and the individual's beliefs will be dependent upon the validity of the assertions of the authorities. The authority may be correct; the authority may be honestly mistaken; the authority may deliberately falsify the facts for his own ends.

All this does not imply, however, that facts offered by the authority will be taken over by the individual wholly, blindly, and undigested. Not only will the individual's wants be of great importance in governing his acceptance of the facts offered by the authority, but other factors will also play a determining role. Among these are the factors that determine who will and who will not be accepted by the individual as an authority or reliable source of information.

We can illustrate the general point under discussion here by some data from a study by Cottrell and Eberhart [1948]. In this study an attempt was made to discover something about people's sources of information about the atomic bomb. Among the findings were the following: (1) The number of sources of information a person had was closely related to his education and income; (2) people with better than average education and income tended to consider magazines their most trustworthy sources; (3) the poorly informed tended to trust the radio more than the newspapers, whereas the well-informed trusted them equally; (4) the radio was trusted because it reported the news quickly; magazines because of their detailed accounts.

Although the above generalizations tell us more about the cultural determinants of authority selection than about the psychological determinants, nevertheless they indicate the complexity of the factors that are responsible for such selection.

CREATION, INVENTION, AND DISTORTION OF FACTS. In Chapter 2 we discussed the principle of consonance in cognitive change (see pages 41 to 42). We found that unbalanced cognitive systems tend to change in the direction of increased harmony or consonance. The principle of consonance also operates in attitude formation. Facts are used by the individual to form attitudes consonant with pre-existing, interconnected attitudes (Box 6.2).

The lack of relevant facts and the conflicting facts provided for us by different authorities may force us to create, invent, or distort "facts" which bear little relation to reality, but which support and are congruent with already established attitudes (see Box 6.4).

APPEARANCE AND REALITY. The frequent unreliability of "experts" and authorities may lead one to trust only what he can see, hear, touch for himself. In most instances this dependence upon the senses is fully justified. Hence direct observation can be effective, sometimes, in providing us with "valid" attitudes. Although all this may be true, nevertheless appearances *are* often illusory. The man who appears to be kind and considerate may be cruel; the politician who is seen and heard behaving nobly may be behaving meanly. That is why some people learn to be cautious about mere appearances. This tendency to avoid dependence upon mere appearance may produce a kind of exaggerated skepticism about facts of all kinds. Many people during World War II, for example, dismissed as propaganda the photographs of atrocities in Nazi concentration camps. Having been fooled by World War I propaganda, later exposed as faked, and having learned the value and necessity of being skeptical about appearances, they refused to accept facts which were truly represented by appearance. These people are the gullible skeptics.

BOX 6.4: *When prophecy fails*

The following story appeared in a late September issue of the *Lake City Herald*.

PROPHECY FROM PLANET. CLARION CALL TO CITY: FLEE THAT FLOOD. IT'LL SWAMP US ON DEC. 21, OUTER SPACE TELLS SUBURBANITE

Lake City will be destroyed by a flood from Great Lake just before dawn, December 21, according to a suburban housewife, Mrs. Marion Keech, of 847 West School Street. . . . It is the purport of many messages she has received by automatic writing, she says. . . . The messages, according to Mrs. Keech, are sent to her by superior beings from a planet called "Clarion." These beings have been visiting the earth, she says, in . . . flying saucers. . . . Mrs. Keech reports she was told the flood will spread to form an inland sea stretching from the Arctic Circle to the Gulf of Mexico. At the same time, she says, a cataclysm will submerge the West Coast from Seattle, Washington, to Chile in South America.

Mrs. Keech told her friends and acquaintances about her messages and gradually attracted a small following of believers. Three social psychologists, Leon Festinger, Henry W. Riecken, and Stanley Schachter, joined this movement to study the effect of the disconfirmation of a strongly held belief upon the members. Some members of the group gave up their jobs, others gave away their belongings, and nearly all of them publicly declared their faith in the common deluge. On December 20, the eve of the predicted cataclysm, the believers gathered at the Keech home to be saved from the disaster. Mrs. Keech had received a message late that morning informing her that the group should be ready to receive a Visitor who would arrive at midnight to escort them to a parked flying saucer that would carry them to a place of safety in outer space.

Midnight came but not the Visitor. The believers first sat in intense despair and confusion. Then the prediction and the accompanying messages were re-examined. One explanation after another of the failure of the Visitor to appear was considered and rejected. At about 4:45 A.M., Mrs. Keech called the group to attention and announced she had just received a message. She read aloud:

For this day it is established that there is but one God of Earth and He is in thy midst, and from His hand thou hast written these words. And mighty is the word of God—and by His word have ye been saved—for from the mouth of death have ye been delivered and at no time has there been such a force loosed upon the Earth. Not since the beginning of time upon this Earth has there been such a force of Good and light as now floods this room and that which has been loosed within this room now floods the entire Earth. As thy God has spoken through the two who sit within these walls has He manifested that which He has given thee to do.

A "fact" was created to explain the disconfirmation: the little group of believers had spread so much light that God had called off the flood.

Festinger, L., Riecken, H. W., Jr., and Schachter, S. When prophecy fails. *Minneapolis: Univer. of Minnesota Press, 1956.*

TO RECAPITULATE

The individual who has strong wants that must be satisfied by the development of ap-propriate attitudes will get his facts where he can. Living in a complex world, he is at the mercy of various authorities for much of the cognitive content of his attitudes. These authorities are sometimes unreliable, through ignorance or intent. In addition, the individual himself is frequently unschooled in discerning substance from appearance; and when he does pick up his facts by himself, he again runs the risk of being fooled. Finally, when he can find no facts (either from authorities or at firsthand), he must, so long as there is any functional necessity for the development of an attitude, invent "facts" himself.

All of this suggests that the incidence of superstitions, delusions, and prejudices will be related to the reliability of the authorities we must depend upon (teachers, newspapers, books, telecasts, broadcasts), the range of experiences to which we have been subjected, and the degree to which our major wants are adequately satisfied.

GUIDE 17: *The group affiliations of the individual help determine the formation of his attitudes*

Many of the attitudes of the individual have their source and their support in the groups to which the individual gives his allegiance. His attitudes tend to reflect the beliefs, values, and norms of his groups. And to maintain his attitudes, the individual must have the support of like-minded persons. (For a vivid description of a type of person for whom group influences are said to be all-powerful in the determination of beliefs, values, and attitudes, see Box 6.5.) The deviate cannot long oppose a unanimous majority. In his search for social support, he may proselytize and thus secure followers. If he cannot find or form a group which holds views similar to his own, he will collapse into conformity.

If, therefore, we are to understand fully the development of attitudes in the individual, we must examine the role of his group affiliations—his group memberships and his group identifications.

In discussing the influence of the group upon attitude formation we must anticipate briefly our later discussion of the nature of society and culture (see Chapters 9 and 10). A society is a system of interconnected groups. Every individual in a society is a member of a large, inclusive classification of people called a social class. And every individual is a member of small, face-to-face or primary groups; he is, for example, a member of a family group, a religious group, a friendship or clique group.

As a member of a society, the individual shares in the total culture of the society, in his social-class culture, and in the cultures of his various primary groups. The typical actions of the members of a group make up the explicit culture of the group. These typical ways of acting reflect the determining influence of implicit regulatory patterns—beliefs, values, and social norms.

Having in mind this brief statement of the nature of society and culture, we can now examine the role of the group affiliations of the individual in the development of his attitudes. We start by observing that the members of a group tend to hold similar attitudes. This uniformity of attitudes within a group requires explanation.

GROUP BELIEFS AND ATTITUDE DEVELOPMENT

The uniformity in attitudes among the members of a culture group is due, in part, to the fact that the members of the group come to hold common *beliefs* about objects, people, events, issues, etc. (see Boxes 6.6 and 6.7). The differences between the attitudes of different culture groups result in part from the fact that their beliefs are different. The Russian Ivan acquires certain beliefs about the United States from his culture; his attitudes toward the United States rest upon these beliefs. The American Joe learns a different set of beliefs about the United States, and his attitudes will reflect his different understanding or knowledge.

David Riesman, a social scientist at Harvard University, has described a personality type which he believes is becoming more and more common in the upper middle class of urban America— the *other-directed man.*

> What is common to all the other-directed people is that their contemporaries are the source of direction for the individual. . . . This source is of course "internalized" in the sense that dependence on it for guidance in life is implanted early.
>
> Of course, it matters very much who these "others" are: whether they are the individual's immediate circle or a "higher" circle or the anonymous voices of the mass media; whether the individual fears the hostility of chance acquaintances or only of those who "count." But his need for approval and direction from others—and contemporary others rather than ances-tors—goes beyond the reasons that lead most people in any era to care very much what others think of them. While all people want and need to be liked by some of the people some of the time, it is only the modern other-directed types who make this their chief source of direction and chief area of sensitivity. . . .
>
> Approval itself, irrespective of content, becomes almost the unequivocal good in this situa-tion: one makes good when one is approved of. Thus all power, not merely some power, is in the hands of the actual or imaginary approving group, and the child learns from his parent's reactions to him that nothing in his character, no possession he owns, no inheritance of name or talent, no work he has done is valued for itself, but only for its effect on others. Making good becomes almost equivalent to making friends, or at any rate, the right kind of friends. "To him that hath approval, shall be given more approval."

Riesman's analysis has been criticized by some psychologists and sociologists as an overgeneraliza-tion based on impressionistic data. Two further cautions are in order. First, social historians tell us that conformity behavior is not unique to this era or to urban American society. Second, every age has had an effective number of persons who have held and acted on attitudes that are *counter* to the majority. These people are the agents of social change. Despite these reservations, there are some studies to indicate that "other-directedness" is for some persons an important factor in the development of attitudes.

Riesman, D. The lonely crowd. *New Haven, Conn.: Yale Univer. Press, 1950.*

GROUP VALUES AND ATTITUDE DEVELOPMENT

Within a society and within groups in a society many values are shared. These group values play an important role in the develop-ment and organization of the attitudes of the individual.

CENTRALITY OF VALUES. The relation be-tween the values of individuals and their atti-tudes is not, however, a simple one. For one thing, the degree to which the various value systems of the individual shape the develop-ment and organization of his attitudes ap-pears to be a function of the *centrality* of the value systems. For example, the American people share the value that "all men are cre-ated equal" and should receive equal treat-ment and equal opportunity. This is a good; this is what the American people hold *ought to be.* If for an individual this is a central value, his attitudes toward minority groups may be equalitarian. If for him it is not a central value, he may exhibit discriminatory attitudes toward ethnic and racial groups within the American society.

A study by Smith [1947] is one of the few which has attempted to examine the relation between the values of the individual and his attitudes. The study was carried out to test the generality of the findings yielded by an intensive clinical study of the determinants of attitudes (see pages 182 and 211). A sample of 250 adult men in a New England community was interviewed twice. The first interview was designed to secure a description of each man's attitude toward Russia, especially the nature of the most salient beliefs incorporated in his attitude. The second interview yielded information about each man's personality, including his values. Smith found that the nature of the central values of the individual was important in determining the most salient cognitive components of his attitude toward Russia. For example, 36 per cent of those respondents who held "liberty" to be a central value stressed "the lack of freedom and democracy inside Russia," as compared with only 17 per cent of the rest of the respondents. This proved to be the only important difference between the two groups in their attitudes toward Russia.

ONE VALUE—DIFFERENT ATTITUDES. The relation between values and attitudes is further complicated by the fact that the same value may lead different persons to develop different—even opposing—attitudes. For example, the freedom of the individual is a basic American value. In some individuals, this value leads to a strongly favorable attitude toward labor unions; in other individuals, it leads to an equally strong negative attitude. The functional relation between a single value and the attitudes of the individual is influenced by all his other cognitions, values, and attitudes, by his wants, and by his group affiliations. Because of this, we should not expect to find a simple, univocal relation.

GROUP NORMS AND ATTITUDE DEVELOPMENT

We shall see in Chapter 10 that group norms regulate the activities of the participants in standard behavior events. Group norms not only prescribe what are the "right" actions; they also prescribe what are the "right" attitudes.

People are rewarded if they act correctly; they are rewarded if they hold the "right" attitudes. Acting incorrectly or holding "wrong" attitudes is met with social disapproval. The pressure on the individual to conform is great. In Chapters 11 and 14 we shall discuss in detail the various factors that lead people to conform, in their ways of perceiving, feeling, thinking, intending, and acting, to the standards or rules of the groups with which they identify or affiliate themselves.

Group norms are an important aspect of the total culture of a society and of its various group cultures. The homogeneity of the attitudes found within various social groups reflects, in part, the members' acceptance of the norms of these groups.

GROUP INFLUENCES IN ATTITUDE FORMATION

Students of attitude development have long been aware of the vital role that the membership and reference groups of the individual play in the formation of his attitudes. In this section we shall examine the role of the *primary* or face-to-face groups of which the individual is a member, and the role of his *reference* groups—groups with which he identifies, whether or not he belongs to them.

PRIMARY-GROUP INFLUENCES. Many investigators hold that primary-group influences are a major determinant of attitude development. An illustration is found in the voting study by Campbell, Gurin, and Miller [1954], another part of which we have cited earlier (see Box 5.14, page 174). These investigators sought to determine the extent of homogeneity of political attitudes in three significant primary groups. In post-election interviews, all respondents were asked how their *friends* had voted; married people were asked how their *spouses* had voted, and unmarried people were asked about their *families*; those respondents

BOX 6.6: *Common beliefs . . .*

In 1932 Daniel Katz and Kenneth W. Braly asked 100 Princeton students to give the five traits that they considered most characteristic of ten different ethnic groups. The traits were to be selected from a list of 84 adjectives, but the students were allowed to add trait names of their own choosing if they wished.

In 1950 G. M. Gilbert repeated the Katz and Braly study, using the same procedure, with 333 Princeton students. The following lists present the traits most frequently checked (and the percentage of students checking them) in both 1932 and 1950 as descriptive of three of the ethnic groups.

Trait	*1932*	*1950*	*Difference*
Germans:			
Scientifically minded	78	62	−16
Industrious	65	50	−15
Stolid	44	10	−34
Intelligent	32	32	0
Methodical	31	20	−11
Extremely nationalistic	24	50	+26
Negroes:			
Superstitious	84	41	−43
Lazy	75	31	−44
Happy-go-lucky	38	17	−21
Ignorant	38	24	−14
Musical	26	33	+7
Ostentatious	26	11	−15
Very religious	24	17	−7
Stupid	22	10	−12
Jews:			
Shrewd	79	47	−32
Mercenary	49	28	−21
Industrious	48	29	−19
Grasping	34	17	−17
Intelligent	29	37	+8
Ambitious	21	28	+7

A comparison of the 1932 and 1950 data shows considerable *stability* of ethnic stereotypes. (In the case of the Germans, the stereotype has changed in a negative direction presumably as a result of the atrocities of the Nazis before and during World War II.) The data also demonstrate, however, considerable reduction in the *homogeneity* of ethnic stereotypes. In the 1950 study no trait was assigned to any group by as many as 70 per cent of the students, as was the case in 1932.

Katz, D., and Braly, K. W. *Racial stereotypes of 100 college students.* J. abnorm. soc. Psychol., *1933, **28**, 280–290.*

Gilbert, G. M. *Stereotype persistence and change among college students.* J. abnorm. soc. Psychol., *1951, **46**, 245–254.*

SOCIAL ATTITUDES

The common beliefs of the American people about ethnic and minority groups support common and relatively stable prejudices. A study that demonstrates the communality and stability of the order of preference for ethnic groups among Americans is that of Eugene Hartley, social psychologist at the College of the City of New York.

Using a slightly modified form of the Bogardus social-distance scale (see page 153), Hartley determined the racial preferences of students from eight different colleges and universities chosen because of the diversity of the backgrounds, ethnic stock, socioeconomic status, and professional interests of their students. These institutions were Bennington College, Columbia University, College of the City of New York (Arts), College of the City of New York (Business), Howard University, Princeton University, a state normal school, and a state teachers college. A comparison of the results obtained from these different groups indicates high agreement in their social-distance placements, the correlation coefficients ranging from .68 to .95. In other words, the boys at Princeton, at C.C.N.Y., at Howard University, and at Columbia display the same pattern of racial preferences as do the girls at Bennington, the students at the state normal school and teachers college, and commercial students at C.C.N.Y.

The stability, over time, of the pattern of racial preferences is indicated in Hartley's comparison of his results with those of Bogardus obtained about two decades earlier. Bogardus obtained the preference ratings of a sample of 1,725 Americans, representing a general cross section of the country, for 40 different nationalities and races, including 26 of the groups used in Hartley's study. Hartley has computed that the percentage of students unwilling to admit each of these 26 nationalities to citizenship correlates .78 with the comparable index from the Bogardus study.

This is the "American dilemma" described by the Swedish social scientist, Gunnar Myrdal: the American creed of equal opportunity under the law on the one hand; the existence of widespread discriminatory preferences on the other.

Bogardus, E. S. Immigration and race attitudes. Boston: Heath, 1928.

Hartley, E. L. Problems in prejudice. New York: King's Crown Press, 1946.

who worked with other people were asked how their *work associates* had voted. As the results in Table 6.1 show, the homogeneity of political behavior within the three primary groups examined in this study is remarkably high. For example, when the respondents' friends voted for the Democratic candidate (at least as so reported by him), 83 per cent of the respondents also voted Democratic; when the respondents' friends voted Republican, 84 per cent of the respondents also voted Republican.

THE FAMILY AND POLITICS. The significance of the family in determining political attitudes is also seen in the large-scale panel studies of the determinants of voting behavior carried out by Lazarsfeld, Berelson, and Gaudet [1944] in Erie County, Ohio, during the 1940 presidential campaign and by Berelson, Laz-

arsfeld, and McPhee [1954] in Elmira, New York, during the 1948 campaign. (The panel technique involves the repeated interviewing of a small sample.) Between two-thirds and three-fourths of the voters voted for the party of their fathers. This may be due, in part, to the fact that parents and children generally belong to the same social class and religious groups. In the Elmira study, however, it was found that the votes of persons whose social-class position conflicted with their family background (e.g., upper-middle-class persons with Democratic parents, or working-class persons with Republican parents) were as often determined by the family group as by the larger social-class group. In their study of a national sample of college graduates, Haveman and West [1952] found that high-income

TABLE 6.1: RELATION BETWEEN 1952 VOTING BEHAVIOR OF THE INDIVIDUAL AND MEMBERS OF HIS PRIMARY GROUPS [Adapted from Campbell, Gurin, and Miller, 1954]

VOTE OF PRIMARY GROUP	HOW RESPONDENTS VOTED, PER CENT		
	Republican (Eisenhower)	*Democratic* (Stevenson)	*Other*
How spouses voted:			
Democratic	11	88	1
Republican	93	7	0
How families voted:			
Democratic	20	79	1
Republican	91	8	1
Split	41	54	5
How friends voted:			
Democratic	17	83	0
Republican	84	15	1
Evenly split	47	50	3
How work associates voted:			
Democratic	20	78	2
Republican	76	24	0
Evenly split	55	43	2

college graduates who came from Democratic families either tended to remain Democrats or, if they broke with the political tradition of their families, reported themselves to be "Independents." College graduates from Republican families were found to be much less likely to change their political preferences.

MECHANISMS OF PRIMARY-GROUP INFLU-ENCES. There can be little question that the attitudes of people stem in part from their primary-group affiliations. However, the complex and subtle means by which the group influences the individual are not revealed by correlational studies such as those reviewed above. The homogeneity of attitudes within primary groups may be interpreted in at least four different ways. First, and this is the most common interpretation, group pressures for conformity may *induce* homogeneity among members of a group. A second possible interpretation is that individuals tend to *seek out* groups in which the prevailing attitudes are congenial. Just as individuals "tune in" on propaganda which supports their established attitudes, so may individuals search for groups which support their existing attitudes. Third, the members of primary groups tend to be *exposed to the same information*—both because they share a common subculture and because they are important sources of information for one another. Finally, new members of a group *take on* the attitudes of the group as a means of "buying acceptance" by the group (see Box 6.8).

It is possible that all four of the above processes operate simultaneously. To evaluate the significance of correlational studies and to understand the role and limitations of primary-group influences require a closer analysis of the fundamental psychological processes involved.

Groups do not operate by simply "giving" attitudes to individuals. The influence of the family, the school, the church, or neighborhood companions is more indirect and complex. Each group operates not in a piecemeal fashion, but in terms of a pattern of influ-ences. These group influences create and limit the situations for the individual out of which arise his cognitions, feelings, and action tendencies which become organized into his attitudes.

The relation between the influence of cul-tural pressures and the resulting attitudes is so complex that in some instances the effect of primary groups can be seen to account for the rise of an attitude in the individual that is in opposition to the attitude of the primary group. Thus the behavior of the parents may induce the child to revolt against parental authority. His rejection of parental authority, in turn, may express itself through the adop-tion of attitudes toward God or militarism or alcohol that are directly (and perhaps delib-erately) opposed to those held by the parents. In such cases, of course, the relation between parents' and children's attitudes will be nega-tive; in other cases, the relation will be posi-tive. Therefore, the mere existence of a low correlation, or even of no correlation at all, tells us very little about the actual mechanics of the influence of parents' attitudes upon their children.

Although the effect of group influences on the formation of attitudes is indirect, complex, and limited by the wants of the individual, a proper recognition of group influences is nonetheless essential if we are to understand the conditions that must be fulfilled before an individual's attitudes can be changed. The significance of this will be shown in the next chapter.

REFERENCE-GROUP INFLUENCES. The mem-bership groups of the individual shape the formation of his attitudes only in so far as the individual identifies with them, that is, uses them as reference groups. Nonmembership groups may also function as reference groups for the individual and importantly influence his attitude development.

For example, the son of an unskilled worker who aspires to middle-class status will tend to accept middle-class values and attitudes. His

middle-class outlook will embrace such diverse objects as sexual practices and political issues. Upward mobile, he will reject the values and attitudes of his lower-class family (see page 334).

SALIENCE OF RELIGIOUS REFERENCE GROUPS. Rossi and Rossi [1961] have studied the sali-ence of religious leaders as reference individ-uals in "Bay City," an industrial community in Massachusetts.

Each respondent was asked to designate the individuals and groups he would look to for advice and guidance in making up his mind on local issues. These were taken to be his *potential* reference individuals and groups. He was also asked whether or not these poten-tial reference individuals had been "helpful" in making up his mind in a recent local elec-tion. The answers to this question were taken to indicate his *actual* reference individuals or groups.

The results of the survey are given in Table 6.2. Parochial school Catholics are most likely to cite religious leaders as both potential and actual reference individuals. Further, it can be seen that all Catholics are more likely to turn to their religious leaders for guidance on educational issues than are Protestants. The table also shows that the potential influ-ence of the Catholic clergy is greater than their actual influence.

For another study of the salience of reli-gious reference groups, see Box 6.9.

TO RECAPITULATE

The group affiliations of the individual play a vital role in the formation of his attitudes. Both the membership groups with which the individual affiliates and the nonmembership groups to which he aspires to belong are im-portant in shaping his attitudes.

But the individual does not passively ab-sorb the prevailing attitudes in the various groups with which he affiliates. Attitudes, like cognitions, develop selectively in the process of want satisfaction. The individual will pick

TABLE 6.2: PERCENTAGES CITING RELIGIOUS LEADERS AS POTENTIAL AND ACTUAL REFERENCE INDIVIDUALS [Adapted from Rossi and Rossi, 1961]

	Religious leaders as potential reference individuals on educational issues	*Religious leaders as actual reference individuals on school board elections*
Parochial school Catholics	53	24
Public school Catholics	34 ⎫	
Public school Protestants	22 ⎭	18

BOX 6.8: *Combat veteran and green recruit*

During World War II, the Research Branch of the Information and Education Division of the War Department carried out a monumental series of studies of the morale attitudes of American soldiers. These studies are reported in the four volumes of *The American Soldier*.

In Volume II, entitled *Combat and Its Aftermath*, appears a study of (1) soldiers who were members of divisions composed entirely of green troops (i.e., troops without combat experience), (2) soldiers who served as green replacement members in Division A composed of combat veterans, (3) combat veterans in Division A. The willingness for combat of these three groups was ascertained through the following question: "Which of the following best tells the way you feel about getting into an actual battle zone?"

The answer categories were as follows (the first three being considered to indicate willingness for combat):

_____I want very much to get into it just as soon as possible.
_____I'm ready to go anytime.
_____I'd like to go before it's over, but I don't think I'm ready yet.
_____I hope I won't have to go but if I do I think I'll do all right.
_____I hope I won't have to go because I don't think I would do very well.
_____No opinion.

The following table summarizes the answers obtained.

	N	*Per cent indicating willingness*
Division A veterans	605	15
Division A replacements	427	28
Inexperienced divisions	9,850	48

Note that the green replacement members of Division A are midway between troops in inexperienced divisions and the veterans of Division A in willingness for combat. This finding is understandable when one knows that the common attitude of veterans toward combat was that "war is hell." The authors comment:

and choose among the attitudes offered to him those which are want-satisfying. And every individual affiliates with many groups, which may endorse congruent or incongruent attitudes. The effect of group influences on the formation of attitudes is thus indirect and complex.

GUIDE 18: *The attitudes of the individual reflect his personality*

We have seen that one of the effects of group influences upon attitude development is to produce uniformity of attitudes among the members of various social groups. But in the midst of uniformity we have also seen diversity. A major factor making for diversity that we have not yet discussed is the existence of personality differences among individuals.

The examination of the role of personality in the organization and functioning of attitudes has a long history. Early students of the problem tended to seek for rather simple personality correlates of attitudes. For example, Vetter [1930] and Dexter [1939] studied the role of such personality traits as introversion-

---

Probably the strongest group code (among combat men) was the taboo against any talk of a flag-waving variety. The core of the attitude *among combat* men seemed to be that talk that did not subordinate idealistic values and patriotism to the harsh realities of the combat situation was hypocritical and a person who expressed such ideas, a hypocrite.

Green replacements motivated to affiliate themselves with the combat veteran group adopted a negative attitude toward combat. The dominant unfavorable attitude of the veteran group about combat is accepted by the green replacement as his "social entrance ticket" to the combat division. Additional data on Division A are available which furnish a partial check on this interpretation. If the attitudes of replacements in veteran companies of a division were affected by the attitudes of their veteran associates, we should find that replacements who joined companies in which relatively favorable attitudes toward combat existed would themselves develop favorable attitudes toward combat, and that those who joined companies in which the common attitude of veterans was unfavorable would develop unfavorable attitudes toward combat.

A survey of the attitude toward combat of veterans in Division A had previously been made in January, 1944, prior to the main influx of replacements. The results of this survey describe the common attitudes prevailing in the companies of the division when the replacements were being assimilated.

The 36 companies of the division were ranked according to the percentage of veterans in them who expressed a favorable attitude toward combat in the January survey. Group I consisted of the nine companies in which the percentage of *veterans* expressing favorable attitudes was the highest; group III consisted of the nine companies in which the percentage of *veterans* expressing favorable attitudes was lowest; group II included the intermediate companies. The attitudes of the *green replacements* toward combat in each of these three groups, as determined in the April survey, are as follows: group I, 40 per cent; group II, 28 per cent; group III, 24 per cent. We see that a markedly higher percentage of green replacements who joined group I companies than green replacements who joined group III companies came to develop favorable attitudes toward combat.

Stouffer, S. A., Lumsdaine, A. A., Lumsdaine, M. H., Williams, R. M., Jr., Smith, M. B., Janis, I. L., Star, S. A., and Cottrell, L. S., Jr. The American soldier, vol. II, Combat and its aftermath. Princeton, N.J.: Princeton Univer. Press, 1949.

Philip Converse and Angus Campbell, of the Survey Research Center of the University of Michigan, report evidence on the question of the effect of salience of religious reference groups upon the vote.

They examined the votes of Catholics and non-Catholics in congressional races in the 1956 campaign which pitted a Catholic candidate against a non-Catholic candidate. Voters have been found to be relatively uninformed about the congressional candidates for whom they vote. In their analysis, Converse and Campbell restricted their comparison to voters who were able to recall the name of the candidate for whom they voted, on the assumption that these respondents would be most likely to be aware of the religious-group membership of the candidate.

The following table gives the votes for Catholic candidates in races in which they were running against non-Catholic candidates of three groups of voters: (1) Catholic voters who had a high degree of identification with their church; (2) Catholic voters who had a low degree of identification with their church; (3) non-Catholic voters. Degree of identification was measured by combining responses to the following two questions:

"Would you say you feel pretty close to Catholics in general or that you don't feel much closer to them than you do to other kinds of people?"

"How much interest would you say you have in how Catholics as a whole are getting along in this country? Do you have a good deal of interest in it, some interest, or not much interest at all?"

| | CATHOLIC IDENTIFICATION | | TOTAL | NON-CATHOLIC |
	High	*Low*	CATHOLIC	VOTERS
U.S. House of Representatives	85%	69%	77%	51%
U.S. Senate	86	57	70	49

The data in the above table show that Catholic voters favored Catholic candidates by an increment of 20 to 25 per cent over a non-Catholic group equated to the Catholic group in all other relevant respects. Remember that this table is restricted to those voters most likely to be aware of the candidate's religious affiliation. The data for *all* Catholic voters, including those for whom salience of religious group membership is low (because they are not aware of the candidate's religious affiliation), show Catholic candidates favored by only a 12 per cent increment over a non-Catholic control group.

The data in the table also reveal that Catholics who have a high degree of identification with their Catholic religious group "vote Catholic" to a greater degree than Catholics with a low degree of identification.

Converse, P., and Campbell, A. Political standards in secondary groups. In D. Cartwright and A. Zander (Eds.), Group dynamics. (Rev. Ed.) Evanston, Ill.: Row, Peterson, 1960.

extroversion and ascendancy-submissiveness in the development of "conservatism-radicalism." Such pioneering studies suffered from inadequate measurement both of personality traits and of attitudes.

Later studies came to place greater stress on the search for more *general* personality patterns which could help account for attitudes. We will review a few of such studies that have been concerned with religious attitudes, ethnocentric attitudes, political attitudes, and internationalist attitudes.

PERSONALITY AND RELIGIOUS ATTITUDES

French [1947] made a careful attempt to characterize the differentiation, clarity, intensity, and integration of the religious attitudes held by each of her subjects. She found that some of her subjects had highly organized religious attitudes, characterized by considerable differentiation and integration among the parts of the attitude system, relatively few unconscious components, low emotional intensity, and the like. Other subjects had much less highly organized religious attitudes.

French also undertook an exhaustive analysis of the general personality make-up of each subject by the use of over 20 tests and devices. These included the Thematic Apperception Test, the Allport-Vernon Study of Values, intensive interviews, written autobiographies, the Scholastic Aptitude Test, and other measures of intellect. Subjects who had highly organized religious attitudes—regardless of whether they were religious, agnostic, or atheistic—proved to be noticeably different in personality structure from the subjects who had less highly organized religious attitudes. French summarizes some of her data as follows:

> The "highs" may be described as . . . persons who consciously recognize and accept both strengths and weaknesses as parts of their selves. The "less highs," on the other hand . . . are persons who accept only what is good as part of their selves and who suppress or repress what is bad.

PERSONALITY AND ETHNOCENTRISM

Probably the most extensive study of the relation between attitudes and personality dynamics is that of Adorno et al. [1950]. These investigators were guided by the over-all hypothesis that "the political, economic and social convictions of an individual often form a broad and coherent pattern . . . and . . . this pattern is an expression of deep-lying trends in his personality."

The authors first examined the organization of anti-Semitic attitudes. They posed this question: Do various beliefs and feelings about Jews constitute a unitary attitude? To answer the question, they constructed five scales to measure their respondents' beliefs about (1) the "offensiveness" of Jews; (2) their "threatening" character; (3) their "seclusiveness"; (4) their "intrusiveness"; (5) the need for "segregation" of Jews. The intercorrelations among these scales were found to be relatively high, ranging in a student sample from .74 to .85. The authors concluded that beliefs and feelings about Jews form a fairly consistent attitude system.

The investigators next examined the question of whether anti-Semitism is a specific attitude or an aspect of a more inclusive general attitude of rejection of all minority groups. An *ethnocentrism* scale was developed which consisted of three subscales to measure attitudes toward Negroes, toward minority groups other than Jews and Negroes, and toward the United States as an in-group as contrasted with other nations as out-groups. The intercorrelations among the three subscales were high, ranging in different samples from .74 to .83. This was taken as evidence that ethnocentrism is also a fairly consistent attitude system. The relation between anti-Semitism and ethnocentrism in a sample of college students was examined, and the correlation was found to be .80. The authors concluded that ethnocentric attitudes, including anti-Semitism, "form a broad and coherent pattern," thus confirming the first half of the over-all hypothesis of the study.

Is this pattern "an expression of deep-lying trends in his [the individual's] personality"? This question was approached in two ways. First, a scale was constructed to measure ways of feeling and thinking assumed to characterize people who have a readiness to accept an antidemocratic ideology. This scale was called the F (Fascism) scale. The first form of the F scale correlated .65 with ethnocentrism. In later forms, purified to increase the power of the scale to predict ethnocentrism, the correlations were higher, form 4 showing a correlation of .77. The investigators tentatively concluded that "the conception of a potentially fascistic pattern can be considerably extended, and . . . the hypothesis of central personality dispositions which give rise to this pattern is lent considerable support."

The second and main approach to the study of the personality correlates of ethnocentrism involved the use of an intensive clinical interview which covered such topics as vocational aspirations and work attitudes, religious attitudes and behavior, family background, parent-child relationships, pattern of sexuality, personal relationships, educational interests, political attitudes and opinions, and attitudes toward minority groups. Eighty persons were interviewed, 45 subjects who were extremely high on anti-Semitism ("Highs") and 35 who were low ("Lows"). This sample was quite heterogeneous. It included psychiatric patients, undergraduate students, merchant-marine student officers, prison inmates, divinity students, unemployed war veterans, professional women, medical students, university extension students, and summer school students. An attempt was made to balance the Highs and Lows in terms of age, sex, political and religious affiliations, and national or regional background, but they were not matched for education.

The interviews were rated by independent judges on each of a large number of categories which covered (1) factual material, such as childhood events; (2) attitudinal measures, such as attitudes toward the role of self, parents, opposite sex; (3) interpretative dimensions. The rating categories used were based on specific hypotheses about the personality correlates of ethnocentrism. The judges who rated the interviews had not interviewed the subjects and were not informed about their prejudice scores. The interviewers, however, did have prior knowledge of the prejudice scores of their subjects.

Analysis of the mean ratings of the Highs and Lows on the various categories revealed that the two groups differed significantly on

a large number of personality variables as predicted by the guiding hypotheses. The major differences between the two groups are shown in Box 6.10.

The authors summarize their conclusions regarding the relation between ethnocentric attitudes and personality trends as follows:

The most crucial result of the present study, as it seems to the authors, is the demonstration of close correspondence in the type of approach and outlook a subject is likely to have in a great variety of areas, ranging from the most intimate features of family and sex adjustments, through relationships to other people in general, to religion and to social and political philosophy. Thus a basically hierarchical, authoritarian, exploitive parent-child relationship is apt to carry over into a power-oriented, exploitively dependent attitude toward one's sex partner and one's God and may well culminate in a political philosophy and social outlook which has no room for anything but a desperate clinging to what appears to be strong and disdainful rejection of whatever is relegated to the bottom. . . . Conventionality, rigidity, repressive denial, and the ensuing breakthrough of one's weakness, fear and dependency are but other aspects of the same fundamental personality pattern, and they can be observed in personal life as well as in attitudes toward religion and social issues. . . .

On the other hand, there is a pattern characterized chiefly by affectionate, basically equalitarian, and permissive interpersonal relationships. This pattern encompasses attitudes within the family and toward the opposite sex, as well as an internalization of religious and social values. Greater flexibility and the potentiality for more genuine satisfactions appear as results of this basic attitude.

BY WAY OF CRITICISM. Hyman and Sheatsley [1954] have pointed out a number of methodological weaknesses in the foregoing study that lead them to question the authors' interpretation of their findings.

First, sampling biases in the selection of subjects may have led to an overstatement of the degree of organization of attitudes and of the relation of attitudes to personality variables. The subjects, other than college students, were members of formal groups. As Hyman and Sheatsley point out, members of organized groups may be expected to show more organization of their attitudes than nonmembers because of the influence of the group ideology. We may also expect to find a closer relation between attitudes and personality in group members because of the common personality characteristics that initially led the different members to join the same group. Moreover, college students who comprised the rest of the sample, may be expected to show a more interconnected attitude constellation than the general population and to relate their attitudes to personality. Hyman and Sheatsley cite a study by Srole [1951] in which the correlations between prejudice and F-scale scores in three different educational groups were compared. In the low-education group the correlation was negligible; in the high school group, it was moderate; in the college group, it was sizable.

Second, the subjects were relatively homogeneous in sociocultural background, thus minimizing the role of social and cultural factors in the development of prejudice. Third, these findings on extreme Highs and Lows may not permit generalizations to less extreme individuals. Fourth, the correlation

BOX 6.10: *Personality and prejudice*

T. W. Adorno, Else Frenkel-Brunswik, Daniel J. Levinson, and R. Nevitt Sanford, University of California psychologists, in their study of "The Authoritarian Personality," intensively interviewed 45 persons who scored in the top quartile of the cases on anti-Semitism or ethnocentrism scales and 35 persons who scored in the bottom quartile. These two extreme groups were found to differ significantly in the following personality characteristics and childhood experiences:

HIGH ETHNOCENTRIC SCORERS	LOW ETHNOCENTRIC SCORERS
Personality differences	
Rejects socially unacceptable impulses as part of self	Accepts socially unacceptable impulses as part of self
Externalizes socially unacceptable impulses (fear, weakness, sex, and aggressive feelings) through projection	Internalizes and ruminates about socially unacceptable impulses in self
Holds conventional values and rules—conventional admiration of parents	Holds more intrinsic and socially constructive values—realistic appraisal of parents
Power-oriented in personal relationships	Affectional and love-oriented in personal relationships
Rigid personality organization	Flexible personality organization
Differences in childhood situation	
Harsh, threatening parental discipline	Reasonable parental discipline
Parental love conditional upon display of approved behavior	Unconditional parental love
Hierarchical family structure	Equalitarian family structure
Concerned about family status	Unconcerned about family status

Adorno, T. W., Frenkel-Brunswik, E., Levinson, D. J., and Sanford, R. N. The authoritarian personality. *New York: Harper, 1950.*

BOX 6.11: *Personality and education*

Herbert H. Hyman, psychologist, and Paul Sheatsley, sociologist, in their critique of the methods used in the study of "The Authoritarian Personality," report the following differences in responses to items taken from the F scale among three different educational groups.

| | PERCENTAGES AGREEING | | |
SCALE ITEM	College education	High school	Grammar school
The most important thing to teach children is absolute obedience to their parents	35	60	80
Any good leader should be strict with people under him in order to gain their respect	36	51	66
Prison is too good for sex criminals. They should be publicly whipped or worse	18	31	45
There are two kinds of people in the world: the weak and the strong	30	53	71
No decent man can respect a woman who has had sex relations before marriage	14	26	39

Note that these differences in responses to the F-scale items seem to parallel the differences found by Adorno et al. among their prejudiced and unprejudiced subjects. That is, in general, the college group responds to these items in a manner similar to that of the unprejudiced; the grammar school group, in a manner similar to that of the prejudiced.

Hyman and Sheatsley comment:

> We are certainly not implying that ethnocentrism is caused by lack of education or that formal education determines basic personality structure, but we contend that the significance of these personality variables to the problem of ethnocentrism seems dubious in the light of the known correlation with education of many of the indices employed, and the failure to take account of this factor in the analysis of the two groups.

Hyman, H. H., and Sheatsley, P. B. The authoritarian personality: a methodological critique. In R. Christie and Marie Jahoda (Eds.), Studies in the scope and method of "the authoritarian personality." Glencoe, Ill.: Free Press, 1954.

between scores on the ethnocentrism scale and scores on the later revisions of the F scale cannot be accepted as valid evidence of a relation between ethnocentrism and personality trends because the F scale was purified to increase its power to predict scores on the ethnocentrism scale. Fifth, the relation between ethnocentric attitudes and personality factors was, in the main, established through intensive clinical interviews with high-scoring and low-scoring subjects. The interviewers knew the attitude-scale scores of their subjects before the interview and thus they may have

systematically biased the interview data.

Perhaps the most serious further criticism of the study advanced by Hyman and Sheatsley is that the differences between the high-scoring and low-scoring subjects in personality trends may be due to uncontrolled differences between the two groups in amount of formal education. Representative sample surveys of the adult American population have revealed differences between educational groups in traits similar to those which differentiate the Highs and Lows (see Box 6.11).

Support for the criticism that uncontrolled

educational differences may possibly be a vitiating variable is provided by a study by Martin and Westie [1959]. In this study, a random sample was drawn of 100 blocks in the city of Indianapolis which contained no Negro residents. Every second household in these blocks was visited. An adult member of the household was tested on a short prejudice scale which served as a screening device. Of the 420 subjects who completed the screening scale those scoring high or low were then given a more intensive attitude test. On this latter test, 41 persons were found who could be labeled "Tolerant," and 59 who could be labeled "Prejudiced."

The Tolerant and Prejudiced subjects were then compared with respect to 25 social and personality variables. The scores of these two groups on some of the personality measures are presented in Figure 6.2. Note that the findings support the results reported in the study of "The Authoritarian Personality." However, a comparison of the amount of education of the two groups revealed that the Tolerants had a significantly higher educational status than the Prejudiced. The mean number of years of schooling of the Tolerants was 14.8, whereas the mean of the Prejudiced was only 11.6.

Despite the methodological weaknesses in the study of "The Authoritarian Personality," the work is an impressive achievement, guided by systematic theory and illumined by psychological insights into the function of prejudice for the prejudiced. Furthermore, a review of studies using the California F Scale during the period from 1950 to 1955 [Titus and Hollander, 1957] reveals more proof than disproof of the hypothesis that repression and projection are functionally related to racial prejudice. It seems to be fairly well established that ethnocentric attitudes may be expressions of "deeper" personality trends. (For one of the studies which confirms the findings of "The Authoritarian Personality," see Box 6.12.)

Allport and Kramer [1946] have estimated that "at least four-fifths of the American population lead mental lives in which feelings of group hostility play an appreciable role." Are we to conclude, then, that all this widespread prejudice is essentially a defense of the self? Certainly not. The "pathology of prejudice" is but a small part of the story of prejudice. For most persons prejudice may mainly represent conformity to community norms (see Box 6.13).

PERSONALITY AND POLITICAL ATTITUDES

McClosky [1958] has made an intensive study of the personality make-up of the extreme political conservative in America. A 12-item Conservatism scale was first constructed, the items reflecting the kinds of social and political beliefs traditionally found in the credo of conservative political philosophies. Table 6.3 shows that persons scoring

TABLE 6.3: PERCENTAGE OF EXTREME CONSERVATIVES AND LIBERALS ENDORSING CONSERVATIVE ITEMS [After McClosky, 1958]

| | AGREEMENT, PER CENT | |
ITEMS	Liberals	Extreme conservatives
Duties are more important than rights	32	63
You can't change human nature	30	73
The heart is as good a guide as the head	22	58
No matter what people think, a few people will always run things anyway	33	63
Few people really know what is in their best interest in the long run	43	77

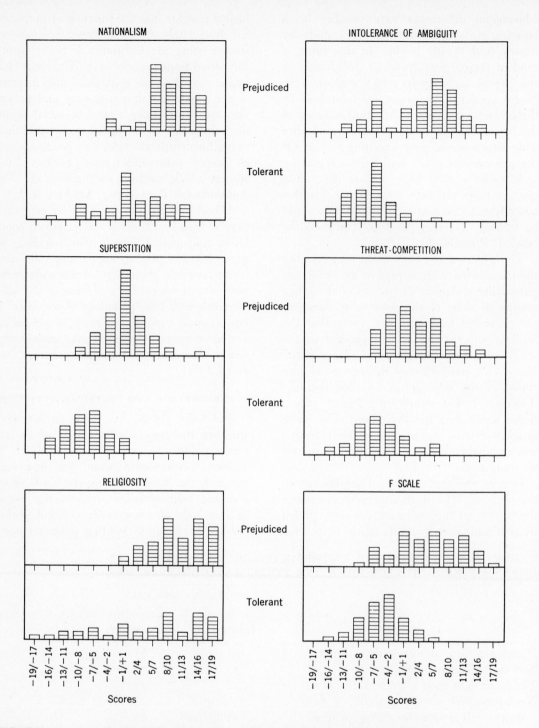

FIGURE 6.2: Distributions of comparative attitude and personality scores of tolerant persons and persons prejudiced against the Negro. [Martin and Westie, 1959.]

Howard P. Smith and Ellen W. Rosen when at Bennington College experimentally asked whether the personality make-up of the "nationalist" may closely resemble the authoritarian personality described by Adorno et al. A W scale designed to measure the general attitude of "world-mindedness" was used in the study. Two illustrative items in the scale are:

We should be willing to fight for our country without questioning whether it is right or wrong. (Scored minus)

All national governments ought to be abolished and replaced by one central world government. (Scored plus)

From a group of 193 summer school students the 20 subjects with the lowest scores (L-W group) and the 20 subjects with the highest scores (H-W group) were selected for further study. These two groups were highly similar in age, sex, education, socioeconomic status, and place of residence.

Each student was given a standardized interview designed primarily to measure attitudes toward world affairs and toward his parents. Each student also completed the F scale and a number of paper-and-pencil personality tests designed to measure 12 personality variables that had been found to differentiate high and low authoritarian subjects.

As expected, the H-W subjects had a significantly lower mean score on the F scale (49.6) than did the L-W subjects (91.3). The differences between the H-W and L-W subjects on the 12 personality traits and parent-child variables that were measured were consistent with the differences between high and low authoritarians found by Adorno et al. Some of these differences are shown below.

	MEAN SCORES	
	H-W	*L-W*
Personality traits:		
Self-expressiveness	23	6
Equalitarianism	18	9
Stereotypy	21	65
Independence	27	8
Compliance	13	45

	NUMBER OF SUBJECTS	
	H-W	*L-W*
Parent-child variables:		
Criticism of parents	12	6
Strict discipline	5	13
Obedient reaction	3	13

The investigators interpret their findings as follows:

The results indicate that the world-mindedness dimension is closely (and inversely) related to the dimension of authoritarianism and it is parsimonious to consider them as slightly different aspects of the same basic personality structure. . . .

Smith, H. P., and Rosen, Ellen W. Some psychological correlates of world mindedness and authoritarianism. J. Pers., 1958, 26, 170–183.

BOX 6.13: *Apartheid*

The importance of cultural norms in the development of racial prejudice is brought out by studies of racial prejudice in the Union of South Africa and in the United States carried out by Thomas F. Pettigrew of Harvard University.

In his South African study, Pettigrew administered to 620 white undergraduates at the English-speaking University of Natal three scales which measured authoritarianism, social conformity, and negative attitudes toward native (black) Africans.

These students showed considerable prejudice against native Africans. For example, 69 per cent agreed that "manual labor seems to fit the native mentality better than more skilled and responsible work."

Despite their extreme prejudice, these South African students were *not* more authoritarian than the less prejudiced American college students. This suggests that personality factors such as authoritarianism cannot completely account for the intense prejudice of the South African students.

The importance of sociocultural factors in the development of prejudice in this group is made clear by a number of additional findings. First, the students who were born on the African continent were significantly more prejudiced toward black Africans than were students not born on the continent. And yet the two groups did not differ in authoritarianism. Second, students who supported the Nationalist party—the extreme pro-*Apartheid* party—were significantly more prejudiced than were their fellow undergraduates. Again, these two groups did not differ in authoritarianism. Finally, the white Afrikaner-speaking students were significantly more hostile toward the black Africans than were the English-speaking students; but, on the other hand, the English-speaking students were considerably more prejudiced toward the African *Indian* than were the Afrikaner-speaking students. Thus one-fifth of the English-speaking students said they "wish someone would kill all of them [South African Indians]."

In his American study Pettigrew interviewed white adults living in four small Southern towns (where the Negro population ranged from 10 to 45 per cent) and white adults living in four roughly comparable towns in New England (where the Negro population was less than 1 per cent).

The Southern sample was considerably more anti-Negro than the Northern sample but was *not* more authoritarian. In the Southern sample, cultural conformity as indicated by churchgoing is associated with anti-Negro attitudes. In the North, Protestant churchgoers tended to be more tolerant than nonattenders.

Prejudice apparently reflects cultural norms. Personality factors alone are not sufficient to explain prejudice.

> Pettigrew, T. F. *Personality and sociocultural factors in intergroup attitudes, a cross-national comparison.* J. Conflict Resolution, *1958, 2, 29–42.*

as extreme conservatives on the scale endorse far more frequently than do liberals a variety of statements often thought to mirror a "conservative" outlook. (The items in Table 6.3 were not, of course, in the final scale.) The scale appears, then, to have some degree of "internal" validity.

The Conservatism scale and 52 other scales, constituted to measure other attitudes and personality factors, were administered to a cross-section sample of 1,211 persons in the twin cities of Minneapolis and St. Paul. The subjects were divided into four groups—liberal, moderate liberal, moderate conservative, extreme conservative—on the basis of scores on the Conservatism scale.

One of the clearest findings in the study was that conservatism is not the political doctrine of the intellectual elite. On the contrary, as the first part of Table 6.4 shows, conservative attitudes tend to characterize the uninformed, the poorly educated, and the unintelligent. The Awareness scale is a measure "of . . . the clarity of one's grasp of the social process, past and present. It serves, to some extent, as a crude intelligence test. The same can be said, though less authoritatively, for the Intellectuality scale, which measures the degree to which intellectual habits have been formed and are perceived as attractive." (In Table 6.4, "high" means a score in the top third of the scale named; "low" means a score in the bottom third.)

McClosky also developed a number of scales to measure interpersonal response traits and other personality traits which govern the individual's social behavior. Table 6.4 shows that the extreme political conservatives tend to fall at the "undesirable" end of the distribution of every one of these social traits. As McClosky comments:

Conservatism, in our society at least, appears to be far more characteristic of social isolates, of people who think poorly of themselves, who suffer personal disgruntlement and frustration, who are submissive, timid, and wanting in confidence, who lack a clear sense of direction and purpose [anomie], who are uncertain about their values [alienation], and who are generally bewildered by the alarming task of having to thread their way through a society which seems to them too complex to fathom.

On scales designed to measure "clinical" or "psychiatric" personality traits, the extreme conservatives also come out badly. As Table 6.4 shows,

The extreme conservatives are easily the most hostile and suspicious, the most rigid and compulsive, the quickest to condemn others for their imperfections or weaknesses, the most intolerant, the most easily moved to scorn and

TABLE 6.4: PERCENTAGES OF CONSERVATIVES AND LIBERALS CHARACTERIZED BY VARIOUS TRAITS [After McClosky, 1958]

Trait	Liberals	Moderate liberals	Moderate conservatives	Extreme conservatives
Grade school education only	9%	14%	29%	49%
Scoring low on awareness	9	25	45	66
Scoring low on intellectuality	7	20	34	56
Low on dominance	9	19	37	51
Low on social responsibility	12	25	36	62
Low on self-confidence	18	23	32	35
High in anomie	4	16	30	59
High in alienation	11	20	27	45
High in bewilderment	9	20	34	57
High in guilt	16	18	28	47
High in hostility	18	37	46	71
High in contempt for weakness	8	18	29	55
High in ego defense	11	20	38	60
High in intolerance of human frailty	8	16	23	54

disappointment in others, the most inflexible and unyielding in their perceptions and judgments. Although aggressively critical of the shortcomings of others, they are unusually defensive and armored in the protection of their own ego needs. Poorly integrated psychologically, anxious, often perceiving themselves as inadequate, and subject to excessive feelings of guilt, they seem inclined to project onto others the traits they most dislike or fear in themselves.

It might be thought that these marked personality differences are mostly a function of the sharp educational and status differences between the liberals and extreme conservatives in the sample. But McClosky points out that "the differences remain almost as large even when we control for these factors."

McClosky interprets the connections between conservatism and personality variables as follows:

> The connection does not seem surprising, so soon as one thinks about it. The extreme emphasis on order and duty; the elaborate affection for the tried and familiar; the fear of change and the desire to forestall it; the strong attachments to the symbols and rituals of in-group culture; the hope for a society ordered and hierarchical in which each is aware of his station; the unusual concern for law, authority, and stability—all these can easily be understood as doctrinal expressions of a personality pattern that has strong need for order and tidiness; that adjusts only with difficulty to changes in the environment; that cannot bear the uncertainty of questions left open, and requires answers; that is made uncomfortable by the give-and-take of free inquiry and the open society; that yearns for consensus, harmony of values, unequivocal definitions of the norms, and conclusive specification of the sources of authority.

> It may seem ironic, in light of these traits, that conservatives also tend to exhibit the submissive, indecisive, retiring, and somewhat spiritless demeanor noted in our discussion of the social-psychological variables. I cannot pretend to follow, if indeed anyone can, the com-

plex threads by which these several personality configurations are somehow held together. One can, nevertheless, observe (without explaining it) that persons who feel inadequate and who for one reason or another dislike themselves are often the quickest to aggress against others and to demand perfection of them. Similarly, by a process which psychologists have labelled "reaction formation," the disgruntled often seem to venerate the very society which frustrates them. It is almost as though, disliking themselves, they seek solace and support in an over-defense of society and in the over-institutionalization of life. Conservatives make a fetish of community, although it is apparent that in many ways they are more alienated from the community than most. . . . In the same vein, although the intensity of their patriotism exceeds that of any other group, their faith in democracy (American or otherwise) is lowest of the four groups, while their scores on the totalitarian, elitist, and authoritarian values (which, for the most part, the American creed rejects) are the highest of the four.

CONSERVATISM AND POLITICAL PARTISANSHIP. Of the relations between conservatism and more specific political attitudes, McClosky writes:

> The correlation(s) between them tend, however, to be fairly low, suggesting that for the present, at least, many Americans divide in their party preferences, their support of candidates, their economic views, their stands on public issues, or their political self-identifications without reference to their beliefs in liberalism or conservatism. The latter have influence, of course, especially among some of the more articulate groups; for the general population, however, political divisions of the sort named appear to be more affected by group membership factors than by personality.

These findings are supported by the work of Campbell et al. [1960], who applied McClosky's Conservatism scale to a national sample. These investigators found conservatism to show a patchwork of negative, positive, and indeterminate relations with various issues of social welfare and domestic policy. Further, there was no correlation between conservatism and party identification. Campbell et al. conclude, "In short, if we focus upon the total range of individuals represented in the national electorate, we find almost no correlation between a general disposition that we would expect to be of prime political relevance and variation in issue attitudes or partisanship."

For the rank-and-file citizen, political attitudes mainly reflect primary-group influences. There is little or no connection between his stand on specific political and social issues, his party identification, his political behavior, and his more general attitude toward change— his conservative or liberal ideology.

PERSONALITY AND INTERNATIONALIST ATTITUDES

The intensive study by Smith, Bruner, and White of personality factors associated with attitudes toward Russia (cited on page 182) throws further light on the role of attitudes in the functioning of the personality of the individual. These investigators conclude that an attitude toward an object, such as Russia, may, for some persons, represent a transformed version of ways of coping with a personality difficulty. The object is reacted to in a manner that is related to the inner problem. In so doing, the individual "externalizes" the difficulty and thus reduces his anxiety.

Bjørn Christiansen, a Norwegian psychologist, has studied the role of personality in the formation of attitudes toward foreign affairs [1959]. His subjects were 167 applicants to and students of the Military Academy and the Naval Academy in Oslo.

The first step in the investigation was to determine whether a person's characteristic way of responding to his simple daily conflicts—his interpersonal response traits—will be generalized to international conflict situations. Christiansen constructed scales to measure the direction and form of "blaming reactions" in everyday life situations (the ER scale) and in the area of foreign affairs (the IR scale).

The items of the two scales were so constructed that the six alternative answers could be assumed to measure two general forms of reaction to conflict (Threat-oriented or Problem-oriented) and, for each of these, three general directions of reaction to conflict (Outwardly directed, Inwardly directed, or Passively directed). Table 6.5 shows the design of the multiple-choice items and the identifying symbols.

A sample item from the ER scale (with the identifying symbols indicated) follows.

21. A friend absent-mindedly puts a lighted cigarette on your table and burns a large hole in the cloth and on the tabletop. *In which of the following ways would you be likely to react?*

TABLE 6.5: SCORING CATEGORIES FOR THE ER AND IR SCALES [After Christiansen, 1959]

| DIRECTION OF REACTION | FORM OF REACTION | |
	Threat-oriented	*Problem-oriented*
Outwardly directed	Blame ascribed to others (E)	Problem solving demanded or expected of others (*e*)
Inwardly directed	Blame ascribed to oneself (I)	Problem-solving activity imposed upon oneself (*i*)
Passively directed	Blame implied in emphasizing forgiveness or absolution (M)	Problem solving expected or trusted to take place by itself, with time (*m*)

(a) Reproach him, tell him to look what he is doing another time. [E]

(b) Ask him to compensate for the damage or see that it is repaired. [e]

(c) Be annoyed with myself for not having paid more attention. [I]

(d) Be sorry for my friend, offer to fix myself. [i]

(e) Say it was just an accident, such things can happen to anybody. [M]

(f) Take it calmly. [m]

The following is an example of an item from the IR scale.

26. A Russian radio station starts jamming Norwegian wave-lengths used for broadcasting to Norwegians abroad. *How would you prefer Norway to react?*

(a) Take the matter calmly; wait and see. [m]

(b) Protest and retaliate on Russian broadcasts in Norwegian. [E]

(c) Change the wave length. [i]

(d) Demand an explanation and bring the matter before an international forum. [e]

(e) Wonder what reasons the Russians might have for disturbing these broadcasts. [I]

(f) Do nothing; such things can be due to pure accident. [M]

The ER and IR scales were administered to the subjects and the correlations of scores from both scales for each of the scoring categories of Table 6.5 were computed, as shown in Table 6.6. It appears that for several of the categories there is a moderate degree of consistency between the way the individual re-

TABLE 6.6: CORRELATIONS BETWEEN SCORING CATEGORIES ON THE ER AND IR SCALES [Christiansen, 1959]

Scoring category	r
E	.42
e	.19
I	.44
i	.15
M	.08
m	.30

acts to everyday life conflicts and the way he reacts to international conflicts. Especially noteworthy is the consistent tendency to blame others—the Outwardly directed, Threat-oriented reaction (E).

In order to follow up this significant finding, Christiansen next investigated the relation between *latent* aggression in the individual and his tendency to react aggressively to international conflict situations. A projective device— the Blacky Pictures [Blum, 1950]—was used to secure a measure of the number of conflicts among the basic psychosexual impulses of the individual as psychoanalytically conceived (e.g., oral, anal, and phallic impulses). The assumption here was that the amount of latent aggression in the individual is related to the number of such conflicts. The correlation between number of conflicts revealed in the Blacky Pictures Test and the E category on the IR scale was found to be .33, suggesting that latent aggression in the person is associated with his tendencies to blame others in international problems.

Christiansen hypothesized that the relations he had obtained among the blaming-others reaction (to international problems), latent aggression, and the everyday hostile reaction tendency would be even greater among individuals who were more highly "nationalistic" in their outlook. He developed a scale designed to measure the tendency to see one's own country as superior to the rest of humanity. After giving this scale to his subjects he divided them into three subgroups—those scoring in the highest, middle, and lowest thirds of the distribution of scores on the scale. He then recomputed for each subgroup separately the correlations he had previously obtained.

As Table 6.7 shows, the correlations between the blaming-others reaction in international conflicts and this same tendency in everyday situations increases consistently as one goes from the least to the most "nationalistic." The same is true of the correlation with

TABLE 6.7: CORRELATIONS BETWEEN THE E CATEGORY OF THE IR SCALE AND OTHER MEASURES FOR THREE SUBGROUPS ON THE "NATIONALISM" SCALE [After Christiansen, 1959]

| | CORRELATION BETWEEN E ON IR SCALE AND: | |
SUBGROUPS ON "NATIONALISM" SCALE	Latent aggression score from Blacky Pictures	E on ER scale
Least nationalistic	.18	.23
Moderately nationalistic	.26	.55
Most nationalistic	.56	.62

latent aggression. As Christiansen comments, "A certain degree of nationalism seems to be a prerequisite for the displacement of aggression on to the international sphere."

Finally, Christiansen undertook to determine how effectively the individual's destructive reaction to international problems could be predicted from a combination of three of his measures: (1) aggressive reaction in everyday problems (E on the ER scale), (2) latent aggression (Blacky Pictures), (3) "nationalism." The multiple correlation of these three measures and an index of destructive reactions to international problems was found to be .66. Christiansen concludes, "Our data therefore support the assertion that *destructive tendencies in foreign affairs do not represent any isolated aspect of the individual personality,* but are linked with other dynamic and cognitive aspects."

GENERAL COMMENTS

The individual tends to accept as his own those attitudes which are of a piece with his personality. This is true of such varied attitudes as ethnocentrism, religious attitudes, political attitudes, and attitudes toward foreign affairs.

The personality of the individual, however, is not a perfectly integrated system, and the individual may take over attitudes that are inconsistent or contradictory because of the different teachings of his authorities in different areas, because of conflicting group affiliations, and because of conflicting wants. Man can and does serve many masters.

CHAPTER GUIDES AND GLOSSARY

GUIDE 15: *Attitudes develop in the process of want satisfaction*
GUIDE 16: *The attitudes of the individual are shaped by the information to which he is exposed*
GUIDE 17: *The group affiliations of the individual help determine the formation of his attitudes*
GUIDE 18: *The attitudes of the individual reflect his personality*

authoritarian personality. A cluster of traits found in some persons. It includes high degree of conformity, dependence upon authority, overcontrol of feelings and impulses, rigidity of thinking, ethnocentrism.
ethnocentrism. A generalized attitude which pre-

disposes the individual to reject members of groups other than his own and to exalt the superiority of his own group, especially his ethnic and national groups.
membership group. A group of which an individual is a member and in which he has

face-to-face relations with other members of the group.

prejudice. An unfavorable attitude toward an object which tends to be highly stereotyped, emotionally charged, and not easily changed by contrary information.

primary group. Two or more persons in intimate, face-to-face association. The most important primary groups are the family, friendship, and work groups. They are primary in the sense of their enduring influence upon the individual.

ATTITUDES, AS ENDURING RESIDUALS OF THE EXPERIENCES OF THE *individual, tend to constrict, conserve, and stabilize his world. But men cannot live completely autistic lives in worlds of their own making. The world "outside" does move, and all men, in varying degree, are responsive to changes in the world about them. As they strive to catch up with this changing world, they find themselves— with ease or with difficulty, with ready acceptance or with extreme reluctance—changing their attitudes. This is the individual and psychological accompaniment of social change, social upheaval, and the rise and fall of societies and cultures.*

To know how attitudes change or can be made to change is a theoretical and practical problem of great moment. This is especially true in periods of economic, social, scientific, technological, and political transformation. Whatever else the future may hold in store for the world, it is clear that change—rapid change—in all these aspects will occur. And so we end our systematic study of attitudes with the problem of the changing of attitudes—perhaps the most urgent psychological problem in our world today.

7: THE CHANGING OF ATTITUDES

THERE ARE TWO MAJOR KINDS OF ATTITUDE change. Much of the research upon attitude change has been instigated by individuals and organizations concerned with eliminating "undesirable prejudices." For this reason, attitude change has most generally come to mean a change in the sign of the existing attitude (from positive to negative or negative to positive) or a decrease in the initial amount of positivity or negativity. This type of change we will term *incongruent* change because the

direction of change is toward the sign opposite that of the original attitude. Thus, when the National Conference of Christians and Jews seeks to eliminate religious prejudice, it seeks to make people *less* anti-Semitic. To take another example: when a pacifist organization seeks to change a *pro*-militaristic attitude to an *anti*-militaristic attitude, its objective is to produce what we call incongruent change.

The second major type of attitude change we will term *congruent* change because the

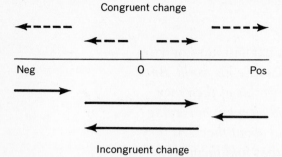

Congruent change

Neg   O   Pos

Incongruent change

FIGURE 7.1: A graphic representation of congruent and incongruent attitude change. Congruent change (dashed arrows) is defined as an *increase* in the positivity of an originally positive attitude or an *increase* in the negativity of an originally negative attitude. Incongruent change (solid arrows) is defined as a *decrease* in the positivity of an originally positive attitude or a *decrease* in the negativity of an originally negative attitude. The decrease may or may not be large enough to reverse the sign of the original attitude.

direction of change is congruent with the sign of the existing attitude. Congruent change may involve an increase in the negativity of an existing negative attitude (e.g., changing a mild anti-American attitude into a strong anti-American attitude) or an increase in the positivity of an existing positive attitude (e.g., changing a mild pro-American attitude into a strong pro-American attitude).

For a graphic portrayal of congruent and incongruent attitude change, see Figure 7.1.

The principles of attitude change may not be the same for both the congruent and the incongruent types of change. We venture the following two hypotheses, recognizing that the evidence concerning them is sparse:

1. Congruent change is always easier to produce than incongruent change, other things being equal.

2. Congruent change is relatively easier the more extreme, multiplex, consistent, interconnected, consonant, want-serving, and centrally valued the attitude.

The modifiability of an attitude depends upon the characteristics of the attitude system, and the personality and group affiliations of the individual

The attitudes of the individual, once formed, differ in their modifiability—their susceptibility to change. And the modifiability of an attitude depends both upon certain characteristics of the pre-existing attitude and upon certain characteristics of the individual who holds the attitude.

ATTITUDE CHARACTERISTICS AND MODIFIABILITY

It appears that of the attitudinal characteristics we examined in Chapters 5 and 6, the most important in determining attitude modifiability are the following seven: (1) extremeness, (2) multiplexity, (3) consistency, (4) interconnectedness, (5) consonance, (6) strength and number of wants served by the attitude, and (7) centrality of the value to which the attitude is related.

EXTREMENESS. A commonly accepted principle is that more extreme attitudes have lower susceptibility to change than do less extreme attitudes. As we have seen (pages 156 to 157), extreme attitudes are held with a greater degree of intensity or confidence than are less extreme attitudes, and hence may be expected to be more resistant to change. Tannenbaum [1956] was perhaps the first to put this principle to direct experimental test. He found, as anticipated, that the mean amount of attitude change induced by a persuasive communication is inversely proportional to the degree of extremeness of the original attitude, i.e., the more extreme the attitude, the smaller the change. As can be seen from Figure 7.2, extreme initial attitudes (e.g., those with mean values of 6 or 42) were changed on the average by a little less than one unit, whereas less extreme attitudes (e.g., those with scores of 18 or 30) showed a mean change of over three units.

We must, however, accept these findings with some qualification. Tannenbaum exposed some of his groups of subjects to favorable and some to unfavorable communications toward the attitude object. In Figure 7.2 the amount of change in attitude is an averaging of changes in both favorable and unfavorable directions; in other words, congruent and incongruent changes are combined. This procedure assumes that the two kinds of change are equivalent. Yet there is good reason to believe that there may be a significant difference in these two kinds of change. To reduce an extreme attitude (incongruent change) by a given amount may be much harder than to further strengthen an extreme attitude (congruent change) by the same amount, assuming, of course, that there is still room for such further strengthening. With less extreme attitudes the difference in the ease of inducing congruent and incongruent change may be much less pronounced.

MULTIPLEXITY. The modifiability of an attitude may be expected to vary with its degree of multiplexity. A simplex attitude will be relatively more susceptible to incongruent change than will a highly multiplex attitude. A person whose anti-American attitude embraces one "fact," to wit, the American people support European colonialism, may change his attitude when confronted with evidence that this belief is false. If, however, his anti-American attitude includes many other "facts" as well (e.g., America is a capitalist country, is militaristic, is materialistic), he may accept the evidence that Americans are not in favor of colonialism but still hold to his anti-American attitude.

In contrast, we may expect to find that attitudes with a high degree of multiplexity are relatively easier to move in a congruent direction than are simplex attitudes. This would

appear to be especially true of the cognitive component of the attitude. There is more possible relevant additional information (e.g., America's wealth, its missile programs, its automobiles, its television shows) which can be integrated into an existing multiplex anti-American belief structure, reinforcing its sign and thus moving it toward a more extreme anti-American position. The more multiplex attitude can find more grist for its mill.

CONSISTENCY. We have seen that there is a moderately strong trend toward consistency among the components of an attitude system. A consistent attitude system tends to be a stable one; the components mutually support one another. An inconsistent system is, in contrast, relatively unstable because of the dissonance among its components and, hence, may be more easily changed in the direction of increased consistency. This may be particularly true of congruent change. (For an experimental study of cognitive consistency and attitude change, see Box 7.1.)

INTERCONNECTEDNESS. The amount and nature of the interconnectedness of an attitude with other attitudes are important in determining how easily the attitude can be modified. For one thing, attitudes which are tied

FIGURE 7.2: Curve showing the mean amount of attitude change produced by persuasive communications in subjects whose initial attitudes varied from extremely unfavorable (6) to extremely favorable (42). [Adapted from Tannenbaum, 1956.]

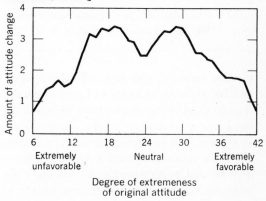

BOX 7.1: *Attitude consistency and attitude change*

William J. McGuire, a psychologist at the University of Illinois, guided by Heider's balance theory (see page 41) and Festinger's theory of cognitive dissonance (see page 261), formulated the following hypothesis: A persuasive communication will produce changes in attitude not only toward an explicit target issue but also toward logically related issues (unmentioned in the communication), in such a way that increased internal consistency will result.

One hundred and twenty high school seniors and college freshmen were used in the experiment. Their attitudes toward sets of logically related issues were measured by the use of a questionnaire that included 16 sets of three syllogistically related propositions. To illustrate, one set of propositions used was as follows: (1) *Students who violate any regulation that has been made to safeguard the lives and property of other students will be expelled.* (2) *The regulations against smoking in the classrooms and corridors were made to safeguard the lives and property of the student.* (3) *Students who violate the regulations against smoking in the classrooms and corridors will be expelled.* Agreement with the first two propositions would logically imply agreement with the third. The three propositions making up any one syllogism appeared in different parts of the questionnaire, randomly intermixed with propositions from other syllogisms.

The subjects were asked to indicate the extent of their *adherence* to each proposition. After the first administration of the questionnaire, the students were given 16 messages, each of which argued for the truth of one of the propositions in each of the 16 syllogisms. The messages, attributed to a competent and dependable source, were rational appeals, presenting arguments based on factual evidence.

The opinion questionnaire was then administered a second time, and finally, one week later, the questionnaire was given a third time.

Analysis of the responses to the first questionnaire revealed a significant amount of initial inconsistency among the attitudes held by the subjects.

Immediately after the presentation of the persuasive messages there was a change in attitudes not only on the explicit target issues but also on logically related issues. These related issues, it must be remembered, had not been mentioned in the messages. The change in attitudes toward the related issues, however, fell short of the amount needed for complete logical consistency. But during the following week the influence of the messages continued to seep down to the related issues. Thus, immediately after the presentation of the messages, attitudes toward logically related issues showed only 52 per cent of the amount of change required for complete logical consistency; one week later this figure had risen to 91 per cent.

McGuire, W. J. Cognitive consistency and attitude change. J. abnorm. soc. Psychol., *1960,* **60,** *345–353.*

to other attitudes with high affective loadings will be relatively resistant to forces applied to change them in an incongruent direction, because the emotionality in the entire cluster, as it were, will be mobilized to resist change. Thus an attitude toward a specific religion may be tied to an attitude toward one's parents; the love for one's father, now long dead, may sustain one's continued devotion to his religious faith.

In addition, the presentation of information opposing one attitude may call forth "defensive" cognitions from related attitudes. For example, if a person who is opposed to the foreign-aid program of this country is confronted with evidence of its effectiveness in

SOCIAL ATTITUDES

creating a favorable image of America, his connected reactionary and isolationist attitudes may defend him against change. Beliefs about bureaucratic mismanagement and waste, the corruption of foreign nations, and the need to conserve our resources to build a strong military defense may become more salient and these older beliefs of his will be mobilized in support of his negative attitude toward the foreign-aid program. Thus the presentation of information in opposition to an attitude may have a boomerang effect. It may, as it were, arouse "sleeping cognitions" (see page 45). In contrast, if an individual's attitude toward the foreign-aid program is cut off from all his other attitudes, information about its effectiveness may cause his negative attitude to crumble.

On the other hand, we should expect interconnected attitudes to be relatively more susceptible than isolated attitudes to influences making for congruent change. Here the emotionality and beliefs of related attitudes will become mobilized as forces making for change. The isolated attitude, in contrast, has no related attitudes to push it toward change.

CONSONANCE OF ATTITUDE CLUSTER. Our speculations about the differential susceptibility of interconnected and isolated attitudes to forces making for incongruent and congruent change assume that some degree of consonance characterizes attitudes interconnected to form a cluster. For the ease of changing an attitude which is part of a cluster will vary with the degree to which it is consonant with the other attitudes in the cluster. Attitudes which exist in a state of consonance will tend to be relatively immune to forces making for incongruent change, as compared with dissonant attitudes. For example, suppose that you, a Democrat, respect President Kennedy and support his tariff program. To weaken your support of Kennedy's tariff program would be relatively difficult because your positive attitude is supported by consonant positive attitudes toward Kennedy and the Democratic party. On the other hand, if your attitude toward Kennedy's tariff program is dissonant with your attitudes toward Kennedy and the Democratic party (you, a Kennedy man and a Democrat, oppose the program), it would be relatively easy to move you in the direction of supporting the program.

Attitudes which are consonant with other attitudes in a cluster should, on the other hand, be relatively easier to move in a congruent direction than attitudes which are in a dissonant relation with other attitudes. Thus your liking for Kennedy and for the Democratic party would reinforce appeals aimed at strengthening your lukewarm support of his policies. In contrast, if you reluctantly support a program espoused by disliked Kennedy, the leader of the despised opposition, it will be relatively difficult to make you a vigorous proponent.

Balance theory (see pages 41 to 42) would predict that an attitude which is in a state of imbalance with other attitudes in a cluster will tend to move in the direction that will balance the system. The resulting change in the system will typically be that which requires a minimum of cognitive reorganization—the least amount of "cognitive work." Osgood [1961] has termed this process "psycho-logic."

> Thus if we like Ike and he happens to praise some congressman from Timbuktu, the minimum restructuring is toward making the relatively unknown congressman a more favorable figure. But if Khrushchev were to comment on this congressman's . . . ideas—a type of assertion popularly known as the "kiss of death"—then psychologically—but not logically—there would be pressure toward discounting these ideas. The fact that psychologic may sometimes lead to valid conclusions does not validate the process.

STRENGTH AND NUMBER OF WANTS SERVED. We have seen that attitudes, once formed, may serve not only the original wants involved in their formation, but other wants as well (see pages 181 to 182). The resistance of an attitude to change depends partly upon the strength and number of the wants served. An attitude that serves strong and multiple wants (a "multiservice" attitude) is especially important in the psychological economy of the individual, and will be prized by him. An attitude based on strong and multiple wants, therefore, will be relatively immune to incongruent change. For example, an anti-Catholic attitude that is the main prop supporting a person's self-esteem—thus serving a whole cluster of his central wants—will be very difficult to eradicate. If, on the other hand, a propagandist were interested in inducing congruent change in this multiservice anti-Catholic attitude (i.e., seeking to make the person *more* anti-Catholic), he might have a relatively easy task. The reason is simple: the individual whose prejudice serves a major want or many wants is easily induced to become still more prejudiced in order to experience still greater want satisfaction.

CENTRALITY OF RELATED VALUES. Many of the attitudes of the individual reflect his values—his conception of what is "good" or desirable (see pages 192 to 193). An attitude that stems from a value that is basic to the individual and strongly supported by his culture will be difficult to move in an incongruent direction. For example, the value "an eye for an eye, a tooth for a tooth" may be the basis for a strong, positive attitude toward capital punishment. It is doubtful that the most persuasive counterargument, supported by a mass of evidence on the ineffectiveness of capital punishment as a deterrent, could change such an attitude from support to rejection of capital punishment. Such arguments and evidence are likely to be seen by the person as irrelevant to the basic concept of *justice* involved in his attitude. However, we should expect to find that the more central the value-base of an attitude, the more susceptible would the attitude be to *congruent* change. "Facts," in other words, indicating that capital punishment is a deterrent to murder could

readily increase the strength of the pro-capital punishment attitude.

PERSONALITY AND MODIFIABILITY

The modifiability of attitudes, Guide 19 asserts, is determined not only by their characteristics but by certain attributes of the persons who hold them. The relation between an individual's personality and the modifiability of his attitudes is a complex one which has been little studied.

INTELLIGENCE. Individual differences in intelligence help determine differences in rate of attitude change. For example, when one citizen arrives more quickly at a new attitude toward a complex issue—such as medical care for the aged, or national sovereignty in a missile age—than does another citizen, it may be due to the fact that the first citizen is more intelligent than the second. He can better comprehend and evaluate the opposing arguments. The second citizen may remain confused and leave the problem to the "experts," saying, "It's too much for me."

In a study cited earlier (see page 175) Hyman and Sheatsley pointed to the large number of chronic "Know Nothings" in the American population. They comment: "There is something about the uninformed which makes them harder to reach, no matter what the level or nature of the information." This "something" may be, in part, lack of intelligence. The chronic "Know Nothings" may be the intellectual "Have Nots."

A study by Swanson [1951] supports this interpretation. He examined the relation between intelligence and amount of information about government activities. His results indicate that "intellectual ability is the most important trait for predicting who learns from this class of news, and . . . understanding the news about government imposes an intellectual task of significant dimensions upon the individual." His data are portrayed in Figure 7.3.

On the other hand, less intelligent persons, *once reached by the propagandist,* may be less able to evaluate his material critically and hence may be more susceptible to the propaganda. And, as we shall see later (page 526), there is experimental evidence that the less intelligent person is more conforming to the attitudinal pressures of his group.

GENERAL PERSUASIBILITY. In a monograph by Janis et al. [1959] evidence is presented in support of a personality factor of *general persuasibility*. Such general or "unbound" persuasibility is defined as a readiness to accept social influence regardless of the communicator and the topic, content, medium, and circumstances of the communication.

In contrast to general or unbound persuasibility, there are also various "bound" persuasibility factors, which refer to predispositions to be susceptible to influence by *specific* kinds of communications only. For example, one type of bound persuasibility, called "topic-bound," includes a readiness to accept or reject a given point of view on a particular *topic*, e.g., aggressive treatment of malefactors (see Box 7.2). A second type refers to a susceptibility to be influenced by communications which contain particular *kinds of appeals,* particular *kinds of arguments,* and other specific stylistic features.

The method of systematic variation is one way of measuring general persuasibility. In this method, a large and varied sample of persuasive communications which represent a wide range of topics, appeals, arguments, communications, media characteristics and situations is presented. If there is a general factor of persuasibility, or a set of general factors, attitude changes induced by the various communications used should be positively correlated. That is, persons who are highly influenced by any one of the communications should tend also to be highly influenced by each of the others, regardless of the topic, the content, and other characteristics of the communications.

Using this method of systematic variation, Janis and Field [1959a] studied individual differences in attitude changes produced by a

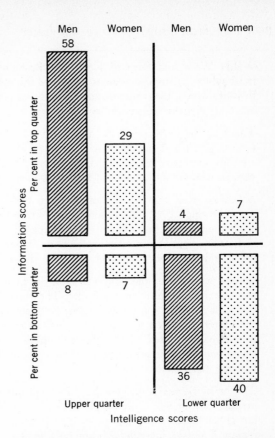

FIGURE 7.3: Relation between intelligence and information about government activities. Note the high correlation between intelligence and information for both men and women. [Swanson, 1951.]

sample of ten different communications, five pro and five anti on five different topics. A factor analysis of the intercorrelations among the attitude-change scores yielded what these investigators took to be a general persuasibility factor, combined with one or more specific persuasibility factors. However, as Katz [1960] points out, the correlations are relatively low and it would appear that if there is a general persuasibility factor it is not a potent one.

Many investigators have observed significant sex differences in persuasibility. Two findings consistently reported are of interest. First, females are found to be more persuasible than males. Second, the correlations be-

BOX 7.2: *Hate propaganda for the hater*

Walter Weiss and Bernard J. Fine of Boston University have studied some of the personality traits which predispose persons to accept the strict and harsh treatment of juvenile delinquents. In other words, their interest was in studying personality correlates of topic-bound persuasibility—one type of bound persuasibility.

These investigators tested the assumption that a message designed to induce aggressive attitudes toward juvenile delinquents will be more effective with persons who are high in hostility and who are extrapunitive (tend to discharge their hostility by aggressing against others) than with persons who are intrapunitive (tend to aggress against themselves).

A "before-after" research design was used with college students. The "before" measures included the following: (1) The Rosenzweig Picture-Frustration Study—a projective measure of extrapunitiveness. (2) Five Thematic Apperception Test (TAT) cards useful in yielding measures of hostility. (3) A nine-item opinion questionnaire. Four of the questions were concerned with juvenile delinquency; the other five were "filler" items.

Several weeks after the administration of these tests, a report on juvenile delinquency was presented to the experimental subjects. The report urged *strict discipline* and *harsh punishment* as the most effective way to deal with the problem. A questionnaire given after the presentation of the report contained ten opinion questions on the topic of juvenile delinquency. Of these, four were the items used in the "before" opinion questionnaire and six were new items. A control group was not exposed to the report on juvenile delinquency; in all other respects, it was treated like the experimental group.

The mean opinion scores on the "after" questionnaire for the control subjects and for the experimental subjects who scored high or low on the Rosenzweig, the TAT, and on both of these tests, are given in the following table. The possible range of opinion scores is from −10 (maximum *leniency* toward juvenile delinquents) to +10 (maximum *punitiveness* toward juvenile delinquents).

EXPERIMENTAL SUBJECTS

CONTROL SUBJECTS	Extrapunitiveness		Hostility		Extrapunitiveness and hostility	
	Low	High	Low	High	Low	High
−6.86	−4.00	+1.39	−2.26	+0.28	−4.64	+4.69

Except for the experimental group scoring low on both the Rosenzweig and the TAT measures, the means of all other experimental groups were significantly higher than that of the control group. Thus the communication seems to have been effective for five of the six experimental groups.

The differences between means of the low and high scorers in the three experimental groups were all significant. The combined Rosenzweig-TAT measure yielded the largest difference between the low and high scorers.

Persons with strong aggressive impulses are more susceptible to "hate propaganda" than are persons with a low amount of aggression.

Weiss, W., and Fine, B. J. Opinion change as a function of some intrapersonal attributes of the communicatees. J. abnorm. soc. Psychol., 1955, 51, 246–253.

tween personality measures and persuasibility are higher among males than among females. (For example, Janis and Field [1959b] report that whereas feelings of personal inadequacy are associated with persuasibility in male subjects, in female subjects the correlation is almost zero.) This is commonly interpreted as meaning that in the American society, the culture demands of females greater compliance with prestigeful sources of information and a pattern of smooth, harmonious social relationships. The influence of this culturally prescribed female sex role is assumed to outweigh in females the influence of personality differences upon persuasibility.

Linton and Graham [1959] administered a large battery of personality tests to a group of high school students in their attempt to tease out personality correlates of persuasibility. Their results are summarized in Table 7.1. In this table, "Changers" are students whose attitudes were changed in the direction of a communication; "Nonchangers," those who seemed to be unaffected by the communication; "Negative changers," those who showed a boomerang effect—changing their attitude in the direction opposed to the communication.

SELF-DEFENSIVENESS. There is considerable evidence that people who are highly self-defensive cling tenaciously to attitudes that bolster their self-esteem. It will be recalled that extreme political "conservatives" tend to be insecure, defensive individuals (see pages 209 to 210). It may be expected, therefore, that it would be very difficult to "liberate" them. That this is indeed the case we shall see later in this chapter.

COGNITIVE NEEDS AND STYLES. Kelman and Cohler [1959] proposed that persons who are high in "need for cognitive clarity" would react strongly to new information which challenges their existing attitudes. As Kelman [1961] puts it, "They would be made uncomfortable by the incongruity produced by such a situation." The nature of their reaction, however, would depend upon their characteristic "cognitive style." An individual who typically reacts to ambiguity by seeking clarification and understanding (a "clarifier") would, it was predicted, tend to be open to the challenging new information and his attitudes would therefore tend to change in an incongruent direction. On the other hand, a person who typically reacts to ambiguity defensively, by simplifying his cognitive world and excluding disturbing elements (a "simplifier"), would be likely to shut himself off from the challenging information and thus resist incongruent change.

Measures of cognitive need and cognitive style were obtained on a group of college students. The group was then given a persuasive communication which presented some challenging information about American education. Change in attitudes toward the message of the communication was measured on two occasions: immediately after the communication under conditions of salience, and six weeks later under conditions of nonsalience.

As predicted, high-cognitive-need clarifiers showed more incongruent change than did high-cognitive-need simplifiers. The latter, in fact, changed in a negative direction, i.e., showed congruent change. The difference between the two groups was small under conditions of salience but became significant under conditions of nonsalience. The investigators interpret this finding as due to a difference between clarifiers and simplifiers in the tendency to "internalize," i.e., to accept social influence because the induced change is compatible with one's system of values. Among the subjects who were low in need for cognitive clarity, no consistent differences between clarifiers and simplifiers were found.

GROUP AFFILIATIONS AND MODIFIABILITY

Everything that we have said in the previous chapter about the role of group affiliations in attitude development (see especially page 196) would lead us to expect that the modifiability of an attitude will be related to

TABLE 7.1: SOME PERSONALITY CORRELATES OF PERSUASIBILITY [After Linton and Graham, 1959]

Test	Changers	Nonchangers	Negative changers
Inner-other direction measure	Need for social approval, participation, and security; succumb to peer-group conformity pressures	Concern with self-expression, creative strivings, personal achievement, freedom from social restrictions; resist peer-group pressures	No trend
	Ideological focus on people and adjustment in short-run situations	Ideological focus on ideas and principles	
Authoritarian questionnaire	High respect for parental authority	High respect for parental authority	Reject parental authority
	Harsh condemnation of social deviates		Nonpunitive toward social deviates
	Anti-intraceptive values	Intraceptive values	
	Admiration for power	Little admiration for power	Moderately low admiration for power
			Cynical
	Little projection		Tend to project
Personality questionnaire	Feel inadequate and inferior	Feel adequate	Feel physically inadequate
	Little assertiveness	Wish for assertion and independence	Rebellious toward authority and convention
			Expressions of hostility
Rorschach	Weak, passive self-image	Strong, active, assertive self-image	Strong, active, assertive self-image
	Not critical of self or others	Much self-analysis, self-concern	Hypercritical

the degree of group support which the attitude has. We will have occasion to refer to this relation several times in this chapter.

VALUE OF MEMBERSHIP. Attitudes that reflect the norms of a group which is highly valued by the individual are markedly resistant to change, as a study by Kelley and Volkart [1952] shows. In that study, an adult visitor made a short speech before 12 Boy Scout troops in which the emphasis of the Boy Scout organization upon camping and woodcraft was criticized. In other words, the Boy Scout norm that it is desirable to have knowledge of the forest and that it is good to be able to live in it was discredited. Before and after this speech, the 12 troops were given a scale to measure attitudes toward camping and forest activities as compared with the activities of city living. In addition, a measure of the degree to which the boys valued membership in their troops was secured before the speech. The results are summarized in Table 7.2.

Note that there is a consistent tendency for the amount of change in the direction sought by the communication to decrease with increase in valuation of membership. Note also that the *net change* column (change in the direction sought by the speech minus opposite change) reveals that whereas the low-valuation members tend to change in the direction of the speech, the high-valuation members tend to change in the opposite direction. In other words, the high-valuation members tend to conform *even more closely to the group norm* after it has been attacked than before.

TO RECAPITULATE

Attitudes, once formed, differ in their modifiability—the ease with which they can be changed. The major determinants of attitude modifiability are the characteristics of the pre-existing attitude, the personality of the individual, and his group affiliations.

Other things being equal, congruent change will be easier to induce than incongruent change. The relatively greater ease with which congruent as compared with incongruent change can be brought about is a function of the extremeness, multiplexity, consistency, interconnectedness, consonance, and the want-serving function and value-relatedness of the attitude.

Attitude modifiability depends in part on the level of intelligence of the individual. Moreover, some individuals seem to be characterized by a general trait of persuasibility, tending to be susceptible to all kinds of persuasive communications; other individuals may be characteristically resistant to persuasive communications. The cognitive need and style of the person influence his readiness to accept change.

Attitudes which have strong social support through the group affiliations of the individual are difficult to change. If a person values his membership in a group, he will tend to cling to the attitudes endorsed by the group in order to maintain his status.

GUIDE 20: *Attitude change is brought about through exposure to additional information, changes in the group affiliations of the individual, enforced modification of behavior toward the object, and through procedures which change personality*

Formation and change are not separate stages in the lives of attitudes. They are, rather, continuous phases in growth which we have separated arbitrarily for purposes of ex-

TABLE 7.2: ATTITUDE CHANGE, FOLLOWING CRITICAL SPEECH TOWARD CAMPING, IN BOYS HAVING DIFFERENT INITIAL VALUATIONS OF BOY SCOUT MEMBERSHIP [After Kelley and Volkart, 1952]

Initial valuation of membership	Per cent change in direction of speech	Per cent net change
1 2 } (low)	51.2	12.3
3	45.2	19.0
4	37.1	−5.7
5 (high)	29.6	−22.2

position. The principles of attitude formation and the principles of attitude change must, therefore, be consistent with one another. We have seen in Chapter 6 that the particular attitudes of the individual are jointly determined by the information available to him, his various group affiliations, and the structure of his personality. It follows that changing the attitudes of the individual will be brought about through manipulation of these same factors.

Attitudes, as we have seen, are used by the individual in constructing a meaningful, orderly, and stable world. We should expect, then, that in so far as additional information tends to change, enlarge, or constrict the individual's world, such information will tend to become incorporated into existing attitudes. As this happens, the original attitudes undergo change.

The attitudes of the individual, formed as he interacts with other persons in his groups, reflect the beliefs, norms, and values of his groups. As he moves into new groups with different belief systems, different norms, and different values, his attitudes will tend to show accommodating changes.

It is sometimes possible to push people into changing their attitudes by *coercing* them to modify their behavior toward the object. The process of "change by fiat" is little understood. Undoubtedly many factors are at work. First, the individual is "force-fed" additional information. This may correct autistic distortion (see page 123). Second, the forced modification of the action tendency component may bring about corresponding changes in the other components of the attitude system through the operation of the principle of consistency (see page 143). The degree to which enforced modification of behavior will produce attitude change will be importantly influenced by the circumstances of enforcement and by the personality of the individual.

The importance of personality factors has been and will continue to be a recurrent theme throughout our discussion in this chapter. Attitudes serve the personality in various ways. And the personality of the individual, in turn, influences his attitudes. The functional interconnections between attitudes and personality are intricate and pervasive. The modification of attitudes by changing the personality they serve is a relatively new approach to the problem of changing attitudes.

Guide 20 is a synopsis of the major factors governing attitude change, each of which will be discussed in the following guides of this chapter.

GUIDE 21: *The direction and degree of attitude change induced by additional information is a function of situational factors and of the source, medium, form, and content of the information*

We shall use the term "information" to include all sources of experience with an attitude object. Thus broadly defined, it includes both the kind of formal information provided by educational and propaganda agencies and the kind of informal information one picks up in talking with other people about an attitude object or in one's direct experiences with the object.

Whatever the type of information, the nature of the situation in which this information is received can play an important—or even decisive—role in determining whether the information will be effective in bringing about an attitude change.

SITUATIONAL FACTORS

Three characteristics of the communication situation have been subjected to scientific study: the effect of group versus solitary exposure, the effect of private versus public commitment after exposure of a communication, and the effect of group decision.

GROUP VS. SOLITARY LISTENING. Although there is little or no supporting evidence, it is commonly thought that the most effective radio and television broadcasts are those which are addressed to arranged audiences rather than to isolated individuals. The success of Father Coughlin, a reactionary rabble-rouser who flourished during the economic depression of the 1930s, appears to have been built on carefully organized group radio listening. Goebbels, the German propagandist, staged dramatic mass meetings for his Führer, Hitler. Inkeles [1950] in his study of "Public Opinion in Russia" reports that the Soviets make extensive use of personal presentations to organized groups. Mass communications are superimposed upon these "in-person" presentations.

Brodbeck [1956] has studied the role of small groups in mediating the effects of propaganda. She determined the initial attitudes of her subjects toward wire tapping and their degree of confidence in the attitudes they held. The subjects, in small groups, then heard a speech which attacked the attitudes held by most of the members of the group. After the speech, their attitudes and confidence levels were again measured. The subjects were told that they might be chosen to participate in a discussion of the topic, using a one-way intercommunication system by means of which one could either talk to or listen to another person, but could not do both. The attitude of each subject toward wire tapping was then made public and each subject was asked to indicate his first, second, and third choices for both listening and speaking partners. After the choice questionnaires had been collected, the subjects were told that there was so much overlapping in choices that the one-way intercommunication system was too difficult to arrange. Hence they were invited to engage in free group discussion of the problem. After the discussion, their attitudes toward wire tapping were measured for a third time.

Those subjects who were in disagreement with the speech tended to choose as persons to whom they would like to listen, persons who agreed with their own position more often than did members of the group who agreed with the speech. This finding suggests that persons whose confidence in their attitude toward an issue has been shaken by new information will try to obtain social support for their attitude by seeking out and listening to persons who agree with them. Analysis of the effect of the group discussion upon the disagreers showed that those who had chosen to listen to persons who *agreed with them* returned to their initial confidence level more frequently than did those who had chosen to listen to persons who *disagreed with them*. Presumably the former "listened selectively" during the discussion (i.e., attended to the arguments of proponents of their own position and turned a deaf ear to their opponents), with the result that confidence in their position was restored.

The results of this study suggest that group listening may counteract the effects of a communication if there is a split in opinion among the members of the group and the members are allowed to discuss the issue.

A study by Mitnick and McGinnies [1958] complements Brodbeck's work. Their results suggest that discussion of a communication by groups who are *solidly antagonistic* to it lowers the effectiveness of the communication. They studied the effects upon groups of high school students of a film on racial tolerance. Some of the groups consisted solely of highly prejudiced students, others of persons low in prejudice. One half of all the groups were shown the film without opportunity for discussion; the other half were permitted to discuss it.

Table 7.3 shows that the film significantly reduced prejudice in highly prejudiced students in the "film-alone" condition. In the "film-discussion" condition, however, the effect of the film was much smaller. Apparently the discussion tended to counteract the effect of the film. Examination of the transcripts of the discussions showed that the highly prejudiced students spent most of the discussion period expressing their antipathies toward Negroes. In contrast, the low-prejudice groups tended in their discussion to examine the general problem of group prejudice raised by the film. Thus, as we see in Table 7.3, there was a tendency for their discussions to reinforce the effects of the film.

Now what will be the effect of group listening if the group is so planned that an overwhelming majority is in favor of the position advocated by the communication? The studies of yielding or conformity behavior which we will discuss in some detail in Chapter 14 indicate that a small dissident minority is pulled in the direction of majority opinion. Thus a situation in which a communication is addressed to a group largely composed of persons favorable to the communicator's position will greatly increase the effectiveness of his communication upon the dissident minority. The majority will express its approval of the position of the communicator in various ways: through applause, nodding of the head, smiling, etc. A study by Kelley and Woodruff [1956] offers some experimental support for this point. College subjects who heard prestigeful members of their college group applaud a speech which opposed their pre-existing values and attitudes (the experimental group) shifted slightly more in the direction of the speech than did a control group which was told that the applauding audience was a group of townspeople. Further, the experimental group included a higher percentage of subjects who showed a large amount of change: 63 per cent of the experimental subjects exhibited more change than the median amount of change of all subjects, whereas only 30 per cent of the control subjects did so.

Demonstrations by paid professional claques are used to generate audience approval of performers. And in the days of professional mourners, the deceased was dispatched with appropriate sorrow generated by paid mourners who depressed the congregation into appropriate weeping and wailing.

COMMITMENT. The device of requiring people to commit themselves publicly to a change in attitude has long been used by propagandists. It is assumed that if a person makes his stand public, he will be less likely to change his position as a result of counterpropaganda. For example, revivalist preachers invite converts to come forward to acknowledge their acceptance of God in the belief this will discourage backsliding.

The effect of commitment on the stability of changes in attitude has been studied by several investigators. In general, *public* commitment has been found to be an effective procedure; *private* commitment (making a decision which remains unknown to anyone but the individual) has been found to be ineffective (see Box 7.3).

GROUP DECISION. Lewin and his associates [1952] were the first to study the effect of group decision upon the action and attitudes of individuals. Their objective was to change strongly held, traditional food preferences. The first study attempted to increase the consumption by groups of housewives of beef hearts, sweetbreads, and kidneys—meats which they generally rejected. Two methods were used. In some groups, a lecturer gave an attractive talk on the dietary value and economy of these meats, and provided recipes for

TABLE 7.3: INFLUENCE OF GROUP DISCUSSION ON EFFECTIVENESS OF A PRO-TOLERANCE FILM [After Mitnick and McGinnies, 1958]

| | MEAN REDUCTION IN PREJUDICE SCORE | |
| | Low-prejudice | High-prejudice |
CONDITION	subjects	subjects
Film-alone	4.9	14.7
Film-discussion	7.5	7.6

their preparation. In other groups, the same information was given in a discussion in which the housewives took part. After the discussion, the housewives were asked to indicate by a show of hands whether they intended to serve the new meats. In a follow-up study, it was found that only 3 per cent of the housewives in the lecture groups had served one of the meats, as compared with 32 per cent of the housewives in the discussion groups. In this study, as in the following study, the subjects were asked to make individual decisions in a group setting. They were not asked to reach a consensus as a group.

In a second study, farm mothers who had their first child in the state hospital at Iowa City received, before discharge from the hospital, information about the value of feeding their infants orange juice and cod-liver oil. The traditional practice had been to give this

BOX 7.3: *Stand up and be counted*

One of a series of studies carried out as part of the Yale Communication and Attitude Change Program is the study by Carl I. Hovland, Enid H. Campbell, and Timothy Brock of the effect of individual commitment upon the resistance of changed attitudes to counterargument.

Two communications on the same issue were presented successively to 69 junior and senior high school students. The topic of the communications was "The reduction of the legal voting age to 18 years—the current draft age." One communication was strongly in favor of the proposed change; the other, strongly in favor of retaining the present minimum voting age of 21 years.

Opinions on the topic were measured twice during the experimental session (once after the first communication and once after the second). The opinion measure taken after the first communication was based on a scoring of essays written by the students in response to a request to write a short paragraph stating their own frank opinion on the issue.

In the *public commitment* groups the subjects were asked to sign their names to their statements and were told that their opinions would be printed in full in the next week's issue of the school newspaper. In the *private commitment* groups the subjects were not asked to sign their papers and were told that their papers would be kept anonymous.

The following table gives the percentage of subjects in the public and private commitment groups who showed changes in opinion as a result of hearing the second, counterpropaganda communication.

	Public commitment group	*Private commitment group*
Change in direction of counterpropaganda	14%	41%
Change in direction opposed to counterpropaganda	11	9
No change	75	50

The data show that the groups who made a public declaration of their position were less susceptible to counterpropaganda than the subjects who stated their position anonymously. The effect of public commitment is to fix the attitudes of the individual so that he is relatively resistant to change.

Hovland, C. I., Campbell, Enid H., and Brock, T. The effects of "commitment" on opinion change following communication. In C. I. Hovland et al., The order of presentation in persuasion. New Haven, Conn.: Yale Univer. Press, 1957.

information individually in a talk with a nutritionist. Students of Lewin carried out a study to compare the effectiveness of this traditional procedure with a group-decision method in which mothers were gathered in groups of six to receive the same information in a discussion. Toward the end of the discussion, they were asked to state publicly whether or not they intended to give their infants orange juice and cod-liver oil.

The results secured in follow-up studies two and four weeks later are shown in Figures 7.4 and 7.5. The effectiveness of the group-decision method was clearly far greater than that of the lecture method.

The exploratory studies of Lewin and his associates do not reveal the specific factors responsible for the superiority of the group-decision method. A study by Bennett [1955] was the first to attempt to disentangle the relative contribution of such factors as lecture versus discussion, decision versus no decision, degree of publicity of commitment to adopt the recommended practice, and degree of actual or perceived consensus in the group. Bennett concluded that the act of making a

decision and the degree of perceived consensus in the group, in combination, were sufficient to account for the results of Lewin's group-decision experiments. Group discussion and public commitment were found to be no more effective than the lecture method and private commitment, respectively. (Bennett's finding that public commitment is ineffective in changing attitudes is the one negative result in all the studies of public versus private commitment.)

Bennett's conclusion that group discussion, as such, is no more effective than the lecture method is questioned by a study of Pennington, Hararey, and Bass [1958]. These investigators found that opinion change was greater when discussion was allowed than when no discussion took place. Decision making was also found to be effective in causing opinion change, but this factor did not have as large an effect as discussion. In interpreting the conflicting findings of the studies of Bennett and of Pennington et al., it should be pointed out that in Bennett's study the subjects were asked to make *individual* decisions in a group setting, whereas in the Pennington et al.

FIGURE 7.4: Percentage of mothers found on follow-up, two and four weeks after "group decision" or individual instruction, to have given their infants cod-liver oil. [Lewin, 1952.]

FIGURE 7.5: Percentage of mothers found on follow-up, two and four weeks after "group decision" or individual instruction, to have given their infants orange juice. [Lewin, 1952.]

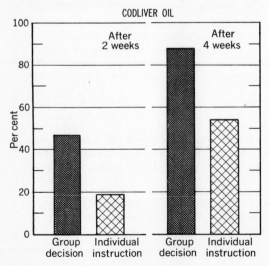

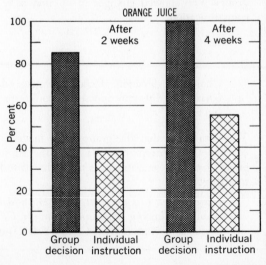

study, the subjects were asked to come to a *group consensus.* Discussion may be more effective than the lecture method when a consensus is sought, but no more effective when the members of a group are asked to make individual decisions.

SOURCE OF INFORMATION

A communication, as we have often pointed out, is an interpersonal behavior event. It would seem clear, then, that whether or not a communication is effective in changing attitudes will depend very much upon how the communicator is perceived by his audience. And there is ample experimental evidence in support of this. Studies have determined that, among other characteristics, the *credibility, attractiveness,* and *group affiliations* of the communicator, as perceived by the audience, are important in determining his effectiveness.

CREDIBILITY. Hovland and Weiss [1951] studied systematically the effect of an individual's evaluation of the propagandist upon his effectiveness. In their study, college students were given communications to read, half of which were attributed to sources that the students regarded as trustworthy and half of which were attributed to untrustworthy sources.

Two alternative communications were prepared, one presenting the affirmative and one the negative position on the issues. The two versions presented an equal number of facts and used essentially the same material. For each version, one trustworthy and one untrustworthy source was used.

Marked differences in the *immediate* effects of trustworthy and untrustworthy communications on opinions were found. Twenty-three per cent of the subjects changed their opinions in the direction advocated by the communicator when a trustworthy communicator was used; less than seven per cent changed when an untrustworthy communicator was used. These differences were not due to differences in attention or comprehension, since

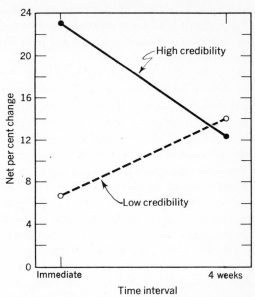

FIGURE 7.6: Curves showing net per cent attitude change induced by a communication when it was attributed to a communicator of high credibility and the same communication when it was attributed to a communicator of low credibility. Immediately after the communication, the subjects exposed to the high-credibility communicator showed a much larger net change than did the subjects exposed to the low-credibility communicator. After an interval of four weeks, the difference between the two groups had disappeared. The high-credibility group showed a loss of about 50 per cent, whereas the low-credibility group showed an increase in agreement with the communication. This "sleeper effect" is presumably due to the fact that with the passage of time, the identity of the communicator becomes less salient in the minds of the subjects and is "detached" from the communication. [Hovland and Weiss, 1951.]

the same amount of information was learned whether the communication was attributed to a trustworthy or to an untrustworthy communicator.

This "obvious" finding is not the whole story. An analysis of the "sleeper effect" of these communications revealed a more interesting result (see Figure 7.6). Compared with immediate opinion changes, there was, over a four-week interval, a *decrease* in amount of agreement with the trustworthy source and an *increase* in amount of agreement with the untrustworthy source.

One hypothesis advanced to explain this paradoxical finding rests upon the assumption that with the passage of time the identity of the communicator becomes less salient than the content of the communication. Persons who were initially suspicious of the communicator and who therefore tended to reject his message should, as awareness of the untrustworthy communicator decreases over time, be increasingly influenced by the message itself. On the other hand, persons who were initially disposed to accept the message because of the trustworthiness of the communicator should show decreasing acceptance of the message as their awareness of the trustworthy communicator decreases over time.

ATTRACTIVENESS. Tannenbaum, in a study cited earlier (see page 217), has found that the amount of positive attitude change is directly proportional to the degree of attractiveness of the communicator. The attractiveness of the communicator was measured through the use of the semantic-differential

FIGURE 7.7: Curve showing the relation between original attitude toward the communicator and amount of attitude change induced. The amount of positive attitude change increases directly with increase in the degree of attractiveness of the communicator. [Adapted from Tannenbaum, 1956.]

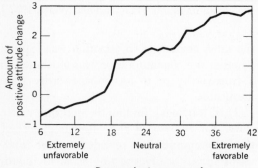

technique (see page 167). The ratings of the subjects on the following six evaluation scales were secured: fair-unfair, dirty-clean, tasty-distasteful, good-bad, pleasant-unpleasant, worthless-valuable (see Figure 7.7).

Tannenbaum's results also indicate that the propagandist incurs disfavor when he advocates a position opposed to the original attitude of his audience and that he gains approval when he advocates a position in accord with the original attitude of his audience. In Figure 7.8 the relation between original attitude toward the object and mean amount of shift in attitude toward the communicator is shown.

GROUP AFFILIATIONS. To be effective, a propagandist (or anyone who would change attitudes) must have "membership character"—he must be seen by the members of his audience as "one of us." Thus Inkeles, in the study cited earlier (page 227), reports that when the Russian Communist Party faced the problem of carrying out agitation on a large scale, careful thought was given to what a successful agitator (i.e., "educator") should be like. The Russians concluded, according to Inkeles, that:

> The successful agitator is . . . the man who knows not only how each person in his shop works, but also how he lives, what his family is like, what his living conditions are, and whether or not he needs advice on one or another personal problem. The agitator is told that "only in the event that the agitator stands in close contact with the people" does he actually win for himself authority and respect.

Studies carried out in various societies indicate that the person who occupies a position of influence in the word-of-mouth communication system—the "opinion leader"—is seen as "one of us" by the persons whom he influences. In the panel study of voting behavior carried out in Elmira, New York, by Berelson, Lazarsfeld, and McPheee (see page 195), opinion leaders were found in similar proportions on every socioeconomic and occupational level. This suggests that people talk to and are influenced by persons who are more or less like themselves.

In a study by Katz and Lazarsfeld [1955], opinion leaders or "influentials" in Decatur, Illinois, were identified by the following procedure. A sample of 800 women was interviewed twice. In both interviews, each woman was asked whether friends or acquaintances had recently asked her advice about each of four topics: marketing, fashions, movie-going, and public affairs. In the second interview each woman was also asked: "Compared with other women belonging to your circle of friends, are you more or less likely than any of them to be asked your advice on marketing?" This question was repeated for each of the other three topics. A woman was considered an opinion leader on a given topic if she said that her advice was sought by her friends or acquaintances.

These investigators found that for marketing, fashions, and movie-going, there was no appreciable concentration of opinion leaders in any one socioeconomic level. In the area of public affairs, however, there was a slight concentration of opinion leaders in the highest socioeconomic level. The evidence suggested that influence tends to flow from persons in this group to persons of lower status.

It would appear from the above studies that *who* says what is as important as what is said.

THE MEDIUM

The effectiveness of propaganda is influenced not only by who the propagandist is but by the *medium* (radio, television, newspaper, magazine, word-of-mouth, etc.) which is used. Considerable research has been done on this problem, and in this section we will compare mass-media appeals with personal appeals.

MASS-MEDIA VS. PERSONAL INFLUENCE. There seems to be almost universal agreement that personal influence is more effective than the influence of the various mass media in

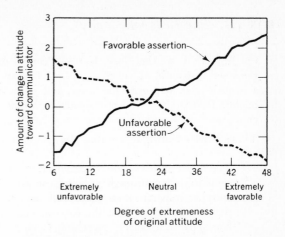

FIGURE 7.8: Curves showing the relation between original attitude toward an object and amount of change in attitude toward the communicator. Note that communicators making favorable assertions about an object suffer a loss in approval on the part of persons holding initially unfavorable attitudes toward that object and enjoy a gain in the approval of persons holding initially favorable attitudes. Conversely, communicators making unfavorable assertions about an object gain in the approval of persons initially opposed to the object and suffer loss of approval among persons initially favorable to the object. [Adapted from Tannenbaum, 1956.]

changing attitudes. (For an illustration of the "planned" use of personal influence in political propaganda, see Box 7.4.)

Lazarsfeld, Berelson, and Gaudet, in a study cited earlier (see page 195), found personal influence much more effective in inducing changes in voting decisions than the mass media. They suggest that the greater effectiveness of personal influence is due to the greater flexibility of face-to-face persuasion. The mass media had, in fact, only small effects upon actual vote decisions and even smaller effects upon *changes* in vote decisions. The ineffectiveness of mass media over short periods of time is due largely to the fact that people tend to select information which is congruent with their existing attitudes. Most people, most of the time, "tune in" on palatable

BOX 7.4: *The Reds take a city*

On June 28, 1950, the North Korean People's Army captured Seoul, capital of South Korea, and remained in control of the city until their hasty withdrawal on September 28. Wilbur Schramm, a sociologist at Stanford University, and John W. Riley, Jr., a sociologist at Rutgers University, made a field study of the propaganda techniques used by the Communists while controlling the city.

These social scientists report that great reliance was placed upon word-of-mouth propaganda.

The Communists made a special effort to reinforce the propaganda of the formal media of communication through personal contacts. The first wave of occupation soldiers had apparently had special training in this aspect of propaganda. A Seoul businessman described their conduct thus: "At the earliest stage of their occupation, every soldier behaved himself like a political officer, preaching Communism outside and inside his barracks at off times and being very friendly toward the people. They tried to leave the unpleasant duties of arrest and search to their agents." This careful friendliness and the studied use of every contact with the South Korean people to advance the cause of Communism, a fact widely reported, is evidence of the fine attention to propaganda detail which characterizes the sovietized state. . . .

Meetings, however, were the most important devices for word-of-mouth sovietization, as it revealed itself in Korea in the summer of 1950. Almost every personal account of the occupation emphasizes the great number of meetings. "We were forced to attend meetings every morning at seven," reported a beer wholesaler. "If we were absent we were supposed to receive 'training.' Sometimes we had to attend meetings four or five times a day."

Riley, J. W., Jr., and Schramm, W. The Reds take a city. New Brunswick, N.J.: Rutgers Univer. Press, 1951.

propaganda. (For an instance in which this tendency toward self-selection of propaganda was partially circumvented, see Box 7.5.)

Katz and Lazarsfeld, in the study cited above, have compared the relative impact of personal influence and mass media on such personal decisions as the purchase of food and other household goods, the choice of motion pictures, and fashion changes. In all three types of decisions, personal influence played a greater role than did any of the mass media (see Figure 7.9).

The greater effectiveness of face-to-face influence does not mean that the mass media are not important in the flow of communication in a modern society. One of the major hypotheses of the study by Katz and Lazarsfeld, in fact, was that of "the two-step flow of communication." This was first stated by Lazarsfeld, Berelson, and Gaudet as follows: "Ideas often flow *from* radio and print *to* the opinion leaders and *from* them to the less active sections of the population."

If this "two-step" hypothesis is valid for opinion leadership in the areas of marketing, movie-going, and fashions, the opinion leaders should be found to be more highly exposed to the various mass media than nonleaders. And this was found by Katz and Lazarsfeld to be the case. In a modern society, communications tend to flow from the various mass media to opinion leaders and from them, by word of mouth, to other people (see Figure 7.10). Despite the name, mass media do not depend only upon direct influence on the mass for their effectiveness.

TELEVISION AND POLITICS. In Campbell, Gurin, and Miller's study of political behavior, to which we have referred earlier (see Box 5.14, page 174, and page 193), an intensive analysis was made of factors influencing voting decisions in the 1952 presidential campaign. A national post-election sample of 1,714 persons of voting age was interviewed about the media (newspapers, radio, television, and magazines) through which they had "paid attention to the campaign." (This aspect of their study is presented in a separate report [Campbell, Gurin, and Miller, 1953].)

The first finding of importance was that during the 1952 campaign the American peo-ple went out of their way to follow the campaign on television. At that time only about 40 per cent of the homes in the United States had sets but 53 per cent of the population saw political programs on television.

Although fewer people watched the campaign on television than read about it in newspapers or heard it on the radio, television was most often named as the source of "most information" about the campaign.

Among persons who actually watched the campaign on television, 59 per cent considered television their most important information source. Nearly all of these persons were exposed to other media as well. In sharp con-

BOX 7.5: *The Great Debate of 1960*

In the 1960 American presidential election campaign, the television industry provided a means for correcting, at least in part, autistic distortion due to the tendency of people to insulate themselves from the propaganda of the opposition. For the first time in presidential election campaigns, the opposing candidates confronted one another face-to-face in a series of debates on television. In their debates, Vice President Richard M. Nixon, the Republican candidate, and Senator John F. Kennedy, the Democratic candidate, attracted the largest audience in the history of television. It was estimated that the debates were watched by sixty to seventy million people.

The effect of the debates on the political attitudes of the viewers is difficult to assess. Robert F. Kennedy, the brother and campaign manager of John F. Kennedy, the winning candidate, told newsmen after the election that the "debates won for us." Without the debates, he added, "it wouldn't have been close." This view is supported by the results of an American Institute of Public Opinion poll of November 5, 1960. A national adult sample of Americans was asked: "Which man did a better job in the TV debates?" The distribution of responses was: Kennedy, 42 per cent; Nixon, 30 per cent; even, 23 per cent; undecided, 5 per cent.

The central significance of the debates, however, is that they provided a built-in corrective for the self-selection of propaganda—the tendency for people to expose themselves to propaganda with which they already agree. Supporters of Nixon and Kennedy alike were exposed not only to the propaganda of their man and their party, but also to the propaganda of the other man and the other party.

Some observations by students of Nathan Maccoby, psychologist at Stanford University, suggest that the "built-in" corrective for selective attention which the debates provided was only partially effective. Maccoby's students observed television viewers in their homes and found a tendency for persons not to attend to the opposition candidate. While he was speaking, viewers of the opposition "tuned him out" through conversation, beer drinking, and other distracting activity. As in McGuire's study (see page 242), even in a captive audience, selective self-exposure to information can take place.

Maccoby, N. Personal communication to the authors.

FIGURE 7.9: The relative effectiveness of different kinds of influence in inducing decisions. Decisions induced are: to change from one brand of household product to another—Marketing Shifts; to change from one style of hair-do, make-up technique, or clothing style to another—Fashion Changes; to decide which movie to attend—Motion Picture Selections.

Each bar represents a particular kind of influence. The three categories within each bar are defined as follows: "Effective Exposure" refers to persons who mention a given influence, claim it played a specific role (e.g., taught them something or directed them toward something), and further state it was the *most* important factor in their decision. "Contributory Exposure" refers to persons who mention a given influence and claim it played a specific role, but do *not* report it was the most important factor in their decision. "Ineffective Exposure" refers to persons who mention a given influence, but do not acknowledge that it played *any* role in their decision. The Index of Effectiveness given beside bar is a measure of the relative effectiveness of each type of influence. It is the ratio of effective exposure to a particular medium to total exposure to that medium. The higher this ratio, the greater the relative effectiveness of any given medium. For example, in Marketing Shifts, radio advertising is much more effective (.25) than newspaper advertising (.07). [After Katz and Lazarsfeld, 1955.]

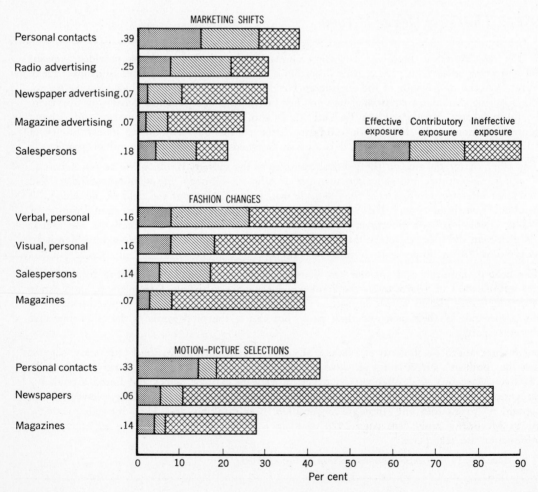

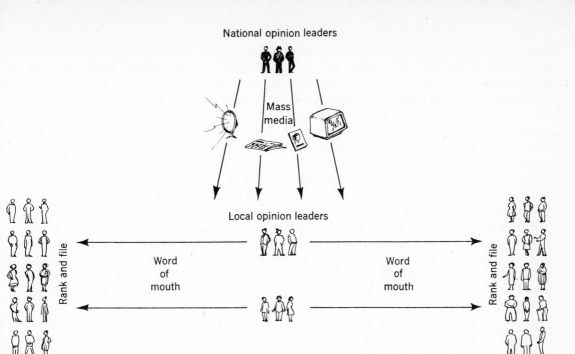

National opinion leaders

Mass media

Local opinion leaders

Rank and file

Word of mouth

Word of mouth

Rank and file

FIGURE 7.10: A schematic portrayal of the two-step flow of communication within a society. Information flows vertically from national opinion leaders via the various mass media down to local community and neighborhood opinion leaders. From the local opinion leaders, it flows horizontally via word of mouth to the rank-and-file members of the community.

trast, among those who followed the campaign in newspapers (79 per cent of the population), only 28 per cent judged it their most important source of information. As Campbell, Gurin, and Miller note, although their findings are not clear evidence as to how television affected political attitudes, their data do indicate that it was an important source of information.

A study by Simon and Stern [1955] suggests that television has little if any direct influence on the *vote*. These investigators made a detailed analysis of the vote in Iowa for the elections of 1944, 1948, and 1952 on a county-by-county basis. Their data revealed no relation between the pattern of voting and concentration of television ownership.

Bogart [1958] cites a study by Seibert of the influence of television on voters' evaluations of the candidates in the 1952 presidential cam-

paign. In this study, nine mail questionnaires were sent at nine different phases of the campaign to a panel of voters in fourteen counties in the metropolitan Cincinnati and Dayton areas, including the rural regions. One of the most significant findings of the study was the demonstrated power of television to attract viewers who were opposed to the political candidate. In this predominantly Republican region, the Republican television programs were viewed more frequently than the Democratic programs. Nevertheless, more Republicans than Democrats watched the speeches of the Democratic candidate. This finding suggests that television viewers do not restrict their viewing to political propaganda programs with which they already agree (see, in this connection, page 233).

The data also revealed that television was a potent means for creating favorable impressions of Stevenson (the Democratic candidate). Both at the beginning and at the end of the campaign, Eisenhower (the Republican candidate) was rated higher than Stevenson on every trait of personality measured except humor and speaking ability. However, Stevenson's position relative to Eisenhower improved during the campaign on every trait except humility and aggressiveness. The increases in the personality ratings of Stevenson were greater among television watchers in the panel than among the panel as a whole. This suggests that his television appearances were directly responsible for the increased favorability of his image. It should be added that Eisenhower's failure to make comparable gains may have been partly due to the "ceiling effect." His popularity at the outset of the campaign was so great that it was difficult for him to become even more popular.

Seibert felt that "it appears reasonable to conclude that it was in these areas [personality traits], rather than in the area of issues, that television contributed the most to the final election results."

FORM AND CONTENT OF INFORMATION

In this section we will consider the *what* and *how* of information. Our concern will be with matters of content, form or style, and organization and procedure.

INFORMATION AND INSTRUMENTAL VALUE. Peak [1955] has directed a program of research on attitude change which is based upon the following assumption: "An attitude toward any object or situation is related to the ends which the object serves, i.e., to its consequences. This we have called the *instrumental relation*."

It follows from this assumption that attitude change should result from changes in expected satisfaction from the goals served by an attitude or from changes in the instrumental relations believed to exist between the attitude object and the goal. A study by Carlson [1956] was designed to test the latter

hypothesis. In this study, an attempt was made to change attitudes toward the housing segregation of Negroes by presenting experimental subjects with persuasive arguments that "allowing Negroes to move into white neighborhoods" would be a means of attaining four important goals: American prestige in other countries; protection of property values; equal opportunity for personal development; being experienced, broad-minded, and worldly-wise.

The arguments proved to be effective. As compared with control subjects, a significant proportion of the experimental subjects changed toward seeing the instrumental value of Negro housing integration for realizing the four goals. Moreover—and this was the crucial finding—the attitudes of the experimental subjects toward Negro housing became significantly more favorable as compared with the attitudes of the control group.

As Figure 7.11 shows, the relation between initial attitude and amount of attitude change was found to be curvilinear. Those subjects whose initial attitude was moderate changed significantly, whereas extremely prejudiced and extremely nonprejudiced persons did not change systematically. The smaller proportion of positive attitude changes among the extremely nonprejudiced may be explained by the fact that they were already very favorable and hence did not have room to move toward a more positive attitude (the "ceiling effect"). The failure of the extremely prejudiced persons to move may reflect the fact that in the case of extreme attitudes, *incongruent* change is difficult to produce (see page 217).

The work of Peak and her students suggests an important principle for the propagandist: *A communication that induces new beliefs about the instrumental or means attributes of an object will be more effective than one that does not have that advantage.* The good propagandist will attempt to design his message to change *beliefs* about the object of the attitude. This requires that the propagandist tailor his propaganda to hit those beliefs of his audience which support the attitude.

AMOUNT OF CHANGE ADVOCATED. Which is more effective—extremely stated or moderately stated propaganda? The first study to present clear-cut data on this question is that of Hovland and Pritzker [1957]. The opinions of college students on 12 different topics were first secured. Some of the topics used were the following: Washington or Lincoln the greater president? Married or single women better teachers? Likelihood of cancer cure within five years? The topics did *not involve deep-rooted attitudes in which the subjects had a high degree of self-involvement.* One month later, a communication handtailored for each student was presented. This communication cited an authority who was respected by the individual student. On some of the issues he expressed opinions that differed *only slightly* from the opinions held by the student; on other issues he expressed opinions that differed *somewhat more*; and on still others he was alleged to differ *markedly* from the student's opinions.

After receiving the communication, the students again expressed their own opinions on the 12 topics. It was found that the larger the change advocated, the greater the change produced: a mean shift of 0.88 scale unit when a slight change was advocated; 1.25 when a moderate change was advocated; 1.75 when a marked change was advocated. This relation was found to be much the same for individuals holding extreme opinions and for those holding less extreme opinions.

Weiss [1958] confirmed these findings. In his experiment, he studied the relation between the *judged* position of an anonymous communicator and the amount of opinion change. The topic used was the treatment of juvenile delinquents. Weiss found significantly greater opinion change among the audience members who *attributed* a more extreme position to the communicator than among the members who had been exposed to the very same communication but had judged it as less extreme.

As Hovland and Pritzker have pointed out, the generality of these findings may be limited. If the issue is one in which the individual is deeply involved, results opposite to the above findings may hold. In such cases it may be that the greater the discrepancy between the stand advocated by the communicator and the position of the subject, the smaller the amount of change which will be produced. (See Box 7.6 for a study which confirms the prediction of Hovland and Pritzker.)

As a matter of fact, *boomerang effects* (changes in a direction opposite that advocated) may be expected to occur when there is a marked discrepancy between the position of the communicator and the position of the subject. The propagandist who attacks an attitude toward an issue in which a person is deeply involved is attacking an attitude which is a part of the individual's self-concept (see

FIGURE 7.11: The relation between degree of extremeness of original attitude and percentage of subjects showing positive attitude changes. [Adapted from Carlson, 1956.]

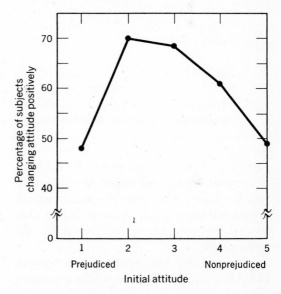

BOX 7.6: *The teetotalist and the tippler*

Carl I. Hovland, O. J. Harvey, and Muzafer Sherif, as part of the Yale Communication and Attitude Change Program, collaborated on a study concerned with the effect of amount of change *advocated* in propaganda upon the amount of attitude change *obtained* on an issue in which people are deeply involved.

The controversial issue chosen was prohibition and repeal in Oklahoma—a "dry" state at the time of the study. Shortly before the study began, a referendum to repeal the prohibition laws had lost by a narrow margin.

People who were known to have taken definite stands on the issue and who were personally involved in the controversy were selected. A total of 183 "drys" was secured from W.C.T.U. groups, the Salvation Army, a divinity school, and denominational colleges. It proved to be difficult to get "wets." Twenty-five were finally secured from persons known to the experimenters. An unselected group of 290 college students was also secured for comparative purposes.

In the first experimental session, measures of the subjects' attitudes toward prohibition were obtained. From one to three weeks later, a "wet" communication was presented to extreme dry subjects and to a subsample of the unselected subjects. A moderately "wet" communication was presented to wet, dry, and unselected subjects.

After the presentation of the communication, attitudes toward prohibition were again measured. The following table presents the percentage of subjects in the various groups who showed opinion change. As predicted by the investigators, subjects whose own positions deviated widely from the position advocated in the communication changed very infrequently.

GROUP	CHANGE TOWARD COMMUNICATION	NO CHANGE	CHANGE AWAY FROM COMMUNICATION
	Wet communication		
Drys	27.5%	49.3%	23.2%
Unselected	52.2	23.9	23.9
	Dry communication		
Wets	24.0	56.0	20.0
Unselected	40.2	33.4	26.4
	Moderately wet communication		
Drys	31.6	49.1	19.3

Hovland, C. I., Harvey, O. J., Sherif, M. Assimilation and contrast effects in reactions to communication and attitude change. J. abnorm. soc. Psychol., *1957*, **55**, *244–252*.

page 79). It is "his" attitude. The advocate of extreme change will therefore be resisted, and the target of the propaganda, in defending his self-esteem, may be driven still further away from the position advocated by the propagandist.

ONE-SIDED VS. TWO-SIDED PRESENTATIONS. Should a propagandist present only arguments in support of his position, or should he acknowledge and refute counterarguments? This problem was first investigated by Hovland, Lumsdaine, and Sheffield [1949] in their studies of training and indoctrination films used by the American Armed Forces during World War II. Communications dealing with the question of an early end of the war with

Japan after the surrender of Germany were presented to two experimental groups of soldiers. One group was given a one-sided, 15-minute talk presenting only the arguments for the position that the war with Japan would be a long one because of the resources of Japan. The second group was given a two-sided communication. Here the original 15-minute talk was continued with an additional four minutes which stressed the advantages of the United States and the weaknesses of Japan. Before and immediately after hearing the talks, both groups of subjects were asked to estimate the probable length of the war with Japan.

Figure 7.12 shows that the amount of net change was different for the two types of presentation for subjects with different initial positions. The two-sided presentation was more effective for men who initially held the opposed opinion that the war with Japan would be a short one (less than two years). For men who initially favored the position of the communication, the one-sided presentation was more effective. In our terms, a two-sided presentation was found to be more effective in inducing *incongruent* change; a one-sided presentation was found to be more effective in producing *congruent* change.

A second finding was that better educated men were influenced less by the one-sided than by the two-sided presentation. On the other hand, the less well educated men were more influenced by the one-sided argument. Here is a possible interpretation of these findings: A person who values his own independence of judgment and his own intellectual competence may view the acceptance of a one-sided communication as incompatible with maintaining his self-esteem. Among better-educated persons—those who would tend to value their intellectual competence more highly than less well educated—this would be especially true, and therefore a one-sided argument would be relatively ineffective in producing incongruent change in better-educated persons.

Lumsdaine and Janis [1953] have compared the relative effectiveness of one-sided versus two-sided presentations in "inoculating" an audience against the effects of later counterpropaganda. Their study was conducted several months before President Truman (in September, 1949) announced that Russia had exploded its first atomic bomb. Two forms of a persuasive communication were prepared in which the same communicator took the position that Russia would be unable to produce large numbers of atomic bombs for at least five years. The one-sided version contained

FIGURE 7.12: The amount of net attitude change induced by one-sided and two-sided communications. Subjects included those who initially held a position opposed to the communication and those who initially favored the position advocated. [Adapted from Hovland, Lumsdaine, and Sheffield, 1949.]

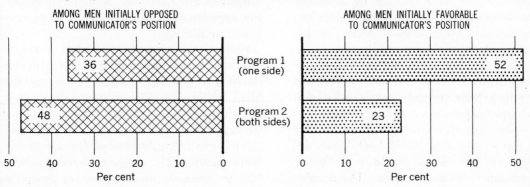

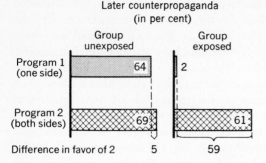

FIGURE 7.13: The net change in a positive direction induced by a one-sided and a two-sided communication. For the groups not exposed to later counterpropaganda there was little difference in the effectiveness of the two types of communications. However, the groups exposed to the two-sided communication were definitely more immune to later counterpropaganda than were the groups exposed to the one-sided presentation. [Lumsdaine and Janis, 1953.]

only the arguments that supported the conclusion. The two-sided version contained the same arguments as the one-sided version and was presented in a similar manner, but certain opposing arguments were also woven into the relevant sections of the two-sided communication.

Four groups of high school students were used. The initial opinions of the subjects had been determined several weeks before the communications were presented. Two groups were given the one-sided version and the other two the two-sided version. The effects of the communications were assessed by a second questionnaire given about a week after the presentation of the communications. Just before the administration of the postcommunication questionnaire, two of the groups (one which had received the one-sided version and one which had received the two-sided version) were exposed to a second communication—intended as *counter*propaganda—that took the position that Russia had already developed the A-bomb and would be producing large numbers within two years. The remain-

ing two groups were not exposed to this counterpropaganda.

The main question in the final questionnaire designed to measure the effect of the original communication was: "About how long from now do you think it will be before the Russians are really producing *large numbers* of atomic bombs?" The results are given in Figure 7.13. For the two groups who were not exposed to counterpropaganda, there was little difference in the effectiveness of the two forms of the original communication. For subjects who had been exposed to the later counterpropaganda, however, the original two-sided presentation was definitely superior to the one-sided version in inducing an irreversible effect. The authors speculate that a person who has been exposed to a two-sided communication not only is familiar with the counterarguments, but has been led to a positive conclusion in a context containing the negative arguments. They conclude, "In effect he has been given an advance basis for ignoring or discounting the opposing communication and, thus 'inoculated,' he will tend to retain the positive conclusion."

CONCLUSION DRAWING BY COMMUNICATOR, BY AUDIENCE. As we have stressed earlier (page 24), facts do not speak for themselves. The same facts may mean different things to different people. We should, therefore, expect that the propagandist would be more effective in securing comprehension and acceptance of the intended interpretation of his facts if he himself pointed out the desired conclusion. For experimental evidence on this important point, see Box 7.7.

ORDER OF PRESENTATION. When a propagandist writes a speech, he is faced with the question of how best to order his arguments. Shall he present positive arguments before negative arguments? Shall he present the sweet first and the bitter second, or *vice versa?*

McGuire [1957] addressed himself to the latter question. He sought to determine how best to persuade an audience to accept a

BOX 7.7: *Facts do not speak for themselves*

As part of the Yale Communication and Attitude Change Program, Carl I. Hovland and Wallace Mandell compared the relative effectiveness of conclusion drawing by the communicator versus conclusion drawing by the audience.

A taped speech on "Devaluation of Currency" was prepared in which the appropriate conclusion, from the evidence presented, was that it would be desirable to devaluate American currency. In the group of subjects for whom this conclusion was *explicitly drawn by the communicator,* the effectiveness of the speech was much greater than for a second group *left to draw its own conclusion.* The percentage of subjects showing attitude changes in the two groups is given in the following table.

Direction of change	Conclusion not drawn by communicator	Conclusion drawn by communicator
In agreement with communicator	30.7%	51.2%
Opposed to communicator	11.4	3.3

In a later study, D. L. Thistlethwaite, H. de Haan, and J. Kamenetzky of the University of Illinois were unable to confirm these findings, using as the issue the wisdom of the United States policy of limited war in the Korean conflict. These investigators suggest that the positive results obtained by Hovland and Mandell may have been due to the fact that some subjects perceived one of the two opinion items used to be a measure of what the speaker said rather than a question on the subject's personal opinion. This item read as follows: "Devaluation of the dollar as a method of manipulating the American economy should be used: (*a*) In a situation such as exists at present; (*b*) If the situation starts to become worse; (*c*) Only if things become very much worse; (*d*) Only in an extreme emergency; (*e*) Never."

This interpretation was suggested by the finding of Thistlethwaite, de Haan, and Kamenetzky that *comprehension* of the intended conclusion was greater when the conclusion was explicitly stated by the communicator, but that *agreement* with the conclusion was not greater.

An alternative explanation of these conflicting results may be suggested. The issue used by Thistlethwaite, de Haan, and Kamenetzky (the wisdom of the United States policy of limited war in the Korean conflict) had been widely discussed in the mass media, and the arguments, pro and con, had been spelled out in simple terms. In contrast, Hovland and Mandell's issue (the devaluation of the currency) is a complex economic problem about which most people understand very little. It may be that conclusion drawing by the communicator is more effective only when the issue discussed is complex.

Hovland, C. I., and Mandell, W. An experimental comparison of conclusion-drawing by the communicator and by the audience. J. abnorm. soc. Psychol., 1952, 47, 581–588.

Thistlethwaite, D. L., de Haan, H., and Kamenetzky, J. The effects of "directive" and "nondirective" communication procedures on attitudes. J. abnorm. soc. Psychol., 1955, 51, 107–113.

future educational program, some features of which were seen as desirable by the audience and some as undesirable. He predicted (and his study confirmed his prediction) that when desirable features were presented first and undesirable second, greater agreement would result than when the features were presented in the reverse order.

This prediction was based on the following argument:

It would seem that after receiving the earlier undesirable messages, the subject can be thought of as saying to himself, "What this man says appears to be true, but I find it unpleasant and so I am not going to listen to him any more." . . . The subject who . . . receives earlier desirable messages can be thought of as saying to himself, "This man's comments are pleasant and worth listening to and so I shall pay close attention to him." Thus he receives more of the source's later arguments and as a result is influenced by them . . . even with a presumably "captive" audience, the device of selective self-exposure to information can operate.

Closely related to McGuire's question, and one which has stimulated research, is the following: Is change of attitude more effectively produced by first arousing a fear before presenting facts calculated to allay the fear, or is the reverse order more effective? One experimental answer to this question is that the fear-fact sequence is more effective than the fact-fear sequence (see Box 7.8).

INTENSITY OF THREAT. Whether the propagandist uses the fear-fact or the fact-fear sequence, he is making the implicit assumption that the use of fear, or threat, *is* effective in inducing attitude change. How valid is this assumption?

Janis and Feshbach [1953] studied the effects of three different intensities of fear-arousing appeals in an illustrated lecture on dental hygiene given to three matched groups of high school students. The major differences in the content of the three appeals are shown in Table 7.4.

The immediate effect of these three different intensities of fear arousal showed that adherence to the recommended behavior was *inversely* related to the intensity of fear arousal. The mild fear appeal produced a 37 per cent net change in the direction sought; the moderately intense fear appeal, a 22 per cent net change; and the extremely intense fear appeal, only an 8 per cent net change.

One week later the subjects were exposed to counterpropaganda which contradicted the dominant theme of the first message. The effect of this counterpropaganda is shown in Table 7.5.

The investigators suggest that the reason for the ineffectiveness of the intense fear appeal may have been that it aroused anxiety which was reduced by the subject's becoming hostile toward the communicator, thus leading to rejection of his message.

The use of fear or threat in appeals designed to change attitudes must, it would seem, be managed with caution. A little fear

TABLE 7.4: NUMBER OF DIFFERENT TYPES OF THREATS IN THREE FEAR APPEALS
[After Janis and Feshbach, 1953]

Type of threat	Strong appeal	Moderate appeal	Minimal appeal
Pain from toothaches	11	1	0
Cancer, paralysis, blindness, or other secondary diseases	6	0	0
Having teeth pulled, cavities drilled, or other painful dental work	9	1	0
Having cavities filled or having to go to the dentist	0	5	1
Mouth infections: sore, swollen, inflamed gums	18	16	2
Ugly or discolored teeth	4	2	0
"Decayed" teeth	14	12	6
"Cavities"	9	12	9
Total number of threats	71	49	18

BOX 7.8: *Fear-fact or fact-fear?*

Arthur R. Cohen, a psychologist at Yale University, addressed himself to the following question: Which order of presentation is more effective in changing attitudes: fear arousal followed by information designed to allay the fear, or the presentation of the comforting information before the fear-arousal information?

At the time Cohen carried out his study, the issues of grading and grading reforms were being widely discussed on the Yale campus. Several articles had appeared in the university newspaper discussing the "abundance of high grades" at Yale, the attitudes of the administration and the faculty toward the situation, and the possibility of new and tougher systems of grading.

During a class meeting, students answered a long opinion questionnaire. One of the items embedded in the questionnaire was designed to elicit their attitudes toward grading "on the curve." Approximately one month later the students were divided into two groups. Each group attended different discussion sections in which they were introduced to a speaker who was there to discuss grading problems. The speaker was identified as a member of the psychology department and chairman of a committee concerned with evaluating grading problems.

Two orders of presentation were employed—the Fear-Fact sequence and the Fact-Fear sequence. In the Fear-Fact sequence the speaker first made vague statements to the effect that the rise in grades at Yale had resulted in a good deal of confusion, uncertainty, and resentment, and that there undoubtedly would be an eventual lowering of grades. Fear arousal was followed by an informative talk on grading "on the curve." The speaker concluded that grading on the curve was a system whereby "academic standards are maintained, the discriminatory ability of the faculty is maximized, and the individual student is given a great deal of consideration." The informative talk could thus be seen as providing a means for allaying the fears aroused in the first part of the communication.

The group which received the Fact-Fear sequence heard the informative talk first and the fear-arousal talk second.

Immediately after hearing the talk, the subjects completed an opinion questionnaire containing the same item about grading on the curve which they had answered one month earlier. Three months later, a final opinion questionnaire concerning grading on the curve was administered.

The results are given in the following table. In reading the table, keep in mind that the higher the mean attitude scale score, the more favorable the attitude.

	MEAN ATTITUDE SCALE SCORES	
	Fear-fact sequence	*Fact-fear sequence*
One month before speech	4.47	3.72
Immediately after speech	6.29	3.33
Three months after speech	5.90	3.67

Before the communication, the difference between the two experimental groups was not significant. Immediately after the communication, the Fear-Fact group is significantly more favorable to grading on the curve, and this difference persists over a three-month period. The Fact-Fear group does not, in fact, change in its opinion.

Cohen, A. R. Need for cognition and order of communication as determinants of opinion change. In C. I. Hovland et al., The order of presentation in persuasion. *New Haven, Conn.: Yale Univer. Press, 1957.*

TABLE 7.5: EFFECT OF DIFFERENT DEGREES OF FEAR APPEAL ON REACTIONS TO SUBSEQUENT COUNTERPROPAGANDA, IN TERMS OF NET PERCENTAGE OF CHANGE [After Janis and Feshbach, 1953]

TYPE OF CHANGE	NET PERCENTAGE CHANGE		
	Strong appeal group	*Moderate appeal group*	*Minimal appeal group*
Acceptance of counterpropaganda	30	28	14
Rejection of counterpropaganda	38	42	54
No change	32	30	32
Net change	−8	−14	−40

may be a good thing; a lot of fear may be a bad thing.

TO RECAPITULATE

Whether new information will change attitudes depends upon the nature of the communication situation, the characteristics of the communicator, the medium of the communication, and the form and content of the message.

Three characteristics of the communication situation which influence the effectiveness of the propagandist are group versus solitary listening, public versus private commitment to the position advocated, and group decision versus the lecture method. Group listening is more effective than solitary listening if the majority of the group is in favor of the position of the communicator; it is less effective if the majority is opposed. A public declaration of one's acceptance of the position advocated makes one relatively immune to counterpropaganda. The group-decision method has been found to be more effective in changing attitudes and action than the lecture method.

Who says what is often as important in determining the effect of a message as is its content. To be effective, the propagandist must be seen as a member of the group he is trying to influence—he must be seen as an "insider"; he must also be seen as credible and attractive.

While word-of-mouth messages are more potent than mass-media messages, the mass media nevertheless play an important role in the process of social influence and social change by influencing the word-of-mouth opinion leaders in the community.

The content and form of the message are also important. Numerous content and form variables have been subjected to experimental study; among them are the amount of change advocated, one-sided versus two-sided presentation, conclusion drawing by the communicator versus no conclusion drawing, the order of presentation, and the intensity of the threat in the appeal.

GUIDE 22: *The effectiveness of new group affiliations in inducing attitude change is a function of the characteristics of the group and the nature of the individual's membership in the group*

When an individual affiliates himself with a new group, he tends, as a "social entrance ticket," to adopt the attitudes prescribed by the values and norms of the group. This is well illustrated in Watson's [1950] study, in which she interviewed 45 adults who had reported that their attitudes toward Negroes or Jews had undergone marked change at some time in their lives. Almost half of her subjects reported that among the experiences closely preceding their change in attitude had been the joining of a new group. A large number of other subjects said that their change in attitude followed a change in place of residence—and this presumably had brought about membership in a variety of new groups.

The changing of attitudes is influenced by all the changing group relations of the individual. For one thing, the changes in his *membership* groups play a role. It will be recalled that the membership groups of an individual are those groups in which he has direct, face-to-face relations with other members (page 193). For another thing, changes in the *reference* groups (page 197) of the individual (those groups with which he identifies) may change his attitudes. (For an ingenious experiment that reveals the influence of both the membership and reference groups of the individual upon attitude change, see Box 7.9.)

CHARACTERISTICS OF THE GROUP

The studies we have reviewed show that changes in the group affiliations of the individual often bring about changes in his attitudes. But all new group affiliations are not, of course, equally effective in inducing attitude change. The power of a group to modify the attitudes of new members is, in part, a function of certain characteristics of the group. We will examine the following group characteristics in this connection: (1) the nature of the group norm; (2) constraints upon leaving the group; (3) the effectiveness of the monitoring system of the group.

GROUP NORMS. In our present discussion, we anticipate the more detailed treatment of norm enforcement in Chapter 11. The term *group norm* is defined as a rule which states the attitudes and actions expected of members under given circumstances and which specifies the consequences of compliance and noncompliance. A rule of behavior, to be a norm, must be accepted by a majority of the group.

Note that norms prescribe both how the members of a group are expected to act and how they are expected to think.

Norms that have to do with attitudes and actions that are of central importance to the group will be rigidly enforced. Deviation from such central norms is heresy and will not be tolerated. The new member must perforce conform and adopt the approved attitudes (if he does not already have them) or suffer expulsion.

CONSTRAINTS UPON LEAVING GROUP. In voluntary groups, the *cohesiveness,* or over-all attractiveness of the group to its members, provides the source of the group's "policing power" over its members. We would therefore expect that the greater the cohesiveness of a group, the greater the amount of conformity to its norms. The new member who finds his new group attractive will, in other words, tend to change his attitudes to conform with the group norms.

A nonvoluntary group, that is, one which persons are constrained to join and which they cannot leave because the costs of leaving are too great (e.g., a labor union), may have "absolute" power over its members. Punishment for the nonacceptance of group norms can be forcefully applied, and if the monitoring system of the group is effective, there will be a high degree of conformity among the members.

EFFECTIVENESS OF MONITORING. Unless agents of the group can maintain surveillance over the members and thus detect and punish deviant behavior, the impact of norms may be greatly reduced.

The effectiveness of the monitoring system of a group is influenced by the visibility of the behavioral expressions of an attitude. If an attitude is usually expressed in private behavior only, the group cannot effectively monitor the members to enforce compliance with the norm prescribing the "proper" attitude. Argyle [1957] found significantly more social influence in a public as compared with a private situation. He gave two-person groups the task

BOX 7.9: *Houses, co-eds, and attitude change*

Alberta and Sidney Siegel, while at Stanford University, undertook a field experiment to test the assumption that both the reference and membership groups of a person affect his attitudes.

A dormitory group (a *membership* group) of 28 college freshman women served as subjects. At the end of the year, these students all listed a high-status "Row house" (former sorority houses located on "Fraternity Row") as their first choice in drawing for a residence during the sophomore year. Thus they shared a common reference group (the Row house group). Nine of these students were successful in drawing for a Row house and lived in a Row house throughout the year. The other nineteen spent the year in a non-Row house.

At the end of the sophomore year, the students were again entitled to participate in the drawing for a residence if they wanted to change their residence for the junior year. If a student took part in this drawing, the house she listed as first choice was assumed (by the experimenters) to identify her reference group. If a subject did not take part, the house in which she was currently living was taken to be her reference group.

The subjects were classified into three groups: Group A: Subjects who had successfully drawn for a Row house and who did not try to draw out at the end of the sophomore year. Group B: Subjects who unsuccessfully drew for a Row house for the sophomore year and who tried again for a Row house after living in a non-Row house during the sophomore year. Group C: Subjects who unsuccessfully drew for a Row house for the sophomore year and who chose to remain in a non-Row house after living in one during the sophomore year.

The following table summarizes the membership and reference groups of the A, B, and C subjects.

Group	Original reference group	Membership group	Reference group
A	Row	Row	Row
B	Row	Non-row	Row
C	Row	Non-row	Non-row

Girls living in Row houses were known to be more authoritarian (as measured by the E-F scale;

of coming to agreement in their judgment of a picture. One person in the group (a confederate of the experimenter) sent a standard series of messages to the naïve person. These messages were designed to be the extreme opposite of the judgments of the naïve subject. In the public condition, the naïve subject made his final judgment in a face-to-face meeting with the confederate; in the private condition, he made his final judgment in an anonymous report to the experimenter. The results are given in Table 7.6.

PLURALISTIC IGNORANCE. If the behavior of the members of a group cannot be effectively monitored, a state of *pluralistic ignorance* may result in which "no one believes, but in which everyone believes that everyone else believes." In an early study of "Elm Hollow," a rural community, Schanck [1932] found that the Methodist Church was dominant. The norms of this church prohibited card playing, smoking, and drinking. When Schanck first investigated the attitudes of the people in Elm Hollow through interviews and questionnaires, the answers of nearly everyone reflected the norms of the church. Before he had left the community, however, he had played cards and had drunk hard cider with many individ-

see page 201) than girls living in non-Row houses. It was further known that on this campus there was a general decline in authoritarian attitudes from the freshman to the sophomore year.

It was predicted that (1) *Group A would show the least change.* The individuals in this group spent the sophomore year in a group typically high in authoritarianism. This membership group (Row-house group) also served as their reference group. Thus their initial attitudes were reinforced. (2) *Group C would show the greatest change.* As sophomores the individuals in this group were members of a group that was typically low in authoritarianism. They also changed their reference group from a Row to a non-Row house, i.e., from a group that was typically high to one that was typically low in authoritarianism. (3) *Group B would show an intermediate amount of change.* The individuals in this group were members of a group that was low in authoritarianism but they identified themselves with a reference group that was typically high.

A comparison of the E-F scores of the subjects obtained during the freshman year with scores obtained at the end of the sophomore year confirmed the hypotheses: Group A decreased the least in authoritarianism; group C decreased the most; group B changed an intermediate amount. The influence of the *membership* group by itself upon attitude change was studied by comparing the amount of change in group A who lived in a Row house during the sophomore year with the amount of change in groups B and C who lived in non-Row houses. Decrease in authoritarianism should be greater in groups B and C combined than in group A. This hypothesis was confirmed.

The influence of the *reference* group by itself in inducing attitude change was examined by comparing the amount of change in groups A and B combined, for whom the Row house had always been the reference group, with the amount of change in group C, whose reference group shifted from the Row-house group to the non-Row-house group. As predicted, the decrease in authoritarianism was greater in group C than in groups A and B combined.

The attitudes of the girls were determined by the groups they belonged to, by the groups they wanted to belong to, and by the combined influence of these two kinds of groups.

Siegel, Alberta E., and Siegel, S. *Reference groups, membership groups, and attitude change.* J. abnorm. soc. Psychol., *1957,* **55,** *360–364.*

uals—behind locked doors and drawn blinds. Each individual believed that he was virtually alone in rejecting the norms of the church.

Pluralistic ignorance results in public lip service to the norms of a group, and private recalcitrance. In such a state, the norms of the group have been termed "ideal" or "fictitious" norms; the norms which govern the deviant private behavior have been termed the "real" or "actual" norms of the group. This distinction overlooks the fact that both sets of norms—the "ideal" and the "real"—do govern behavior. Here again we have a situation in which imbalance among the "affective cog-

nitions" of a person can be maintained because it is want-satisfying (see Box 2.11, page 43). For the Elm Hollowers to refrain from

TABLE 7.6: PERCENTAGE OF SUBJECTS CHANGING OPINION IN PUBLIC VS. PRIVATE CONDITION [Adapted from Argyle, 1957]

Change	*Public condition*	*Private condition*
Toward partner	53.6	23.2
No change	34.5	72.6
Away from partner	11.9	4.2

card playing and drinking would make for consonance with their "public" attitudes—but what a dull and drab orthodoxy!

CHARACTERISTICS OF THE MEMBERSHIP

Not all members of a group are alike in their membership character. And the degree to which new members of a group accept the attitudes prescribed as appropriate by the norms of the group is partly determined by membership characteristics. In this section we will discuss three such membership characteristics and the manner in which they affect the power of the group to shape the attitudes of members: (1) the status of the new member; (2) the degree to which the new member values membership in the group; (3) the perceived legitimacy of the group norms.

STATUS OF MEMBER. Homans [1950] summarizes as follows a number of studies on the relation between a person's popularity in a group and the extent of his living up to the group norms: "To rank high in his group, a man must live up to all of its norms, and the norms in question must be the actual or sanctioned norms of the group and not just those to which the group gives lip service."

It should be noted, in passing, however, that studies of the relation between status and conformity to the norms of a group leave a basic question unanswered: Does a high-status member achieve his rank by conforming, or does he conform to maintain his high status?

A new member of a group, unsure of his status, may conform—indeed, overconform—to win popularity. The marginal status of the social climber is probably responsible for his oft-observed social orthodoxy. The middle-class man who has "struck it rich" and who aspires to upper-class status will be painfully proper. The aristocrat, secure in his elite status, will be casually comfortable in violating norms to suit his convenience.

The relation between status and reputation for compliance with group norms may, then, be curvilinear; that is, the amount of compliance

with group norms may increase with higher status to a certain point and then, with still higher status, it may decrease. An illustrative study will be cited.

Hughes [1946] has described a work group in which a clique of long-service workers had established a standard production rate with which new workers were required to comply. Hughes observed that once a new worker had become accepted by the group, there was less pressure to conform to the standard production rate. "Apparently a girl who is socially well established in the group can consistently break the rate a little with only mild teasing as punishment. But outsiders who break the rate are severely punished by ridicule and scorn; if they persist, and if associations are important to them, they may be forced off the job."

A study by Sherif [1951] of boys in an experimental summer camp revealed that the most unpopular boys in the group conformed more closely than the more popular boys to the norms of the group. This finding may reflect both the ability of the more popular boys to deviate, without fear of punishment from the group norms, and the use of compliance by unpopular boys to try to win greater acceptance.

Whether a man will change his attitudes when he changes groups depends—it would seem—on his status in his new group.

VALUATION OF MEMBERSHIP. The study by Kelley and Volkart cited earlier (see page 224) shows that the resistance to change of a group-anchored attitude increases with the degree to which membership in the group is valued. Their findings suggest also that new members of a group will take on the attitudes prescribed by a group more readily if membership is highly valued by them. If the group is unimportant to a new member, he will more readily assume the risk of rejection for deviance.

LEGITIMACY OF NORM. The impact of a group norm upon a new member will be influenced by his beliefs about the legitimacy of the norm. If he believes a particular norm of the group to be an improper intrusion upon his personal freedom or privacy, he may resist the group.

In a national study of the 1956 presidential election, Converse and Campbell [1960] examined the influence of the political norms of four types of groups—Catholics, Jews, Negroes, and labor unions—upon the votes of their members. The members were asked whether or not they felt it was "all right" for organizations representing the group to support relevant legislation and political candidates. A substantial relation was found between belief in legitimacy of the political group norm and voting for the party (viz., Democratic) predominantly favored by the group. Of those with "strong" belief in legitimacy of the norm, 65 per cent voted Democratic; of those with "weak" belief, only 41 per cent voted Democratic. It was also found that members with a high degree of identification with the group tended to feel more strongly that its political activity was legitimate than did members who were less closely identified. However, for comparable amounts of identification, there still remained the above relation between belief in norm legitimacy and voting in accord with the group.

As Converse and Campbell point out, the beliefs of members about the legitimacy of political norms will be influenced by perceived congruence between personal and group political positions. In other words, belief in legitimacy could be a result rather than a cause of conformity to the group political norm. However, there is evidence to suggest that the "legitimacy questions" were measuring values which are independent of personal political preferences. For example, members of the two religious groups—Catholics and Jews—were much more prone to say that political pressures from their groups were illegitimate than were members of labor unions and Negroes. This was interpreted as reflect-

ing the American doctrine of the separation of church and state.

THE BENNINGTON COLLEGE STUDY. The most complete study of the relation between the nature of the individual's membership in a group and the effectiveness of the group in changing his attitudes is the Bennington College study by Newcomb [1943]. This study is historically important as the first major study to use the method of repeated interviews of a sample of subjects to study change in attitudes over time (the panel method).

The Bennington College community at the time of the study (1935–1939) was new (the study was begun during the first year in which there was a senior class) and geographically isolated. The students were drawn largely from urban, upper-income families whose social attitudes were conservative. The members of the teaching staff were predominantly liberal, deeply concerned about social issues, and felt a responsibility for encouraging the students to take an active interest in social and political problems.

In this college community, most of the students shifted in their social attitudes from conservatism as freshmen to liberalism as seniors. For example, the straw votes of the students in the 1936 presidential campaign revealed a substantial difference between freshman and senior students. As Table 7.7 shows, 62 per cent of the freshmen voted for Landon, the Republican candidate; in sharp contrast, only 15 per cent of the upperclassmen voted for him. Roosevelt secured only 29 per cent of the freshman vote, but captured the majority of the votes of the upperclassmen. The votes for the Socialist and Communist party candidates increased from 9 per cent among freshmen to 30 per cent among seniors. Note also that the political preferences of the freshmen closely resembled the preferences of their parents, whereas the upperclassmen sharply diverged from their parents.

Attitudes toward nine specific social and economic issues were measured yearly during

TABLE 7.7: PREFERENCES OF STUDENTS AND PARENTS (BY SCHOOL YEAR) FOR PRESIDENTIAL CANDIDATES IN 1936 CAMPAIGN [After Newcomb, 1943]

CANDIDATES	FRESHMAN		SOPHOMORE		JUNIOR AND SENIOR	
	Students	*Parents*	*Students*	*Parents*	*Students*	*Parents*
Landon (Republican)	62%	66%	43%	69%	15%	60%
Roosevelt (Democratic)	29	26	42	22	54	35
Thomas (Socialist) or Browder (Communist)	9	7	15	8	30	4

the four years of the study. The mean trend was again from freshman conservatism to senior liberalism. This trend was not, however, found in all students. Some students changed markedly; others changed not at all; still others reversed the group trend.

Newcomb's search for the factors associated with these individual differences led him to study intensively 24 liberal and 19 conservative seniors. In interviews, they were asked questions about the resemblance between their own attitudes and the attitudes of class majorities and leaders, about their parents' attitudes and the resemblance of their own attitudes to them, etc. Personality data were also obtained from the personnel office of the college and from the college psychiatrist.

From his study of these two extreme groups, Newcomb concluded that the reasons the attitude changes occurred in some students and did not occur in others had to do with the relation of the student to the college community and her relation to her family.

The liberal seniors were found to be highly motivated to achieve independence from their families and to achieve leadership and prestige in the college group (prestige in this college community being accorded liberal students). In other words, identification with the college group and conformity to its norms had instrumental value for these students (see Box 7.10).

The conservative seniors were generally self-defensive in personality make-up because of feelings of personal inadequacy. Those who had very low self-esteem defended themselves by withdrawal and were thus not influenced by the college community. Those with somewhat higher self-esteem defended themselves by actively resisting community influence to maintain their family ties (see Box 7.11).

BY WAY OF CAUTION. It should be emphasized that Newcomb's finding that the effect of college experience is to move students in the direction of liberalism holds only for a liberal college. In a conservative college, we should expect to find the majority of the students moving in the direction of increased political-economic conservatism. College students, as is well known, are drawn preponderantly from conservative middle-class families. Thus the family and the conservative college would tend to reinforce each other in support of conservatism. The occasional student from a liberal family may show increased conservatism if he is motivated to reject his family and to identify with the conservative college community; or increased liberalism, if he clings to his family and insulates himself from the influence of the college. This points to the danger of characterizing a "liberal" or a "conservative" as having such and such a personality pattern.

Moreover, the political-economic liberalism of the majority of the Bennington College upperclassmen should not be interpreted as due solely to their strivings for group acceptance and status. The faculty provided the students with new information about political

SOCIAL ATTITUDES

and economic issues and events, and stimulated them to think seriously about the problems facing "a depression-torn America and a war-threatened world." Undoubtedly the attitudes of many students changed because of changes in their cognitions. The general liberal "atmosphere" of the college community was important, however, in influencing the way in which the students *interpreted* the new information; facts, as we have repeatedly said, do not speak for themselves. For example, the facts about Franco, the Spanish *Caudillo*, tended to make Bennington College students (a preponderantly Protestant and liberal college) anti-Franco; the same facts, when presented to students in a Catholic and conservative college, as Newcomb points out, reinforced their pro-Franco attitudes.

TO RECAPITULATE

The attitudes of an individual tend to change as he moves into new groups or changes his group allegiances. The effectiveness of a group in leading a new member to adopt the "group line" is determined, in part, by the centrality of the group norm relating to the attitude, the degree to which the new member is free to leave the group, and the effectiveness of the policing power of the group. If a group cannot police its members effectively because deviant attitudes can be expressed privately, a state of pluralistic ignorance may develop.

Certain characteristics of the person's membership also determine the power of the group to force him to comply with the group norms. If a new member feels insecure in his status, he will be more likely to take on the approved attitudes to gain approval and enhance his status. The degree to which the new member values his membership in the group will also determine its power over him. And only if the new member accepts as legitimate the group norm which prescribes a particular attitude will the norm effectively regulate his behavior.

GUIDE 23: *The effectiveness of enforced modification of behavior in inducing attitude change is a function of the circumstances of the enforcement and the reaction of the individual to it*

The thesis of the sociologist Sumner [1906] is quoted even today in support of the proposition that one cannot bring about changes in attitudes and behavior by law or by force: "Legislation cannot make mores" and "stateways cannot change folkways." This thesis has been invoked most recently in the United States by persons who are opposed to the integration of public schools as required by the Supreme Court decision of May 17, 1954.

Both theory and experience challenge the validity of this venerable position. Numerous studies of the effect of enforced change in behavior toward an attitude object clearly indicate that substantial attitude changes may thus be brought about. In this section we will examine the influence of two types of enforced modification of behavior upon attitudes: (1) intimate contact with minority-group members, forced upon the individual by law or by circumstances; (2) the required playing of a role in which attitudes contradictory to the actual attitudes of the individual must be publicly expressed.

ENFORCED CONTACT AND ETHNIC ATTITUDES

Enforced contact with the object of an attitude may strengthen or weaken an existing attitude, may produce congruent or incongruent change. Familiarity may breed love or hate. Enforced contact may also change the intensity of an attitude, even if its valence remains unchanged (see Box 7.12).

Enforced modification of behavior owes its effectiveness to several factors. First, enforced contact with members of minority groups tends to correct autistic distortion (see page 123). When Negroes and whites live together in the same neighborhoods and apartment houses, the whites will have an opportunity to meet and know Negro people. This may correct invalid, stereotyped beliefs which support prejudiced attitudes. Second, when there is a need to put up with or come to terms with a "negative" object, there is also a tendency to seek to discover favorable aspects about that object. A white neighbor of Negroes may insist that "Negroes aren't so bad after all," in situations where the white finds himself on the defensive because he lives in a "mixed" neighborhood. Although this may be at first only a rationalization, it may, because of the trend toward attitude consistency (see page 143), eventually become an integral part of the belief and feeling components of the individual's attitude toward Negroes.

IN THE ARMY. During World War II an opportunity arose to test the effect of enforced contact between Negroes and whites—contact

BOX 7.10: *The liberal community creates liberals . . .*

Theodore M. Newcomb, a social psychologist at the University of Michigan, studied the effect of membership in a liberal college community (Bennington College) upon the political attitudes of the students. An examination of those students who changed in the direction of the liberal majority showed that liberal attitudes served a dual function: they were a means of securing independence from conservative parents and of gaining prestige in the college community.

The following excerpts from interviews with five liberal students illustrate these dual functions:

I accepted liberal attitudes here because *I had always secretly felt that my family was narrow and intolerant, and because such attitudes had prestige value.* It was all part of my generally expanding personality—*I had never really been part of anything before.* I don't accept things without examining things, however, and I was sure I meant it before I changed.

It didn't take me long to see that liberal attitudes had prestige value. But all the time I felt inwardly superior to persons who want public acclaim. Once I had arrived at a feeling of personal security, I could see that it wasn't important—it wasn't enough. *So many people have no security at all. I became liberal at first because of its prestige value.* I remain so because the problems around which my liberalism centers are important. What I want now is to be effective in solving the problems.

Every influence I felt tended to push me in the liberal direction: my underdog complex, *my need to be independent of my parents, and my anxiousness to be a leader here.*

I came to college to get away from my family, who never had any respect for my mind. Becoming radical meant thinking for myself and, figuratively, thumbing my nose at my family. *It also meant intellectual identification with the faculty and students that I most wanted to be like.*

Of course there's social pressure here to give up your conservatism. I'm glad of it, because for me this became the *vehicle for achieving independence from my family.* So changing my attitudes has gone hand in hand with two *very important things: establishing my own independence and at the same time becoming a part of the college organism.*

Newcomb, T. M. Personality and social change: attitude formation in a student community. New York: Dryden, 1943.

SOCIAL ATTITUDES

which was opposed by the whites. At one point in the war there was urgent need for combat replacements in the European Theater of Operations. Because of manpower shortage, the American General Staff adopted a new policy with regard to the utilization of Negro combat troops. Instead of attempting to form all-Negro infantry units, Negro soldiers who volunteered for combat were formed into platoons led by white commissioned and noncommissioned officers and assigned to 11 white combat divisions.

Attitude surveys were made by the Research Branch of the Army's Information and Education Division [1952] both before and after the institution of this policy. The first survey showed that the majority of the white soldiers and two-thirds of the white officers who were to lead the Negro soldiers were opposed to this mixing of troops. Nevertheless, the General Staff went through with its decision. Two months after the Negro troops had joined the white outfits, a second survey indicated that (1) 77 per cent of the white officers had be-

. . . except when it doesn't: **BOX 7.11**

Those students in Newcomb's study who did *not* change in the direction of the liberal majority were found to reject the college community or to isolate themselves from its influence and to maintain their dependent affiliation with their parents. The following excerpts from interviews with five conservative seniors illustrate the conflict between "family and faculty" which these conservative students faced, and their resolution of the conflict in favor of the family.

I wanted to disagree with all the noisy liberals, but I was afraid and I couldn't. *So I built up a wall inside me against what they said. I found I couldn't compete, so I decided to stick to my father's ideas. For at least two years I've been insulated against all college influences.*

I've come to realize how much my mother's happiness depends on me, and the best way I can help her is to do things with her at home as often as I can. This has resulted in my not getting the feel of the college in certain ways, and I know my general conservatism is one of those ways. But it has not been important enough to me to make me feel particularly left out. If you're genuine and inoffensive about your opinions, no one really minds here if you remain conservative.

I'm all my mother has in the world. It's considered intellectually superior here to be liberal or radical. This puts me on the defensive, as I refuse to consider my mother beneath me intellectually, as so many other students do. Apart from this, I have loved every aspect of college life.

Family against faculty has been my struggle here. As soon as I felt really secure here I decided not to let the college atmosphere affect me too much. Every time I've tried to rebel against my family I've found out how terribly wrong I am, and so I've naturally kept to my parents' attitudes.

I'd like to think like the college leaders, but I'm not bold enough and I don't know enough. So the college trend means little to me; I didn't even realize how much more conservative I am than the others. *I guess my family influence has been strong enough to counterbalance the college influence.*

Newcomb, T. M. Personality and social change: attitude formation in a student community. New York: Dryden, 1943.

BOX 7.12: *Contact and attitude intensity*

Louis Guttman and Uriel G. Foa of the Hebrew University in Jerusalem have shown that contact with the members of a group may affect the intensity of attitudes toward the group, although the valence of the attitude may remain unchanged.

A cross-section survey of the attitudes of the Israeli population toward the government's civil servants was carried out. A Guttman scale of four items (see pages 154 to 155) was the instrument used to measure valence. The intensity of the attitude was also measured (see pages 156 to 157). In addition, each respondent was asked: "In recent months did you have occasion to come in contact with officials in government offices?" Four alternatives were provided: much contact, some contact, almost no contact, no contact at all.

No relation between extent of contact and valence of attitude toward civil servants was found. However, as the following table shows, the *intensity* of the attitude does increase with contact, both for persons with favorable and for persons with unfavorable attitudes.

Level of contact	Median intensity percentile
Much contact	63
Some contact	58
Almost no contact	39
No contact at all	40

The investigators suggest the following possible interpretation of this observed relation between contact and intensity. Beliefs about government officials are based primarily on two sources of information: direct contact and indirect contact (word of mouth and mass media). Those persons who have little or no opportunity for direct contact derive their attitudes from persons who have had more contact. Since their attitudes are thus acquired at second hand, the attitudes tend to be less intense.

This study illustrates the importance of measuring not only valence but intensity in studying attitude change.

Guttman, L., and Foa, U. G. Social contact and an inter-group attitude. Publ. Opin. Quart., *1951,* **15**, *43–53.*

come more favorable to the mixed companies and none had become less favorable; (2) more than 80 per cent thought that the Negro soldiers had been good combat soldiers and that white and Negro soldiers were getting along well with each other; (3) only 7 per cent of the white soldiers in mixed companies said that they disliked very much the policy of mixing Negroes and whites, whereas 62 per cent of the soldiers in companies which had remained "pure white" were opposed to the policy. Attitudes *can* be made to obey orders!

IN THE HOUSING PROJECT. Deutsch and Collins [1951] have compared Negro-white relations in two types of housing projects—integrated projects in which families were assigned to apartments without regard to race, and segregated projects in which Negro and white families were assigned to different buildings or to different areas in the project. A sample of 100 white and 25 Negro housewives was interviewed in each of four projects—two integrated projects and two segregated projects.

One of the basic hypotheses of the study was that living in an integrated project will result in more frequent and more intimate interpersonal relations between Negroes and whites than will living in a segregated one. The data strongly confirm this hypothesis. More than 95 per cent of the housewives in the two integrated projects said that a person who moved into the project would "be likely to get to know . . . colored people in the project." In the two segregated projects, in contrast, only about 25 per cent of the women felt that there was any likelihood of getting to know colored people. Twenty-seven per cent of the women in one integrated project and 62 per cent of the women in the other indicated that at least one of the women they "know best" was a Negro. None of the women in the segregated projects counted Negro people among those they knew best.

What was the effect of the frequent and intimate contact between Negro and white women in the integrated projects? The many different measures of attitude toward the Negro obtained by Deutsch and Collins all indicate that the housewives in the integrated projects became much less prejudiced than the women in the segregated projects. The net gains for the women in the two kinds of projects (per cent of housewives reporting favorable changes minus per cent reporting unfavorable changes) are shown in Table 7.8.

It is clear that the net gains are far greater in the integrated projects than in the segregated. Deutsch and Collins were able to show that this difference could not be accounted for by assuming that the differences existed before the women moved into the projects.

Separate measures of the three attitude components were secured through interview questions and rating scales. The data indicate that the experience of living in an integrated project produced changes in a positive direction in all of the three components—in beliefs about Negroes, in feelings about Negroes, and in action tendencies toward Negroes. Although the changes in attitude seem to have been greater toward Negroes living in the project than toward Negro people in general, there was evidence of considerable change in attitude toward the latter also.

These investigators sum up their work and the results of related studies as follows:

Prejudices are likely to be diminished when prejudiced people are brought into situations that compel contact between them and the objects of prejudice, provided:

(a) that the behavior of the objects of prejudice is such as not to conform with the beliefs of the prejudiced. That is, the Negroes with whom the prejudiced person has contact are not "lazy," "ignorant," "delinquent," etc.

(b) that the intimacy and amount of contact with objects of prejudice not conforming to the stereotypes of the prejudiced are such as to result in experiences which are sufficiently compelling to resist marked perceptual and memorial distortion.

(c) that the contact takes place under conditions which make the nonconforming behavior seem relevant to the basis on which the objects of prejudice are grouped together. Thus, if a Negro attendant is seen to be clean

TABLE 7.8: ATTITUDE CHANGE AND ENFORCED CONTACT [Data from Deutsch and Collins, 1951]

INITIAL ATTITUDE	INTEGRATED HOUSING PROJECTS, PER CENT OF NET GAIN		SEGREGATED HOUSING PROJECTS, PER CENT OF NET GAIN	
	Koaltown	Socktown	Bakerville	Frankville
Highly unfavorable	71	78	26	19
Moderately unfavorable	46	61	18	2
Favorable	13	28	15	−18

and honest, there may be little effect on stereotypes if the perception of cleanliness and honesty is connected primarily with the requirements of the situation, with the classification of the individual as an attendant rather than as a Negro or Negro attendant.

(d) that the prejudiced person has values or is exposed to social influences (e.g., democratic values or the social influences emanating from a policy of an official, public body) which would strongly conflict with the unabashed retention of unrationalized prejudices.

ON THE JOB. Intergroup contact in a work situation seems to be much less effective in inducing changes. Harding and Hogrefe [1952] found that significantly more white department-store employees who had worked with Negroes on an equal-status basis were willing to do so again than were those who had never worked with Negroes. However, no changes in other action tendencies toward Negroes, or in feelings toward Negroes, were observed.

These results are reminiscent of a form of anti-Semitism that the Jews in New York term "five o'clock shadow." Jewish and non-Jewish business associates who work together in harmony and friendship during business hours part and go their separate ways as soon as five o'clock strikes. The non-Jew would rarely think of inviting his Jewish business associate to become a member of his club, to be his house guest, or to have his children mix socially or intermarry with the children of his Jewish associate.

REACTION TO ENFORCING AGENT. Changes in behavior toward an attitude object are not forced upon an "empty organism." How the individual is affected by the required modification of his behavior, forced upon him by external authority, will be influenced by the kind of person he is, especially by the way he characteristically reacts to authority. A study by Mussen [1950] documents this point. He examined the effect of membership in a nonsegregated summer camp upon the attitudes of white children toward the Negro. The white boys' attitudes were measured just before they left home for camp and again, four weeks later, at the end of the camp period. Personality measures and data on adjustment to camp life were also obtained.

Comparison of the pre-camp and post-camp mean attitude scores indicated striking individual differences in attitude change. Twenty-four of the 106 boys showed a significant decrease in prejudice, but 27 showed an increase.

How are we to account for these marked differences among the boys in response to the camp experience? They all experienced enforced contact with Negroes in a camp where the adult camp leaders upheld the norm of racial equality and tolerance. Why did 24 of the boys accept the official norms of the camp group? Why did 27 reject them? Mussen's personality and social-adjustment data indicate that a boy's acceptance or rejection of the norm of the camp group was a function of his identification with the group. Identification with the group, in turn, was found to be associated with enduring personality trends. (Here is a dramatic illustration of the importance of psychological factors in determining how individuals will respond differently to an identical social situation.)

Mussen writes:

> From the point of view of social adjustment in the camp situation, those whose prejudice decreased were generally more satisfied with the camp, complained less about interpersonal relations, and liked the vast majority of their fellow campers. They were better accepted by other boys, formed fewer but probably more intimate friendships, and were judged to be better at "relating" to others. It may be assumed that the camp experience was a rewarding one for them; that they therefore accepted the social norms of the new situation, and became less prejudiced.

The boys who increased in prejudice showed "great needs to defy authority, and strong aggressive feelings. However, they felt that the expression of aggression led to punishment, retaliation, restraint and prohibition." The boys who decreased in prejudice revealed a different pattern. They "had relatively few aggressive needs and less feeling that punishment and retaliation follow the expression of aggression."

THE EFFECT OF REQUIRED ROLE PLAYING

People often find themselves in situations in which norms of behavior require them to act toward members of a minority group or toward other attitude objects in a way that is opposed to their private attitudes. The prejudiced professor is constrained to be polite to a Jewish colleague or a Negro student; the bigoted businessman must, if he is to survive, attract and serve customers of all races, creeds, and colors; the ethnocentric white guest must show a modicum of politeness to a Negro whom he finds is a fellow guest in the home of his host. The culturally defined roles of professor, businessman, and guest prescribe behavior toward minority-group persons which is opposed to the private attitudes of the prejudiced professor, the bigoted businessman, the ethnocentric guest. Will their private attitudes be affected by the public attitudes which they are expected to express? This question is our concern in this section.

SOME EXPERIMENTAL ILLUSTRATIONS. In a laboratory study of the influence of role playing upon attitudes toward the Negro, Culbertson [1957] administered pre-experimental attitude scales to a sample of subjects to measure the valence of their attitude toward Negro-white housing integration and of their generalized attitude toward Negroes. She then divided her subjects into groups of six, each group consisting of three role players and three observers. Each observer was instructed to watch a particular role player.

The role players were told that a marked increase in the number of Negroes in a nearby community was expected because of a new

defense plant. An integrated housing policy had been adopted, and an educational program was planned to minimize the danger of interracial tensions and antagonisms. In playing the role, the subject was instructed to advocate a specific theme for the educational program which was completely in favor of residential integration. Following the role-playing session, the original attitude scales were again administered.

The results of the study are given in Table 7.9. Note that a significantly larger percentage of role players than observers became more positive toward integration. Note also that a higher percentage of observers shifted than did control subjects who had not observed the role-playing session. Finally, note that the effect of the specific role-playing experience also spread to the subjects' generalized attitudes toward the Negroes.

For another example—in this case an example of how role playing may change beliefs—see Box 7.13.

The influence of playing a role in which one publicly expresses attitudes opposed to one's private attitudes may, it seems, lead the individual to adopt the attitudes he publicly espouses. (In this connection see the discussion on page 228 concerning the effects of public commitment.) "Playing the game" may leave permanent effects.

If the role player is rewarded by approval, he will more readily shift in the direction of

TABLE 7.9: ROLE PLAYING AND ATTITUDES TOWARD THE NEGRO [After Culbertson, 1957]

| | PER CENT POSITIVE CHANGE | |
GROUP	Attitude toward housing integration	Generalized attitude toward Negro
Role players	66.7	76.1
Observers	42.9	56.8
Controls	11.1	21.1

BOX 7.13: *Saying is believing . . .*

Irving L. Janis and Bert T. King, while members of the staff of the Yale Communication and Attitude Change Program, studied the effect of role playing upon change in beliefs.

In the first study, students were asked to give an informal talk based on an outline given them by the experimenters, arguing in favor of a position which differed from their actual beliefs. In two of the three issues used in the study, the role players changed more in the direction advocated in the talk than did a group of passive control listeners. On the third issue, the two groups showed about the same amount of change. The students who had presented talks on this issue expressed dissatisfaction with their performance. They tended to adhere more closely to the proposed outline, made few attempts to reformulate the main points, to give illustrative examples, or to present additional arguments.

These findings suggested two possible explanations of the effect of role playing upon beliefs.

1. The "improvisation" hypothesis: A person's beliefs will be changed if he is stimulated to think of new arguments and appeals in order to convince others to adopt a point of view.

2. The "satisfaction" hypothesis: Satisfaction with performance in role playing provides a special reward that reinforces the beliefs expressed in playing the role.

These two hypotheses were investigated in a second study. Here male college students (after having been given an opinion test on the subject of military service) were randomly assigned to various experimental groups, and were exposed to the same persuasive communication. The communication argued that (1) over 90 per cent of all college students would be drafted within one year of graduation; (2) the majority of college students would be required to serve at least three years in the Armed Forces (one year longer than the period then required).

Two different groups of role players were used: The subjects in group A had to make an impromptu talk, without using the communication, immediately after reading it. In giving their talks, the subjects were asked to play the role of a sincere advocate of the point of view expressed in the communication. The subjects in group B were given a much easier task which was expected to lead to a feeling of satisfaction with their performances. They were instructed merely to read the fully prepared script aloud.

The subjects in group B, as anticipated, were found to be much more satisfied with their performance than the subjects in group A. Hence the "satisfaction" hypothesis would predict more change in group B. The "improvisation" hypothesis would make the opposite prediction.

The net opinion change is shown in the following table.

Estimates of:	*Improvisation group A*	*Satisfaction group B*
Length of service for draftees	41%	27%
Chances of being deferred	44	26

"It seems plausible," the investigators conclude, "that there is a lowering of psychological resistance whenever a person regards the persuasive arguments emanating from others as his 'own' ideas."

Janis, I. L., and King, B. T. The influence of role-playing on opinion-change. J. abnorm. soc. Psychol., 1954, 49, 211–218.

King, B. T., and Janis, I. L. Comparison of the effectiveness of improvised versus non-improvised role playing in producing opinion changes. Hum. Relat., 1956, 9, 177–186.

William A. Scott, a social psychologist at the University of Colorado, has studied the effects of rewarding the verbal expression of attitude upon attitude change.

In one study, pairs of students were selected from different psychology classes to debate one of three different issues toward which they had earlier expressed their attitudes. Both members were required to argue for the position *contrary* to the one they preferred. The winner of the debate was determined by the vote of the class. However, the experimenter actually manipulated the class vote so that a predetermined member of each pair "won." Later attitude tests showed that the "winners" changed in the direction of the position which they had defended in the debate. The "losers" did not change significantly as compared with a group of control subjects who made up the audience. Indeed, as the data in the following table indicate, there is some slight suggestion that the initial attitudes of the "losers" may have been *reinforced*. (In reading this table, positive mean change is a change in the direction advocated in the debate; negative mean change is a change in the direction opposite to that defended in the debate. Attitude change was measured on a seven-point scale.)

	"Winners"	"Losers"	Controls
Per cent of subjects changing in direction opposed to initial opinion	58	19	31
Mean change in scale position	+1.25	−.17	+.31

In a later study, Scott confirmed these results and further found that the attitude changes in the debate winners persisted for at least 10 days.

These results suggest that role playing will induce attitude change only if the individual receives reward for publicly espousing a view at variance with his private attitudes. Again we are reminded of the important role of wants in the development and change of attitudes.

Scott, W. A. *Attitude change through reward of verbal behavior.* J. abnorm. soc. Psychol., *1957,* **55,** *72–75.*

Scott, W. A. *Attitude change by response reinforcement: replication and extension.* Sociometry, *1959,* **22,** *328–335.*

the attitudes he expresses in playing his role; if he is not rewarded by approval, he will not so readily shift (see Box 7.14). It would appear, in other words, that role playing tends to result in a shift of attitude when there is *social support* for such a shift.

A THEORY OF COGNITIVE DISSONANCE

Festinger [1957] has developed a theory of *cognitive dissonance* which has a number of interesting consequences for attitude change. The cognitive dissonance theory holds that two cognitions ". . . are in dissonant relation if, considering those two alone, the obverse of one element would follow from the other." For example, the belief that all human beings are equal in the sight of the Lord and the belief that Negroes should not be allowed to worship in one's church are in dissonant relation since the *obverse* of the second belief follows logically from the first. The theory further holds that dissonance, ". . . being psychologically uncomfortable, will motivate the person to try to reduce dissonance and achieve consonance."

The direct applicability of this theory to the

phenomena of attitude change through enforced modification of behavior and through role playing is obvious. If, through either of these means, the individual is led to express outwardly an attitude which is discrepant from his actual private attitude, then a state of dissonance is created in him. This uncomfortable state can be reduced in various ways, one of which is to shift the inner attitude so that it corresponds more closely with the outward expression. (For a study which indicates some unexpected consequences of such dissonance between inner belief and overt action, see Box 7.15.)

BOX 7.15: *Twenty pieces of silver*

If you want to buy a man's beliefs, how much should you pay him? This question was explored by Leon Festinger and J. M. Carlsmith, social psychologists at Stanford University. The following derivations of the theory of cognitive dissonance proposed by Festinger were tested.

1. If an individual is forced to act in a manner which is contrary to his private attitude, he will experience dissonance.

2. If the "external" forces which compel him to act contrary to his attitude are overwhelmingly *strong,* the total magnitude of dissonance will be *minimal;* if the forces are *weak*—just barely strong enough to induce him to act—the dissonance will be *maximal.*

3. One way to reduce dissonance is for the individual to change his attitude to correspond with his action. Since the pressure to reduce dissonance is a function of the magnitude of the dissonance, *attitude change should be greatest when the force used to induce the action is just minimally sufficient.*

Three groups of 20 undergraduate students each were used as subjects. In the "One-Dollar condition," the subject was first required to perform repetitive and monotonous tasks. He was then hired by the experimenter as an "assistant" and paid one dollar to tell a waiting fellow student that the tasks were enjoyable and interesting. In the "Twenty-Dollar condition" the subjects were hired for twenty dollars to do the same thing. Control subjects merely performed the monotonous tasks.

A postexperimental interview was held to learn the subjects' attitudes toward the tasks. The interviewer was identified as a member of the psychology department who was conducting a study of the experiments in which elementary psychology students were required to serve as subjects. The true purpose of the interview was to get valid expressions of the subject's private attitudes.

The results confirmed the theory. The One-Dollar subjects had persuaded themselves that the tasks were really interesting and enjoyable. The Twenty-Dollar subjects had not changed their private opinions (as checked against the control group).

In simple terms, the results of this study may be interpreted as follows. If a man is paid to act contrary to his beliefs and if the bribe is small, he will say to himself: "I have been bought for a paltry sum." To assuage his feeling that he is a "cheap bribe," he will tend to come to believe that he acted the way he did, not because of a paltry sum but because he really believed in what he did. On the other hand, if he has been bought for a large sum, he will tend to explain his conduct by saying to himself: "No one could resist such a great sum—*everyone else would do the same,*" and therefore he will not find it necessary to counter the threat to his self-image by changing his attitudes.

Festinger, L., and Carlsmith, J. M. *Cognitive consequences of forced compliance.* J. abnorm. soc. Psychol., *1959,* **58,** *203–210.*

SOCIAL ATTITUDES

TO RECAPITULATE

Enforced modification of the actions of an individual toward an object may come about in two ways: the individual may be thrown into intimate contact with the object by law or by circumstances; he may be coerced by authority, by social mores, or by a reward to play a role in which he expresses an attitude contradictory to his actual attitude.

The effectiveness of enforced contact in producing attitude change depends upon the circumstances of the enforced contact and upon the reaction of the individual to the enforcing authority. Role playing may produce change if the individual sees that the attitude he publicly expresses is socially supported.

The theory of cognitive dissonance holds that the attitude change produced by enforced modification of action results from the uncomfortable state of dissonance which is aroused when an individual publicly says or does something counter to his private attitude. One way of reducing this state of dissonance is to change the attitude privately held to make it conform with the attitude publicly expressed.

GUIDE 24: *The effectiveness of personality change techniques in producing attitude change depends upon the appropriateness of the techniques to the function of the attitude for the personality*

As we have seen, the attitudes held by the individual are "used" by him in various ways: they may aid him in his search for meaning, they may be means of satisfying his wants, they may enable him to maintain his self-concept. By holding prejudicial attitudes, the bigot is able to defend himself against unacceptable impulses of a hostile, aggressive, or

sexual nature by projecting them onto members of minority groups. (See the discussion of the functional nature of prejudice, pages 182 to 186). As Ackerman and Jahoda [1956] point out in their study of anti-Semitism in persons undergoing psychoanalytic therapy:

> The mechanism of projection permeates the entire personality of the anti-Semite. . . . For the anti-Semite, the Jew is a living Rorschach blot. His alleged and actual qualities are so manifold and so inconsistent, so ambiguous and indeterminate, that the anti-Semite sees whatever he needs to see in the Jew.

In recent years there has been increasing interest in examining the possibility of changing social attitudes by changing personality. For an earlier study illustrating the use of a standard psychotherapeutic technique with "problem children" and resulting changes in racial attitudes, see Box 7.16.

PRIDE AND PREJUDICE

In a series of studies, Katz and his associates have studied the role of self-insight and self-defensiveness in racial attitudes and in the changing of racial attitudes. In one study Katz, Sarnoff, and McClintock [1956] compared the effectiveness of a factual informative appeal and a self-insight procedure. They found that unfavorable attitudes toward the Negro were not appreciably changed by the factual, informative appeal. As these investigators comment:

> Attempts to change the ego-defensive individual which are based upon the logic [of rational appeals] may actually reinforce his old attitudes. These appeals really assume either (a) the individual is interested in a more accurate and more complete knowledge of the world, or (b) he is primarily concerned with maximizing the satisfaction of his conscious needs. If, however, he is primarily concerned with avoiding a direct facing of his own internal conflicts, then he will protect himself from such a possibility the moment he senses an attempt to make him change. . . . The

BOX 7.16: *Tolerance through therapy*

Virginia M. Axline conducted a series of play-therapy sessions for seven-year-old "problem children" who were either extremely withdrawn or aggressively antisocial. In these permissive or nondirective play sessions, the children were subject to few rules and were able to express their feelings and impulses with little fear of punishment. One therapy group was made up of Louise, Perry, Robbin, and June. June was a Negro child; the other three were white children.

In one of the sessions, Perry and Louise were painting. June turns and holds up a small table from the doll house. "This is a cocktail table." As she reaches over she jars Robbin's arm and he spills the tray on which he was carrying "the drinks."

"Oh, for Christ sake," he shouts, "you Goddam nigger. You spilled the tray! This makes me so goddam mad I could spit on you!"

June draws back. Her face clouds over. "I am not a nigger!" she shouts. "What are you then?" Robbin demands. June looks about her unhappily. "I-I-I am a person!" she says.

There is absolute silence in the playroom. All three children turn and look at June.

"Oh," says Robbin. There is still another silence. Robbin looks down at the floor. He goes over and sits down on the edge of the sand box. He puts his hand down in the sand, idly sifts it through his fingers. June stands still in the middle of the room staring at Robbin. He looks at her again. "I'm sorry, June," he says finally.

"That's all right," June says. There is once more quietness in the room. June turns her back to the others—goes over to the doll house things and sorts through them until she finds a little Negro doll. She holds it in her hand and looks at it. Robbin still sits on the edge of the sand box watching June with an odd expression on his face.

June picks up a white doll, holds the white doll and the Negro doll side by side, looks at them for a long time. She picks up one of the doll house beds and places the white doll in it very carefully. Then she glares at the Negro doll. She lays it on the table, grabs the wooden hammer and pounds the doll viciously. "Get rid of the old nigger!" she shouts. "Dirty old nigger. Black, hateful old nigger."

Robbin stands up quickly and looks at her. "June!" he says. "June! She is a person!"

"Oh," says June in a tone of distress, "I'm sorry." She picks up the Negro doll. She looks at Robbin again. "Could I—" she asks, then hesitates. "What?" Robbin asks. "Could I put her in the same bed with the—pretty doll?"

Robbin comes over and looks at the white doll in the little bed and at the Negro doll in June's little brown hand. He considers it for a long time. Perry and Louise leave their painting and come over, too. They all gather around June, who is still holding the little black doll.

"Is there—is there another bed?" Perry asks. "Everyone should sleep in a bed of his own. No two people should ever sleep together."

resistance generated to protect the ego results in a blanket rejection of the change situation . . . and an emotional reinforcement of the attitude. Though we recognize the importance of resistance in other contexts, we have slighted its role in attitude change. Hence, persuasion and propaganda can have negative rather than positive effects.

"I sleep with my sister," Louise says, "and that's all right!"

Robbin stoops down and sorts through the toy furniture. He finds another bed. June watches him silently. There are tears in her eyes.

"Here is another bed," Robbin says to June. She stretches the doll out toward him. Robbin does not touch the doll.

Perry reaches out a hand to take the bed. Robbin pulls it out of his reach. He glares at Perry. "You keep outa this," he says roughly.

Then he looks at June and asks her very gently, "Where does she want to sleep, June? Does she want a bed all her own? Or does she want to sleep with the white girl?"

June will not commit herself. She blinks back her tears and continues to hold the Negro doll out to Robbin. Finally he takes it, places it in the bed alone, quickly removes it, throws the empty bed across the room with violence and places the Negro doll in the bed with the white one. June smiles radiantly.

"Why did you do that?" Perry asks. "I know why," Louise says. "I'm glad you did, Robbin."

"Why did you?" Perry demands again.

Robbin shrugs his shoulders and sits down on the edge of the sand box.

"I know why he did," Louise says. "You didn't want June to cry. Isn't that why?" "No," Robbin says, shaking his head. "Well, I think you're crazy," Perry says, and goes after the other doll bed. He brings it back and reaches for the Negro doll. Robbin grabs his arm.

"You let that alone!" he yells. "You keep your hands off." "They should each have their own bed!" Perry shouts. "Let them alone," Robbin shouts. "Let them alone!"

The group splits up again. Robbin crawls into the sand box and sits with his back to the others. June sits down at the table and rolls a ball of clay in her hands. Louise and Perry return to their painting. None of the children speaks. When it is time to go they leave quietly. June walks back to the schoolroom with Perry and Louise and they talk happily together. Robbin walks back alone—hanging his head.

In later play-therapy sessions, other "racial" conflicts arose and were resolved. After the seventh session, however, they had disappeared. They all seemed to have accepted one another. This change in ethnic attitudes, according to the investigator, carried over in the classroom.

These findings, while dramatic, must be interpreted with caution. It is not clear that the play-therapy sessions have produced changes in personality—a general decrease in amount of hostility. An alternative interpretation might be that the "enforced contact" between the Negro child and the white children led to specific changes in the racial attitudes of the white children.

Axline, Virginia M. Play therapy and race conflict in young children. J. abnorm. soc. Psychol., *1948,* **43**, *300–310.*

The investigators describe the self-insight procedure as follows:

In the first part of this presentation, we described in general terms the dynamics of scapegoating, projection, and compensation with respect to the development of anti-minority attitudes. We then presented a case history of a college girl to illustrate how these mechanisms of defense were basic to her ethnic prejudices.

This interpretative material was found to be effective in producing more tolerant attitudes toward the Negro in persons who were low and moderate in self-defensiveness. Those subjects who were high in self-defensiveness were not, however, appreciably changed. This was interpreted as due to resistance: the material was assumed to be so threatening to a highly self-defensive person that it was rejected. The high "ego-defender" needs, and needs badly, to keep her prejudice to preserve her pride.

It was also found that the self-insight material, as predicted, had a greater effect, over time, than did the informational material. The prediction of a "sleeper effect" (see page 231) for the self-insight procedure was based on the notion that "deeper" changes in the personality would be produced by this material and that these changes would take longer to occur.

The assumption that the reduction in prejudice produced by the self-insight procedure resulted from a breakthrough in self-defensiveness was based on three arguments: First, the nature of the material was deliberately planned to describe the functional nature of prejudice. Second, the changes produced by this material showed, as predicted, a sleeper effect, thus suggesting that "deeper" personality changes were involved. Third, as predicted, persons high in self-defensiveness were most resistant to the self-insight material.

However, in another study in this series, Stotland, Katz, and Patchen [1959] gave some of their subjects case material which applied, not to prejudice toward minority groups, but to prejudice toward townspeople around the college which the person in the case history attended. This material was not effective in bringing about significant changes in attitudes toward the Negro. Case material which was explicitly relevant to prejudice against minority groups was again found to be effective. This finding, and the failure of Katz and his coworkers to confirm consistently their prediction that persons with a moderate degree of self-defensiveness will be more susceptible to change through self-insight material than persons low in self-defensiveness, raises a question. Is the reduction in prejudice brought about through the self-insight material a result of personality change, or is the change due to a direct, frontal attack on the attitude itself?

In the study by Stotland, Katz, and Patchen a procedure was used with some subjects which was designed to appeal to the desire to be self-consistent. It consisted of material which ". . . described the advantages of consistent behavior in avoiding difficulties. It introduced dramatic examples of foolhardy behavior to illustrate the effects of irrationality. . . . There was emphasis, too, on the importance of self-understanding in achieving a rational, consistent approach to the world."

It was found that the material designed to produce self-insight was most effective when accompanied by this appeal to self-consistency. A number of subjects changed their attitudes because they came to recognize the inconsistency of prejudice existing in the kind of persons they were or believed they were. The process seemed to be more one of increased self-understanding than one of increased insight into the defensive nature of prejudice.

Multidetermination of attitude change and attitude persistence

The free man in society, unlike the subject man in the psychological laboratory, lives in a world in which all the factors that make for attitude change or attitude persistence are simultaneously active, working together or at cross purposes. The final result—attitude change or attitude persistence—is the product of complex interactions among the various determinants which we have discussed in this chapter.

For clarity of exposition, we have treated these various determinants separately. But here, as everywhere in psychology, interaction is the rule. Men are exposed to new information which may both support and oppose existing attitudes; their goals, in whose service attitudes are formed, may be various and conflicting; the groups with which they affiliate may demand antagonistic loyalties. The change or persistence of their attitudes is the end result of the complex interaction of these diverse, and often opposing, forces.

AN ILLUSTRATION

It is now generally believed by pediatricians and child psychologists that many feeding problems in infants are caused by oversolicitous parents who "force-feed" their children. Current doctrine preaches that when a child refuses to eat, the best way to manage the problem is to leave the child alone, to be "permissive" about his eating. Brim [1954] studied some of the factors associated with the attitudinal change involved in acceptance of this permissive approach to feeding problems in infants.

Fifty-seven mothers were chosen for special study from the records of those attending the Child Health Stations (well-baby clinics) of the New York City Department of Health. These mothers met the following criteria: (1) were unemployed and taking full care of child; (2) were not divorced or separated from husband; (3) were either Italian, Negro, or Jewish, and married to a husband of the same cultural background; (4) had an eldest child in good health between the ages of one and one-half and three years; (5) the child was considered a feeding problem, and was forced to eat when he refused food.

The experimenter, playing the role of doctor, interviewed these 57 mothers in the Child Health Stations at one of their regular appointments. The "doctor" suggested to each mother that she adopt permissive behavior as a method of handling food refusals, and gave her a pamphlet which described the permissive-feeding practice in detail.

Reinterviews with 50 of the mothers three to four months later disclosed that 26 did not even try the permissive-feeding practice. Of the 24 who did try it, 16 rejected it after a few trials. Thus only eight of the 50 adopted the practice as their customary way of meeting their children's food refusals. The interview data revealed a number of factors responsible for the enduring change in the behavior of these eight mothers.

PRESTIGE OF DOCTOR. The first factor studied was the prestige accorded to doctors by the mothers. This was measured by asking them to give a general rating of the "helpfulness" of previous advice received from doctors. The relation between prestige of doctors and change in behavior is shown in Table 7.10.

The data suggest that the doctor's prestige was highly important in leading the mother to try the new method. But the data also indicate that the doctor's prestige did *not* affect the extent of adoption among those who tried the new method. Thus, for both higher and lower prestige groups, approximately two-thirds of those who tried the practice were backsliders. What factors, then, led mothers

TABLE 7.10: PRESTIGE OF DOCTOR AND ADOPTION OF PERMISSIVE-FEEDING PRACTICES [After Brim, 1954]

Permissive practice	Higher prestige group	Lower prestige group
Adopted	6	2
Rejected after trial	12	4
Not tried	7	19

who tried the new method to adopt it as a customary practice?

INFORMATIONAL SUPPORT. One factor that was found to be related to the desired change was the informational support which the new practice had in the environment of the mothers. Significantly more of the mothers who did not change reported that they were exposed to "counterpropaganda" against the permissive-feeding practice in what they read or heard. The relation between change and presence or absence of such counterpropaganda is shown in Table 7.11.

It is clear from the data that failing to try the recommended practice was much higher among those exposed to counterpropaganda. Moreover, among those who did try, many more who heard counterpropaganda gave up the practice. None of the eight who were permanent adopters reported such counterpropaganda.

SOCIAL SUPPORT. A second factor found to influence adoption of the new method was the social support it received. The attitudes of the husbands of the subjects toward permissive-feeding practices were ascertained in the interviews with the mothers. The attitudes of the husbands were found to influence somewhat the trying of the new practice, and they were even more important in influencing adoption among those mothers who did try the practice. Thus, as Table 7.12 shows, *all* nine mothers who tried the practice and whose husbands disapproved gave up the practice, whereas among the eleven who tried and whose husbands approved, eight adopted the practice.

(*A word of caution:* Data on the informational support of the permissive practice and on attitudes of husbands toward it were secured from reports by the mothers themselves. Their reports may have been distorted to make them congruent with their own attitudes.)

Attitude change—or lack of change—is, we see, multidetermined.

TABLE 7.11: INFORMATIONAL SUPPORT AND ADOPTION OF PERMISSIVE-FEEDING PRACTICES [After Brim, 1954]

Permissive practice	Exposed predominantly to pro-permissiveness information	Exposed also to anti-permissiveness information
Adopted	8	0
Rejected after trial	7	9
Not tried	8	18

TABLE 7.12: ATTITUDE OF HUSBAND AND ADOPTION OF PERMISSIVE-FEEDING PRACTICES [After Brim, 1954]

Permissive practice	Husbands approved	No reaction	Husbands disapproved
Adopted	8	0	0
Rejected after trial	3	4	9
Not tried	4	10	12

CHAPTER GUIDES AND GLOSSARY

GUIDE 19: *The modifiability of an attitude depends upon the characteristics of the attitude system, and the personality and group affiliations of the individual*

GUIDE 20: *Attitude change is brought about through exposure to additional information, changes in the group affiliations of the individual, enforced modification of behavior toward the object, and through procedures which change personality*

GUIDE 21: *The direction and degree of attitude change induced by additional information is a function of situational factors and of the source, medium, form, and content of the information*

GUIDE 22: *The effectiveness of new group affiliations in inducing attitude change is a function of the characteristics of the group and the nature of the individual's membership in the group*

GUIDE 23: *The effectiveness of enforced modification of behavior in inducing attitude change is a function of the circumstances of the enforcement and the reaction of the individual to it*

GUIDE 24: *The effectiveness of personality change techniques in producing attitude change depends upon the appropriateness of the techniques to the function of the attitude for the personality*

cognitive dissonance. A theory, developed by Festinger, which asserts that an individual experiences discomfort when he holds logically inconsistent cognitions about an object or event, and that he is thus motivated to reduce the dissonance through cognitive and attitudinal changes.

congruent attitude change. A change in the valence of an existing attitude in the direction of its original sign, e.g., an increase in the negativity of an existing negative attitude or an increase in the positivity of an existing positive attitude.

incongruent attitude change. A change in the valence of an existing attitude in a direction opposite to its original sign, e.g., from negative to positive or a decrease in negativity.

negative attitude change. A change in attitude in the direction opposite to that advocated by a persuasive communication. Negative change is often referred to as the "boomerang effect."

net attitude change. The mean amount of positive change produced by a persuasive communication minus the amount of negative change produced. Net change may also be calculated by subtracting the percentage of persons showing negative change from the percentage showing positive change.

persuasibility, bound. A predisposition in the individual to be influenced by *specific* kinds of persuasive communications only. For example, "content-bound persuasibility" is a susceptibility to be influenced by communications which contain particular kinds of appeals, particular kinds of arguments, and other stylistic features.

persuasibility, general. A general readiness in the individual to accept and be influenced by persuasive communications regardless of the specific nature of the communicator and the topic, content, medium, and circumstances of the communication.

pluralistic ignorance. A condition in which the members of a group incorrectly believe that "everyone else" in the group holds a certain attitude, whereas they themselves do not.

positive attitude change. A change in attitude in the direction advocated by a persuasive communication.

Part Three: THE SOCIAL

AND CULTURAL

HABITAT

MAN'S GREATEST ACHIEVEMENT AND THE SIGN THAT ABOVE *all others distinguishes him from the great ape is language. We learn how to think, to feel, to judge through the aid of and within the constraints imposed upon us by the words, idioms, and syntax of our language. The experiences, dreams, and wisdom of past generations are subtly and ineradicably preserved in language. And it is through language that the dead are enabled to collaborate in the education of the living, and in the transformation of man, the ephemeral biological unit, into man, the historic person. Language makes possible the communication of meanings and the sharing of experiences among a people, enabling them to form an enduring society and to create and transmit a distinctive culture.*

Because of all this we start Part Three of our book—the study of the development and role of society and culture in social behavior—by first turning to language, man's crowning glory.

8: LANGUAGE AND COMMUNICATION

MAN IS A TALKING ANIMAL. HE HAS BUILT A world of words and he lives in this world as he lives in a world of things and persons. His responses to words and his use of words have much in common with his responses to and use of people and things. He uses words as tools to control his own behavior and the behavior of other persons (see Boxes 8.1 and 8.2). The outstanding characteristic of this speech tool is its *social* nature. For it is primarily through speech and language that men communicate to one another their thoughts, feelings, and intentions.

Even the first, fragmentary, incomplete sentences of the child who is learning to speak testify to the *interpersonal* nature of speech, although the degree to which the speech of young children is truly social has been a matter of debate among psychologists. The Swiss psychologist Piaget [1926] distinguished two functions of speech for the child: the social and the egocentric. In social speech, "the child addresses his hearer, considers his point of view, tries to influence him or actually exchange ideas with him." In egocentric speech, "the child does not bother to know to whom he is speaking, nor whether he is being listened to. He talks either for himself or for the pleasure of associating anyone who happens to be there with the activity of the

In his major work, *Purposive Behavior in Animals and Men*, Edward C. Tolman, long a psychologist at the University of California, Berkeley, characterized speech as ". . . but a 'high-faluting' 'tool' not differing in essence from other tools such as 'strings,' 'sticks,' 'boxes,' and the like."

It is to be emphasized that . . . speech . . . is a tool-behavior. This is quite obvious in the case of a command. What happens in a command . . . is that by means of it the speaker causes one of his fellows to do something. Instead of the former having to take the latter by the scruff of the neck and actually push him through the desired act, the speaker by means of a command accomplishes the same result. . . .

Conversely, now, what, it must be asked, is speech to the listener? It is a set of *signs*. Speech, when heard, is a set of immediately presented objects which the hearer thereupon takes as signs for some further environmental stimulation . . . the heard words are the sign-objects and the environmental stimulation, which is proclaimed, is the significate or signified-object. . . .

To sum up, whereas to the speaker, speech is like an extension of arms and hands and pointing apparatus; to the listener it is like an extension of eyes and ears or other sensory apparatus.

Tolman, E. C. Purposive behavior in animals and men. *New York: Century, 1932.*

moment." And after observing a very few children, Piaget concluded that social speech seldom appears until the age of seven.

Repetitions of Piaget's study by other investigators have not confirmed his findings. Miller [1951], who has summarized these investigations, concludes that the bulk of the child's speech—approximately 90 per cent—is social. The work of the Russian psychiatrist Vigotsky [1939] suggests that even the so-called "egocentric" monologues described by Piaget are really directed toward *others*. When Vigotsky placed a child whose speech showed all the characteristics of egocentric speech—babblings, short and incomplete sentences—among deaf-and-dumb children, or in isolation, or in a very noisy room, the amount of the child's talk dropped off considerably. Vigotsky interpreted this as indicating that the child believes his babbling speech *is* understood by others, and when external conditions make communication impossible or difficult, he stops speaking. The child, we must remember (see Box 2.1, page 18), does not clearly differentiate *his* perception of the world from the world as perceived by others. He acts as if everyone else perceives what he perceives, and understands what he understands, including his highly idiosyncratic language. This tendency, as we shall see, is not completely restricted to the child, and lies at the bottom of many failures of communication. But the significant thing, according to the best experimental data available, is that speech—all speech—is a form of interpersonal behavior.

It is precisely because speech is the most common form and medium of interpersonal behavior that the study of language is of major importance for the social scientist. For it is the mutual apprehension of the experience of the other which communication by language makes possible. And this mutual apprehension facilitates joint social action, makes possible the formation of societies, and brings about the creation and transmission of cultures. In this chapter, therefore, we shall examine the communicative role of language, and how language is related to the personality and beliefs of people and to the formation of cultures and societies. The chapter will thus set the stage for the following two chapters, which deal with society and culture.

GUIDE 25: *Communication—the interchange of meanings among people—occurs mainly through language and is possible to the degree to which individuals have common cognitions, wants, and attitudes*

Our study of communication and language can best be started with an examination of the functions of words, which make up the vocabulary of a language.

THE FUNCTIONS OF WORDS

Words function in three different ways: as *symbols* of objects, as *attributes* of objects, and as *objects* themselves.

WORDS AS SYMBOLS. A word is said to be a symbol, that is, something that stands for or represents an object other than itself. The word "ball" is clearly not identical with the object "ball"; as stimuli they are clearly different. Yet the word "ball" does somehow stand for or represent the object "ball" in that the word can evoke reactions that are *related to* the object.

The object represented by a word symbol may be a discrete thing—a ball, a chair, or an H-bomb; or it may be a complex pattern of external or internal stimuli—the warmth of the sun upon the face or the throbbing pain of a toothache. The object of a symbol may even be another symbol. When the stenographer taking dictation writes down the symbol ⌒ , this stands for the word "organization," which in turn stands for the object "organization."

A word stands for what we have agreed it shall stand for. There is no necessary relation between word and object. The relation is a matter of social convention. Any object may be signified by any one of a large number of

---

BOX 8.2: *Speech and self-control*

When we speak we stimulate and influence not only other persons but ourselves as well, and the individual also speaks to himself and thus directs his behavior. In the mature individual, self-directed speech is silent speech. But in the young child, self-directed speech is not yet completely internalized. Lorimer has given us an example of how a child uses speech to control his own behavior.

A child of about eighteen months was warned not to put her hand into a certain open chest and not to take out things in the chest. The inhibition was clearly established but the original impulse was strong. For ten enormous minutes I watched with fascination the battle between the impulse and the inhibition, as the little hand reached forward toward the things in the chest and withdrew to the verbal accompaniment "no, no, no!" uttered by the child herself. Then the battle subsided, called to a close by the distraction of other interests.

Through the "high-faluting tool" of speech the individual takes himself by the scruff of his neck and pushes himself around.

Lorimer, F. The growth of reason. *New York: Harcourt, Brace, 1929.*

different words, although some words, because of their sounds, rhythm, or other physiognomic characteristics, seem more appropriate for certain objects than do other words. As Thorndike [1946] points out:

> How many of these ten words would Arabs, Finns, or Chinese define correctly from merely hearing them—*blob, chatter, chuckle, flick, giggle, ping, slap, swish, thump, yap?* . . . a slight, even imagined similarity of a word's sound to its meaning may make the meaning easier to get and remember. If it seems as fit and proper that maladroit persons should bungle and ebullient persons blurt, as that dogs should bow-wow and cannon boom, then mere sounds of bungle and blurt may help to carry their meanings as much as do the mere sounds of bow-wow and boom.

For an experimental examination of Thorndike's suggestion, see Box 8.3.

Once a society has agreed upon a particular word to signify an object, the association tends to become, for the members of the society, a *psychologically* necessary association. We tend to feel that the word "sidewalk" is the only *proper* way to refer to that object. Any other word, such as *trottoir,* for that object seems silly. The word-object association is also *socially* necessary. The members of the society are constrained to use the agreed-upon word. The capricious use of any other word for the object will block communication and the individual will be hindered in making his wants known to others. This does not mean, of course, that all words have *invariant* meanings, as we shall see later in this section when we discuss the influence of context on meanings of words.

WORDS AS ATTRIBUTES OF OBJECTS. The ability to use words as symbols is a mark of language sophistication. Piaget [1929] and Vigotsky [1939] report that children frequently perceive the name of an object as an inalienable attribute of the object. The name—like size, color, and shape—is seen as part of the object; it belongs to the object. The name and the object are one. (For illustrations of this perceptual tendency, see Box 8.4.)

Nor is this tendency confined to children. Preliterate peoples often believe that if an enemy practices evil magic upon the name of a man, the man will be injured. One must guard carefully one's name that it may not become known to one's enemies.

As the semanticists delight in pointing out, the notion that there is a direct and necessary relation between the thing and the word, between an object and its name, is the source of much difficulty and confusion in thinking. That names and words are seen as inalienable attributes of objects can be used effectively by the advertiser and propagandist. Just as scoundrels can wrap themselves in the American flag, so can they wrap themselves in "O.K." words.

WORDS AS OBJECTS. Man's words are part of his real world. They are perceived as existing in their own right, and are responded to directly. One of the reasons for the frequent misinterpretation of the function of words in our behavior is the belief that since words are symbols, therefore all language behavior is somehow "substitute" or "vicarious" behavior. But all that we know about our perception of words indicates that words are often perceived in the same immediately meaningful way in which we perceive other objects. When we hear a sudden loud noise, we react immediately to that noise; we are startled or frightened by the noise itself, not merely by the noise as a "sign" of something else. In much the same way do we adjust to words. When we hear a word or a sentence, we often react directly and immediately to it as we would to any other object in our real world. The function of a word in an individual's behavior is similar to the functions of other equally real objects in his behavior. It is an object to which he listens and adjusts as a pedestrian must adjust to a speeding automobile; it is an object that he uses in speech as a rider uses the automobile to get about.

THE SOCIAL AND CULTURAL HABITAT

BOX 8.3: *Sound and sense*

According to some students of language, there are words whose meaning is determined by their very sounds. These are the familiar onomatopoetic, or "echoic," words which seem to imitate the sound of the objects to which they refer—such as the word "quack" when used to refer to the call of the duck.

Roger W. Brown, A. H. Black, and A. E. Horowitz, while at Harvard University, did a study which suggests that there may be sound-meaning linkages which are the same for all men and that these linkages are found in all languages.

These investigators began with a list of 21 pairs of English antonyms chosen because of their familiar sensory nature (e.g., "warm-cool," "heavy-light"). The list was translated into Chinese, Czech, and Hindi by native speakers of the three languages, who also recorded their pronunciations of the words.

The experimental procedure which was used may be illustrated by an example. The subjects (86 Harvard and Radcliffe students who knew no Chinese, Czech, or Hindi) heard the recorded pronunciation of the Chinese words *tuǹ* and *K'uài*, and were asked to guess which word meant *sharp* and which meant *blunt*. The same procedure was followed for the other 20 pairs.

The over-all percentage of correct matches for the 21 pairs was 62 per cent for Chinese, 62 per cent for Czech, and 61 per cent for Hindi. The chance level of guessing is, of course, 50 per cent. It is clear, therefore, that even when completely ignorant of a language, persons can recognize, slightly better than by chance, the meanings of words expressive of simple, sensory qualities.

The percentage of correct matches for each pair of words in each of the three languages was separately computed. There was found to be a better than chance matching for the great majority of the pairs. However, the pairs varied widely in ease of correct matching, and in some of the pairs in some of the languages the matching was even *poorer* than chance. This is shown, for example, in some of the following 5 of the 21 pairs. The correct answers are indicated by the italicized word in the English pair, which corresponds to the top word in the foreign pair in each case, e.g., "blunt" is *tuǹ, tupy, gothil;* "bright" is *liang, svetly,* and *chamakdar.* The number preceding each foreign pair is the percentage of correct matches.

	English	*Chinese*		*Czech*		*Hindi*	
1.	sharp-*blunt*	70	tuǹ	83	tupy	83	gothil
			K'uài		špičatý		tez
2.	*bright*-dark	90	liang	77	svetly	90	chamakdar
			aǹ		tmavy		dhundhala
3.	*bad*-good	64	huai	57	zlý	31	kharab
			haǒ		hodný		achha
4.	soft-*hard*	83	Káng	96	tvrdý	64	sakht
			joú		měkký		narm
5.	*sweet*-sour	51	t'ién	25	sladký	70	mitha
			suān		kyselý		khatta

It would seem from this study that sounds may play some role in determining the meaning of words in all languages.

Brown, R. W., Black, A. H., and Horowitz, A. E. Phonetic symbolism in natural languages.
J. abnorm. soc. Psychol., *1955,* **50**, *388–393.*

Jean Piaget, the Swiss child psychologist, reports the following conversation with a child:

Could the sun have been called "moon" and the moon "sun"?—No—Why not?—Because the sun shines brighter than the moon. . . . But if everyone had called the sun "moon" and the moon "sun" would we have known it was wrong? *Yes, because the sun is always bigger, it always stays like it is and so does the moon.*—Yes, but the sun isn't changed, only its name. Could it have been called . . . etc.?—*No. . . . Because the moon rises in the evening, and the sun in the day.*

Vigotsky, the Russian psychologist, tells us this story:

A peasant listened to two students of astronomy talking about the stars. Finally the peasant said: "I can see that with the help of instruments men could measure the distance from the earth to the remotest stars and find their position and motion. But what puzzles me is: How in the devil did you find out the names of the stars?"

Piaget, J. The child's conception of the world. *New York: Harcourt, Brace, 1929.*
Vigotsky, L. S. Thought and speech. Psychiatry, *1939,* **2,** *29–54.*

These considerations mean that man lives in a world of word objects as truly as he lives in a world of thing objects. An individual listening to a speaker or reading a pamphlet is immersed in the special real world created by the words and sentences as truly as he is living in a real world created by chairs, tables, and sidewalks. Man can often alter another's world by introducing *words* in the other's environment, just as he often can through introducing cows, automobiles, and buildings. The possibility is suggested, therefore, that by changing an individual's environment via words, we can accomplish the same kinds of changes in his behavior as we can by changing his environment through the manipulation of other objects. It is because of this that language can be effective in changing attitudes, in arousing wants and emotions, and in inducing changes in behavior.

While we have emphasized the functional similarity between words and other objects, there are some important differences—differences that are of particular significance in understanding the unique power of words as persuasive tools. In the first place, words are not limited by the same temporal and spatial factors that limit other objects. The speaker can, through words, immerse the hearer in one environment and a moment later change that environment completely. Perceptions evoked by words can be greater in number and more varied in kind than those evoked by other objects. Almost any word can be experienced in juxtaposition with any other word, and thus novel and bizarre perceptions can be more easily evoked. It is these qualities which give to speech events their unique power. But other than that, speech is effective or ineffective in controlling behavior in the very same way that other environmental changes are effective or ineffective.

THE MEANING OF MEANING

Guide 25 defines communication as the interchange of meanings between persons. The "meaning of meaning" is one of the most venerable problems in philosophy. More recently, psychologists too have come to recognize the central importance of meaning in psychology and many of them have turned their attention to this age-old problem.

We will follow Brown [1958] in defining meaning as ". . . the total disposition to make use of or react to a linguistic form." There are a great many different components in the meaning evoked by a word or a sentence. As Brown notes, "A man might give all his productive years to spelling out the . . . meaning of a single utterance and find the task unfinished in the end."

DENOTATIVE VS. CONNOTATIVE MEANING. Many writers have distinguished between the denotative and connotative meanings of a linguistic form. The *denotative* meaning of a word is that to which the word points. Denotation is the explicit identification of the referent.

The language of mathematics and of science is designed to be exclusively a denotative language—a "thing language." The attempt in science is to build a language in which the terms have invariant, pointing meanings.

In the general language of a society, on the other hand, most of the words also have *connotative* meanings. Connotative meaning refers to the wider penumbra of ideas and feelings and action tendencies which cluster about a word, to the implicit and the attitudinal components of the meaning.

Two words may have precisely the same denotative meaning but quite different connotative meanings. For example, consider the words call-girl and whore. Both point to the same object, but the emotional overtones evoked by the two words are quite different. And action, as every propagandist knows, is mightily influenced by emotion.

In the case of many words, the connotative meaning is far more important than the denotative meaning. What, for example, are the denotative meanings in the following excerpt from a speech by E. E. Cox of Georgia in the United States House of Representatives, June, 1937?

I warn John L. Lewis and his communistic cohorts that no second carpetbag expedition into the Southland, under the Red banner of

Soviet Russia and concealed under the slogans of the CIO, will be tolerated. If the minions of the CIO attempt to carry through the South their lawless plan of organization, if they attempt to demoralize our industry, to corrupt our colored citizens, to incite race hatreds and race warfare, I warn him here and now that they will be met by the flower of Southern manhood and they will reap the bitter fruits of their folly.

Stuart Chase [1938], who cited this utterance as a "Horrible Example," commented:

The honorable gentleman from Georgia gives us a rendering of Southern oratory with all stops out. In one sense it is meaningless balderdash. Yet in another it is pregnant with tragic meaning. Mr. Cox is calling on all the old gods of the South with his war cries of "carpetbag," "race warfare," "flower of Southern manhood," to crush labor unions. John L. Lewis is identified with both Moscow and the hated Yankee carpet baggers of post-Civil War days. There is more than a hint of the flaming cross of a new Ku Klux Klan that will take law enforcement into its own hands.

Similar war cries, devoid of denotative meaning but "pregnant with tragic [connotative] meaning," today fill the angry air of many communities in the American South as the die-hard segregationists seek to oppose the law of the land. And such cries fill the air in many African nations as the embattled white champions of apartheid seek to stem the rise of the colored natives.

THE MEASUREMENT OF MEANING

Until psychologists, with their bent for measurement, became interested in the problem of meaning, it might have been said that meaning was like the weather—everyone talked about it but no one did anything about it.

Osgood and his associates [1957] have done something about it. The *semantic-differential* rating instrument, which we discussed briefly as an attitude-measuring device (see page

168), was originally designed to measure the connotative meaning of concepts.

The basic assumption underlying the semantic differential is that some of the important components of the meaning of a concept can be measured by securing ratings of the concept on a number of bipolar adjectives. Each set of bipolar adjectives is called a *scale* on the semantic differential. The following is a typical set of instructions for subjects used in studies by Osgood and his associates.

> The purpose of this study is to measure the *meaning* of certain things to various people by having them judge them against a series of descriptive scales. In taking this test, please make your judgments on the basis of what these things mean *to you*. On each page of this booklet you will find a different concept to be judged and beneath it a set of scales. You are to rate the concept on each of these scales in order.
>
> Here is how you are to use these scales:
> If you feel that the concept at the top of the page is *very closely related* to one end of the scale, you should place your check-mark as follows:
>
> fair X __ : __ : __ : __ : __ : __ unfair
>
> OR
>
> fair __ : __ : __ : __ : __ : __ X unfair
>
> If you feel that the concept is *quite closely related* to one or the other end of the scale (but not extremely), you should place your check-mark as follows:
>
> strong __ : X : __ : __ : __ : __ weak
>
> OR
>
> strong __ : __ : __ : __ : X : __ weak
>
> If the concept seems *only slightly related* to one side as opposed to the other side (but is not really neutral), then you should check as follows:
>
> active __ : __ : X : __ : __ : __ passive
>
> OR
>
> active __ : __ : __ : __ X : __ : __ passive
>
> The direction toward which you check, of course, depends upon which of the two ends of the scale seem most characteristic of the things you're judging.
>
> If you consider the concept to be *neutral* on the scale, both sides of the scale *equally associated* with the concept, or if the scale is *completely irrelevant,* unrelated to the concept, then you should place your check-mark in the middle space:
>
> safe __ : __ : __ : X : __ : __ : __ dangerous
>
> IMPORTANT:
>
> (1) Place your check-marks *in the middle of spaces,* not on the boundaries.
>
> THIS   NOT THIS
> __ : __ : __ : X : __ : __ X
>
> (2) Be sure you check every scale for *every* concept—*do not omit any.*
> (3) Never put more than one check-mark on a single scale.
>
> Sometimes you may feel as though you've had the same item before on the test. This will not be the case, so *do not look back and forth* through the items. Do not try to remember how you checked similar items earlier in the test. *Make each item a separate and independent judgment.* Work at fairly high speed through this test. Do not worry or puzzle over individual items. It is your first impressions, the immediate "feelings" about the items, that we want. On the other hand, please do not be careless, because we want your true impressions.

Osgood assumed that connotative meaning is multidimensional—that there are a number of different components of meaning. As we have earlier seen (page 167), factor-analytic studies by Osgood and Suci and by others have isolated three dimensions or factors of meaning: (1) the evaluative factor, which is most prominently identified by such scales as good-bad, valuable-worthless, pleasant-unpleasant; (2) the potency factor, which is most prominently identified by scales such as strong-weak, large-small, heavy-thin; (3) the activity factor, which is most prominently identified by such scales as active-passive, fast-slow, sharp-dull. The evaluative factor, which appears to measure the valence of attitudes (see our discussion on page 169), is the most important of the three factors.

The meaning of a concept as measured by the semantic differential is the pattern or profile of scores on the various scales. An illustrative example is provided by a study of the meaning of the concept of mental illness and of the concepts of various social roles reported by Nunnally [1959]. He administered a semantic-differential form to a panel of 200 persons, chosen to represent the population of the United States on a number of demographic characteristics. The scale profiles for three concepts are shown in Figure 8.1. Note that "neurotic man" is viewed as relatively foolish, dangerous, sad, unpredictable, and tense as compared with "old man" and "me." Nunnally also found that psychotic disorders are thought of as different from neurotic disorders in that "psychotic man" is rated more strong, less predictable, and more dangerous than "neurotic man."

Studies of the semantic differential by Osgood and others associated with him indicate that it is a highly reliable measure. It appears to be a useful measure of three important dimensions of connotative meaning. The technique does not, however, measure all the dimensions of connotative meaning. To illustrate: Nunnally reports that the profiles for "mother" and "father" are highly similar for most persons. But, assuredly, the full connotative meanings of mother and father differ for most persons.

LEARNING AND MEANING

The central role of *learning* in the acquisition of meaning is suggested by our definition of the term. But this important point merits emphasis. The meaning we acquire concerning a chair, say, is dependent in large measure upon our experiences with and use of chairs. We may have used chairs as things to sit on, as stepladders, as weapons, as fuel, as temporary tables. Each one of these uses has added to the meaning which chair as an object has for us.

Our interpretations of *words* may also vary tremendously. Many words have quite varied meanings which reflect our own past experiences with them. Thus the word "chair" may have such varied meanings as a thing to sit on, a desired academic position, or an office in a political organization.

MEANING DIFFERENCES ACROSS CULTURES. The importance of differences in experience

FIGURE 8.1: Semantic-differential profiles for the concepts Me, Old Man, and Neurotic Man, based on the mean ratings of 200 subjects. [Nunnally, 1959.]

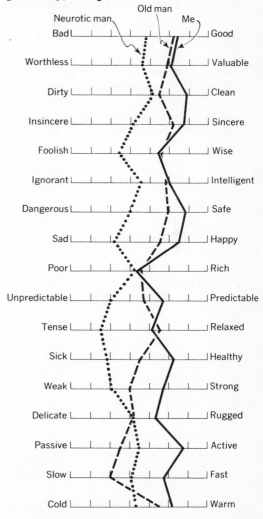

in determining differences in the meanings of words becomes of crucial concern when we seek to understand the nature of communication among people of different cultures or even subcultures. Frequently we find that these cultural differences create well-nigh insurmountable barriers to communication.

Margaret Mead [1949] has suggested, for example, that the experiences of males and females in our culture are so different that the meanings of such words as "mother," "love," and "marriage" are different for men and women. As a result, it may be difficult for men and women to communicate accurately with one another about these matters. For a study of sex differences in the meaning of fairly simple and common words, see Box 8.5.

The experiences of the various ethnic and

BOX 8.5: *Sex and sense*

Florence L. Goodenough, a child psychologist who was at the University of Minnesota for many years, used the free-association method to study sex differences in the meaning of words. This method consists in presenting a list of stimulus words to a subject with the instruction to respond to each word with the first word he thinks of.

Goodenough collected a list of 240 homonyms for use as stimulus words. (A homonym is a word identical with another in sound but differing in meaning; e.g., *bow* and arrow, *bow* in hair.)

The 240 stimulus words were presented to 400 male and 400 female subjects as a "test to see how quickly you can think." In analyzing the data, the responses were classified "in terms of the specialized meaning . . . selected by the subject as the basis for his response." The responses of the subject were tabulated by age and sex separately. Examples of age and sex differences in homonymic meanings are given in the following table.

STIMULUS WORD *bow*

	Reference to hair or hair ribbon		Reference to archery	
AGE GROUP	*Male*	*Female*	*Male*	*Female*
18–22	0%	20%	42%	6%
17–18	0	13	64	32
15–16	0	27	63	20
13–14	0	22	65	22
11–12	0	10	32	12

STIMULUS WORD *file*

	Reference to wood or metals		Reference to fingernails or manicuring	
AGE GROUP	*Male*	*Female*	*Male*	*Female*
18–22	6%	0%	16%	32%
17–18	15	0	16	29
15–16	14	2	16	36
13–14	24	5	12	39
11–12	4	0	12	18

Goodenough, Florence L. The use of free association in the objective measurement of personality. In Studies in personality contributed in honor of Lewis M. Terman. New York: McGraw-Hill, 1942.

social-class groups within our society are so different that many words have come to have a special significance. For example, the word "work" may have quite different meanings for members of the lower class and for members of the middle class. For a member of the lower class "work" may symbolize an unpleasant but necessary means of securing food and shelter; work, in itself, is neither interesting nor desirable. For the middle-class person, "work" may symbolize a means to such goals as enhancement of one's prestige, realization of one's talents, etc., and for him work may be satisfying and desirable in itself. People from these two classes, in discussing the subject of "work," may really be talking about different things, although believing all the time that they are talking about the same thing.

The difficulty of establishing accurate communication among individuals and groups with different past experiences and learning has proved a problem for those interested in reducing conflicts among ethnic and racial groups in the American society (see Boxes 8.6 and 8.7).

Communication between members of different national cultures is even more fraught with difficulties. Margaret Mead [1947] has commented upon the different meanings which the word "compromise" carries for an Englishman and an American.

> In Britain, the word "compromise" is a good word, and one may speak approvingly of any arrangement which has been a compromise, including, very often, one in which the other side has gained more than fifty per cent of the points at issue. . . . Where, in Britain, to compromise means to work out a good solution, in America it usually means to work out a bad one, a solution in which all the points of importance (to both sides) are lost.

In his report to the American people on his meeting of June, 1961, with Mr. Khrushchev, the Soviet leader, President Kennedy noted that

> . . . the Soviet and ourselves give wholly different meanings to the same words—"war,"

"peace," "democracy," and "popular will." We have wholly different views of right and wrong, of what is an internal affair and what is aggression, and above all, we have wholly different concepts of where the world is and where it is going.

For illustrations of the "wholly different meanings" the Soviets and ourselves give the same words, see Box 8.8.

CONTEXT AND MEANING

As we know, cognitions are determined by much more than the "traces" of past experience. Present contexts interact with past traces to determine the nature of the present cognition. People can and do, therefore, interpret words in entirely novel ways, depending upon the situation and the present psychological state of the individual. To understand the meaning of a word, then, we must know, in addition to the individual's experience with it, the present context—verbal and nonverbal—in which the word is used.

VERBAL CONTEXT. Words do not, of course, stand alone. In most languages, they are combined to form phrases, sentences, or larger "utterance units." In the study of how words are combined to form larger units, linguists are concerned with syntax. Syntax is basic to the understanding of linguistic meaning, i.e., meaning as related to structure, for it is the syntactical arrangement which determines the meaning of an utterance.

Consider these two sentences: *The first man's hat. The man's first hat.* The difference in meaning between these two sentences clearly has to do with the different arrangements of the same set of words within the two sentences. And the meaning of the individual words in the sentences changes when the words are ordered in different ways. Every word occurs in a context of other words, and the meaning of a word depends upon the pattern of these other words.

If an external verbal context is not supplied, the individual will provide his own *internal* verbal context. An experiment by

Arthur L. Campa, a scholar in modern languages at the University of Denver, has provided us with the following illustration of a communication failure due to language barriers.

Take the case of Juan in a school somewhere in the Southwest. He has a certain amount of "amorpropio" which is mistranslated as "pride," and then because it does not mean the same in English, Juan is said to have a "false pride." One day he gets into trouble with Pedro, one of his schoolmates and, there being no word for "compromise" in their vocabulary nor in their culture-content, they resort to physical arguments. The teacher insists that Juan "apologize" to Pedro for what he did. "Go on," she insists, "apologize to him." Again Juan doesn't know what to say, because there is no word in Spanish for it, nor does the apologizing custom exist. The teacher is assuming that just as words are linguistically translated, so are cultural patterns. She continues, "Tell him you're sorry." This he refuses to do because he is a product of a realistic culture, loath to change the realism of the past by the instrumentality of mere words. So he stays after school for being stubborn, disobedient and generally incorrigible. Juan still doesn't know the meaning of "apology," but if he is intellectually curious he may look up the word in a Velasquez dictionary where he will find it mistranslated linguistically as "apologia." Not knowing this half dollar word he looks it up in the Academy dictionary where he finds to his amazement the following definition, "Discurso en alabanza de una persona" (an utterance in praise of a person). Now he is mad at the teacher!

Campa, A. L. Language barriers in intercultural relations. J. Communication, *1951, 1, 41–46.*

Mosier [1941] illustrates the importance of the internal verbal context in determining meaning. He read a list of words and word phrases to subjects who had been instructed to rate each word for favorableness or unfavorableness on an 11-point scale ranging from 1 (means most unfavorable), through 6 (means neither favorable nor unfavorable), to 11 (means most favorable). After the subjects had made their ratings, the list of words was read a second time and the subjects were asked to write down what they had thought about when they rated each word.

Of the 296 words and word phrases in the list, 28 yielded marked bimodality in the ratings of favorability and unfavorability. For example, the phrase "completely indifferent" had modes at 1 and 6. Analysis of the associations of the subjects revealed two different verbal contexts: persons and objects. A com-

pletely indifferent *person* is judged highly unfavorable; a completely indifferent *object* is judged quite neutral.

NONVERBAL CONTEXT. The nonverbal context is also of obvious importance in determining the meaning of words. The *external* nonverbal context includes the facial expressions of the speaker, his gestures and actions, the objects in the situation, the ongoing activity—in fine, the total situation in which the utterance is heard by the individual.

It is also well known that the *internal* nonverbal context—the emotional and motivational state of the individual—is important in determining the meaning of words.

THE SIGNIFICANCE OF CONTEXT. For the student of social behavior, the important lesson to be drawn from our discussion of the effects of external and internal contexts upon the meaning of words is this: The same word may have different meaning for different people and different meaning for the same person at different times (see Box 8.9).

Church [1961] has emphasized the importance of the "behavioral context" in determining the meaning of an utterance.

It is in trying to decipher the semantics of utterances detached from their behavioral contexts that students of meaning have gone astray. Instead of asking what a statement, considered as an objective entity, means, we might better ask what this individual means (or intends) when he says thus-and-so, *and* what this statement uttered by so-and-so means to this listener. It is obvious that we have removed meaning from the level of the word to that of the utterance. Words do not have

BOX 8.7: *The clock that walks*

In his study of the Spanish-speaking people of the American Southwest, Lyle Saunders of the University of Colorado School of Medicine points out that "inability to speak a common language presents an almost insuperable barrier to communication and makes difficult the achieving of a wide range of mutually satisfactory relationships between Anglos and Spanish-speaking people."

Like other elements of culture, language for most of us is so taken for granted that frequently we are not aware of the clues it provides for understanding our own behavior and that of other people. It is not without significance, for example, that, as Arthur Campa has pointed out, in English a clock runs, while in Spanish it walks (*el reloj anda*). Such a simple difference as this has enormous implications for appreciating differences in the behavior of English-speaking and Spanish-speaking persons. If time is moving rapidly, as Anglo usage declares, we must hurry and make use of it before it has gone. If time walks, as the Spanish-speaking say, one can take a more leisurely attitude toward it. If an English-speaking workman arrives late at his job with the excuse that he missed the bus, the language he uses indicates that he was the active agent in his failure to make connection with the bus and he, therefore, is responsible for the lateness. A Spanish-speaking workman, in the same circumstances, would not say that he missed the bus but that the bus left him. The active, and therefore culpable, agent was the bus, not the workman, and he cannot blame himself nor does he expect to be blamed for his late arrival. The Anglo foreman, however, who knows that people miss buses, is not likely to be sympathetic to the notion that the fault lies with the bus, particularly if he also is told that the workman's clock was "walking" a bit slowly.

In the repetition and proliferation of small differences such as these lies the basis of large misunderstandings between people of different cultures. Unable to understand in terms of the concepts of his culture, that buses leave people, that objects lose themselves, that automobiles wreck themselves, that dishes break themselves by falling away from people, that diseases are the manifestation of the will of God, the English-speaking person reaches into his box of categories and brings out concepts in terms of which his experiences make sense to him. And thus the Spanish-speaking people come to be labeled as untruthful, or irresponsible, or lazy, or superstitious, or are assigned some other stereotyped characteristics. Thereafter their behavior is "understood," but not in a way that is conducive to the establishment of either deeper and more accurate levels of understanding or mutually satisfactory relationships between members of the two groups.

Saunders, L. Cultural differences and medical care. New York: Russell Sage Found., 1954.

BOX 8.8: *Communist words—capitalist words*

Hadley Cantril of the Institute for International Social Research, Princeton, New Jersey, has studied the techniques used by Soviet leaders to control the minds of the Russian people. He believes that the study of the official Soviet language can throw light on the control techniques used by the Soviet leaders because of their explicit assumption "that an individual's thought and action are guided and molded by language and words and that, therefore, no inconsistencies or conflicts of meanings can be tolerated."

Cantril therefore consulted Soviet dictionaries and encyclopedias to learn the official meanings given words. Some of his findings are given below. For contrast, we have added the American meanings as given in standard American dictionaries.

	Soviet meaning	*American meaning*
Individualism	"The-individual-as-a-member-of-a-collective"	"The pursuit of individual rather than common or collective interests"
Freedom	"The recognition of necessity"	"Exemption from necessity, in choice and action; as, the freedom of the will"
Charity	"Help granted hypocritically by representatives of the dominant class in societies of exploiters to a certain fraction of the disinherited sectors of the population in order to deceive the workers and to divert their attention from the class struggle"	"An act or feeling of affection or benevolence"
Initiative	"Independent search for the best way to fulfill a command"	"Self-reliant enterprise; self-initiated activity"

Cantril, H. Soviet leaders and mastery over man. New Brunswick, N.J.: Rutgers Univer. Press, 1960.

meanings, but functions. The "meanings" assigned to words by dictionaries are abstractions drawn from the ways words function in various contexts. It is true that a single word can constitute an utterance, as in "Yes," "Why?" "Never," and so forth; but again the meaning of the one-word utterance comes from its behavioral context. By itself, the utterance "Wood" does not make much sense; as an answer to the question "What is your house built of?" it is perfectly coherent. We must also, of course, grant status as utterances to nods, gestures, grunts, grimaces, and whatever other devices people use in communicating

with each other. We must draw a distinction, however, between conventional *signs,* which have a single fixed meaning regardless of context, and *symbols,* which convey information and vary in meaning according to context. In some cases, of course, an utterance can be both sign and symbol: a forefinger against the lips has the sign-value "Quiet!" but it can also convey that the signaler wants to surprise somebody, that the person to whom it is addressed was about to say something dangerous, that there is something important to be heard that would be drowned out by speech, and so forth. We are saying here that what has long been

THE SOCIAL AND CULTURAL HABITAT

treated as a logical problem is in fact a psychological one, that the problem of meaning is the problem of how meaningful utterances come to be uttered by a speaker and comprehended by a listener.

A WORD OF CAUTION. We must, however, be careful not to overemphasize the variant meanings of words. The people of a culture who speak a common language must and do communicate with one another; they must and do understand what others mean when they use words. Many words of the common language come to have a relatively invariant meaning which makes mutual understanding possible. Strictly speaking, of course, these words owe their meaning to particular individuals having particular experiences with them. But they are invariant in the sense that these experiences are so common to all the people of the culture that the meaning of the words no longer depends upon specific contexts. Thus each culture has "bad" or "good" words, "happy" or "sorrowful" words. The relative invariance of these words is of interest for the understanding of the effect of words upon behavior. Words, if they are to be the means of social intercourse, cannot mean simply whatever they are "paid to mean," as Humpty Dumpty would have it.

COMMUNICATION AND COMMON COGNITIONS, WANTS, AND ATTITUDES

With an understanding of the nature of the meanings of words and of some of their determinants, we are now in a position to examine the nature of the communication

---

BOX 8.9: *"I love you"*

Joost A. M. Meerloo, a psychiatrist and social psychologist at Columbia University, has pointed out the varieties of meanings which the simple statement "I love you" may carry.

This is no essay on love and no profound treatise on the variations of feelings of tenderness. I only want to show how much semantic difficulty there is in the expression "I love you"— a statement that can be expressed in so many varied ways. It may be a stage song, repeated daily without any meaning, or a barely audible murmur, full of surrender. Sometimes it means: *I desire you* or *I want you sexually*. It may mean: *I hope you love me* or *I hope that I will be able to love you*. Often it means: *It may be that a love relationship can develop between us* or even *I hate you*. Often it is a wish for emotional exchange: *I want your admiration in exchange for mine* or *I give my love in exchange for some passion* or *I want to feel cozy and at home with you* or *I admire some of your qualities*. A declaration of love is mostly a request: *I desire you* or *I want you to gratify me*, or *I want your protection* or *I want to be intimate with you* or *I want to exploit your loveliness*.

Sometimes it is the need for security and tenderness, for parental treatment. It may mean: *My self-love goes out to you*. But it may also express submissiveness: *Please take me as I am*, or *I feel guilty about you, I want, through you, to correct the mistakes I have made in human relations*. It may be self-sacrifice and a masochistic wish for dependency. However, it may also be a full affirmation of the other, taking the responsibility for mutual exchange of feelings. It may be a weak feeling of friendliness, it may be the scarcely even whispered expression of ecstasy. *"I love you"*—wish, desire, submission, conquest; it is never the word itself that tells the real meaning here.

Meerloo, J. A. M. Conversation and communication. *New York: Int. Universities Press, 1952.*

---

process. In large degree, of course, we have anticipated this analysis already. In this sense we are here merely summarizing and applying our previous analysis to the communication process.

A simple definition of communication would refer to the use of symbols to achieve common or shared information about an object. While the most important medium of communication among human beings is language, other symbols may be used. A shrug of the shoulders, a thumbs-down movement, a nod or a wink can also serve as symbols which convey ideas.

Communication is a process which usually involves interaction between the communicating individuals. The response evoked in the recipient of a communication becomes in turn a stimulus for the communicator to which he responds with a communication. In a communication event, each person's communications are at once both responses and stimuli. The ball is bounced back and forth between the players in the conversational game.

In social interaction man is guided by his interpretation of the meaning of the words and actions of the other. As Davis [1949] puts it:

> The essential feature of communication is that one person infers from the behavior of another . . . what idea or feeling the other person is trying to convey. He then reacts not to the behavior as such but to the inferred idea or feeling. The other person then reacts to his response in terms of the idea or feeling —the meaning—behind it.

When we communicate with each other, we do not respond only to the words we hear. We are always "hearing between the lines"— we are always listening with the "third ear." We are always trying to get inside the skin of the other person.

JUDGING THE ACCURACY OF COMMUNICATION. Communication accomplishes its purpose accurately if the message is interpreted in the same way by the communicator and by the recipient of the communication. If similar interpretations have been made, each participant conveys his thinking and feeling about the object of communication to the other. This does not mean that the participants must *agree* in their thinking about the object of communication. They may be in disagreement, but if each accurately apprehends the thoughts of the other, communication has been successfully established.

How may the communicator assess the accuracy of his communication? Clearly the only possible way is to observe the response of the recipient. If I point to the moon and say, "Look at the moon," and you turn your eyes skyward in that direction, your action leads me to conclude that I have communicated accurately. (But my inference may be wrong; it may turn out that you thought I had said, "Look at the plane," and it was a plane, not the moon, toward which your gaze was directed.)

The testing of the accuracy of communications involving *thoughts* and *feelings* is, however, even more difficult. Here the communicator must lean mainly upon the nature of the communicative response of the other to his own communication. If you respond to my communication about my feelings toward some object ("The moon tonight really sends me") with a look of puzzlement, or with what I judge to be an irrelevant or inappropriate remark ("Sends you what?") I infer that the communication has not been accurate. If you make no response, I have no means of testing the accuracy of the communication.

AIDS AND BARRIERS TO COMMUNICATION. Because of our emphasis on the role of individual experience and *internal* as well as external context in determining the meaning of a communication, it may be asked how any two persons can ever communicate accurately with each other about anything. The meaning of many words seems to be exquisitely personal. It is at this point that we have recourse to that part of Guide 25 which emphasizes the role of communality of wants, beliefs, and attitudes in making communication possible. Two people can communicate accurately in so far as they have each experienced comparable (though never identical) wants, have each faced comparable problems, and have each arrived at comparable solutions to these problems. Masserman [1946], in discussing this very point, writes:

As a specific illustration, the word for hunger "means" almost the same in any language, since all individuals have experienced the elemental biologic need to which it refers; in contrast, the connotations of "food" begin to vary much more widely from culture to culture. Similarly, symbols with more complex and contingent motivational referents such as "home," "family," "work" and so on (not to mention ethereally elaborate concepts such as "truth," "beauty," "religion," or "the good life") must necessarily have ever wider ranges of meaning among individuals with necessarily different experiences and social backgrounds. Indeed, we hardly need language to communicate experiences of direct biodynamic significance: thus, we can accurately discern pain, fear or rage in each other or in animals with no expressions at the verbal level at all. Conversely, as the experiences become more specialized to the individual and group, their communication becomes at best only approximately "understood' by those not personally acquainted with them. . . . Disparities of connotation also increase rapidly as social and cultural gaps among individuals and groups become wider; indeed, such difficulties in inter-personal and inter-group communications have constituted barriers to human understanding and fellowship that are of transcendent (and sometimes tragic) importance.

Thus the mutual assumption that accurate communication is being accomplished and that the other is perceiving exactly one's thinking, feeling, etc., may not be valid. In this case we have *pseudo-communication*. Pseudo-communication may occur without either person being aware that he is not communicating accurately. Pseudo-communication

is frequently the source of interpersonal difficulties (see Box 8.10).

From our previous analyses we know that there are two major reasons for such pseudo-communication: (1) the different experiences of the communicators with words; (2) the idiosyncratic perceptions by the communicators of the general situation in which the communication is taking place. We have already discussed the first of these reasons at some length, and it needs no further elaboration. The second, however, may need further illustration.

IDIOSYNCRATIC PERCEPTIONS AND PSEUDO-COMMUNICATION. A communication is never perceived in isolation; it is always perceived in terms of the context of which it is a part (see Guide 3, page 30). Thus the way in which the communication situation (including the communicator) is perceived by the individual, together with the individual's system of related perceptions, will influence his interpretation of the communication. This can sometimes lead to inaccurate communication.

Roethlisberger and Dickson [1939] report an interview which was secured in the course of studies carried out in the Hawthorne Works of the Western Electric Company.

One of the women interviewed (Mrs. Black) had the reputation of being a "chronic kicker."

Shortly after the interview began, Mrs. Black said: *"Say, you know, that Mr. Jones* [group chief] *is not so good.* . . . He gives you the awfullest looks. I don't think he's such a good boss. You know, Mr. Smith [former group chief] is so different. He comes around you all the time and says little jokes and makes you feel good, but Mr. Jones is kind of mean like. He's so mean looking."

Interviewer: "You mean it's just his looks?"

Mrs. Black: "Well, he talks that way too. If it happens that just one coil is bad—by gosh, that happens once in a while—he comes over and wants to know why it happened. Gee, he has to tell you all about it. . . . You know, with Mr. Smith when things would go wrong

E. Shouby, a psychologist who has studied Arabic life and culture and whose native language was Arabic, has provided us with an instance of cultural misunderstanding due to linguistic differences. Shouby observes:

The Arabic language abounds with forms of assertion, *tawkid,* and of exaggeration, *mubalaghah.* There is the common *n,* ending words that are meant to be emphasized; there is also the doubling of the sounds of some consonants to create the desirable stronger effect; there are also the frequent words *inna* and *kad,* used to emphasize a large number of sentences; and there are such forms of assertion as the repetition of pronouns and certain other words to get across their meanings or significance. Besides these grammatical types of overassertion are the numerous stylistic and rhetorical devices to achieve even further exaggeration. Fantastic metaphors and similes are used in abundance, and long arrays of adjectives to modify the same word are quite frequent. Though gradually developing in the direction of brevity, the style of Arabic prose is still too florid (as judged by the standards applicable to English prose) to be considered factual and realistic. . . .

The full psychological explanation of these phenomena of assertion and exaggeration cannot be dealt with here, but it should be obvious that once such a linguistic tradition has been established, it cannot fail to produce far-reaching results. . . . Its implications (applicable to both literate and illiterate) are two. In the first place, the Arabs are forced to overassert and exaggerate in almost all types of communication, as otherwise they stand a good chance of being gravely misunderstood. If an Arab says exactly what he means without the expected exaggeration, other Arabs may still think that he means the opposite. This fact leads to misunderstanding on the part of non-Arabs who do not realize that the Arab speaker is merely following a linguistic tradition. Secondly, we have the corollary of the first: the failure of the Arabs to realize that others mean exactly what they say if it is put in a simple, unelaborated manner; even repetition may not be enough for an Arab to realize that the communication cannot perhaps mean the opposite of what the speaker intends. . . .

The writer once had the opportunity of observing an illustration of this twofold reaction to a linguistic condition when he listened to the confidential report of two friends: an English girl and an Arab youth. The girl complained that her Arab friend (*a*) was pestering her with his attentions and declarations of love; and (*b*) refused to take "No" for an answer when she made it perfectly clear that she was not interested in him at all. The Arab confided (*a*) that the English girl was encouraging him to make love to her; and (*b*) that he had so far shown only a little interest and admiration. Both were strictly honest and truthful even to their conscious selves, but they did not know what a contrast could be created between Arab overassertion and exaggeration and British tact and understatement.

Shouby, E. The influence of the Arabic language on the psychology of the Arabs. Middle East J., *1951,* **5,** *284–302.*

you'd just feel like telling him, but not with Mr. Jones. You'd sooner suffer than tell him. . . . It seems that he just likes to hurt people. He just wants you to know that he's the boss, I guess. . . .

"I've always had a lot of trouble. You know, I've had to help my mother a lot because

things aren't so good at home. I have a step-father, and he's a mean man. Gosh, he's the meanest man I ever heard of. Gee, and my mother is the sweetest woman! She's got to take so much dirt from him; I feel so sorry for her. That's why I stayed home as long as I did. I wanted to help her."

After a lengthy discussion of the family situation, Mrs. Black, at the end of the interview, commented:

> "You know, I think the reason that I can't stand Mr. Jones is because every time I look at him he reminds me of my stepfather."

This interview furnishes us with a clear illustration of the influence of the external, nonverbal context upon the interpretation of communication. Mrs. Black interpreted the communicative acts of Mr. Jones as hostile because she perceived Mr. Jones as "mean looking."

ANXIETY AND PSEUDO-COMMUNICATION. If a communication situation, for whatever reason, arouses anxiety in an individual, the primary goal of his communication may become the reduction of anxiety, rather than the accurate transmission of ideas. The communicative acts of the anxious person become "face-work"—operations designed to protect the self. The anxious person may use any of the defense mechanisms which we have discussed in Chapter 4 (see pages 119 to 124).

Sullivan [1954] has pointed to the frequency with which anxiety blocks accurate communication in the psychiatric interview.

> Unless the interviewee is revealing data bearing on his aptitudes for living, on his successes, or on his unusual abilities as a human being, the operations of the self-system are always in opposition to achieving the purposes of the interview. That is, it always opposes the clear revelation of what the interviewee regards as handicaps, deficiencies, defects, and what not, and it does not facilitate communication except in the realms where that which is communicated clearly enhances his sense of well-being, his feeling of making a favorable impression.

In interpersonal behavior events other than the psychiatric interview, anxiety similarly tends to impair accurate communication. Whenever an individual feels threatened, he will use words to conceal himself from the other person and from himself.

TO RECAPITULATE

Joint action in the interpersonal behavior event is accomplished through communication—the interchange of meanings between the persons involved. Communication occurs mainly through language.

Words function in three ways: as symbols of objects, as attributes of objects, as objects themselves. Words have both denotative and connotative meanings.

The meaning of any utterance is determined by the experiences of the individual with words and by the total context in which the utterance is heard—the external and internal verbal and nonverbal contexts.

Accurate communication—mutually correct understanding of the meanings of the utterances of each participant in a communication event—is possible to the degree that each has experienced comparable wants, has faced comparable problems, and has arrived at comparable solutions of these problems.

If two persons have had different experiences with words or if they perceive the communication context differently, the meaning of an utterance will differ for them. Pseudo-communication, a failure to exchange meanings accurately, will result. Because of the different experiences of persons who live in different cultures, accurate communication across cultures is difficult to achieve, and misunderstandings often occur. An important and ubiquitous barrier to accurate communication is anxiety.

GUIDE 26: *Language reflects both the personality of the individual and the culture of his society and in turn helps shape personality and culture*

It would seem that the language behavior of the individual, like other central aspects of his behavior, necessarily reflects basic features of his personality. And his language behavior, having been developed in the context of his particular culture, necessarily reflects basic features of that culture. Conversely, it would seem that the specific language which the individual uses helps determine his mental processes and thus helps govern the development of his personality; and, similarly, the language of a people can be expected to have significant influence on the development and change of their culture. These relations among language, personality, and culture are intricate and as yet but little understood. Thus Guide 26 should perhaps better· be phrased as a series of questions: Does the individual's speech behavior tell us something about his personality? Does language influence the person's cognitive processes? Does language mirror culture? Does language mold culture?

SPEECH AND PERSONALITY

The notion that a man's linguistic style reflects and reveals his personality is an ancient belief. "Speak that I may judge thee," said Ben Jonson.

A number of investigators, principally in Germany and in America, have made very detailed analyses of speech style. A study by Sanford [1942a] may be cited as typical of this work. He recorded 11 samples of the free or extemporaneous speech of two subjects, Chatwell and Merritt, who were among 20 experimental subjects intensively studied by a group of personologists at the Harvard Psychological Clinic. An analysis of the speech samples of his two subjects enabled Sanford to summarize their style of speech. As to Merritt:

Thus, Merritt's speech is *complex, perseverative, thorough, uncoordinated, cautious, static, highly definitive,* and *stimulus-bound.* If we go one step further toward synthesis and generalization, we might conceive of his whole style as *defensive* and *deferent.* Most of his verbal behavior seems to reflect a *desire to avoid blame or disapproval.* He is cautious and indirect, rarely making a simple or bold statement. Once he makes a judgment he explains it and presents all aspects of it, leaving little to the auditor's imagination and little for the auditor to question. His concern for the adequacy of every response results in a re-examination of the response and this, in turn, brings about roughnesses in his discourse. His disinclination to venture out "on his own" makes him feel more comfortable in the stimulus-bound situations.

As to Chatwell:

In his verbal behavior Chatwell is *colorful, varied, emphatic, direct, active, progressing always in a forward direction.* His responses are *well coordinated,* more *evaluative* than *definitive, closely interconnected,* and somewhat *enumerative.* He covers *extensive* areas, verbally, and is *disinclined to consider details or precision of reference.* His speech is *confident, definite, independent.* In general, he appears to use speech not so much to describe the external world and its relations as to *express his own individuality and to impress the auditor.*

Sanford comments: "From what we know of personality we might well expect that the individual's verbal and nonverbal behavior are all of a piece and that we can, if we are clever, see the latter in the former. Studies of style are likely to have psychodiagnostic value."

Sanford's characterizations of the speech styles of Merritt and Chatwell do read like personality descriptions. But we need further to know whether Merritt's "cautious speech" indicates a generalized trait of cautiousness, and whether there is behavioral evidence for a ". . . disinclination to venture out 'on his own.'"

THAUMATURGY OF WORDS. A semantic movement led by Korzybski [1941], once influential in America, put forth claims that complex personality characteristics could be assessed by analyzing speech characteristics. Korzybski developed a theory of psychoneurosis based

THE SOCIAL AND CULTURAL HABITAT

on poor habits of speech. "The hypothesis, stated broadly, maintains that the individual who applies rigid Aristotelian classwords to a world which is not rigid and not Aristotelian will sooner or later run afoul of the inevitable misfit between his words and the world" [Sanford, 1942b].

Korzybski assumed that poor speech habits are the *cause* of personality maladjustment. The causal relation may, of course, run the other way: the personality disturbance may produce poor speech habits. The overemphasis upon the power of speech in determining behavior, which characterizes the writings of the semanticists, reminds one of Masserman's discussion of the "thaumaturgy of words."

> The sounds produced by the human voice reach so deeply into the formative layers of experience that at times they appear to have almost magical effects. For that matter, nearly all animals try to influence their environment by cries, howls and other vocalizations—certainly human children do. And when food, warmth, protection and other wants are satisfied through the medium of such sounds, the child further cultivates and refines its vocalizations in accordance with the requirements of its milieu, i.e., it acquires a "language" endowed with apparently magic potentialities for satisfying wants. This fantastic belief in the covert powers and uses of words and word-systems is, then, found almost everywhere—in the incantations and prayers of savage religions, in the "secret" languages (pig Latin, Opish, "Double Dutch," etc.) of adolescents and clinically, in the ardor with which the neurotic patient importunes the psychiatrist for some particular brand of verbal magic.

Sanford [1942b] has summarized the work on the relation between speech and personality as follows:

> All along the line there are data, reasonable arguments, insights and hunches, adding up to the conviction that by his words a man may be known. We can accept it as a fact that speech and personality are related. But before we can get to the bottom of this relationship there are many bridges to cross.

LANGUAGE AND CULTURE

Two different sets of relations have been postulated to exist between language and culture. It has been suggested, on the one hand, that the language of a people is determined by, or *reflects,* their culture; and, on the other hand, that the language of a people, however it may originate, *determines* or molds their culture.

LANGUAGE—THE MIRROR OF CULTURE. It has long been assumed that the language of a people mirrors their culture, that it can be regarded as the crystallized thought of a people.

It seems safe to assume that the language of a people does reflect their dominant concerns and interests. Thomas [1937] has pointed out that in the Arabic language there are about six thousand names associated in some way with "camel." Similarly, Boas [1938] has pointed to the very large variety of words for "snow" among the Eskimos. "In the life of the Eskimo *snow* means something entirely different as falling snow, soft snow on the ground, drifting snow or snowdrift. Fresh water ice, salt water ice, an iceberg, play quite different rôles in their life and all these are designated by distinctive terms."

In his study of "Englishmen, Frenchmen, and Spaniards," De Madariaga [1929] has suggested that the language of a people is a key which unlocks their culture. For example, the words "fair play," *"le droit,"* and *"el honor"* are the keys to these three cultures. As another example, in his discussion of English he writes:

> There is a deep satisfaction in the thought that English—the language of the man of action—is a monosyllabic language. For the man of action, as we know, lives in the present, and the present is an instant with room for no more than one syllable. Words of more than one syllable are sometimes called in English

"dictionary" words, i.e., words for the intellectual, for the bookworm, for the crank, almost for the un-English. They are marvellous, those English monosyllables, particularly, of course, those which represent acts. Their fidelity to the act which they represent is so perfect that one is tempted to think English words are the right and proper names which those acts are meant to have, and all other words but pitiable failures. How could one improve on splash, smash, ooze, shriek, slush, glide, squeak, coo? Who could find anything better than hum or buzz or howl or whir? Who could think of anything more sloppy than slop? Is not the word sweet a kiss in itself and what could suggest a more peremptory obstacle than stop?

For another example of how language provides insights into a culture, see Box 8.11.

The lower and upper classes in most societies speak a different language. Bernstein [1959], as we shall soon see, finds that the "public" language of the poorly educated British lower class is poles apart from "formal" English (see Box 8.12 for an American example). It may well be that these distinctive social-class languages reflect distinctive class differences in ways of thinking.

LANGUAGE—THE MOLDER OF CULTURE. We now turn to a question which has long interested linguists and philosophers: What is the effect of language upon the way a people think and deal with objects and events in their world?

More than one hundred years ago, Von Humboldt suggested that the structure of the language of a society (the vocabulary and grammar of the language) influences the people's conception of the world. Sapir [1929] has restated these early ideas in his classic formulation of the problem of language and culture:

> Human beings do not live in the objective world alone, nor alone in the world of social activity as ordinarily understood, but are very much at the mercy of the particular language

BOX 8.11: *Language—the key to culture*

Roland W. Force, curator of oceanic archaeology and ethnology, Chicago Natural History Museum, and his wife, Maryanne Force, have studied figures of speech in the language of the Palauan people. The Palau Islands are among the islands of Micronesia in the Western Pacific.

The Forces assume that the figures of speech of a language are ". . . 'home-made' models which help people to define their universe and its workings, and which enable them to render the abstract concrete." The analysis of the figures of speech of a language thus provides insights into various aspects of a culture, as the following examples from the language of the Palauans show.

Maternal descent . . . is emphasized in preference to paternal descent. . . . The positive values which accrue to the term for mother are readily seen in superlative expressions. Largest or oldest is *delal a klou* (literally, 'mother of large or old'); and highest is *delal a ngarabub* (literally, 'mother of up'). This usage reflects an important organizational bias.

To Palauans a beautiful woman is a "comet." An illegitimate child is a "child of the woods or brush." The term for ocean current (*omtelub*) has come to be used to describe repetitive accusations. A Palauan born in a given village is said to be the "meat" of a certain nut (*techel a miich*) of that village. This expression illustrates one's extremely close relationship to his place of birth. . . . To Palauans, the first child is *ketingek* (literally, "my first child") from the expression *ketingel a du* (literally, "first fruit of the banana tree"). In contrast, the youngest child is called the "tail of the fish."

Force, R. W., and Force, Maryanne. Keys to cultural understanding. Science, 1961, 133, 1202–1206.

BOX 8.12: *Two languages—two images?*

Sociologists Leonard Schatzman and Anselm L. Strauss examined social-class differences in speech in interviews (transcribed from tape recordings) with persons who had survived an Arkansas tornado.

Respondents were classified as *middle class* (one or more years of college education and annual incomes greater than $4,000) and *lower class* (no schooling beyond grammar school and annual incomes of less than $2,000). Interviews of ten middle-class and ten lower-class white respondents (matched for age, residence, etc.) were selected for study.

Analyses of these interviews revealed striking class differences:

1. *Perspective.* Almost without exception, lower-class descriptions were given as seen through the respondent's *own* eyes. The middle-class person, on the other hand, described the acts of others as the *others* saw them. Even descriptions of his own behavior were frequently portrayed from the point of view of the other.

2. *Ability to take listener's role.* Lower-class persons showed a relative insensitivity to differences between their perspective and that of the interviewer. There was much surnaming of persons without identification; terms like "we" and "they" were used frequently without specifying the referents. The middle-class respondent recognized much more fully the difference between his perspective and that of the interviewer and used many devices to supply context and to clarify meaning.

3. *Organizing framework.* The lower-class respondents, with one exception, did not give long, well-organized accounts of their experiences. Their organizing frames were segmental or limited in scope. They tended to wander off into a detailed account of a particular incident, with the incident in turn providing the framework for an account of other events, with logical or temporal connections between the incidents often obscure.

In sharp contrast, the middle-class respondents, without exception, used over-all frames to organize their entire account.

It might appear, therefore, that the lower-class respondent perceives in concrete terms, has specific, concrete cognitions, and that his speech reflects this mode of thought. However, as the investigators ask:

> Does his [the lower-class person] speech accurately reflect customary "concrete" modes of thought and perception, or is it that he . . . is unable to convey his perception? . . . one concludes that speech does in some sense reflect thought. The reader is perhaps best left at this point to draw his own conclusions. . . .

Schatzman, L., and Strauss, A. L. *Social class and modes of communication.* Amer. J. Sociol., *1955,* **60,** *329–338.*

which has become the medium of expression for their society. It is quite an illusion to imagine that one adjusts to reality essentially without the use of language and that language is merely an incidental means of solving specific problems of communication or reflection. The fact of the matter is that the "real world" is to a large extent unconsciously built up on the language habits of the group. . . . We see

and hear and otherwise experience very largely as we do because the language habits of our community predispose certain choices of interpretation.

Sapir's thesis has by no means been accepted universally. Linguists, anthropologists, and social psychologists are in disagreement regarding its validity. It remains, however, a lively and important question even today. Should this thesis prove to be valid, the study of the structure of languages could become a powerful means for gaining understanding of differences in social behavior among the different peoples of the world.

ARGUMENTS PRO. Whorf [1956] has defended the thesis that people in different cultures perceive the world in basically different ways. The evidence which Whorf gives in support of this thesis is entirely linguistic, that is, he assumes that differences in language structure indicate differences in ways of perceiving and organizing reality.

To illustrate, Whorf notes that in the Eskimo language there are three words for three different kinds of snow for which there are no single-word equivalents in the English language. This he interprets as indicating that the Eskimo discriminates between the three different kinds of snow, whereas English-speaking people are unable to make this distinction.

Whorf also assumes that the grammatical categories of a language are indicative of cognitive categories. Thus, for example, in the Hopi language, there are two grammatical categories which are strange to English-speaking people. The first Hopi category includes names only for temporary events (e.g., lightning, flash, spasm); the second category contains names only for long-term events (e.g., man, house, lifetime). Whorf concludes that the Hopi organize their world on a dimension which English-speaking people overlook.

A number of other linguists and anthropologists have attempted to relate linguistic structure to behavior. For example, Bernstein [1959] has described the language which he asserts is spoken by relatively uneducated persons in England. He calls this a "public" language as distinguished from the so-called "formal" language said to be used by better educated middle- and upper-class people.

On the assumption that "Language is . . . one of the most important means of initiating,

synthesizing, and *reinforcing* ways of thinking, feeling and behavior," Bernstein enumerates the following characteristics of "public" language and discusses their effects upon the person's thinking:

1. *Short, grammatically simple sentences, often unfinished, with syntactically poor construction.* This characteristic impedes the communication of ideas and relations which require a precise formulation. The crude, simple verbal structure of the language points to a possible difficulty in talking about complex processes.

2. *Simple and repetitive use of a small number of conjunctions (so, and, then, because).* This means that logical modification and stress can only be expressed crudely. The use of a small number of conjunctions also means that a wrong conjunction is often used, or an approximate term is constantly substituted for a more exact logical distinction.

3. *Rigid and limited use of adjectives and adverbs.* This severely reduces individual qualifications of objects (nouns) and individual modifications of processes (adverbs).

4. *Frequent use of personal pronouns (we, you) as subjects rather than impersonal pronouns (one, it).* This prevents the speaker, Bernstein argues, from objectifying the experience he is talking about. The use of "one" as a subject permits the speaker to make the subject general and impersonal.

5. *Frequent use of statements formulated as implicit questions which set up a "sympathetic circularity" ("It's only natural, isn't it?").* According to Bernstein, this "discourages further analysis of the event and processes which provoked it and so discourages the search for reasons. . . . Curiosity is therefore limited in such a way as to enhance the solidarity of the social relationship."

6. *Frequent tendency for reason and conclusion to be confounded to produce a categoric statement ("Do as I tell you.").* This has important cognitive and social implications. "When this form of communication takes

296

place between parent and child the reasons for the required change of behavior are rarely or only briefly given and so a possible range of behavior and, more importantly, learning will not occur . . . the frequency of, and dependency upon, the categoric statement . . . limits the range of behaviors and learning, and conditions types of reaction and sensitivity toward authority."

7. *Frequent use of traditional, idiomatic phrases.* This means that the speaker of a public language "tends to attach his feelings to social counters or tags which maximize the solidarity of the social relationship at the cost of the logical structure of the communication, and the specificity of the feeling. For traditional phrases, idioms, etc., tend to operate on a low causal level of generality in which . . . symbols are employed, aimed at maximizing the emotive rather than the logical import."

8. *Implicit meaning.* For Bernstein the fact that a public language is one of implicit meaning is its most important characteristic, the determinant of the other characteristics. "If some of the characteristics are examined— short, grammatically simple, syntactically poor sentence construction; inappropriate verbal forms; simple and repetitive use of conjunctions; rigid and limited use of adjectives and adverbs; selection from a group of traditional phrases: the very means of communication do not permit, even discourage, individually differentiated cognitive and affective responses."

ARGUMENTS CON. Whorf's assumption that language differences are necessarily indicative of cognitive differences has been severely criticized by several writers. Brown and Lenneberg [1954] question Whorf's conclusion that the lack in the English language of words for the Eskimos' three different kinds of snow indicates that English-speaking people are not able to discriminate these differences. They argue that English-speaking people may also be able to make the discrimination, but for them, however, the difference may be a differ- ence which makes no difference. English- speaking people, therefore, have not troubled to invent separate names. The assumption that differences in grammatical structure necessarily indicate differences in cognition is similarly attacked.

In his review of the relation of language to culture, Hoijer [1953] concludes:

The fact of the matter, then, is not that linguistic patterns inescapably limit sensory perceptions and thought, but simply that, together with other cultural patterns, they direct perception into certain habitual channels. . . . there is much in the thesis we have outlined that requires testing; the work . . . serves only to rough out a hypothesis on the relation of language to culture, not conclusively to demonstrate it.

THE EXPERIMENTAL QUESTION. To demonstrate a relation between the structure of the language of a people and their characteristic ways of seeing and ordering the world requires that the question be pared down to experimental size. This involves the formulation of testable hypotheses regarding the relationship between specific linguistic measures and specific cognitive processes, such as particular ways of perceiving, remembering, etc. *The question whether linguistic differences indicate cognitive differences cannot be answered merely by collecting instances of linguistic differences and then inferring cognitive differences.* The question can be answered only by determining whether a relation does or does not exist between a measure of language structure, on the one hand, and an *independent* measure of some nonlinguistic cognitive process, on the other hand.

An illustration may clarify this point. Lenneberg and Roberts [1956] tell us that in Portuguese "the temperature continuum is cut into *quente* and *frio* (intermediary words such as *tepido* or *caldo* are rarely used in colloquial speech). Any stimulus above the cut elicits word A (*quente*) and any stimulus below it elicits word B (*frio*). In English two cuts are made through the same continuum so that three groups emerge—a (hot), b (warm), and c (cold)." (See Figure 8.2.) We would certainly not be safe in directly inferring that these linguistic differences produce corresponding differences in the perception of the temperature of objects. The need for experimentally *testing* this inference should be obvious. And the method for testing it would be to secure and compare independent measures of the thermal perceptions of monolingual Portuguese- and English-speaking subjects.

EXPERIMENTAL STUDIES OF LANGUAGE AND COGNITION

In this section, we shall examine a few of the studies which have tackled the language-cognition problem. Some of these have been carried out within single-language communities, and it may seem, at first glance, that such *intralinguistic* studies can have little or no relevance to the general thesis that language affects behavior. However, if it can be shown that the structure of a single language affects the way its users cognize their world, we would have good reason to believe that two groups of people who use languages which are structurally different will see their worlds differently. In the remaining studies, an *interlinguistic* design has been used. In this design, the nonlanguage behavior of subjects from different language communities is compared. Observed differences in behavior are then attributed to differences in the vocabularies or structure of the languages of the subjects.

INTRALINGUISTIC STUDIES. A study by Brown and Lenneberg [1954] is directly relevant to the language-cognition problem. These investigators were interested in the relation between the verbal codability of colors and their perceptual recognition. A measure of the codability of each of 24 colors for English-speaking persons was first secured by showing patches of these colors to subjects and asking them to name them. Some patches were immediately given the same single-word name by the subjects; these had high codability scores. Other patches produced blocking of the naming response and were assigned compound word names which varied from subject to subject; these had low codability scores.

Four of the 24 colors for which codability scores had been previously secured were shown to another sample of subjects, who were then asked to pick out these colors from a large number of other colors. The question at issue was: Will the subjects be able to *recognize* the more readily codable colors more correctly than the less readily codable colors? The answer was positive—colors which are easily and readily coded (colors with simple, common names) are recognized more correctly than colors which are not easily and readily coded.

Brown and Lenneberg also obtained data from a Zuñi Indian group. The results showed a relationship between codability and recognition similar to that obtained in the English-speaking group. In the Zuñi color vocabulary, the colors we call orange and yellow have the same name. The Zuñis frequently confused orange and yellow colors in the recognition task, whereas English-speaking subjects were never observed to make this error.

Brown's [1958] examination of the influence of parts of speech of the English language upon the cognitions of preschool children also suggests that there is some language determinism. For the details of this study, see Box 8.13.

FIGURE 8.2: How a physical-stimulus continuum, e.g., temperature, may be divided in different ways by different languages. [Adapted from Lenneberg and Roberts, 1956.]

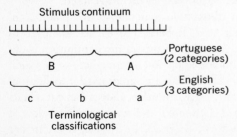

Stimulus continuum

B   A   Portuguese (2 categories)

c   b   a   English (3 categories)

Terminological classifications

BOX 8.13: *What is "sibbing?"*

Roger Brown, a psychologist at Massachusetts Institute of Technology, speculated as follows:

> A child who had *absorbed* the semantics of the noun and verb would know the *first time* he heard the word *dog* that it was likely to refer to an object having characteristic size and shape whereas *running* would be likely to name some animal motion. The part-of-speech membership of the new word would operate as a filter selecting for attention probably relevant features of the nonlinguistic world. It seemed to me that one could learn whether children experience any such filtering of attributes by introducing them to newly invented words assigned to one or another part of speech and then inquiring about the references the words seemed to make.

Recordings of the play conversations of preschool children led Brown to conclude that children give nouns and verbs proper grammatical treatment. The children also made differential grammatical use of *mass* nouns (e.g., dirt, snow, milk, and rice) as distinguished from *particular* nouns (e.g., barn, house, and dog). (We speak of *a* barn or *a* house; and we speak of *some* milk or *some* rice, not *a* milk or *a* rice.) Brown therefore decided to work with these three classes of words: the particular noun, the mass noun, and the verb.

In the experiment three sets of four pictures each were used. In one of the sets, for example, the first picture showed a pair of hands performing a kneading motion, with a mass of red confetti-like material which filled to overflowing a blue-and-white striped container. The three critical features of the picture were the kneading motion, the mass of confetti, and the container. The motion would commonly be named with a verb (e.g., kneading), the mass with a mass noun (e.g., confetti), and the container with a particular noun (e.g., container). Brown assumed that his preschool children would have no easily available specific names for any of these three features. Each of the remaining three pictures in this set exactly reproduced one of the three critical features of the first picture, but differed in the other two features.

The child was shown the first picture in conjunction with an artificial word which would be identified by the experimenter as either a verb, a mass noun, or a particular noun. Three such words were used: *niss, sib,* and *latt.* If the word was to function as a verb, the experimenter would begin by asking: "Do you know what it means to sib?" "In this picture you can see sibbing. Now show me another picture of sibbing" (presenting other three pictures of the set). If the stem was to function as a particular noun he began: "Do you know what a sib is?" and proceeded in consistent fashion. If the word was to function as a mass noun he began: "Have you ever seen any sib?" and went on accordingly.

Each child was presented with all three sets of pictures and heard each of the words—one of them as a particular noun, another as a mass noun, and the third as a verb. The combinations of word, part-of-speech membership, picture set, and order of presentation were all varied randomly.

The results showed that there was a high degree of appropriateness in the choice of pictures. When the new word was introduced as a verb, 10 of the 16 children pointed to the picture of action. When the new word was identified as a particular noun, 11 of the 16 chose the picture of an object. When the word was introduced as a mass noun, 12 of the 16 selected the picture of a mass substance.

This experiment indicates that the class of a word serves to make more salient those objects or events whose names fall in that particular class. Had these children not known the grammar involved, their perception could not have shown this selectivity.

Brown, R. Words and things. Glencoe, Ill.: Free Press, 1958.

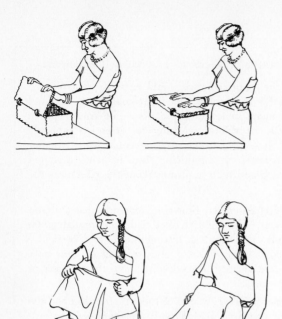

FIGURE 8.3: The pictures for item 20 of Carroll's test. The linguistic basis for this item is that in the Hopi language there is a verb, *'u'ta*, which means "to close an opening"; in contrast, placing a cover on something to protect it from dust or damage is represented by different verbs. In the English language, the verb *cover* is used whether an opening is being covered or not, and *close* is used when an opening is more or less exactly fitted with a lid or other special stoppage. On this basis, Hopis should tend to group the first and third pictures together; Anglos, the second and third pictures. [Carroll and Casagrande, 1958.]

INTERLINGUISTIC STUDIES. In some of the studies of the effect of language upon behavior, an interlinguistic design has been used, that is, the nonlinguistic behaviors of the speakers of two *different* languages have been compared.

Carroll [Carroll and Casagrande, 1958] studied the effect of structural differences between the Hopi and English languages upon perception. In the Hopi language, the verbs for various kinds of physical actions have structures quite different from the corresponding verbs in the English language. To illustrate, we will consider item 20 in Carroll's test, the pictures for which are presented in Figure 8.3. In Hopi there is a verb, *'u'ta*, which means "to close an opening." This verb is used to denote placing covers on open boxes, closing lids, closing holes in tubes or walls, etc. In contrast, the verb *na: kwapna* or *nonoma* is used to represent placing a cover on something for protection against dust or damage.

In the English language the verb *cover* is used whether we are covering an opening or not; the verb *close* is used to refer to the special case where an opening can be fitted more or less exactly with a lid or top. It was predicted, therefore, that Hopis, when asked to decide which of the three pictures went together, would choose the first and third pictures, whereas white Americans would match the second and third.

Seventeen items similar to item 20 were administered to 14 Hopi adults and 28 white Americans—12 adults comparable in education to the Hopis and 16 graduate students. The results of the study are summarized in Table 8.1. The results for all 17 items reveal only a slightly greater tendency for the Hopi subjects to make the expected "Hopi" response of pairing the first and third pictures as compared with the two Anglo groups. Re-examination of the purely linguistic data revealed five items which Carroll had reason to believe were poor or invalid items. When these were

TABLE 8.1: "HOPI" AND "ANGLO" RESPONSES OF THREE GROUPS [After Carroll and Casagrande, 1958]

	"Hopi" response: first and third pictures	"Anglo" response: second and third pictures	Neutral response: first and second pictures
17 items:			
Hopi (N = 14)	29.0%	52.9%	18.1%
Rural Anglos (N = 12)	22.6	58.3	19.1
Educated Anglos (N = 16)	24.0	57.5	18.5
12 selected items:			
Hopi (N = 14)	34.0	47.6	18.4
Rural Anglos (N = 12)	21.5	59.0	19.5
Educated Anglos (N = 16)	18.8	63.9	17.3

weeded out, the data for the 12 remaining items provided stronger support for the Whorfian thesis. The findings thus lend some support to the hypothesis that language affects behavior. However, the findings are not impressive confirmation of the hypothesis; they may best be regarded as "suggestive" and as indicating that we have at hand a promising technique for examining the influence of language upon behavior.

In Casagrande's study [Carroll and Casagrande, 1958] an attempt was made to demonstrate that the grammar of a language influences behavior. In the Navaho language, it is obligatory, when using verbs of *handling*, to use the particular one of a set of verbs that denotes the shape or other essential characteristic of the object handled. Because of this peculiarity in the grammar of the Navaho language, it was predicted that Navaho-speaking Navaho children would learn to discriminate the *form* attributes of objects at an earlier age than would English-speaking Navaho children.

A test procedure called "Ambiguous Sets" was developed. Ten pairs of objects were used, each pair differing significantly in two respects, e.g., color and size, color and shape, size and shape. The child was presented with these pairs of objects, one pair at a time, and was then shown a third object similar to each member of the pair in only one of the two relevant characteristics. The child was asked to say which of the pair went best with the comparison object. For example, set O consisted of a yellow rope and a blue stick. The child was then shown a blue rope. He could choose either the blue stick (a color choice) or the yellow rope (a form choice). The subjects were 59 Navaho children for whom Navaho was the dominant language, 43 Navaho children for whom English was the dominant language, and 47 white American children.

The results are shown in Table 8.2. Note that the Navaho-dominant Navahos make the "Navaho" choice ("a") significantly more frequently than do the English-dominant Navahos. The differences between the two groups are large and striking.

This finding seems to lend substantial support to the hypothesis that language structure influences behavior. Unfortunately, the neatness of the results yielded by comparing Navaho-dominant and English-dominant Navahos is disturbed by the test behavior of the white American children. Their choices are slightly more "Navaho" than the choices of the Navahos themselves. The investigator argues that upper-middle-class white American

TABLE 8.2: RESULTS OF THE "AMBIGUOUS SETS" EXPERIMENT [After Carroll and Casagrande, 1958]

SET	ATTRIBUTES CONTRASTED	COM-PARISON MODEL	ALTERNATIVE CHOICES "a"	"b"	PER CENT OF "a" CHOICES Navaho-dominant Navahos	English-dominant Navahos	White American children
O	Form, color	Blue Rope	Yellow Rope	Blue Stick	70.7	39.5	83.0
P	Form, color	Yellow Rope	Blue Rope	Yellow Stick	70.7	39.5	80.7
H	Form, color	Blue Stick	Yellow Stick	Blue Cylinder	71.2	44.2	76.6
N	Form, color	Blue Stick	Yellow Stick	Blue Oblong Block	72.4	44.2	82.9
I	Shape, size	Small Blue Cube	Medium Blue Cube	Small Blue Sphere	79.7	60.5	72.4
L	Shape, size	Small Blue Cylinder	Large Blue Cylinder	Small Blue Oblong	59.4	44.2	82.9
K	Shape, color	Medium Blue Cube	Medium White Cube	Medium Blue Pyramid	45.7	39.5	70.2
G	Size, color	Medium Blue Cube	Medium Yellow Cube	Small Blue Cube	21.0	23.2	74.4
J	Size, color	Medium Blue Cube	Medium White Cube	Large Blue Cube	15.2	14.0	55.3
M	Size, color	Medium Blue Cube	Medium Black Cube	Small Blue Cube	59.3	30.2	74.4

children may not be a fair control group because their early and continued play with toys of the form-board type may impress them with the importance of form as compared with a "secondary" quality like color. This study illustrates a major difficulty besetting the interlinguistic approach—the difficulty of securing adequate control groups, i.e., control groups that differ from the experimental group in language training only.

SOME GENERAL COMMENTS. These studies suggest that language and cognition are related. Whorf's thesis, drawn from his cross-cultural studies, that different language communities conceive reality in different ways is thus lent support. But much work remains to be done to further our understanding of the influence of language upon behavior.

The most reasonable interpretation of the relation between language and cognition would appear to be that in the history of a *culture,* the characteristic features of the language and of the thinking of the people develop together, both being influenced by the physical environment of the group and by its history.

In the history of the *individual,* we have to reckon with the fact that he is born into a society which has a language with such and such a vocabulary and such and such a grammar. From birth, he hears this peculiar language spoken by everyone around him. He learns to speak a language which, for example, has single-word, agreed-upon names for certain objects and only phrases, inconsistently applied, for other objects. We would guess that for the new member of the society, those objects which are readily namable will tend to stand out as figures and be perceptually available, whereas less readily namable objects will have background quality and will be less prominent in the perceptual world of the individual. In the history of the individual, his language may well help to shape his picture of the world and influence his social actions.

TO RECAPITULATE

The relations between the language of an individual and his personality, like the relations between language and culture, are intricate and little understood.

It seems to be clearly established that speech and personality are related. The speech of a person reflects his personality—his cognitive style and personality dispositions. But to what extent one is the cause or the effect of the other remains to be worked out.

Language, a most important part of any cul-ture, is a key to the nature of the total culture. It can be seen as the crystallized thought of a people.

Philosophers, linguists, and anthropologists have long been interested in a question of major import for the social psychologist. Does the language of a person influence the way he comes to perceive and understand his world? This question can be answered only by determining experimentally whether differences in linguistic structure, i.e., differences in vocabulary or syntax, influence non-linguistic cognitive processes. The final answer is not yet in. The few experimental studies which have been carried out suggest a mild form of linguistic determinism. The structure of a language does, it would appear, serve to make salient for the individual certain objects and events in his world.

GUIDE 27: *Language makes possible the growth and transmission of cultures, the continuity of societies, and the effective functioning and control of social groups*

It would be difficult indeed to overstate the importance of language in the affairs of man. Language makes possible the growth and transmission of cultures and it is through the tool of language that members of a society are enabled to cooperate in solving the problems of communal living. A complex society could not develop without a symbolic language.

Hallowell [1953] has well stated the critical role of language in the transmission of cultures and in the operation of human societies.

Neither a human society nor a human personality can be conceived in functional terms apart from systems of symbolic communication. Symbolic communication is the basis on which a common world of meanings and values is established and transmitted in human societies. Communication . . . is a necessary condition for the operation of human societies in their characteristic form.

Since even a most highly evolved primate, like the chimpanzee, cannot master a human language and there is no evidence that at any subhuman level the graphic and plastic arts exist, extrinsic symbolic systems as media of communication are an exclusively human creation. They provide man with the central vehicle that has been used to build up culturally constituted modes of existence for himself. The transmission of culture . . . is the over-all unifying factor in the temporal continuity of man from generation to generation. And, since man has been able to develop, live by, and transmit different images of the world and himself, rather than adapt himself to some given existential reality in an "objective" sense, distinct cultural traditions become the differential attributes of discrete human societies.

SPECIAL LANGUAGES

Within our own society and within our own culture we can see how language operates to preserve special cultures. This is apparent when we examine the so-called *special languages,* characterized by Hiller [1933] as follows:

By the term "special language" we mean a language which is employed only by groups of individuals placed in special circumstances. The language of the law is a case in point. In the exercise of their profession lawyers employ a language very far removed from that of ordinary speech; it is a special legal language. Another example can be found in ecclesiastical language. A special language is often used in addressing the Deity. . . . All forms of slang are special languages. Students, artisans, and thieves all use a language of their own. . . . They all have this in common . . . when their structure is examined they are found to be the outcome of a common tendency to adapt the language to the functions of a particular group.

From his study of special languages Lewis [1948] concluded that their development within the larger language community is a phenomenon found throughout the history of language. "Whenever men are organized into groups for the purpose of specific action, they tend to develop a language foreign in some measure to the language of the larger society in which they move."

And as Box 8.14 suggests, if a member of a group uses his special language in talking with an outsider, he may experience a perilous communication failure.

THE SPECIAL LANGUAGE OF SOLDIERS. Elkin [1945] has analyzed the special language of the American soldier in World War II. He divides the distinctive language of the soldier into two categories: *fashion expressions,* or those expressions found in local units or for a brief time throughout the Army; and *habitual expressions,* or those expressions learned and used by all soldiers throughout their Army career.

The most common fashion expressions were those that became popular among units stationed in foreign countries. For example, among American soldiers stationed in England, the following expressions for prostitutes became fashionable: "torches," "queens," and "Piccadilly Commandos." Elkins concludes that fashion expressions are an outgrowth of the adjustment of the group to new phenomena and new situations. In addition, the use of such distinctive language expressions creates a feeling of greater solidarity among the men.

The habitual expressions of the American soldier reflect the self-image of the soldier and his attitude toward the Army authority system. Elkins believes that major changes in the self-image that result from the Army experience are reflected in the special language of the soldier. The individual soldier comes to identify himself with the Army; he comes to feel a sense of freedom from the restrictions of civilian life; he comes to perceive himself as strong and virile. Corresponding to each of these new emphases in the soldier's perception of himself are certain habitual language expressions.

Thus the perception of the solidarity of the

In his witty autobiography, Dr. Frederic Loomis, a physician, tells the following story:

I learned something of the intricacies of plain English at an early stage in my career. A woman of thirty-five came in one day to tell me that she wanted a baby but that she had been told that she had a certain type of heart-disease which might not interfere with a normal life but would be dangerous if she ever had a baby. From her description I thought at once of mitral stenosis. This condition is characterized by a rather distinctive rumbling murmur near the apex of the heart, and especially by a peculiar vibration felt by the examining finger on the patient's chest. The vibration is known as the "thrill" of mitral stenosis.

When this woman had been undressed and was lying on my table in her white kimono, my stethoscope quickly found the heart-sounds I had expected. Dictating to my nurse, I described them carefully. I put my stethoscope aside and felt intently for the typical vibration which may be found in a small but variable area of the left chest.

I closed my eyes for better concentration, and felt long and carefully for the tremor. I did not find it and with my hand still on the woman's bare breast, lifting it upward and out of the way, I finally turned to the nurse and said: "No thrill."

The patient's black eyes snapped open, and with venom in her voice she said: "Well, isn't that just too bad? Perhaps it's just as well you don't get one. That isn't what I came for."

My nurse almost choked, and my explanation still seems a nightmare of futile words.

Communication between members of different subcultures may be fraught with peril.

Loomis, F. Consultation room. *New York: Knopf, 1939.*

self with other soldiers is reflected in such expressions as "GI" and "Buddy," which help mark off soldiers from officers, civilians, and any other group. Feelings of freedom from social restraint are manifested in the pervasive profanity which characterizes the talk of soldiers. The soldier's perception of himself as strong and virile is revealed in such expressions as: to be on the ball, to blow one's top, to sweat out, to bitch, to take off, to hit the sack, to shack up.

THE FUNCTIONS OF SPECIAL LANGUAGES. Special languages, like the language of the total society, are the product of the common experiences of the members of the group and reflect their distinctive concerns and problems. The special language of the group facilitates communication about matters of common interest and, at the same time—as we have just seen in the case of the language of soldiers—reinforces feelings of group solidarity.

Sullivan [1947] has insightfully commented upon the "solidarity creating power of a common tongue."

Let me now suggest something of the wide spread of significance in speech as speech rather than as spoken words and sentences. Some of you may recall from childhood the experience of first encountering a person whose dialect was not the accustomed one. Or, perhaps, you may recall the first hearing of a conversation in a foreign tongue.

If some such experience is recaptured, let us compare it with the general experience of children with strangers. When the stranger speaks in the accustomed dialect—quite aside from the extensive significance of other nonverbal factors in everyone's speech—the insecurity felt by the child is diminished. The familiar diaphonic progressions convey some reassurance as to the *naturalness* of the stranger. He is not some awesome creature from the autistic world blended out of dreams and longings and tales of wonder that one has been told.

This unity in one's dialect-group, which presently spreads to include one's language-group, is by no means restricted to the era of childhood. Many Americans who go to Europe and move among peoples in the use of whose tongue they are not competent, show the same

BOX 8.15: *A "steamshovel" is a "derrick" is a "tractor"*

Muzafer and Carolyn W. Sherif, social psychologists at the University of Oklahoma, have observed the development of a "special language" in a laboratory situation.

Twenty-seven children of kindergarten age took part in the experiment in groups of two and three. The children in each group were shown a toy which was completely new to them and hence was nameless. The toy—a model basket-loader—was one which could be used in cooperative play. To secure the toy, it was necessary to request it from the experimenter. No particular name had to be used to designate the toy; it could be obtained by any request which differentiated it from other available toys. Each group was observed in four sessions on different days.

The experimenters considered that a name for the toy had been standardized by a group when (1) it had been used by each child at least three times in succession with no other intervening name being used; (2) each child in the group responded to the name accurately when it was used by the experimenter in an individual testing session.

The names standardized by the different groups were different. Group 1 adopted the name "big green thing"; group 2, "derrick"; group 3, "steps"; group 4, "erector"; group 5, "tractor"; group 6, "steamshovel."

The process of standardizing a name for the toy is described by the investigators as follows:

> One child, typically the one who most frequently initiated activity in the play situation, gave a name to the unnamed toy in his efforts to coordinate group play around it. The name for the object was useful to him in assuming a directive role in play activities. Therefore, when the other children used different words and phrases to refer to the toy, he tended to correct them verbally. For example, if one said "that big, big thing," he would respond "you mean _____," giving the label he had used. Eventually other children responded and sometimes corrected others. When a name was thus standardized, it was used consistently in play activities and in every case responded to accurately when later used by the experimenter outside of the group setting.

> Members of the different play groups had great difficulty in communicating with each other about the toy. For example, a member of Group 6, which standardized the name "steam-shovel" for the toy during one of the play sessions said to the experimenter: "J_____ in Group 2 said yesterday you didn't have no steam-shovel in here when they came in to play. Didn't you?" Group 2, of which J_____ was a member, had standardized the name "derrick" for the toy.

We see that groups standardize names for objects that are important to the activities of the group, thus making possible accurate communication among the members of a group.

Sherif, M., and Sherif, Carolyn W. The standardization of names. A neglected problem in the study of symbolic behavior. Unpublished manuscript, 1949. Summarized in M. Sherif and C. W. Sherif, An outline of social psychology. (Rev. ed.) New York: Harper, 1956.

THE SOCIAL AND CULTURAL HABITAT

factor in the attitudes that they manifest. The people whom they encounter are not invested with as complete a set of human traits as are even the more obnoxious of our acquaintances at home. These foreigners are not quite human. One feels emancipated correspondingly from some or many of the restraints that govern one in life at home. One does odd things—sometimes durably regrettable things—that have never occurred to one before. There is an attenuation of our conventional inhibition because we do not recognize these strangers as fully human and do not accord them the same critical attitudes towards us that we have accustomed ourselves to live with.

The solidarity creating power of a common tongue is most important.

For an experimental study which illustrates the development of a special language and its functions for the group, see Box 8.15.

A SPECULATION

The part language has in the recording and the transmission of culture in literate societies gives the scribes of the society a critical role. It is the literate segment of society which can, in a sense, decide what to record and what to transmit. It is of interest to speculate that in the very process of *transmitting* the culture of a society from one generation to another, the literate transmitters may, because of the selective nature of cognition, *change* various aspects of the culture in their own image. The historian, in recording the past for his fellows, may *recreate* their past for them. Man may both make and remake his history.

CHAPTER GUIDES AND GLOSSARY

GUIDE 25: *Communication—the interchange of meanings among people—occurs mainly through language and is possible to the degree to which individuals have common cognitions, wants, and attitudes*

GUIDE 26: *Language reflects both the personality of the individual and the culture of his society and in turn helps shape personality and culture*

GUIDE 27: *Language makes possible the growth and transmission of cultures, the continuity of societies, and the effective functioning and control of social groups*

communication. The interchange of meanings between people, primarily accomplished through the use of conventional symbols.

connotative meaning. The feelings and attitudes associated with a symbol.

denotative meaning. All of the objects, events, or instances to which a word points or refers.

language. Any set or system of vocal or written symbols, used in a more or less uniform way by the members of a community.

meaning. The entire set of cognitions, feelings, and action tendencies evoked by a symbol.

pseudo-communication. Failure to apprehend the meanings of a communication of another person as intended, frequently without knowledge of either person.

special language. The language of a group within a larger community which reflects the functions of the group and which differs in some degree from the language of the larger community.

symbol. Anything that is intentionally used to stand for or represent something else. The major kinds of symbols are intentional gestures and words.

WE HAVE SOUGHT TO ANALYZE SOCIAL BEHAVIOR IN TERMS OF THE
wants, cognitions, interpersonal response traits, and attitudes of
individuals. *This emphasis on the individual, with due recognition
of the importance of the social context in which he functions,
distinguishes most social psychologists from most sociologists.
Recognition of the importance of the social context requires that we
try to explain, with precision, what we mean by it. And it is at this
point that the social psychologist has recourse to the work of the
sociologist.*

*The individual is born into a social enterprise which is a going
concern with different positions and roles, for some of which he
must be trained and into which he will be fitted as he lives out his
days. This societal structure helps impart a distinguishing and
perduring flavor to the individual's wants, cognitions, interpersonal
response traits, values, and attitudes. It is the influence of distinctive
social habitats which distinguishes the American from the
Frenchman, from the Ghanian, from the Chinese. It is this
influence which makes biological man into social man. And it is to
the study of the structure of the societies of men that we
now turn.*

9: SOCIETY

FROM BIRTH TO DEATH MAN LIVES OUT HIS
life as a member of a *society*. And to live in a
society is to be under constant, all-pervasive
social influence (see Box 9.1). For the central
characteristic of a society is that it is an *organized* collectivity of *interacting* people whose
activities become centered around a set of
common goals, and who tend to share *common beliefs, attitudes,* and *modes of action.*

Modern industrial societies are large and
highly complicated groupings of people. To
study "society as a whole"—without further specification—would be unmanageable.
Smaller units of analysis are necessary, and
such units are readily available. The most
cursory look at any modern society reminds us
that it is composed of many *communities*, and
of organizations and smaller groups within

BOX 9.1: *The interpersonal child*

In their pioneering study of psychological ecology, Roger G. Barker and Herbert F. Wright of the University of Kansas present data which illustrate nicely the pervasive influence of the social situation—even among children.

Studying the psychological living conditions of children in Midwest (a community of 707 persons in central United States), they secured complete records of one day's behavior in the lives of each of eight children. When these day records were analyzed into *behavior episodes,* a total of 7,751 behavior episodes were coded from the eight records.

Among other questions, the investigators were interested in learning the extent to which face-to-face relations with other persons figured in the daily lives of the children.

The episodes were classified into three categories: (1) *Social episode,* where the child acts in relation to another person or persons. (2) *Potentially social episode,* where at least one other person is present but to whom, however, the child does not react. (3) *Nonsocial episode,* where the child is alone.

The following table reveals that the lives of these children were predominantly social. Although the figure of 85 per cent is inflated by the fact that the psychologists were always around to observe the child, the investigators conclude that even if the observer had been an "invisible man," unavailable to the children as an object of action, the percentage of social episodes would still have been very high—perhaps 60 per cent.

Episodes	Median per cent
Social	85
Potentially social	16
Nonsocial	1

The social episodes were analyzed to determine the frequency of "closed-action circuits," i.e., episodes in which the person toward whom the child acted responded in turn to the child. As the following table reveals, the median per cent of closed-action circuits was 80; the range was from 75 to 89 per cent.

Percentage of social episodes with closed-action circuit

Child	MC	JS	DT	MR	RB	ME	DC	CG	Median
Per cent	89	75	78	86	81	80	87	80	80

These results give quantitative evidence that interpersonal behavior events fill the waking hours of the child.

Barker, R. G., and Wright, H. F. Midwest and its children. Evanston, Ill.: Row, Peterson, 1954.

communities—friendship, family, work, and other types of groups—which have an internal structure of their own.

In complex societies the integration of individuals into society, the control of society over the person's attitudes and behavior, is determined primarily in the community. The following quotation from Murdock [1949] well expresses the views of social scientists on this matter:

> Since it is mainly through face-to-face relations that a person's behavior is influenced by

his fellows—motivated, cued, rewarded and punished—the community is the primary seat of social control. Here it is that deviation is penalized and conformity rewarded. It is noteworthy that ostracism from the community is widely regarded as the direst of punishments and that its threat serves as the ultimate inducement to cultural conformity. Through the operation of social sanctions, ideas and behavior tend to become relatively stereotyped within a community, and a local culture develops. Indeed, the community seems to be the most typical social group to support a total culture.

For purposes of analysis we use the smaller units—communities, organizations, groups—when studying society. But for purposes of exposition, in this chapter, we use the term "society" to cover all organizations and groups within this complex system.

GUIDE 28: *The coordination and control of the activities of the members of a society are achieved through systems of positions and roles*

As we study a society we discover that perhaps the major characteristic which makes its communities and groups (business firm, family, etc.) effective in controlling the behavior of the individual is that each community and group develops a system of well-defined "psychological niches" for which individuals are specially trained, and into which they are fitted. The study of these niches, how they help determine the psychological development of the person, and the ease with which individuals can move from one niche to another, is the major concern of this chapter.

POSITIONS

At least five different ways of classifying people seem to be commonly involved in giving organization and structure to a society: (1) age-sex groupings, (2) biological or family (kinship) groupings, (3) occupational group-

ings, (4) friendship and interest groupings, (5) status groupings. Within each classification, a number of different categories are recognized. These categories are termed *positions*. Within the age-sex grouping, for example, at least seven positions seem commonly to be differentiated: infant, boy, girl, adult male, adult female, old male, old female. In many societies even more positions within the age-sex system of classification are recognized.

Each individual necessarily occupies a position in each of these main systems of classification. Thus any given person at any given time may be designated as a young man, son, student, class president, etc. Many of his positions change as he grows older, develops new interests and skills, takes a job, gets married, and so on. Some positions he occupies "automatically," e.g., by virtue of the family into which he is born or his age; other positions he achieves through his individual accomplishments.

The contribution that a position makes to the objectives and purposes of the community represents the *function* of the position. Thus the function of the position of teacher is to train the young in the ways of the community. The beliefs shared by the members of a community regarding the functions of the various positions represent one part of the ideology of the community (see page 349). The function of a position as defined in the ideology of a community may or may not correspond to its function as interpreted by an outside observer—by a sociologist or a social psychologist, for example.

ROLES

For every recognized position there is an expectation widely shared by members of the community of what *should be* the behavior of persons who occupy that position. What a typical occupant of a given position is expected to do constitutes the *role* associated with that position.

A role can be seen as encompassing, among other things, the duties or obligations of the position. Thus a doctor is expected to treat the sick who come to him, to be emotionally neutral, to be expert in the diagnosis and treatment of diseases, to value health, to refrain from gossip about his patients, to avoid public criticism of his colleagues, to conduct himself with "professional propriety" in his relations with nurses.

A role can also be seen as encompassing the rights of the position. The rights of a position are defined in part by the roles of related positions. Thus the rights of the doctor are defined in part by the roles of patient and nurse. The patient is expected to follow the orders given him by his doctor, to pay promptly for the services which he receives, to abstain from self-medication; the nurse is expected to carry out all the doctor's orders, to accept his judgment on medical matters, and so on.

Clearly the system of roles which regulates the relations between the doctor and persons in related positions minimizes conflict and makes for effective interpersonal functioning. The doctor knows what is expected of him and what to expect of his patient; the patient knows what is expected of him and what to expect of his doctor. Each can thus guide his behavior appropriately with respect to the other.

ROLES ARE INTERDEPENDENT. The role associated with any given position in a group is necessarily defined in relation to the roles of other related positions. The role of patient, for example, is defined in terms of the role of doctor. When the role of doctor changes, the role of patient changes too. Thus the change in the role of doctor brought about by the development of medical specialization has resulted in corresponding changes in the role of patient. The traditional role of a general practitioner included the expectation that he would have an intimate and friendly interest in a patient as a person; the role of a patient included the expectation that he would have a friendly and personal relationship with his doctor. The role of a medical specialist is defined primarily in terms of impersonal expertness in diseases of a particular organ system; the role of a specialist's patient is primarily that of a stranger suffering from such and such disease of a particular organ system.

ROLES ARE "FAMILIES OF EXPECTANCIES." The expectancies making up a role are not restricted to actions; they also include expectancies about motivations, beliefs, feelings, attitudes, and values. Thus the role of doctor not only includes expectancies about actions (a doctor is expected to comport himself with dignity); it also includes expectancies about his wants and goals (he is expected to maintain a continuing interest in furthering his knowledge of medicine and improving his skills as a doctor), his feelings (he is expected to be emotionally neutral in his relations with patients), his attitudes (he is expected to be opposed to "socialized medicine"), his values (he is expected to value science as the means of increasing man's knowledge about diseases and their treatment). We may thus think of a role as a "family of expectancies."

ROLES REFER TO STANDARD SITUATIONS. Roles prescribe the behaviors expected of people in specified positions operating in specifically defined or standard situations, e.g., the minister in the church. Suppose Mr. Arbuthnot were, for the first time, to meet his minister, not in church, but in the locker room of his country club. There may be an initial awkwardness and unpatterned fumbling in the relations between the two. Mr. Arbuthnot may wonder whether to offer the minister a drink and whether to avoid telling a racy story. The minister may also be uncertain about what behavior to display. Should he retain his ministerial dignity or be a hail-fellow-well-met? Neither Mr. Arbuthnot nor his minister can readily identify the salient role of the other in this "nonstandard" situation and thus anticipate his behavior. Hence the interpersonal behavior of the two cannot be guided by such anticipations.

The importance of the situation for the

recognition of roles reflects the influence of context upon perception. We always perceive the behavior of a person in a context. And this context influences our perception (see Guide 3, page 30).

MULTIPLE POSITIONS AND ROLES

Every person at one and the same time occupies a position within each of the different systems whereby his society classifies and places its members. Everyone, in other words, occupies a number of different positions and therefore has a number of different roles.

Multiple positions and multiple roles are typical of all people (see Box 9.2).

The place of the individual in each of these systems determines in part how he is treated by his fellows. People receive different treatment from their fellows, depending upon their position in the various systems of the community. Thus boys are treated differently from girls; uncles are treated differently from grandfathers; priests are treated differently from politicians; upper-class boys are treated differently from lower-class boys.

The differential treatment given persons

BOX 9.2: *From clerk to Grand Imperial Lizard*

Ralph Linton, for many years a leading American cultural anthropologist, was one of the pioneers in the study of the effects of culture upon personality. In his writings on this subject, he made much of the concepts of status (i.e., position) and role. The following excerpt illustrates the multiple positions a person may occupy during the course of a day and the many roles he may play:

Let us suppose that a man spends the day working as a clerk in a store. While he is behind the counter, his active status is that of a clerk, established by his position in our society's system of specialized occupations. The role associated with this status provides him with patterns for his relations with customers. These patterns will be well known both to him and to the customers and will enable them to transact business with a minimum of delay or misunderstanding. When he retires to the rest room for a smoke and meets other employees there, his clerk status becomes latent and he assumes another active status based upon his position in the association group composed of the store's employees as a whole. In this status his relations with other employees will be governed by a different set of culture patterns from those employed in his relations with customers. Moreover, since he probably knows most of the other employees, his exercise of these culture patterns will be modified by his personal likes and dislikes of certain individuals and by considerations of their and his own relative positions in the prestige series of the store association's members. When closing time comes, he lays aside both his clerk and store association statuses and, while on the way home, operates simply in terms of his status with respect to the society's age-sex system. Thus if he is a young man he will at least feel that he ought to get up and give his seat to a lady, while if he is an old one he will be quite comfortable about keeping it. As soon as he arrives at his house, a new set of statuses will be activated. These statuses derive from the kinship ties which relate him to various members of the family group. In pursuance of the roles associated with these family statuses he will try to be cordial to his mother-in-law, affectionate to his wife and a stern disciplinarian to Junior, whose report card marks a new low. If it happens to be lodge night, all his familial statuses will become latent at about eight o'clock. As soon as he enters the lodge room and puts on his uniform as Grand Imperial Lizard, in the Ancient Order of Dinosaurs, he assumes a new status, one which has been latent since the last lodge meeting, and performs in terms of its role until it is time for him to take off his uniform and go home.

Linton, R. The cultural background of personality. *New York: Appleton-Century, 1945.*

THE SOCIAL AND CULTURAL HABITAT

who occupy a particular position, e.g., "boys," is guided by the role expectations held by the members of the community. This expectation of how boys should act guides the training or socialization of boys. When an American boy plays with dolls, he is punished by ridicule: "Look at the sissy." When he plays football, he is rewarded by praise: "He's *all boy,* isn't he!"

In short, every individual learns that such and such behaviors are expected of him as an occupant of such and such a position. That is, he learns the role associated with the position. In his ways of perceiving, thinking, feeling, striving, and acting, he is influenced by the expectancies of his fellows, backed up by the big stick of rewards and punishments wielded by members of his society.

This is not to say that the way in which a given individual *performs* a given role is identical with the way in which other individuals perform the role. It is a truism, but an important one, that individuals differ in their role performances. The source of these differences reflects the differences among individuals in the basic psychological factors—cognitions, wants, interpersonal response traits—which we examined in Part One. What we are saying here is that the range of differences in the behavior of individuals who occupy a given position is restricted by the fact that they are exposed to a more or less uniform social environment; society (i.e., other people) expects them to behave in such and such a way, and rewards conformity and punishes nonconformity.

GUIDE 29: *Every society has status systems, the most pervasive of which is social class; social class significantly determines the social environment and power of the individual*

In every community people are recognized as differing in status, some being perceived as of superior status, others as of inferior status. In highly developed, complex communities, a multiplicity of elaborate and permanent status systems is found. Within each of these systems persons are rank-ordered in terms of prestige or social worth. One of the most pervasive status systems is that of *social class.*

MEASUREMENT OF SOCIAL CLASS

The concept of social class has been variously defined by social scientists, depending upon their theoretical persuasion and their research interests. The definitions reflect the methods used in their research. Three methods have been used to measure the social-class system of communities: (1) the objective method; (2) the subjective method; (3) the reputational method.

THE OBJECTIVE METHOD. In the objective method the social scientist first decides (on the basis of theory or research experience) what objective characteristics are likely to discriminate most sharply among the different patterns of social behavior which he conceives of as "class" behaviors. The objective characteristics most frequently used (in studies of the class structure of the United States) are amount of income, amount of education, and type of occupation. Such data are easily available for the country as a whole. Thus the U.S. Bureau of the Census furnishes us with the data necessary to describe the stratification of the United States by income, education, and occupation (see Figure 9.1).

The second step is to give every individual in the community scores on the selected characteristics. The third step is to classify the persons in the community on the basis of their scores, or on some combined index of their scores, on the chosen characteristics. For example, a high score might be designated "upper class," a low score "lower class," etc.

THE SUBJECTIVE METHOD. In the subjective method the investigator defines social class in terms of how the members of the community *see themselves* in the status hierarchy. To illustrate: In 1940, the American Institute of

Public Opinion carried out a study of the social-class structure of American society. A national sample was asked this question: "To what social class in this country do you think you belong—the middle class, the upper, or the lower?" The distribution of responses was as follows:

	Per cent
Upper class	6
Middle class	88
Lower class	6

These results were widely interpreted by editorial writers and political pundits as showing that the American society is one big middle-class society. On the other hand Centers argued that the term "lower class" is not a flattering term and that many people would therefore be reluctant to use it to designate their own class as differentiated from the "middle class." The term "working class," Centers believed, would be more acceptable. Hence, in 1945 Centers [1949] asked a national sample of 1,100 white male adults the following question: "If you were asked to use one of these four names for your social class, which would you say you belonged in: the middle class, lower class, working class, or upper class?" The results are given below:

	Per cent
Upper class	3
Middle class	43
Working class	51
Lower class	1
Don't know	1
Don't believe in classes	1

From these figures, it would seem that a majority of American adult males place themselves in the working class; they apparently do not think of themselves as members of "one big middle-class society."

The Survey Research Center at the University of Michigan carried out a survey study in 1952 in which a national sample of respondents was asked about their class identifications [Converse, 1958]. As Table 9.1 shows, there

FIGURE 9.1: Stratification of U.S. families by income, 1959. [Source: Current Population Reports, Consumer Income. Washington, D.C.: U.S. Bureau of the Census, January 5, 1961, Series P-60, No. 35, derived from Table B.]

Stratification of U.S. population (25 years old and over) by education, 1959. [Adapted from Current Population Reports, Population Characteristics. Washington, D.C.: U.S. Bureau of the Census, February 4, 1960, Series P-20, No. 99.]

Stratification of employed population of United States by occupation, 1958. [Adapted from Current Population Reports, Labor Force. Washington, D.C.: U.S. Bureau of the Census, 1959.]

FAMILY INCOME (IN PER CENT)

$15,000 and over	3
$10,000–14,000	9
$5,000–9,999	43
$3,000–3,999	22
Under $3,000	23

EDUCATION (IN PER CENT)

College	18.2
High school	40.8
Less than high school	38.9

OCCUPATION (IN PER CENT)

Professionals, managers, officials, and proprietors	25
Clerical, sales, and skilled	33.7
Semiskilled and unskilled	41.2

appeared to be, as compared with 1945, a sizable shift from choice of middle class to choice of working class. Unfortunately, it is not possible to determine whether this shift represents a true change in choice of class or is due to differences in the sampling methods employed by Centers and by the Survey Research Center. Centers used a sampling method, known as the quota control method, in which the upper-income groups are overrepresented. The Survey Research Center data probably present a truer picture of the class identifications of the American people.

THE REPUTATIONAL METHOD. The reputational method of measuring social class was developed by W. Lloyd Warner and his associates in studying the social-class structure of various American communities. In this method the definition of social class is in terms of how the members of a community place *each other* in the status system of the community.

In *Social Class in America,* Warner, Meeker, and Eels [1949] describe in detail how the reputational method works. Intensive interviews are held with selected informants (members of the community, chosen because they are knowledgeable about the workings of the community). The interviews are analyzed to yield reputational ratings of the social-class position of an individual.

By the use of this method Warner and his associates have described the class structure of three American communities: "Yankee City," a town in New England with a population of approximately 17,000; "Old City," a Southern town of about 10,000; and "Jonesville" (also called "Elmtown"), a town of about 6,000 in Illinois.

In all three communities, a social-class hierarchy was found to exist. The distinguishing characteristics of the different class levels can only briefly be given here.

The upper-upper class is the "aristocracy of birth and wealth." It is made up of "old families" who live on "old money." The lower-upper class is similar to the upper-

upper, but is made up of "new" families who live on "new" wealth. The upper-middle class is the third of the three higher classes, which together comprise the "level above the common man." This stratum is occupied by the more substantial businessmen and professional workers in the community. They are often leaders in the community.

The "level of the common man" is made up of the lower-middle class and the upper-lower class. Members of the lower-middle class are characteristically small businessmen, clerical and other white collar employees, and some skilled workers. The upper-lower class is composed of some skilled workers, semiskilled workers, and small trades people.

The lower-lower class is the nonrespectable group in the community. It is the "level below the common man." This group is perceived by the superior classes to be immoral. Its members live in the deteriorated sections of the community and are largely semiskilled and unskilled workers. A disproportionately large percentage of public-relief cases come from this group.

The relative size of the six social classes in Yankee City and Jonesville is quite similar (see Table 9.2), save for the fact that in Jonesville the lower-lower class is smaller and the upper-lower and lower-middle groups are

TABLE 9.1: SUBJECTIVE CLASS IDENTIFICATION OF WHITE AMERICAN MALES [After Converse, 1958]

Class	University of Michigan survey, 1952 N = 666	Centers's survey, 1945 N = 1,097
Lower class	2%	1%
Working class	59	51
Middle class	35	43
Upper class	1	3
Reject idea of class	1	1
Don't know, not ascertained	2	1

TABLE 9.2: CLASS STRUCTURE IN YANKEE CITY AND JONESVILLE [Based on data from Warner and Lunt, 1941; Warner et al., 1949]

Class	Yankee City percentage of population	Jonesville percentage of population
Upper-upper	2% ⎫	3%
Lower-upper	2 ⎭	
Upper-middle	10	11
Lower-middle	28	31
Upper-lower	33	41
Lower-lower	25	14

correspondingly larger. In the two relatively old communities—Yankee City and Old City —the upper-class groups were found to be differentiated into "old" families (the upper-upper) and "new" families (the lower-upper). In Jonesville, a smaller and younger community, the upper-class group was not so differentiated and only five class strata were found. Because of the different rural-urban ratio in the South and the effect of the Negro-white caste system upon class structure, the distribution of the classes in Old City is somewhat different from the distributions found in Yankee City and Jonesville.

Kornhauser [1953] has summarized a number of criticisms of Warner's reputational method. First, the method is applicable to small communities only. In a metropolitan community, the inhabitants are anonymous except to their intimates. Hence the information required by the reputational method cannot be obtained. This is a serious limitation of the method. Second, some critics contend that Warner has described the social-class structure, not as it actually exists in small communities, but as it is perceived by the upper-middle- and upper-class residents who were his principal informants. Why, these critics ask, are six social-class divisions more "real" than the three or four that are recognized by the lower class? (See Box 2.2,

page 19.) Third, the procedures have been criticized as being imprecise and as not leading to reproducible results by other investigators.

SOCIAL CLASS AS SOCIAL ENVIRONMENT

The interest of the social psychologist in social class stems from the fact that social class significantly determines the social environment of the individual. For, as we have seen in Parts One and Two, the individual's cognitions, wants and goals, interpersonal response traits and attitudes are heavily conditioned by his social environment. And inasmuch as these factors determine the social actions of the individual, the social psychologist must pay attention to social class. As Davis and Havighurst [1946] have pointed out:

> The social class system maintains cultural, economic, and social barriers which prevent intimate social intermixture between the slums, the Gold Coast, and the middle-class. We know that human beings can learn their culture only *from other human beings,* who already know and exhibit that culture. Therefore, by setting up barriers to social participation, the American social-class system actually prevents the vast majority of children of the working classes, or the slums, from learning any culture but that of their own groups. *Thus the pivotal meaning of social class* to students of human development is that it defines and systematizes different learning environments for children of different classes. [See Box 9.3.]

The degree to which social class limits intimate social interaction between persons has been the subject of many studies, all of which indicate that people generally restrict most of their intimate social relations to members of their own class (see Box 9.4). When we first meet a stranger, we frequently spend considerable time, each in our own manner, applying our own criteria, in an attempt to determine the class status of the stranger. We must do this so as to know just how intimate we may become with him, and the appropriate way

BOX 9.3: *Social class among the five-year-olds*

Psychologists Robert R. Sears and Eleanor E. Maccoby of Stanford University and Harry Levin of Cornell University have studied child-rearing practices in mid-twentieth-century America.

The mothers chosen for the study lived in two suburbs of a large metropolitan area in New England. All had children enrolled in public school kindergartens; all were born in America and were living with American-born husbands. Their social-class position was determined by combining a measure of the occupational level of the husband with a measure of income. Using this index, they were divided into two social-class groups: middle class (professional, business, white-collar occupations) and working class (blue-collar occupations).

Through individual interviews, information was obtained on the child-rearing practices of the mothers. These various practices were then scaled and rated.

Some of the differences between middle-class and working-class mothers in their child-training practices (for children up to the age of five years) are shown in the following table.

| | PERCENTAGE RATED HIGH | |
PRACTICE	*Middle* class	*Working* class
Severity of toilet training	15	26
Sex permissiveness	53	22
Permissiveness for aggression toward parents	19	7
Pressure for conformity with table standards	23	39
Pressure for neatness and orderliness	43	57
Extent of father's demands for instant obedience	53	67
Importance of child's doing well at school	35	50
Use of ridicule	31	47
Use of physical punishment	17	33

The investigators summarize:

These are fairly radical differences. It must be kept in mind that we are comparing here not two fully discriminable groups, such as men and women, but two halves of what some observers would consider a homogeneous population—a sample of the American people. Evidently the sample is not as homogeneous as that nationalistic label implies.

Sears, R. R., Maccoby, Eleanor E., and Levin, H. Patterns of child rearing. *Evanston, Ill.: Row, Peterson, 1957.*

to treat him. However, as we shall later see, people can *move* from one class into another, that is, they can change their social environment.

The three methods of measuring social class which we have discussed can be seen, therefore, as representing three approaches to the description of the social environment of the individual.

SOCIAL ENVIRONMENT AND "OBJECTIVE" SOCIAL CLASS. Persons in the same occupational group, or in the same income group, or in the same educational group tend to live in the same neighborhoods and to interact more closely and frequently with one another than with members of different occupational, income, or educational groups. Hence, objective measures of social class may be interpreted as

BOX 9.4: *Who cliques with whom?*

August B. Hollingshead, a sociologist at Yale University, was associated with W. Lloyd Warner in the 1941 study of the social structure of "Elmtown," a small town (pop. 5,200) in southern Illinois. He studied the effect of social-class position upon the clique relations of the boys and girls enrolled in the one high school in the town.

All the boys and girls in the high school were categorized by him within five social classes— I to V. Sixty-three per cent of all clique ties were between members of the same social class; 33 per cent were between members of two adjacent classes; only 4 per cent were with students separated by two class lines. There were no clique relations between class I and II and class V students. Thus boys and girls who belonged to the top and bottom classes in the social structure of Elmtown were isolated from one another; there were no intimate, face-to-face relations between them in the informal friendship or clique groups of the high school.

The dating relations in the high school closely paralleled the clique relations. Of all the dates the students had in one month, 61 per cent were with a member of the same class; 35 per cent were with a member of an adjacent class; only 4 per cent were with a member of a class separated by two class lines. There were no dates between class I and II's and class V's. The percentages of dates within and across social classes are shown in the following figure, for boys and girls separately. For example, 54 per cent of the dates of class I and II boys were with class I and II girls; 8 per cent were with class IV girls.

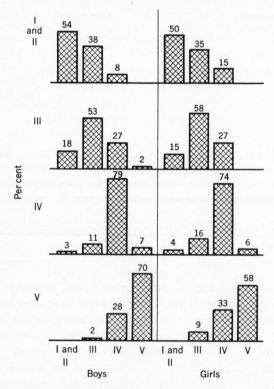

Hollingshead, A. B. Elmtown's youth. *New York: Wiley, 1949.*

indirect measures of the social environment of the individual. A high-level executive is expected as part of his role as executive to live in an elite neighborhood; a laborer is expected to live in a lower-middle-class neighborhood. The laborer cannot afford to live in an elite area; the executive cannot afford *not* to live in an elite area. The demonstration that objective measures of the social class of the individual provide good measures of his social environment has recently been elaborated by Tryon in a series of studies [1955a, 1955b, 1959]. These studies represent a new departure in psychosociological analysis and will be treated in detail in the next section.

SOCIAL ENVIRONMENT AND "SUBJECTIVE" SOCIAL CLASS. The subjective measure of class position may be viewed as a measure of the social environment to the extent that the individual tends to restrict his social relations to members of the class group with which he identifies himself. Inasmuch as this group is composed for the most part of individuals who do similar work and have similar ways of thinking and feeling about things, this seems a reasonable assumption, and one for which there is empirical evidence as well.

Centers [1949], in the study cited earlier (see page 314), asked the members of each subjective class group which of 11 occupational groups belonged to their class. Middle-class persons listed predominantly business, professional, and white-collar occupations; working-class persons listed predominantly manual work occupations. As Figure 9.2 reveals, however, there is considerable overlap between the two classes. Many middle-class persons included manual workers in their class, and many working-class persons included business, professional, and white-collar workers in their class.

The rather blurred differentiation between the middle and working classes with respect to occupational composition led Centers to suspect that other criteria of class distinction might be important. Each person was therefore asked: "In deciding whether a person belongs to your class or not, which of these other things do you think is most important to know: who his family is; how much money he has; what sort of education he has; or how he believes and feels about certain things?" Table 9.3 gives the distribution of the responses obtained to this question. Forty-seven per cent answered, "How he believes and feels about certain things."

These findings suggest that a subjective social class is a "real group" for the members of the class; it exists for them. It is a group which is made up of people who do similar work and who have a similar set of beliefs, attitudes, and values. A person tends to affiliate with those who are like him in work ways and in ways of thinking and feeling.

SOCIAL ENVIRONMENT AND "REPUTATIONAL" SOCIAL CLASS. The reputational method is a direct measure of the social environment of the individual. This method (assuming the validity of the reports of the informants) tells us with whom the individual exchanges visits, plays, worships, etc.

SOCIAL AREAS

The existence of social classes means, as we have seen, that people live in different social environments. It is also true that the physical surroundings in which people live reflect these differences in their social environments. When

TABLE 9.3: CRITERIA FOR OWN CLASS MEMBERSHIP OTHER THAN OCCUPATION [After Centers, 1949]

Criterion	Percentage of respondents
Beliefs and attitudes	47.4%*
Education	29.4
Family	20.1
Money	17.1
Other answers	5.6
Don't know	9.1

* Percentages add to more than 100 because some respondents gave more than one answer.

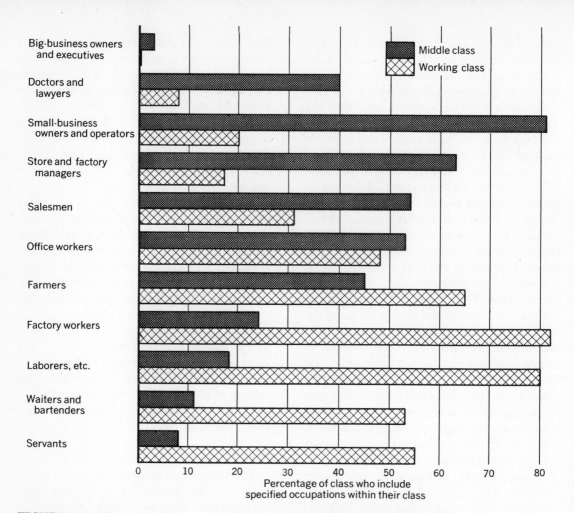

FIGURE 9.2: The occupational composition of the working and middle social classes as specified by members of these two classes. The length of each bar represents the percentage of people in the working and middle class, respectively, who include the given occupational group in their class. [Adapted from Centers, 1949.]

one travels through such metropolitan areas as Chicago, New York, the San Francisco Bay Area, Los Angeles, one is immediately struck by the sharp and dramatic contrasts between the slums and the Gold Coasts, between the downtown caves of the apartment dwellers and the scattered houses of the suburbanites. Clearly the slum dweller lives in a different physical *and* social world from the Gold Coaster; the apartment dweller in a different physical *and* social world from the suburban-

ite. The problem is to describe these different worlds in a systematic, quantitative, meaningful way. The *Social Area method*, developed by Tryon, is designed to do just this.

THE IDENTIFICATION OF SOCIAL AREAS. Essentially, Tryon is concerned with identifying the neighborhoods of various social strata—objectively defined—which make up a metropolitan community. These neighborhoods he calls *social areas*.

Tryon's method of identifying social areas

320   THE SOCIAL AND CULTURAL HABITAT

may be described by following him in his analysis of the Bay Area metropolitan community in California. The Bay Area is composed of San Francisco and the East Bay cities from San Leandro to Richmond. For census purposes the U.S. Bureau of the Census uses as its smallest enumerative unit the *census tract*. The Bay Area is composed of 243 such tracts.

The first step Tryon took in identifying social areas was to secure (from the 1940 census reports) for each of the 243 census tracts 33 objective demographic and ecological characteristics. For each characteristic, the score of each census tract was expressed as a percentage. To illustrate: The score of a tract on "Owner occupied" is the percentage of all homes in the tract which are occupied by the owners.

Fifteen of the 33 demographic measures could be grouped into three relatively independent clusters within each of which the measures were highly intercorrelated. These, Tryon has termed S, Socioeconomic Independence; A, Assimilation; and F, Family Life. The meaning of these three clusters is given in Figure 9.3—the Demography Sphere.

The Demography Sphere is a mathematical device which graphically illustrates two things: the intercorrelations among the variables which cluster together, and the correlations among clusters. Each demographic measure is a point on the surface of the sphere, and points that lie close together are highly correlated. Thus S, the dimension of financial and occupational attainment, includes such demographic characteristics as number of residents with college education, number of people employed in

FIGURE 9.3: Demography Sphere showing the intercorrelations among the demographic variables which make up three clusters: F, Family Life; A, Assimilation; and S, Socioeconomic Independence, and the intercorrelations among these three clusters. Each demographic variable is represented by a point on the surface of the sphere, and points lying close together are highly correlated. [Tryon, 1959.]

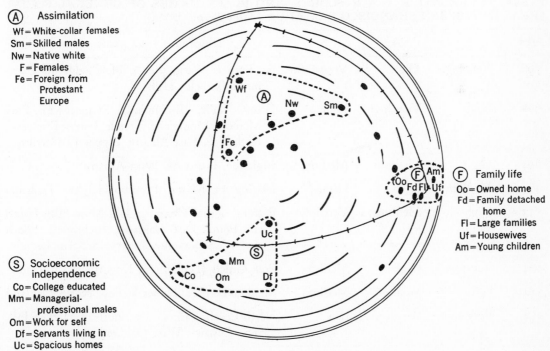

Ⓐ Assimilation
Wf = White-collar females
Sm = Skilled males
Nw = Native white
F = Females
Fe = Foreign from
      Protestant
      Europe

Ⓕ Family life
Oo = Owned home
Fd = Family detached
      home
Fl = Large families
Uf = Housewives
Am = Young children

Ⓢ Socioeconomic
   independence
Co = College educated
Mm = Managerial-
      professional males
Om = Work for self
Df = Servants living in
Uc = Spacious homes

FIGURE 9.4: A map of the social structure of San Francisco Bay Area. The map shows how the eight general social areas of this metropolitan community are distributed in space. Note that people living in physically separated neighborhoods may, nevertheless, be living in the same social area. [Adapted from Tryon, 1955a.]

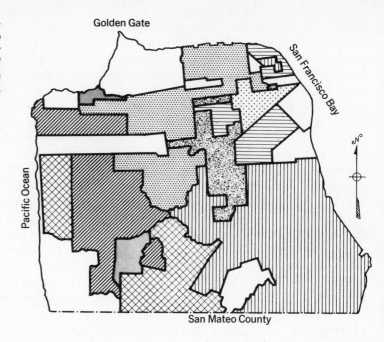

TABLE 9.4: RELATIVE F A S SCORES AND PLACE NAMES OF GENERAL SOCIAL AREAS IN THE SAN FRANCISCO BAY AREA [After Tryon, 1955a]

Area	F	A	S	Illustrative local place names
768	Very high	High	Very high	St. Francis Wood, Sea Cliff, Piedmont, Claremont, Berkeley Hills
666	High	Very high	High	Forest Hills, Richmond, Stonestown, Park Merced, Montclair, Trestle Glen, Elmwood, Rockridge, East Albany, Upper El Cerrito
654	High	Medium	Medium	Ingleside, Fruitvale, West Albany
466	Medium	High	High	Marina, Ft. Mason, Presidio Heights, Temescal
533	High	Medium	Very low	Potrero, Bernal Heights, Gold Mine Hill, Hunter's Point, East Oakland, Richmond, South and West Berkeley, Emeryville, San Leandro
164	Very low	High	Medium	Polk Gulch, Tenderloin, Downtown Oakland
344	Low	Medium	Medium	Mission District, Hayes Valley, North Oakland
224	Very low	Very low	Low	North Beach, Chinatown, South of Market, Fillmore District, West Oakland

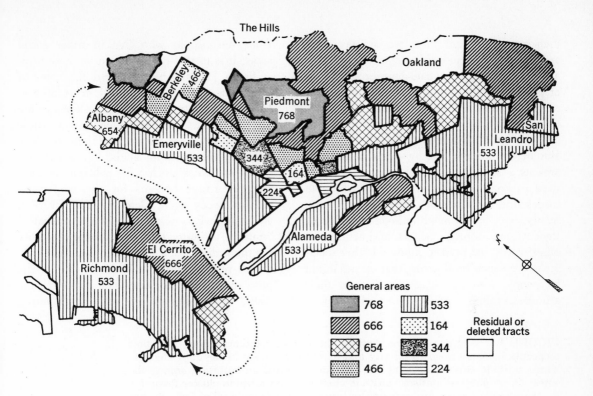

General areas

▨	768	‖‖‖	533
⧄	666	⣿	164
⊠	654	▦	344
⣿	466	☰	224

Residual or deleted tracts ☐

managerial-professional work, spaciousness of homes, etc. These several points, as can be seen, lie close together to form the S cluster. The S cluster is some distance from both the A and F clusters. Cluster A is the dimension of degree of acculturation to the old American, white culture. Cluster F refers to the organization of persons around family living.

Each tract can now be assigned a score on each cluster. Social areas are then made up by grouping together those tracts which have the same pattern of scores on the three clusters. Thus tracts which may be widely separated *geographically* but are similar on their F A S scores are grouped to make up a single social area. In this manner, eight social areas were identified (see Table 9.4). Tryon describes the four most distinctive areas as follows:

> Primary area 768 is the familiar "high-quality" area, called for brevity, *The Exclusives.* Area 164 consists of the group *The Downtowners:* nonfamily older residents,

native-white, variably educated, salaried white-collar workers. Area 533 is *The Workers:* a family-oriented area, with more poorly educated, skilled and semiskilled workers living in single-family homes of low value but frequently owner-occupied. Area 224 consists of *The Segregated,* little cities within the city, the crowded national and racial minority sections, low in family life as defined, unassimilated, and in poor economic circumstances.

The social structure of the San Francisco Bay Area is mapped in Figure 9.4. This map shows how the eight social environments making up the San Francisco Bay Area are distributed in space. Note that people who live in physically separated neighborhoods within a metropolitan community may, nevertheless, be living in the same *social* environment or habitat.

SOCIAL AREAS AS SUBCULTURAL AREAS. Suppose we identify an individual as an inhabitant of a particular social area. What can we then say about him? First, we can say what are his own most probable demographic characteristics. Second, we can describe the kinds of people he will most commonly meet in his neighborhood, in terms of their age, education, ethnic origins, occupation, family status, and the kinds of homes in which they live. But before we can validly think of a social area as a social or cultural environment we need to know whether we may also be able to describe the kinds of people he will commonly meet in his neighborhood in terms of their values, attitudes, beliefs, and actions. In other words, we need to know whether social areas are *subcultural areas,* that is, inhabited by people who are relatively alike in their attitudes, values, and actions and different

from the people who live in other social areas. It is to this question that we now turn.

Tryon [1955b] has analyzed the votes of people in the different social areas of San Francisco on city and state propositions in the 1954 election. The associations among these different votes are shown in Figure 9.5, the Attitude Sphere. Thus at the left is a cluster of five variables labeled P—political attitudes favoring fringe benefits for city employees, aid for needy aged, Democrat for governor, etc. A high P is taken by Tryon to indicate a "statism" attitude: the state has responsibility for the individual; a low P indicates an "individual responsibility" attitude: no aid to the individual from the state. The cluster to the right, T, consists of five attitudes favoring

FIGURE 9.5: Attitude Sphere showing the intercorrelations among the votes of people in San Francisco on city and state propositions in the 1954 election. Three attitude clusters account for most of the common variation among the votes: P, a "political statism" attitude cluster; T, an attitude cluster favorable to taxes and community enterprise; and E, an "ethnic-religious" cluster. [Tryon, 1959.]

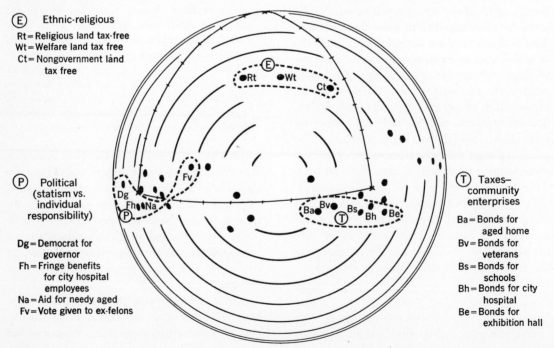

(E) Ethnic-religious
Rt = Religious land tax-free
Wt = Welfare land tax free
Ct = Nongovernment land
    tax free

(P) Political
    (statism vs.
    individual
    responsibility)

Dg = Democrat for
    governor
Fh = Fringe benefits
    for city hospital
    employees
Na = Aid for needy aged
Fv = Vote given to ex-felons

(T) Taxes—
    community
    enterprises

Ba = Bonds for
    aged home
Bv = Bonds for
    veterans
Bs = Bonds for
    schools
Bh = Bonds for city
    hospital
Be = Bonds for
    exhibition hall

community enterprise. The upper cluster of three variables, E, is also one of state support (by tax relief) of churches, religious and ethnic welfare institutions, etc. This Tryon calls the Ethnic-Religious attitude.

Now comes the critical question. Are these three *attitude clusters* of Figure 9.5 correlated with the three *demographic clusters* of Figure 9.3? The answer seems to be yes. For example, Tryon found he was able to predict with a high level of accuracy the P votes of social areas from their F A S profiles. The correlation between the F A S scores of social areas, derived from 1950 census data, and their P vote in 1954 was .90. The accuracy of the prediction of the other votes, on a social-area basis, was somewhat lower, but still impressive.

It appears, then, that social areas differentiated on demographic variables are to a considerable degree inhabited by different subcultural groups. The different social areas of people in a metropolitan community differ in such cultural elements as work skills and knowledge, patterns of family living, and political attitudes. Social areas may therefore be said to be subcultures, each having a particular and distinctive share of the total culture.

STABILITY OF SOCIAL AREAS. The stability of social areas over time is clearly an important question. If the pattern of demographic characteristics which defines a social area is ephemeral, changing substantially and rapidly with the passage of time, any statement about a given social environment is of limited value in accounting for the social behavior of people who are born and grow up in a spe-

cific area. Social areas, to be useful for the psychological understanding of the individual, must remain constant over long periods of time.

What are the data? Tryon [1955b] has correlated the 1940 F A S scores of the census tracts in the Bay Area with the F A S scores derived from the 1950 census. Let the reader look back upon the decade from 1940 to 1950. During this period, America entered into a global war which brought in its wake vast changes in the American society; millions of people were uprooted and relocated; a tremendous industrial expansion was pushed to supply the guns, the planes, the ships, and all the other matériel needed to wage war. The lives of most Americans were profoundly affected.

Despite this upheaval in the American society, the census tracts remained remarkably stable in their scores on the three clusters. As Table 9.5 shows, the correlations between the 1940 scores of census tracts on the three clusters and the 1950 scores are without exception above .90. We may conclude, then, that social areas, in the Bay Area at least, do provide a constant and predictable *milieu* for their inhabitants.

The constancy of the social areas over the decade from 1940 to 1950 is *not due to the fact that the same persons inhabited the areas during this period.* The U.S. Bureau of the Census has estimated that the mean turnover of persons in the tracts of the Bay Area for the year 1949–1950 was about 20 per cent. If, as Tryon points out, the turnover rate was the same in each of the nine preceding years,

TABLE 9.5: CORRELATIONS BETWEEN 1940 AND 1950 F A S SCORES [Tryon, 1955b]

	F	A	S	Number of tracts
Bay Area				
(including San Francisco)	.99	.94	.92	237
San Francisco (alone)	.98	.93	.94	110

about 90 per cent of the individuals living in an average tract in 1950 would be persons different from those who lived in that tract in 1940. Thus these social areas remained constant despite a thoroughgoing turnover in their individual inhabitants.

STABLE HABITAT—UNSTABLE MAN. As we shall see in the next section, there is a considerable amount of vertical social mobility in all the modern industrial societies. People are continuously moving up and down the various status systems. This, it should be noted, is not inconsistent with Tryon's finding that social habitats are remarkably stable over time despite an almost complete turnover of the inhabitants. It simply means that as people move out of a particular social area, other people, similar to them in their demographic and psychological characteristics, move in.

TO RECAPITULATE

The coordination and control of the activities of the members of a society are achieved through systems of positions and roles. Positions—which are different categories within such classifications as age-sex groupings, occupational groupings, etc.—involve a series of specific rights and obligations recognized by the community.

What a typical occupant of a given position is expected to do in standard situations constitutes the role associated with that position. Roles are interdependent; thus the system of roles helps to make for effective social interaction. The individual typically has multiple positions and multiple roles, and these determine in part how he is treated by his fellows.

In all highly developed, complex societies a number of elaborate and permanent status systems exist in which persons are rank-ordered in prestige or social worth. Of these one of the most pervasive is the social-class system. Three major methods have been used to measure the social-class positions of the members of a community: the objective method, the subjective method, and the reputational method.

The pivotal meaning of social class for the social psychologist is that it helps determine the individual's social environment and thus influences the particular kind of cultural training he receives.

Metropolitan communities are made up of social areas—groups of neighborhoods, not necessarily contiguous, which are similar in demographic and ecological characteristics. Social areas are inhabited by persons who tend to be similar in their political and other attitudes, and they are remarkably stable over time, despite the high rate of turnover of their inhabitants.

GUIDE 30: *The openness of status systems to vertical social mobility is determined by functional requirements of the society; mobility has both positive and negative consequences for the individual and for the group*

The members of every society occupy various positions in the status systems of their society—social class, wealth, occupation, power, etc. The status systems in different societies are not all equally "open" or "closed," but vary in accessibility according to the specific nature and functional requirements of the society.

The movement of individuals from one position to another, higher or lower in status, is termed *vertical social mobility*. The importance of vertical social mobility for the student of social psychology is that in moving up or down the status hierarchy, the individual moves into different social environments.

AMOUNT OF MOBILITY

Lipset and Bendix [1959] have reviewed comparative data on the amount of social mobility in modern industrial societies in the Western world. Their findings run counter to the common notion that America, the land of opportunity, is an open society with a considerable amount of mobility, whereas the old countries of Europe are closed societies which offer individuals little opportunity to rise in status. They conclude that there is widespread and more or less equal social mobility in all Western countries (see Box 9.5).

Lipset and Bendix also question the common notion that America itself, as it grows older, is becoming more and more a closed society, offering fewer and fewer opportunities for upward movement in the status structure. The available evidence indicates little or no change in amount of upward social mobility from the early nineteenth century to the present (see Box 9.6).

These findings pertain to modern industrial societies only. The reason that widespread social mobility characterizes every modern industrial society is probably to be found in the increasing demand for more professional, technical, and managerial workers as a result of technological advances. The established upper strata cannot meet this increasing demand from within their ranks alone and must, perforce, recruit from the lower strata. Those persons born into upper strata who lack the motivation and the abilities to succeed in professional, technical, and managerial jobs will gravitate downward. This "functional need" for social mobility can become effective only when, among the members of the various strata of society, a want for achievement and status can be inculcated. In modern industrial societies, where we find social mobility, we also find strong "status striving"—at least among the middle classes (see Boxes 9.7 and 9.8).

In a pre-industrial society which has little need for an increasing number of highly trained professional and technical workers a large amount of social mobility does not occur. It is for this reason that the feudal society, for example, is often referred to as a static society.

The degree of social mobility in a society depends not only upon the functional requirements of the society, but also upon the personality characteristics of the people who inhabit it. Whatever the sources of status-striving personality traits, it is only in societies which have an abundant number of "status-striving-prone" personalities that we find a great deal of mobility.

THE COSTS OF MOBILITY

It has commonly been assumed by political philosophers who espouse equalitarian principles that high social mobility is a good thing for the individual and for society. We have already seen that a modern industrial society does benefit tremendously from social mobility. Without it, in fact, modern industrial societies could not function. And there are many possible benefits which may accrue to the individual from upward mobility, quite aside from material gain.

However, as Lipset and Bendix point out,

To assume as much [namely, that high mobility is a good thing] is to ignore the abundant evidence of the social and psychic cost of a high degree of social mobility: a cost that is probably high in terms of the combativeness, frustration, restlessness and other ills that are engendered. . . . In saying this we do *not* imply that the price is *too* high, for we lack the proper standards of comparison. . . . More explicit empirical research on the gains and losses accruing from different rates of social mobility can certainly increase our understanding more than can a tacit assumption that the higher the mobility rate the better things are. . . .

Actually, some research has been done on this problem. Let us examine several of the studies.

PSYCHOLOGICAL COSTS. Stouffer et al. [1949], in various studies of the attitudes of American soldiers in World War II, found that "the

BOX 9.5: *Myth I: the frozen society of Old Europe*

Seymour M. Lipset and Reinhard Bendix, sociologists at the University of California, Berkeley, have analyzed considerable data on social mobility in their book *Social Mobility in Industrial Society*. In one of the studies reported in that volume, Lipset and Hans L. Zetterberg present the comparative indices of upward and downward *occupational* mobility (for nonfarm populations) in various countries. The data, shown in the following table, make two important points. First, all the countries are characterized by a high rate of mobility. From one generation to another, one-quarter to one-third of the population moves upward from working class to middle class or downward from middle class to working class. Second, the total mobility rate is much the same in all the countries.

COUNTRY	UPWARD MOBILITY *Sons of manual workers moving up into nonmanual occupations*	DOWNWARD MOBILITY *Sons of nonmanual workers moving down into manual occupations*	TOTAL VERTICAL MOBILITY *(Men moving across manual-nonmanual line in either direction)*
United States	33%	26%	30%
Germany	29	32	31
Sweden	31	24	29
Japan	36	22	27
France	39	20	27
Switzerland	45	13	23

The amount of *social-class* mobility was studied by examining the rates of interclass marriage. High rates were found in all of the Western countries for which data were available. Moreover, studies carried out in Britain, France, and Sweden agree in showing that the number of marriages across class lines is about the same in all Western countries.

Lipset and Zetterberg summarize their findings by quoting from an early essay on social classes by Schumpeter:

[The] assumption as to the insurmountability of class barriers for individual families does not accord with the facts. The persistence of class position is an illusion, created by the slowness of change and the great stability of class character as such and of its social fluid. Class barriers *must* be surmountable, at the bottom as well as at the top . . . there is constant turnover. Entries and exits occur continually—the latter directed both upward and downward. Class composition is forever changing, to the point where there may be a completely new set of families. . . . The process always goes on, though at times extremely slowly and almost imperceptibly, impeded by legal and other barriers which every class, for obvious reasons, seeks to erect. For the duration of its collective life, or the time during which its identity may be assumed, each class resembles a hotel or an omnibus, always full, but always of different people.

Lipset, S. M., and Bendix, R. Social mobility in industrial society. Berkeley: Univer. of California Press, 1959.

Schumpeter, J. Imperialism and social classes. New York: Meridian Books, 1955.

THE SOCIAL AND CULTURAL HABITAT

In the book by Lipset and Bendix appears a study by Bendix and Frank W. Howton which examines the popular notion that in the early period of American history, business leaders frequently came from families of small farmers and manual workers, but that today only the son of a business tycoon has much chance of becoming a business leader.

These investigators have analyzed the social origins of samples of American businessmen born between 1771 and 1920. Their findings are given in the following table together with the findings of two other studies—one by Suzanne Keller and the other by Mabel Newcomer.

[KELLER]

	PERCENTAGES OF BUSINESS LEADERS WHOSE FATHERS WERE:		
ESTIMATED YEAR OF BIRTH OF BUSINESS LEADERS	Businessmen	Wage earners and office workers	N
1820	47	8	254
1855	50	4	168
1900	57	12	348

[BENDIX-HOWTON]

	Businessmen and gentry farmers	Farmers and manual workers	N
1785	65	12	125
1815	63	13	89
1845	69	11	360
1875	73	8	380
1905	74	7	143

[NEWCOMER]

	Wealthy	Medium	Poor	N
1849	46	42	12	118
1873	36	48	16	253
1898	36	52	12	342

The data point to two conclusions. First, the clear majority of American business leaders do come from relatively well-to-do families. Second, *this has always been true.* The proportion of business leaders coming from working-class families has always been small and has remained quite stable during the course of American history.

If the American society is relatively rigid and closed today, it is no more so than it was one hundred years ago.

Lipset, S. M., and Bendix, R. Social mobility in industrial society. Berkeley: Univer. of California Press, 1959.

Keller, Suzanne. The social origins and career lines of three generations of American business leaders. Unpublished doctoral dissertation, Columbia University, 1953.

Newcomer, Mabel. The big business executive. New York: Columbia Univer. Press, 1955.

BOX 9.7: *Status and striving*

Elizabeth Douvan, a social psychologist at the University of Michigan, speculated that in middle-class children the achievement want is more generalized than it is in working-class children and, hence, is less likely to vary with changes in the reward offered for achievement.

The subjects were high school students in a medium-sized Midwestern community. Their social-class position—middle class or working class—was determined by using two indices: (1) an index based on occupation of father—an objective measure of class (see page 313), and (2) a subjective measure (see page 314) in which the student was asked to which class he belonged. Those students for whom the two indices were in agreement were designated appropriately as of the middle-class or of the working-class group. Those for whom the two indices were in disagreement (predominantly children, of working-class fathers, who identified with the middle class) were designated "marginals."

One half of the children in each of the three social class groups were randomly assigned to a "no-reward" and one half to a "money-reward" condition. In the reward condition they were told that $10 would be given to any student whose over-all score on the experimental tasks reached a certain value.

An anagrams and a motor task were then administered. All children were caused to "fail" through announcing a falsely high average for "high school students in your city." The assumption here is that "failure" arouses the achievement want.

The children were then given the McClelland need-achievement test (see Box 3.7, page 90). The following table shows the results.

	MEAN NEED-ACHIEVEMENT SCORES	
CLASS	No reward	Money reward
Working	4.89	8.06
Middle	7.56	8.30
Marginal	7.71	7.85

Note that in the no-reward conditions, the working-class subjects have a low mean need-achievement score as compared with middle-class children. This confirms Rosen's finding (see Box 9.8). In the reward condition, however, the level of achievement motivation for the working-class subjects is as high as that of the middle-class children. The money reward aroused strong success strivings. The middle-class children show the same scores in both conditions. Their achievement want seems to be more consistent and dependable.

The "marginals" (members of the working class oriented toward the middle class) resemble the middle-class subjects in consistency of achievement motivation.

Douvan, Elizabeth. Social status and success strivings. J. abnorm. soc. Psychol., 1956, 52, 219–223.

less the promotion opportunity afforded by a branch or combination of branches, the *more favorable* the opinion tends to be toward promotion opportunity." For example, the promotion rates in the Military Police "were about the worst in any branch of the Army." And yet the men in the Military Police felt much less frustrated about chances for promotion than men in the Air Corps, where the promotion rate was conspicuously high. A second

Many explanations have been offered for the common observation that upward mobility is greater among middle-class persons than among members of the lower class. Sociologist Bernard C. Rosen tested the thesis that this difference is due to the differences in the *achievement motives* and *achievement values* of the two social classes.

The sophomores of two large public high schools in the New Haven area were assigned to one of five social classes through the use of an index based on occupation of main wage earner in family, education of parents, and place of residence. Five sophomores, drawn randomly; were taken from class I (the highest status group), 25 from class II, and 30 each from classes III, IV, and V.

Achievement motivation was measured through the use of the McClelland technique. Class differences in achievement motivation are shown in the following table. The differences are, it will be seen, both substantial and consistent.

ACHIEVEMENT MOTIVATION SCORE	SOCIAL CLASS			
	I and II	*III*	*IV*	*V*
Below median of total group	17%	57%	70%	77%
Above median of total group	83	43	30	23

Rosen next studied class differences in achievement-oriented values. He constructed a questionnaire to measure three of the orientations in Kluckhohn's schema (see Box 10.7, page 350) which were taken to reflect achievement values: (1) the activistic approach to mastering the physical and social environment, (2) the future orientation, (3) the individualistic relation to one's kin.

The differences between the social classes in the obtained achievement value scores (shown in the following table) were strikingly large and consistent.

ACHIEVEMENT VALUE SCORE	SOCIAL CLASS			
	I and II	*III*	*IV*	*V*
Below median of total group	23%	30%	67%	83%
Above median of total group	77	70	33	17

Rosen concludes: "Middle class children are more likely to be taught not only to believe in success, but also to be willing to take those steps that make achievement possible: in short, to embrace the achievement value system which states that given the willingness to work hard, plan, and make the proper sacrifices, an individual should be able to manipulate his environment so as to ensure eventual success."

Rosen, B. C. The achievement syndrome: a psycho-cultural dimension of social stratification. Amer. soc. Rev., 1956, 21, 203–211.

example: the better-educated soldiers were found to be more disgruntled about chances for promotion, despite their notably higher promotion rate.

Stouffer and his associates attempt to explain this paradox by the concept of *relative deprivation*. A high rate of mobility leads to high hopes of promotion with the result that

BOX 9.9: *Hope, frustration, and morale*

While at the University of Connecticut, Aaron J. Spector tested the following aspect of the theory of relative deprivation: "On failing to achieve an attractive goal, an individual's morale will be higher if the possibility of achieving that goal had been perceived to be low than if it had been perceived to be high."

Thirty-six groups of college sophomores of four men each were formed. Each group worked on two military intelligence tasks. One-half of the groups ("High Expectation") were told that *three* out of the four men in the group would be promoted from corporal to top sergeant after the first task was completed. The remaining half of the groups ("Low Expectation") were told that *one* out of the four men would be promoted. None of the subjects in any of the groups was in fact promoted.

After the completion of the second task, a six-item morale scale was administered to the subjects. The six items measured the following components of morale: (1) the group's attractiveness to its members; (2) satisfaction with the first task; (3) desire to remain a member of the group; (4) satisfaction with the promotion system; (5) evaluation of the group's productivity; (6) satisfaction with the second task.

The following table shows the mean scores of the High and Low Expectation groups for each of the six questions. Lower scores indicate more favorable morale attitudes.

Morale item	Low expectation groups	High expectation groups
1	2.83	3.30
2	2.77	2.75
3	2.52	3.10
4	2.87	3.60
5	3.29	3.90
6	2.71	3.25

Responses of the Low Expectation groups were more favorable than those of the High Expectation groups on five of the six questions.

The hypothesis of the study is thus supported: When high hopes are frustrated, discontent is greater than when low hopes remain unfulfilled.

*Spector, A. J. Expectations, fulfillment, and morale. J. abnorm. soc. Psychol., 1956, **52**, 51–56.*

the men are more likely to feel frustrated in their present positions and critical of their chances for promotion. (For an experimental study of the hypothesis of relative deprivation, see Box 9.9.)

Another kind of "psychological price" paid for social mobility is described in the Hollingshead and Redlich [1958] study of the relations between social class and mental illness in the New Haven community. They report some of the differences between men who were *born* into the class of skilled workers and those who had *moved up* into this class from the lower class of unskilled workers:

The former [those born into the class] are satisfied with their "way of life" and are not making sacrifices to get ahead. They have a sense of personal dignity and self-esteem which sustains them in their "life position"; they also identify themselves with the working class in significantly larger numbers. On the other hand, 77 per cent of the 31 per cent who moved upward . . . have "sacrificed" to better themselves. . . . These strivers are less satisfied with their accomplishments and roles in the community, also they expect more from the future than stable persons who tend to be content with things as they are.

Hollingshead and Redlich also found that within the upper class in the New Haven community, the families of *arrivistes,* as compared with members of the "core group" whose money was "old," were more prone to exhibit "conspicuous consumption, insecurity and family instability. Thus, we find divorces, broken homes, and other symptoms of disorganization in a significantly large number of new [upper class] families."

However, we must sound a note of caution. Not all upward mobile people are "sick, sick, sick." Investigators have found that the upward mobile person may be self-accepting, self-confident, and psychologically healthy (see Box 9.10.)

BOX 9.10: *The aspiring adolescent*

Elizabeth Douvan and Joseph Adelson of the University of Michigan have used the social-survey method to study some of the psychological accompaniments of upward and downward mobility strivings in adolescent boys.

Their data were secured from a national-sample survey of boys in the 14-to-16-year age range. Each boy (whose father was either a white-collar worker or a skilled manual worker) was given a personal interview which lasted from one to three hours.

Each boy was classified as upward mobile, stable, or downward mobile by determining whether his occupational aspiration was higher than, equivalent to, or lower than his father's occupation.

The interviews revealed sharp differences between the upward- and downward-aspiring boys in a number of motivational and personality characteristics. The upward-aspiring boy was found to be unusually lively and energetic; the downward aspirer, inactive and apathetic. The upward aspirer stressed interest of work in judging the attractiveness of a job; the downward aspirer, job security. The upward-oriented displayed a long-term time perspective; the downward-oriented, a short-term perspective.

A set of projective pictures was used to measure degree of internalization of personal standards. The pictures showed an adolescent boy in conflict between a promise made to his parents (e.g., to be home at a certain time) and pressure from his friends (e.g., to stay out late). The subjects were asked what the boy would do and how he would feel about it. In both the upward and downward groups, two-thirds of the boys said that the boy would go home. However, the upwards more often had the boy go home because "he promised" or because "his parents trust him." The downwards more often said he would go home because of a fear of parental punishment. The investigators conclude from these and other findings that the upward-oriented have internalized personal controls in contrast to the downward-oriented, who show a tendency to externalize standards and to rebel against them.

The upward striver was found to show a greater independence of the family than the downward. The downward aspirer was more dependent on his parents, although he showed signs of rebellion against them. And, finally, the upward striver showed high self-acceptance and social confidence. The downward-oriented was more ambivalent toward himself and more unsure in social situations.

Douvan, Elizabeth, and Adelson, J. The psychodynamics of social mobility in adolescent boys. J. abnorm. soc. Psychol., *1958,* **56**, *31–44.*

SOCIAL COSTS. In their studies of promotions in the Army during World War II, Stouffer and his associates advanced the hypothesis that "one factor which hardly would have failed to enter to some extent into the judgment of an officer in selecting a man for promotion was his conformity to the officially approved military mores." Three different longitudinal studies of the careers of enlisted men were carried out to test this hypothesis. The three studies were consistent in showing that men who conformed to the established norms of the Army *subsequently* received a proportionately larger number of promotions than did other soldiers. It was found that when the men in the three samples were rank-ordered according to their scores on a scale of attitudes of conformity, "the men whose attitudes were most conforming were the men most likely to be promoted subsequently."

As Merton and Kitt [1950] point out, the norms of the enlisted men were often at odds with the official norms of the Army. This means that conformity to official Army norms represented nonconformity to the norms of the group of enlisted men.

The early adoption of the norms of a status group to which the individual aspires aids the rise of the individual to that group. To *anticipate* the beliefs and values of the group one aspires to seems to help one achieve membership in that group. This is clearly the meaning of the Army studies we have examined. *Anticipatory socialization* (to use Merton's term) is a means for moving up in the status system. And anticipatory socialization may show itself in many subtle and unanticipated ways (see Box 9.11).

While anticipatory socialization is of functional value for the individual in that it serves to facilitate his upward mobility, it is quite possible that it is *dysfunctional* for the group or organization to which the individual belongs. Anticipatory socialization may destroy

BOX 9.11: *Social mobility and sexual conduct*

In the monumental study of sexual behavior in the American male by Kinsey and his associates, we find revealing data on the relation between social mobility and sexual conduct.

In their sample of 2,945 American males, a considerable amount of occupational mobility was found. About 39 per cent of the subjects stayed in the occupational class of their fathers, 21 per cent moved downward, and 40 per cent rose to positions higher than those occupied by their fathers. These data are congruent with those reported by Lipset and Zetterberg (see Box 9.5). The sexual histories of males who stayed in the occupational class of their fathers were then compared with the histories of males who moved out of their father's class into a higher or lower class.

Figure 9.6 shows that there are marked differences in the sexual patterns of the 16-to-20-year-old males in three occupational classes. The semiskilled-labor group has a relatively low frequency of masturbation and a relatively high frequency of premarital intercourse. In the professional group, this pattern is reversed. The lower-white-collar group shows a transitional pattern.

But note this: A person born into the skilled-labor class who *ultimately* moves into the professional class shows a youthful sexual pattern congruent with the *class into which he will eventually move!* Similarly, if a person born into the skilled-labor class ultimately locates in the unskilled-labor class, his pattern of sexual conduct closely resembles the pattern of persons born into that class. Here we have, as it were, "anticipatory sexual socialization."

Kinsey, A. C., Pomeroy, W. B., and Martin, C. E. Sexual behavior in the human male. Philadelphia: Saunders, 1948.

THE SOCIAL AND CULTURAL HABITAT

PARENTAL OCCUPATIONAL CLASS

SUBJECT OCCUPATIONAL CLASS
Semiskilled labor

Masturbation Nocturnal emissions Premarital intercourse

Day labor
Semiskilled labor
Skilled labor
Lower white collar

Lower white collar

Semiskilled labor
Skilled labor
Lower white collar
Upper white collar

Professional

Skilled labor
Lower white collar
Upper white collar
Professional

FIGURE 9.6: For explanation, see Box 9.11.

the morale of the group *from* which the individual hopes to move. As Merton and Kitt point out:

> From the standpoint of the larger social system, the Army as a whole, positive orientation toward the official mores would appear to be functional in supporting the legitimacy of the structure and in keeping the structure of authority intact. . . . But manifestly, much research needs to be done before one can say that this is indeed the case. It is possible, for example, that the secondary effects of such orientations may be so deleterious to the solidarity of the primary groups of enlisted men that their morale sags. . . . Does the personal "success" of conformists (promotion)

only serve to depress the morale of the others by rewarding those who depart from the in-group mores?

For one answer to the question raised by Merton and Kitt, see Box 9.12.

STATUS DISCREPANCIES

Individuals seldom have exactly the same rank in all the status systems of the community, and often they occupy widely discrepant positions. The existence of such status discrepancies has been widely recognized. Such terms as *"nouveaux riches,"* "upstart," "social climber," "old family," "parvenu," "poor but genteel" indicate awareness of discrepancy be-

BOX 9.12: *Education—defection*

At the end of World War II, the Labor Party assumed power in England. Among other social reforms instituted by the Labor government, the educational opportunities of English children were greatly expanded. Under the postwar system, children who pass the "eleven-plus" examinations at a high level are accepted for the "grammar schools," which offer the classical, university preparatory curriculum. Children who do less well on the examinations are steered into the "modern" and the "technical" schools, which offer a terminal, general education and vocational training.

Recently, a branch of the Labor Party in Birmingham, ideologically strong supporters of increasing the opportunities of the people for upward social mobility, officially stated that "from Labour's point of view, the objection to the grammar school system was that it had the effect of taking the brightest children of the working class and in effect de-classing them by separation from children in the modern schools. Eventually, they get white-collar jobs and upon marriage go to live in the outer suburbs and vote Tory."

tween positions in the economic and social status systems.

What happens when an individual's status in two or more hierarchies differs? Benoit-Smullyan [1944] approached this question through his status-equilibration hypothesis:

> As a result of status conversion processes which are normally at work in every society, there exists a real tendency for the different types of status to reach a common level, i.e., for a man's position in the economic hierarchy to match his position in the political hierarchy and for the latter to accord with his position in the hierarchy of prestige, etc.

But the various status systems of a community may not be equally open, thus blocking movement toward status equilibration. For example, though we have seen that the occupational status system in America is relatively open, there is some evidence that the *upper social class* in America has become a more or less closed group. Thus, in a study of "Philadelphia Gentlemen," Baltzell [1958] made a trend analysis of the rate of admissions to the *Social Register* for the city of Philadelphia. The *Social Register* is a listing of the upper-upper social class in metropolitan American cities which is produced yearly by the Social Register Association. A person is considered a candidate for membership only after three members have certified that he is a person with whom they have regular and intimate associations (a precursor of Warner's reputational method!). Baltzell found an increase of 68 per cent in the number of families listed in the *Social Register* in the decade 1900–1910. Admission rates declined sharply in each succeeding decade. Between 1930 and 1940, the increase was only 6 per cent. Baltzell suggests that "this upper class has developed into a more or less closed group over the years and that status within it is less and less achievable, or sought after." Hence a new Philadelphia millionaire on the upper rung of the economic-status ladder may find his entry into the upper-class social group blocked.

Status discrepancy may be a source of severe frustration for the individual (see page 117). These individual frustrations may culminate in major social upheavals. As Lipset and Bendix point out, "Political literature, in fact, contains many suggestions that class discrepancies—e.g., low social status and relatively high economic position—predispose individuals and groups to accept extremist political views." The revolutionary fervor of the French *bourgeoisie* in the eighteenth century is thought to have developed when they were denied recognition and social status by the aristocracy. Various political scientists have suggested that the middle-class Germans embraced the Nazi movement because they feared the threat of downward mobility. Extremist political attitudes may develop when the security of a group is threatened or when the status strivings of an ascending group are blocked.

TO RECAPITULATE

In every modern industrial society there is a considerable amount of vertical social mobility—people are constantly moving up and down the various status systems of the society. Comparative studies indicate that the amount of social mobility is approximately equal in all the Western societies. Historical comparisons further suggest that the American frontier has become neither more nor less closed in the last hundred years.

Upward social mobility is not an unmixed good. The upward mobile individual may pay costs in the form of insecurity and tension; society may pay costs in the form of reduced group solidarity.

Discrepancies between the ranks of an individual in the various status systems of a community—the occupational, the power, the economic, and the social-class systems—may be a source of severe frustration for the individual, predisposing him to adopt extremist political attitudes.

THE SOCIAL PLACE OF THE INDIVIDUAL

Consider what guesses you can make about what manner of man Mr. Arbuthnot is as you successively learn the following facts:

1. Mr. Arbuthnot is an American.
2. Mr. Arbuthnot is white.
3. Mr. Arbuthnot is an older-age person.
4. Mr. Arbuthnot is married and a father.
5. Mr. Arbuthnot has a high income.
6. Mr. Arbuthnot is senior partner in a brokerage firm.
7. Mr. Arbuthnot lives in St. Francis Woods, which is an "exclusive" social area of San Francisco.
8. Mr. Arbuthnot is an Episcopalian and a member of the Pacific Union Club.
9. Mr. Arbuthnot is a member of the upper-upper class.

As each additional fact about Mr. Arbuthnot became known to you, you probably found yourself increasingly able to make guesses about what manner of man he is. The reason is that you were able to fix more and more precisely his social place—you were able to describe more and more exactly his social habitat. And to know an individual's social habitat increases your ability to make estimates about his psychological characteristics—his cognitions, wants, attitudes, values, and actions. For the social place of the individual largely determines *his particular participation in the total culture of his society*. The total culture of a complex society is too complex and too rich for any one individual to participate in it in its entirety, to share all of its beliefs, norms, values, and actions.

Thus the men in a society will have certain skills and knowledge; they will hold certain attitudes and values; they will entertain certain goals. The women will have different skills, different attitudes and values, different goals. We may then speak of the male culture and the female culture. Similarly, there are age cultures, occupational cultures, class cultures, and many other "part cultures"—as many cultures as there are distinctive "parts" in a society. It is precisely because of this that we have first studied the way in which the members of a society can be partitioned before turning our attention to the study of culture—the concern of our next chapter.

CHAPTER GUIDES AND GLOSSARY

GUIDE 28: *The coordination and control of the activities of the members of a society are achieved through systems of positions and roles*

GUIDE 29: *Every society has status systems, the most pervasive of which is social class; social class significantly determines the social environment and power of the individual*

GUIDE 30: *The openness of status systems to vertical social mobility is determined by functional requirements of the society; mobility has both positive and negative consequences for the individual and for the group*

objective method of measuring social class. A method for measuring the social-class positions of the members of a community in which class indices are based on such objectively measurable characteristics as income, education, occupation.

position. A category or place in a system of social classification, e.g., the age-sex system, recognized by a community. For example, "adult male" is a position in the age-sex system. Each individual occupies multiple positions, associated with each of which is its role.

reputational method of measuring social class. A method for determining the social-class positions of the members of a community on the basis of how they are socially placed by other members of the community.

role. The pattern of wants and goals, beliefs, feelings, attitudes, values, and actions which members of a community expect should characterize the typical occupant of a position. Roles prescribe the behavior expected of people in standard situations. The various roles in a group are interdependent.

social area. A concept associated with the work of Tryon which refers to two or more neighborhoods in a metropolitan community, not necessarily contiguous, which possess highly similar demographic characteristics. There is evidence that the members of social areas share similar political and other attitudes. Social areas tend to be highly stable over time.

social class. A division of a society, made up of persons possessing certain common social characteristics which are taken to qualify them for intimate, equal-status relations with one another, and which restrict their interaction with members of other social classes. The pivotal meaning of social class for social psychology is that an individual's social-class position largely determines his social environment.

social mobility, vertical. The movement of persons upward or downward in the various status systems of the community. The total rate of vertical mobility in a society indicates the degree of "openness" of the society.

socialization, anticipatory. The taking over by the individual of the beliefs, values, and norms of a higher or lower status group in which he seeks membership but does not yet belong.

society. An organized collectivity of persons, made up of a network of interconnected groups and organizations, which constitutes the structure of the society.

status. The rank of a position or an individual in the prestige hierarchy of a group or community.

status discrepancy. Any difference between the rank of an individual in one status system and his rank in another status system. For example, a labor leader may have a high rank in the power status system and a relatively low rank in the social-class status system.

subjective method of measuring social class. A method for measuring the social-class positions of the members of a community by determining the social class with which they identify.

THE HIGH-CROWNED TEETH WITH THEIR COMPLEX GRINDING
surfaces of the horse who grazes on grass and the incisors of eohippus who browsed on leaves testify to the principle that an animal's evolution and way of life reflect his habitat. For in the history of the world, as grassy prairies and savannas became more plentiful, only those early horses who, through the development of high-crowned teeth, were able to change their design for living from nipping leaves to munching grass inherited the earth. In man, unlike the horse, this relation between environment and behavior is a reciprocal one. Man's culture both reflects his environment—physical and social—and in turn shapes it. Man moves mountains and causes the desert to bloom; and man forms and re-forms his society in his cultural image.

Once again we must step across the border into a neighboring social science. Just as we turned to the sociologist for aid in our analysis of society, so in this chapter we turn to the anthropologist for help in our analysis of culture.

10: CULTURE

IN THE PRECEDING CHAPTER WE EXAMINED the structure of society in order to specify with some precision what is meant by social environment. By fixing the person in his social niches—by knowing his place in his society—we are enabled to describe the pattern of his social interactions. But knowing with whom an individual interacts is only part of the story. We must also know the significant consequences of such interactions. People who consistently interact with one set of individuals acquire from them one set of life-ways; people who live among a different set of individuals acquire a different pattern of life-ways. To complete our analysis of the social environment we must therefore add to our description of the *who* of social interaction an analysis of *culture*—the *how* and the *what* of social interaction.

Kroeber [1948] has vividly indicated the wide range of behaviors which the American individual learns from his culture:

That he speaks, say, English and not Chinese is the result of where he is born or raised;

that is, of which language forms part of the culture in which he grows up. Similarly with his being a Christian instead of a Buddhist, casting his vote in November, observing Sunday, celebrating New Year on January 1, instead of in February, eating with a fork and not with chopsticks, and bread and butter in place of rice, tucking his shirt in and not out (in Kipling's day at least), saying hello to his parents instead of using honorifics, steering a tractor and not a lightly shod wooden plow, writing with letters instead of a thousand logograms, and so on endlessly. In fact, the mass of what any person receives from his culture is so great as to make it look at first glance as if he were nothing but an individual exemplar of his culture, a reduction of it abbreviated to the scope of what one personality can contain.

The massive impact of different "designs for living" upon the individual is indicated by the cultural molding of his perception, memory, and attitudes (see Boxes 10.1, 10.2, and 10.3).

A convenient shorthand way of referring to the training in the life-ways of a society which the new member acquires through social interaction is to speak of the "effect of culture upon the individual." But let us be clear that in so speaking we are merely using a convenient abstraction to point to the myriad ways in which various people (who have themselves learned the ways of the group from others) train the new individual in the approved ways. There is no single *thing* called "culture" which influences a person.

The relation between culture and the individual is not a one-way affair. The lines of

BOX 10.1: *The whole-perceiving Samoan*

The Rorschach Ink-blot Test is the most widely used projective technique for the study of personality. It consists of a series of ten ink-blots, on each of which the subject tells what he perceives. His mode of perceiving the blots is assumed to reveal broad personality trends.

Numerous studies employing the Rorschach have revealed striking cultural differences in modes of perceiving. For example, an early study by Bleuler and Bleuler showed that desert Moroccans give a much larger number of fine-detail responses than do Europeans.

Card VII in the Rorschach series is shown below. A popular response for European subjects is "two women talking." An illustrative Moroccan response was to interpret the tiny, scarcely observable irregularities on the two protrusions at the top of the blot (see arrow) as an alignment of Arab riflemen opposed by a row of Christian warriors.

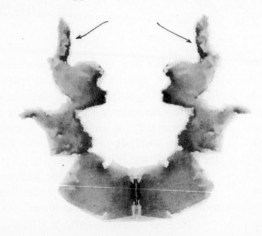

influence run both ways. Culture influences the person in a massive and pervasive way and thus makes for the stability of a society and the continuity of its culture; the person also influences his culture and thus makes for social change.

GUIDE 31: *In coping with their common problems the members of a society try various solutions, certain of which become firmly established and are transmitted to successive generations as the culture of that society*

The culture of a society consists, in part, of a particular set of arrangements for solving the problems of the members of the society. Some of these problems are special ones peculiar to the members of a particular society. Others are universal problems common to all human beings—such as meeting the biological needs of the members, training the young, caring for the sick. There are, of course, many different possible arrangements for solving these problems. From among these possible arrangements, one society adopts one set; a second society, a different set. This is another way of saying that no two cultures are identical (see Box 10.4).

The particular set of cultural arrangements adopted by a society is influenced by physical environmental factors (climate, topography, natural resources, etc.). A people living in an arid land, raising sheep and other animals for

---

In the record of a European or American subject, such responses are not common; an over-emphasis on such fine-detail responses is interpreted as an indication of a compulsive tendency or as an indication of mental disorganization.

Cook reports that the Samoans tend to make even fewer fine-detail responses than do Europeans and Americans; they tend rather to give "whole" responses, making use of the entire blot, e.g., perceiving it as a map or an animal. Samoans also differ markedly from European and American subjects in making numerous responses to the white spaces in the blots, which they perceive as figure rather than ground. In card VII the middle white space might be seen as an island.

In the records of European and American subjects, well-organized "whole" responses are taken as indicative of abstracting ability, and are said to be more characteristic of the intelligent, creative individual. And responses to white spaces are interpreted as indicating resistiveness, negativism, or stubbornness.

These differences in modes of perceiving suggest the influence of cultural factors. In Moroccan art and religion, great importance is attached to fine details; among the Samoans, white is a highly valued, symbolic color. These cultural differences in modes of perceiving do not necessarily mean that the Moroccan is compulsive or mentally disorganized; nor do they mean that the Samoan is intelligent and creative and negativistic. First, it is a question whether there really *is* a consistent relation between modes of perceiving and other aspects of personality among Europeans and Americans on whom the Rorschach was standardized. Second, even should the Rorschach prove to be valid for Europeans and Americans, it may not be equally valid in other cultures.

Bleuler, M., and Bleuler, R. Rorschach ink-blot tests and social psychology. Charact. & Pers., *1935*, *4*, 99–114.

Cook, T. H. The application of the Rorschach test to a Samoan group. Rorschach Res. Exch., *1942*, *6*, *51–60*.

BOX 10.2: *The detail-remembering Nape*

An early study by S. F. Nadel has provided us with a demonstration of the power of cultural influences upon style of memory functioning in the individual.

He presented school children from the Nape and from the Yoraba tribes in Africa with the tasks of repeating from memory a story which was read to them and of describing from memory the contents of pictures they had just seen.

The Nape children tended to list the discrete items in the story and the objects in the pictures in serial order, showing little or no organization or integration of the items. Their responses were detailed, piecemeal listings of the separate items. In sharp contrast, the Yoraba children integrated the elements, emphasizing the general meaning and structure of the story and the pictures in their reports.

Nadel points out that these differences between the two culture groups in their styles of remembering have their parallels in other aspects of the two cultures. For example, the gods of the Nape have relatively discrete, isolated functions. The gods of the Yoraba, in contrast, occupy positions with well-known authority and responsibility in an integrated and clearly defined status structure.

Nadel, S. F. A field experiment in social psychology. Brit. J. Psychol., 1937, 28, 195–211.

---

food, will tend to develop a total culture consonant with a nomadic life; a people living in a fertile land will tend to lead a sedentary life, tilling the soil and raising corn, grains, and other crops, and will develop a total culture appropriate to such a life. Man, however, is not a passive victim of his physical environment. Within limits he can act on it and transform it to suit his ends. A society's culture, in other words, is not entirely determined by the "given" physical environment. As Hodgen [1952] writes:

> The historically important thing in regard to natural resources is man's attitude toward them. It was not the availability of iron that created the Iron Age in Britain, nor the presence of coal that ushered in the Industrial Revolution, but the initiative of certain men at particular moments in time in finding a use for these mineral riches of the earth. The modifications or changes that have taken place in mechanical contrivances follow and tangibly employ prior modifications and changes in the purposes of human tool-makers and tool-users. The conversion of an agricultural parish in England into an industrialized community, the adoption of a new tool, or the incorporation

of a new technique of production into a small, local cultural system has occurred early or late in time, here or there in space, as dictated by human will. Human geography demands as much knowledge of human beings as of geography.

The culture of a given society is also influenced by contacts with other cultural groups. Just as there is congruence between the "physical surround" and culture, so is there congruence between the "social surround"—the neighboring cultures—and the culture of any given society (see Box 10.5). The borrowings of one society from the culture of another are not, however, blind and random scavengings of odd bits and pieces. A society borrows only those cultural ways that are seen by its members as helpful in solving the problems they face; that are seen, in other words, as means of reaching their goals.

In saying that a society adopts a given set of arrangements, we are speaking abstractly. The arrangements which are finally developed by a group are the historical product of the interactions of tens of thousands of individuals in a particular physical environment in

Under the general direction of Bradford B. Hudson, a social psychologist at Rice University, a comparative psychological study of young people in America and in the Middle East was carried out by an intercultural research group.

Levon H. Melikian, a psychologist at the American University of Beirut, Lebanon, was one member of the research group. He examined authoritarianism in the relatively authoritarian culture of the Middle East and in the relatively nonauthoritarian culture of the United States. The main aspects of the Middle Eastern way of life have been described by George Gardner, another member of the research group, as follows:

> In the first place, the presence of tribal organization throughout the [Middle Eastern] area serves to intensify the authoritarian bonds of family. Marriages are closely arranged by the parents; the young couples remain closely tied to the parental families; and young men tend to make their way in the world through the channels of nepotism. In the second place, formal schooling has only recently been emphasized as a necessity and consequently illiteracy in the area still averages about 70–80%, reaching well above 90% in most rural areas. In the third place, the quality of the religious life of the area emphasizes submissiveness under the overruling hand of God and leads to considerable emphasis on acceptance as an approved attitude toward the vicissitudes of daily living. In the fourth place, the nomad, almost absent from the American scene except possibly in the form of migratory workers, is an important cultural factor, in addition to the far more numerous villager and city dweller. . . . And in the fifth place, the strong emphasis on in-group loyalties, epitomized by the familiar phrases, "our people," or "one of us," as contrasted with all others, has led to a faulty development in the individual's sense of responsibility to the larger community.

The California F (fascism) Scale, a measure of the degree to which a person accepts an authoritarian ideology, was administered to samples of high school and college students in the Middle East and in the United States. The following table summarizes the results.

Group	N	Mean
United States:		
Protestant males	667	55.8
Protestant females	673	57.2
Catholic males	221	59.1
Catholic females	99	59.4
Egypt:		
Moslem males	443	68.2
Moslem females	301	67.6
Christian males	143	67.0
Christian females	79	65.2

Both Moslems and Christians in the Middle East score significantly higher on the F scale than do Americans. The attitudes of the individual reflect the influence of his culture, and serve to perpetuate the culture.

Gardner, G. H. *The Arab Middle East: some background interpretations*, J. soc. Issues, *1959*, **15**, *no. 3*.

Melikian, L. H. *Authoritarianism and its correlates in the Egyptian culture and in the United States*. J. soc. Issues, *1959*, **15**, *no. 3*.

George P. Murdock, anthropologist at Yale University, employed what is known as the cross-cultural method (see page 361) in a study of family, kinship organization, and the regulation of sexual conduct and marriage. For this analysis he had data on 118 societies in North America (mainly Indian tribes), Africa, Oceania, Eurasia, and South America. With the exception of a Chinese group and a group of New England whites (the Connecticut Yankees) the preliterate peoples of the earth constituted the sample.

Murdock's data reveal considerable diversity among the various peoples of the world in the restrictions placed upon sexual behavior. As the following table shows, only three societies in the sample of 118 seem to have a general taboo against all sexual intercourse outside of marriage. These are the Connecticut Yankees and the Ashanti and Timne of West Africa.

Sex taboos	*Number of societies*
Permissive premarital unchastity	49
Freely or conditionally permitted adultery	3
Sexual intercourse permitted with privileged kinship relation before or after marriage	23
Two or all three of the above	40
Generalized sex taboo outside of marriage	3

Murdock comments:

Our own culture includes a blanket taboo against fornication, an over-all prohibition of all sexual intercourse outside of the marital relationship. To a member of our society, consequently, sex itself seems the obvious focus of sex regulation. . . . To the overwhelming majority of the peoples of the world, the point of departure for the regulation of sex is not sexual intercourse *per se* but one or more other social phenomena with respect to which sex is important, notably marriage, kinship, social status, reproduction, and ceremonial. . . . To few peoples is sex an evil, albeit a necessary one, and thus to be confined exclusively within the limits of the one social relationship vested with the responsibility for reproduction.

Murdock, G. P. Social structure. *New York: Macmillan, 1949.*

the day-by-day business of living and working together in the society. Such arrangements are not consciously and systematically sought.

Once the group accepts a given arrangement, once the arrangement becomes the typical means of coping with a problem, it is transmitted to new members of the society as the "approved" way, and very frequently as the only "decent" or "civilized" way. The failure to recognize the diverse ways in which the various peoples of the world have tried to cope with the universal problems of living, and the failure to realize that there is not *one*

but *many* "decent" or "civilized" ways of doing things, makes for misunderstanding and conflict (see Box 10.6).

GUIDE 32: *The culture of a people consists of their distinctive modal patterns of behavior and the underlying regulatory beliefs, values, norms, and premises*

What makes up a culture—of what does a culture consist? In answering this question, it

THE SOCIAL AND CULTURAL HABITAT

BOX 10.5: *The un-American*

Ralph Linton, the American cultural anthropologist, has given us an amusing but telling account of the extent to which one culture may borrow from other cultures.

Our solid American citizen awakens in a bed built on a pattern which originated in the Near East but which was modified in Northern Europe before it was transmitted to America. He throws back covers made from cotton, domesticated in India, or linen, domesticated in the Near East, or silk, the use of which was discovered in China. All of these materials have been spun and woven by processes invented in the Near East. He slips into his moccasins, invented by the Indians of the Eastern woodlands, and goes to the bathroom, whose fixtures are a mixture of European and American inventions, both of recent date. He takes off his pajamas, a garment invented in India, and washes with soap invented by the ancient Gauls. . . .

He puts on garments whose form originally derived from the skin clothing of the nomads of the Asiatic steppes, puts on shoes made from skins tanned by a process invented in ancient Egypt and cut to a pattern derived from the classical civilizations of the Mediterranean, and ties around his neck a strip of bright-colored cloth which is a vestigial survival of the shoulder shawls worn by the seventeenth-century Croatians. Before going out for breakfast he glances through the window, made of glass invented in Egypt, and if it is raining puts on overshoes made of rubber discovered by the Central American Indians and takes an umbrella, invented in southeastern Asia. Upon his head he puts a hat made of felt, a material invented in the Asiatic steppes.

On his way to breakfast he stops to buy a paper, paying for it with coins, an ancient Lydian invention. At the restaurant a whole new series of borrowed elements confronts him. His plate is made of a form of pottery invented in China. His knife is of steel, an alloy first made in southern India, his fork a medieval Italian invention, and his spoon a derivative of a Roman original. He begins breakfast with an orange, from the eastern Mediterranean, a cantaloupe from Persia, or perhaps a piece of African watermelon. With this he has coffee, an Abyssinian plant, with cream and sugar. Both the domestication of cows and the idea of milking them originated in the Near East, while sugar was first made in India. After his fruit and first coffee he goes on to waffles, cakes made by a Scandinavian technique from wheat domesticated in Asia Minor. Over these he pours maple syrup, invented by the Indians of the Eastern woodlands. As a side dish he may have the egg of a species of bird domesticated in Indo-China, or thin strips of the flesh of an animal domesticated in Eastern Asia which have been salted and smoked by a process developed in northern Europe.

When our friend has finished eating he settles back to smoke, an American Indian habit, consuming a plant domesticated in Brazil in either a pipe, derived from the Indians of Virginia, or a cigarette, derived from Mexico. If he is hardy enough he may even attempt a cigar, transmitted to us from the Antilles by way of Spain. While smoking he reads the news of the day, imprinted in characters invented by the ancient Semites upon a material invented in China by a process invented in Germany. As he absorbs the accounts of foreign troubles he will, if he is a good conservative citizen, thank a Hebrew deity in an Indo-European language that he is 100 per cent American.

Linton, R. The study of man. New York: Appleton-Century-Crofts, 1936.

BOX 10.6: *Time and trouble*

Cultural differences in norms and values may lead to failure of communication and to conflict. Many of the clashes between the various national delegates to the United Nations Educational, Scientific and Cultural Organization (UNESCO) have been traced to the different cultural orientations of the delegates.

Ina Telberg, a journalist, has provided us with the following illustration.

One of the most deeply rooted, and largely unconscious, features of any culture is what the psychologists call the *time perspective*. Within the United Nations, at least three different time perspectives operate.

"Gentlemen, it is time for lunch, we must adjourn," announces the Anglo-Saxon chairman, in the unabashed belief that having three meals a day at regular hours is the proper way for mankind to exist.

"But why? We haven't finished what we were doing," replies—in a puzzled manner that grows rapidly more impatient—an Eastern European delegate, in whose country people eat when the inclination moves them and every family follows its own individual timetable.

"Why, indeed?" placidly inquires the Far Eastern representative, hailing from a country where life and time are conceived as a continuous stream, with no man being indispensable, with no life-process needing to be interrupted for any human being, and where members of electoral bodies walk in and out of the room quietly, getting a bite to eat when necessary, talking to a friend when pleasant; but where meetings, theatre performances, and other arranged affairs last without interruption for hours on end, while individuals come and go, are replaced by others, meditate or participate as the occasion requires, without undue strain, stress, or nervous tension.

As one or the other group persists in its own conception of the time perspective, as the Anglo-Saxons demand that the duration of meetings and conferences be fixed in advance and that meals be taken regularly at fixed hours, and as the Russians sit irritated and the Latins puzzled and the Secretariat frantic—as this condition continues, mutual friction grows, murmurs of "unreasonableness" are heard around the room; and, when the issue under discussion is an important one, overt accusations are hurled across the room of "insincerity," "lack of a serious approach to the problem," and even "sabotage."

Telberg, Ina. *They don't do it our way.* Courier *(UNESCO), 1950, 3, no. 4.*

is first important to distinguish between the *explicit* and the *implicit* culture. The explicit culture consists of directly observable regularities in the verbal and nonverbal behavior of the members of a society. The implicit culture consists of the beliefs, values, norms, and premises which the anthropologist infers or invents to explain observed regularities in behavior and to explain the patterning of seemingly unrelated bits of behavior.

EXPLICIT CULTURE

Culture is as people do. It must be realized, however, that the culture of a society as described by an anthropologist is not a description of the behavior of any actual member of the society. Rather, it is a "statistical" statement—it is a description of the behavior of the *typical* or *modal* member of the society. The explicit culture of a group consists, then,

THE SOCIAL AND CULTURAL HABITAT

of the typical patterns of behavior of a people.

We shall take as the simplest discriminable bit of cultural behavior a unit which we will term the *standard behavior event*. A standard behavior event is the pattern of behavior of typical individuals in a situation standard in a culture. All the standard behavior events taken together comprise the explicit culture of a society. By far the most important class of standard behavior events is the *standard interpersonal behavior event*, which may be defined as the system of reciprocal role behaviors, in a given standard situation, of two or more persons who are typical members of their respective positions. A doctor interviewing a patient, a lawyer conferring with a client, a teacher lecturing to a class, a father disciplining his son—these are examples of standard interpersonal behavior events in the American culture.

AN EMPIRICAL ILLUSTRATION. A study by Riley and Riley [1954] illustrates the standard interpersonal behavior event. These investigators administered to 2,500 New Jersey high school students a questionnaire which read as follows:

Suppose you were taking a test and the student sitting beside you asks you the answers to some of the questions. You are sitting way in the back of the room so most of the students won't be apt to notice what you do.

The students were asked to indicate whether or not they would refuse help in each of four situations:

(a) The student is your best friend; the teacher is out of the room and won't find out.

(b) The student is not a particular friend; the teacher is still out of the room.

(c) The student is not a particular friend, but the teacher is in the room. If she sees you cheating she will disapprove though she won't openly punish you.

(d) The student is not a particular friend, but the teacher is in the room and will lower your grade if she sees you cheating.

The actions selected in the four role situations are shown in Table 10.1. Consider first the right-hand column of the table. Note that 18 per cent of the subjects would refuse to give help in all four situations; 29 per cent would help their best friend but refuse in all other situations; 27 per cent woud help if the teacher is not in the room; 10 per cent would refuse only if punished by a lowering of the grade; the remaining 16 per cent would refuse help in none of these four situations. The figures in the right-hand column provide a means for classifying or ordering individuals according to their disposition to act honestly or, to put it differently, to help a fellow student.

Our interest here is not in classifying or ordering persons, however. These data provide a second set of ratings which apply to the *situations*. Consider the totals given in parentheses at the foot of each column. In the first

TABLE 10.1: ACTIONS SELECTED IN FOUR ROLE SITUATIONS [Riley and Riley, 1954]
+ indicates respondent would refuse to help fellow student to cheat

(a) Best friend	(b) Fellow student	(c) Teacher disapproves	(d) Teacher punishes	Per cent of total subjects
+	+	+	+	18
....	+	+	+	29
....	....	+	+	27
....	....	....	+	10
....	....	....	....	16
(18%)	(47%)	(74%)	(84%)	

column, only 18 per cent would refuse help; in the second column, 47 per cent would refuse help (both the 18 per cent who would refuse in all four situations and the 29 per cent who would help their best friend but refuse otherwise), etc.

Each of the four situations in the questionnaire places the subject in a standard interpersonal behavior event. He is asked to make a choice of action in these behavior events, which include one or more other persons. The other persons expect him to behave in a certain way and they will respond in a certain way to the particular action that he chooses.

Consider situation (b), which includes another student as the other person. The other student requests help. In other words, he has the expectation that the subject, a fellow student, will offer help. The other student's expectation of help must be taken into account by the subject in choosing what action to take. Note that the subjects are almost evenly divided between those who would help the other student (53 per cent) and those who would refuse help (47 per cent). This illustrates a principle of basic importance. The role behavior of an individual is determined jointly by the individual's enduring predispositions to act and by the expectations and sanctions of other persons who are enacting complementary roles.

Now, let us go on to situation (c). Again we have a role relation involving the subject student and the student who expects help. In addition, however, a second other person is involved, the teacher. The teacher expects the subject student to refuse help and will punish nonconformity by disapproval. The percentage of students who would refuse help increases from 47 to 74 per cent. This marked shift is due to the presence of the teacher who has such and such expectations and sanctions.

This illustration demonstrates that the actions of an individual in a standard interpersonal behavior event are influenced by the expectations and sanctions of persons occupying related positions. Table 10.2 schematically represents the interpersonal controls which govern the course of action when student B asks help of student A.

We would emphasize that action in the standard interpersonal behavior event is determined jointly by the individual's own predispositions—his cognitions, motivations, interpersonal response traits, and attitudes—and by the expectations and sanctions, as apprehended by the individual, of other persons in the behavior event who are enacting complementary roles. Both the characteristics of the individual and the way in which other persons respond to him as a taker of a given role

TABLE 10.2: A SCHEMATIC REPRESENTATION OF THE STANDARD INTERPERSONAL BEHAVIOR EVENT [After Riley and Riley, 1954]

From A's point of view:	From B's point of view:
(i) A perceives himself in role of student.	B perceives himself in role of student.
(ii) A perceives B in role of fellow student.	B perceives A in role of fellow student.
(iii) A perceives B's expectations and takes them into account.	B expects A to choose a certain action.
(iv) A chooses an action (to help or not to help B).	B perceives A's choice of action.
(v) A expects B to respond to the action taken in a certain way.	B perceives A's expectation and takes it into account.
(vi) A perceives B's response which has a significance for him as either a reward or a punishment for his own action.	B responds to A's action.

must be taken into account in seeking to understand his behavior.

IMPLICIT CULTURE

Anthropologists are now becoming increasingly interested in studying the implicit patterns *for* behavior which are assumed to underlie and determine the observed regularities in the explicit behavior of a people. Implicit culture is an anthropological term, akin to the social psychologist's concept of psychological factors—cognitions, wants, interpersonal response traits, and attitudes. Implicit culture can then be defined (in psychological terms) as the *modal* cognitions, wants, interpersonal response traits, and attitudes in a society.

We can conveniently discuss the implicit culture of a society in terms of cultural beliefs, cultural values, cultural norms, and cultural premises.

CULTURAL BELIEFS. In every society there is a set of cultural beliefs which in large measure defines the implicit culture of that society and sets it off from those of other societies (see Box 10.7).

The belief system of a society includes all of the cognitions—ideas, knowledge, lore, superstitions, myths, and legends—shared by most members of the society and by the typical occupants of the various positions in the society.

Myth and legend constitute a very important body of folklore in every society. They provide a basis for the continuity of social life and of culture. Through them the world is given order and meaning. Our own myths and legends are as real a part of our belief system as any other part. What Malinowski [1926] said about myth among simple, preliterate peoples is equally true of us, members of a complex, literate society.

Myth as it exists in a savage community, that is, in its living primitive form, is not merely a story told but a reality lived. It is not of the nature of fiction, such as we read today in a novel, but it is a living reality, believed to have once happened in primeval times, and continuing ever since to influence the world and human destinies. The myth is to the savage what, to a fully believing Christian, is the Biblical story of Creation, of the Fall, of the Redemption by Christ's sacrifice on the cross. As our sacred story lives in our ritual, in our morality, as it governs our faith and controls our conduct, even so does his myth for the savage.

Studied alive, myth is not symbolic, but a direct expression of its subject-matter; it is not an exploration in satisfaction of a scientific interest, but a narrative resurrection of a primeval reality, told in satisfaction of deep religious wants, moral cravings, social submissions, assertions, even practical requirements. Myth fulfills in primitive culture an indispensable function: it expresses, enhances, and codifies belief; it safeguards and enforces morality; it vouches for the efficiency of ritual and contains practical rules for the guidance of man. Myth is thus a vital ingredient of human civilization; it is not an idle tale, but a hard-worked active force; it is not an intellectual exploration or an artistic imagery, but a pragmatic charter of primitive faith and moral wisdom.

CULTURAL VALUES. Action in standard behavior events is also influenced by the values of our typical persons. A value is an especially important class of beliefs shared by the members of a society or by typical occupants of all the various positions in the society, concerning what is desirable or "good" or what ought to be. For example, the typical American values human equality; the typical physician holds health to be desirable; the typical lawyer believes in "due process"; the typical teacher entertains the idea that intellectual competence is an "ought to be." Values are both positive and negative; the positive values are the "desirables"; the negative values, the "undesirables."

The dominant values in a culture may be

Florence R. Kluckhohn, an anthropologist, has stated the assumption that there are a limited number of basic human questions for which all people at all times and in all places must find answers: (1) What is the dominant modality of the *relationship of man to other men?* (2) What is the significant *time dimension?* (3) What is the valued *personality type?* (4) What is the relation of *man to nature?* (5) What are the *innate predispositions* of man?

To each of these five basic questions there appear to be the three possible answers as given in the following table.

Question	Possible answers		
Modality of relationship among men	Familialistic	Collateral	Individualistic
Time dimension	Past	Present	Future
Valued personality type	Being	Being-in-becoming	Doing
Man's relation to nature	Man subjugated to nature	Man in nature	Man over nature
Innate predispositions	Evil (mutable or immutable)	Neither good nor bad (mutable or immutable)	Good (mutable or immutable)

To clarify the scheme depicted in the table, let us see how Florence Kluckhohn contrasts the answers of Spanish-Americans with those of Anglo-Americans to the five basic questions of man.

Where the Anglo-American stresses Individualism, the Spanish-American puts his primary emphasis upon a combination of the Lineal [familialistic] and the Collateral. The semifeudal *patron-peon* system of Mexicans . . . has neither permitted nor required very much independent behavior of most people. Or, to phrase this another way, whereas the Anglo-American is quite systematically trained for independent behavior, the Spanish-American or Mexican is trained for dependence.

---

ascertained in a number of ways. Williams [1951] has indicated five different kinds of relevant data:

Suppose we assert that cleanliness is a major value in American society. We could establish or refute such a statement by recording the following types of observations: (1) In this society, people often choose between activities that promote cleanliness and other types of activity (for example, cleaning house *versus* going to church or enjoying leisure). A great deal of time and effort is lavished on washing hands, taking baths, preparing clean clothes, scrubbing and sweeping, collecting and disposing of trash, and so on. (2) Newspapers and magazines devote much space to news, articles, and advertising dealing with cleanliness, and ways of promoting it in various areas of life. (3) Comments asserting or implying a bias in favor of cleanliness are extremely common, not only in response to direct questioning but in the form of unprompted statements. (4) Analysis of a wide sampling of spoken and written materials reveals an extraordinary number of instances that assume "cleanliness is desirable" as an implicit concept underlying the assertions. (Thus, in the frequent articles on new housekeeping methods, there are many that never make the value statements directly.) (5) Children are approved and otherwise rewarded for cleanly behavior, but meet frowns, censorious speech, minor deprivations, and physical chastisement for certain violations of

The American dominant *time* orientation has been noted to be Future, that of the Spanish-Americans, Present. We show a vague awareness of this difference when we often refer to Mexicans in general as being a *mañana* [tomorrow] people. Yet how very much bound by our own cultural values we are when we interpret *mañana* to mean that a Mexican will always put off until tomorrow what should be done today. Tomorrow in a highly specific sense is meaningless to the Spanish-American or Mexican. He lives in a timeless present, and as one Mexican scholar phrased it: "The Mexican never puts off until tomorrow what can be done *only* today."

Consider, too, the vast difference between the Spanish-American Being orientation and the American emphasis upon Doing or accomplishing. Doing things in the name of accomplishment is not usual Spanish-American behavior. That which "is" is in large part taken for granted and considered as something to be enjoyed rather than altered.

Our own and the Spanish-American's definition of the *man-nature* relationship are likewise poles apart. We set out to conquer, overcome, and exploit nature; they accept the environment with a philosophical calm bordering on the fatalistic. And seldom in Spanish-American culture does one find evidence of our own historical view of human nature as Evil but Perfectible. Their view would appear to be much more that of human nature as a Mixture of the Good and Bad.

Florence Kluckhohn's generalizations about the Anglo-American and Spanish-American cultures are based primarily upon her impressions as a social scientist rather than upon systematic data. Nevertheless, her schema outlined in the table above may provide valuable insight into cross-cultural comparisons.

Kluckhohn, Florence R. Dominant and variant value orientations. In C. Kluckhohn, H. A. Murray, and D. M. Schneider (Eds.), Personality in nature, society, and culture. New York: Knopf, 1953.

this pattern. Although the rewards and punishments may be less obvious in later life, adults, too, face sanctions for conduct disregarding this value.

What the person recognizes as desirable—his values—are not necessarily his *desires*. As people grow up and become "culture-broken," the desirables tend to become desired—values become goals. (For an exploratory study of the influence of group values upon the goals of the individual, see Box 10.8.)

CULTURAL NORMS. Behavior in standard behavior events is also regulated by cultural norms. These are the rules or standards, accepted by the members of a society and by the typical occupants of a position, which specify the details of appropriate and inappropriate behavior in a standard behavior event. The norms may also specify the reward for appropriate behavior and the punishment for improper behavior.

Norms are divided into *folkways* and *mores*. Norms are termed folkways when conformity to them is not considered vital to the welfare of the group and when the means of enforcing conformity is not clearly defined. Thus, in American culture, a folkway specifies that a man shall wear a tie on formal occasions. If a man does not do so, he may be considered a boor, but his nonconformity is not regarded

BOX 10.8: *Cultural values and personal goals*

Glen Rasmussen and Alvin Zander, social psychologists at the University of Michigan, report one of the few research studies which have tried to examine the part that group values play in shaping the goals of the individual.

Eighty-five teachers in six different high schools were studied. As a first step, the investigators determined the friendship or clique group within the faculty to which each teacher belonged. Then, a 16-item questionnaire on values regarding teacher behavior (e.g., the desirability of experimenting with new teaching methods or sticking to the tried and true) was given to each teacher with the request that he answer the questions from three different points of view. First, he answered the questions as he thought the members of *his friendship group* would answer them. Second, he answered the questions as he thought the members of the *other group* on the faculty to which he did not belong would answer them. And third, he marked the questions to indicate what *he* would ideally like to do; that is, to describe his goals as a teacher.

The degree of similarity between the individual's goals and the values of his friendship group (the first and third sets of answers) is given by a correlation coefficient of .46. This modest-sized correlation indicates that though there is an appreciable relation between group values and individual goals, there is at the same time considerable room for individual deviation from the group values.

It was found—as might be predicted—that the correlation between the individual's goals and the values of the group to which he did *not* belong (the second and third sets of answers) did not reach a statistically significant level.

Another result of interest: the teachers were asked to select the eight items among the sixteen which they believed their friendship groups regarded as *most important*. The correlation between individual goals and group values on these eight most important items was substantially higher than the correlation for the relatively unimportant items.

This study presents interesting findings, but it can also serve to illustrate some of the difficulties in doing research in social psychology. As the investigators note, values of the group were measured by asking the teachers to tell what the other members of the group believed. The group values thus measured are "attributed" values. And there is a possibility that in reporting the values of the group, the teachers were, to some extent, attributing their *own* goals to the other members, such attribution thus accounting for the moderate correlation found between group values and individual goals.

Rasmussen, G., and Zander, A. Group membership and self-evaluation. Hum. Relat., *1954, 7, 239–251.*

---

as having important consequences for the group. And the punishment for his nonconformity is informal, variable, and often mild. He may be frowned upon, or talked about, or perhaps socially rebuffed; sometimes, on the other hand, he may not even be aware that he is being "punished."

Mores are norms which specify behavior of vital importance to the society and which embody its basic moral values. The prohibition against bigamy is one of the mores in the American culture. Another of the mores is that the man must provide for his wife and children; failure to do so can be a cause for legal action.

The mores are actively enforced by the members of the society, either through legal action or through social sanction. Thus, in many communities in the southern United States, the "right" attitude is to favor educating Negro and white children in separate public schools, and a white individual who transgresses this norm by advocating integrated schools is severely punished. The punishment may take the form of "firing" him from his job, boycotting his place of business, jailing him for minor traffic offenses, etc.

Some norms are set down in the legal code, which details the violations of a law, establishes the means for deciding whether the violation has been committed, specifies the penalties for each type of violation, and designates the agents to enforce the law. The crucial relation between law and social mores has been expressed by Hutchins [1961] in the following passage:

> The law is a great teacher. It is . . . the way in which newly discovered moral truth is disseminated among the population and incorporated in the conscience and mores of the community. The popular notion that law reflects the mores is, as countless historical examples show, often the reverse of the truth. Law helps make the mores. Law-making is the process by which the members of the political community learn together what the mores should be.

The mores of most cultures in the world are associated with the religious beliefs which are common in the culture. The rewards for conformity and the punishments for nonconformity are commonly believed to be meted out by supernatural powers. The rewards and punishments may be immediate or they may be delayed until some distant time. The expectation of delayed punishment may arouse strong feelings of guilt in the deviant believer: "I have sinned and I am unworthy."

CULTURAL PREMISES. The implicit culture includes many premises about the world which remain unverbalized. These premises are tacit generalizations which may be thought of as "the metaphysics of the people." They are likely to be revealed only through the analytic work or intuitive speculation of the social observer who suspects that a set of seemingly unrelated actions is meaningfully patterned (see Box 10.9).

INSTITUTIONALIZED WAYS

The basic elements of a culture—the standard behavior events and their associated regulatory patterns—are frequently organized into larger *patterns* which are well-established and accepted as a fundamental part of culture. These larger patterns we will term *institutionalized ways*.

Institutionalized ways may be thought of as a system of standard behavior events, together with their associated beliefs, values, and norms, which represent a society's solution to one of the main problems of living. Among the more important institutionalized ways are those which concern themselves with procreation, distributing goods and services, satisfying aesthetic needs, training the young, enforcing the mores, disposing of the dead, and propitiating the gods.

In any institutionalized way, the bits which make it up (the constituent standard behavior events) are interrelated to form a coherent, organized system. We may illustrate this by examining the institutionalized mating ways in two societies: (1) the Kurtatchi, a community of Melanesian people in the Solomon Islands (see Table 10.3); (2) the middle-class North Americans (see Table 10.4).

Examination of the mating ways of the Kurtatchi and of Americans reveals that the two societies have developed different solutions of the problem of arranging for the mating of men and women to reproduce young. More importantly, however, it will be seen that in both the Kurtatchi and the Americans, the institutionalized mating way consists of an ordered, integrated series of standard behavior events, directed toward the goal of mating. In each of these standard behavior events, the participants perform their respective roles as prescribed by the culture, thus setting the stage for the succeeding event.

PATTERNS OF CULTURE

A culture, like a personality, has both content and *pattern*. Just as the mere listing of the separate traits of an individual does not describe his personality, so the mere listing of the separate institutionalized ways of a society does not describe its culture. Two cultures, just as two personalities, may contain highly similar elements and still be extremely unlike one another in pattern.

The full significance of any single institutionalized way in the pattern of a culture can be seen only when that way is viewed in the total matrix of its relations to other ways. And changes in one way will tend to bring about changes in other related ways in the cultural system. For example, Linton and Kardiner [1952] describe the effects of the change from dry to wet rice cultivation in the Tonala society on the island of Madagascar. The establishment of permanent irrigated rice fields resulted in permanent villages. These settled villages were much less self-contained than the mobile villages of the era of dry rice culti-

BOX 10.9: *Evil premises*

Clyde Kluckhohn, the cultural anthropologist, spent many years studying the culture of the Navaho. Among the Navaho, witchcraft was widely practiced. However, when Kluckhohn, in the early days of his study, asked 11 Navaho about witchcraft, seven denied knowing anything about it. On a later occasion, Kluckhohn asked 25 additional Navaho about witchcraft. Sixteen of these denied any knowledge.

These observations led Kluckhohn to believe that he had isolated one bit of an important behavior pattern typical in this culture. He proceeded to relate it to other bits of behavior which, on the surface, seemed unrelated: care in hiding one's feces; care in preventing others from securing anything else that comes from one's body, such as hair, nail clippings, and sputum; secretiveness about one's personal name. Kluckhohn concluded that these different bits of behavior were determined by a single, implicit pattern: "fear of the malevolent intentions of other persons." It is dangerous to reveal to a stranger knowledge of witchcraft; it is dangerous to permit a stranger to secure one's feces or one's hair and nail clippings; it is dangerous to reveal one's name to a stranger. For to do so gives the stranger power to harm one. The Navaho can rarely verbalize this belief; it is an "unspeakable."

Are there "unspeakables" in our own American culture? Most of us would probably deny it. But an unbiased anthropologist from another land who studied our culture as Kluckhohn did the Navaho's might piece together the following seemingly unrelated acts: many American hostesses go to elaborate lengths to avoid having thirteen guests for dinner; many American people perform ritualistic, propitiatory acts after breaking a mirror; many Americans go out of their way to avoid walking under a ladder; many Americans are made slightly uneasy when a black cat crosses their path.

Our visiting anthropologist might then ask himself: Does the typical American entertain the implicit premise that there is a supernatural, evil force to which one can expose himself if he engages in certain seemingly harmless acts? Is this premise of "sinister magic" an "unspeakable" in the American culture?

> *Kluckhohn, C. Patterning as exemplified in Navaho culture. In* Language, culture and personality: essays in memory of Edward Sapir. *Menasha, Wis.: Sapir Memorial Publ. Fund, 1941.*

vation, and a change from independent villages to a tribal organization took place.

This change in an agricultural way brought about changes in the patterns of native warfare. The defense of a permanent village, in contrast to a mobile village, required more powerful defenses, which involved large expenditures and permanent upkeep. Further, slaves, who were of no significance in the dry rice economy, now became important. Slavery, in turn, gave rise to new ransom techniques. With the growth in the solidity of the tribal organization, the old tribal democracy disappeared. The next step was a King at the head.

Cultures, like personalities, vary in the degree to which they are integrated. The more "simple," preliterate cultures may have been more highly integrated than the complex, literate cultures of modern industrial societies. In the latter cultures, we find many inconsistencies and contradictions among the component parts. These cultural strains complicate the adjustment of the individual to his culture and make for personal conflict. (See our discussion of frustration and the social environment, page 119.)

INDIVIDUAL AND CULTURE— A MANY-FACETED RELATION

The individual and his culture are complexly related. He may act as a creature of the culture of his group, and also as a carrier, a manipulator, a creator of his culture.

As a *creature* of culture, the individual displays conformity. He is strongly motivated to behave appropriately in every situation. As a *carrier* of his culture, the individual plays a more active and positive role. He strives to exemplify the desirability of the sanctioned ways and to teach them to others.

The *manipulator* of culture uses the common attitudes, values, and patterns of behavior to advance his own interests. In the role of *creator,* the individual serves as a vehicle for cultural change. Cultures change as the result of the actions of specific individuals who are

able to challenge the *status quo* and bring about innovations.

The chief value of this description of the different roles which the individual may play in relation to his culture is to emphasize that the relation between an individual and his culture is an active, give-and-take relation.

TO RECAPITULATE

Men in all societies must solve a number of problems if the society is to survive and endure: the biological needs of the members must be met, the young must be socialized, the sick must be cared for, the dead must be disposed of, the gods must be propitiated, etc.

Each society adopts a particular set of arrangements for solving its problems which become traditional arrangements, transmitted from generation to generation.

In analyzing the content of culture, the smallest discriminable unit is the standard behavior event. The total set of such events makes up the explicit culture of the society. The actions of persons in these events are regulated by beliefs, values, and norms, which constitute the implicit culture of the society.

Standard behavior events do not exist as isolated events. They are organized to form larger patterns—institutionalized ways. These ways are the arrangements a society has developed to solve its various problems. The total pattern of ways, together with their associated regulatory patterns, make up the culture of the society.

Methods for the study of culture and the comparison of cultures

The anthropologist faces complex problems of analysis and of synthesis as he goes about the task of constructing a map of the culture of a people (see Box 10.10). In his work, he has recourse to a number of different methods of study. The main ones that we shall con-

TABLE 10.3: MATING WAYS AMONG THE KURTATCHI . . .

Occasion	Standard behavior events
Betrothal, when both are children, the girl often a baby.	Father of boy presents spear hung with string of ceremonial currency made of shell disks to mother of girl. Betel mixture chewed.
First visit of mother of boy to mother of girl. Soon after betrothal above.	Aromatic plants brought by mother of boy to decorate girl. Betel mixture chewed.
Visit of boy's mother to take back girl for her first visit. When girl is about 7 or 8 years old.	Paint for head of girl brought by boy's mother. Betel mixture chewed.
Visit of girl's mother to see her daughter in mother-in-law's hut 3 or 4 days after visit above. Girl remains with mother-in-law for a month or more.	Food and areca nut provided by boy's mother for girl's mother and accompanying women.
Request for handing over of ceremonial currency, usually at first signs of breast development.	Girl's mother sends food, including pig meat, to boy's mother, the pig being a hint that it is time to produce the currency.
Boy's mother collects ceremonial currency from her brother and other male relatives.	Boy's mother sends pieces of pig to relatives who are expected to help provide the currency.
Visit of boy's people to girl's people to hand over currency, and to bring back girl for long visit. As soon as enough currency has been collected.	Agreed amount of ceremonial currency handed over for division among the girl's relatives. One string given as personal gift, secretly, by boy's mother to girl's mother. One string given by girl's mother to boy's relatives "to pay for the boy."
During the next few years girl spends much time with her mother-in-law, returning to her mother only for occasional visits.	
Special visit of girl and her relatives to boy's mother to pay for the front end of the house with its verandah, usually reserved for men.	Girl's mother and relatives bring menak and live pig to boy's relatives, and small amount of ceremonial currency.
Marriage ceremony. Usually not until boy has taken off upi (special headgear worn by boys during adolescence) and girl has been through her first menstruation ceremony.	Exchange of ceremonial baskets of taro. Much food given by bride's mother to bridegroom's relatives.

SOURCE: After Blackwood, 1935, and Herskovits, 1949.

sider are the field method, content analysis, and the cross-cultural method. In addition, various ancillary techniques, e.g., projective tests and attitude scales, may be used. The statistical method of factor analysis may be used to isolate the primary dimensions of culture content.

THE FIELD METHOD

The major method for the study of culture

Occasion	Standard behavior events
Betrothal, arranged by young man and young woman, when both are adults.	Jeweled engagement ring presented by young man to young woman. Young man ceremonially places ring upon third finger of left hand of young woman and couple exchange lip kisses. Public announcement of betrothal.
Engagement period of some months or years.	"Showers" are given for young woman by her female friends, who present gifts to young woman for use in her home after marriage. Young woman collects clothes for use after marriage. Young man and young woman visit with families of each other and send gifts to families on birthdays and feast days. During the period of engagement, intimate association with other persons of the opposite sex on the part of both the young man and the young woman is unsanctioned. During this period, petting—pre-coital sexual play with mutual erotic arousal—is sanctioned if engaged in with discretion.
Bachelor dinner. Usually night before marriage ceremony.	A ceremonial feast to which friends of young man are invited to memorialize the end of unmarried status of young man. Much drinking of alcoholic beverages and sexual talk.
Marriage ceremony. Usually in a house of worship.	Religious rite in which couple mutually exchange vows of marital fidelity. Bride is dressed in symbolic white clothing and is attended by female relatives and friends. She is "given in marriage" by her father. The young man places a ring on the third finger of the left hand of the young woman which symbolizes her position as a sexually taboo, married woman. In what is known as a "double ring ceremony," the young man and woman present the symbolic ring to one another.
Wedding reception. Usually in house of parents of bride or in feast house (hotel, club, etc.) rented for purpose.	Ceremonial feast attended by kin and friends of young man and young woman. Much food and alcoholic beverages consumed. Wedding cake is cut by bride and groom together. Guests accept pieces of wedding cake as good luck omens. Bride tosses bouquet of flowers worn at marriage to unmarried, virginal female attendants. Female attendant who catches it is believed to be next female to marry. The father of the young woman is expected to pay all the costs of the ceremonial wedding feast.
Hazing.	Rice thrown at newly married pair as they leave reception; old shoes and signs announcing newly married status of couple appended to vehicle in which they leave reception for place of honeymoon.
Honeymoon.	Period of seclusion for newly married pair in which young man and young woman engage in sanctioned sexual intercourse for the first time. Achievement of sexual intercourse during honeymoon legally consummates the marriage.

BOX 10.10: *The Kula*

Bronislaw Malinowski, the cultural anthropologist, has provided us with an example of the task facing an anthropologist when he sets out to describe the culture of a people.

Malinowski studied an exchange system called the Kula, which is carried on by a number of tribes inhabiting a ring of islands in British New Guinea in the Western Pacific. The ring of islands forms a closed circuit along which two articles, red shell necklaces and white shell bracelets, are constantly being carried in opposite directions by the men who take part in the Kula. When the two articles meet on their travels around the circuit, they are ceremoniously exchanged. Malinowski notes that the Kula is a complex institution which is regulated by a system of traditional rules. It unites a rather large number of tribes and associated with it is a complex system of interconnected ritualistic ceremonies and supporting and secondary activities. However, the individuals who participate in the Kula

> . . . have no knowledge of the *total outline* of any of their social structure. They know their own motives, know the purpose of individual actions and rules which apply to them; but how, out of these, the whole collective institution shapes, this is beyond their mental range. Not even the most intelligent native has any clear idea of the Kula as a big, organized social construction, still less of its sociological functions and implications. If you were to ask him what the Kula is, he would answer by giving a few details, most likely by giving his personal experiences and subjective views on the Kula, but nothing approaching the definition just given here. Not even a partial coherent account could be obtained. For the integral picture does not exist in his mind; he is in it, and cannot see the whole from the outside.

> The integration of all the details observed, the achievement of a synthesis of *all* the various, relevant symptoms, is the task of the Ethnographer. First of all, he has to find out that certain activities, which at first sight might appear incoherent and not correlated, have a meaning. He then has to find out what is constant and relevant in these activities, and what accidental and inessential, that is, to find out the laws and rules of all the transactions. Again, the Ethnographer has to construct the picture of the big institution, very much as the physicist constructs his theory from the experimental data. . . .

Malinowski, B. Argonauts of the Western Pacific. *New York: Dutton, 1922.*

is the *field method*. The anthropologist, in carrying on field work, lives closely with the people he is studying. He talks with members of the group; he observes their forms of behavior in the home, in places of work, and in other situations; he attends their rites; he questions them about traditional practices (see Box 10.11). He is a participant observer.

The major field technique is the interview with informants—members of the group who report to the anthropologist on the way of life of their people. Observational and interview data secured in the field may be supplemented by the analysis of biographical and autobiographical materials. These various sources of information are synthesized by the anthropologist in his attempt to delineate the culture of the group.

THE RELIABILITY OF THE FIELD METHOD. Occasional studies in which two anthropologists have studied the same group reveal important discrepancies between their accounts, suggesting that the field method is not free of error. For example, the village of Tepoztlan in Mexico was studied independently by Redfield [1946] and Lewis [1951]. In comment-

THE SOCIAL AND CULTURAL HABITAT

Melville J. Herskovits, a cultural anthropologist at Northwestern University, and his wife, Florence S. Herskovits, have studied the Saramacca tribe of Bush Negroes of Dutch Guiana in South America.

The following account is cited by Herskovits to illustrate the *field method* as used by anthropologists in the study of the culture of a people. It also indicates how voluminous informal notes are later condensed into a short technical paragraph.

We were aroused early after our night of stories. The women were moving about, getting their morning meal before daybreak came to give them light for their harvesting. There was much they had to do. Late that afternoon they would be returning to their villages, for the next day was sacred to the Earth Mother, and no work could be done in the fields. Today, added to the round of harvesting were the preparations for the return to their village. The rice that had been cut during the week would have to be carried there for drying and winnowing, and yams and peanuts and beans were to be brought in. . . .

Soon our men, too, began to stir and, as we came out of our hammocks, Bayo and Angita entered the clearing. They were just returning from the dance at Pa'aha. . . . With Angita was a man we had not seen before, holding a small child by the hand.

"This is Awingu, my brother-in-law," said Angita in explanation. "His eyes trouble him. I brought him to you for medicine."

After an exchange of courtesies demanded by the visit, we turned to the child. "Is this your child, Awingu?" we asked.

His answer came promptly. "No, he is not my child. He is my wife's child. I made him. . . ."

Just then our cook came up with a small present for the child, but, since he would not take it from his hands or ours, Angita gave it to him.

"Thank you, father," he said to Angita.

Angita looked down affectionately at the youngster. "Two, three years more, Awingu and he will be ready to go and live with his father at Gankwe. Do you remember your father at Gankwe? It was he who showed you how to make a gun from a reed. And you made it well. . . ."

"This is not your child, Awingu," we took the occasion to remark when we were saying goodbye. "Yet he seems to like you very much."

"*Ma, tye! Ma Neng'e!*—Mother of all Negroes! What would you have? I am his father! . . ."

The discussion then continues with a description of how, on various occasions, three different women claimed the man named Angita, who was a fine wood-carver, as a son, and how social reality resolved this biological impossibility and thus yielded further understanding of Bush Negro kinship.

Later that day when our boat found itself abreast of the dugout which Angita was poling, we lost no time in questioning him.

"Angita," we called, "is the woman who gave us the rice your mother?"

He nodded.

"But what of Tita, who said she was your mother, too?"   (*Continued*)

He was a quick-witted lad and he saw at once what we had in mind. He said with a laugh, "You are asking about my true, true mother, the one who made me? It is not this one, and it is not Tita, who made me. It is Kutoi."

"But who are the other two?"

"They are her sisters."

Herskovits tells us that this experience would be reported in a monograph describing the culture of the Bush Negroes in a summary statement which might read as follows:

The social organization of the Bush Negroes is unilateral, descent being counted on the maternal side, with controls within the family exercised by the mother's eldest brother. Kinship nomenclature is classificatory, mother and mother's sisters being called by the term "mother," father and father's brothers being called "father." Biological parents have no distinguishing appellation, being identified by a child as the parent "who made him."

Herskovits, M. J. Man and his works: the science of cultural anthropology. *New York: Knopf, 1949.*

Herskovits, M. J., and Herskovits, Florence S. Rebel destiny: among the Bush Negroes of Dutch Guiana. *New York: McGraw-Hill, 1934.*

ing on the difference between his report and the earlier account by Redfield, Lewis notes:

The impression given by Redfield's study of Tepoztlan is that of a relatively homogeneous, isolated, smoothly functioning, and well-integrated society made up of a contented and well-adjusted people. His picture of the village has a Rousseauian quality which glosses lightly over evidence of violence, disruption, cruelty, disease, suffering, and maladjustment. We are told little of poverty, economic problems, or political schisms. Throughout his study we find an emphasis upon the cooperative and unifying factors in Tepoztecan society. Our findings, on the other hand, would emphasize the underlying individualism of Tepoztecan institutions and character, the lack of cooperation, the tensions between villages within the municipio; the schisms within the village and the pervading quality of fear, envy, and distrust in inter-personal relations.

The occasional appearance of discrepant reports on a group which has been studied by two different anthropologists suggests the need

for systematic studies of the reliability of the field method designed to reveal sources of observer biases. Anthropologists are, of course, aware of the need for such methodological studies, but little systematic work has been undertaken. The cost of assigning different field workers to make independent and parallel studies of the same society is one consideration which has hindered reliability studies. The few scattered and more or less accidental studies of interobserver variation (such as the one referred to above and the Mead [1935] and Fortune [1939] studies of the New Guinea Arapesh) suggest the need for caution in accepting the report of a single field worker.

CONTENT ANALYSIS OF CULTURE

Content analysis is a research technique, systematized by Berelson [1952], which permits an objective, systematic, and quantitative description of the manifest content of a communication. The use of this technique involves a number of discrete steps.

The content analyst first defines the universe or population of communications which he will examine. For example, he might decide to examine all editorials in the *New York Times* for a given year. He next selects the unit of analysis to be used in counting content elements. The unit may be the word, the sentence, the paragraph, or the item, i.e., the entire textual unit. The next and most critical decision the analyst must make is to choose appropriate analytic categories. Categories that have been used include subject-matter categories, pro-con categories, value categories, etc.

Once the population has been specified, the unit of analysis selected, and the analytic categories determined, quantitative content analysis can be carried out. Qualitative or interpretative analysis is sometimes used to illuminate or supplement quantitative findings. An example of the use of content analysis in the description of a single "culture" is given in Box 10.12.

In the application of the method of content analysis to the study of culture change and the comparative study of cultures, the assumption is made that the content of the popular communications (magazine stories, plays, movies, radio serials, novels, etc.) in a society "expresses" or "reflects" the modal attitudes, values, mores, etc., of the members of that society. (Such use of content analysis in the comparative study of cultures is illustrated in Box 10.13.)

Berelson [1954] questions the validity of certain applications of content analysis to the study of culture:

It is difficult to know under what conditions inferences can be validly drawn about the total population or only about the particular audiences [of the mass communication]; to what extent they refer to the audience proper or to the producer's [of mass communication] conception of the audience or to the producers themselves as (atypical) members of the audience. . . . In short, the whole relationship between the content and the audience characteristics allegedly "reflected" in it is far from

clear. At the least it is far from a one-to-one relationship, and this fact in itself is a cautionary note against the over-interpretation of content data.

THE CROSS-CULTURAL METHOD

The *cross-cultural method* is designed to discover similarities and differences among cultural patterns in a sizable sample of societies. In this method each society is assigned a "score" on each of a number of selected cultural dimensions. This score is the modal practice or belief, etc., in the society. The scores of the various societies are then compared.

The potentialities of the cross-cultural method, long in use by anthropologists, have been significantly increased by the creation of the Human Relations Area Files. This is a cooperative enterprise among a number of universities to collect and process ethnographic data on a world-wide sample of societies. As described by Whiting [1954], "Processing consists of working up a complete bibliography of the major sources on a society. . . , classifying or coding each paragraph according to a standard outline. . . , duplicating the paragraphs on 5 x 8 cards, and distributing them in the appropriate categories in a file."

Murdock [1949] has reported on the usefulness of the cross-cultural files in his study of "social structure" (see Box 10.4):

The author began the present study . . . by formulating a schedule of the data needed . . . and by abstracting such data from the files of the Cross-Cultural Survey. . . . In a very few weeks he was able in this way to assemble the relevant materials for 85 societies. . . . This number, though large, still fell short of the cases required for reliable statistical treatment, and the author set out to secure further information by the usual methods of library research. Eventually he secured data on 165 additional societies, making a total of 250 in all. The labor required to secure these additional cases was immense, consuming well over a year of research effort or more than ten times that spent in obtaining the original 85 cases.

BOX 10.12: *The classroom culture*

Irvin L. Child, Elmer H. Potter, and Estelle M. Levine of Yale University applied the content-analysis method to the study of the "classroom culture."

The investigators selected for content analysis samples of stories from the general third-grade readers published since 1930. Altogether, 914 stories were analyzed.

The unit used in the content analysis of the stories was the *thema,* defined as "a sequence of psychological events consisting of (1) a situation or circumstances confronting a person, (2) the behavior (internal and external) with which the person responds, (3) the consequences of the behavior as felt by the person himself." In the 914 stories 3,409 themas were identified and analyzed.

The following table shows the percentages of reward, of punishment, and of absence of consequence for a few of the categories of behavior found in the stories. The treatment of the various categories of behavior reflects, of course, the cultural norms of the American society. The classroom culture is a microcosm of the total culture.

Category of behavior	Behavior rewarded	Behavior punished	Behavior neither rewarded nor punished
Gaining information	86%	9%	5%
Affiliation	82	8	9
Helping others	82	5	12
Achievement	80	10	9
Social approval	79	13	8
Dominance	74	16	8
Acquisition	64	31	3
Aggression	35	52	11
Self-consciousness, shyness	8	74	18
Laziness, inattentiveness	1	91	8

The investigators noted a number of general emphases running through the whole series of categories which could be presumed to have implications concerning the impact of the classroom culture on the motivational development of the child.

For example, effort or work as a means of reaching goals was repeatedly rewarded. "Here certainly are some of the forces leading to the development of a motive to work or put forth effort." A second emphasis was on the acquisition of skills, or the importance of learning. Finally, a distinction was emphasized between satisfying wants in socially approved ways, which tends to be rewarded, and satisfying them in socially disapproved ways, which tends to be punished. For example, in the case of retaining behavior, nonselfish retaining such as saving money is rewarded; selfish retaining is punished.

Child, I. L., Potter, E. H., and Levine, Estelle M. Children's textbooks and personality development: an exploration in the social psychology of education. Psychol. Monogr. 1946, 60, no. 3 (whole no. 279).

Moreover, the results were both quantitatively and qualitatively inferior. . . .

The cross-cultural method has been used to test hypotheses derived from culture theory and, in recent years, to test hypotheses from psychological theory. Thus Whiting and

Child [1953] used the cross-cultural method to test their hypothesis that a high degree of frustration and punishment experienced by a child in the course of the socialization of a particular "system" of behavior (e.g., oral, anal, sexual, aggression, etc.) would lead to enduring anxieties associated with that system which would be reflected in his adult behavior. Specifically, they took as an index of such enduring anxiety in a given system the tendency of adults to attribute the causes of illness to that particular system of behavior.

Data on prevailing child-training practices and prevailing adult beliefs about the causes of illness were collected on 75 societies distributed over the world. The results confirmed the hypothesis. Thus, for example, in cultures where the children are severely frustrated and punished with respect to sexuality there is a tendency for the adults to believe that illnesses result from violations of sexual taboos; and, as another example, in cultures where toilet training is severe (i.e., the anal "system"), anal explanations of illness tend to predominate.

BOX 10.13: *By their plays ye shall know them*

Donald V. McGranahan and Ivor Wayne sought to compare the national character of Germans and Americans by making a content analysis of the 45 most popular plays produced in the two countries in 1927, a year in which both countries were political democracies enjoying a period of economic prosperity. The investigators justify their procedure as follows:

Our first assumption in this study is that popular drama can be regarded as a case of "social fantasy"—that the psychological constellations in the dramatic work indicate sensitive areas in the personalities of those for whom the work has affect; their needs, assumptions, and values are expressed ("projected") in the drama. The successful play must be attuned to the audience.

They found the German plays were considerably more ideological, philosophical, historical, and social-minded than the American ones. The personal crimes and sins which posed the basic problems in the American plays were frequently excused or justified in the German plays. In the German plays, society was pictured as responsible—not the individual. In the American plays, virtue triumphed; in the German plays, success was won through power and ruthlessness. The good side usually won in the American plays because a person in a position of power changed his mind. In German plays, conflicts were more frequently resolved through power techniques. The investigators conclude:

The data of this study . . . lend support to the theory that there are real and persistent German-American psychological differences—or, if you will, differences in "national character." . . . it is not difficult to see how Germans could be led into National Socialism [Hitler's Nazi party] with its peculiar combination of power politics and folk idealism.

It should be noted that these conclusions—however plausible they may be—are based on a method which makes two assumptions of questionable validity: (1) Dramatists are accurate judges of the values, attitudes, and wants of the theater-going public. (2) Theater-goers constitute a random sample of the general population.

McGranahan, D. V., and Wayne, I. German and American traits reflected in popular drama. Hum. Relat., *1948, 1, 429–455.*

TABLE 10.5: SIX DIMENSIONS OF CULTURE [After Cattell, 1949]
Loading indicates correlation of each variable with factor concerned

Loading	Variable
	FACTOR 1: SIZE
.63	Large gross area
.65	Many political assassinations
.63	Many cities over 20,000 per 1,000,000 population
.61	Large gross population
.52	Many riots and local rebellions 1837–1937
.52	Many different language groups
.47	Late increase in industrial production
.46	High ratio of divorces to marriages
	FACTOR 2: CULTURAL ASSERTION
.78	Many cities over 20,000 per 1,000,000 population
.64	High ratio of white- to blue-collar occupations
.63	High frequency of political clashes with other countries 1837–1937
.62	High frequency of participation in wars 1837–1937
.62	High number of Nobel Prizes in Science, Literature, Peace
.60	High frequency of treaties (all kinds) with other countries
.57	Large gain in area 1837–1937
.46	Many ministries maintained for government
.45	Early increase in industrial production
.40	High creativity in science and philosophy
.35	High musical creativity
.35	High real standard of living
	FACTOR 3: ENLIGHTENED AFFLUENCE
.73	Low death rate from tuberculosis
.70	Large gross area
.67	High expenditure of tourists abroad
.55	High real standard of living
.51	High real income per head
.42	High expenditure (all sources) on education
.40	High musical creativity
.39	High percentage of men eminent in art
.37	High sugar consumption per head
.36	Low degree of government censorship of the press
	FACTOR 4: THOUGHTFUL INDUSTRIOUSNESS
.63	Low frequency of political assassinations
.50	High percentage of population in trade unions
.46	Many Nobel Prizes in Science, Literature, Peace
.41	High creativity in science and philosophy
.38	High ratio of white- to blue-collar occupations
.36	High percentage of population of Protestant affiliation

Loading	Variable

FACTOR 5: BOURGEOIS PHILISTINISM

.76	Tendency to save money from earnings
.55	High percentage of eminent men eminent in commerce and industry
.46	Low death rate from heart disease
.42	Tendency to have more than one political party
.39	High legal marriage rate
.37	Low percentage of eminent men eminent in art

FACTOR 6: CULTURAL DISINTEGRATION

.49	High death rate from syphilis
.48	Severe restriction of divorce
.48	Low percentage of population of Mohammedan religion
.42	High death rate from typhoid fever
.42	Many miles of railroad per head
.35	High death rate from tuberculosis
.34	Low density of population

ANCILLARY TECHNIQUES

Anthropologists, particularly those interested in the relations between culture and personality, have in more recent years turned to a number of auxiliary techniques which serve to supplement the major methods we have briefly described. Among these are projective tests (see Box 10.14) and standardized attitude scales (see Box 10.15).

FACTOR ANALYSIS OF CULTURE

Cattell [1949] has attempted to discover the primary dimensions of culture through the use of the method of factor analysis—a method originally designed to isolate psychological factors in the individual (see page 107).

Cattell began by selecting 69 contemporary nations which have existed ". . . during the past century, with sufficient continuity of form and for a sufficient length of time to permit reliability of historical data." For each of these 69 national cultures, Cattell then secured data from bibliographical and documentary sources on 72 different variables. The 72 variables which he used included measures of various aspects of the total society, of

internal structure and relationships, and of population characteristics.

The 2,556 intercorrelations among the 72 variables were then computed and the resulting matrix factor analyzed. The factor analysis yielded 12 factors. Of these, the six factors described in Table 10.5 are of most interest to us. The "loadings" given in the table are the correlations of each variable with the factor in question.

In the first factor—Size—it is of interest that many political assassinations, riots, and local rebellions, and a high ratio of divorces to marriages are positively associated with size of country. Cattell interprets this finding as indicating that "sheer size is connected systematically with difficulty of organization and movement."

Cattell interprets the second factor—Cultural Assertion—as essentially a psychological one. "Countries high in this factor show, in addition to urbanization and a high ratio of skilled to unskilled occupations, sustained self-assertion both in cultural and in international affairs. They are sociable as opposed to seclusive countries. . . ."

Enlightened Affluence indicates ". . . ease

of living accompanied by good order and foresight." The association between wealth and high expenditure on education, high musical creativity, and low degree of government censorship of the press may be both a consequence of affluence and a cause of affluence.

Through the six variables defining Thoughtful Industriousness, Cattell finds ". . . a consistent theme of reasonableness in social relations, an objective scientific attitude in cultural matters, and a society organized for intelligent citizens. . . . The factor is thus essentially one determined by culture habits of fair-minded, intelligent reasoning and freedom from emotional, prejudiced thinking in social affairs."

A Babbitt would be comfortable in a culture which scored high on the factor of Bourgeois Philistinism. As Cattell notes,

A single glance suffices to recognize these as the pattern of "bourgeois" culture, or the "Philistine" virtues of Victorian laissez-faire society, as defined, for example, by Samuel Butler and praised by Samuel Smiles. It comprises thrift, industry, postponement of marriage, cautious decorum and comfort, . . . sentimentalism rather than the stark emotions of art, and the combination of reflective liberalism and powerful commercial interests which produces a multiplication of political parties.

The final factor—Cultural Disintegration—is interpreted as ". . . not merely a factor of poor morale, but of poor morale associated with cultural contradictions, i.e., a lack of integration either through cultural decay or through a melting pot of cultural formation." The locus for this inference is mainly the high death rates ". . . connected with moral depravity, poor social organization, and individual irresponsibility."

Cattell's study is a pioneering attempt to apply a statistical technique to the analysis of the content of culture. Similar factor analyses of the ethnographic variables on the cultures of the world which are in the Human Rela-

tions Area Files might prove of value to the student of culture.

TO RECAPITULATE

In delineating the culture of a society, the anthropologist may use a number of different methods of study.

The major anthropological approach is the field method, in which the anthropologist lives closely with the people he is studying. In constructing a picture of the culture, he makes use of observations of behavior in a wide variety of the major areas of living and interviews selected informants to elicit their conceptions of various cultural arrangements. Occasional instances in which two anthropologists have studied the same culture through the field method suggest that the method may yield discrepant results.

The method of content analysis—a technique for describing in a systematic manner the manifest content of communications—has been applied to the study of culture. Its use for this purpose is based on the assumption that the manifest content of such cultural products as books, plays, movies, etc., sheds light on basic beliefs and values of the culture. The validity of the use of content analysis in the study of culture change and in the comparative study of cultures has been questioned.

In the cross-cultural method, each society is assigned a score on each of a number of selected cultural dimensions (the mode of the society). The patterns of scores of various societies can then be compared to discover similarities and differences among the societies.

A number of auxiliary techniques have come to be used to supplement the major anthropological methods, especially by anthropologists interested in the relations between personality and culture. Among these are the projective test technique and the attitude scale.

Though the method of factor analysis may hold promise as a way of identifying the main

Walter Goldschmidt and Robert B. Edgerton, anthropologists at the University of California, Los Angeles, have experimented with a projective technique for the study of cultural values.

The test was given to 44 adult male members of the Menomini Indian tribe in northern Wisconsin. Earlier work had shown that the Menomini can be classified into five categories which represent a rough continuum of degree of acculturation to the white culture: Native Oriented, Peyote, Transitional, Lower Status Acculturated, and Elite Acculturated.

Each of the eleven test pictures presented a choice between the values accepted by the different subgroups on the reservation. Two questions were asked of the respondents: What is happening in the scene? What should the actors do?

Of the 11 pictures five gave positive results, that is, the descriptions given by the subgroups were an appropriate reflection of their cultural values. Card 2 in the series is reproduced below.

It was anticipated that the Native Oriented and the Peyote, who value "taking it easy," would approve the fishing, whereas the Elite Acculturated, who value work, would condemn it. These predictions were confirmed. Sample stories told were as follows:

Elite Acculturated. "These are just damn lazy fishermen. That one don't care to fish at all and the other can hardly hold up the pole. They better be careful they don't fall asleep and fall in the river. These other guys are going to work. It could be a factory or a mill." [What should they do?] "Those fishing should get up and go to work with the others. Being lazy will never help. I worked hard and went to school and studied and got a good job that requires specialized training and once I got this job all the lazy guys who wouldn't go to school on a bet want to know why I got a good job. They don't know nothing or understand what it is like to work hard and study for a position, but they want to make just as much money as somebody who has had specialized training. They try to drag down anybody who gets ahead." *(Continued)*

Native Oriented. "Fishing, huh? Two people, a man and boy. Kinda sleepy fishing. Just taking life easy, not trying to catch fish. Maybe it's a father and his boy. Other men are going to work. Looks like in the morning. Maybe that is like the mill they are working in." [What should the fishermen do?] "Fish, and in a while they'll go home. They better just enjoy life." [What should the workers do?] "Go to work. After work, they can enjoy life too."

Goldschmidt, W., and Edgerton, R. B. *A picture technique for the study of values.* Amer. Anthropologist, *1961,* **63,** *26–47.*

dimensions for the description of culture, it has not yet been widely used.

The culture of an American town

Barker and Wright's [1954] study of life in "Midwest"—a town in Kansas with a population of 707—is the first attempt to describe in a comprehensive, quantitative way the psychological living conditions of people in a small American town. The study is a valuable, pioneering effort to apply the techniques of social psychology to the description of the *explicit* culture of a community. The results clearly indicate the ubiquitous, pervasive effects of culture upon behavior. Almost all of the time of the people of Midwest is spent in settings in which their behavior is modified by cultural forces. This is culture at work.

Because of the importance of the Barker and Wright study we shall discuss it in some detail.

BEHAVIOR SETTINGS

The first task of the investigators was to identify and define an analytic unit which would be suitable for the task of describing "psychological living conditions." The major unit adopted was the *behavior setting.* (This concept is equivalent to our concept of standard interpersonal behavior event.) This unit was defined as a discriminable pattern of be-

havior involving two or more persons and behavior objects which is independent of particular individuals, and which is attached to a particular place, objects, and time. An example is the Presbyterian worship service—a pattern of interacting behaviors which takes place in a particular room in a particular church building at a particular time with particular behavior objects, e.g., pulpit, pews, hymnals, etc., arranged in a particular design. The worship service persists relatively unchanged year after year despite a complete turnover of the persons involved in the service.

The investigators identified and enumerated all the behavior settings in Midwest publicly recognized by the community. This involved a content analysis of the public literature produced in the town during one year— the town newspaper, school programs and schedules, church bulletins, placards, handbills, etc.—to secure all possible "public" behavior settings. Of the 2,030 behavior settings thus identified, 1,445 were family behavior settings in homes of the community (e.g., holding a "baby shower" for expectant mothers), and 585 were community behavior settings in public places (e.g., Presbyterian worship service).

DYNAMICS OF BEHAVIOR SETTINGS. Before further discussion of the results of the survey of behavior settings of Midwest, we might refer to Barker and Wright's observation that there were often abrupt and marked changes in the behavior of individuals as they passed from one behavior setting to another. They illustrate this point by describing the well-known changes in the behavior of children during a school day. Table 10.6 summarizes the behavior patterns of children of the second grade as they pass from the behavior setting, Classroom before School, through the settings Academic Activities, Playground, and Music Class. The same children display these different behavior patterns in these different behavior settings day after day. Year after year different second grade children display similar patterns of behavior in the behavior settings of the school. In the words of the authors, "Behavior settings coerce behavior and vice versa."

OCCUPANCY TIME

After enumerating these behavior settings, the investigators attempted to describe them in an objective and workable manner. They chose six descriptive variables, one of which was *occupancy time*. The occupancy time is the total number of hours Midwest residents spent in a setting during the survey year. This was computed by multiplying the number of times the setting occurred during the survey year, by the number of persons who entered the setting at each occurrence, by the time in hours these persons spent in the setting. For example, Presbyterian Worship Service had an occupancy time of 3,750 hours; Baby Shower, an occupancy time of 308 hours.

The primary locus of the behavior of people in Midwest was in the home. During the survey year, they spent 5,130,000 hours in family settings, 1,030,658 hours in community settings, and 330,620 hours in settings outside the boundaries of the town (foreign settings).

The occupancy time of these three classes of behavior settings for different age groups, expressed as mean number of hours per day per person, is given in Figure 10.1. The amount of time spent in family settings decreased sharply from infancy to adolescence. In the adult and aged groups, family settings again were dominant.

Community settings were also important in the lives of Midwesterners. The inhabitants of the town spent 25 per cent of their waking hours in community settings. Males, white

BOX 10.15: *Does Uncle Sammy run?*

Ralph H. Turner, sociologist at the University of California, Los Angeles, constructed Guttman scales to measure preoccupation with competitiveness and preoccupation with social acceptance. The two scales were found to meet the usual standards of reproducibility (see page 155). The two scales were administered to samples of American and English college students to check the widespread notion that Americans are a peculiarly competitive people who, at the same time, paradoxically strive to be liked by everyone.

Turner found no differences of note between American and English college students on either of the two scales. In both national samples, competitiveness scores were higher for men than for women. Contrary to expectation, however, women did not show a greater preoccupation with social acceptance than men.

Turner suggests that the similarities in the social and economic structure of the American and English societies may produce similar preoccupations with competitiveness and social acceptance. The "closed" Englishman conceals his preoccupations; the "open" American reveals his preoccupations.

Turner, R. H. Preoccupation with competitiveness and social acceptance among American and English college students. Sociometry, 1960, 23, 307–325.

TABLE 10.6: PATTERNS OF BEHAVIOR OF THE SAME CHILDREN IN DIFFERENT BEHAVIOR SETTINGS [Barker and Wright, 1954]

	BEHAVIOR SETTING			
	Classroom, before school	*Academic activities*	*Playground*	*Music class*
Milieu	Second grade classroom, 8:30–8:50 A.M. Monday through Friday	Scheduled periods for work; books, paper, pencils, etc.	School playground at recess; swings, teeter, balls, etc.	Scheduled period in music room; piano, music books, etc.
Behavior pattern	Unorganized activity; free locomotion; medium tempo, noise, and energy; cheerful mood; large variety of behavior	Organized activity; little change in positions; slow tempo, noise, and energy; serious mood; limited variety of behavior	Unorganized or partly organized activities; fast tempo, loudness, and vitality; exuberant mood; large variety of behavior	Organized activities; variation in tempo, noise, and energy; medium cheerfulness; little variety of behavior, singing predominant

FIGURE 10.1: Average time spent in family, community, and foreign behavior settings by the different age groups in "Midwest," Kansas. [Adapted from Barker and Wright, 1954.]

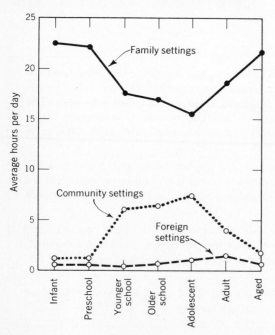

persons, and members of social class I (upper middle) spent more time in community settings and less time in family settings than females, Negro persons, and members of social classes II and III (lower middle and upper lower, respectively).

The 585 community behavior settings fell into 107 categories. A few varieties were found to take up a large proportion of the total occupancy time. Thus, as Table 10.7 shows, 70 per cent of the occupancy time was spent in 16 varieties of settings. The Occupancy Index of a given setting is the percentage of total time in community settings spent in that setting.

ACTION PATTERNS

Another important variable used to describe behavior settings was *action patterns*, which are the functions of behavior settings, e.g., eating for nutritive purposes at a church social, playing games for recreational purposes at a church social, etc. Table 10.8 presents the 13 action patterns identified, together with the

THE SOCIAL AND CULTURAL HABITAT

TABLE 10.7: VARIETIES OF COMMUNITY BEHAVIOR SETTINGS WHERE MIDWEST
RESIDENTS SPENT THE GREATEST AMOUNT OF TIME [Barker and Wright, 1954]

Variety of setting	Prominent behavior characteristics	Occupancy Index (per cent of 1,030,658 hours)
School classes	Formal teaching and learning	12.4
Trafficways	Traveling between behavior settings	7.5
Grocery, locker, and feed stores	Buying and selling food	5.7
Motor vehicle sales and service	Buying, selling, and repairing automobiles, trucks, and equipment	5.4
Drug, variety, and department stores	Buying and selling clothing, household accessories, and medicines	5.1
Indoor entertainments	Attending and producing public entertainments	4.8
Restaurants and taverns	Eating, drinking, and preparing food in public cafes and taverns	4.5
Government and school offices	Office work	4.0
Home appliance, hardware, implement, and furniture store	Buying, selling, and repairing home and farm equipment	3.8
Attorneys, insurance, and real estate offices	Legal work, buying and selling insurance and real estate	3.3
Indoor athletic contests	Attending and participating in indoor athletic contests	2.9
Building contractors and material suppliers	Buying and selling materials and equipment, and erecting and altering buildings	2.9
Hotels, rooming houses, and nurseries	Providing temporary lodging	2.3
Telephone and electric offices	Providing and maintaining telephone and electric service	2.0
Barbers and beauticians	Providing and securing hairdressing	1.8
Hallways and cloakrooms	Going from one setting to another within buildings. Putting on and removing outdoor garments	1.3
Total		69.7

Occupancy Index and the Prominence Index of each. The Prominence Index was determined by a rating procedure in which an action pattern of primary importance in a large number of behavior settings where Midwesterners spent a large amount of time was given a high index score.

The most prominent action pattern in the community settings of Midwest was Social Contact. The next most prominent action pattern was Recreation. As the investigators note: "Sociability and play formed the behavioral background of almost all the community behavior settings of Midwest. Midwest was, above all, a social town and one where having some fun was widespread. Midwesterners carried their social and recreational life into almost all behavior areas of the town."

TABLE 10.8: OCCUPANCY INDEXES AND PROMINENCE INDEXES OF ACTION PATTERNS [After Barker and Wright, 1954]

Action pattern	Occupancy Index	Prominence Index
Social contact	27	1,053
Recreation	14	294
Business	30	270
Earning a living	29	203
Education	15	195
Government	10	70
Religion	4	60
Aesthetics	6	48
Nutrition	9	36
Physical health	7	7
Orientation	3	6
Personal appearance	2	4
Philanthropy	....	....

Work (Business and Earning a Living) action patterns were also prominent, work settings consuming more than one-third of the public time of Midwesterners. Education was next in prominence. Formal teaching and learning in Midwest were not restricted to children; about 40 per cent of the settings which featured formal teaching and learning were devoted to adults.

After education, four action patterns had approximately the same degree of prominence in Midwest: Government, Religion, Aesthetics, and Nutrition (dining in public places). Action patterns concerned with Physical Health, Orientation (asking for information), Personal Appearance, and Philanthropy had the lowest levels of prominence in Midwest.

MIDWEST'S CULTURAL LANDSCAPE

This study of the psychological living conditions of the people of Midwest can be called, as indeed Barker and Wright do call it, a study in *psychological ecology,* concerned as it is with the "behavioral landscape" of Midwest. In so far as this is true, the study gives us a picture of the salient characteristics of the cultural milieu of Midwest children. It is in this milieu that the children of Midwest become socialized—a milieu sketched by Barker and Wright as follows:

In 1951/52, the variety of behavior settings available to Midwest children was limited; it was only a part of the total range occurring in American culture. . . . A Midwest child on a Sunday afternoon could not visit an aquarium, ride in a subway, eat pizza in an Italian restaurant, or attend a chamber music concert. Opportunities for highly specialized training and experience were not available in the town.

The actual variety of psychological situations and behavior in which individual Midwest children engaged was, nevertheless, great. It may have been greater than that of children living in cities. A highly literate and technologically advanced segment of American life was represented in Midwest. Because this rich segment occurred within a small geographical area, because there was relatively little specialization within the behavior settings, and because there was pressure to enter many settings, Midwest children participated in a wide range of psychological situations and they engaged in a great diversity of behavior. . . .

Midwest provided its children with a general behavioral context in which sociability, play, work, and education dominated the behavioral landscape.

Occupational and social class subcultures in American society

In a society as complex as the American society, there are a number of subcultures or part-cultures with more or less characteristic and distinctive designs for living. The major subcultures in the American society are the ethnic, social class, and regional subcultures. In addition, occupational subcultures exert a profound influence over the life careers of individuals.

The importance of these various subcultures in molding the behavior of their members can be illustrated by indicating the impact of social-class membership upon the individual. As we have seen (page 315), each social class carries and maintains a more or less distinct culture. The share of an individual in the American culture will be determined partly, then, by the social-class group to which he belongs. If he belongs to the upper social class, he will receive one cultural curriculum; if he belongs to the lower class, he will receive a different curriculum. The two curricula will have in common only the universals in the American culture. And even the supposed "universals" will actually be somewhat different: the specific form of the American language (diction, pronunciation, grammar) used by the individual will vary by social class; so also will the clothes he wears; the house he lives in; and even his conception of proper child rearing. The American culture is, then, perhaps more appropriately called the American *cultures*.

OCCUPATIONAL SUBCULTURES
AND CHILD-REARING PRACTICES

Miller and Swanson [1958] collaborated in a study of the relation between occupational status in the American society and child-rearing practices. A representative sample of 582 mothers living in the Detroit area was interviewed.

Among other things, the investigators were interested in examining the differences between entrepreneurial and organizational families in ways of child rearing. A family was classified as entrepreneurial if the husband met any one of the following criteria: (1) was self-employed; (2) received at least half of his income from profits, fees, or commissions; (3) worked in a small-scale organization, i.e., one having only two levels of supervision. Organizational families were those in which the husband worked for someone else in an organization of at least moderate complexity (three or more supervisory levels) and got most of his income from salary or wages.

The investigators describe the world of entrepreneurial parents as one in which maintaining and improving one's status requires doing and saying the right thing at the right time. Controlled, rational behavior and the denial of momentary impulses to achieve long-term goals are required for success in the competitive world of the entrepreneur. Success in the world of the entrepreneur also requires that one must be independent and able to take risks to capitalize on opportunities. People and things must be actively and boldly manipulated.

The world of organizational parents is more secure and relaxed. To function smoothly in an organization requires that the individual cooperate with and accommodate to others, subordinating himself willingly to authority. The behavior of the "organization man" is governed to a considerable degree by the external controls exercised by his fellows and superiors in the organization.

These considerations led the investigators to predict that entrepreneurial mothers would be more likely than organizational mothers to use child-rearing practices which emphasize self-control and an active, manipulative approach to life. A comparison of entrepreneurial and organizational mothers with respect to various training practices gave general support to this prediction. Thus it was found that entrepreneurial mothers are significantly more likely than organizational mothers to:

Give delayed attention to a crying baby or give no attention.

Feed the baby on a schedule.

Use symbolic punishments.

Use harsh means to stop the child who sucked parts of his body.

Say that the child did not touch his sex organs.

Say the parents felt it necessary to do something when the child touched his sex organs.

Feel it good to leave a child at home frequently with a competent woman while the mother shops or visits because the mother benefits.

Agree that a child should be on his own as soon as possible to solve his own problems.

Child-rearing practices tend to reflect and to perpetuate the way of life of the family.

CLASS SUBCULTURES AND
MECHANISMS OF DEFENSE

In other studies, Miller and Swanson [1960] investigated the relations among social class, methods of child rearing, and means of resolving inner conflict. Their sample consisted of 112 white boys in the seventh to the ninth grades whose families originally came from northern and western Europe. The social-class position of the boys was determined by means of a weighted composite of father's occupation and education. The distribution of social classes in the sample was: upper middle, 24; lower middle, 35; upper working, 34; and lower working, 19.

In one study, Miller and Swanson predicted that boys in the middle class would be more inclined toward repression than would boys in the working class. They defined repression as "the tendency to remember more successes, or completed tasks, than failures, or incompleted tasks, in a test in which the subjects were highly motivated to succeed." Sixteen short, timed tests (verbal, drawing, motor speed, perceptual, attention), described as tests of ability to succeed, were individually administered. The time limits were arbitrarily so arranged that only one half of the tasks could be completed. After the testing session the boys were asked to recall as many of the tasks as they could. If a boy remembered more completed than uncompleted tasks, an inclination to repress failures was assumed to be operative.

The results are given in Table 10.9. Note that middle-class boys were significantly more inclined to repress failures than were working-class boys.

In a second study, Miller and Swanson tested the prediction that middle-class boys

TABLE 10.9: SOCIAL CLASS AND RELATIVE RECALL OF COMPLETED AND UNCOMPLETED TASKS [After Miller and Swanson, 1960]

Recalled	Working-class boys	Middle-class boys
More completed tasks	15	30
Equal number of completed and uncompleted tasks	13	13
More uncompleted tasks	21	14
	49	57

TABLE 10.10: SOCIAL CLASS AND DEFENSES AGAINST OVERT AGGRESSION [After Miller and Swanson, 1960]

	No. of working-class boys	No. of middle-class boys
Increased defense against aggression	12	26
No increased defense against aggression	29	21
	41	47

would be more inclined to inhibit the direct expression of aggression than would working-class boys. The boys wrote endings for three stories; the experimenter then aroused the hostility of the boys; they then wrote endings for three more stories. In each story, an adult does something to a boy which, although well-intentioned, is very frustrating and tends to make the boy angry. For example, in one story, Don, whose art teacher has helped him to become a talented artist, works for a month on a painting for an art contest and does an exceptionally fine piece of work. The teacher, who has always criticized Don for his sloppiness, inadvertently puts the painting on a table covered with glue and in removing it rips it beyond repair.

Hostility was aroused by telling the boys that their mothers as a group felt that "their sons were once attractive children with bright futures and were now neither providing the pleasures of the past nor fulfilling their early promise."

Three criteria were used to identify defenses against aggression: (1) The main character in the ending written by the subject must not express his anger directly; (2) he must distort his interpretation of the frustrating act of the adult; and (3) the distortion must result in socially acceptable behavior. The number of these defenses was counted in the stories told by each boy, before and after arousal of hostility.

Table 10.10 shows that after the arousal of hostility the sons of white-collar workers exceeded the sons of blue-collar workers in making increased use of defenses against the direct expression of aggression.

CLASS SUBCULTURES AND SOCIAL CONDUCT

A number of studies have indicated that high-status persons in the American society are much more active in formal community organizations than are low-status persons (see Box 3.8, page 92).

The results of a study by Brown [1953] are typical of the findings on this problem. He interviewed two samples of persons in three Pennsylvania rural communities who had been identified by "key informants" as the most active and the most inactive participants in community organizations. The relation between three objective indices of status of these persons and the amount of their participation in community activities is shown in Table 10.11. It will be seen that high-status persons are much more active in the community than are low-status persons.

Analysis of the interview data suggested that high-status persons felt they were *expected* to assume a leadership role in community organizations and to participate actively. In a second study, Brown interviewed 69 persons to determine whether the members of a community *do* have role expectations about participation in community activities of persons occupying different status ranks. He found the rank order of occupations on being expected to take part in organizations was: business men, professional men, farm owners, skilled workers, clerks, laborers, tenant farmers. The better-educated people were expected to be more active than the less educated. And high-income people were expected to be more active than low-income people.

The American core culture

Few anthropologists have attempted to describe the universals in the American culture—those cultural elements which most Americans share. The task is a staggering one because of the overwhelming diversity and complexity of the American culture. In this section we will briefly describe one attempt to develop a quantitative measure of degree of acculturation to the American core culture.

In a study of the relations between acculturation and illness, Ruesch, Jacobsen, and Loeb [1948] developed a scale for measuring

TABLE 10.11: ACTIVE AND INACTIVE COMMUNITY PARTICIPA-
TION AND STATUS [After Brown, 1953]

Status indices and categories	Inactive per cent	Active per cent
Family income group:	(N = 212)	(N = 278)
Lowest income	53	22
Middle income	37	36
Highest income	10	42
Total	100	100
Grades of schooling completed:	(N = 255)	(N = 336)
Eight or less	63	24
Nine to eleven	18	13
Twelve	14	37
More than twelve	5	26
Total	100	100
Occupation of male respondents or husbands of female respondents:	(N = 271)	(N = 338)
Professional	2	13
Farmer	39	36
Proprietor	4	21
Clerical	1	9
Skilled and semiskilled laborer	35	18
Unskilled laborer	19	3
Total	100	100

degree of conformity to the American core culture, defined as ". . . general attitudes and orientations which are shared by the majority of Americans."

The scale consists of 24 items. On each item, the individual is rated on a four-point scale for degree of his conformity to that aspect of the core culture. Scale point 4 indicates complete conformity; scale point 1 indicates the greatest deviation from the American core culture. The descriptions of the scale categories were based upon anthropological and sociological studies of the American culture and upon personal observations of the authors.

The 24 items in the scale and the response to each which indicates complete conformity to the American core culture (i.e., scale point 4 responses) are given below.

1. *Nativity:* Native-born of native-born parents.

2. *Culture of origin:* Born and educated in the American culture.

3. *Attitude towards American culture:* Unaware of cultural differences. American culture only one known to individual. No interest in going abroad.

4. *Attitudes towards parents and family structure:* Parents are primarily friends and guides rather than punitive authority. Matriarchal family structure or authority evenly divided between parents.

5. *Religion:* Member of any of large Protestant denominations.

6. *Name:* First, middle and last name according to Anglo-Saxon use.

7. *Mother tongue:* American, English, Scottish, Irish, Canadian-English, New Zealandish–English.

8. *Accent:* No discernible accent.

9. *Reading:* Reads American papers and books only, exclusive of foreign professional publications.

10. *External appearance:* Style of dress reflects American local standards and fashions; posture, relaxed, casual and informal; gestures, minimal; physical culture conforms to American ideals of slender, youthful appearance.

11. *Choice of menu:* Protein eater.

12. *Preparation of food and use of condiments:* Quickly prepared dishes; no sauces; no spices; catsup and other condiments added at time of meal. Food served in large pieces. Leftovers thrown away.

13. *Attitude towards food:* Food is nourishment, but provides no particular sensual gratification. Convenience and expediency greatest concern. Emphasis on food hygiene, vitamins and calories.

14. *Non-alcoholic drinks:* Coffee, milk, fruit juices, cola drinks, milk shakes.

15. *Drinking habits and alcoholic beverages:* No separation of sexes for alcohol consumption. Cocktails before dinner, highballs after dinner. Preference for cocktails made of whiskey, gin, rum. Beer with food.

16. *Recreation:* Passive, non-organized types of relaxation; spectator sports and gambling enjoyed. No separation of sexes except for occasional hunting or fishing trips of men and sewing and knitting of women.

17. *Characteristic personal traits:* Sense of humor, casual, warm, conformist, playful, fair, vivacious, healthy, good sport, happy-go-lucky, self-sufficient, tough.

18. *Ideal traits wished for:* Relaxed, democratic, casual, successful, easy-going, energetic, fair-minded, tough, flexible, cheerful, enterprising, non-argumentative, resourceful.

19. *Attitudes toward women:* Women emancipated; they vote and work. Status not related to marriage. Women considered equal to men.

20. *Attitudes towards public and success:* Winning the public is of prime importance. Success measured in terms of money and popularity.

21. *Residence:* Resides in areas determined by class membership. If member of lower class, less separation from minority ethnic groups than if member of middle or upper class. Mixes with neighborhood group.

22. *Associations:* If a joiner, belongs to American type of lodge, club, or association without ethnic slant. Same friends as in childhood. No members of minority ethnic groups among close friends.

23. *Festivities and special occasions:* Celebrates official or local holidays of American character, e.g., Thanksgiving, Fourth of July, July 24 (Mormon holiday), etc.

24. *Music:* Prefers popular American music: jazz, jitterbug, musical comedy, swing, boogie-woogie, Bing Crosby, Negro spirituals, etc.

The investigators interviewed three kinds of samples of individuals—native-born of American parentage, native-born of mixed or foreign parentage, foreign-born—and rated the individuals on the 24-item scale. The results are shown in Table 10.12, together with similar data from Barker and Wright on the parents of 12 children in Midwest. Note that this latter group proves to be the most highly ac-

TABLE 10.12: MEAN SCORES OF SELECTED GROUPS ON SCALE OF ACCULTURATION TO AMERICAN CORE CULTURE [Adapted from Ruesch, Jacobsen, and Loeb, 1948; Barker and Wright, 1954]

	N	Mean scale score
Parents of Midwest children	24	93.4
Native-born of American parentage	25	90.4
Native-born of mixed or foreign parentage	25	85.4
Foreign-born	25	78.7

culturated to the American core culture—obtaining a mean score value of 93.4 as compared with a theoretical maximum of 96. Note also that though the foreign-born are the least acculturated, they too show a very substantial degree of acculturation—mean score value of 78.7 as compared with a theoretical minimum of 24.

Culture change

The culture of a society is not a static construction in time and space; it is, rather, in a state of constant change. As members of the culture question traditional solutions and invent new solutions to problems of living which they and their fellows face, the culture changes. As we have said, man is the originator of his culture; he is also a creative changer. Any description of a living culture is, to some degree, a time-bound description.

AN ILLUSTRATION—INFANT TRAINING

Bronfenbrenner [1958] has provided us with an interesting analysis of changes in infant-training practices among middle-class American mothers in the period between 1930 and 1955. This study of change in an institutionalized way is important for two reasons. First, the infant is introduced to his culture by the way his mother feeds him, weans him, and manages his toilet training. The "culture of the nursery" may have long-enduring effects upon the individual. Second, we have in this study, as we shall see, an illustration of culture change brought about by changes in the beliefs of opinion leaders—child psychologists and psychiatrists—communicated to the public, among other ways, through a government bulletin.

Bronfenbrenner's analysis was prompted by a controversy regarding the relative permissiveness in infant training of working-class and middle-class mothers. In 1940 Davis and Havighurst [1946] studied social class and color differences in child rearing among samples of Chicago mothers. They found impressive evidence that middle-class mothers ". . . place their children under a stricter regime, with more frustration of their impulses than do lower-class parents." For the next eight years, this conclusion was commonly accepted as a valid statement of class differences in socialization practices. And many social scientists indulged in a sentimental revolt against their own middle-class backgrounds, identifying with the reportedly gentle, permissive, psychologically free, and healthy working class.

In 1948–1949, however, Sears, Maccoby, and Levin [1957] made a study of child-rearing practices which in general contradicted the Davis and Havighurst findings: these investigators found middle-class mothers in Boston were "more permissive" than lower-class mothers. (For further details of the Boston study, see Box 9.3, page 317.)

The Chicago and Boston investigators differed in their interpretations of their contradictory findings. Bronfenbrenner has attempted a "reappraisal" of the issue. He assembled all available studies of social-class differences in infant-training practices, published and unpublished, done during the period from 1930 to 1955. These data he has examined for time trends. Part of his analysis is summarized in Table 10.13.

Bronfenbrenner concludes:

> All these figures on timing point to the same generalization. In the earlier period, middle-class mothers were exerting more pressure; they weaned their children from the breast and bottle and carried out bowel and bladder training before their working-class counterparts. But in the last ten years the trend has been reversed—it is now the middle-class mother who trains later.

INSTITUTIONALIZED WAYS—BELIEFS AND NORMS. Bronfenbrenner notes that these trends are given significance by Wolfenstein's [1953] content analysis of successive editions of *Infant Care*, a bulletin published by the U.S.

378

TABLE 10.13: TIME TRENDS IN CLASS DIFFERENCES IN TOILET-TRAINING PRACTICES [After Bronfenbrenner, 1958]

M indicates middle class began or completed training earlier than lower class; L indicates the reverse

Sample	Year of study	Beginning of bowel training	Ending of bowel training	Beginning of bladder training	Ending of bladder training
National	1931		M		M
National	1932		M		
Chicago	1940	M	M	M	L
Detroit	1942	M	M	L	M
Detroit	1945	L		M	
Eugene (Oregon)	1947–1948	L	M	L	L
Boston	1948–1949	M	L		
New Haven	1950–1951	L			
Palo Alto	1951	L			

Children's Bureau. Bulletins published in the period 1929–1938 Wolfenstein characterizes as follows:

> . . . a pervasive emphasis on regularity, doing everything by the clock. Weaning and introduction of solid foods are to be accomplished with great firmness, never yielding for a moment to the baby's resistance. . . . bowel training . . . must be carried out with great determination as early as possible . . . the main danger which the child presented at this time was that of dominating the parents. Successful child training meant winning out against the child in the struggle for domination.

In the next decade, however, "all this was changed":

> The child became remarkably harmless . . . His main active aim was to explore his world. . . . When not engaged in exploratory undertakings, the baby needs care and attention; and giving these when he demands them, far from making him a tyrant, will make him less demanding later on. At this time mildness is advocated in all areas: thumbsucking and masturbation are not to be interfered with; weaning and toilet training are to be accomplished later and more gently.

Bronfenbrenner concludes:

> Our analysis suggests that the mothers not only read these books [Spock, B., *Baby and Child Care* and similar volumes] but take them seriously, and that their treatment of the child is affected accordingly. Moreover, middle-class mothers not only read more but are also more responsive; they alter their behavior earlier and faster than their working-class counterparts.

The world does move; culture does change.

CHAPTER GUIDES AND GLOSSARY

GUIDE 31: *In coping with their common problems the members of a society try various solutions, certain of which become firmly established and are transmitted to successive generations as the culture of that society*

GUIDE 32: *The culture of a people consists of their distinctive modal patterns of behavior and the underlying regulatory beliefs, values, norms, and premises*

content analysis. A method for the systematic and quantitative description of the manifest content of a communication. It consists in discovering and tabulating the frequency with which certain specified elements occur. The method has been used to describe culture by analyzing the manifest content of books, movies, and other communications within the culture.

core culture. That part of the total culture of a society which is shared by all members of the society.

cross-cultural method. A method for making comparative studies of different cultures. Each society in the sample is assigned a score (the mode of the society) on each of a number of selected cultural dimensions. The patterns of scores of the various societies may then be compared to discover similarities and differences.

cultural beliefs. All the cognitions—ideas, knowledge, lore, superstitions, myths, and legends—shared by the members of a society or by the typical occupants of various positions in the society.

cultural norms. The rules or standards which specify appropriate and inappropriate behavior in standard behavior events. A norm also specifies the rewards for appropriate behavior and the punishments for inappropriate behavior. Norms include *folkways* and *mores.*

cultural premises. Tacit assumptions held by members of a society about the nature of persons, objects, and events in their world. Such unverbalized generalizations may underlie and integrate seemingly unrelated actions of members of the society.

cultural values. An especially important class of beliefs shared by the members of a society, or by the typical occupants of various positions in the society, of what is desirable—what ought to be—and what is undesirable.

culture. The pattern of all those arrangements, material or behavioral, which have been adopted by a society as the traditional ways

of solving the problems of its members. Culture includes all the *institutionalized ways* and the implicit *cultural beliefs, norms, values,* and *premises* which underlie and govern conduct.

explicit culture. The typical and distinctive patterns of behavior of a people. These patterns are ascertained by noting regularities in the actions of members of the society.

field method. The major method for the study of culture. The anthropologist lives closely with the people he is studying. His data are secured by observation of the behavior of members of the culture and by interviews with selected informants.

folkways. A class of cultural norms which specify behavior in those standard behavior events regarded by society as of relatively minor importance. The punishment for nonconformity to folkways is informal and variable.

implicit culture. The total set of cultural beliefs, values, norms, and premises which underlie and determine the observed regularities in behavior making up the *explicit culture.*

institutionalized way. A system of standard behavior events, together with their associated regulatory patterns, which represents the arrangement of a society for solving a problem of living.

mores. A class of norms which specify proper behavior in standard behavior events of vital importance to the members of a society. Violation of mores is drastically punished, often through legal action.

standard behavior event. The pattern of behavior of a typical individual in a situation standard in a culture. The most important class is the *standard interpersonal behavior event* which is defined as the system of reciprocal role behaviors in a given standard situation of two or more persons who are typical members of their respective positions.

subculture. That part of the total culture of a society which is distinctive of a segment of the society, e.g., an ethnic group, a social-class group, a regional group.

Part Four: GROUPS, ORGANIZATIONS, AND THE INDIVIDUAL

WE STARTED OUR STUDY OF SOCIAL PSYCHOLOGY BY EXAMINING
the basic psychological determinants of behavior; we then
considered how these psychological factors interact to produce and
change attitudes; finally, we described language, society, and
culture—the major dimensions of man's social cosmos. In this
manner we have traced the development of sensate man into
thinking and wanting man, into valuing man, into social man.

In this last part of the book, we examine social man behaving in
his own immediate fragment of society. For man does not live in a
cosmos; he lives in a microcosm. Every society consists of many and
varied groups and organizations. These groups and organizations
catch up each one of us; and no matter what our weaknesses and
strengths, predilections and aversions, each of us is influenced and
constrained by our groups. Each of us also helps form and re-form
our groups. We begin this final study, then, by examining the most
common and basic characteristics of the groups and organizations
within whose grooves the individual moves, and by whose
enforcement agents he is pushed around.

11: GROUPS AND ORGANIZATIONS

EVERY INDIVIDUAL, AT LEAST IN OUR PRESENT complex societies, is a member of many different social groups—groups which are vitally significant to his individual welfare. These groups are usually divided into two categories: *psychological groups* and *social organizations*. A brief definition and characterization of these two kinds of social groups may suggest how and why the influence of each of these two types of social groups on the individual differs.

A psychological group may be defined as two or more persons who meet the following conditions: (1) the relations among the members are *interdependent*—each member's behavior influences the behavior of each of the others; (2) the members *share an ideology*—a set of beliefs, values, and norms which regulates their mutual conduct. This ideology is developed as the members of the group work together on common tasks, and, in time, this ideology becomes, to some degree, peculiar to them as members of the group and sets their group apart from other groups. There are many kinds of groups which meet these criteria; families, friendship circles, political clubs; work, educational, religious, neighborhood, and recreational groups.

Many such groups are functionally related to other groups and, taken together, form *social organizations*. A social organization may be defined as an integrated system of interrelated psychological groups formed to accomplish a stated objective. A political party with its many local political clubs, leader cliques, friendship circles, etc., is clearly seen to be a social organization within this definition. So too is a factory with its many work gangs, labor-union locals, junior-executive clubs, friendship groups, and plant baseball teams.

The influence upon the individual of the various psychological groups to which he belongs is determined by certain characteristics of these groups: their specific ideologies, their structures, and the position of the individual within those structures. Similarly, every social organization has its own characteristics. The ideology, structure, and behavior of the constituent groups in an organization are influenced by these superordinate characteristics of the organization.

In this chapter, then, we shall examine the ideology, structure, and functions of both the psychological groups and the social organizations which form the social habitat of man. But first, we must look at methods for the study of groups.

Methods for the study of the structure and functioning of groups

Shortly after World War II, there was a pronounced increase in the experimental investigation of the structure and behavior of psychological groups. This "new" research interest of the social psychologist was notably spurred by the ingenious theoretical and experimental ideas of Kurt Lewin [1951]. Under the name of "group dynamics," Lewin and his associates initiated a research program which still engages the attention of many social psychologists, and much of the research work we will refer to in this and the following chapters derives directly from this program.

Characteristic of most of this work is the use of the experimental method, in which different group variables are systematically manipulated under controlled conditions. Whether carried out in the laboratory or in a natural setting in the field, such studies require careful description and quantitative measurement of relevant dimensions of group structure and functioning. Basically, there are two ways to do this. First, there are the *observation* methods. Here trained observers watch the group in action and make systematic records of what they see. Second, there are *self-report* methods. Here, as the name implies, group members themselves report on, or rate, various group characteristics.

OBSERVATION METHODS

In using the observational approach, there are two principal ways of recording the relevant information: (1) In the *rating-scale method* an expert observer assigns numerical scores to specified dimensions or categories of behavior. (2) In the *category-system method* he codes the behavior into separate categories.

RATING SCALES. Rating scales may be used to secure quantitative measures of the behavior of individual members of a group, the activities of the group as a whole, changes in the situation of the group, and other kinds of data.

In using rating scales to measure group behavior the observer may rate specific dimensions of behavior periodically throughout the course of group activity, or he may make his ratings after the group activity has ended. An example of the latter is the scale developed by Fouriezos, Hutt, and Guetzkow [1950] to rate the amount of self-oriented-need behavior displayed by each member of a conference group. Self-oriented-need behavior was defined as "behavior directed primarily to the satisfaction of the need itself, *regardless* of the effect on the attainment of the group goal." The 11-step scale ranged from 0 ("No expression of self-oriented need") to 10 ("All behavior of the self-oriented-need type").

There is some evidence that ratings yielded by this scale have empirical validity. For example, in using the scale in a study of conference groups, it was found that groups which were high in self-oriented-need behavior tended to perceive themselves as less unified than low self-oriented-need groups. (This study will be discussed in Chapter 13; see page 478.)

Sometimes it is convenient to secure a complete permanent record of the behavior of a group, which may be done by transcribing or by filming the activities of the group. These records of the total activity of the group may then, at a later time, be rated by trained judges (see the study by Davitz, Box 4.11, page 127).

CATEGORY SYSTEMS. In using a category system, the observer classifies or codes the actions of the members of the group into separate categories. The nature of a category system, e.g., the kinds of categories used, the number of categories, the range of applicability of the system to different kinds of groups, depends upon the theoretical orientation of the investigator and his research interests.

One of the best-known and most widely used category systems is that developed by Bales [1950] which he has called "interaction process analysis." Bales set out to develop a standard set of categories for classifying interaction that could be used to study *any* group regardless of its history, its function, or its composition. The categories are meant to constitute a mutually exclusive, logically exhaustive system. Table 11.1 shows the 12 categories in the system.

An observer, equipped with this category system, has the task of classifying each act of every member of the group into one of the 12 categories. The unit of observation "is

TABLE 11.1: OBSERVATION CATEGORIES IN THE BALES CATEGORY SYSTEM [Adapted from Bales, 1950]

A. EMOTIONALLY POSITIVE RESPONSES
1. *Shows solidarity,* raises others' status, gives help, reward
2. *Shows tension release,* jokes, laughs, shows satisfaction
3. *Agrees,* shows passive acceptance, understands, concurs, complies

B. PROBLEM-SOLVING RESPONSES: ANSWERS
4. *Gives suggestion,* direction, implying autonomy for other
5. *Gives opinion,* evaluation, analysis, expresses feeling, wish
6. *Gives orientation,* information, repeats, clarifies, confirms

C. PROBLEM-SOLVING RESPONSES: QUESTIONS
7. *Asks for orientation,* information, repetition, confirmation
8. *Asks for opinion,* evaluation, analysis, expression of feeling
9. *Asks for suggestion,* direction, possible ways of action

D. EMOTIONALLY NEGATIVE RESPONSES
10. *Disagrees,* shows passive rejection, formality, withholds help
11. *Shows tension,* asks for help, withdraws out of field
12. *Shows antagonism,* deflates others' status, defends or asserts self

the smallest discriminable segment of verbal or nonverbal behavior" which the observer can classify. A simple sentence is a single unit; complex sentences always contain more than one unit. Because nonverbal behavior is continuous and cannot be easily broken up into units, the observer scores the nonverbal behavior of all the members at 1-minute intervals.

Bales [1952] has given us a concrete example which will illustrate the use of the method.

The chairman brings the meeting up to

date with a few remarks. He says, "At the end of our last meeting we decided that we would have to consider our budget before laying out plans in greater detail."

The interaction observer looks over the set of twelve categories and decides that this remark is most relevant to the problem of orientation and, specifically, that it takes the form of an "attempted answer" to this problem, and so he classifies it in Category 6. The observer has already decided that he will designate the chairman by the number 1, and each person around the table in turn by the numbers 2, 3, 4, and 5. The group as a whole will be designated by the symbol 0. This remark was made by the chairman and was apparently addressed to the group as a whole, so the observer writes down the symbols 1–0 in one of the spaces following Category 6 on the observation form. In this one operation, the observer has thus isolated a unit of speech or process which he considers a proper unit for classification, has classified it according to its quality, identified the member who performed the act, and the person or persons to whom it was directed.

Later in the meeting, the following interactions took place:

Finally the chairman says, "Well . . . what do you think we should do about that piece of equipment?" The observer scores 1–0 in Category 9. Member 2 says, "I think we should get it." The observer scores 2–0 in Category 4. As Member 2 begins to support the suggestion, Member 3 breaks in with a counterargument and the discussion begins to grow heated, with more disagreement. Presently the observer notices that Member 5, who has said little up to this point, sighs heavily and begins to examine his fingernails. The observer puts down a score under Category 11.

In the meantime, Member 3, the chronic objector, comes through with a remark directed at Member 2, "Well, I never did agree about hiring that dead-head secretary. All she's got is looks, but I guess that's enough for Joe." The others laughed at this. The observer scores the first and second remarks under Category 12 as showing antagonism, and scores the

laugh which follows as tension release in Category 2.

And so it goes. As the members of the group interact with one another in working toward a solution of their problem, the observer categorizes each act, and also identifies the actor and the object or objects of the act.

The Bales category system provides a number of scores that describe quantitatively the functioning and structure of groups. The distribution of the total number of acts among the twelve categories can be computed for a group, and plotted in the form of a group profile which shows the relative frequencies of the twelve types of interaction.

An illustrative comparison of the profiles of two 5-man groups which worked on Bales' standard human-relations problem is shown in Figure 11.1. Note that the Satisfied group achieved a higher rate of suggestions and more often responded to these with agreement, rather than with negative reactions and questions, than did the Dissatisfied group. Bales reports that the profile which would be secured by averaging these two illustrative profiles is a more or less typical profile for larger samples of discussion groups. Giving orientation, opinion, and suggestions is almost always found to be more numerous than asking for orientation, opinion, or suggestions. Similarly, the positive reactions of showing agreement, tension release, and solidarity are usually found to be more numerous than the negative reactions of showing disagreement, tension, and antagonism.

Various index scores can also be derived. For example, the ratio of the number of acts in category 7, "Asks for orientation," to the number of acts in this category plus those in category 6, "Gives orientation," provides a measure of orientation difficulty.

Another kind of category system has been developed by Carter and his associates [1951a, 1951b] to study leadership in small laboratory groups. Because nonverbal tasks were used, the system includes many nonverbal behavior categories. The categories are given in Table 11.2.

RATING METHODS VS. CATEGORY SYSTEMS. In the study cited above, Carter et al. have examined the relation between ratings and category scores. After observers had coded the behavior of the members of a group using the category system, they were asked to rate each member on fifteen personal traits and four group-oriented traits. The correlations between trait ratings and category scores were all positive. When the reliabilities of the two scores were high, the agreements were found to be highest. These results suggest that under ideal circumstances rating scales and category systems yield comparable data. This ideal is difficult to reach, however, and the investigator is usually faced with the choice of using one or the other method. The nature of the problem and the research resources available will be determining factors. In general, the category method seems to be more reliable than rating methods, but it is also more costly.

PARTICIPANT OBSERVATION. Rating scales and category systems have been developed and used in the study of groups under more or less controlled conditions. The study of "natural" groups, observed under uncontrolled conditions, raises new problems of observation. The natural group is mobile and engages in a variety of behaviors not under the control of the investigator.

The method of *participant observation* has been used by various investigators to study groups in their natural settings. In this method the observer participates with the group in its various activities. A continuing record of the frequency and kinds of interactions among the members of the group is made. From these data, a picture of the organization of the group is constructed.

Perhaps one of the most extensive uses of this method was made by Whyte [1943]. He spent three and one-half years in a slum district in Boston, living as a quasi-member of various street-corner groups, participating in

their day-by-day activities. The members of the group knew that he was a graduate student interested in learning what life in a congested urban neighborhood was like. Whyte [1951] describes his role as follows:

FIGURE 11.1: The distribution of the total number of acts among the 12 categories in the Bales category system—called a profile—for two 5-man groups who worked on a discussion problem: a "Satisfied" and a "Dissatisfied" group. [Based on data from Bales, 1952.]

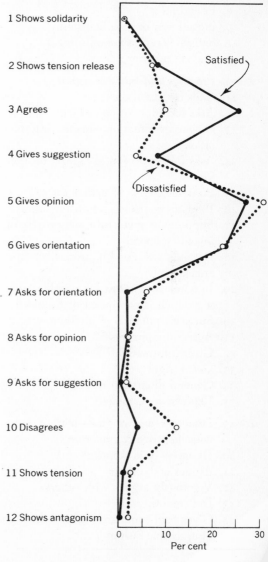

TABLE 11.2: LIST OF MAJOR AND MINOR OBSERVATION CATEGORIES IN THE CARTER CATEGORY SYSTEM [Carter et al., 1951a]

MAJOR CATEGORIES	MINOR CATEGORIES

MAJOR CATEGORIES

1–19. *Shows a personal feeling of*
  1. Aggressiveness or anger
  2. Anxiety or insecurity
  3. Attention or readiness
  4. Confusion
  5. Cooperativeness
  6. Deference
  7. Dissatisfaction
  8. Formality or reserve
  9. Friendliness
  10. Negativism or rebelliousness
  11. Satisfaction or accomplishment
  12. Status (superior)

20–39. *Proposes and initiates action*
  21. Calls for attention
  22. Asks for information or facts
  23. Diagnoses situation—makes interpretation
  24. Asks for expression of feeling or opinion
  25. Proposes course of action for self
  26. Proposes course of action for others
  27. Supports or gives information regarding his proposal
  28. Defends self (or his proposals) from attack
  29. Initiates *action* toward problem solving which is continued or followed
  30. Supports proposal of another
  31. Agrees or approves
  32. Gives information
  33. Gets insight
  34. General discussion re task
  35. Expression of opinion

40–49. *Disagrees and argues—with a somewhat negative connotation*
  40. Disagrees or is skeptical
  41. Argues with others
  42. Vigorously argues with others
  43. Deflates others
  44. Gives bald commands or prohibits (in disagreeable fashion)

MINOR CATEGORIES

50–59. *Leader roles in carrying out action*
  50. Gives information on how to carry out action
  51. Praises, commends, rewards
  52. Expresses a desire that something be done
  53. Asks for assistance for others
  54. Asks for assistance for self
  55. Integrates group behavior

60–69. *Follower and "worker" roles in carrying out action*
  60. Follows suggestions or directions
  61. Offers to help or helps
  62. Imitates others
  63. Asks for permission
  64. Collaborates with others
  65. Answers questions
  66. Performance of simple work unit (group-oriented)
  67. Performance of simple work unit—an independent effort
  68. Passively helps

70–79. *Abortive or nonproductive behavior re problem*
  70. Initiates action which is not followed or continued
  71. Verbal interplay without outcome
  72. Listens, but does not express self or enter in

90–99. *Miscellaneous*
  90. Stands around doing nothing
  91. Engages in "out of field" activity
  92. Engages in incidental conversation while working

It is well to play a semidetached role: to join in social activities, to bowl, to play ball, to eat and drink together, and so on, but still to have it recognized that you are interested in research. Of course that does not mean interrupting people in the middle of a ball game or a wake for an explanation of the proceedings; it does mean discussing the event thoroughly after it is over. The observer's role must be such that these discussions will be accepted and even welcomed. . . .

They did not expect me to behave just like them. . . . On the other hand, it was extremely important that I accepted with interest everything they did and whatever they said.

One of Whyte's studies [1941] was based on observations of the members of the Cornerville Social and Athletic Club. Whenever he went into the rooms of the club, he observed the spatial groupings of the members. These observations were recorded in maps. The map in Figure 11.2 shows the kind of data yielded by the observations. Through the analysis of a number of such maps, Whyte found he was able to place most of the men in the club in the subgroups to which they belonged.

The status of a man in his subgroup—his power to influence the activities of the group—was, however, not revealed by these maps. The investigator, therefore, made records of who originated action for two or more other members. He gives the following examples as illustrations:

Seven men are standing in the club room, in groups of two, two, and three. Individual X comes in and the three little groups immediately reform into one larger group, with the seven men remaining silent while X talks, and each man seeking to get the attention of X before he himself speaks.

X says, "Let's take a walk." We then observe the group setting out for a walk. Or A says to X, "Let's go to the Orpheum." X says, "Naw, that picture is no good." No change in group activity. Then B says to X, "Let's go to the State." X says, "O.K." The group is then off to the State.

Some of the fellows are sitting around a table in a cafeteria having their evening coffee—

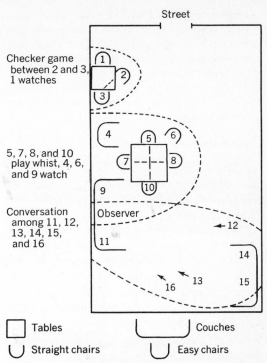

FIGURE 11.2: An example of a positional map—a technique used by Whyte in his study, through the method of participant observation, of the structure of informal groups or gangs of boys in "Cornerville," a slum area in a large Eastern city. The map shows the spatial positions of the members of the Cornerville Social and Athletic Club in their clubroom on one occasion. On the basis of a number of such maps, Whyte was able to determine the subgroups existing within the larger group. Direction in which chair and couches face indicates direction in which men face. Arrows indicate direction in which standing men face. Dotted lines enclose those interacting. [Whyte, 1941.]

ands. A leaves the group to sit down for a few minutes with people at a nearby table. X remains at the original table, and the conversation continues much as it did when A was present. On another occasion, the same people are present in the same spatial arrangement in the cafeteria, but this time it is X who gets up and goes over to another table. The conversation at X's former table noticeably slows down and perhaps breaks up into two's and three's. The men talk about what X could be doing over at the other table, and their attention is frequently directed to that table. If X stays away beyond a given point in time, we may observe his friends picking up their chairs and moving over to the other table with him.

Observations along these lines establish that X characteristically initiates action for this group, that he is the leader of the group (Whyte, 1951).

SELF-REPORT METHODS

Two principal self-report methods have been developed and applied to the study of groups: the *field-interview* method and the *sociometric* method.

FIELD-INTERVIEW METHOD. As we have seen (page 356), anthropologists have relied mainly upon the field-interview method in the study of culture. Investigators who have been trained in anthropology or sociology have also made extensive use of the field-interview technique to study various aspects of group behavior. The method is particularly useful in describing the ideology of a group.

In the method of participant observation the interview is commonly used as an ancillary method. For example, Whyte [1943] reports the following remarks by Doc, leader of the Nortons:

> On any corner you would find not only a leader but probably a couple of lieutenants. They could be leaders themselves, but they let the man lead them. You would say, "They let him lead because they like the way he does things." Sure, but he leans upon them for his authority. Many times you find fellows on a corner that stay in the background until some situation comes up, and then they will take over and call the shots. Things like that can change fast sometimes.

Whyte concluded from this interview material, supported by behavioral observations and interviews with the leaders of other groups, that the leader does not deal with his followers as an undifferentiated group.

The study by Koos [1946] of "Families in Trouble" (for a summary of this study, see page 449) is another illustration of the use of the interview method in the study of groups.

SOCIOMETRIC METHOD. The sociometric method of studying group structures was developed by Moreno [1934]. As originally used by him, the objective of this method was to establish the pattern of *feelings* of acceptance and rejection, of like and dislike, that exists among the members of a group. The method involves asking each member of a group to name privately the other persons in the group with whom he would like, and with whom he would *not* like, to engage in some particular activity, e.g., living with as a roommate, working with, spending leisure time with.

The sociometric method has been extended to include other ways of discerning the interpersonal relations among people, beyond what is revealed in their reported feelings about others. Thus we may record the frequency of contact (or the total duration of contact) between pairs of individuals. Where such contacts are largely voluntary, it is assumed that their frequency provides a good measure of group structure. Loomis [1941], for example, has made an elaborate sociometric study of a New Mexican village. He ascertained the frequency of visiting, eating meals together, and lending farm equipment among the families. Such data, together with data on feelings, make it possible to construct a *sociogram* which pictures for the whole group all the patterns of mutual like, dislike, and indifference, and the patterns of interaction. It is easy for the investigator to see at a glance what the sociometric structure of a group actually is— the cliques, the people who are much liked and disliked and by whom, the social isolates, etc. (For a special use of the sociogram, see Box 11.1.)

Proctor and Loomis [1951] have provided us with a hypothetical example of how a sociogram may be used to select cohesive work groups. They ask us to suppose that a sociometric questionnaire has been given to a research team of ten atomic scientists. The questionnaire reads as follows: "It has been suggested that an evaluation of the progress which this research team has made be prepared by a committee. If you are chosen as one member of this committee, whom else (if anyone) would you choose to collaborate with you? Name as many as you wish. Whom (if anyone) would you dislike working with? Again name as many as you wish."

The patterns of choices, rejections, and indifference are pictured in the sociogram in Figure 11.3. Proctor and Loomis infer that the subgroup composed of 1, 2, 3, 4, and 5 should be given the opportunity for much cooperative work; 6 and 7 should collaborate; 8 should work independently or with 10; 9 should be

BOX 11.1: *Top leaders at the UN—who saw whom in a hurry?*

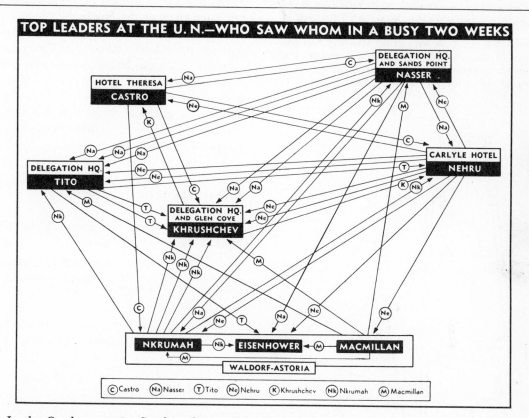

In the October 2, 1960, Sunday edition of the *New York Times,* the pattern of visiting among some of the top leaders of the world was portrayed by means of a sociogram. The period was a busy two weeks during the 1960 meeting of the General Assembly of the United Nations—a meeting which owed its importance to the presence of such national leaders as Khrushchev of the U.S.S.R., Eisenhower of the U.S., and Macmillan of Great Britain.

Khrushchev was a busy host indeed: he was visited on three occasions by Nkrumah of Ghana; Nasser of Egypt called upon him twice; Nehru of India, twice; Tito of Yugoslavia, twice; Castro of Cuba, once; Macmillan of England, once. And Khrushchev journeyed forth to call upon Castro and Nehru.

Eisenhower received the visits of Nkrumah, Macmillan, Tito, Nasser, and Nehru in his suite at the Waldorf-Astoria. He did not leave his hotel to confer with other leaders.

assigned either to subgroup 1, 2, 3, 4, and 5 or to subgroup 6 and 7, preferably the latter. The assumption underlying these decisions is that a large number of mutual choices between pairs of individuals in a group will make the group more satisfying to the members.

An especially interesting sociometric pattern has to do with power. It can be ascertained which individual or individuals in the group occupy positions in which they can be particularly influential. Figure 11.4 shows the sociogram of a "powerful" individual as contrasted with that of a merely "popular" person.

Numerous scores and indexes have been developed to analyze sociometric data. Some of these indexes are designed to describe the sociometric status of the individual, others to describe the group as a whole, and still others to describe the individual in interaction with other members of the group.

To illustrate index analysis, we shall present several indexes (taken from Proctor and Loomis) which can be used to describe group structure. Positive expansiveness (desire to associate with other persons) of the individual p, in a group of N persons, where p is allowed an unlimited number of choices, is measured by the index

FIGURE 11.3: A sociogram showing the pattern of choices and rejections in a group of 10 atomic scientists for collaboration in writing a report. [Proctor and Loomis, 1951.]

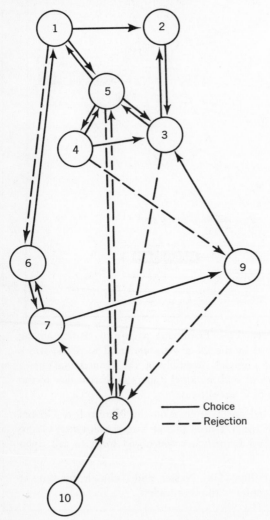

$$\text{Positive expansiveness of } p = \frac{\begin{array}{c}\text{number of}\\\text{choices } p \text{ makes}\end{array}}{N - 1}$$

The expansiveness of a group may be measured by the following index:

$$\text{Group expansiveness} = \frac{\begin{array}{c}\text{total number of choices}\\\text{made by group}\end{array}}{N}$$

Group cohesion and group integration may be measured by the following indexes:

$$\text{Group cohesion} = \frac{\begin{array}{c}\text{number of}\\\text{mutual choices}\end{array}}{\begin{array}{c}\text{total number of possible}\\\text{mutual choices}\end{array}}$$

$$\text{Group integration} = \frac{1}{\begin{array}{c}\text{number of isolates}\\\text{(individuals receiving}\\\text{no choices)}\end{array}}$$

——— Choice
– – – Rejection

TO RECAPITULATE

Methods for the description and measurement of the structure and function of groups fall into two major classes: observation methods and self-report methods.

The two major observation methods—the rating-scale method and the category-system method—have been widely used in the study of the functioning of laboratory, problem-solving groups. The method of participant observation has been applied to the study of groups in their natural setting.

The major self-report methods are the field-interview method and the sociometric method. The field-interview method is often used to supplement the method of participant observation. It is especially useful in the study of the group ideology. The sociometric method, in its original form, yields a description of the pattern of likes and dislikes among the members of a group. The extension of the method to secure reports of frequency of visiting, eating meals together, etc., makes it possible to portray the pattern of interaction among the members of a group. Sociometric data may be represented graphically in a sociogram. The construction of sociometric indexes is another way of treating the data to describe the individual's sociometric status and various aspects of the group structure.

The methods which have been developed for the study of groups have yielded important findings and generalizations about groups—their ideology, their structure and functioning. We now turn to an examination of these findings and generalizations.

GUIDE 33: *A group comes into being to achieve the wants of its members; in the course of interaction the members develop a group ideology which regulates their attitudes and actions and influences their satisfactions*

An individual's membership in a particular group may come about through external circumstances that compel or enforce his mem-

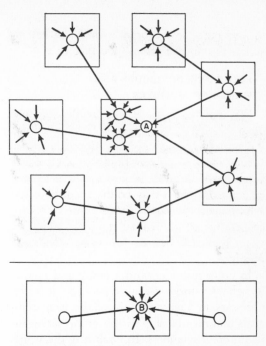

FIGURE 11.4: Sociometric diagrams showing a "powerful" and a "popular" person. A is directly chosen by four individuals who in turn are chosen by many others both inside and outside their groups; thus A is in a highly influential position; B is more popular, being directly chosen by seven individuals, but is less influential, since those who chose B are not themselves chosen. [Adapted from Moreno, 1934.]

bership. Thus a child is, through biological chance, a member of a given family group; a soldier may become a member of a military unit by being drafted; a man may be forced to join a labor union. Or the individual may freely choose his group memberships. He marries into a family, enlists in a specific military service, voluntarily decides to join a labor union. Whether membership is externally imposed or freely chosen will undoubtedly determine the part which group membership plays in satisfying the individual's wants.

It is also noteworthy that the attractiveness of a particular group to the individual is partly a function of the difficulties that he had to overcome, or the ordeal which he had to suffer, to join the group (see Box 11.2).

FUNCTIONS OF GROUPS AND WANTS OF MEMBERS

For most groups we can safely say that group membership serves a function for the individual. Through it he satisfies his wants. It may serve to provide food and shelter and sexual satisfaction. It may protect him against external threats. It may be the avenue for the achievement of social goals which require cooperative effort. It may serve the affiliation want and the desires for recognition and prestige.

In order to understand a group and predict its behavior under various conditions, it is first necessary to have a picture of the wants and goals that membership in this group serves for its different members. In analyzing the wants served by group membership we must keep several cautions in mind: (1) The wants and goals that a given group serves for some of its members may differ from those it serves for other members (see Box 11.3). (2) The apparent or avowed wants of group members are not always the real wants, and, therefore, the apparent or avowed functions of groups are not always the real functions. (3) The wants currently served by a group may differ from the wants served by the same group in times past.

DIFFERENTIAL SATISFACTION OF WANTS. We have seen that some group members are members involuntarily; the group may or may not meet *their* wants. We also know that some members have more influence in making group decisions than others. We can therefore anticipate that we will find that most groups serve to meet the current wants of its *dominant* members more adequately than those of its less dominant (or rank-and-file) members. The distribution of dominant and nondominant members varies for different groups (e.g., compare democratic with autocratic groups), but the dominant members are better served.

POWER AND BELONGINGNESS WANTS. Perhaps the most generally valid statement that can be made about the nature of the functions of groups is that *all groups serve to meet the power want of some of the members and the belongingness want of most of the members.* Every group, even though there may be no formal recognition of leadership, provides roles for its various members which differ in amount of power. In so far as this is true, every group will provide for the gratification of the power want of some of its members.

While the power want characterizes many people, the desire to belong to some activity or group larger than one's self, to be "accepted," to be a part of something significant, characterizes most people in society (see pages 89 to 93). This powerful want frequently motivates the "joining" activities of people. By joining a union the individual worker seeks to gain not only his economic goals but also to satisfy his want to "belong." The member of a church, of a college fraternity, of a scientific association, of the Knights of Columbus, of the American Veterans Committee—all these may find gratification of this want in their various groups.

The feeling of group belongingness importantly determines the individual's feeling of self-worth: his "subjective status" reflects his objective status in his groups. It is inevitable that the group identifications of the individual become an important part of his extended self, for this valued object is the product of the interactions of the individual with the members of his various primary groups (see pages 79 to 80). The groups of the individual become "My groups right or wrong" and attacks upon them may be defended as vigorously as attacks upon the self (see Box 11.4).

CREATION OF NEW WANTS. Man's wants are not static; they grow and develop as the individual changes (see pages 72 to 76). Group

BOX 11.2: *Ordeal by shame*

It is a common belief that persons who go to a lot of trouble to secure something tend to value it more highly than persons who get the same thing with little or no effort.

Social psychologists Elliot Aronson and Judson Mills, while at Stanford University, carried out an experiment to answer two questions: (1) Is this common belief true? (2) If true, how can it be explained?

Aronson and Mills ask this specific question: "Is severity of initiation positively related to group preference when motivation for admission is held constant?"

Festinger's theory of cognitive dissonance (see page 261) would predict a positive relation for the following reasons. A person's attitude toward a group is usually mixed—the group has both desirable and undesirable features. The knowledge that one has gone through a severe initiation ceremony to join the group is dissonant with the knowledge that the group has certain undesirable characteristics. This dissonance can be reduced by coming to think that the initiation was not so bad after all or by overestimating the attractiveness of the group. If the initiation was, in fact, very severe, the second stratagem is more likely to be used.

To test this prediction, Aronson and Mills randomly assigned 63 college women, who had volunteered to participate in a series of group discussions of the psychology of sex, to one of three experimental conditions: A Severe Initiation condition, a Mild Initiation condition, and a Control condition. The two initiation conditions were presented as "screening devices to rule out women who could not talk about sex without embarrassment." In the Severe Initiation condition, the women read aloud to a male experimenter 12 obscene words and two vivid descriptions of sexual activity from contemporary novels. In the Mild condition, the women read aloud five words related to sex which were not obscene. In the Control condition, the women were not required to read anything.

Each subject then listened to a tape recording of what was ostensibly an ongoing discussion by the group which she had just joined. The discussion was deliberately made as dull and worthless as possible.

At the end of the recording the subjects were asked to rate the discussion, and the women whose voices they heard during the discussion, on 14 different semantic-differential evaluative scales, e.g., dull-interesting, intelligent-unintelligent (see page 167).

The means of the sums of the ratings are given in the following table. (The higher the score, the more favorable the evaluation.)

Item rated	Control	Mild initiation	Severe initiation
Discussion by the group	80.2	81.8	97.6
Discussion group members	89.9	89.3	97.7

Note that those women who had undergone embarrassing initiation perceived the group as more attractive than did those who had undergone a mild initiation or no initiation. There was no difference between the latter two groups.

Aronson, E., and Mills, J. *The effect of severity of initiation on liking for a group.* J. abnorm. soc. Psychol., *1959, 59, 177–181.*

BOX 11.3: *Many minds with many thoughts*

The wide variety of individual goals that a group may serve is illustrated by some of the reasons people attend human relations workshops and conferences, as listed by J. R. Gibb, G. N. Platts, and L. E. Miller:

    to relieve boredom
    to get inspiration and stimulation
    to have a trip, holiday, or a rest
    to meet people in their field or with their interests
    for educational purposes
    for status or prestige—to impress friends at home
    because their expenses are paid
    because they are expected to
    to shop in the town where the conference is held
    to get away from a tense home situation
    to meet friends
    to put across an idea, to lobby, to influence
    to get a job
    because they "have gone every year"—it's expected
    because their boss or organization requires it

The persons who sponsor the workshop or conference also have a wide variety of goals:

    to inspire and stimulate organization members
    to disseminate information
    to get at the grass-roots member and his ideas
    to train people to work together
    to improve human relations
    to bring people together who have similar interests and problems
    to put across an issue, to lobby, to influence
    to bring national and local groups together
    because they are expected to
    because "it has always been done"

Gibb, J. R., Platts, G. N., and Miller, L. E. Dynamics of participative groups. *St. Louis: J. S. Swift, 1951.*

membership may change the individual by providing him with new experiences, thus inducing new wants. The new wants that are created through group membership are many and varied.

Among the socially most important wants that a group can induce is the member's dedication to the survival of the group. This is especially true for the dominant members and is in part responsible for what has been called the "grewsome immortality" of groups. In the normal process of socialization, the continued existence and growth of his groups become identified with the continued existence and welfare of the individual himself. Consequently, members seek to ensure the continued existence of their groups, and in many instances this want overrides the other wants satisfied by the group. The existence of such a driving want on the part of members often results in a *conscious effort to increase the functions of the group.* Sometimes this effort is in the nature of a defensive tactic in recognition of the fact that the unique wants

GROUPS, ORGANIZATIONS, AND THE INDIVIDUAL

which the group has served are no longer important for most of its members and the group faces possible disintegration.

WANTS AND MULTIPLE-GROUP MEMBERSHIP. Though every group may serve multiple wants for the individual, no one group can satisfy *all* of his wants and goals. This means that he is perforce a member of many different groups. His loyalty to these various groups and to their members may often be divided and conflicted (see pages 495 to 500).

The pressures toward multiple-group membership arise from at least three sources: (1) the very multiplicity of the constantly devel-

---

BOX 11.4: *Martyrdom in the laboratory*

In two experiments, Wallace E. Lambert, Eva Libman, and Ernest G. Poser of McGill University studied the effect of religious rivalry upon the individual's ability to endure pain.

In their first experiment 40 Jewish and 40 Protestant college women served as subjects. They were randomly assigned to experimental and control groups. In individual testing sessions, the amount of pain each subject could endure was established. A sphygmomanometer (an instrument for measuring blood pressure) with sharp, hard rubber projections sewn into the inner surface of the cuff was used. The cuff was placed on the upper arm of the subject, and the pressure was gradually increased until the subject pronounced the pain intolerable. The index of intolerable pain was millimeters of Hg on the sphygmomanometer gauge, which was, of course, a measure of the pressure exerted by the hard rubber projections on the subject's upper arm.

After the limit for intolerable pain had been established, the subject was told that a retest would be made in 5 minutes to determine the reliability of measurement. The experimenter then casually added, if the subject were Jewish, that Jews can endure less pain than non-Jews. The Protestant experimental subjects were told that Protestants can take less pain than "other groups." The controls were told only that a retest would be made in 5 minutes.

The intolerable pain limits of the Jewish experimental subjects increased significantly on the retest. Neither the Jewish controls nor the Protestant experimental and control subjects showed any change in pain tolerance scores on retest.

The investigators concluded that the Jewish experimental subjects were motivated by the allegation of Jewish inability to endure pain to disprove the allegation. The Protestant experimental subjects, when the experimenter had unfavorably compared Protestants with "other groups," may not have been aroused sufficiently because of failure to specify a particular "rivalrous" religious group.

To test this interpretation, a second experiment was carried out. Between the first and second measures of the limit for intolerable pain, the Jewish experimental subjects were told that Jews as a group can take less pain than Christians; the Protestant experimental subjects were told that Christians can take less pain than Jews. In this second experiment, the intolerable pain limits of *both* the Jewish and the Protestant experimental subjects were found to have significantly increased.

These findings suggest that, in part, the extended self of the individual is made up of the groups with which he is identified. Attacks upon his groups are responded to as attacks upon the self, and this effect is powerful enough to increase the willingness and capacity of the individual to suffer intense pain.

Lambert, W. E., Libman, Eva, and Poser, E. G. *The effect of increased salience of a membership group on pain tolerance. J. Pers., 1960, **28**, 350–357.*

oping wants and goals of the individual; (2) the trend toward specialization of group function which restricts the want-satisfying power of any single group; (3) the inability of a given group to modify itself rapidly enough to continue to satisfy the changing wants of the individual in a fast-changing world.

There are, on the other hand, certain countertendencies to the growth of multiple-group membership. We have already discussed one of these—the deliberate attempt of the dominant members of a group to increase the functions of the group and thus make unnecessary multiple-group membership. Another arises from the attempt of the individual to escape from conflicts growing out of competing memberships, and from the emotional pull toward making a single group the focus of loyalty and identification. Witness the closely knit group of teen-age girls who strive "to do everything together."

The dominant member, or leader, of a group may tend to have fewer significant group memberships than the rank-and-file member. Thus the church leader—the priest, minister, or rabbi—may find his religious group a means for expressing his entire personality, and it becomes the object of all his aspirations and strivings. Unlike the rank-and-file member, the priest does not find it necessary to belong to another group in order to earn his living—the church provides. He does not have to seek out other groups to satisfy his wants for power, for affiliation, for self-expression—the church provides. Thus his loyalties and identifications can be more focused, his conflicts less bothersome.

GROUP GOALS

No matter how various may be the wants that lead persons to affiliate with a group, the effectiveness and viability of the group require that the majority of its members come to agree on the goals they will strive for while in common association. These *group goals* are, of course, held by individual members of the group, and display all the characteristics of individual goals. They are group goals only in the sense that they form in and are shared by persons joined together in a group.

"UNIQUE" AND "ACCESSORY" GROUP GOALS. Because almost every group comes into being as a social device to meet certain *specified* wants of its members, we can categorize groups in terms of their major, or "unique," group goals. Thus we can speak of friendship groups, religious groups, family groups, or political groups. However, such a functional analysis can be misleading. Groups often accrue to themselves "accessory" goals as they continue to exist over time. These accessory goals may sometimes be unrelated to the unique goals of the group and may even completely overshadow them to the point where the unique goals disappear entirely.

Douglass' [1926] analysis of the changing functions of the Protestant Church in the United States presents a good illustration of this phenomenon. In 357 Protestant churches which he examined he found that there existed 33 different kinds of nonreligious "church activities." Among these were general social events, Boy Scout activities, orchestras and bands, girls' clubs, dramatic clubs, gymnasium classes, sewing classes, domestic science classes, employment offices, visiting nurse associations, day nurseries, dispensaries and clinics, and civics and economics classes. These activities represent a change in the very nature of the functions of these religious organizations. Religious organizations have always concerned themselves with nonreligious institutionalized ways—with medicine, farming, warfare, education, etc.—but always in a *religious* sense. That is, since the supernatural entity was all-powerful, the healing art could not be effective without divine help; the fields could not be sown or harvested without religious rites and ceremonies; wars could not be conducted without the blessing of the priest and the presence of the Cross. But the picture that Douglass presents is that of a religious organization concerning itself with *nonreligious functions in a nonreligious manner* (see Box 11.5).

Perhaps the major reason for the accretion of accessory group goals lies in the fact that as the wants and goals of its members change, the functions of the group must show corresponding changes if the group is to survive. It is therefore necessary, in any functional analysis of a group, to examine both its accessory and unique group goals.

INDIVIDUAL WANTS AND GROUP GOALS. It is clear that a person will work for a group goal only if he believes that its achievement will satisfy his own wants. One way that the meshing of individual wants with group goals has been studied is through the use of the "Zeigarnik effect," so-named because of Zeigarnik's [1927] finding that if a person is motivated to do a series of tasks and if he completes only part of them, his memory for the incompleted tasks will be better than his memory for the completed ones. Memory is assumed to be activated by systems which remain in a state of "tension" because of lack of completion, and completion of a task is assumed to reduce the "tension system" related to the task.

Lewis [1944] and Lewis and Franklin [1944] were the first to use the Zeigarnik effect to study interdependency between individual wants and group goals. These investigators found that when a person's incomplete tasks were completed by a *coworker*, the person's recall of these coworker-completed tasks was about equal to recall of tasks completed by the person himself. Thus apparently the completion of a task by a partner can reduce the level of tension related to the task as much as does completion by oneself. For a group goal, it is immaterial which group member actually reaches the goal.

In a later study, Horwitz [1954] extended the use of the Zeigarnik effect in investigating motivation to strive for group goals. Five-person groups, each representing a college sorority, competed with one another on a series of group tasks. About halfway through each task, the members voted (by secret ballot) to determine whether the group should complete it. For one-third of the tasks, the experimenter announced the vote was against continuing them ("No" tasks); for the remaining tasks, the experimenter announced the vote was in favor of continuing them ("Yes" tasks). Some of the "Yes" tasks were interrupted shortly after the vote ("Y-I" tasks); the remainder were completed by the group ("Y-C" tasks).

BOX 11.5: *A unique church—with all accessories*

Mr. Andrew Mackerel, pastor of the People's Liberal Church of Avalon, Connecticut, a fictitious exurbanite community, describes his church:

> Our church is, I believe, the first split-level church in America. It has five rooms and two baths downstairs—dining area, kitchen and three parlors for committee and group meetings. . . . Upstairs is one huge all-purpose interior, divisible into different-sized components by means of sliding walls and convertible into an auditorium for putting on plays, a gymnasium for athletics, and a ballroom for dances. There is a small worship area at one end . . . in back of this building is a newly erected clinic, with medical and neuro-psychiatric wings, both indefinitely expandable. Thus People's Liberal is a church designed to meet the needs of today, and to serve the whole man.

De Vries, P. The Mackerel Plaza. *New York: Little, Brown, 1958.*

Recall of the "Y-I" tasks was significantly better than recall of either the "Y-C" or the "No" tasks. Horwitz interprets this result to mean that when the group consensus is to complete a task, a tension is induced in the individual for the group to reach its goal which remains active until the task is completed. If the group vote is against continuing the task, no tension is induced.

Further analysis of the data showed that the engagement of the individual's wants by the group goals was not dependent upon her own vote. A girl who voted against continuing would subsequently accept the decision of the group to do so, and become motivated toward completion of the task. This acceptance of the group consensus, despite initial opposition, may in part reflect the fact that the girls in each group were members of the same sorority, competing with other sorority groups.

FACTORS DETERMINING ACCEPTANCE OF GROUP GOALS. Studies of the relation between worker morale and productivity emphasize the importance for the acceptance of group goals of the *perceived relevancy* of the group goals to individual wants. The members must, in other words, see the group goals as want-satisfying. Despite a widespread tendency to assume that high morale means high productivity, and low morale means low productivity, the evidence indicates that employee morale bears little or no consistent relation to productivity [Brayfield and Crockett, 1955]. The production goals set by management may be simply irrelevant to the wants of the workers. In so far as this is true, management is definitely limited in attempting to transmute its own goals into *group goals* for the work group.

In a factor analysis of the reasons for worker satisfaction, Kahn [1951] isolated four independent factors: (1) satisfaction with the material rewards of the job (its present and future pay, its opportunities for learning and promotion); (2) satisfaction with the work (the extent to which the job is challenging, is interesting, and provides status); (3) satisfac-

tion with the company as an organization (working conditions and company operations); and (4) satisfaction with the competency of supervisors, technicians, and leaders. Note the importance of the wants for "self-actualization" and for satisfying interpersonal relations.

There are some indications that the degree to which management provides for the satisfaction of such wants determines the acceptance of the production goals of management by workers. For example, Seashore [1954] found that work groups which perceived the company as providing a "supportive setting" tended to set high production goals, whereas work groups which perceived the company as not providing a supportive setting tended to restrict production. Similarly, Greer [1955] found, among infantry rifle squads in a field exercise, that group cohesiveness was related to performance effectiveness only in those squads in which the men were "highly adjusted to the Army."

Both theory and empirical research indicate that the *clarity* of the goals of a group also influences their acceptance by the members. In an experiment by Raven and Rietsema [1957] goal clarity was experimentally manipulated by giving subjects varying knowledge of the final group product. The task of the subjects was to cut figures to build a board house, ostensibly as part of a team. The members of the "clear goal" groups were told how each individual's contribution would contribute toward the final structure. The "unclear goal" group members were merely given specific assignments without being told how their individual activities meshed with the product to be completed. The investigators found that "the subject who had a clear picture of his group goal and group path experienced greater feelings of group belongingness, particularly as manifested in an involvement with the group goal and in sympathy with group emotions. He was also . . . more willing to accept influence from his group than subjects who were unclear about the goals and paths of their group."

A group with high *cohesiveness* is one in which the members are highly attracted to the group. Such a group should be able to secure a relatively high degree of acceptance of any type of group goal which is set for the group. Further, since the members of cohesive groups are highly interdependent, sanctions to secure compliance can be more effectively applied to deviant members.

Schachter et al. [1951] experimentally tested the hypothesis that cohesiveness makes for greater acceptance of a group goal. Two sets of laboratory groups were first established — high-cohesion groups and low-cohesion groups. This was done by two different sets of instructions. These groups were then given the task of cutting large rectangles from heavy cardboard to make checkerboards. The goal of high productivity was established for one half of the high- and low-cohesion groups and the goal of *low* productivity for the other half of these two sets of groups. The investigators found that high cohesiveness promoted the acceptance of a group goal of restricted production; that is, when the goal was low production, the output of the high-cohesion groups was significantly less than that of the low-cohesion groups. These investigators did not, however, obtain significant differences between high- and low-cohesion groups when the goal was high production, perhaps because they were already at the task ceiling.

Berkowitz [1954] repeated the study, using a task with a supposedly higher ceiling. He did find that high cohesiveness promoted the acceptance of high-production as well as low-production goals: "Members of cohesive groups will tend to conform to the perceived group standard—by raising their production if the standard is for high production or lowering it, or not increasing as rapidly, if the standard is for low production. . . ."

When the members of a group are invited by their leaders to *participate in setting the group goals*, acceptance of the goals is increased (see pages 479 to 482). It is likely that many factors are responsible for this effect. Through their participation in goal setting, the members may see more clearly the relevance of the goals to their personal wants. Participation may also increase the clarity of the group goals. In participating, the members may publicly commit themselves. And public commitment to the goals of a group should, for the reasons we have discussed in considering public commitment in attitude change (see pages 228 to 229), result in greater acceptance. Finally, as Bennett (see page 230) found, the perception that a particular decision has been made by a large majority of a group is a major determinant of the individual's acceptance of that decision.

CHANGES IN ACCEPTANCE OF GROUP GOALS. As the members of a group work together at their common tasks, individual acceptance of the goals of the group will change with the perceived probability of success. If an individual comes to believe that his group is unable to realize its goals, he will tend to give up the group goals and seek satisfaction of his wants through other means. If, on the other hand, the group is perceived as successfully moving toward its objectives, the individual's wants will become more and more fully engaged with the goals of the group and acceptance will become more and more complete.

Related to this is the study by Rosenthal and Cofer [1948] of the effect of an indifferent and neglectful member upon group performance. Small groups of college students were given a series of trials on a dart-throwing task. The groups were motivated to reach or exceed the fictitious score made by a group of government workers. The experimenters "planted" in the experimental groups an assistant who performed at an average level but who displayed an indifferent and neglectful attitude. A control group, containing no such member, was also used. Individual levels of aspiration were secured and after several trials the group was asked to decide upon a satisfactory group score. It was found that the experimental groups experienced much more difficulty in agreeing upon a group level of aspiration than did the controls. Moreover, the individual levels of aspiration in the experimental groups were consistently higher than were the group levels. The effect of the indifferent and neglectful attitudes of the "stooge" (despite the fact that he actually performed at an average level) was to decrease the level of confidence of the experimental subjects in the probability of attaining the group goal. These findings suggest that when there is impairment of group functioning, members of a group will tend to give up group goals for individual goals.

GROUP IDEOLOGY

In the course of interacting with one another, the members of every enduring group come to develop a *group ideology*. The group ideology consists of common beliefs, common values, and common norms (see pages 349 to 353).

The double role of ideology—the directing of action designed to satisfy wants, and the creating of new goals which must be realized—becomes particularly important if we are to understand the influence of the group upon the individual. We have seen that the wants which induce people to affiliate themselves with a group may vary. However, the existence of a common ideology tends to minimize behavior differences due to different wants of different members. A common ideology does this by creating a core of *common wants* among the members and by inducing a *common method of expressing different wants*.

To argue, as some do, that the official ideology of a formal group is merely a network of rationalizations and myths to justify the existence of the group is to misunderstand the multitude of functions that ideology plays in group behavior. It is true that a group ideology may be more clearly related to the wants of the dominant members of the group than to the wants of the other members, and that *part* of the ideology may properly be described as "rationalization," but, as we shall see, in no case can a group ideology be dismissed as of little consequence for the understanding of group behavior.

DEVELOPMENT OF GROUP BELIEFS. The members of every stable group share a set of ideas, knowledge, and lore about matters relevant to the common goals of the group members. These *group beliefs* are part of the ideology of the group.

There are several reasons why group beliefs exist. In the first place, most people join a group to satisfy common wants, and common wants will come to result, to a certain extent, in a communality of beliefs. In the second place there are many different groups which can satisfy the same wants, and people have a free choice among them. The reason that a specific one of these groups is joined is frequently that the belief system of the chosen group is most congruent with the already existing beliefs of the individual. Thus there is an initial selective factor which helps ensure a common set of beliefs among the diverse members of a group. In the third place, as was indicated in Chapter 6 (see especially page 188), many of our beliefs are based upon facts and information given to us by "authorities." Almost all groups have their own authorities or "experts," especially in the person of the leader (see page 429). The expertness of the leader is frequently one of the attractions of a group and one of the reasons why particular groups are joined by individuals. In so far as the members of a group receive their facts from the same expert, or authority, the different members will tend to acquire common beliefs. Finally, in so far as the members of any group are constantly exposed to a common and specifically limited range of information (through group-controlled, group-approved, group-censored propaganda and educational media), we must expect a common set of beliefs and judgments to form. This is a consequence of the processes (see the discussion on page 32) which determine the individual's judgment as a function of the range of the stimulus objects to be judged. As Tresselt and Volkmann [1942] have pointed out:

> Each person in a group says what he does not only because he has been persuaded by argument, induced by reward, compelled by pressure, guided by his own past beliefs, or influenced by the voiced opinions of other people. He says it also because he faces a restricted range of social or non-social stimulation, and this range has determined his scale of judgment.

As a result of the reasons for group beliefs, most members of various groups will have individual belief systems which overlap greatly with those of their fellow members. These group beliefs are extremely resistant to change. Some of the reasons for this have been discussed in Chapter 7. Primarily these reasons derive from the fact that the very essence of a group belief is its *integrating nature* (see page 349). There is also the fact that group membership provides effective social support for a group-belief system (see Guide 19, page 216). Finally, there is the factor of coercion. Many psychological groups and all social organizations possess enforcing agents or enforcing techniques. Most groups and organizations extend their coercive activities to the *beliefs*, as well as the actions, of their members; and as we have seen in Chapter 7 (Guide 23, page 253), coercive force applied to the individual may frequently result in effective control of his beliefs.

The resistance of group beliefs to change is of profound social importance. To understand the role of groups in social change, we must give proper weight to the static nature of group beliefs, to the forces that inhibit cognitive change among the members of groups

and that eventually tend to result in cultural lag and dysfunctional behavior (sociologically or technologically viewed).

THE "INSTITUTIONAL FICTION." A common group belief found among the members of almost any organized and enduring group is the belief that the group transcends the immediate members of the group, or the real property of the group, or even the space and time coordinates in which the group seems to exist. This belief has been dubbed the "institutional fiction." A university, our commencement orators never tire of telling us, is "something more" than its students and faculty and buildings and laboratories and books; a nation is "more than" its inhabitants and its rocks and rills.

The very process of *perception* predisposes the individual to regard his group as existing in this superordinate manner. When a person perceives several people acting together or praying together or working together or fighting together, certain perceptual properties will be present that are absent when we attend to the individuals one at a time. Not only do we perceive these "group properties" because we see many individuals in proximity who have significant traits in common and who behave in coordination, but also the material properties possessed by many groups (buildings, uniforms, weapons, prayer books) serve as environmental supports that predispose us toward perceiving the group as a unitary reality. But to argue that because the group is *perceived* as supraindividual, it therefore exists "out there" as superordinate, is to confuse perceptual reality with objective reality. Organizing discrete events into a unitary perception is an achievement of the *perceiver* (see page 20).

There are also *motivational* factors which reinforce the institutional fiction—the belief that an institution has an existence "of its own." We have seen that members of a group tend to identify themselves with the group. If identification is to serve its functions, that with which the person identifies must be greater than the person himself—it must have virtues beyond any of his own virtues or the virtues of his obviously imperfect fellow members. Only a superlative group, in other words, can be a wholly satisfying object for a person's identification. Because of this, many members of a group have a need to consider their group to be the best of all possible groups, possessing virtues above and beyond those of any of its members, all-righteous in its aims, and, in the long run, all-conquering. However inaccurate or invalid these beliefs may be, they play an important and often decisive role in determining the behavior of the individual.

GROUP VALUES. An important part of the ideology of a group is the set of values shared by the members. Values, as we have seen (page 349), refer to beliefs about what objects and actions are good and desirable and what objects and actions are bad and undesirable.

Values should, of course, be distinguished from wants. It is a commonplace that an individual may want what he knows is bad and fail to want what he knows is good. As Heider [1958] has suggested, values tend to be perceived by the individual as independent of his wants—as impersonal and objective requirements imposed by the group and therefore possessing suprapersonal validity. For the individual member, the values of the group are a property of the group. The values of a group, like the larger belief system, reflect the group goals. A boys' play group may have the value of "fair play"; a college fraternity, the value of "blood brotherhood"; a research group, the value of "freedom of inquiry."

GROUP NORMS. Another important part of the ideology of a group consists of norms or rules of behavior. The norms of a group flow from its values. Norms, as we have seen (page 351), specify those actions in particular circumstances which are proper and those actions which are improper. The norms of a group also specify the rewards for adherence and the punishment for nonadherence.

Some norms of a group specify the behavior expected of all members of the group; other norms specify the behavior of particular members of the groups who occupy particular positions within the group—that is, role behavior (see Box 11.6). The norms of formal groups may be codified in the form of written rules; the norms of informal groups are seldom if ever so codified.

Festinger [1950] suggests that the factors responsible for the emergence of group norms are of two kinds. First, individuals in their drive for understanding seek to validate their beliefs. In the case of beliefs which cannot be empirically tested by checking with the facts or by applying a logical test of correctness, validity must be based on consensual agreement: what everyone believes, must be true. In their search for understanding, the members of a group seek and enforce unanimity. If *all* "right-thinking" men (the members of your group) believe that racial segregation is divinely approved, this is *true* as tested by "social reality"; therefore all must so believe. Segregation becomes a group norm. A heretic who violates this norm is punished.

Second, some degree of uniformity in attitudes and action is necessary if the group is to maintain its identity. And if the group is to survive, the interactions among the members must be coordinated to make it possible for the group to solve its problems. Norms regulating the conduct of the members are, therefore, instrumental to the success and survival of the group (see Box 11.7).

NORM SENDING. The process of norm enforcement has been termed "norm sending" by Rommetveit [1955]. As Thibaut and Kelley [1959] have pointed out, three processes are involved in norm sending: (1) stating the rule specifying the desired behavior and the consequences of adherence and nonadherence; (2) maintaining surveillance over the members of the group to determine whether or not they adhere to the rule; (3) administering rewards for adherence and punishments for

GROUPS, ORGANIZATIONS, AND THE INDIVIDUAL

BOX 11.6: *The code of the frat rat*

The following account of the social norms of the fraternity elite on the campus of a large Pacific Coast university was obtained in an interview with "one wise young informant," the son of one of the authors of this book. This informant had achieved some objectivity about the fraternity culture as a result of graduation from the university. As in some other anthropological investigations, the validity of findings based on the report of one informant may be questioned. To a harassed ethnographer-father, however, this account seems to have face validity. A word of caution: the old order is changing as a result of the effect of the "population explosion" on scholastic standards. This account describes the norms of the fraternity elite, circa 1960.

WHICH HOUSE, YOUNG MAN?

The houses in the fraternity system form a hierarchy of social worth; some are recognized as "big" houses, others as "bad" houses.

RUSHING

Each house in the system has a set of criteria which young men must satisfy to become pledges. Rich houses seek rich young men; athletic houses seek athletes; etc.

PLEDGE CONDUCT

The pledge is expected to perform certain jobs, e.g., cleaning the house, "hashing." Pledges are also required to answer the phone and to carry matches and pocket change for the use of active members. Failure to meet these requirements is punished by "tubbing," "swatting," or extra work. These punishments are termed "harassing activities."

MYSTICS

The pledge is required to learn the songs, rituals (secret dogma and handgrips), and rules of his fraternity which bind the members together in the complete harmony of true brotherhood.

STUDYING

A casual attitude toward academic work is expected of the frat rat. Studying in the library is "out"; it is the habitat of "apes"—minority-group members.

SPEECH STYLE

The frat rat is expected to speak the "special language" of his house; this language is loaded with ugly vulgarisms designed to reinforce a self-image of toughness and cynical sophistication.

DRINKING

The frat rat is expected to drink heavily.

DRESS

The frat rat is expected to conform to the style of the moment, e.g., "Ivy."

SOCIAL BEHAVIOR

Loud, rude, and drunken behavior is expected of the frat rat in the football rooting section and at house parties.

DATING

The particular house of the frat rat specifies the girls he is expected to date: certain fraternities date certain sororities only. Pledges are expected to date sorority girls only.

SEXUAL BEHAVIOR

Exploitative sexual conquests are expected of the frat rat. The badge of male virility is proudly worn; or, perhaps, it is only brandished in talk.

BOX 11.7: *Persuading the deviate*

Leonard Berkowitz and R. C. Howard, social psychologists at the University of Wisconsin, have tested the hypothesis that pressures toward uniformity among the members of a group will be greater the more interdependent the members.

Four- or five-person groups were given the case history of a labor-management dispute that had supposedly been adjusted by a mediation board. In one half of the groups a high degree of interdependence among the members of the group was created by announcing that prizes would be given to the best *groups* (High Interdependence). In the remaining half of the groups the subjects were told that prizes would be given to the best *individuals* (Low Interdependence). The subjects were then asked to predict the decision of the board by choosing one of 11 alternatives, ranging from a decision which placed the entire blame on the company and imposed a heavy fine on the company to a similar decision against the union. The subjects were told they were to make two predictions: one immediately after reading the case history and a second after an interchange of opinions among the members of the group.

The subjects could communicate with one another only by exchanging notes. The experimenter collected the notes giving their first prediction, and delivered previously rigged notes to each subject. In this manner the experimenter caused each group member to believe that one of his fellow members (the "deviate") was four steps away from his own prediction, another member was one step away, and the remaining members held identical opinions. A 10-minute "discussion" period (via notes) was then held. The number of words in each message was counted and taken as a measure of "pressure"—since each message attempted to persuade the recipient to change his vote. Previously prepared notes were again substituted for the real notes and the notes, as delivered, indicated that the deviate would not change his mind; the notes from the other members were neutral in content. The experimenter also manipulated the final prediction of the members of the group. The deviate remained four steps away: the other members gave opinions identical with that of the subject.

The mean number of words sent by the subjects are summarized in the following table.

	High Interdependence groups	Low Interdependence groups
Mean number of words sent to average group member	22.1	20.7
Mean number of words sent to deviate member	64.2	55.3

As the table shows, a greater number of words was sent to the deviate than to the average group member. Moreover, a greater proportion of words was sent to the deviate in the High Interdependence groups.

After each group had completed the task, the subjects were asked to indicate on a nine-point scale the extent to which they would want each person to join them in a new group. The data showed that the deviate member was more strongly rejected in the High Interdependence groups than in the Low Interdependence groups.

When the members of a group strive to satisfy their individual wants through group goals, a deviant member is coerced and deviant behavior is punished.

Berkowitz, L., and Howard, R. C. Reactions to opinion deviates as affected by affiliation need (n) and group member interdependence. Sociometry, 1959, 22, 81–91.

nonadherence to produce the desired consequences. Norms regulating behavior directly *relevant* to the objectives of the group are more strongly enforced than other norms. For example, in industrial work groups, norms regulating output are vigorously enforced; in criminal gangs, violation of the norm proscribing "squealing" may be met with death.

Roethlisberger and Dickson [1939] have described how the members of a work group attempt to enforce the group norm of a "day's work." They recount the following illustrations of the ways in which members of the group who violated the norm by overproducing were punished.

W6 and W2 were the first in output and it was toward them that most of the group pressure was directed. W6 was designated by such terms as "Shrimp," "Runt," "Slave." Sometimes he was called "Speed King," a concession to his wiring ability. W2 was called "Phar Lap," the name of a race horse. W1 was nicknamed "4:15 Special," meaning that he worked until quitting time. W5 was also called "Slave" occasionally.

One of the most interesting devices by which the group attempted to control the behavior of individual members was the practice which they called "binging." This practice was noticed early in the study. The observer described it as follows:

W7, W8, W9, and S4 were engaged in a game which they called "binging." One of them walked up to another man and hit him as hard as he could on the upper arm. The one hit made no protest, and it seems that it was his privilege to "bing" the one who hit him. He was free to retaliate with one blow. One of the objects of the game is to see who can hit the hardest. But it also was used as a penalty. If one of them says something that another dislikes, the latter may walk up and say, "I'm going to bing you for that." The one who is getting binged may complain that he has been hurt and say, "That one was too hard. I'm going to get you for that one."

In addition to its use as a penalty and as a means of settling disputes, binging was used

to regulate the output of some of the faster workers. This was one of its most significant applications and is well illustrated in the following entry:

W8 (to W6): "Why don't you quit work? Let's see, this is your thirty-fifth row today. What are you going to do with them all?"

W6: "What do you care? It's to your advantage if I work, isn't it?"

W8: "Yeah, but the way you're working you'll get stuck with them."

W6: "Don't worry about that. I'll take care of it. You're getting paid by the sets I turn out. That's all you should worry about."

W8: "If you don't quit work I'll bing you." W8 struck W6 and finally chased him around the room.

Obs. (a few minutes later): "What's the matter, W6, won't he let you work?"

W6: "No, I'm all through though. I've got enough done." He then went over and helped another wireman.

As we have seen (page 250), the perceived legitimacy (relevance) of a norm influences the degree to which it is accepted. If, for example, the members of a church group do not believe that political activity is a legitimate function of the church, norms which regulate political beliefs and prescribe how to vote may be rejected. In an experiment by Schachter [1951], the relation between relevance of task to the group's function and norm sending was experimentally studied. In some groups the activity assigned the group corresponded to the purposes of the group; in other groups, it had nothing to do with the purposes of the group. Schachter found that in the former groups greater pressure toward uniformity was exerted upon deviant members. Also the deviant was assigned to a low-status committee (a measure of rejection) to a far greater extent in the task-relevant than in the task-irrelevant groups.

The effect of variation in group *cohesiveness* upon pressure toward uniformity in two-person groups has been studied by Back

[1951]. The experimental task was the interpretation of a set of three pictures. After the two members of each group had independently interpreted the set of pictures, they were brought together to discuss their interpretations. The discussion was presented as an opportunity to improve their interpretations. The subjects were told that the final product would consist of their independent interpretations. The necessity for reaching agreement was specifically denied. Cohesiveness was experimentally manipulated in three ways: (1) the subjects were informed that the other member of the group had been selected by means of a personality questionnaire so that he would be highly congenial (for high cohesiveness) or uncongenial (for low cohesiveness); (2) the outcome of the task was made important to the subjects (for high cohesiveness) or unimportant (for low cohesiveness); (3) the value of belonging to the group was stressed (for high cohesiveness) or minimized (for low cohesiveness). In addition, a negative treatment was employed in which attraction to the partner, the outcome of the task, and the interest of the task were all depreciated by the experimenter to reduce cohesiveness.

Back found that in the high-cohesive groups there were more attempts to influence the partner in an effort to reach agreement. Reports of the subjects confirmed the high pressure toward uniformity in these groups. Moreover, in the high-cohesive groups, the members actually changed more toward the positions of their partners than in the low-cohesive groups. Cohesiveness, in short, increases pressures toward uniformity in groups.

GROUPS AND COMMON ACTION PATTERNS

The emergence of group goals and a group ideology leads the members of a group to display *common action patterns*. In this section, therefore, we must concern ourselves with this attribute of the behavior of group members.

Not all patterned action is determined by an individual's group membership. We must distinguish between patterned action that can properly be called group-determined and that which is more general in origin. The first of these is the patterned behavior which is *peculiar to members of a given group;* the latter is the patterned behavior which is *displayed by most members of a given culture.* Instances of group-determined patterned behavior would be the ritual of Mass in the Catholic Church, the secret handclasp of a college fraternity, the cadenced step of soldiers on the march, the parliamentary procedures corresponding to the special bylaws of a group. Culturally determined patterns include such acts as tipping one's hat when meeting a woman, handshaking, driving on the right side of the road, the wearing of trousers by men and of skirts by women. Most groups induce two kinds of common action patterns among their members: patterns which all members show in common, and patterns which differentiate members occupying different positions. Thus the foreman has a different action pattern from the worker, the minister from the parishioner, the head of the family from the child.

ACTION PATTERNS AND FUNCTIONAL SIGNIFICANCE. Many social scientists, in discussing group-determined action patterns, distinguish between "technological" patterns and "ritualistic" or "ceremonial" patterns. This distinction is presented clearly in an illustration that Benedict [1935] gives in her discussion of ritual:

> Ritual according to the accepted usage of the term does not include acts of routine provision of physical necessities. Traditional ways of building a house or of grinding and leaching acorns may be elaborating and exacting, but they are technological and not ritualistic. Ritual is always extra-necessitous from the technological point of view: it has reference, for example, to the act of killing slaves to bury under the house posts or to fertility ceremonies that employ the symbolism of eating or of impregnation to further the growth of fields.

This distinction is, however, of doubtful psychological validity. To a social scientist who has his own beliefs, based on modern technology, as to what does and what does not determine a firm foundation for a house, killing and burying a slave underneath the house post may seem extra-necessitous; but to the person who carries out these rituals and who has a different set of beliefs about house construction, such action may be just as utilitarian and just as necessitous as any other in building the house. Rituals, ceremonies, or any other standardized action pattern which is group-determined, must be seen as organically related to the goals of the group.

PATTERNING OF ACTION. While all group-determined action patterns can be seen as functional, we must understand why such actions show the high degree of communality of patterning that they do among different members of the same group. Perhaps the major reason lies in the fact that patterning is frequently demanded by the very nature of the group's goals. Typically, many of the primary goals sought by the members of a group require coordinated action. Thus the work patterns in a modern industrial plant must display a minimum of individual differences if production is to proceed "efficiently." The actions of the individual soldier must likewise be standardized if the army is to achieve its objectives.

Another compelling force toward standardization of action derives from the fact that groups are frequently the repository of the expert skills and knowledge required to achieve certain goals. Groups also provide for communicating a new skill developed by one member to the other members. Any single group member, therefore, by availing himself of a *common fund of knowledge,* will end with ways of doing things that are similar to the ways of others in the group. Furthermore, the different members of groups have access to the same material possessions of the group (tools, equipment, etc.), and these common tools impose a certain uniformity upon the actions of the person using them.

In addition, the knowledge that he is going through a specialized and elaborate pattern of behavior in common with the other members of "his" group can go a long way toward satisfying the individual's want to identify with something larger than himself. The participation in the same ritual in common with his fellows serves as not-to-be-denied evidence to the participant and to others that he does "belong" and that he is accepted. The youngster who gets his first job in the factory not only performs his particular work task in the patterned way but also gets great satisfaction through adopting the same dress, carrying the same kind of lunch box, and walking along with the same stride as his fellow workers.

DIFFERENTIATED ROLE PATTERNS. As we have said, the norms of a group not only prescribe that the members display common action patterns as members of the group, but also prescribe the role-behavior patterns of persons holding different positions in the group. This is especially true for larger and more formal groups. As a group becomes larger, the number of specialized positions and "appropriate" role patterns increases. A set of rules and regulations specifying the conduct of members vis-à-vis other members becomes at the same time more and more standardized and more and more differentiated. Intermember communications and relations become increasingly depersonalized. This is a characteristic feature of a *bureaucracy,* whether it be a business, educational, military, religious, or governmental bureaucracy.

The term bureaucracy is a label and not an epithet. Merton [1940] has described the structure of a bureaucracy as follows:

A formal, rationally organized social structure involves clearly defined patterns of activity in which, ideally, every series of actions is functionally related to the purposes of the organization. In such an organization there is integrated a series of offices, of hierarchized statuses, in which inhere a number of obligations and privileges closely defined by limited and specific rules. Each of these offices contains an area of imputed competence and responsibility. Authority, the power of control which derives from an acknowledged status, inheres in the office and not in the particular person who performs the official role. . . . The system of prescribed relations between the various offices involves a considerable degree of formality [which] is manifested by a more or less complicated social ritual. . . . Ready calculability of others' behavior and a stable set of mutual expectations is thus built up.

The effects of membership in a bureaucracy on the individual will be discussed in Chapter 14 (see page 502.)

TO RECAPITULATE

Through his various group memberships, the individual satisfies many of his wants. The power want of high-status members is especially well served by group membership, as is the affiliation want of rank-and-file members. In addition, it is through working with others in groups that individuals achieve many of the social goals essential to the survival of a society. Changes in the wants of the individual may come about as a group provides the individual with new experiences.

The members of a group, no matter how various the wants that led them to affiliate with the group, must come to agreement about the goals they will strive for as a group. These group goals consist of both the unique and the accessory goals of the group.

Acceptance of the goals of a group is facilitated if the group goals are seen as relevant to the satisfaction of the wants of the members, if the goals are clearly stated, if the group is cohesive, and if the members participate in setting the group goals. Over time, acceptance of group goals changes with the perceived probability of satisfying individual wants through group membership.

An ideology—a set of common beliefs, common values, and common norms—develops in every enduring group. This ideology impor-

tantly influences the behavior of the members of the group. The acceptance of the norms of a group depends upon the perceived appropriateness of the norms, the cohesiveness of the group, the characteristics of norm enforcement.

Common action patterns come to be displayed by the members of a group as group goals and a group ideology emerge in the course of member interaction. These standardized action patterns have functional value for the group. Role-differentiated action patterns also come to be displayed by members occupying different positions in the group.

GUIDE 34: *In all groups, the positions, roles, and powers of the members become differentiated and organized into a system—the group structure—which influences the functioning of the group and the satisfactions of the members*

An account of how an enduring group with a more or less stable "group structure" evolves from a collection of strangers is our first concern in this section.

THE BEGINNINGS OF GROUP FORMATION

There is a considerable body of evidence that mere spatial proximity may help lead to the formation of enduring groups. Festinger, Schachter, and Back [1950], in their study of a housing community for married veteran students, found that friendship groups were most often made up of next-door neighbors. In the two projects in the community, 60 and 76 per cent respectively of all sociometric choices were made of next-door neighbors. The most popular persons were those who lived in apartments that opened directly onto the stairways of the buildings, and who were, therefore, more likely to meet people. Furthermore, in those housing units that opened onto a court, the people who lived in centrally located units were most likely to receive choices. Relatively few choices went to persons who lived in end and corner units.

Various studies indicate that as time goes on, mere spatial proximity becomes less important as a determinant of group formation. Thus, Loomis and Beegle [1950], in their study of a farm-relocation colony, found that friendship groups were initially made up of settlers who lived close together. (The settlers had been randomly assigned their holdings in the new colony and were not, therefore, previously acquainted with one another.) These friendship groups were important in influencing the decision of the settlers to stay or leave the colony. Most of the persons who left had lived in a particular geographical region in one colony and had visited one another frequently. Two years after the founding of the colony, when many members of the dissatisfied group had left, a reexamination of the social groups indicated that physical proximity was no longer an important determinant of group formation.

As for other factors influencing the formation of groups, various studies have pointed to the importance of such obvious factors as kinship ties, ethnic-group membership, religious-group membership, age, sex, and similarity in values and attitudes.

ATTITUDES AND GROUP FORMATION. In one of the first studies in social psychology in which living groups were expressly created to meet the requirements of the research design, Newcomb [1960] offers some experimental evidence in support of the generalization that similarity in attitudes is a very effective group-inducing factor. His general interest was in studying the changes in relations, over time, between interpersonal attraction and similarity of attitudes. Because he wished to start with a base line of zero interpersonal attraction, he had to find a collection of persons who were complete strangers. It was also necessary to provide a research setting in which regular

and repeated observations could be made. These requirements were met by renting a student house. Male students who had transferred to the University of Michigan from other colleges and universities were offered the opportunity, several weeks before their planned arrival at the university, of living rent-free in the house for a full semester, if, in return, they would serve as experimental subjects. During this 16-week period, Newcomb systematically observed the development and change in the patterns of different forms of attraction among the men. Two collections of 17 students each were studied.

One of Newcomb's findings was that perceived degree of agreement in attitudes was of considerable importance in group formation. One of the two 17-man collections was found to develop into three relatively distinct groups. Newcomb describes these three groups as follows:

(1) a 5-man clique whose members ranked 2, 3, 4, 5, and 9 in . . . nonauthoritarianism; all were "liberal" in politics and in religion (they included two Jews, two Protestants, and a Catholic); all were in the arts college (rather than in engineering), and all were proud of their "intellectual" interests; four of the five were Easterners; in Spranger values they are, as a group, high in aesthetic, social, and theoretical values, and low in economic, political, and religious.

(2) a 3-man clique whose members ranked 7, 12, and 16 in nonauthoritarianism, together with a semi-isolate "hanger-on" who ranked 17; the three central members were all veterans, and three of the four were in engineering; their interests were "practical" ones; in Spranger values they are, as a group, high in economic and religious values and low in political.

(3) a 3-man clique whose members ranked 10, 11, and 13 in nonauthoritarianism; all were Midwestern, small-town Protestants, two of whom were in engineering; in Spranger values they are, as a group, distinctive only in being low in theoretical values.

Newcomb adds:

> The remaining five subjects included four rather extreme isolates, and one who was marginal between the first and second of the above cliques. This latter person ranked 1 in nonauthoritarianism, and fully shared the intellectual interests of the first clique; two of the members of the second clique were his roommates and, as one of the youngest House members, he admired their maturity and was "protected" by them.

GROUP STRUCTURE

In Newcomb's groups (see especially the second clique with its hanger-on) embryonic group structures were already apparent. Had these groups endured, more clearly defined systems of positions would doubtless have emerged (see page 310). Each of the various positions that come to be recognized by the group has a specialized function that contributes in some way to the objectives of the group. The emergence of a differentiated system of positions introduces order and regularity into the interactions of the members of the group as they work together on the tasks of the group. This differentiated system of positions constitutes the *structure* of the group. Associated with each position is its role (see pages 310 to 312), which prescribes the behavior of the person having the position toward persons having related positions.

In defining different positions, the members of a group promote the stability and effectiveness of the group. The group may successfully survive despite changes in the particular individuals holding different positions. The observations of boys' camp groups made by Sherif et al. [1954] suggest that the leader position and the bottom positions in the group structure are usually the first to become stabilized. These investigators report a good deal of jockeying for lieutenant positions near the leader.

In all groups, the different positions which are set up differ in status (see Box 11.8). Persons holding high-status positions enjoy greater rewards, both material and nonmaterial, than low-status members; they enjoy certain privileges and powers not accorded other members; they exercise the functions of leadership. In Figure 11.5 we have a graphic representation of the structure of a group.

RIGIDITY AND STEEPNESS. Groups and organizations vary considerably in structural *rigidity*. At one extreme are highly formal groups and organizations in which there is an integrated system of positions, with the rights and duties of each, or its role, closely defined by written rules and regulations. The behavior of the persons holding various positions is determined by these rules and regulations—idiosyncratic behavior is discouraged. Two persons holding the same position will tend to fill it in very much the same impersonal way—they act "by the book." At the other extreme are highly informal groups, such as friendship and play groups, in which the positions and their associated roles are only loosely defined. In such groups the behavior of the members reflects to a high degree their personalities;

FIGURE 11.5: Hierarchical structure of the Nortons, a neighborhood gang studied by the method of participant observation. [Whyte, 1943.]

THE NORTONS, SPRING AND SUMMER 1937

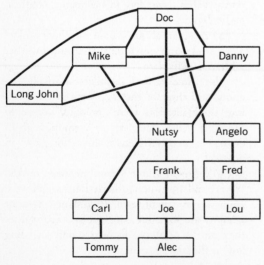

GROUPS, ORGANIZATIONS, AND THE INDIVIDUAL

BOX 11.8: *Who's who in the kitchen*

William F. Whyte, a sociologist at Cornell University, carried out a field study of "Human Relations in the Restaurant Industry." Whyte points out that every work group has a status system. The various jobs into which the work of the group is subdivided have different prestige value in the eyes of the workers, and the supervisor of the group must know the status system of his group to cope effectively with problems in human relations.

Whyte's description of the work groups in the kitchen of the Mammoth Restaurant well illustrates the complex factors which determine an organized status system.

Whyte observed first that the work situations in the kitchen were socially ranked. At the top was the range where all the cooking was done. The most highly paid and most skilled positions were found at the range. Next came the salad station, which also dealt in finished foods of high prestige. Next in order of status were the chicken-preparation and meat-preparation stations. Toward the bottom of the hierarchy were the chicken-cooking and vegetable-preparation stations. At the very bottom was the fish station.

The larger stations had a status system of their own. For example, the vegetable-preparation station consisted of eight women. The tasks of the women in order of status were as follows: One and Two were the vegetable cooks. Three divided her time between cooking and preparing vegetables. Four was in charge of preparation under the direction of One and occasionally did some cooking. Five, Six, Seven, and Eight did no cooking. This status pattern had developed as a result of the formally specified division of labor (e.g., cooking duties versus non-cooking duties) and personal factors. (Seven and Eight were older women who worked sitting down, thus giving the younger workers the opportunity to organize and direct the work.)

The influence of status was seen in the assignment of different vegetables to the women, for vegetables, it seems, differ markedly in social standing. Such decorative or luxury vegetables as parsley, chives, and celery are at the top. Green beans head the regular vegetables, followed by spinach and carrots. Next to the bottom are potatoes. Onions are considered the most undesirable of all because of their odor.

Higher-status workers tended to work on higher-status vegetables. When all the women were working on the same vegetable, the higher-status workers handled later stages in the process of preparation (e.g., dicing carrots instead of scraping them). This brought them closer to the social pinnacle of the kitchen—the range—and put them in a position to criticize the work of those handling the earlier stages.

The working supervisor of the fish station was one of the most skilled and valuable workers in the kitchen. Yet her station stood at the bottom of the status hierarchy because the other workers considered the fish station an odorous, dirty, and unpleasant place to work.

Whyte, W. F. Human relations in the restaurant industry. New York: McGraw-Hill, 1948.

the requirements of the positions are of little importance. Two persons holding the same position may act in two quite different ways.

Groups and organizations also vary in the *steepness* of the status hierarchy. In some groups and organizations, there is a high degree of concentration of status and power at the top. Control is in the hands of a small "power elite." In other groups and organizations, status and power are more widely diffused throughout the membership.

It is particularly in social organizations that these kinds of structural differences have important consequences for the individual. We will, therefore, discuss group structure as it is found in the social organization.

THE SOCIAL ORGANIZATION

Argyris [1957] points out that the basic property of a formal organization is its functional foundation. An organization is formed to accomplish a particular objective, and its structure reflects the conception of the planner of how this objective may best be achieved. The underlying assumption of the planner is that the members of the organization will, within limits, behave as the formal structure requires them to behave. Simon [1955] suggests that this assumption is, by and large, validated by the behavior of men in organizations:

> Organizations are formed with the intention and design of accomplishing goals; and the people who work in organizations believe, at least part of the time, that they are striving toward these same goals. We must not lose sight of the fact that however far organizations may depart from the traditional description ... nevertheless most behavior in organizations is *intendedly rational behavior*. By intended rationality I mean the kind of adjustment of behavior to goals of which humans are capable —a very incomplete and imperfect adjustment, to be sure, but one which nevertheless does accomplish purposes and does carry out programs.

The structure of most social organizations reflects the consensual experience and assumptions about human nature of organization planners. A number of "organizational principles" have been enunciated, among which are (1) task specialization, (2) chain of command, (3) span of control, and (4) minimal number of levels.

TASK SPECIALIZATION. The first assumption of the organization planner is that specialization of work increases the efficiency of the organization. In the design of industrial jobs, the criterion of minimizing costs is satisfied by specializing jobs to reduce skill requirements and time of learning.

CHAIN OF COMMAND. Task specialization leads to a multiplicity of groups, each performing a highly specialized task. Hence it is necessary to control, direct, and coordinate the constituent groups within the organization. This is done by ordering the groups in a hierarchy of authority in which the group on top directs and controls the groups on the bottom through prescribed channels of communication. Figure 11.6 shows the chain of command in an organization.

SPAN OF CONTROL. The principle of span of control holds that organizational and administrative efficiency are increased by limiting a leader to no more than five or six subordinates with interlocking work. The available evidence suggests that the concept of span of control is adhered to rather closely by most American business and industrial organizations.

MINIMAL NUMBER OF LEVELS. The concept of span of control has been criticized by Simon [1947] and others because it violates the organizational principle ". . . that administrative efficiency is enhanced by keeping at a minimum the number of organizational levels through which a matter must pass before it is 'acted on.'" Increasing the "administrative distance" between individuals by multiplying the number of levels creates communication problems for the top executive. The flow of messages to him becomes so heavy that he is forced to base his decisions upon summaries prepared by his subordinates.

BY WAY OF CRITICISM. McGregor [1960] has pointed out that these traditional principles of organization ". . . fall considerably short of being like the laws of physics." This is true for many reasons; McGregor cites the following three as especially significant:

1. The principles were primarily derived from an examination of such models as the Army and the Roman Catholic Church which differ in many important ways from industrial organizations. The notion that there are universal organizational principles is implicitly assumed.

2. Traditional organization theory overlooks the importance of political, social, and

economic factors in shaping organizations and in influencing management practices. The world of today resembles only faintly the world of a half century ago. The increased standard of living, the higher level of education, the spread of unionism, and the increased size and power of the Federal government in the United States today all deeply affect the functioning of industrial organizations. Technological changes, furthermore, have brought about all manner of changes in all types of organizations.

3. The principles of classical organization theory are based on a number of assumptions about human nature that are at best true only in part. McGregor asserts that the following set of assumptions guides the conventional organization planner:

a. The average human being has an inherent dislike of work and will avoid it if he can.

b. Because of this human characteristic of dislike of work, most people must be coerced, controlled, directed, threatened with punishment to get them to put forth adequate effort toward the achievement of organizational objectives.

c. The average human being prefers to be directed, wishes to avoid responsibility, has relatively little ambition, wants security above all.

Our discussion of the principles of motivation should suggest that these assumptions are of dubious validity. In Chapter 14 (see especially page 503), we will examine the effect on the rank-and-file members of organizations planned by traditional organization planners who are guided by this conception of human nature.

Organization planners would reply to McGregor's criticism, "Better some plan than none." They would argue that a rational plan is more logical, humane, economical, and efficient than building an organization planlessly and haphazardly. (Some of the consequences of planless growth are given in Box 11.9.)

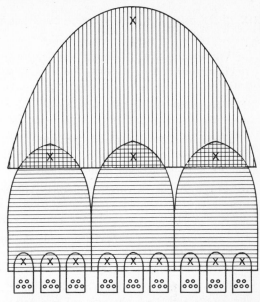

FIGURE 11.6: **The hierarchical structure of an organization. X symbolizes the official leaders at various levels in the organization. Orders and instructions flow from top leaders through intermediate leaders down to the front-line leaders who direct the primary work groups. The leaders below the top level have overlapping group membership, being members of both a superordinate and a subordinate group. Through their "linking-pin" function, they serve to integrate and coordinate the various groups in the organization to accomplish the goals of the organization. [After Likert, 1961.]**

STATUS SYMBOLS. In many groups and organizations, symbols are created and used to denote the various status ranks in the organizational structure. In an army, insignia of rank and the style of the uniform are the clearly visible symbols of status. Status symbols serve as cues which enable the members of an organization to perceive the status of other persons accurately and thus guide their behavior appropriately. (For an amusing example of how refusal to "wear" a status symbol resulted in difficulty for an individual and confusion for others, see Box 11.10.) Status symbols may also function to strengthen the feeling of identification with the organization. Status symbols come to be prized for them-

In Washington, D.C., one day not long ago, a quasi-governmental agency was established to conduct social science research. The official head of this organization was a retired military officer who played a do-nothing role with respect to organizational planning.

The growth of this organization was observed over a period of two years by a social scientist. He has summarized his major findings in the following six principles.

I. *The Principle of Symbiotic Accretion.* In a planless organization, the creation of a sinecure for a political favorite makes it necessary to create and staff a second, related position to protect the political favorite from ennui and loneliness.

II. *The Principle of Ascribed Status.* The political favorite is granted supervisory status and upon him are conferred all the perquisites of such status, including a fitting title (e.g., Chief), the appropriate status symbols, and a properly high salary.

III. *The Principle of Artificial Growth.* To rationalize the granting of supervisory status to the political favorite, it is necessary to add persons to the staff of the organization in the number required to form a section of sufficient size to justify an additional supervisor.

IV. *The Principle of Negative Value.* The size of the housekeeping or service group supported by the research staff—the primary working group—tends to vary *inversely* with the functional value of the service group. (The Principle of Negative Value results from the empire-building tactics of the service chief and from the reflex tendency of the official head to correct a dimly sensed malfunctioning of the organization by making the service group "bigger and better.")

V. *The Principle of Grewsome Immortality.* The planless organization achieves a "grewsome immortality" because it creates and justifies positions for numerous liaison and administrative persons in a higher echelon of the governmental bureaucracy who have the continuing function of explaining to their superiors in a still higher echelon why the planless organization is not functioning effectively.

VI. *The Principle of Rationalized Respectability.* The various liaison and administrative persons in the higher echelons of the governmental bureaucracy who are responsible for overseeing and directing the planless organization become bound together in a silent conspiracy of guilt which they assuage by inventing and believing the fiction that the organization will someday, somehow, become respectable.

selves alone. For example, the following account of the scramble for status symbols among American corporation executives was reported in *Time* [1955]:

In the hierarchy of U.S. business, a big problem is the question of executive prerogatives. Who eats in the executive dining room? Who gets the best office? And when does a man rise high enough to rate a rug on his floor? The scramble for the perquisites of rank is the butt of a thousand jokes, often leads to ludicrous situations. But to corporations themselves, the scramble is no joke. . . .

In many companies executives continuously play the game of "one-upmanship," the gentle art of being a jump ahead of colleagues in acquiring everything from better ashtrays to air conditioners. In general, the president and board chairman, who get the best of everything anyway, are rarely involved; the struggle takes place among the vice-presidents, and below. A few years ago, a Dallas company set up a new subsidiary with five brand-new vice-presidents installed in identical offices. Everything was peaceful until one used his expense account to replace his single-pen set with a two-pen set. Within four days all five worked their way up to three-pen sets. . . . A big Chicago oil company caused a major crisis a few years ago when it bought a new type of posture chair to test on a few of its executives.

Those left out were so miserable that one man, to save face, bought a chair with his own money and smuggled it into the office.

Corporation executives are not alone in

BOX 11.10: *The Mrs. was amiss*

When Doris E. Fleischman was married to the noted public relations counselor Edward L. Bernays, she was resolved, as an ardent feminist, to preserve her personal identity. But after 26 years of marriage as Miss Fleischman, she capitulated and became Mrs. Bernays.

The following excerpts from her account illustrate how her stubborn insistence upon retaining her maiden name complicated her social life.

Our first daughter was born in the fashionable obstetry of Miss Lippincott, on Madison Avenue. The latter accepted woodenly the news that I was "Miss" and my husband "Mr." However, she wept when she presented the birth certificate and whispered: "Do I have to put in illegitimate? . . ."

Every note to teacher presents a problem, since teacher should not be misled into thinking that dual names indicate a broken home . . . progressive educators adopt watchful attitudes towards children of split marriages. Cards, contracts, excuses for lateness all must be signed Miss with a coquettish parenthetical Mrs. for identification. The same awkwardness applies to our relationship with the various doctors and dentists who take care of them. . . .

While life at home has presented the greatest hazards to Lucy Stonerism, travel is not altogether smooth, either. Registering in a hotel in the United States leads to battles, withdrawals or confusion. Reactionary room clerks are not always easy to indoctrinate when rooms are scarce. We have developed various subterfuges. For instance, my husband once tried to solve the difficulty by registering "Mr. Bernays and wife (Miss Fleischman)." We were billed for three persons in one room that time, and made to feel decidedly immoral besides.

Morality seemed often to be drawn into the use of separate names, especially in Europe. I can remember a leering conductor on a train from Vienna to Prague, who wished us all happiness when he left us alone in one compartment with two passports. Using my own name was a good deal of fun in France in the early twenties. There was a puzzled *homme du monde* in Paris, who couldn't understand why any married woman should want to pass herself off as single. He assured me that men are far more interested in married than in maiden ladies. Why should I sacrifice the opportunities that awaited me as Mrs., but would be denied me as Miss? . . .

Occasionally, use of my own name has given me a sense of separate individuality. Once at a cocktail party, a beautiful woman attached herself to my husband and after a few minutes of intense presymbolic conversation looked indignantly at me as if to say, "I saw him first—why don't you scram?" I did, of course, to my husband's delight, since he didn't want to be saddled with a Mrs. at that point. And one evening at a public dinner, a fascinating Economics Professor urged, "Let's get out of here and have some fun. You don't have to wait for that so-and-so who brought you."

Fleischman, Doris E. Notes of a retiring feminist. Amer. Mercury, 1949, 68, 161–168.

scrambling for status symbols. Research scientists also covet their status symbols, be they degrees, titles, academic gowns, or uniforms (see Box 11.11).

FORMAL AND INFORMAL ORGANIZATIONS. The principles of organization which we have discussed guide the organizer when he sits down to draw a blueprint of an ideal organiza-

BOX 11.11: *The lab coat as a status symbol*

No one seems to be immune to the allure of the status symbol. The following satire was published in *Science* as an "editorial" and represents a critical, and amusing, self-examination of the foibles of research scientists by F. E. Warburton.

A neat, white, knee-length coat is universally recognized as the uniform of the scientist. The lab coat's primitive function as a utilitarian garment, protective against the dermolytic and vestidemolitive hazards of the laboratory, has bit by bit been replaced by its function as a status symbol. Just as we recognize a bishop by his mitre, or a burglar by his mask, we recognize a scientist by his lab coat. But in recent years the lab coat has become more than a mere workaday uniform. The soldier peels potatoes, cleans his rifle, and even fights his battles in his uniform; the modern scientist rarely works in his lab coat. When work is unavoidable, he will be found in his shirtsleeves, in a coarse brown smock, or in plastic. His lab coat, clean, pressed, possibly even starched, hangs safely behind the door, to be worn only when he is lecturing or greeting official visitors. Like spurs and shakos, the lab coat has been promoted to a new role; it is rapidly becoming, not merely the uniform, but indeed the dress uniform of the scientist.

Dress uniforms are worn solely for symbolic and ceremonial reasons, not for practical purposes. Nevertheless, their once-useful features are conscientiously preserved; an infantryman's sleeve buttons, or the spiked helmet of an uhlan, are examples. The lab coat is fraught with potentialities for such symbolic survivals. Detachable buttons were highly functional on garments subject to the vicissitudes of frequent vigorous laundering. The modern lab coat should of course be safely dry-cleaned, but the Chinese puzzles formerly used to hold the buttons in place might well be retained, and even elaborated into conspicuous ornaments —no longer detachable, of course. The utilitarian lab coat always bore stains characteristic of the work of its wearer. These could be symbolized by chevrons or flashes of suitable color; purple and red (hematoxylin and eosin) for the histologist; black and orange (sulfuric acid and bichromate) for the chemist; greenish yellow and scarlet (pus and blood) for the pathologist; blue and brown (ballpoint and coffee) for the statistician. Compact patterns of small holes or a bit of fringe on the cuff might be other symbols reminiscent of the days when lab coats were worn in the lab. Vertical as well as horizontal status could be shown by such insignia; undergraduates would wear unadorned white; graduate students might claim the right to a single, grey, grime-colored insigne; Ph.D.'s would wear the colors of their specialties, and Nobel prize-winners, like admirals-of-the-fleet and field marshals, would be privileged to blossom out in creations of their own tasteful design.

These developments cannot be pressed; they must evolve slowly, guided by tradition and respect for the past. But they should be taken seriously. Scientists have momentarily achieved a position of high prestige, but in a democratic society (as in any other) prestige without symbols is but fleeting, while symbols without prestige may endure forever.

Warburton, F. E. Malpighii, the newsletter (circulation 18) of the Malpighian Society of Montreal, vol. 2, no. 2, 14 Jan., 1960.

tional structure. However, if there is lack of congruence between the norms and goals of the organization and the wants of the members, an *informal organization* will very likely develop to satisfy their wants and to protect them against reprisals from top management. An informal organization may also arise if the formal organization proves to be inefficient in achieving the goals of the organization (see Box 11.12). This informal organization consists of all the patterns of interpersonal and intergroup relations that develop within the formal organization. It includes the cliques and friendship groups formed by the mem-

BOX 11.12: *Going out of channels*

Edwin E. Ghiselli, an industrial psychologist at the University of California, Berkeley, has studied the formal and informal structure of a small food manufacturing company. The chart below is based on his study.

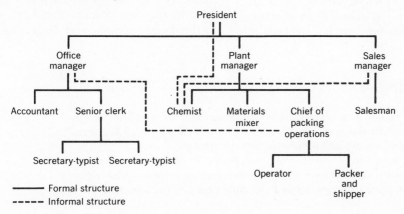

Both the president of the organization and the sales manager were interested in product development and therefore worked directly with the chemist. In working directly with the chemist, the president is "going out of channels" since the formal structure prescribes that he communicate with the chemist through the plant manager. In working with the chemist, the sales manager is assuming a function not formally assigned to him but he takes it on because it satisfies his interest in product development.

The office manager found it convenient to work directly with the chief of packing operations in handling orders and billing customers. In working with the chief of packing operations, the office manager is also going out of channels.

Thus, the study of the discrepancy between formal and informal organization can sometimes reveal weaknesses in an organization and suggest wants in members not satisfied by their roles as formally defined.

The formal structure apparently did not satisfy the wants of the president and the sales manager, nor did it make for efficiency in matters concerned with orders and billings. Under the circumstance, an informal structure developed which had little relation to the formal blueprint—almost everyone from president down went out of channels.

Ghiselli, E. E., and Brown, C. W. Personnel and industrial psychology. (2nd ed.) New York: McGraw-Hill, 1955.

bers. The ideology and structure of the informal organization is a powerful influence on the behavior of the members of the organization.

Bakke [1950] has emphasized that the informal and formal activities of an organization together constitute the social system which influences its members. He writes:

> As factors in influencing human behavior, the formal and informal systems *are not separable*. . . . Without denying the danger of inconsistency and conflict between the formal and informal systems, we would suggest that the social system to which participants in an organization react, and which is an effective determinant of their behavior, is a synthesis of

both formal and informal elements. People do not live in the midst of one, now the other, set of elements. They experience the system as a whole, a whole which is continually, though slowly, being modified by the daily adjustments of participants.

TO CONTINUE

As we have seen, a differentiated system of positions and roles characterizes every enduring group and organization. The emergence of leadership and followership positions and roles is of especial importance to the functioning of a group and the satisfaction of its members. In the next chapter, therefore, we turn to the social psychology of leadership.

CHAPTER GUIDES AND GLOSSARY

GUIDE 33: *A group comes into being to achieve the wants of its members; in the course of interaction the members develop a group ideology which regulates their attitudes and actions and influences their satisfactions*

GUIDE 34: *In all groups, the positions, roles, and powers of the members become differentiated and organized into a system—the group structure—which influences the functioning of the group and the satisfactions of the members*

category-system method. A method for describing the structure and functioning of a group in which an observer classifies the actions of the members into a set of mutually exclusive categories.

cohesiveness. The over-all attractiveness of a group to the members. Cohesiveness has been measured in various ways. One procedure is to ask each member to rate the degree to which he would like to remain a member. The mean rating is taken as a measure of cohesiveness.

formal organization. The differentiated system of interrelated groups, positions, and roles which is designed by the organization planner as the most efficient arrangement for accomplishing the objectives of the organization. The formal organization specifies the lines of authority and control and the official channels of communication among the groups and individuals in the organization.

group goal. An objective of a group accepted by most of the members of the group.

group goal, accessory. A secondary objective of a group as agreed to by most of the members. Accessory group goals develop as the group leaders strive to satisfy the changing wants of the members.

group goal, unique. The primary or major objective of a group as agreed to by most of the members.

group ideology. The set of beliefs, values, and norms shared by a majority of the members of a group. The ideology of a group is formed in the process of group interaction and, once formed, serves to regulate the behavior of the members.

group structure. The differentiated system of positions and roles of a group. The structure of most groups is hierarchical: the positions within the group are ordered in status and power from high to low.

informal organization. The patterns of interpersonal and intergroup relations that develop within the formal organization. The informal organization includes the cliques and friendship groups. An informal organization tends to develop when the formal organization proves to be inefficient or when it fails to satisfy important wants of the members.

institutional fiction. The belief, shared by the members of a group, that the group transcends the immediate members and the real property of the group. The group is perceived as a supraindividual entity. The institutional fiction is, in part, a product of the organizing and integrating nature of cognition and the want of the individual for a satisfactory object of identification.

participant observation, method of. A method for studying the structure and functioning of groups in their natural settings in which the observer lives intimately with the members of the group, participates in their various activities, and makes a continuing record of the content and pattern of group interaction.

psychological group. Two or more persons whose relations are interdependent and who share an ideology which is, to some degree, peculiar to the members of the group.

rating-scale method. An application of the rating method to the study of group functioning. An observer assigns a numerical score to certain specified dimensions of individual or group behavior. For example, the cooperativeness of each member and of the group as a whole might be rated on a seven-point scale.

social organization. An interrelated, integrated system of psychological groups formed to accomplish a stated objective.

sociogram. A graphic method for portraying, among the members of a group, the pattern of choices and rejections, likes and dislikes, secured through the sociometric method.

sociometric method. A method developed by Moreno to describe the pattern of acceptance and rejection that exists among the members of a group. Each member of the group is asked to specify privately his choices and rejections of persons for some specified activity. The method has been extended to include other ways of studying the pattern of interpersonal relationships, e.g., frequency of contact. The results of the sociometric study of a group may be graphically portrayed in a *sociogram.*

status symbol. Visible marks of the status of the various positions in a group or organization. Status symbols serve as cues which enable the members of a group or organization to perceive the status of other members accurately and thus guide their behavior appropriately. Status symbols come to be prized for themselves as symbols of success.

WHEREVER TWO OR MORE PEOPLE ARE GATHERED TOGETHER, *there will we find a leader. With the very formation of a group, some members are almost certain to take a more active role than others, to be preferred to others, to be listened to with more respect than others, to be dominant over others. This is the beginning of the differentiation of group members into leaders and followers. As the group continues to grow, and especially as it becomes more stable, a more definite and established leadership-followership hierarchy appears. And as this happens the role of the leader becomes more crucial for the functioning of the group.*

If, as we have asserted, the individual lives out his life within the context of groups, then it is true to say that he lives out his life under the influence of leaders: foremen, supervisors, officers, chiefs, chairmen, presidents. Who his leaders are and how they lead determine in large measure his fate and the fate of his groups. It thus becomes crucial, if we are to understand the social behavior of man, to understand the dynamics of leadership and group change. This is the concern of the present chapter.

12: LEADERSHIP AND GROUP CHANGE

JUST AS THE VARIETY OF MEN AND THE GROUPS they compose is great, so is the variety of their leaders and leadership behavior. While leadership of some kind is found among all groups, the individual who emerges as leader and his "style" of leading will, as we shall see, reflect the special circumstances of his emergence into leadership, the nature of the group within which he functions as leader, and the personality attributes not only of him but also of his followers. It is all of this which makes

it clear that the problem of defining leadership and identifying who is the leader of a group is not a simple one. Before turning to the study of leaders and leadership, it is therefore necessary to clarify how one does define and identify a leader—obviously we must be able to recognize the leader before we can study him.

DEFINING AND IDENTIFYING THE LEADER

There are two principal ways to identify the leaders of a group: (1) we may ask the members of the group whom they regard as most influential in directing the group (self-report method; see page 390); (2) we may ask observers of the group to name the members who seem to exert influence over their fellow members, or to record the relative frequency of effective influence-acts of the members of the group (the observation method; see page 384).

The criterion common to the two methods of identifying leaders is the *influence* which the individual has on his fellows. In our discussion of leadership we shall therefore define leaders as those members of the group who influence the activities of the group. This is a deceptively "simple" definition. There are at least three corollaries of this definition—corollaries which are sometimes neglected in discussions of leadership.

First, by this definition *all* members of the group are, at least to some degree, leaders. This is so simply because every member, to some degree, must of necessity influence the activities of other members in the group. Leadership, in other words, is a quantitative variable, not an all-or-none matter. Properly, we should speak not of leaders versus followers, but of the amount of leadership vested in any given person. Those members of the group who *outstandingly* influence the group may conveniently (and somewhat arbitrarily) be termed the "leaders," and we shall do so throughout this chapter. In using the term "leader," therefore, we are using a shorthand term, and our so-called "leaders" differ only in amount of influence from the other members of the group.

The second corollary is that leadership acts are interpersonal behavior events—instances of interaction. Like all forms of interaction, leadership works two ways: the leader influences the follower and the follower, in turn, influences the leader. Haythorn [1956], for example, found that the behavior of leaders was, to a significant degree, a function of the attitudes of the members of the group. When the behavior of leaders with authoritarian followers was compared with that of leaders with equalitarian followers (the two groups of leaders being matched with respect to authoritarianism as measured by the F scale; see page 201), it was found that the leaders of authoritarian groups tended to behave like authoritarian leaders and the leaders of equalitarian groups, like equalitarian leaders.

The third corollary is simply that we must differentiate between the leader as the individual who has a significant amount of influence and the official *head* of a group who may have very little influence. Not all *formal* leaders, in other words, are *actual* leaders.

We must keep all of these qualifications in mind as we now turn to a closer examination of the social psychology of leaders and leadership.

GUIDE 35: *The emergence of leadership and its functions in a group are determined by the structure, situation, and tasks of the group*

We have already pointed out that leaders, by virtue of their central position in the group, play important roles in shaping group goals, ideology, structure, and the common activities of the group members. We shall now see that the relationship is reciprocal, for it is the structure, situation, and tasks of the group which determine how leadership emerges and what functions it serves.

EMERGENCE OF LEADERSHIP

In general, as we have indicated, influence in a group tends to become lodged in one or relatively few persons, rather than spread evenly among all the members of the group. This is particularly true as the group becomes older and more stable. The natural history of this change in concentration of leadership can vary tremendously from group to group. In this section all we can hope to do is to indicate some *critical* points or episodes in the growth and functioning of a group, and some significant characteristics of its members which seem to speed up the emergence of such concentration of leadership and which determine the *pattern* of concentration.

LEADERS AND GROUP COMPLEXITY. As a group becomes larger, as it acquires more and more functions and accessory group goals (see page 398), a *hierarchy* of leadership develops. At the top of the hierarchy are the primary leaders; then appear successive layers of secondary and tertiary leaders, and so on; at the bottom of the hierarchy are the followers. It should be clear that the development of such a hierarchy involves a delegation or *spreading* of leadership. It is sometimes assumed that a leadership hierarchy implies concentration of leadership in the hands of one man. This, obviously, is not true. Large and complex groups and organizations necessitate a *number* of leaders and provide the conditions for the emergence of many leaders (see Box 12.1).

LEADERS AND CRISES. The emergence of leaders is particularly demanded in situations when progress toward the group goal is blocked or when the group suffers external threats to its security. In such cases there is likely to be lack of understanding on the part of the group membership as to what steps to take to achieve the goal or to ward off the danger. If at this point, for whatever reason, an individual in the group is *perceived by the group as a means to the goal* because of his personal characteristics—bravery, skill, knowledge, self-confidence, or anything else—he is then likely to emerge as leader.

The degree of threat faced by the group and the difficulty of its task will influence not only the emergence of leadership, but also the distribution of leadership. In a crisis situation strong focused leadership seems to occur (see Box 12.2). Historical analyses of the rise of dictatorships have shown that they arise in

crisis situations which require sudden changes in government. Demagogues seeking political power may create crises as a means of taking over control and may continue to make crises to retain control.

Leighton [1945] studied the "governing of men" in the miniature society of a Japanese relocation camp during World War II. He describes the blind, apathetic compliance of the Japanese-Americans under the stresses induced by the sudden disruption of established patterns of living and the isolated, idle life of the internment camp. They seemed ready to follow any would-be leader. Power was lying in the camp streets for anyone to pick up.

If the problems confronting the group are of great difficulty, the leadership functions become distributed among a number of persons. With tasks of lesser and lesser difficulty, leadership tends to become more and more concentrated, but below a certain level of difficulty, with very easy group tasks, leadership may again become more distributed. The task is so easy that "everyone" can do the job.

LEADERS AND GROUP INSTABILITY. Internal threat, as well as external threat, offers a prime opportunity for the emergence of leadership. Conflicting forces among subgroups can sometimes be brought into equilibrium by a powerful leader, who thus achieves a "balance-of-power" status. With the unification of the group, the subgroup leaders are displaced by the over-all leader.

Crockett [1955] offers empirical evidence that divided groups provide a good breeding ground for the usurpation of the roles of old leaders and the emergence of new leaders. As one phase of the Conference Research Project of the University of Michigan, he studied the emergence of new leaders in 72 conference groups in business, governmental, and industrial organizations. Groups in which the members held *divergent* opinions about the goals of the group and the means for reaching these

GROUPS, ORGANIZATIONS, AND THE INDIVIDUAL

BOX 12.1: *Division of leadership*

William F. Whyte, a sociologist at Cornell University, has illustrated, in his study of the restaurant industry, the implications of growth in the size of an organization for the delegation of leadership.

Tom Jones, restaurant man, begins with a small, short-order restaurant. He has two employees, but there is no division of labor—all three work together as cooks, countermen, and dishwashers. (Stage 1)

Stage 1

M – Manager
C – Customers
W – Workers

The restaurant flourishes and Jones moves to larger quarters and hires additional workers. He now has a staff of cooks, dishwashers, and waitresses. We see the beginning of the division of labor. Jones himself is, however, still the only supervisor, but the beginning of division of labor confronts him with a problem which he did not have in Stage 1. The smooth functioning of the organization requires that the work of waitresses, cooks, and dishwashers be coordinated. (Stage 2)

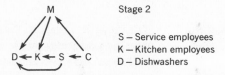

Stage 2

S – Service employees
K – Kitchen employees
D – Dishwashers

The business continues to grow and Jones moves to still larger quarters. The increased size of the business makes it impossible for him to supervise all the work. He hires a service supervisor and a food-production supervisor. One of his employees is placed in charge of the dishroom, as a working supervisor, and a checker is added to the staff to total checks for the waitresses and to see that the food is served properly. With increase in the size of the organization has come specialization of both work and leadership functions. There are now four "leaders": the manager, the two supervisors, and the checker. (Stage 3)

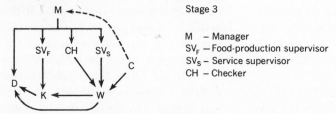

Stage 3

M   – Manager
SV_F – Food-production supervisor
SV_S – Service supervisor
CH – Checker

One more step in the division of labor is taken in the interest of efficiency of operation. Up to this point, the cooks have been serving the food directly to the waitresses. These two functions are divided so that both can proceed more efficiently. A service pantry is set up as a relay station between cooks and waitresses. This adds one more group of workers to the organization, and a second level of supervision is added to cope with the problems created by increasing size and specialization. *(Continued)*

Tom Jones, the erstwhile short-order cook, is now a top-management official and "dishes out" orders to second-line "leaders" rather than food to customers. (Stage 4)

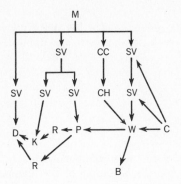

Stage 4

M — Manager
SV — Supervisor
CC — Cost control supervisor
CH — Checker
C — Customer
W — Waitresses
B — Bartender
P — Pantry workers
K — Kitchen workers
R — Runners
D — Dishwashers

Whyte, W. F. Human relations in the restaurant industry. *New York: McGraw-Hill, 1948.*

goals generated informal leaders significantly more often than groups which were agreed upon their means and goals.

LEADERS AND FAILING HEADS. New leaders are likely to emerge when the official head of the group, the formal leader, does not adequately perform the functions of leadership, e.g., as policy maker, expert, planner, and executive. The study by Crockett, cited above, indicates this clearly. In 83 per cent of the groups whose formal head did not fulfill the functions of leadership, another member of the group took over these functions. In comparison, in only 39 per cent of the groups in which the formal leader performed effectively did a new leader emerge.

Katz, Maccoby, Gurin, and Floor [1951] have reported a similar finding in their study of railroad section gangs. The men were asked, "Is there some one man in the section who speaks up for the men when they want something?" The results indicated that when the foreman, the official head, did not assume this leader function effectively, another leader emerged.

LEADERS AND WANTS. Like any member, the potential leader seeks achievement of the group goals and seeks also the satisfaction of accessory wants. But what marks off the leader from the nonleader is the strength of certain kinds of wants in him that are especially well served by the leadership role. Primary among such wants are wants for power, prestige, and material gain (see Box 12.3). Only if there are members of the group who have such wants in sufficient degree can we assuredly expect that a leader will emerge. If the group is rich in "leader potential," distributed leadership may be a possible solution; if the group has very few members with such potential, more highly focused leadership will emerge; if there are no such members, no leadership will emerge and the group may disintegrate.

In other words, to understand the emergence of leadership we must consider not only the factors in the group situation and in the perceptions and wants of the followers, but also the psychology of potential leaders. We cannot have leaders without followers; we cannot have leaders without leaders.

426

BOX 12.2: *Leadership in a laboratory crisis*

Robert L. Hamblin, while at the University of Michigan, carried out a laboratory investigation of the effects of a "crisis" upon leadership.

Twenty-four 3-person groups of college students were asked to play a modified shuffleboard game for about 30 minutes. They were told that they were to learn the special rules of the game by trying out different procedures. A red light would flash on a light board every time a rule was violated; a green light, every time a score was made.

The game was presented as a test of ability to analyze a rather complex situation, and the groups were told that they were in competition with high school students who had earlier participated in a similar experiment and that comparative cumulative scores would be posted at the end of each of the game's six 5-minute playing periods.

Each time a player suggested a procedure for testing a rule or suggested a possible rule, he was given an "influence-attempt score." If the attempted suggestion was adopted by the group, he was given an "accepted influence score." Two measures for each player for each playing period were then calculated: an *influence ratio* and an *acceptance rate*. The influence ratio was the number of influence-attempt scores of an individual divided by the average of the influence-attempt scores of the other two group members. The acceptance rate was the proportion of a subject's influence attempts which were accepted.

By the end of the first three playing periods, the average group had learned most of the rules of the game and was enjoying a comfortable, albeit fictitious, lead over the high school competitors. In the fourth playing period, 12 of the groups (crisis groups) were exposed to a "crisis" by an unannounced change in the rules of the game. Procedures that had been legal were now made illegal and vice versa. As soon as the players learned a new rule, it was again changed. The members of the crisis groups were unable to make a single score during the last three periods. The remaining 12 groups (control groups) continued to play under the original rules.

The results indicated two things. First, leaders have more influence in a time of crisis than in a time of noncrisis. The members of a group accept leadership when faced with a crisis. The following figures show the mean influence ratios and mean acceptance ratios for high influencers in the crisis and control groups, by playing periods.

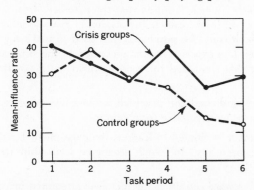

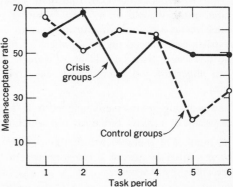

Second, a group rejects its old leader and replaces him with a new leader if the old leader does not quickly and decisively meet the crisis. Whereas 9 of the 12 crisis groups replaced their original leaders, only 3 of the control groups ever changed their leaders.

Hamblin, R. L. Leadership and crisis. Sociometry, 1958, 21, 322–335.

THE FUNCTIONS OF LEADERS

The complexity of the role that the emerging leader must play may best be indicated by reviewing briefly the manifold functions of the position. As will presently be shown, the specific functions of leaders vary somewhat in importance with the kind of group being led; leaders functioning in an "authoritarian" group may stress certain functions, whereas leaders in a "democratic" group may stress others. However, whatever the nature of the group, all leaders must serve to some degree many different functions. Many of the functions of group leaders apply also to leaders of organizations.

THE LEADER AS EXECUTIVE. The most obvious role of the leader in any group is as the top coordinator of the activities of the group. Whether or not he assumes the direct role of determining the policies or objectives of the group, it is almost invariably his responsibility to oversee the execution of these policies.

In his executive capacity the leader does not himself ordinarily carry out the necessary work; he assigns it to other group members. Occasionally, a person in a leadership role suffers from an inability to delegate responsibility and authority; he feels the necessity of becoming personally involved in each group activity. This produces either (or both) of two difficulties in group functioning. Either the leader becomes a bottleneck or he prevents the development of task responsibility on the part of other members and their involvement in the work of the group.

THE LEADER AS PLANNER. The leader often assumes the role of planner—deciding the ways and means by which the group shall achieve its ends. This may involve both the determination of immediate steps and the long-range planning of the future steps to the

BOX 12.3: *Motivation to lead*

John K. Hemphill of the Educational Testing Service has reported an experimental study of why people attempt to lead.

In the experiment, several four-man groups were assigned to a "high" reward condition. These groups worked on a "manufacturing problem" which required that the members organize themselves as a toy manufacturing concern to operate their business for maximum profit. Tinkertoy parts were placed on a "supplier's" table which could be purchased and used to make toys. The toys could then be sold at a "buyer's" table. The experiment was presented to the subjects as an important and interesting research project that simulated the manufacturing of goods for profit.

The remaining groups were assigned to a "low" reward condition in which the task was presented as a pretest of a trivial Tinkertoy test which might be more suitable for children.

The number of times each individual group member attempted to lead on the experimental task was measured by use of a category system (see page 385) in which attempted leadership acts were tallied by observers.

The results showed clearly that under the "high" reward condition the members attempted many more leadership acts than under the "low" reward condition.

Men will strive for leadership to achieve goals of importance to them.

Hemphill, J. K. Why people attempt to lead. In L. Petrullo and B. M. Bass (Eds.), Leadership and inter-personal behavior. *New York: Holt, Rinehart & Winston, 1961.*

GROUPS, ORGANIZATIONS, AND THE INDIVIDUAL

goal. And frequently the leader is the sole custodian of the plan. He alone knows the entire pattern; other group members are apprised only of segments—often apparently unconnected—of the whole plan.

THE LEADER AS POLICY MAKER. One of the most important of all leader functions is the establishment of group goals and policies. In general, group goals and policies may arise from three sources:

1. From "above," that is, dictated by authorities superordinate to the given group, such as commands passed down from higher military echelons to lower, or policies established at the top level of an organization and unquestioningly accepted as directives at lower levels. However, even when policy originates from above, the lower-level leaders are frequently consulted in establishing policy.

2. From "below," that is, dictated by the decision of the group membership as a whole. When goals and policies are determined from below, the leader still has a responsibility for guiding the discussion and thus is intimately involved in policy making.

3. From the leader himself when he has autonomy to make policy decisions.

No matter, then, what the source of policy may be, involvement in policy making remains one of the leader's most important functions.

THE LEADER AS EXPERT. The leader is often distinguished as a source of readily available information and skills. With a high degree of specialization of function, of course, leaders of formal groups come to lean more and more heavily upon technical assistants and advisers. In many informal and spontaneous groups, on the other hand, it is often the man who demonstrates the greatest technical knowledge, relevant to the group's goals, who becomes the leader. Thus, on a camping expedition the guide may come subtly to assume the leadership of the group. Whenever group members are dependent upon the person with technical knowledge, there is likely to be a polarization of power around him, and he may exploit this power to consolidate his role as leader.

THE LEADER AS EXTERNAL GROUP REPRESENTATIVE. Since it is manifestly impossible for all members of a large group to deal directly with other groups and other people outside the group, the leader characteristically assumes the role of representative of the group in its external relations. He is the official spokesman for the group. Not only are the outgoing communications of the group channeled through him; so are the incoming communications. He is in this special sense what Lewin has called a "gatekeeper."

THE LEADER AS CONTROLLER OF INTERNAL RELATIONS. More than any other member, the leader governs the specific details of group structure and by so doing he may function as the controller of in-group relations. There are types of groups, as we shall presently see, in which internal relations are primarily channeled through the leader himself; there are others in which the leader is remote from all but a few special group members; there are still others in which the leader is "one of the boys."

THE LEADER AS PURVEYOR OF REWARDS AND PUNISHMENTS. Particularly significant from a member's point of view is the leader's power to apply rewards and punishments, which enables him to exercise control over the group members. Sometimes the rewards and punishments are concerned with relatively external things, e.g., when a gang divides stolen loot or when a worker is given an unpleasant task by his foreman. Often, however, the rewards and punishments have to do directly with the role of the individual in the group—he may be promoted to a more important position in the group hierarchy; he may be given special honors; he may be reduced in status or deprived of a coveted position. In extreme disciplinary action, he may be ousted or killed.

THE LEADER AS ARBITRATOR AND MEDIATOR. Somewhat associated with the leader's function as a purveyor of rewards and punishments is his role as an arbitrator and mediator of intragroup conflict. It is his task to act as both judge and conciliator. It is within the power of the leader to reduce or to encourage factionalism within the group, depending upon what personal aims he seeks to achieve.

THE LEADER AS EXEMPLAR. In some kinds of groups the leader may serve as a model of behavior for the group members thus providing them with a concrete indication of what they should be and do. A military leader who bravely precedes his troops into battle serves as such an exemplar; so does the leader of the church who must, at least in his public life, exemplify all the moral virtues he would inculcate in the church members.

THE LEADER AS SYMBOL OF THE GROUP. Group unity is likely to be enhanced by any factor that makes the group a distinct entity. To this end a group may equip itself with various identifying paraphernalia—badges, uniforms, names, etc. The leader plays something of a similar role by providing a kind of cognitive focus for group unity, e.g., the Royal Family of Great Britain. The leader as a symbol provides for group continuity in still another way, in that he may exist in "office" over a prolonged period, even though there is a complete turnover among the rank-and-file members of the group (e.g., the tenure of the president and faculty of a college as compared with that of the students).

THE LEADER AS SUBSTITUTE FOR INDIVIDUAL RESPONSIBILITY. Not uncommonly in certain types of groups, the leader plays an extremely important role for the individual member in relieving him of responsibility for personal decisions and acts that he wishes to avoid. In return for allegiance, the leader frees the individual from the necessity of making decisions. Instead of endeavoring to clear up areas of cognitive confusion for himself, the individual puts his trust in the leader and lets him make the decisions. Fromm [1941] has written

cogently about the tendency of people to delegate critical responsibilities to their leaders in their "escape from freedom."

THE LEADER AS IDEOLOGIST. The leader may in some circumstances serve functions far more extreme in their implications than some of those described above. Sometimes it is the leader who furnishes the ideology of the group; he serves as the source of the beliefs, values, and norms of the individual members. The "official" ideology of a group, as we have indicated, frequently reflects the thinking of the leadership more closely than the thinking of the rank-and-file membership. The official ideology, no matter how discrepant from the beliefs of individual members, will tend to filter down and influence them. This will be particularly true where the leader controls the flow of information into the group.

THE LEADER AS FATHER FIGURE. A number of the preceding functions of the leader are incorporated in a more general emotional role of father figure for the individual member. The leader serves as a perfect focus for the positive emotional feelings of the individual; he is the ideal object for identification, for transference, for feelings of submissiveness. When the leader does not immediately seem to fill these needs, the followers may sometimes "remake" him to fit their needs (see Box 12.4). There seems to be no doubt of the central importance of the father-figure role in accounting for the power of certain leaders in special circumstances.

THE LEADER AS SCAPEGOAT. The ambivalence of attitudes toward father figures in general is markedly true of leaders. Just as the leader may constitute an ideal object for positive emotional feelings, so may he serve as a target for the aggressions of the frustrated, disappointed, disillusioned group. This is the opposite side of the coin: to the extent that the leader assumes responsibility, he may, in the event of failure, expect to be blamed.

PRIMARY AND ACCESSORY LEADERSHIP FUNCTIONS. The various functions of leadership

BOX 12.4: *Followers: creators of leaders*

During World War II, H. L. Ansbacher, a psychologist at the University of Vermont, was a member of a staff of social scientists who studied the attitudes and reactions of German prisoners of war to Allied propaganda. The bulk of the data was obtained by anonymous questionnaires administered to recently captured soldiers.

Beginning in November, 1943, each succeeding group of prisoners was asked, "Do you have confidence in the Führer?" Confidence in Hitler persisted at a high level throughout the period from November, 1943, to January, 1945, despite the fact that during this period Germany had met with continuous military reverses. Why did the German people continue to believe in a leader who was leading them from bad to worse?

Analysis of the attitudes of a group of 643 German soldiers captured in September, 1944, throws light on this question. In this group, 65 per cent expressed confidence in Hitler, 19 per cent reported no confidence, and 16 per cent did not answer.

Of the 65 per cent who expressed confidence in Hitler, only a minority accepted all his views. The majority of his followers held views which were sharply divergent from the policies proclaimed by him.

Ansbacher interprets this finding as follows:

> As confidence in Hitler was found in spite of basic disagreement, the object of the confidence was no longer the real totalitarian leader as manifested in his writings, speeches, and deeds, but a leader of the follower's own creation. . . . He was a leader who knew the war was lost, in spite of the fact that he still promised victory many months after this poll was taken; who would consequently take the necessary steps to end the war, all propaganda to the contrary notwithstanding; and who did not expect his soldiers to fight to the last bullet under all circumstances, although he had given explicit orders to that effect. He was a Hitler who at least in these respects was reasonable, compromising, humane—which the real Hitler was not. The imagined Hitler was the expression of the motives of the majority of his followers. . . .

> The extraordinary confidence in Hitler during 14 months of continuous reversals finds its explanation in the phenomenon that the object of confidence was at least in part a social-psychological creation, rather than a complete reality.

Ansbacher, H. L. Attitudes of German prisoners of war: a study of the dynamics of national-socialistic followership. Psychol. Monogr., 1948, 62, no. 1.

discussed above may be classified into *primary* and *accessory* functions. The primary functions include those essential to the exercise of leadership: executive, planner, policy maker, expert, external group representative, controller of internal relations, purveyor of rewards and punishments, arbitrator and mediator. The accessory functions are those a leader may assume or may be assigned by the group by virtue of his leadership position: exemplar, external symbol of the group, substitute for individual responsibility, ideologist, father figure, and scapegoat.

The distinction between primary and accessory leadership functions is somewhat arbitrary and depends upon the objectives of the group. The primary functions of the leader of a religious group, for example, include the functions of exemplar and symbol of the group—functions we have termed accessory.

And with changes in the objectives of a group, the primary functions of the leader may change.

PATTERNS OF LEADERSHIP FUNCTIONS. Although leadership tends in any group to serve all the functions we have discussed above, the degree of importance of each function, the pattern of interrelations of functions, and the particular manner in which each function is carried out depend upon the type of group. In informal and temporary groups, many or most of the functions of leadership have no opportunity to emerge, whereas in more stable and formal groups of long duration, in such groups and organizations as the family, political parties, business organizations, military units, *all* the leadership functions may be important.

TO RECAPITULATE

The leaders of a group or organization—those members who outstandingly influence the group—emerge early in the life of the group or organization. The emergence of leaders is facilitated by a number of factors: increase in the size and complexity of the group; blockage to the achievement of group goals; external and internal threats that confront the group with a crisis; failure of the official head; the availability of members strongly motivated to attempt leadership.

The complexity of the leadership role is clearly brought out by an analysis of the numerous functions which all leaders, in varying degrees, must serve. These various functions—the leader as executive, planner, policy maker, expert, external group representative, controller of internal relations, purveyor of rewards and punishments, arbitrator and mediator, exemplar, symbol of the group, substitute for individual responsibility, ideologist, father figure, scapegoat—may be classified into primary and accessory functions. The pattern of salient functions and the way they are carried out depend upon the type of group.

GUIDE 36: *The characteristics of a leader, and the type of leadership he displays, reflect the goals and norms of the group and the leader's personality*

Having seen how leadership emerges in a group and the functions it fulfills, we turn now to the question of *who* fills the leadership role and *how* he carries out its functions. Different leaders perform the role in different ways; there are many types or "styles" of leadership. We begin our discussion of types of leadership by examining individual differences in the way leaders discharge their functions.

DIMENSIONS OF LEADERSHIP BEHAVIOR

A factor-analytic study by Halpin and Winer [1957] suggests that most of the individual differences in the performance of leaders can be accounted for by postulating two relatively independent dimensions of leadership behavior: (1) "consideration" and (2) "initiating and directing." "Consideration" behavior is primarily concerned with *motivating* the members of a group to accept the group goals and to work at the group tasks, and with *maintaining internal harmony* and member satisfaction. "Initiating and directing" behavior is primarily concerned with specifying *ways and means* for accomplishing the goals of the group and *coordinating* the activities of the several members.

A leader who receives a high score on the "consideration" dimension is member-oriented: he displays consideration toward the members, rewards good work, stresses the importance of harmony and satisfaction in internal relations, remains easily approachable, accepts suggestions from the group, and invites participation in planning and goal setting. A leader who earns a low score on this dimension punishes members for poor work, displays little consideration for the feelings of the members, acts without consultation, does not accept suggestions, and does not explain his actions.

When a group faces a difficult problem, the dimension of "initiating and directing" becomes of special importance. This kind of behavior serves many of the primary leadership functions we have listed: policy making, planning, executing, etc. A leader who receives a high score on this dimension is one who tries out new ideas on members, makes his attitudes clear to the membership, makes sure his role in the group is understood, requires that standard procedures be followed in any work task, maintains definite standards of performance.

In the study by Halpin and Winer of the leader behavior of air-crew commanders, it was found that the two factors of "consideration" and "initiating and directing" together accounted for 83 per cent of the differences in their leader behavior.

The isolation of these two primary dimensions of leadership behavior suggests that if a leader is successfully to exert influence and move a group toward its goals, he must motivate the members and maintain harmony and satisfaction, while at the same time directing and coordinating the efforts of the group.

TASK AND MAINTENANCE SPECIALISTS. In most groups, especially those with an official head, the above two functions must be assumed by the same head if he is to lead effectively. The failure of the head to fulfill one or the other of the functions may give rise to an unofficial or informal leader who takes over the neglected role. In "headless groups," where there is no official leader, the two functions are often assumed by two *different* emergent leaders—a "task specialist" and a "maintenance specialist."

This is nicely illustrated in Bales's [1953] study of small discussion groups. Thirty 5-man experimental groups were used. Each group, which met four times, was required to arrive at a single solution of a human-relations prob-

lem acceptable to all the members. After each of the four sessions, each member was asked to rank-order all the other members on four scales: who contributed best ideas? who did the most to guide the discussion? whom do you like? whom do you dislike?

Bales found that at the end of the *first* meeting of the group the best-liked member tended to be judged most frequently as having had best ideas and as having given most guidance to the discussion (the "like" choices coinciding with choice for "best ideas" and "guidance" to the extent of 64 and 41 per cent, respectively). By the end of the *fourth* meeting, however, the "like" choices coincided much less frequently with choices for "best ideas" or "guidance" (11 and 18 per cent, respectively). Over the four meetings of the group, the top-ranking man on "best ideas" and "guidance" was, on the average, the *most disliked* man. The most liked man was usually ranked only second or third on "best ideas" and "guidance."

Bales concludes that the group elevates to leadership positions two complementary leaders: a "task specialist" and a "social-emotional specialist." The task specialist is selected because he is seen as having the best ideas and as doing the most to guide the discussion. He concentrates on the task of the group, playing an aggressive role in moving the group toward a solution. He thus tends to incur hostility and is disliked. Concurrently, a second man emerges as a leader. Chosen as highly liked, he is the "social-emotional specialist" who concerns himself with solving the social-emotional problems of the group, resolving tensions and conflicts within the group to preserve group unity. Thibaut and Kelley [1959] have termed the latter kind of leader a *maintenance specialist* because his function is to maintain the interdependence of the members and thus ensure the survival of the group.

The differentiation of the leadership role into task and maintenance specialists appears to be a primitive and widespread phenomenon. Zelditch [1955] studied, in 56 different societies, role differentiation in the basic family unit (a family group consisting of one male adult, one female adult, and their offspring). He found that characteristically throughout the 56 societies, families showed a differentiation into the task specialist and maintenance specialist roles. Typically, the male adult was found to be the task specialist; the female adult, the maintenance specialist.

AUTHORITARIAN AND DEMOCRATIC LEADERSHIP TYPES. Perhaps the most prominent and socially significant typology of leadership is the authoritarian-democratic distinction. At the outset it should be emphasized that these terms are used simply as a convenient way of distinguishing two very different types of leadership. Whether the particular names authoritarian and democratic are the most precise ones is questionable, and it is wise to be cautious in assuming these two types are directly descriptive of the kinds of leadership to be found in what are called, in the world today, democracies and authoritarian states. Nonetheless, we do feel some confidence that what we shall describe as authoritarian leadership is more like that found in dictatorship states, and democratic leadership more like that found in democracies.

Another caution should be indicated. Most of the research evidence bearing on the differentiation between these two types of leadership has been obtained *in our democratic culture*. It is entirely possible that similar studies in other cultures might yield different results. But even granting this possibility, the significance of these data is not diminished. The fact is that in our own culture all types of leadership are to be found, from the most extremely authoritarian to the most extremely democratic. It is of the highest relevance, therefore, to compare the effectiveness of these two leadership types as they operate within our culture.

AUTHORITARIAN LEADERSHIP. The authoritarian leader wields more absolute power than the democratic leader; he alone determines policies of the group; he alone makes major plans; he alone fully knows the succession of future steps in the group's activities; he alone dictates the activities of the members and the pattern of interrelations among the members; he alone serves as the ultimate agent and judge and as the purveyor of rewards and punishments. Hence, the fate of each individual within the group is in his hands.

The authoritarian leader deliberately develops these absolute functions and actively resists changes in them. The techniques by which he reinforces and protects his leadership status are various. By preventing individual members from participating in the setting of the group goals and by imposing what often seem to them irrelevant subgoals, the autocratic leader guarantees that his guidance will be indispensable for the long-term functioning of the group. Under this type of control, the involvement of individual members is segmental and dependent, and the group goals are unclear (see page 400).

The authoritarian leader encourages a segregated group structure in which intercommunication among the members is held to a minimum and wherever possible the avenues of intercommunication are through the leader or are under his immediate supervision. This may have unfortunate effects upon the group as a whole. For one thing, there is less opportunity for the development of close interpersonal relations among all group members, and this lessens the attractiveness of the group. For another thing, the withdrawal of the leader (for whatever reason) may precipitate chaos in the group. With the leader as keystone removed, the group structure may simply fall apart, since there is little else in the way of cohesive forces among the remaining group members.

The sociometric picture of an authoritarian group is therefore likely to be star-shaped (see page 444), with the leader at the center of the radial strands and with few circumferential relationships among the followers.

In very small face-to-face groups the authoritarian leader may be personally related to each of the members in this fashion. As the group grows larger, however, the leader perforce becomes more remote from the rank and file, and a hierarchical organization tends to develop in which the authoritarian leader is directly in contact with the second-rank leaders, who in turn are in contact with the next rank, and so on, down to the most subordinate members. But the important point is that the authoritarian leader still is able to retain the star-shaped structure and to minimize the degree of interpersonal relations among the rank and file. Figure 12.1 schematizes this type of structure in very small and in larger groups.

The hierarchical organization of the authoritarian group can be seen, then, as a natural consequence of the aim of the leader to maintain his position of central power. With it automatically comes the development of the leader's personal deputies and lieutenants ("palace guard," "city hall gang," etc.), who seek to maintain and extend their own status at the expense of other group members. And with it comes the development of an internecine struggle for power and rivalrous jockeying for status within the group. This atmosphere is conducive to frustration and aggression and to the rise of intragroup tension and conflict.

DEMOCRATIC LEADERSHIP. The democratic leader does not necessarily differ from the authoritarian leader in amount of power but he does differ in the way he exercises his power. The democratic leader seeks to evoke the maximum involvement and participation of every member in the group activities and in the determination of group objectives. He seeks to spread responsibility rather than to concentrate it. He seeks to encourage and reinforce interpersonal relations throughout the group so as to strengthen it. He seeks to reduce intragroup tension and conflict. He seeks to prevent the development of a hierarchical group structure in which special privilege and status differentials predominate.

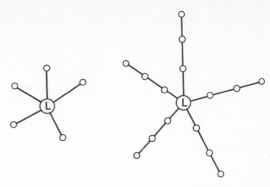

FIGURE 12.1: Structure of authoritarian leadership in small group (left) and larger group (right).

The sociometric picture of democratically led groups tends to be of the form shown in Figure 12.2. Although the leader occupies the position of focal importance in the group, other individuals also are intimately related to one another in both small and larger groups.

In comparison with the authoritarian leader, who tends to be the group "dictator," the democratic leader serves as the "agent" of the group. He seeks wherever possible to carry out the "mandate of the group" or, better, to encourage and facilitate the carrying out of this mandate by the group members themselves. Whereas the authoritarian leader is the keystone of the group, without whom the whole structure may collapse, the democratic leader may judge his success in terms of the degree to which the group is able to go along without him when he temporarily leaves the group.

Many of the above conclusions are based on a study by Lippitt and White (see Box 12.5). The experimental findings of that study would seem to argue for higher task

FIGURE 12.2: Structure of democratic leadership in small group (left) and larger group (right).

BOX 12.5: *The autocrat and the democrat*

In order to investigate some aspects of group functioning under different types of leadership and different types of group "atmosphere," Ronald Lippitt and Ralph K. White, under the general direction of Kurt Lewin, conducted, in 1938, experiments with children's groups. The objective was to set up small, genuine groups of children which were led by adults (experimenters) who adopted two different leadership styles: "authoritarian" and "democratic." The activities of the groups were mask making and other similar tasks. Meetings were held regularly over a period of weeks.

Authoritarian style	*Democratic style*
All determination of policy by the leader.	Policies by group decision.
Techniques and steps for attaining the goal dictated by the leader, one at a time; future direction uncertain to a large degree.	Explanation of over-all process given at first meeting. When technical advice was needed, the leader suggested several alternatives from which choice could be made.
Leader usually dictated work task and work companions of each member.	Members free to choose work companions and division of tasks.
Leader "personal" in his praise and criticism without giving objective reasons. Remained aloof from active group participation except when demonstrating.	Leader "objective" or "fact-minded" in his praise and criticism and tried to be a regular group member in spirit without doing much of the actual work.

Differences in the behavior of the authoritarian and democratic groups were striking. The following are some of the most interesting differences:

1. The authoritarian groups tended to be either more aggressive or more apathetic than the democratic groups. When aggression was expressed, it tended to be directed toward other group members rather than toward the leader. Two scapegoats were the targets of such concentrated hostility that they left the club. In the apathetic authoritarian groups it seemed that the lack of aggression was due merely to repressive influence of the leader; for when he temporarily left the group, aggressive outbursts occurred.

2. In the authoritarian groups there were more submissive approaches to the leader and also more attention-demanding approaches. The approaches to the democratic leader were more friendly and task-related.

3. In the authoritarian groups the relations among group members tended to be more aggressive and domineering than in the democratic groups.

4. Group unity appeared higher in the democratic groups, and subgroups tended to be more stable than in the authoritarian atmosphere, where they tended to disintegrate.

5. Constructiveness of work decreased sharply when the authoritarian leader temporarily absented himself, whereas it dropped only slightly when the democratic leader was absent.

6. Under experimentally induced frustrations in the work situation, the democratic group responded by organized attacks on the difficulty, whereas the authoritarian groups tended to become disrupted through recriminations and personal blame.

Lippitt, R., and White, R. K. An experimental study of leadership and group life. In Eleanor E. Maccoby, T. M. Newcomb, and E. L. Hartley (Eds.), Readings in social psychology. (3rd ed.) New York: Holt, 1958.

motivation under democratic-type leadership than under authoritarian leadership. But the results must be interpreted with caution. Not all the autocratically led subjects (children) in the Lippitt and White experiments reacted poorly to authoritarian leadership. Though most children expressed secret preference for the democratic leader, not all did. The submissive groups seemed perfectly satisfied to take orders. That some of these children came from homes which were autocratic in structure is probably revealing. Even in our culture, it seems, authoritarian leadership may often be accepted.

A number of investigators have noted that workers may *resist* democratic leadership. And Bailey [1953] describes students who have learned to be passively dependent upon the teacher. Bailey's attempts to help them to become more self-responsible by exercising participatory leadership were resisted by the students. They kept insisting that it was his task as the leader to play a directive role. Democratic leadership may in the long run be preferred, but techniques of democratic group behavior may require a process of learning and growth. For example, Singer and Goldman [1954] found that the effectiveness of group discussion in group therapy with schizophrenic patients may increase if the therapy leader begins by using a more directive type of leadership and shifts slowly to a more democratic pattern.

There is some evidence to indicate that people will tend to react with special favorableness to authoritarian leadership patterns when they are emotionally insecure or when they find themselves in an ambiguous and critical social situation. It will be remembered that one of the functions of the leader is to relieve the individual of responsibility for decision making. In this connection the finding of Peak [1945] that proportionally more German Protestants than German Catholics adopted the views and ideology of the Nazi party is relevant. In the United States Strategic Bombing Survey (upon whose data Peak

based her analysis), a total of 2,033 German Protestant civilians and 1,265 German Catholic civilians were interviewed on various beliefs and attitudes. The open-end interview technique (see page 170) was used. Forty-three per cent of the Protestants and 31 per cent of the Catholics were found to have pro-Nazi attitudes. Peak suggests that one of the reasons for this difference might be stated as follows: Among the emotionally insecure German people, in the unstable social order of Germany after World War I, the Catholics could find their security needs met by submitting to the monolithic and authoritative leadership hierarchy of the Catholic Church. Such a leadership is most efficiently designed to provide comfort and security for the emotionally insecure and immature individual, for the confused individual living in a confusing and changing world.

On the other hand, the Protestant did not have so authoritative a leadership in his church and consequently he more often "found solace in the submission to a *Fuehrer* who left little to individual choice and mapped a clear course to salvation." (Peak points out, however, that "it is an interesting question whether members of Protestant Churches would have been more susceptible than Catholics to a fascist appeal in a nation where submission to authority was a less common national tradition and where individuals had been taught to stand on their own feet.")

Peak's more general thesis that stress makes people ready to accept authoritarian leadership has some experimental support. Lanzetta [1953] placed laboratory groups under stress by badgering them to complete the experimental tasks in an unrealistically short time. He found that aggressive individuals were more likely to emerge as successful leaders in groups under stress than in groups under no stress. The relation between stress and style of leadership is complex. A stressful situation may change the leadership style of the incumbent leader. For example, Ziller [1955] found that the *appointed* leaders of groups (the leaders designated by the experimenter), when exposed to uncertainty and risk, became relatively unconcerned about the opinions of their followers and behaved in an authoritarian manner.

THE FOLLOWERS' PERCEPTION OF THE LEADER

What distinguishes the leader from the led? How is the leader *perceived* by his followers?

THE LEADER MUST BE PERCEIVED AS "ONE OF us." Most of the studies of successful leaders suggest that the leader shares certain characteristics with the members of the group. He is perceived as "one of us," and not as an "outsider." It would be difficult in the extreme for the members of a group to identify with an outsider.

Brown [1936] early stressed the point that *"the successful leader must have membership-character in the group he is attempting to lead. . . .* All organized groups with codified regulations stipulate that officers must have membership in the group. . . . Membership-character in the social-psychological sense, however, means more than this. . . . It means that the individual has the pattern of attitudes and reaction tendencies common to the group."

THE LEADER MUST BE PERCEIVED AS THE "MOST OF US." Not only must the leader have membership-character in the group, he must also be seen as incorporating *to a special degree* the norms and values which are central to the group (see Box 12.6).

The role of the leader in relation to the norms of an established group is nicely revealed in a series of three studies of farm leaders. Lionberger [1953] found that farm leaders (farm operators sought out by other farmers as sources of information about farming practices) were innovators of new farming methods. Wilkening [1952] found, in contrast, that farm leaders in the community he studied were *not* innovators. Intensive interviews with the farm leaders revealed a possible explanation for the contradictory findings. Leaders tended to reflect the traditional values and norms of their community. If a community values innovation and change, it will select innovators as leaders. If, on the other hand, the community does not value innovation, the leaders will tend to be conservative.

Marsh and Coleman [1954] subjected Wilkening's hypothesis to empirical test. All farmers in 13 neighborhoods in a Kentucky county were interviewed to determine the extent to which they had adopted 21 practices recommended by government agencies. A practice-adoption score—the percentage of applicable practices adopted—was computed for each farmer. Twenty-nine farmers were named by two or more farmers as sources of information about each of five selected practices. These farmers were designated as leaders. The 13 neighborhoods sampled were divided into a high-adoption area and a low-adoption area on the basis of the mean practice-adoption rates of the farmers living in the communities.

Table 12.1 gives the mean practice-adoption scores of farm leaders and of all farmers in areas of high and low adoption. Note the large difference between the mean practice-adoption scores of leaders in the two areas. And note that in the low-adoption areas the leaders did not stand out from their fellow farmers. Farm leaders, like other leaders, conform to the values and norms of their groups. If farmers value change, their leaders will be "social changers"; if farmers do not value change, their leaders will cling to old ways and resist change.

TABLE 12.1: MEAN PRACTICE-ADOPTION SCORES OF LEADERS AND OF ALL RESPONDENTS IN AREAS OF HIGH ADOPTION AND LOW ADOPTION [After Marsh and Coleman, 1954]

Area	Leaders	All respondents
High adoption	66	48
Low adoption	37	32

To what degree can the leaders of an established group change the values and norms of the group? The "great man" conception of leadership asserts that the leader can impose his wishes upon the group by exercising the power of his office. The alternative view is that the group is stronger than the leader, who must, therefore, conform to the established norms of the group. This view of the role of the leader in relation to the group is illustrated by the story of the French revolutionary leader who, when he saw the mob rush by, said, "I am their leader. I must follow them." The degree to which a leader can influence the norms of an established group is a problem of great interest and importance. At present, no firm answer can be given. However, it appears that to remain a leader, the leader must accept, or seem to accept, the traditions, norms, and goals of the group and assist the group in achieving its purpose (see Box 12.7).

THE LEADER MUST BE PERCEIVED AS THE "BEST OF US." But to accept the central values of the group is usually not sufficient to establish one as a leader. He who would be a leader must not only be like the "most of us," he must, paradoxically, also be the "best of us." He must be the best of us because only as he is perceived as an outstandingly superior person can he serve as an exemplar for the group, and as a father figure. And, more prosaically, he must also be the "best of us" if he is to exercise effective control and coordination of the work of the group. If the leader is not an expert in the tasks facing the group, the goals of the group will not be achieved—or not achieved most efficiently.

Jenkins's [1947] review of leadership among military groups indicated that leaders were superior to the rest of the members of their group in those abilities which were relevant to the group task. This observation of military groups is supported by a number of studies of task groups in the laboratory. One such study is Bales's research on the emergence of leadership in small discussion groups, which we cited earlier (page 433). He found that the members identified as their leader the person judged to have had the "best ideas" in the discussion.

The leader is the "best of us," but he apparently must not be *too much* the "best of us." Hollingworth [1942] found that among children "the leader is likely to be more intelligent, but not too much more intelligent, than the average of the group led." She found that when a discrepancy of more than 30 IQ points existed between the leader and the led, a leader-follower relation either did not develop or quickly disintegrated.

There may be several reasons why too big a discrepancy in intelligence can interfere with leadership. First, the "too intelligent" person may not be perceived as "one of us." Second, his interests may be so remote from the problems of the group that he is not motivated to help the group. Third, problems of communication may arise because of the large gap in intelligence. And, finally, there is some reason to believe that the superior person may seek to introduce innovations that the group is not ready to accept because these innovations challenge the existing ideology, i.e., the superior person may not be the "most of us."

THE LEADER MUST FIT THE FOLLOWERS' EXPECTATIONS. The members of a group may have common ideas about how a leader should behave and what functions he should serve. The members will choose and keep only those leaders who fit these expectations.

Two of the leadership functions which we have earlier discussed—the leader as substitute for individual responsibility and the leader as father figure—suggest that persons will be chosen as leaders who are perceived as capable of satisfying the dependency, affiliation, and other wants of the individual (see Box 12.8).

We see, then, that the personality of the chosen leader depends in part upon the personality of the followers. Milton [1952], for

BOX 12.6: *Parents versus peers*

H. C. Bredemeier, Marcia L. Toby, and Matilda W. Riley, sociologists at Rutgers University, studied in high school students the relation between status and reputation for exemplifying the accepted norms of the middle-class youth and parent cultures.

Status was measured by means of a five-item status scale. The items in the scale were, in order: leader, popular, admired, confided in, and liked.

Adherence to the values of the middle-class youth and parent cultures was measured by means of a questionnaire consisting of a series of 20 sketches of typical high school boys and girls. Each sketch described a particular characteristic or pattern of behavior in a model boy and girl which represented a value of either the youth or the parent culture. Some of the sketches portrayed adherence to the value; others portrayed deviation. Three illustrative sketches follow.

Ritualist value: "Mike and Ella know that not everybody can get top grades. They spend most of their time studying, always get their assignments done on time, and are very reliable and neat in their work. Their motto is that nothing matters as long as you do the best you can." (Parent-supported value)

Fun value: "Dottie and Ed have a great deal of fun with their friends. They spend a lot of time with the gang, going out, studying, playing all kinds of games, and just hanging around." (Youth-supported value)

Mediocrity value: "Helen and Dick are what you would call all-around. They're pretty smart, but not too smart; good-looking but not exactly the movie type. They play on teams but aren't top athletes. In short, they seem to be pretty good at almost everything although not outstanding in any one way." (Value supported jointly by parents and youth)

Each student was asked of each sketch: "Who in your class comes closest to being like this?" This question was designed to measure the reputation of the students for embodying or deviating from centrally important youth and parent values.

The following table shows the relation between the status of the student and his reputation for

example, found that a person's preferences for political figures who were aspiring for the Presidency in 1952 were associated with his degree of authoritarianism. College students with higher scores on authoritarianism (as measured by the California F scale) tended to support the nomination of General Douglas MacArthur, who appeared to them to be a "strong" leader. Nonauthoritarian students, on the other hand, tended to support the nomination of Adlai Stevenson, who seemed to them to emphasize the problem-solving function of leadership.

There is a good deal of evidence to sug-gest that the management of most American business and industrial organizations believes in strong, directive leadership. The "dynamic" leadership sought by management is the auto-cratic leadership studied by social psycholo-gists in the laboratory. Personnel officers, guided by management policy, seek out execu-tives who are able to pressure, coerce, push.

Blau's [1955] study of the bureaucratic structure of a Federal enforcement agency reveals the impact of the formal ideology of the group upon leadership behavior. He reports that despite deliberate attempts on the part of supervisors to minimize social distance

GROUPS, ORGANIZATIONS, AND THE INDIVIDUAL

embodying the values represented by nine sketches. These sketches were selected from the original twenty because they were perceived by the students as representing values outstandingly supported by parents, by fellow students, or by both.

	Low-status student	High-status student
Parent-supported values		
Success-oriented	43%	44%
Ritualist	56	48
Good student	55	46
Youth-supported values		
Popular with opposite sex	17	73
Humor	45	50
Fun	45	81
Jointly supported values		
Mediocrity	43	71
Popular with own sex	37	81
Friendly	43	83

The results indicate that students who had a reputation for adherence to youth-supported and jointly supported values were given high status. Thus 73 per cent of the high-status students had a reputation for being popular with the opposite sex, while only 17 per cent of the low-status students had a similar reputation. On the other hand, there is a slightly negative relation between reputation for adherence to parent-supported values and status in the high school class group. Thus 55 per cent of the low-status students had a reputation for being good students, while 46 per cent of the high-status students had this reputation.

Bredemeier, H. C., Toby, Marcia L., and Riley, Matilda W. Reputation. In Matilda W. Riley, J. W. Riley, and J. Toby, Sociological studies in scale analysis. New Brunswick, N.J.: Rutgers Univer. Press, 1954.

between themselves and subordinates and to practice democratic leadership, the supervisors frequently and unwittingly lapsed into authoritarian leadership behavior. The subordinates also slipped into a dependent, submissive relation to their supervisor despite his requests for increased participation.

"The group's insistence that the supervisor discharge his duty of issuing directives— 'That's what he gets paid for'—serves to emphasize that their obedience to him does *not* constitute submission to his will but *adherence, on his part as well as theirs, to abstract principles* which they have socially accepted."

In other groups and organizations, weak or soft leadership may be approved by the ideology. Thus, strong, pressure-packed leader behavior might not be acceptable to the members of a bird-watching society.

THE PERSONALITY CHARACTERISTICS OF LEADERS

We have discussed how the leader is perceived by his followers. Quite aside from the way he is *seen*, what manner of man is he in reality?

As might have been predicted from our discussion of the relativity of leadership to

BOX 12.7: *Leader versus group*

Ferenc Mérei, a Hungarian social psychologist, studied the following question concerning the relation between the leader and the group: "Does the group follow the leader, or does it force its traditions upon him?"

Twelve groups of young children were formed, homogeneous with respect to sex and age, by selecting children from two day nurseries who tended to be "followers." The groups were placed in separate rooms where they spent 30 to 40 minutes each day. After several meetings, the groups developed "cultures" peculiar to themselves—rules and traditions with respect to order of seating, division of play objects among the members, group ownership of certain objects, ceremonies connected with the use of objects, expressions of belonging together, rituals, and a special group language.

After the group had developed such a "culture," a "leader" was placed in the group. He was a child who was judged by the nursery school teachers to have initiative and directing power, and who more often gave than followed orders, more often was imitated than imitated others, more often was the attacker than the attacked. The leader also was older than the members of the group.

The responses of the groups to 26 such leaders were observed. *In all but one case, the leader was forced to accept the rules and traditions of the group.* The one exception was a group into which on three successive days as many new leaders had been introduced. The group successfully resisted the efforts of these three leaders to change it in rules and traditions. However, the struggle "exhausted the group and it began to weaken," as evidenced by a marked increase in solitary play. The fourth leader introduced into the group was able to reorganize completely this "weakened group"—she gave orders, introduced new rules, and decided what to do and how to play. In all the other groups, although the leader accepted the established rules and traditions, he still managed to play the role of leader by adopting one of these three strategies:

1. *The order giver.* This strategy is illustrated by the behavior of one leader who at first gave orders, made suggestions, and bossed the children in the group. He was avoided and ignored and the group carried on in its traditional way. Suddenly the leader's behavior changed. He joined the group in its activities and learned its rules and traditions. During the second play period, he again gave orders, ". . . . that is, he ordered them to do exactly what they would have done anyway. He appropriated the leadership without being able to change the group's traditions."

2. *The proprietor.* Leadership may express itself through taking possession of the property of the group. The objects continue to be used according to group tradition, but they now "belong" to the leader. This strategy is illustrated by the behavior of an outstanding leader in the large day-nursery group. When placed in a formed group with traditions, he was "swallowed" by the group. He followed the group's activities, accepted its traditions. The group never followed his suggestions. However, his leadership still expressed itself in the group. "The children gave him every object without his asking, and with that acknowledged his authority."

3. *The diplomat.* This type of leader accepts the traditions of the group to change them gradually. This is illustrated by a leader who, when introduced into a group with particularly strong traditions, first tried to suggest new games but was rebuffed. He then joined their traditional games but introduced minute changes and became the leader of the changed games. Later he was able to change more drastically the traditional games of the group.

Mérei, F. Group leadership and institutionalization. Hum. Relat., *1949,* **2**, *23–39.*

sets of tasks and to the followership, there do not appear to be personality traits which unequivocally characterize effective leaders in *all* situations. But there is good evidence that certain traits do tend to characterize effective leaders in a wide variety of situations. In general, leaders are found to be more *intelligent* than their followers (but not *too* much so, as

BOX 12.8: *Follow which leader?*

Fillmore H. Sanford, a psychologist then at Haverford College, studied the follower's role in the leader-follower relationship. He worked with a personality variable—authoritarianism—which both theory and existing evidence suggested should have a great deal to do with the reactions of the individual to leaders. It was expected that authoritarian persons would want strong, directive leadership that "pays off" in material benefits. Equalitarians, on the other hand, should emphasize the leader's ability to do his job and his concern for people.

A representative sample ($N = 963$) of the city of Philadelphia was interviewed in 1949. A group of 80 individuals having annual incomes between $5,000 and $10,000 and at least a high school education was selected from the total sample. The 40 subjects in this subgroup who scored highest on an authoritarian attitude scale were classified as "authoritarians." The 40 scoring lowest were classified as "equalitarians."

Each subject was asked, among other questions, these two questions about President Franklin D. Roosevelt:

1. Now take Franklin D. Roosevelt. Do you think of him as a good leader or a poor leader?

2. What about him made him a good/poor leader?

Each response of the 80 persons to the second question was examined and sorted into the most appropriate one of the following four classes:

1. *Emphasis on democratic leader function.* This category was defined as the tendency of the respondent to think of Roosevelt's function as the leader of a democratic country.

2. *Emphasis on material dependency.* In this category were placed responses which emphasized the material benefits Roosevelt secured for his followers.

3. *Emphasis on power.* In this category were placed responses which emphasized the power or strength of Roosevelt.

4. *Emphasis on personal warmth.* This category was defined as the tendency of the respondent to emphasize Roosevelt's humanity and warmth.

Results. Of the 25 responses which emphasized democratic leader function, 19 were made by equalitarians. Of the 6 responses which emphasized material dependency, 5 were made by authoritarians. The authoritarians and the equalitarians, contrary to expectation, did not differ significantly with respect to emphasis upon power (18 and 13 such responses, respectively). The equalitarians, as predicted, did emphasize Roosevelt's warmth and humanitarian qualities: 12 of the 13 responses which emphasized personal warmth were made by equalitarians.

Sanford's data show that personality factors in the follower play a significant role in determining his reaction to a leader. Though authoritarians and equalitarians alike in Sanford's sample admired Roosevelt, they differed in the reasons they gave for accepting him as a leader.

Sanford, F. H. The follower's role in leadership phenomena. In G. E. Swanson, T. M. Newcomb, and E. L. Hartley (Eds.), Readings in social psychology. (2nd ed.) New York: Holt, 1952.

Leonard Berkowitz, a social psychologist at the University of Wisconsin, has examined the interaction between personality characteristics and the requirements of the leadership role in determining the behavior of leaders.

Forty male college students served as subjects in this experiment. Of these, 10 had "high-ascendant" personalities, 10, "low-ascendant," and 20, "moderately ascendant"—as measured by a battery of personality tests.

In the experiment proper, a number of four-person groups were constituted, each consisting of one high-ascendant, one low-ascendant, and two moderately ascendant subjects. These groups were assigned three different problems which have been used by other investigators in studying the efficiency of different communication nets (see pages 468 to 469). One of the problems was:

A small company is moving from one office building to another. It must move four kinds of equipment: (1) chairs, (2) desks, (3) filing cabinets, and (4) typewriters. How many trucks are needed to make the move in one trip?

Each subject was given two of the eight items of information necessary to solve the problem. The communication net imposed on the groups was the "star" pattern shown below.

In this pattern, A is the central position which can communicate directly with each of the other three persons. The three peripheral positions can communicate only with A. The assumption is that the central position requires ascendant behavior.

In half of the groups, a high-ascendant person was assigned to the central position; in the remaining groups a low-ascendant person occupied the central position.

A content analysis of the messages sent by each position was made. The messages were classified into two categories: (1) *relaying* information received from others; (2) *initiating* communication (e.g., asking for information, proposing a solution to the problem). The assumption made is that

we have already seen). It also seems clearly established by Mann's [1959] review of studies carried out from 1900 to 1957 that leaders tend somewhat consistently to be better *adjusted*, more *dominant*, more *extroverted*, more *masculine*, less *conservative*, and to have greater *interpersonal sensitivity* than rank-and-file members. These differences are, however, not great.

It is of interest to speculate that the personality traits which have been found to characterize leaders may, in part, *develop* in individuals as they act as leaders. The leader role demands dominance, extroversion, interpersonal sensitivity, etc., and these traits may be strengthened in an individual as he copes with the problems of leading a group. It should not be assumed, therefore, that the pattern of traits distinctive of leaders is due solely to the *selection* for positions of leader-the relaying of information indicates passive behavior, whereas the initiation of communications demonstrates a more active role.

The following table shows the percentage of information-relaying messages (i.e., *passive* behavior) sent by the high- and low-ascendant subjects occupying central and peripheral positions, for each of the experimental tasks.

| | HIGH-ASCENDANT SUBJECTS | | LOW-ASCENDANT SUBJECTS | |
TASK	*Central position*	*Peripheral position*	*Central position*	*Peripheral position*
I	45.4%	35.0%	51.6%	62.0%
II	48.4	55.4	48.0	50.4
III	47.2	55.2	36.8	65.0

On task I, the low-ascendant subjects in a peripheral position tended to be more passive than the central high-ascendant subject (62.0 per cent as against 45.4 per cent). That this greater passivity is probably determined by both personality differences and position requirements is suggested by the fact that the low-ascendant peripheral persons sent a significantly higher percentage of information-relaying messages than did the high-ascendant when occupying the same peripheral position (62.0 per cent versus 35.0 per cent).

Most important is the change over time in the behavior of the low-ascendant subjects who occupied the *central* position. On task I, they tended to be more passive than the high-ascendant central subjects (51.6 per cent versus 45.4 per cent). They were even more passive than the high-ascendant subjects in a *peripheral* position (51.6 per cent versus 35.0 per cent). But observe their steady decrease in the level of passivity—from 51.6 per cent to 36.8 per cent. In short, low-ascendant central persons over time came to behave like high-ascendant persons in the central position. (The greater passivity on task III of the central high-ascendant as compared with the central low-ascendant is a chance difference.)

The demands of a central "leader" position tend, over time, to count more in determining the behavior of the individual than his characteristic level of ascendance. People can, to some degree, learn to "make like a leader."

To what extent these preliminary findings in the laboratory can be generalized to real-life groups faced with difficult problems still remains an important question.

Berkowitz, L. Personality and group position. Sociometry, *1956*, **19**, *210–222*.

ship of persons who already exhibit this pattern; the "leader pattern" may be partly the result of learning to be an effective leader. As we shall see in Chapter 14 (pages 501 to 503), there is some evidence that the long-continued performance of such occupational roles as bureaucrat, business executive, and teacher may distinctively mold the personalities of individuals. This may be no less true of leaders in general. The office may make the man. For one study which supports this notion, see Box 12.9.

LEADERSHIP—GENERAL OR SPECIFIC? There are two extreme positions with respect to the question of generality of leadership. One view holds that leadership is *general*—that a person who is a leader in one situation will be a leader in all other situations. The alternative view holds that leadership is *specific* to the task and to the group and that with changes in the task and in other characteristics of the group, leadership will change.

Several studies have demonstrated that there exist sets of tasks in which leadership is relatively constant. Carter and Nixon [1949] observed two-person groups in three different kinds of tasks: an intellectual task, a mechanical assembly task, and a clerical task. The correlation between leadership scores in the intellectual and clerical tasks (both requiring verbal ability) was .64; between leadership scores in the intellectual and mechanical assembly tasks, the correlation was only .40; between leadership scores in the clerical and mechanical assembly tasks, only .30. These correlations suggest two kinds of leadership: "intellectual" leadership and "mechanical assembly" leadership.

In a later study, Carter [1953] studied the same groups in six different tasks: a reasoning task, an intellectual construction task, a clerical task, a discussion task, a motor cooperation task, and a mechanical assembly task. A factor analysis of the intercorrelations between the leadership ratings for each member in each task revealed two clusters of tasks, within each of which leadership demands were general. These were intellectual tasks and tasks involving the manipulation of objects. Carter concluded: "There are probably families of situations for which leadership is fairly general for any task falling in that family, but there will be other families in which the leadership requirements will be fairly independent of those in the first family of situations."

Gibb [1949] obtained an average correlation of .67 among leadership ratings in eight different tasks. The sample of tasks was quite heterogeneous, including, as it did, mechanical construction, intellectual problems, clerical tasks, and a discussion of emotion-laden issues. This correlation supports Carter's conclusion that leadership is neither entirely specific to tasks nor general over tasks. Rather, leadership is general over groups or families of tasks,

(For a more general report, see Box 12.10.)

Research on the characteristics of leaders would be greatly advanced if those clusters of tasks in which leadership is fairly general were clearly identified. It may be found that within each of these clusters of tasks a consistent and particular pattern of traits will be found to characterize leaders. The identification of leader-trait profiles for each established cluster would be of enormous value in the selection and training of leaders.

TO RECAPITULATE

In their leadership performance, leaders vary greatly. Factor-analytic studies suggest that individual differences in leader behavior are largely accounted for by two primary leadership dimensions—"consideration" and "initiating and directing." In some groups, for example, in "headless groups," these two complementary functions are likely to be split between a "maintenance specialist" and a "task specialist."

Studies of authoritarian and democratic types of leadership suggest that democratic leadership promotes acceptance of the group goals and increases cohesiveness and member satisfaction. This finding may, however, be limited to persons who have been taught to value individual autonomy and freedom.

To emerge as leader a person must be capable of being perceived by the group members as "one of us," as the "most of us," and as the "best of us." Moreover, the leader must fit the followers' expectations and wants. Thus democratic followers tend to demand democratic leaders; authoritarian followers, authoritarian leaders.

Studies of the personality characteristics of leaders have failed to uncover any characteristics common to all leaders. Certain traits, such as superior intelligence, ascendance, and dominance, appear to characterize effective leaders in rather a wide variety of situations. Studies of the generality of leadership sug-

BOX 12.10: *The headless group*

During World War II, the Assessment Staff of the Office of Strategic Services developed a situational test, called the "leaderless group discussion test," to measure the leadership potential of candidates for duty in OSS.

The method consisted in asking a group of candidates to discuss a controversial topic for a period of 30 minutes or more with the objective of arriving at a group consensus. No official head was appointed. Observers recorded the attempted leadership acts and the effectiveness of the leader behavior of each participant.

Since World War II, considerable research has been carried out on the technique. In the following summary table of much of this research (compiled by Bernard M. Bass of Louisiana State University), the correlations between amount of successful leader behavior in the "leaderless group discussion test" and successful performance as a leader in "real life" groups are given.

Investigator(s)	Subjects	Correlations	Measure of successful leadership in "real life"
Arbous and Maree (1951)	Administrative trainees	.45, .47, .36	Supervisor's opinions of administrative capacity
Bass and Coates (1952)	ROTC cadets	.51, .68	Supervisor's ratings of leadership potential 6 months after test
		.49	Ratings of leadership potential based on summer-camp performance
		.37	Ratings by peers of leadership potential
Bass and White (1951)	Fraternity members	.44	Ratings by peers of leadership potential in fraternity
Bass et al. (1953)	Sorority members	.39	Ratings by peers of leadership potential in sorority
		.36	Amount of leadership activity outside sorority
		.10	Amount of sorority leadership activity per semester
Carter, Haythorn, et al. (1951)	NROTC cadets	.46	Superior's ratings of performance on summer cruise
Mandell (1950)	Foremen in federal shipyards	.36, .21	Ratings by superiors of success as foremen
Vernon (1948)	Civil Service administrators	.36	Ratings by supervisors of success as Civil Service administrators
Wurster and Bass (1953)	Fraternity pledges	.47	Ratings by peers of leadership potential 6 months after test

Note that the correlations are, without exception, positive, though of only moderate value.

These results support the conclusion that there is some generality of leadership potential over quite different kinds of groups and tasks.

Bass, B. M. Leadership, psychology, and organizational behavior. *New York: Harper, 1960.*

gest that leadership is general over sets or families of tasks. For example, certain members tend consistently to assume the leadership of groups working on intellectual tasks; other members tend consistently to lead the same groups when they are assigned "mechanical" tasks.

GUIDE 37: *Groups tend to undergo self-stabilizing changes in structure and leadership as a consequence of internal conflicts, external forces, and shifts in membership.*

Having reviewed in Chapter 11 some of the principal aspects of the emergence and functioning of groups, and in this chapter, the nature of leadership, we now turn our attention to the *changes* that take place within groups. For groups, like individuals, are almost always under pressure to change. We will examine what kinds of groups tend to change, under what conditions they change, and what the direction of change is likely to be.

STABLE AND UNSTABLE GROUPS

Some groups are highly stable, their structure tending to remain unchanged over considerable periods of time. Other groups are unstable, susceptible to temporary or enduring changes in structure. Groups are especially likely to be unstable during the process of formation or of reformation as the aftermath of some significant change in the external environment. Groups may also undergo change *even in the absence of significant variations in the external situation.* Such instability typically arises out of conflict among individuals and among subgroups *within* the total group.

INTERNAL CONFLICT AND GROUP CHANGE

The sources of internal group conflict are many. Several different subgroups may be seeking to increase their power at the expense of the others; the leader of the group may be trying to broaden his authority, and other members may be trying to displace him; the roles of the various group members may not be harmoniously established; the attitudes of the various members toward group objectives and means of accomplishing these objectives may be in conflict.

The changes in group structure that occur as a consequence of such conflicts seem, in general, to tend in the direction of a reduction of the tensions and, hence, in the establishment of a more stable group. It is as though there were something of the nature of a self-distribution of forces within the group toward an equilibrium state. See, for example, Berrien's [1961] discussion of "homeostasis" in groups and its implications for leadership.

The kinds of changes in group structure that work toward increased stability are many. *Subgroupings* may change, new ones may appear, and there may be mutual adjustments among them until they come into a more balanced relation of power, function, and responsibility. *Dissident elements*—individuals or subgroups—may be forced out of the group altogether, thus producing more harmony within the group. *Leadership* of the group may undergo drastic change, with the old leaders deposed by new and more effective leaders. Important *ideological shifts* may occur, and the group may achieve stability by redefining its goals, its beliefs, and its plans.

These various changes partake of the nature of fundamental or enduring restructurings. But there may also be temporary expedients to reduce the level of tension among the members of a group and the instability of the group. One is *scapegoating*, in which internal group conflicts become manifested (and, apparently, temporarily alleviated) through aggressions focused on certain individuals or subgroups within the group. Another is *external aggression*, in which tensions among group members become expressed in attacks upon out-groups or individuals (see Box 12.11).

BOX 12.11: *Frustration and group aggression*

M. E. Wright studied the influence of frustration upon the group relations and social behavior of 39 pairs of children, ranging in age from three to six years. Eighteen of the pairs were made up of strong friends; 21 pairs, of weak friends.

In an initial free-play session, the children were allowed to play freely with toys for 15 minutes. Frustration was then deliberately induced by placing more attractive toys behind a wire screen. The children were allowed to play only with the other, less attractive toys.

The amount of cooperative and conflict actions in the free-play session and in the frustration session were recorded. In cooperative actions both children strove toward a common goal and helped each other to achieve that goal. In conflict actions the children were aggressive toward each other, the aggression ranging from verbal teasing to physical violence.

Taking all 39 pairs together, cooperative actions showed a significant increase from the free-play session to the frustration session (38.2 per cent to 50.4 per cent), and social conflict showed a significant decrease (14.9 per cent to 6.9 per cent). Externally induced frustration, it seems, *increases* the interdependence and unity of a group.

Further analysis of the data revealed, however, that this increase in cooperativeness and decrease in intragroup conflict was significant only for the 18 pairs of *strong* friends; the 21 pairs of weak friends did not manifest a significant change. It would appear that it is highly cohesive groups which become more interdependent in the face of frustration.

The experimenter—the source of the frustration—was the object of direct aggression by the children during the frustration session. A fivefold increase in hostility was found (from 7 to 37 per cent). There was a corresponding decrease in friendly approaches to him.

As the following table shows, the hostile actions against the experimenter were predominantly *joint social actions* (involving both children of the pair) in both the free-play and frustration sessions. Thus aggression toward a powerful outsider may require social support. Note also that in the free-play session, friendly approaches were predominantly individual. In the frustration session, however, the experimenter has become such a threatening power figure that the children tend to need social support from each other to make even a friendly approach.

	HOSTILE ACTIONS		FRIENDLY ACTIONS	
	Taken jointly	*Taken individually*	*Taken jointly*	*Taken individually*
Free-play session	99%	1%	26%	74%
Frustration session	82	18	51	49

The cohesive groups were more capable of aggressing against the experimenter than were the less cohesive groups. The strong friends made more hostile actions against him (47 per cent of all action) than did the weak friends (31 per cent). Also, the strong friends *physically* aggressed against the experimenter more than did the weak friends. The strong friends hit him with blocks, tore his records, threw him off his chair, scratched him. The weak friends did not go beyond calling him names!

Wright, M. E. The influence of frustration upon the social relations of young children. Charact. and Pers., 1943–44, 12, 111–122.

EXTERNAL FORCES AND GROUP CHANGE

Once internal conflicts have been resolved and a stable group structure achieved, the structure can be expected to exist unchanged until "external" influences are brought to bear upon it. External influences include those arising out of the environment of the group (situational changes), and those arising in connection with a change in the membership of the group.

GROUP CHANGES CAUSED BY SITUATIONAL CHANGES. As the situation in which a group exists undergoes change, there are likely to be significant changes in the group structure. For one thing, external threats or attacks against the group have often been observed to induce such changes. Under the external dangers, group unity may be increased and internal conflicts reduced (again see Box 12.11). Subtly employed by an outside aggressor, external forces can, however, be divisive by splitting some subgroups from others, breeding mutual suspicion and distrust, leading one faction to blame others, etc. This is particularly important in the analysis of group integration or demoralization during a national catastrophe or during international conflict.

For another thing, the group may be required to serve a different function, as a result of a situational change. We have already seen that the group structure relating to one function may differ from that relating to another function. The normal structure of a family group may change drastically as a result of an emergency. After the emergency has passed, the new structure may persist. Some dramatic illustrations are found in the study by Koos [1946] of families living in one block of a New York tenement district. Thus, in discussing the dominance of the father under situational change, Koos writes:

> If, *in the opinion of the family*, the father failed to meet the demands of a trouble situation, a loss of dominance followed in every instance, regardless of the adequacy of the family. This is best illustrated in the Eduardo family, where the Italian-born father prevented the early hospitalization of the daughter, and in so doing, lost his dominance.

The changes in dominance are diagrammed in Figure 12.3.

Koos quotes the older son as describing this change in group structure in the following words:

> The old man is always boss in our place. That's o.k., he's got a right to be the boss. But, Christ, he wasn't the boss after he belted that one around. When he raised hell, and would not let Agnes go to the hospital (and she sure was sick) everybody forgot he was the old man. None of us paid any attention to what he said. . . . Yea, he's boss again, but not the way he was before. If you didn't forget so easy, he'd never been boss again. If she'd a died, we'd have run him out of the house. Hell, he wasn't worth two cents in our family for a while.

GROUP CHANGES CAUSED BY MEMBERSHIP CHANGES. Although it may be argued that a group is defined by the particular people who constitute it and that any change in group membership necessarily means that a different group exists, it is still useful to discuss how groups may appear to persist in much the same way, even when old members leave and

FIGURE 12.3: Change in dominance of father in the family as a result of his failure to meet the demands of an emergency. The biological symbols ♂ and ♀ represent the male and female sexes, the father and mother are designated by the letters (F) and (M), and the siblings by (1), (2), and (3) in order of birth. [Adapted from Koos, 1946.]

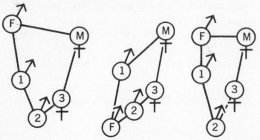

K. Toki, then of the Tokyo Imperial University, did an early study of the relation between the leader and the structure and functioning of his group. In two school classes and one camp group he observed the effect of removing leaders from groups at an early phase and at a late phase in their functioning.

The following protocols illustrate some of his major observations.

Removal of leader, early phase. The experimenter said: "Will everyone join and draw a picture. This doesn't mean that each of you will make a separate drawing but you will consult and assist one another to make a single picture." Shortly afterwards, O. started to draw a picture and the others, encouraged by this, started getting up and appeared as though they wished to get some guidance from him. This was well expressed in the manner in which they looked into O.'s face. Finally, O. started to give guidance. . . . However, at this moment, there was not even a slight idea as to what was going to be drawn. The only thing that had been set down was something like this: ⌂. But there was no doubt that this was a mountain. Then, ten minutes later, the experimenter took O. to another side of the table and said: "Now, leave that drawing to the others and let's make a different drawing together." . . . The other children who were left to themselves immediately lost their power to act and their work stopped. They said among themselves: "What shall we draw now?"—"I'd like to draw a boat. Is it all right, Ot-chan?", etc. But O. not answering, they stood around him not doing anything. When O. would give directions, they would all start working and continue doing so while the directions lasted. Then, they would again come to a stop. After five minutes, the experimenter took O. back to his original place and everything returned to the state which existed before he was removed.

Removal of leader, late phase. O. said in a loud voice: "If it's manual work, I'm good at it. I'm the best one in the class when it comes to doing handicraft." So saying, a strong leader-follower structure was formed. N_1, who was the leader in a previous experiment, was, in this instance, a mere follower. After forty minutes, in the middle of the work, the experimenter said to O.: "You, O., have been doing most of the work so far. From now on, let's have the others do it by themselves." After pacifying O., he was finally led away and at another table, with K. as the center, they were trying to continue their work but it didn't go well and they kept looking toward O., hoping he'd come back. Most of them went back and forth between the tables and were completely uneasy. After five minutes, O. returned to his former place and at this moment, the very feeble, temporary, quasi-leader-follower structure with K. as the quasi-leader was immediately liquidated and all was as it originally was.

Removal of nonleader. Shortly after the beginning of the rabbit-jumping relay, a nonleader, T., shouted out: "I quit," and immediately went over to the experimenter, who was close by. However, nobody paid any attention to this and continued their game with K. as their leader.

Toki, K. The leader-follower structure in the school-class. Jap. J. Psychol., *1935, 10, 27–56.* English summary in E. L. Hartley and Ruth E. Hartley, Fundamentals of social psychology. *New York: Knopf, 1952.*

new ones enter. A military unit may retain the same general structure and may even seem completely unchanged to its members when one of its officers is replaced. There seems to be, in fact, a remarkable amount of substitutability of persons in a group without perceptually appreciable changes in structure. This is particularly true of formal groups in which the role relationships are rigidly prescribed. In informal groups, on the other hand, changes in membership may have marked effects. This is particularly true if the leaders of the group are removed (see Box 12.12).

Sometimes the loss of a member or the entrance of a new one, even in a well-established group, produces considerable change in the group structure. This can again be illustrated by Koos's study. Among the causes of change in family structure Koos lists deaths in families, addition of relatives to families, and the like. Thus:

> In the Walther family, the death of the breadwinner placed the responsibility for family support upon the eighteen-year-old son, who left school and took a shipping clerk's job in order to support his mother and two sisters. Because of his new position in the family as breadwinner, the son felt himself entitled to the headship of the family, which the mother refused to accept. . . . The result for this family was trouble—a trouble which was re-

solved only through the continued pressure by the son and the two daughters which overwhelmed the mother's striving to hold the dominant position in the family.

And again:

> In one family, when Mrs. Mark's mother was taken into the family because another family could no longer care for her, trouble was initiated. The grandmother immediately began to side with her daughter against the son-in-law in small matters which would have been resolved under other circumstances, and troubles resulted.

But even without gain or loss of members, group changes can occur as a consequence of psychological changes within the original members. For example, the sheer aging of members of a group will produce restructuring. In a gang of boys growing up, the group relationships change as the interests and personalities of the members develop differentially and as the special capacities that were important for the teen-age group become relatively less important for the older group.

CHAPTER GUIDES AND GLOSSARY

GUIDE 35: *The emergence of leadership and its functions in a group are determined by the structure, situation, and tasks of the group*

GUIDE 36: *The characteristics of a leader, and the type of leadership he displays, reflect the goals and norms of the group and the leader's personality*

GUIDE 37: *Groups tend to undergo self-stabilizing changes in structure and leadership as a consequence of internal conflicts, external forces, and shifts in membership*

authoritarian leadership. A type of leadership in which the leader plays a strong, directive role in setting group goals and in planning and directing the activities of the members of the group. The authoritarian leader delegates few of the functions of leadership to the members of the group. Authoritarian leadership is to be contrasted with *democratic leadership.*

consideration leadership dimension. One of the two primary dimensions of leadership behavior (the other being the *initiating and directing* leadership dimension). Consideration is primarily concerned with motivating the members of a group to accept the goals of the group and to work for their accomplishment, and with maintaining internal harmony and member satisfaction.

democratic leadership. A type of leadership in which the leader plays a "permissive" role, sharing the functions of leadership with the members of the group by encouraging their participation in goal setting, and in planning and directing the activities of the group. Democratic leadership is to be contrasted with *authoritarian leadership.*

head. The member of a group or organization who is *officially* assigned the responsibility for leading the group. The influence of the head of a group may or may not be accepted by the membership.

initiating and directing leadership dimension. One of the two primary dimensions of leadership behavior (the other being *considera-* *tion*). This dimension is primarily concerned with specifying ways and means for accomplishing the goals of the group and with coordinating the activities of the members.

leader. A member of a group or organization who outstandingly influences the activities of the members of a group and who plays a central role in defining group goals and in determining the ideology of the group.

scapegoating. The focusing of aggressions on certain individuals or subgroups within a group. Scapegoating is likely to occur when a group is in internal conflict or under external threat which may be temporarily alleviated by the displaced aggression.

THE THEME OF THE PRECEDING TWO CHAPTERS HAS BEEN
that groups come into being, develop, change, flourish, or die as a
function of their effectiveness in serving the wants of their members.
Few men can achieve their goals without the help of their fellows—
or so many men stoutly believe. Work, religious, and recreational
activities, even such a traditionally individual enterprise as scientific
research—all of these are increasingly becoming "group projects."
It is clear that the delineation of the effective group—the study of
the factors which increase and decrease group achievement—is a
problem of massive import in our ever more complex and
interdependent society. It is to this problem that we now turn.

13: THE EFFECTIVE GROUP

THE OBJECTIVE OF THIS CHAPTER IS TO EX-
amine the determinants of group effectiveness.
One can study the determinants of group
effectiveness either because of theoretical interest—hoping through such a study to gain
insight into the nature of group functioning—
or because of a straightforward, practical interest in group productivity, efficiency, and well-
being. But no matter why or how we approach
this study we shall find that the problem of
the effectiveness of groups is a complex one.
For one thing, the characteristics of an effective group are complex and varied (see Box
13.1). For another thing, the appropriate
measure of effectiveness varies with the nature
of the group.

MEASURES OF GROUP EFFECTIVENESS

For some groups, the proper measure of
effectiveness is productivity—how many loaves
of bread are baked per day, how many automobiles assembled, how many railroad ties
laid. For other groups, effectiveness is measured by how much satisfaction is engendered
—how many intercollegiate baseball games
are won, successful cocktail parties given, enjoyable poker games or bridge games or rounds
of golf played. For other groups, effectiveness
is determined by creative outcomes—number
of logical problems solved, ideas generated,
works of art produced. And for still other
groups, effectiveness is properly measured by
such less tangible consequences as the intensity of emotional experience the individual
members are helped to achieve, for instance,
in a religious group; the feeling of status
that the wearing of a band's marching
uniform bestows upon the individual; the
sheer satisfaction found in "belonging." It
is perhaps fair to say that the variety of
ways in which group effectiveness can be
measured is limited only by the variety of

Douglas McGregor, an industrial psychologist at the Massachusetts Institute of Technology, draws upon his observations of the management of large companies to characterize a well-functioning, effective, creative group.

1. The atmosphere . . . tends to be informal, comfortable, relaxed. . . .

2. There is a lot of discussion in which virtually everyone participates, but it remains pertinent to the task of the group. . . .

3. The task or objective of the group is well understood and accepted by the members. There will have been free discussion of the objective at some point until it was formulated in such a way that the members of the group could commit themselves to it.

4. The members listen to each other! . . . Every idea is given a hearing. People do not appear to be afraid of being foolish by putting forth a creative thought even if it seems fairly extreme.

5. There is disagreement. . . . Disagreements are not suppressed or overridden by premature group action. The reasons are carefully examined, and the group seeks to resolve them rather than to dominate the dissenter. . . .

6. Most decisions are reached by a kind of consensus in which it is clear that everybody is in general agreement and willing to go along. . . . Formal voting is at a minimum; the group does not accept a simple majority as a proper basis for action.

7. Criticism is frequent, frank, and relatively comfortable. There is little evidence of personal attack, either openly or in a hidden fashion. . . .

8. People are free in expressing their feelings as well as their ideas both on the problem and on the group's operation. . . .

9. When action is taken, clear assignments are made and accepted.

10. The chairman of the group does not dominate it, nor on the contrary does the group defer unduly to him. In fact . . . the leadership shifts from time to time depending on the circumstances. . . . There is little evidence of a struggle for power as the group operates. The issue is not who controls but how to get the job done.

11. The group is self-conscious about its own operation.

McGregor, D. The human side of enterprise. New York: McGraw-Hill, 1960.

groups and by the variety of the wants of the individual.

The problem of measuring effectiveness is further complicated by the fact that the effectiveness of any one group is itself a multidimensional variable. Usually there are *many* primary measures of the effectiveness of any single group. We have seen, in the preceding chapters, that people join groups for various reasons, that the different members of any single group seek and find different wants satisfied by their membership, different satisfactions fulfilled. And sometimes, of course, a group which is extremely effective for some members may be completely ineffective for others. But the problem is even more complicated. Sometimes group effectiveness is measured without any attention to the wants and satisfactions of any of the members of the group. Thus the effectiveness of work groups is often measured by their productivity. Such productivity measures may be meaningful to the man employing the group but may sometimes be completely invalid for the members of the group itself.

There is one caution for the social psychologist to draw from this: When measuring the effectiveness of a group we must always ask ourselves, "Group effectiveness for whom?" By this question we emphasize that our interest in the study of groups derives from our concern with the *individual* in the group.

A framework for study of group effectiveness

Many disciplines, for many reasons, have become involved in research on group effectiveness. Social psychologists, sociologists, business-management research groups, and applied anthropologists have all contributed their talents to this problem. As a result we have accumulated a fairly large mass of data which can be subsumed under the rubric of "the applied psychology of group effectiveness." However, as is true of any series of applied researches (and especially of one which has been conducted by research workers from different disciplines with differing theoretical orientations and with sometimes disparate practical objectives), it is necessary that we first establish a common framework within which these varied studies can be conveniently ordered.

INDEPENDENT-INTERMEDIATE-DEPENDENT VARIABLES

One such guiding framework is provided by the traditional logic of the experimentalist —the logic of the independent-intermediate-dependent variable hierarchy. In this framework each of the manifold dimensions or variables pertaining to the group is classified as an independent, or as an intermediate, or as a dependent variable. These variables are then treated as forming a hierarchy of levels in which one kind of variable—the independent variable—is assumed to be logically and temporally prior to the next type of variable—the intermediate variable—which, in turn, is held to be logically and temporally prior to the final type of variable—the dependent variable. This procedure, as we shall soon see, permits us to organize many different and apparently disparate results into a coherent story.

DEPENDENT VARIABLES. We shall take various measures of group effectiveness and treat them as dependent variables—variables which are governed by the intermediate variables. Examples of dependent variables have already been given: the number of railroad ties laid, the number of problems solved, the total amount of satisfaction with group activities, etc. It is here that we must be alert to the question, "Group effectiveness for whom?"

INTERMEDIATE VARIABLES. Intermediate variables can be seen as group or individual processes which affect the dependent variables. Style of leadership, motivation of the members, friendship relations among the members are typical intermediate variables. These and other intermediate variables are seen as reflecting the influence of the independent variables.

INDEPENDENT VARIABLES. Independent variables are the externally manipulatable "givens" of a group. Certain of these variables are sometimes labeled *structural* variables (e.g., size of group, individual composition of group); others, *task* variables (e.g., nature of task, difficulty of task); and still others, *environmental* variables (e.g., physical setting of the group, functional place of the group within its larger organization). All independent variables, it should be noted, can be manipulated from the outside. Thus the size of a group may be increased or decreased by birth or death of members, by assignment of workers, etc. The group can be given, by an external authority, an easy task or a difficult task to fulfill. The organizational setting of a group may be changed by top management.

Each of these independent variables can serve as the "initiating" event in the system of variables. Thus, for example, the independent variable of individual composition of the group may affect an intermediate variable—style of leadership (see page 434); and style of leadership, in turn, may affect group output—a dependent variable.

In Figure 13.1, the various interrelations among the determinants of group effectiveness are schematically portrayed.

BY WAY OF CAUTION. Unfortunately, the independent-intermediate-dependent classification—like all classifications of complex events—is not without many difficulties. By rigidly adhering to this schema it is not easy or, in some cases, even possible to describe adequately the events which take place in a group. There are three major complications which will temper our use of this classificatory scheme.

In the first place there are *interactions among the variables of any one level*. For example: *size of group*—an independent variable—tends to covary with other independent variables, such as the *group task*. Thus, for certain tasks, the group must of necessity be larger than for other tasks. And, to take another example, the size of a group covaries with the structure of the group. Thus if a social gathering grows too large, it may (often to the consternation of the hostess) tend to change structure by splintering into a number of relatively separate subgroups. There are similar interactions among intermediate variables. We have seen in Guide 36 (page 432) that style of leadership covaries with the cohesiveness of the group. And, finally, dependent variables may influence other dependent variables. An increase in group output, for example, may result in an increase in a member's general feeling of satisfaction with his group membership.

The second complication reflects the fact that there is often a "reverse flow" or feedback of influence in the independent-intermediate-

FIGURE 13.1: The interrelations among the determinants of group effectiveness.

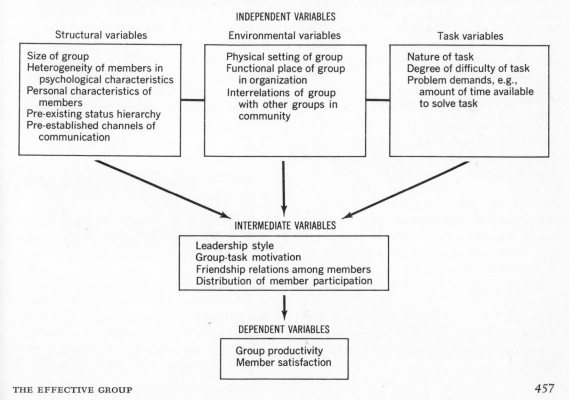

INDEPENDENT VARIABLES

Structural variables

Size of group
Heterogeneity of members in psychological characteristics
Personal characteristics of members
Pre-existing status hierarchy
Pre-established channels of communication

Environmental variables

Physical setting of group
Functional place of group in organization
Interrelations of group with other groups in community

Task variables

Nature of task
Degree of difficulty of task
Problem demands, e.g., amount of time available to solve task

INTERMEDIATE VARIABLES

Leadership style
Group-task motivation
Friendship relations among members
Distribution of member participation

DEPENDENT VARIABLES

Group productivity
Member satisfaction

dependent variable sequence. Changes in dependent variables may produce changes in intermediate or even independent variables. For example, the greater the effectiveness of a social club in putting on dances and plays (usually conceived of as a dependent variable), the greater will become its cohesiveness (an intermediate variable), and the larger will it grow in size (an independent variable) as it attracts new members.

The third difficulty in the use of the schema arises from the fact that it is not always easy to determine which variable is which—independent, intermediate, or dependent. The nature of a given variable may change from time to time, from group to group, and from observer to observer. For example, in a college fraternity, group cohesiveness, being the main *raison d'être* for the group, may be a major *dependent* variable rather than an intermediate one. Or, as we have noted earlier, for the owner of a factory the number of products produced per hour by a work group may be the primary dependent variable; for a working member of the same group good fellowship may be his major objective and he will thus measure group effectiveness (dependent variable) by what his boss would consider an intermediate variable.

A CLASSIFICATION OF GROUPS

We see that any one group's effectiveness can be viewed and evaluated in several ways. Yet every group has one primary criterion of effectiveness. In an assembly-line group, the primary criterion is number of units assembled, although other criteria (e.g., worker satisfaction) are also relevant. In a fraternity group, the primary criterion is amount of satisfaction with the fraternity's activities, although again other criteria are also relevant.

By referring to their primary criteria of effectiveness, and to the purposes for which they were set up, we can classify groups into several main categories: work groups, creative groups, gratification groups, and social-action groups.

To be sure, such a classification is somewhat arbitrary; different categories of groups are possible, and particular groups may not readily fall into any one of these simple categories. But, roughly speaking, most groups do seem to fall into these types, and social organizations, too, can be classified in this way.

The utility of such a typology of groups, i.e., in terms of the *primary* dependent variable, is that it enables us to look for the *particular* independent and intermediate variables that are most crucial in determining the effectiveness of a given type of group, and it helps us to state the functional relations which exist among "chains" of such particular independent, intervening, and dependent variables. For different types of groups the crucial intermediate and independent variables may markedly differ. We shall encounter such important differences in the sections that follow. For example, a medium level of controversy (an intermediate variable) may be favorable to work groups and to social-action groups; a relatively high level of controversy may be favorable to creative groups; and a relatively low level may be favorable to gratification groups. The same thing may hold for the size of a group (an independent variable). Thus gratification and creative groups may be hindered if they grow beyond a small critical size, but this factor may be less important for work and social-action groups.

GUIDE 38: *The effectiveness of a group depends partly upon its structural characteristics—its size, member composition, status structure, channels of communication*

In considering the effectiveness of a group as a function of its structural characteristics, we will discuss the relevant problems and present some of the available data under the following rubrics: (1) size of group, (2) composition of group, (3) status hierarchy of group, (4) the pre-established channels of communication within group. These by no means exhaust the possible independent variables influencing group effectiveness, but these are ones which have been the subject of considerable experimental study.

SIZE OF GROUP

The crude question, "Are small groups or large groups more effective?" can at best yield crude answers. Thus we are not much surprised—nor much helped—to learn from an early study by Köhler [1927] that in a tug of war a bigger group can pull harder than a smaller group. But Köhler also reported the not so obvious finding that total team pull *did not increase in direct proportion to the number of men added*; as each new man (up to 12) was added, each of the members pulled about 10 per cent less hard. This simple experiment suggests that to *understand* the relation between group size and effective performance we must find out *why* the addition of men reduced the output of each member. We have to find out what the increased group size did to the task motivation of each member, to the structure of the group and its cohesiveness, to the way the group was led, etc. In short, following the over-all guiding framework of group variables earlier discussed, we have to investigate how changes in group size may influence certain intermediate variables, which, in turn, may influence the dependent variable of effectiveness.

GROUP SIZE, COHESIVENESS, AND SATISFACTION. Seashore [1954] measured the cohesiveness of 228 work groups in a large factory. He found that smaller groups—groups in the range from four to twenty-two—were, on the average, more cohesive than large groups. (It was also found that the range in cohesiveness of the smaller work groups was greater than that of the larger groups, the smaller groups tending toward either extremely high or extremely low cohesiveness as compared with the larger groups.)

Furthermore, numerous studies show that low group cohesiveness goes with voluntary absenteeism, which may be regarded as an indication of dissatisfaction. Thus, Mann and Baumgartel [1952], in a study of white-collar workers in a public utility company, found that absenteeism increases with decreasing group cohesiveness (see Figure 13.2).

Taking the above findings together we should expect to find that satisfaction with the group is greater in small groups, and this is what studies of absenteeism do suggest. Hewitt and Parfit [1953], for instance, found that the rate of voluntary absenteeism in groups of four was one-third of the rate of absenteeism in groups of 36, and one-fourth of the rate in groups of 128.

These findings of greater dissatisfaction in large groups are not restricted to work groups. Much the same has been found for creative groups. Miller [1950] found larger conference groups to be more disruptive than smaller groups. "Sense of belongingness" in these conference groups correlated −.44 with group size. And lack of opportunity to talk, which correlated highly with group size ($r = .80$), was associated with feelings of frustration.

Hare [1952] compared 5- and 12-person groups of Boy Scouts who were formed to play a "camping game." The boys were told a story about a camping trip which ended in

FIGURE 13.2: How voluntary absenteeism decreases with increased group solidarity. [Mann and Baumgartel, 1952.]

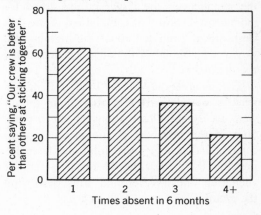

misfortune, making it necessary for each boy to make his way back to civilization alone. The boys were asked to rank ten pieces of camping equipment in order of importance for the return trip. Each group was then asked to decide as a group on the order of importance of the ten pieces of equipment. After a group discussion, the boys again individually ranked the ten pieces of equipment.

Hare found that the 5-person groups arrived at a significantly higher level of consensus after discussion than did the 12-person groups. The larger group was found to limit participation among the members by leading some members to feel that their individual opinions were not important and therefore not worth voicing.

Slater [1958] examined some correlates of group size in a sample of 24 "creative" groups ranging in size from two to seven members. Each group met four times for a discussion of one of four human-relations problems. After each meeting, the members were asked to indicate whether they felt the group was too small or too large for most effective work on the task it was assigned.

Members of the five-man groups expressed complete satisfaction, no one reporting he felt his group was too large or too small. Members of groups larger than five persons reported they felt their groups were disorderly and wasted time, and that the members were too pushy, aggressive, and competitive. Some of the members of the larger groups asked for more central control or complained of the lack of it; others grumbled about the high-handed way in which some of the members dominated the discussion.

The members of groups smaller than five persons complained only that their groups were too small. Observations of the interactions of the members of the smaller groups suggested that they were inhibited from expressing their ideas freely through fear of alienating one another and thus destroying the group.

These various studies of autonomous *ad hoc* groups consistently point to the same conclusion: people tend to be happier in smaller groups. We must, however, be cautious in extrapolating this finding from groups to *organizations*. Members of small organizations may *not* be more satisfied than members of large organizations (see Box 13.2).

GROUP SIZE AND DISTRIBUTION OF PARTICIPATION. Bales and his associates [1951], Stephan and Mishler [1952], and others have secured data on the distribution of participation among members of one kind of creative group—discussion groups. The similar findings of these studies suggest that as the size of the group increases, the most frequent contributor assumes a more and more prominent role in the discussion. The bigger the group, the greater the gap in amount of participation between the most frequent contributor and the other members of the group. Communication, in short, tends to centralize in one person in larger groups. Moreover, the number of persons in a group who contribute less than their proportionate share goes up as the size of the group expands from two to about seven.

How does this affect productivity in creative groups? Gibb [1951] found that the total number of ideas produced increased with increase in group size, though not in proportion to the number of members. Rather, as in the case of Köhler's tug of war, there were diminishing returns from the addition of members. This may be due to the fact that as the size of the group increased, a larger and larger proportion of the group members experienced inhibitions which blocked participation. Gibb also found that if he deliberately undertook to increase inhibitions to participation by formalizing the group procedures, a reduction in the number of ideas contributed was brought about.

A study by Carter and his coworkers [1951a] is also pertinent to this question. They concluded from their study that in the small group "each individual has sufficient latitude

BOX 13.2: *The organization and the man*

Lyman W. Porter, an industrial psychologist at the University of California, Berkeley, has examined the influence of such factors as company size and status in the management hierarchy upon the satisfaction of business managers and executives.

A Management Position Questionnaire was developed to ascertain how persons in management positions viewed their own and related positions. The following table indicates the number of persons in the various levels of management who filled out the questionnaire:

Level 1 (presidents)	114
Level 2 (vice-presidents)	611
Level 3 (plant managers, personnel directors, etc.)	659
Level 4 (department heads, subdepartment heads, etc.)	431
Level 5 (first-line supervisors)	101
	1,916

One section of the questionnaire was designed to measure the degree to which the respondents felt their positions satisfied their wants for security, belongingness, esteem, autonomy, and self-actualization. This categorization of social wants is an adaptation of Maslow's hierarchy (see page 76). In a second section of the questionnaire, the respondents were asked to rank various personality traits in order of their importance for determining success in their positions. These traits fell into two types: "individualistic" traits (forceful, imaginative, independent, self-confident, and decisive) and "conformity" traits (cooperative, adaptable, cautious, agreeable, and tactful).

Porter found that management officials in large organizations (those having more than 5,000 employees) were no more dissatisfied than those in small companies. The large company seems to fulfill a man's need for belongingness, autonomy, and self-actualization as well as a smaller, more intimate company does.

However, there were also significant interactions between the factors of size of organization and level of managerial position in influencing satisfaction. Persons in the *higher* levels of management in *large* organizations were less dissatisfied than persons in the same levels in small organizations. On the other hand, persons in the *lower* levels of management in *small* companies tended to be less dissatisfied than their counterparts in large companies.

Finally, the data indicated that management persons in large organizations consistently thought "individualistic" traits were more important for success as an executive than were "conformity" traits.

The well-publicized picture of the executive of the large company as an Organization Man lost in the friendless maw of a soulless corporation, striving for success by adaptively conforming to authority, may be but another instance of a popular stereotype with but a very small kernel of truth.

> Porter, L. W. *Preliminary summary of a study of management job perceptions.* Ms., Univer. of California, Berkeley, 1962.

or space in which to behave and thus the basic abilities of each individual can be expressed; but in the larger group only the more forceful individuals are able to express their abilities and ideas, since the amount of freedom in the situation is not sufficient to accommodate all the group members."

The constraints upon participation which

persons may experience in large groups will tend to stifle critical evaluation of the ideas presented by the more self-assertive and dominant members. The productivity of creative groups may suffer because of the silence of the majority.

GROUP SIZE AND LEADERSHIP BEHAVIOR. It is clear that style of leader behavior can be significantly affected by size of group. In the study by Carter and his associates referred to above, the correlation between authoritarianism and leadership behavior was found to increase as the size of the group rose from four to eight. Similarly, Hemphill [1950] found, when he compared leader behavior in groups of 30 or fewer members with leader behavior in groups of 31 or more, that in the larger groups the demands upon the leader were greater and leader-centered behavior was tolerated more by the members.

GROUP SIZE AND PRODUCTIVITY. Having examined some of the effects of group size on intervening characteristics of group functioning, we can now look at the over-all relation between size and group productivity. It should be emphasized that, because of the manifold ways in which size affects group functioning, we cannot expect to find simple relations between size and the effectiveness of groups. And complex relations are indeed found, as we turn first to work groups. Marriott [1949] studied output in relation to group size in 251 work groups in two automobile factories. He found a negative correlation between output and group size, groups of less than 10 producing 7 per cent more per man than groups of more than 30. This result, however, may be due to the fact that the group-bonus system (under which his groups worked) becomes ineffective for large groups.

Worthy [1950] has reported that a number of surveys carried out in Sears, Roebuck and Company suggest that both worker satisfaction and operating efficiency tend to decrease with increase in the size of administrative units.

There is, nevertheless, surprisingly little convincing research evidence that small work groups have a higher output per man than large ones.

The relation between group size and productivity has also been studied in creative groups. In a pioneering study, South [1927] compared the performance of groups of three and of six on four different kinds of problems which he classified as "abstract" (bridge problems and a logical reasoning task) and "concrete" (judging emotions from photographs and rating English compositions). Groups of three tended to be faster and equally accurate on the "concrete" problems, while groups of six were faster on the "abstract" problems. South interprets the superiority of the smaller groups on the concrete problems as stemming from the fact that every member of the group had strong initial opinions on these problems, and therefore group consensus could be arrived at only through protracted discussion. This process would presumably require less time in the smaller groups. (Confirmation of this hypothesis has been given by Hare's previously cited study, page 459.) The superiority of the larger groups on abstract problems was presumably due to the greater likelihood of some one member coming up with a solution when a greater number of individuals were at work on the problem.

Another possible advantage of a larger problem-solving group is indicated in a study by Taylor and Faust [1952], who compared the efficiency of problem solving in groups of two and four. The parlor game of "Twenty Questions" was used as the experimental task. Although the performance of groups of four was not found to be superior to that of groups of two, it is significant that groups of four had fewer failures to find the answer in twenty questions. The authors suggest that "increasing the number of participants from two to four reduces the probability of a persisting wrong set resulting in complete failure."

It appears probable that, for any given task,

there is an optimum group size for maximum effectiveness. The optimum size will be a function of the complexity of the task and the degree of heterogeneity of available members in the abilities and skills required by the task. The more complex the task and the more homogeneous the available members, the larger the optimum size. The optimum size for creative groups is probably not large. As we have seen, large groups have difficulty organizing themselves for effective work and constraints upon participation are experienced with increase in size. To sum up, Thelen [1949] proposed that a group should ideally be the smallest possible that contains all the skills required for the accomplishment of the tasks of the group.

COMPOSITION OF GROUP

The effectiveness of a group in reaching its goals is determined by the *individual characteristics* of the separate members making up the group. Effective groups are made up of effective persons.

This, however, is not the whole story of the effect of membership composition upon group behavior. The particular *pattern* or combination of individuals making up a group is also highly important.

GROUPS AND INDIVIDUAL CHARACTERISTICS. A study by Haythorn [1953] throws considerable light on how the characteristics of individual members affect the behavior of the group. In experimental groups assigned discussion and problem-solving tasks, he explored the kinds of individual behavior patterns that facilitate or depress group functioning. Subjects met in groups of four. Membership was rotated so that each subject worked successively in each group and thus the influence of the given individual's behavior could be isolated from that of a particular group. Correlations were computed between the ratings by observers of each subject on each of 12 *behavioral traits* and ratings by group members of the performance of the subject's group. The

behavioral traits of cooperativeness, efficiency, and insight were found to be positively related to smooth and productive group functioning. On the other hand, such individualistic behavior traits as aggressiveness, self-confidence, initiative, interest in individual solution, and authoritarianism tended to reduce group cohesiveness and friendliness. Sociable behavior was found to lower group motivation and competition, but to increase friendliness and interest in social interaction.

Personality attributes of the individual members were measured by means of the Cattell Sixteen Personality Factor Questionnaire. Analysis of these personality measures in relation to the functioning of the group in which the individuals worked revealed consistent and meaningful relations. Maturity, adaptability, and acceptance of others were found to be positively related to effective group functioning; suspiciousness, eccentricity, and coolness toward their fellows tended to impair smooth group functioning.

As we have already pointed out, the qualities of functioning of a group cannot be wholly accounted for by the characteristics of the individual members. The particular *pattern* of characteristics of the membership must be taken into account as well.

MEMBERSHIP PATTERN—HOMOGENEITY. We have seen that persons who are similar in their values, attitudes, and interests tend to form stable, enduring groups (page 411). And there is rather substantial evidence that such *homogeneity* of individual characteristics among the members of a group promotes member satisfaction. For example, Hollingshead [1949] observed that in gratification groups, high school boys and girls ". . . want to associate with people similar to themselves. Here they feel comfortable, for they are 'among my kind of people.' This appeared to be an important principle in the organization of the leisure time activities of each class."

Studies of marital happiness indicate that similarity of interests and attitudes is conducive to a harmonious, satisfying marriage [Terman et al., 1938]. And a study by Preston, Peltz, et al. [1952] showed that couples who are happily married believe themselves to be similar.

In a study by Carter and Haythorn [1956], creative groups which were homogeneous and heterogeneous in authoritarian attitudes were compared. The homogeneous groups, relative to the heterogeneous groups, were found to be more friendly and to have higher morale. The members of heterogeneous groups, conversely, were observed to exhibit more conflict and competition. A greater tendency toward clique formation was also found in the heterogeneous groups. This latter finding was also reported by Gerard [1953].

The homogeneity or heterogeneity of a group also determines its *productivity*. But here it would appear that the *more* heterogeneous the group, the better it is. In other words, the effect of an independent variable upon group functioning varies with the nature of the criterion of effectiveness. Hoffman [1959], for instance, has studied the effect of the degree of homogeneity in personality of the members of a creative group upon the quality of problem solving. His results indicated that heterogeneous groups were superior to homogeneous groups in "inventive solutions."

BY WAY OF CAUTION. It is clear from these studies of the effect of group composition upon task effectiveness that we are here faced with a complex problem. We must ask, "Homogeneity in what characteristics? Heterogeneity in what characteristics? What is the criterion of effectiveness?" It may be the case that homogeneity in certain characteristics facilitates group effectiveness, and that heterogeneity in other characteristics may be facilitating.

A study by Cattell, Saunders, and Stice [1953] is an instance in point. These investigators tested 80 ten-man groups on a wide variety of tasks. Their results suggested that accuracy of group judgments was higher in groups heterogeneous in the personality traits of surgency, radicalism, character integration, and adventuresomeness. But in these same groups, heterogeneity in sensitivity, suspiciousness, and aggressiveness resulted in slowness in decision making and a feeling of blockage of goal achievement.

MEMBERSHIP PATTERN — COMPATIBILITY. Another crucial factor in group composition is the *compatibility* of the members in interpersonal response traits. Schutz [1958] has studied the effect of this factor on group productivity where time pressure was important. He was led to investigate compatibility by his assumption that noncompatible groups dissipate a great deal of time and energy on interpersonal problems. Further, the expression of hostility in the form of such obstructive behavior as unreasonable criticism may greatly reduce group productivity.

A personality scale consisting of items designed to measure power orientation and various interpersonal response traits (e.g., dependence-counterdependence, assertiveness, etc.) was developed and administered to 53 naval recruits. The responses of the recruits to the scale were used by the experimenter to construct Compatible and Incompatible groups. Compatible groups were composed of a focal person around whom the group could form and of members having similar interpersonal orientations. Incompatible groups were composed of two focal persons differing in interpersonal orientation around whom subgroups could form, or of members who differed in interpersonal orientation with no focal person.

The results revealed that the effect of compatibility on productivity increases with increase in task complexity. On a coding problem which required no cooperation among the members, there were no differences between the Compatible and Incompatible groups. A simple intercept problem that had no time limit likewise failed to reveal the effect of compatibility upon productivity.

When the complexity of the intercept problem was increased by imposing time limits, however, the Compatible groups performed significantly better than the Incompatible groups. In contests between the two types of groups, the Compatible groups won seven of eight contests. A plotting problem, which was the most difficult of the three tasks, clearly showed the over-all superiority of the Compatible groups. These findings are summarized in Figure 13.3.

For a study of the effect upon group productivity of the *pattern* of such managerial traits as supervisory ability and style of decision making, see Box 13.3.

STATUS HIERARCHY

As we have seen, the members of any group that exists for any appreciable period of time come to occupy different status positions in the group. The influence that the resulting status hierarchy has upon the effectiveness of group functioning is mediated in part by the pattern of communication established in the group.

STATUS HIERARCHY AND COMMUNICATION PATTERN. Thibaut [1950] deliberately established high- and low-status levels in friendship groups of young boys by favoring some members and discriminating against others. This preferential treatment was found to influence the pattern of communication within the group. The low-status members tended to direct more and more of their communications toward the high-status members as the experimenter continued to favor the latter. Moreover, the proportion of these communications that were aggressive in content decreased. Thibaut concludes that for persons low in a status hierarchy, communication directed toward high-status persons may serve as a substitute for blocked upward movement in the hierarchy. (For a study of this upward-directed pattern of communication in biracial groups, see Box 13.4.)

Kelley [1951] has studied the communica-

tion process in hierarchically organized, small work groups. Eight-man groups were given a task that allegedly required communication among the members to reproduce in one room a geometric pattern that was given in another room. In fact, all members performed the same task in response to standard, pre-prepared communications that were supposedly initiated by other members of the group.

Experimental instructions were used to create high- and low-status subgroups. Furthermore, one-half of each of the two status subgroups were led by experimental instructions to believe that they could move from one group to another; one-half, that they could not move. Thus four subgroups were created: high-status nonmobile, high-status mobile, low-status mobile, and low-status nonmobile.

A content analysis of the communications initiated by these various subgroups was made. Low-status mobile persons more frequently speculated about the nature of the jobs at the other status level than did the low-status nonmobile. This finding supports Thibaut's

FIGURE 13.3: The relation between task complexity and the effect of group compatibility upon task performance on three different tasks. As task complexity increases, the effect of group compatibility on performance becomes greater. The solid portions of the curve indicate the effect of increasing task complexity found for the three different experimental tasks used. [Adapted from Schutz, 1955.]

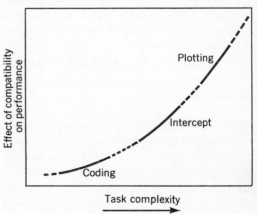

BOX 13.3: *A fine way to run a railroad!*

Edwin E. Ghiselli, an industrial psychologist at the University of California, Berkeley, and Thomas M. Lodahl have shown that the *pattern* of managerial traits in a group is important in determining its operating effectiveness.

Two managerial traits were studied in their experiment: supervisory ability and confidence in decision making. Persons high on the latter trait perceive themselves as active and self-reliant, confident of their ability to make decisions; persons low on the trait see themselves as careful in planning and thoughtful in action, seldom making rash decisions.

Ten 2-person groups, ten 3-person groups, and ten 4-person groups were used in the study. The experimental task was the operation of a model railroad whose track was laid out in a continuous oval with passing sidings. There were two trains on the track, and the task of the group was to run both trains around the track in *opposite* directions as many times as possible during the experimental session. Two sets of identical control panels made it possible for as many as four persons to operate the railroad simultaneously. Since part of the right of way consisted of a single track, the effective operation of the railroad demanded a high degree of coordination among the persons manning the two panels.

Observations of group performance yielded two additional scores for each group: the number of organizational changes and the number of changes in method. An organizational change was defined as (1) any trading of task from one member to another, and (2) any change in the way in which the work was divided among the members. The change-in-method score was obtained by counting the number of times a group changed its method of getting the train around the track. (Two main methods were used. The first was to run both trains simultaneously, using sidings to pass; the second was to run one train for one or more trips, then stop it on a siding, and run the other train.)

Results. Groups having a *single* member who was outstandingly superior in supervisory ability or in confidence in decision making tended to be more productive than groups having *two or more* members who were outstandingly high on these two managerial traits. That is, groups which had a member whose superiority was uncontested in these managerial traits and whose remaining members were thus more homogeneous tended to be the most effective groups.

The investigators suggest that this finding may be due to the fact that such groups went through far fewer changes in organization and methods of operation than did other groups.

The investigators caution that the generality of their findings may be limited. The subjects were college students who were strangers to one another and who were confronted with a new task which required a high degree of cooperation. Similar results may not be found in stable work groups with a developed structure, working on tasks that do not require such a high degree of interdependent effort.

Ghiselli, E. E., and Lodahl, T. M. *Patterns of managerial traits and group effectiveness.* J. abnorm. soc. Psychol., *1958,* **57,** *61–66.*

suggestion that communications may function as a substitute for actual movement. The number of communications irrelevant to the task at hand was greater among the low-status subjects than among the high. This irrelevant talk may, Kelley notes, serve as an escape from the low-status position and task. The status hierarchy also produced restraints affecting the content of communications. The high-status persons addressed few criticisms of their job to low-status persons, and seldom revealed confusion about it to anyone. In comparison with control subjects who were given no in-structions regarding status, both the high- and the low-status persons made few criticisms of persons at the other status level.

Kelley's findings suggest some of the ways in which the status hierarchy of a group can affect communication among the members and thus influence the efficiency of problem solving. For example, the tendency of low-status persons to talk about matters irrelevant to the task may reduce efficiency. And if constraints against criticism of persons at other status levels in the hierarchy reduce the number of critical evaluations of the contributions of members, the effectiveness of the group may suffer.

STABILITY OF STATUS AND GROUP EFFECTIVE-NESS. Heinicke and Bales [1953] have reported findings indicating that groups in which the status hierarchy is *stable* are more effective than groups in which the status relations among the members are fluid. Ten discussion groups made up of five or six persons were observed for at least four successive sessions. In all the groups it was observed that the relative frequency of disagreement, tension, and antagonism tended to reach their maximum values in the *second* session. Heinicke and Bales infer that the members are at this point struggling for status in the group. In four of the ten groups, the amount of conflict dropped in the third and fourth meetings; furthermore, among these four groups the rankings by the members of each other on leadership showed a high degree of agreement at the end of the fourth meeting. These four groups are termed the High Status-Consensus groups, their behavior being interpreted to

BOX 13.4: *Skin color, status, and talk*

Several investigators have found that in all-white groups, the direction of communication is mainly upward in the status hierarchy, i.e., the low-status members address most of their remarks to high-status members. The upward communication of the low-status members has been interpreted as a substitute for blocked upward mobility.

Irwin Katz, Judith Goldston, and Lawrence Benjamin at New York University tested the hypothesis that in biracial work groups the pattern of communication will be similar to the pattern in all-white status hierarchies.

Negro and white male college students were employed to work in groups of four—two Negroes and two whites—on a series of tasks. Initially the men were total strangers. Each group worked a total of 12½ hours. Social interaction among the group members was measured by means of a category system (see page 385).

The results showed that on a substantial number of the communication categories:

1. Whites made more remarks than did Negroes.
2. Whites spoke more to one another, proportionately, than to Negroes.
3. Negroes spoke more to whites than did whites to Negroes.
4. Negroes spoke more to whites, proportionately, than to one another.

The results of this study indicate that the pattern of communication between Negro and white members of a group when they are first thrown into enforced contact with one another is determined by the generally prevailing status differential of Negroes and whites in the American society.

Katz, I., Goldston, Judith, and Benjamin, L. *Behavior and productivity in bi-racial work groups.* Hum. Relat., *1958, 11, 123–141.*

mean that the status struggle ended fairly early in agreement upon a stable hierarchy.

In the other six groups, on the other hand, there was no decrease in conflict in the third and fourth sessions; furthermore, in these groups there was less intermember consensus on leadership ranking. In these so-called Low Status-Consensus groups it is inferred that the power conflict continued to rage and the status hierarchy remained unstable.

The members of the High Status-Consensus groups were found to be more satisfied with their groups and with their solutions of the task. As measured objectively by both the quality and the speed of solutions, they were also more efficient. The investigators suggest that a stable status hierarchy facilitates arriving at a group solution because those members of the group accorded high status by all their fellow members can play a decisive role in adjudicating disputes over what is the "right" or "best" solution. They also suggest that the early solution by the group of the problem of establishing a stable hierarchy frees time and energy for work on the task at hand.

CHANNELS OF COMMUNICATION

By isolating from one another the members of a group which has been assigned a laboratory task, it is possible for the experimenter to control the channels of communication among them to form any desired pattern of communication, or *communication net*. This technique is the one most commonly used in the study of the effect of patterns of communication on group behavior. For example, in a study by Leavitt [1951] five persons, seated around a table, were separated from one another by vertical partitions while working on a problem-solving task. The subjects were allowed to communicate with one another only by passing written notes through slots in the partitions. By varying the slots that were open, any desired network of communication among the five subjects could be established.

THE CIRCLE AND WHEEL. Two of the networks studied by Leavitt—the "circle" net and the "wheel" net—are reproduced in Figure 13.4. In the circle net each person can pass notes to the person on his right or left; in the wheel, member B can exchange notes with all the other members, but they cannot exchange information except by transmitting it through member B.

The circle net is a slightly more highly connected net than the wheel, i.e., in the circle five of the ten possible channels or links are open, whereas in the wheel only four are open. (If all ten possible links were open, we would have 100 per cent *net connectivity*—the "all-channel" structure.) The two nets also differ in the relative *position centrality* of the positions within them—the most central position being that most closely connected with the others. In the circle, the five positions are equally central; in the wheel, position B is more central than the other positions.

In research upon the relative effectiveness of different communication nets in problem-solving groups, the typical procedure is to give each person in the net a part of the total amount of information required to solve the problem. The task of the group is to assemble the various bits possessed by the members to arrive at the solution. To illustrate: In Leavitt's experiment each subject was given five different symbols out of a possible set of six. The task of the group was to discover the one symbol held in common by all five members. Leavitt found that the wheel groups worked faster, needed a smaller number of messages to solve the problem, and made fewer errors than did the circle groups.

Shaw [1954] confirmed Leavitt's finding that wheel groups require less time to solve simple problems. On complex problems, however, the circle groups were *faster* than the wheel groups. Shaw interprets this finding as follows:

> When simple problems are to be solved the availability of information is of primary importance. Thus, the wheel should be faster than the circle because the wheel pattern has the effect of designating which S will perform

the function of identifying the common symbol. As the complexity of the problem increases, however, the possibility of contributions from all members of the group becomes much more important. This is true because some S's are more capable than others of solving such problems quickly, and because part solutions can be delegated to various positions, thereby compensating in part for the effects of "saturation." With complex problems, then, the wheel should be slower than the circle because the *central person becomes saturated* (i.e., because the optimal output level is exceeded) and because it sometimes forces the weakest person in the group to function in the leadership role.

THE "ALL-CHANNEL" NET. Various studies have consistently found the "all-channel" net to require less time and to yield fewer errors than nets of lower connectivity. In these studies [Christie, Luce, and Macy, 1952; Shaw, 1954; Gilchrist, Shaw, and Walker, 1955], the groups were assigned arithmetic problems. Shaw, Rothschild, and Strickland [1957] studied the relative effectiveness of three communication nets in solving two complex human-relations problems. Again the "all-channel" net was more effective, as measured by mean time to reach a decision, than nets of a lower degree of connectivity.

The relative superiority of the "all-channel" net has been interpreted as directly due to the particular topological structure of this kind of net, which permits free communication. Guetzkow and Simon [1955] have proposed an alternative hypothesis: "The imposition of certain restrictions on the communication channels available to a group affects the efficiency of the group performance, not *directly* by limiting the potential efficiency of task performance with optimal organization in the given net, but *indirectly* by handicapping its ability to organize itself for efficient task performance." For a study which offers support for this hypothesis, see Box 13.5.

It seems likely that the net structure both directly and indirectly influences task perform-

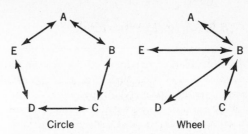

FIGURE 13.4: The circle and wheel networks used in a study by Leavitt of the effects of the structure of communication nets upon group performance. In the circle, each person can communicate with the persons on his right or left; in the wheel, member B can communicate with all the other members, but they cannot communicate with each other without going through B. The wheel network has also been referred to as the star (see Box 12.9, page 444). [After Leavitt, 1951.]

ance. However this may be, the study by Guetzkow and Simon, cited above, and a later study by Guetzkow and Dill [1957] report the following significant finding: Those groups which in organizing their own structure do not come to minimize the number of links in their net take more time to solve their tasks than groups which do. This suggests that the most efficient organizational structure is a minimum linkage system (see page 414).

Three other findings have been consistently reported in studies of problem solving in restricted nets. First, the greater the connectivity of the net, the higher the level of satisfaction in the group. Second, the likelihood of emerging as leader of the group increases with the centrality of one's position in the net. Third, the individual member's satisfaction with his position in the net is similarly related to its centrality: persons occupying central positions in a network have been found by various investigators to be more satisfied than persons occupying peripheral positions.

TO RECAPITULATE

For a number of reasons, the study of the effective group is a difficult scientific enter-

Mauk Mulder of the State University at Utrecht, Holland, has experimentally questioned the assumption that the nature of the communication net in a group determines the effectiveness of the group in solving problems. He advances the alternative hypothesis that "groups with a more centralized decision structure [regardless of their specific communication network] will be capable of better group performance, because the contributions of the individual group members can be integrated by the person in the central 'position' [the leader position]."

In the experiment, circle and wheel communication nets (again see Figure 13.4) were used with 26 groups of university students on five different problems. The following is one of the problems used.

A small company is moving from one office building to another. It must move four kinds of equipment: (a) chairs, (b) desks, (c) filing cabinets, and (d) typewriters. How many trucks are needed to make the move in one try?

The eight items of information needed to solve the problem are that the company owns a total of 12 desks, 48 chairs, 12 typewriters, 15 filing cabinets, and that one truckload can take 12 typewriters, or 3 desks, or 5 filing cabinets, or 24 chairs.

Each subject was given a copy of the statement of the problem and two of the eight items of information. The group was considered to have solved the problem when each subject knew the correct solution.

The degree of "centrality of the decision structure" of a group was measured as follows: A member of a group may function either as a "relayer" or as an "integrator." As an integrator, he may decide to withhold all the messages he receives until he can solve the problem himself. He may then (*a*) send the solution to the other members, or (*b*) send the solution and all necessary information in one message to the other members, or (*c*) send all necessary information in one message to other members.

The Decision Centrality Index of a group (DCI) was computed by first calculating the proportion of messages of types *a*, *b*, and *c* sent by each member. This was done by dividing the number of messages of types *a*, *b*, and *c* sent by each member by the total number of such messages sent

prise. First, the appropriate measure of effectiveness varies with the nature of the group. Second, the effectiveness of any particular group may be variously defined. The two major classes of criteria of group effectiveness are member satisfaction and group productivity.

The examination of the determinants of group effectiveness (the dependent variable) may be facilitated by classifying the determinants into independent variables—structural, task, and environmental factors—and into intermediate variables which are assumed to reflect the influence of the independent variables. Intermediate variables include leadership style, task motivation of members, and friendship relations.

Group effectiveness is partly determined by the interaction of various structural characteristics.

Group size has manifold effects on the functioning of the group. Thus group cohesiveness and member satisfaction tend to be greater in smaller groups; there is evidence that larger groups inhibit participation of some members; style of leadership varies with group size; the relation between group size and effectiveness is complex and variable.

The composition of the group influences its

by the total group. The difference between the person with the highest score and the person with the next highest was then calculated. This difference was the DCI score for the whole net. The DCI thus measures the centralization of decision making in *one* person, the "leader." It may vary from 0 to 1.00.

The relation between degree of centrality of the decision structure and problem-solving effectiveness on the last problem attacked by the groups was analyzed. By this time the groups had stabilized their operating procedures. The Wheel and Circle groups were each divided into two classes—the six more centralized groups (high DCI score) and the six less centralized groups (low DCI score). The findings are shown in the following table.

	Average DCI	Average time to solve in minutes	Average number of errors
Wheel groups:			
More centralized	.85	4.01	0
Less centralized	.17	7.88	5
Circle groups:			
More centralized	.54	5.79	4
Less centralized	.07	8.84	12

It will be seen that both the Wheel and the Circle groups with a more centralized decision structure were faster and made fewer errors than the corresponding groups with a less centralized structure. Note also that the Circle groups with a more centralized structure required considerably less time than the less centralized Wheel groups.

These results indicate that the decision structure of a group is more important than the communication net in determining speed of problem solving. The more centralized the decision structure, the faster the performance of the group.

Mulder, M. Communication, structure, decision structure, and group performance. Sociometry, *1960*, **23**, *1–14*.

effectiveness. Homogeneous groups tend to be more satisfying to their members; whether homogeneity or heterogeneity makes for productivity seems to depend upon the nature of the member characteristics.

Status hierarchy influences group effectiveness through its consequences for the communication pattern among members. A stable status hierarchy makes for group effectiveness.

The all-channel communication net is more efficient and more satisfying to the group members than nets of lower connectivity, perhaps because the latter are handicapped in organizing themselves efficiently.

GUIDE 39: *The effectiveness of a group is determined partly by the nature of the interactions among the members —leadership style, interdependence of motivation, friendship relations*

In terms of our over-all guiding framework for the study of groups, we now turn to an examination of the relations between certain intermediate variables which characterize membership interaction and the dependent variable of group effectiveness. The first such interaction variable that we shall consider is leadership style—how it facilitates or inhibits creativity and work productivity in groups.

LEADERSHIP AND CREATIVE GROUPS

Everything we have said about the functions of leadership (see pages 428 to 432) would suggest that the leader plays a critical role in determining the performance of a group. To be effective, a group must have an effective leader. But what is an effective leader? What distinguishes the behavior of the effective leader from that of a less effective leader?

Some light is thrown on these questions by a study of Maier and Solem [1952] in which the relative effectiveness of two different discussion-group leadership roles was compared. Sixty-four groups were organized, each group being asked to select a representative. In 34 of the groups, the experimenters assigned the representative the role of *discussion leader*; in the remaining groups, he was assigned the role of *observer*. The discussion leaders were instructed to lead a group discussion of the problem. They were told to encourage the participation of all members and to stimulate group activity by asking questions. They were asked to try to get the group to agree on an answer. The observers were told simply to listen to the discussion. Neither the discussion leaders nor the observers were allowed to express their views about the experimental problem. The problem assigned all groups was as follows: "A man bought a horse for $60 and sold it for $70. Then he bought it back for $80 and again sold it for $90. How much money did he make in the horse business?" The members were instructed to record privately their answers to the problem before and after a discussion period of 8 minutes. (Note to reader: The answer is *not* $10.00.)

The two sets of groups were found to give similar answers to the problem before discussion. After discussion, however, the percent-age of correct answers in the leader groups increased to 84 per cent, as compared with 72 per cent correct responses in the observer groups—a statistically significant difference. Analysis of the data showed that the superiority of the leader groups was due mainly to the role of the leader in securing a hearing for minority views. When a minority of one had the correct answer, he had a better opportunity to be heard and to convince others in a leader group than he did in an observer group.

Maier concludes:

> A discussion leader can function to upgrade a group's thinking by permitting an individual with a minority opinion time for discussion. In a leaderless discussion, the majority dominates, and this condition releases social pressure which has an important influence on opinion. Without the right kind of leadership, therefore, a minority cannot effectively compete with the pressure of the majority. When the minority is right, and there is no protection from the leader, a distinct potential contribution is lost; when it is wrong, the minority cannot convince the majority. The leader, in giving the minority a greater voice, can upgrade the end result of a discussion without running the risk of down-grading the end product. The quality of thinking in a democracy is thus dependent on the opportunities it affords minority opinion to be heard.

PARTICIPATORY LEADERSHIP. Pelz [1956] studied the effect of a *participatory leadership* upon research scientists in a large medical research laboratory. In a participatory style of leadership, the leader gives his subordinates a considerable amount of independence in making final decisions. At the same time, however, the leader plays an active rather than a passive role—discussing problems with his subordinates, suggesting leads to be followed, etc. Participatory leadership—akin to democratic leadership—is characterized by two elements: independence of group members, and activity by the leader.

Pelz measured the dimension of independence by getting reports from the scientists on their freedom to make their own decisions, and on the absence of the influence of the chief over their work. Degree of independence was scored on a four-point scale ranging from "dependence" (chief alone makes decisions) to "independence" (subordinate alone makes decisions). Two intermediate degrees of independence were "separation" (neither has much say) and "mutual influence" (both have a say). The degree of activity of the chief was measured by the frequency of contact between chief and subordinates.

Figure 13.5 shows how these two elements of participatory leadership (independence of subordinate and activity of leader), taken together, are related to the scientific performance of the younger members of the research staff of the organization. Scientific performance is *positively* correlated with independence of the subordinate when the subordinate is in frequent contact with the chief (see solid line), but is *negatively* correlated when there is infrequent contact (see broken line). Participatory leadership appears to be more effective than either directive leadership, in which the scientists are dependent on the chief, or laissez-faire leadership, in which the chief plays a hands-off role and does not maintain an active relationship with his subordinates.

In another study in the same laboratory, Baumgartel [1955] found that superior technical competence and strong research motivation were even more important than administrative skill for effective scientific leadership. (This finding is confirmed in the study reported in Box 13.6.) It would seem, then, that the truly outstanding scientific leader should combine all of these—technical competence, research drive, and administrative skill.

LEADERSHIP AND WORK GROUPS

The Survey Research Center of the University of Michigan has conducted a series of studies of leadership behavior in relation to

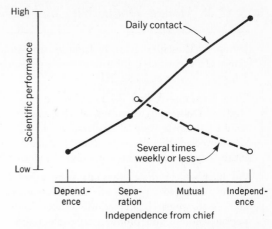

FIGURE 13.5: Scientific performance of younger scientists as related to independence from and frequency of contact with chief. The solid line shows the relation between performance and independence when the chief and scientific worker are in daily contact. The broken line shows the relation when the two have less frequent contact. [After Pelz, 1956.]

job satisfaction and productivity in business and industrial work groups. The three principal studies were carried out in the Chesapeake & Ohio Railway [Katz et al., 1951], the Prudential Insurance Company [Katz et al., 1950; Morse, 1953], and the Caterpillar Tractor Company [Katz and Kahn, 1951]. In summarizing the major findings of this program of research, Kahn and Katz [1953] found that three dimensions of leadership behavior were consistently related to the productivity of work groups: (1) assumption of leader role; (2) closeness of supervision; (3) employee-orientation.

ASSUMPTION OF LEADER ROLE. Supervisors who actively assumed the functions of leadership were found to have consistently better productivity records than supervisors who tended to perform more or less the same functions as the members of the group. The leader cannot, in his role, be "one of the boys." He has special functions (e.g., planning, supervising) to perform, and unless these functions are performed, the output of the group suffers.

BOX 13.6: *Morale, productivity, and leadership*

Irving R. Weschler, Murray Kahone, and Robert Tannenbaum of the Institute of Human Relations, University of California, Los Angeles, collaborated in a study of the effect of leadership on job productivity and morale.

Two divisions—A and B—of the same scientific department in a naval research laboratory were studied. Division A consisted of 28 members; division B, of 38. The leaders of the two divisions differed in their style of leadership. "Division A . . . was headed by a brilliant young scientist, who directed the division along restrictive lines. Division B was headed by an older man, a fatherly type, who directed his division along permissive lines."

All members of these divisions were asked (1) to rate the level of productivity and of morale of their own work group, of their division, and of the laboratory as a whole; (2) to specify their choices for research and administrative leaders of their division and their choices for best-liked person. Morale and productivity were rated on five-point scales which ranged from "very high" (scale value 1) to "very low" (scale value 5).

Seven members of the top administrative staff of the laboratory who were familiar with the two divisions then appraised the level of job satisfaction, morale, and productivity of the two divisions. The following table shows the ratings by these seven superiors and the ratings by the division members themselves.

| | PRODUCTIVITY | | MORALE | |
DIVISION	*Superiors*	*Members*	*Superiors*	*Members*
A	2.71	3.22	3.43	3.42
B	2.86	2.37	2.00	1.95

In the view of the superiors, division A, with low morale, was doing a better job in productivity

(See the discussion of the "initiating-and-directing" dimension of leadership behavior, page 433.)

CLOSENESS OF SUPERVISION. The second dimension of leadership behavior which differentiated high- and low-producing supervisors was closeness of supervision. High-producing supervisors were found to supervise less closely than low-producing supervisors. The latter tended, in various ways, to limit the freedom of the workers to do their jobs in their own way. There is substantial evidence in the findings of these studies that lack of freedom results in dissatisfaction with the job, the supervisor, and the company. Freedom to have a say in determining one's work is, it seems, a strong want. Men will work more productively when they are given some degree of autonomy on the job. Evidence supporting this proposition is furnished by the results of group-decision studies (see page 479). When workers are subjected to overly close supervision, dissatisfaction, poor work motivation, and low production may develop as symptoms of frustration of the "autonomy want."

Another important finding of this research is that the leadership behavior of supervisors reflects the style of leadership at higher management levels in the organization. Supervisors tend to lead in a manner similar to that of their immediate superiors. One significance of this finding for the social psychology of groups is that the behavior of a group in an organization is considerably influenced by the organizational context, and cannot be studied as though the group were an independent,

than division B, and a better job than the low-morale members gave themselves credit for. The permissively led group, B, with high morale, overrated their productivity when checked by the ratings of the superiors.

The sociometric data, summarized in the following table, show that the leader of division A was chosen as a competent research worker (in 39.3 per cent of the choices), but was not perceived as a good administrator and was not liked. The members of division B made a much smaller percentage of choices outside their division for "best administrator" and "best liked" than did division A. This finding is further evidence that the permissively led division was more cohesive and integrated than the restrictively led division.

| | BEST RESEARCHER | | BEST ADMINISTRATOR | | BEST LIKED | |
CHOSEN PERSONS	Division A	Division B	Division A	Division B	Division A	Division B
Division head	39.3%	15.8%	7.2%	26.4%	0.0%	31.6%
Other	39.3	50.0	71.4	57.8	92.8	52.6
Unspecified	21.4	34.2	21.4	15.8	7.2	15.8

The permissive leadership of the older scientist promoted higher morale than did the restrictive leadership of the brilliant younger man, but did not result in greater productivity. Morale and productivity do not necessarily go hand in hand.

Weschler, I. R., Kahone, M., and Tannenbaum, R. Assessing organizational effectiveness: job satisfaction, productivity and morale. In R. Tannenbaum, I. R. Weschler, and F. Massarik, Leadership and organization. New York: McGraw-Hill, 1961.

autonomous unit. The extrapolation of research findings secured from studies of autonomous *ad hoc* groups to stable groups in an organization should be done only with great caution.

EMPLOYEE-ORIENTATION. The third dimension of leadership behavior that is related to productivity is employee-orientation. This refers to a set of attitudes toward workers characterized by concern for them as individuals, interest in promoting their welfare, lack of punitiveness, etc. (See the discussion of the "consideration" dimension of leadership, page 432.) High-producing supervisors were consistently found to be more employee-oriented and less production-oriented than low-producing supervisors. Again the findings of these studies suggest that employee-orientation on

the part of supervisors is in part a reflection of the style of leadership practiced at higher levels in the organization.

For a study which corroborates the findings of the research of the Michigan group, see Box 13.7.

BY WAY OF CAUTION. Employee-orientation can, of course, be overdone. An effective leader must be able to differentiate sharply between competent and incompetent members, and to be critical of the incompetent. As Fiedler [1958], in his studies of leadership and group effectiveness, puts it, the leader

. . . must be willing to reject co-workers who do not adequately perform their jobs. This requires emotional independence and detachment from others. The person who readily forms deep emotional ties with his subordi-

BOX 13.7: *The sympathetic and effective supervisor*

Michael Argyle, a social psychologist at Oxford University, and two associates, Godfrey Gardner and Frank Cioffi, studied the relations between the productivity of work groups and five dimensions of supervisory behavior which earlier studies had shown to be related to productivity. These five dimensions were (1) general versus close supervision, (2) pressure for production, (3) employee-oriented versus production-oriented attitudes, (4) democratic versus authoritarian methods of supervision, and (5) punitive versus nonpunitive attitudes.

Inspection of the correlations among these five dimensions revealed that they formed a consistent and meaningful pattern. Foremen who were described as employee-oriented were democratic and gave general, rather than close, supervision; they also tended to be nonpunitive, and the more democratic their supervisory practices, the less punitive they were. Foremen who tended to give general supervision also exerted less pressure for production than other foremen. Finally, non-punitiveness was found to be associated with the use of little pressure.

Argyle and his associates then proceeded to determine the relations between these five dimensions of foreman behavior and the productivity of their work groups. It was found that the foremen of high-producing work groups tended to use general rather than close supervision and were relatively more democratic and nonpunitive in their supervisory behavior than the foremen of low-producing work groups.

Argyle, M., Gardner, G., and Cioffi, F. *The measurement of supervisory methods.* Hum. Relat., *1957, **10**, 295–313.*

nates, who needs to be liked or supported by his men, will find it difficult to discipline or discharge them, since this may decrease his popularity or cause him to lose their friendship.

Employee-oriented attitudes, in short, do not mean personal attachment to and dependence upon subordinates. They mean, rather, a task-oriented interest in subordinates (see Box 13.8).

WHICH IS CAUSE—WHICH EFFECT? There is, then, substantial evidence that style of supervisory leadership and work productivity are associated. The direction of causality in this relation is, however, not established by correlational studies of the kind we have discussed. There are, in fact, three different possible interpretations of the observed relation: (1) Workers are more productive when supervised in certain ways. (2) Foremen supervise differently when workers are productive. (3) Some underlying common factor or fac-

tors determine both productivity and style of supervision.

Two studies assist us in deciding between the first two of these three possible explanations. Feldman [1937] studied the effects of rotating supervisors among different sections in an office. He found that the productivity of sections changed with the assignment of new supervisors. This finding suggests that style of supervision determines productivity. Jackson [1953] studied the behavior of foremen who were transferred from their original work groups to other groups having a different level of productivity. No change in the style of supervision of the transferred foremen was observed. Apparently group productivity has little, if any, effect on the style of leadership displayed by experienced supervisors.

In the light of these two findings, it seems safe to infer that style of supervision is a *cause* of differences in the productivity of work groups.

GROUPS, ORGANIZATIONS, AND THE INDIVIDUAL

BOX 13.8: *Psychological distance and leader effectiveness*

The research of Fred E. Fiedler, a social psychologist at the University of Illinois, indicates that in a work group the effective leader is one who maintains "psychological distance" between himself and the members of his group, provided that he is supported by his superiors and assistants in the organization.

Thirty-two relatively small consumer cooperatives, members of the Illinois Farm Supply Company, were studied. Each of the cooperatives is owned by the farmers within the county which it serves and has its own board of directors which selects the cooperative's general manager and assistant manager. The general manager is regarded as the formal head of each cooperative.

"Psychological distance" was measured by having the general manager rate his most and least preferred subordinates on various work traits. The bigger the difference between these two ratings, the more "psychologically distant" the manager was taken to be. (The underlying assumption is that the more "distant" the leader, the more likely he is to discriminate sharply between those workers he considers competent and those he considers incompetent.)

Correlations were then computed between a criterion of company effectiveness (net income) and the manager's "psychological distance" score.

When all companies were included in the computation, the correlation was insignificant (.14). When only those companies were used in which the board leader endorsed the general manager, the correlation rose to .39. Finally, when the general manager was both endorsed by the board leader and accepted by his assistant managers, the correlation rose to .70.

Fiedler summarizes the differences between the behavior of "psychologically distant" and "psychologically close" managers as follows:

> Above all, the [psychologically distant] manager . . . saw himself as a professional administrator whose job it was to propose policy to the board and to see that the board decisions were adequately implemented. . . . He held regular staff meetings with his assistant managers, whom he also brought along to board meetings to present reports of the work in their departments. He demanded and got considerable freedom of action from his board, and he gave his assistant managers considerable freedom and responsibility. . . . He wanted ambitious assistant managers, and he felt that they ought to be ready for promotion to a bigger job within three years, even though this would entail more work on his part.

> In contrast, the [psychologically close] manager . . . saw his own job primarily in terms of insuring smooth interpersonal relations with the board, employees, and customers. . . . In general, he showed a strong trend for close informal ties with people. Some of his behavior and attitudes suggested a need of dominating and possessing people. Thus, formal staff meetings were rare, and he insisted on being consulted by his assistant managers on relatively minor decisions since "two heads are always better than one." His assistant managers did not attend board meetings since there were many things which might not be of concern to them, and he felt that an assistant manager should stay a minimum of four years before moving up to a more responsible position.

Fiedler, F. E. The leader's psychological distance and group effectiveness. In D. Cartwright and A. Zander (Eds.), Group dynamics. (2nd ed.) Chicago: Row, Peterson, 1960.

LEADER POWER—REAL OR HOLLOW? In order to throw further light on the specific *manner* in which supervision affects group productivity, Pelz [1952] studied the relations between the practices and attitudes of supervisors and the attitudes and morale of workers in an electric utility company. His study involved several hundred supervisors and several thousand workers.

Holding constant such variables as size of the work group, kind of work, and length of time on the job, Pelz found a considerable number of significant relations between the 50-odd supervisory practices studied and the reactions of the workers. Many of the relations, however, were the opposite of those anticipated. For example, in one such paradoxical instance Pelz found that "giving honest and sincere recognition for a job well done" *depressed* morale in groups of white-collar workers.

Through further analysis of his data, Pelz found that these perplexing findings were due to the amount of power which the leader was perceived by his subordinates to have. When supervisors with "influence upstairs" followed supervisory practices which are generally considered to represent effective leadership behavior, workers tended to respond favorably. When supervisors who lacked influence with their superiors used these same supervisory practices, they either failed to secure a favorable reaction or got a negative reaction from their subordinates.

The leader of a group in an organization, if he is to function effectively, not only must "make like" a good leader—he must also *be* a powerful leader. The trappings and techniques of "good leadership" are not enough. The effective leader must be seen as having influence "up the line" which will enable him to obtain rewards for his subordinates. The amount of influence of a supervisor with his superior is a crucial variable which conditions his effectiveness and power with his subordinates.

GROUP-TASK MOTIVATION AND GROUP PRODUCTIVITY

The effectiveness of a group depends, among other things, upon the willingness of the members to work to achieve the formally specified goals of the group. In problem solving and in work groups, the members are engaged in a common task: they discuss a problem to arrive at a group solution; they work together to make a group product. In short, such groups are assumed to have a single goal and their effectiveness in achieving this goal is determined by the degree to which the members of the group are motivated to work for it.

SELF-ORIENTATION AND GROUP PRODUCTIVITY. The deleterious effects of low "group task motivation" upon group productivity are brought out in a study by Fouriezos, Hutt, and Guetzkow (see page 385). The 72 conference groups studied in the Conference Research Project of the University of Michigan were rated on the extent to which the members expressed self-oriented needs, i.e., motives resulting in behavior "not necessarily directed toward a group goal, or . . . a solution of a group's problems" but ". . . primarily toward the satisfaction of the need itself, regardless of the effect on attainment of the group goal." The experimenters found that the amount of such self-oriented-need behavior correlated negatively with measures of member satisfaction. In other words, groups in which there was a high frequency of self-oriented behavior were relatively dissatisfied with the meeting as a whole, with the decisions arrived at, with the procedures used to reach decisions, and with the chairmanship. These "self-oriented" groups were also high in amount of conflict.

Finally, measures of productivity showed significant inverse relations with amount of self-oriented-need behavior. For example, groups rated high in such behavior tended to complete fewer items on the agenda, although their meetings lasted longer.

478

COOPERATION, COMPETITION, AND GROUP PRODUCTIVITY. The effects of cooperative and competitive situations upon group behavior and productivity have been studied by Deutsch [1949]. Five pairs of matched groups of student subjects were established. One group in each pair was randomly assigned to a "competitive" treatment; the other group, to a "cooperative" treatment. The groups met for a three-hour period each week for six consecutive weeks to work on logical puzzles and human-relations problems. Members of the cooperative groups were told that the group as a whole would be evaluated in comparison with four other similar groups *as a whole*. Members of the competitive groups were informed that each person in the group would be ranked from one to five on the basis of his individual contribution to the solution of the various problems assigned the group.

The cooperative groups were found to be more effective and to show a higher degree of member satisfaction than the competitive groups. In particular, the cooperative groups were characterized by: (1) Higher quantity of production per unit of time as measured by number of puzzles solved and length of recommendations for the solution of the human-relations problems. (2) Higher quality of production as measured by fruitfulness of ideas for handling human-relations problems and by amount of understanding developed in group discussions. (3) Stronger pressure to achieve the group task. (4) Greater division of labor and coordination of efforts. (5) Fewer difficulties in communication with fellow members. (6) Greater friendliness in the discussions. (7) Greater satisfaction with the group and its products. Moreover, observers' ratings of group interaction showed a significantly greater tendency for the members of the cooperative groups to perform such "group functions" as "the maintenance, strengthening, or regulation of the group." Members of competitive groups, in contrast, showed a significantly greater tendency to perform "individual functions," i.e., functions that ". . . are directed toward the satisfaction of the participant's individual needs. They have for their immediate purpose the reaching of an individual goal which is neither task nor group relevant."

INCREASING "GROUP MOTIVATION." It is clear from the foregoing studies that the effectiveness of a group requires that the members be motivated to work at the group task. This poses a central question: *How* can members be motivated to work for the goal of the group? How can they be brought to accept the group goal as their individual goal?

One approach to this question is to make the group members *interdependent* in their work functions. There is some evidence that through the use of division of work techniques, group-goal acceptance is increased (see Box 13.9).

Another approach is through the *group-decision* method developed by Lewin (see page 228) to change the behavior of individuals. This method has also been applied to the problem of securing member acceptance of new group goals. In one of the first of such studies, Coch and French [1948] found that new group goals are more readily accepted when the members of the group participate in setting them than when they are imposed on the group. (See Box 13.10 for a similar but more extensive study.)

Why is group decision a good way to promote the acceptance of new goals? As we have indicated earlier (see page 401), many factors are probably responsible for the effect. The work of Bennett (see page 230) showed that the desired action was adopted more frequently when individuals perceived that there was near-unanimity in the individual decisions made by the group members in favor of the desired behavior. This suggests that the group-decision method is effective because it uses the pressures toward conformity to the norms of a group to bring about conformity to a new norm.

BOX 13.9: *Division of labor and group-task motivation*

Edwin J. Thomas has investigated the effect of division of labor among the members of a work group upon their group-task motivation and productivity.

Thirty-two 5-person groups, composed of women occupying similar jobs in a large private utility company, were used in Thomas's experiment. The groups were seated around a large circular table and were given the task of building miniature houses of cardboard. This task was presented as a test of "general work intelligence." Speed of work was stressed in the instructions.

In one-half of the groups *high interdependence* was created by division of labor. Two of the five steps involved in the task were assigned to each person in the group, as in a double assembly line. Contiguous persons were thus made mutually dependent. In the remaining one-half of the groups, *low interdependence* was created by assigning all five steps in the task to each member of the group. Thus each person was independent of the others in doing her work.

The results indicated that group effectiveness was clearly elevated by this method of increasing the degree of interdependence among the group members. Further analysis suggested that the facilitating effect of the division of work was due largely to its arousal of group-task motivation in the individual members. Indeed, division of work created such a high degree of interdependence that even when subjects (as another part of the experiment) were instructed to work for *individual* goals, most of them said that they worked for *group goals.*

This study, it should be pointed out, still leaves unanswered a number of questions regarding the effects of division of work upon group productivity. Perhaps the most important question is: What *long-term* effects will dividing the work into simple-skill components have upon work motivation and upon productivity? This particular experimental session lasted, of course, but for a short time only.

Thomas, E. J. Effects of facilitative role interdependence on group functioning. Hum. Relat., *1957,* **10,** *347–366.*

The study by Pennington et al. (see page 230) suggests that the discussion of new group goals which is a feature of the group-decision method may help to bring about their acceptance. As a result of group discussion, the clarity of the new group goals may be increased. Their relevance to the wants of the members may become more apparent. The factors determining the effectiveness of the group-decision method are clearly many and varied, and further research is as clearly needed.

FACTORS LIMITING EFFECTIVENESS OF PARTICIPATION. It seems that allowing the members of a group to participate in setting group goals does make for their increased acceptance. The question now is: What factors limit

the effectiveness of participation in the setting of group goals?

A study by French, Israel, and Ås [1960] helps to answer this question. These investigators tried to replicate the original Coch and French study (see page 479) in a Norwegian shoe factory.

Nine 4-man groups were shifted from working on summer footwear to winter footwear. Four of these groups (the control groups) were treated in the traditional manner; the other five (the experimental groups) were permitted to participate in some of the decisions involved in the change-over. The findings revealed no differences between the experimental and control groups in level of production after the change to the new foot-

BOX 13.10: *Change without trouble*

J. R. P. French, Jr., and I. C. Ross, of the Research Center for Group Dynamics, University of Michigan, collaborated with S. Kirby, J. R. Nelson, and P. Smyth, of the Harwood Manufacturing Company, Marion, Virginia, in studying the effect of employee participation in facilitating a program of industrial change. Because few studies of successful, large-scale industrial change have been reported, the work of these investigators is of special interest.

Three of the plants of the Harwood Manufacturing Company, each of which produced similar garments, were to undergo major production changes, such as the reengineering of entire assembly lines. Although labor-management relations in the company had been very good, the workers had always shown resistance to any change in production methods.

A series of approximately 80 meetings was held with the workers in which discussion of all matters pertaining to the proposed changes was encouraged. Engineers, supervisors, and workers discussed the effectiveness of the new methods as they were gradually introduced. Often additional changes were made as a result of the suggestions of the workers.

"Before and after" records of productivity of the two major items manufactured and the turnover rate of employees were used as measures of the degree of adjustment of the workers to the changes. The following tables present the productivity data for one of the plants studied (all three plants gave essentially the same results). A year after the introduction of the changes there was no indication of a decrease in productivity. The productivity on item A remained unchanged, while on item B there was a 10 per cent increase.

| | AVERAGE PRODUCTION IN STANDARD UNITS | |
ITEM MANUFACTURED	*Before change*	*One year later*
A	79	80
B	69	75

The second measure was employee turnover rate. If the changes were resented by the workers, we should find an increase in the number of workers leaving the company. But as the following table shows, the turnover rate *decreased* throughout the period of change. (The changes were begun in 1954 and completed early in 1956.)

Year	1952	1953	1954	1955	1956
Turnover	.703	.623	.320	.282	.248

As the investigators note:

> The radical change in production methods described here brought about results that were highly gratifying to management. The cost of production was reduced; a better product was turned out; production time was shortened; and productive capacity was expanded. . . . To management the minimal nature of the difficulties met with during the change was at least as noteworthy as the economic gains.

> *French, J. R. P., Jr., Ross, I. C., Kirby, S., Nelson, J. R., and Smyth, P. Employee participation in a program of industrial change. Personnel, 1958, 35, 16–29.*

**TABLE 13.1: CORRELATIONS BETWEEN FELT PARTICIPATION IN
DECISION MAKING AND JOB ATTITUDES AND PERFORMANCE**
[After Vroom, 1959]

Group	Ratings of favorable attitude toward job	Ratings of job performance
All supervisors	.36	.20
Supervisors having:		
High independence need	.55	.33
Moderate independence need	.31	.19
Low independence need	.31	.06
Supervisors having:		
High authoritarianism	.03	−.08
Moderate authoritarianism	.35	.28
Low authoritarianism	.53	.28

wear. This result the authors interpreted as due to the irrelevance for production of the decisions that the experimental groups were allowed to make.

However, the experimental groups were found to have greater job satisfaction than the control groups. The positive effects of participation on the job attitudes of the workers were directly related to the perceived legitimacy of participation. Legitimacy was defined as "the extent to which the parties involved consider it right and proper to engage in the decision making process." It was also found that the positive effects of participation upon member satisfaction increased with decreasing resistance to the methods of participation used.

PERSONALITY AND PARTICIPATION. A study by Vroom [1959] indicates that the beneficial effects of participation in group-decision making are limited by the personality of the worker. His subjects were 108 first-, second-, and third-line supervisors in a parcel delivery company. For each supervisor he obtained the following measures:

1. Felt participation—the amount of influence the individual believes he has in decision making
2. Attitude toward job
3. Need for independence

4. Authoritarianism
5. Job performance

The relation between felt participation in decision making and attitude toward the job for subgroups of supervisors differing in need for independence and in authoritarianism is shown in Table 13.1. Taking all supervisors together, there is a significant correlation (.36) between participation and favorable attitude toward the job. But this relationship is appreciably greater for those supervisors high in independence need (.55) and low in authoritarianism (.53). In contrast, high authoritarians and persons with low independence need are far less affected by the opportunity to participate in decision making—the two corresponding correlations being .03 and .31.

The table also shows that felt participation tends to be associated with good job performance among persons who are high in need for independence (.33) and low in authoritarianism (.28). No such relationship exists among those persons low in need for independence (.06) and high in authoritarianism (−.08).

As Vroom notes, studies of participation that ignore the interaction between participation and personality can only yield average statements for all members of the group studied. Such average statements will underestimate the effects of participation upon some

482

persons and overestimate its effects upon others.

FRIENDSHIP RELATIONS AND
GROUP PRODUCTIVITY

Friendship among group members may make for a happy group life—but it need not make for group effectiveness. As Kelley and Thibaut [1954] have pointed out, there seem to be two possible effects of friendship relations upon group productivity. On the one hand, close friendship may reduce constraints upon participation, improve communication, and thus *improve* the effectiveness of the group (see Box 13.11). On the other hand, close friendship relations among the members of a group may lead to the abandonment of the work task of the group in favor of securing satisfaction through purely social activity and thus *decrease* group productivity.

FRIENDSHIP CAN "PRODUCE." Van Zelst [1952] studied the effect of sociometric re-grouping upon the satisfaction, turnover, and output of workers in the building trades. Four groups of carpenters and bricklayers performing identical jobs in a large housing project on the outskirts of Chicago were studied. The members of these groups were accustomed to being assigned to work teams by the construction foreman at the beginning of each work day. Twenty carpenters and 16 bricklayers served as the experimental subjects. These men were assigned work partners on the basis of their expressed preferences for coworkers. (They were given their first or second choice.) The remaining workers—carpenters and bricklayers—served as the controls and were assigned work partners on a purely random basis.

In a pre-experimental base period of 3 months, the experimental and control work groups showed no significant differences in productivity. After the sociometric regrouping, however, sharp differences appeared (see Table 13.2). In the experimental groups job

BOX 13.11: *The case of the changing cage*

Clara B. Richards and Henry F. Dobyns, social scientists at Cornell University, have reported a case study of how administrative restrictions on social activity may affect the satisfaction and productivity of a group of workers.

The group, a voucher-check filing unit in an insurance company, was made up of nine women. For some time, their work area was "the cage"—a wire cage surrounded by filing cabinets and boxes which screened them from the view of the section head. Within the cage, the members of the group worked together smoothly, kept up with the load of work, and, screened from the section head, enjoyed such social activities as chatting, snacking, and playing games.

For reasons of efficiency, the cage was moved to a new location. The new cage was smaller than the old one, and had only one door which opened into the work area of the audit division. Further, in the new cage the filing cabinets were so arranged that the section head could see into the area. In the new cage it was impossible for the workers to stand at the doorway talking with the messenger boys or slip out unobserved to bring in the customary afternoon snack. And the section head ordered the unit chief to restrict the amount of talking.

The workers were very unhappy with their life in the new cage. When the annual inventory of unfiled checks was taken at the end of the year, the unit was found to be several weeks behind schedule. Changes in the culture of this work group, brought about by administrative fiat, had drastically impaired the satisfaction and productivity of its members.

Richards, Clara B., and Dobyns, H. F. *Topography and culture: the case of the changing cage.* Hum. Org., *1957*, *16*, *16–20.*

TABLE 13.2: MEAN SCORES ON JOB SATISFACTION, TURNOVER, AND OUTPUT IN CONTROL AND EXPERIMENTAL WORK GROUPS BEFORE AND AFTER SOCIOMETRIC REGROUPING [After Van Zelst, 1952]

	CONTROL WORK GROUPS		EXPERIMENTAL WORK GROUPS	
	Before	*After*	*Before*	*After*
Job satisfaction	39.7	39.3	38.5	44.8
Turnover rate	2.3	3.7	2.7	0.3
Index of labor cost	3.59	3.49	3.66	2.87
Index of materials cost	3.30	3.32	3.34	3.14

satisfaction increased, turnover dropped to almost a zero level, and output increased substantially. On all of these measures, the experimental groups surpassed the controls.

The chief construction engineer in his report to management stated:

> Savings due to this psychological procedure have exceeded those of any previous work saving device or any combination of five previous work saving methods. Financial benefits are such that we are now constructing every 29th building entirely free from labor and material costs. Even greater financial gains would occur were it possible to evaluate monetarily savings due to the great reduction in turnover.

Other studies suggest that social isolation on the job may lessen satisfaction and productivity. For example, in a study of "The Man on the Assembly Line," Walker and Guest [1952] rated jobs according to their "mass production characteristics," e.g., noise, repetitiveness, restricted opportunity for movement, etc. Absenteeism and turnover (extremely high throughout the automobile industry) were nearly twice as high among workers whose jobs were judged to possess such "extreme mass production characteristics." The central fact for our consideration here is that workers on such jobs often reported that *social isolation* from their fellow workers in such mass production jobs was an important reason for their job dissatisfaction.

Here again we note the multiplicity of wants—social as well as economic—that must be served in the workplace (see page 86).

FRIENDSHIP MAY NOT "PRODUCE." Horsfall and Arensberg [1949] studied four 7-worker teams in the "bottoming room" of the ABC Shoe Company. Each team performed the same series of machine operations on shoes. They found that the more efficient teams indulged in substantially lower amounts of social activity than did the less efficient teams. They comment:

> Much has been said about increasing group give-and-take in order to increase production: the most efficient teams indulged least in social activity. This does not mean that there should not be any interaction. The question is to define quantitatively how much is optimum for a given group under what conditions of leadership.

BUT REMEMBER. As we have pointed out (page 457), there are interactions among the variables of any one level in our schema for the study of group effectiveness—independent, intermediate, or dependent. The influence of friendship relations upon the productivity of a work group will be influenced by the quality of the leadership and the degree to which the members accept the task goals of the group—variables which themselves may be functionally related. Under a weak leader, the members of a group may not fully accept the task goals of the group and may abandon them in favor of satisfying social activities when the task proves difficult. On the other hand, if the task goals of the group are accepted by the members because of the effectiveness of the leader or other factors which we have discussed above, satisfying friendship relations may facilitate productivity.

TO RECAPITULATE

Group effectiveness depends, in part, upon intermediate variables—such characteristics of group interaction as the style of leadership, the interdependence of member motivation, and the amount and quality of friendship relations.

The quality and style of leadership are critically important in determining the effectiveness of both creative and work groups. Dimensions of leadership behavior which have consistently been found to promote group effectiveness include assumption of the functions of the leader, general rather than close supervision (participatory leadership), and employee-orientation. The leader's effectiveness suffers, however, if his concern for his subordinates interferes with his disciplinary function.

The effectiveness of a group in accomplishing its functions is obviously dependent upon the willingness of the members to work for the group goals. Motivational interdependence seems to be increased if the members are made interdependent in their work functions and if they are given a voice in decisions which affect their work.

Studies of the influence of friendship relations among the members of a group upon its productivity suggest that friendship relations tend to increase productivity if the members, for whatever reason, have accepted the task goals of the group. If they have not been accepted, sociability may become the primary goal.

CHAPTER GUIDES AND GLOSSARY

GUIDE 38: *The effectiveness of a group depends partly upon its structural characteristics—its size, member composition, status structure, channels of communication*

GUIDE 39: *The effectiveness of a group is determined partly by the nature of the interactions among the members—leadership style, interdependence of motivation, friendship relations*

communication net. The pattern of channels of communication among the members of a group. In a free, face-to-face group the kind of net that evolves is determined by the status hierarchy, the nature of the group task, and other variables. In restricted communication nets, some of the channels among the members of the group are closed.

net connectivity. The degree to which the communication links among the members of a group are open. In the "all-channel" net all possible links are open. This is a completely connected net.

participatory leadership. A style of leadership in which the leader plays an active consulting and advising role but gives subordinates a considerable amount of independence in making final decisions.

position centrality. The degree to which a position in a communication net is connected with the other positions. The most central position is the one most closely connected with the others.

WHO WE ARE AND WHAT WE DO IS IN LARGE MEASURE DETERMINED *by the people with whom we interact—the people with whom we work, play, live, worship. But groups—whether they be work, recreational, family, or religious groups—affect the members who comprise them differentially. For one thing, every group makes different demands of its different members. For another thing, some people are more resistant to group pressures and demands (the hard-core independents and the deviants) than are others (the easy conformists). The ideal relation between individual and group has not been fully formulated, either by the social scientist or by the many cultures and ideologies which have attempted the task. In this final chapter of our book we review the data and theories which social psychology can bring to bear upon this major concern of modern man. We examine the effects of the confluence of the two great forces which shape all human thought and action—the subtle manifestations of the unique personality of the individual and the massive impact of the group.*

14: THE INDIVIDUAL IN THE GROUP

FOR BETTER OR FOR WORSE, THE INDIVIDUAL is always and forever a member of groups. It would appear that no matter how "autonomous" and how "strong" his personality, the commonly shared norms, beliefs, and practices of his groups bend and shape and mold the individual. And the phrase "for better or for worse" is no mere traditional literary embellishment. In so far as we can tease out the separate influences of the individual's personality and the forces of the group we find that sometimes group membership inhibits man, constricts his creativity, and prevents self-fulfillment (see Box 14.1). But we also find that sometimes the individual can best express his individuality and can most fully develop his originality within the security of his "own" group (see Box 14.2). Perhaps we should write: For better *and* for worse.

And, for better and for worse, groups are composed of inviolably different people. No matter how monolithic the structure of a group, no matter how ancient its traditions, no group is immune to the changes brought about through the interactions of its members —each of whom is a living affirmation of the ubiquity of individual differences.

Many ethical, ideological, legal, philosophi-

486

cal, and religious questions are inevitably raised when we consider the nature and degree of interdependence of the individual and the group. Is responsibility for the activities of a group personal, or is it collective? This, for example, was one of the issues raised when the infamous Eichmann was tried before the "Judges of Israel," for the mass slaughter of Jews under the Nazi regime. And what of the minister who refuses to permit Negroes to worship in his church, because he will not violate the beliefs and practices of his parishioners? Is his behavior justified? And what of the national leader who demands that individuals give up their lives in order that their group—the nation—shall survive? Is this demand defensible? These and many other questions have been raised and answered—and raised and answered again as each society attempts, and fails, to come to a final resolution of the problem of the relation between the individual and the group. The final resolution—which has yet to be achieved by any modern society—is one which will maximize the individual's freedom of choice, release his creativity, and secure for him the many other values of individualism while still enabling the society to function as a stable and effective collectivity.

The social psychologist does not presume, of course, to have final answers to any of the questions we have raised. Indeed, he does not feel that he is especially equipped to comment on most of the ethical, juridical, philosophical, and ideological questions involved. When the social psychologist confronts the problem of the individual in the group he usually addresses himself to two major questions.

The first question deals with the "basic personality" of the individual. To what degree do the role behaviors which the individual is forced to enact within his groups reflect a basic inviolate personality, and to what degree is his basic personality the creature of his group roles? The answer to this question involves some fundamental questions about the nature of personality, as the following quotation from Gordon Allport [1961] indicates. In defending his approach to the study of personality, Allport writes that his convictions lead him

. . . to resist the current fashion in social science that would reduce personality to a matter of roles, to interpersonal relations, to incidents within the sociocultural system. Important as culture and society are, they should not be allowed to eclipse the internal coherent system that is the essence of personality. It is true, of course, that personality is fashioned in, and expresses itself in, a social milieu. Yet it is also a self-contained system, and as such merits study in its own right.

For Allport, then, the individual's behavior in the group is partly determined by a basic personality which is, in a sense, *beyond* group control. For some theorists, on the other hand, personality simply mirrors group influences.

The second question which the social psychologist has been raising with increased vigor in recent years concerns itself with the nature and extent and consequences of individual-group conflict. What happens when the individual's privately held beliefs and behavior tendencies come into conflict with his group's commonly held beliefs and practices? This is the question of *group pressure*, of *conformity*, of *independence*, of *deviancy*. These words are, of course, loaded with value connotations. Thus our youth is sometimes castigated for being "overconformist," or for being "too deviant." Phrases like "group pressure" have evil overtones for people raised in a democracy. The resolution of this question of individual-group conflicts interests not only the social psychologist; it is of major concern to all members of society.

In this chapter we shall seek to survey the data available on both these questions concerning the behavior of the individual in the group, and to examine the tentative answers which the social psychologist can now give.

In 1939 a new "group think" technique called "brainstorming" was introduced by Osborn in the advertising agency of Batten, Barton, Durstine, and Osborn. It was subsequently widely used in a large number of major corporations, and in various governmental and military agencies.

The four basic rules of brainstorming, in which men work on a problem as a group, are:

1. No ideas are criticized.
2. "Freewheeling" is encouraged. The more farfetched and wild an idea, the better.
3. Quantity of production is stressed. The larger the number of ideas, the greater the probability of getting a winner.
4. "Hitchhiking" is encouraged. Participants are urged to improve the ideas of others and to combine ideas to form new and more complex ones.

For twenty years, brainstorming was a fad without a single adequate test of its effectiveness. Then Donald W. Taylor, a psychologist at Yale University, and two of his graduate students, Paul C. Berry and Clifford H. Block, attacked the problem.

In their study, 96 Yale juniors and seniors who had worked together in a course in personnel administration were used as subjects. One half of the students were randomly assigned to four-person groups; the remaining half were used as individual subjects.

These students were presented with three problems: the "Tourists Problem" (how to get more European tourists to come to this country); the "Thumbs Problem" (what practical benefits or difficulties would arise if people were born with an extra thumb on each hand); the "Teachers Problem" (what measures might be taken to ensure that the schools of 1970 with an inflated enrollment will continue to provide effective instruction). Both group and individual subjects were instructed in the rules of brainstorming and then proceeded to brainstorm each problem for

We start with the first question—the question of the relations between role behavior and personality.

GUIDE 40: *The roles which the individual performs in his various groups both reflect and enduringly shape his personality*

As we have previously seen (page 310), the individual's position in any lasting group is coordinate with a specific role. The elder statesman of a group, in order to continue to occupy that position, is constrained to play the *role* of "elder statesmen." And the same is true of the "virtuous wife," the "outspoken critic," the "faithful follower." Each of us, in

each of our groups, has his position and its corresponding role.

The relation between the way we enact the role we are cast in by virtue of our position in a group and the kind of person we are is a *reciprocal* one. That is, the way in which we play our group role is determined, to some degree, by our "original" personality make-up. But the continued performance of this role— a role, it must be repeated, which the group expects and enforces upon us—eventually affects our basic personality, reinforcing certain traits, extinguishing others.

Successful business executives, for example, seem to display a rather high degree of uniformity in personality (see Box 14.3). Our analysis would suggest that this uniform "business-executive personality" most likely occurs for two reasons: (1) Business execu-

12 minutes. Complete transcripts of all discussions were taken and analyzed for all the different solutions proposed for the problems.

Nominal, or fictitious, groups were then formed by randomly dividing the subjects who had worked as individuals into "four-person groups."

As the following table shows, the mean number of ideas produced by these nominal "groups" was considerably greater than the mean number produced by the real, face-to-face groups on all three problems.

	Tourists	Thumbs	Teachers
Real groups	38.4	41.3	32.6
Nominal groups	68.3	72.6	63.5

The number of original and qualitatively superior ideas produced by the nominal groups was also found to be greater than those produced by the real groups.

The findings of this study indicate that brainstorming, far from aiding creative thinking, may actually inhibit creative thinking. In explanation, Taylor suggests that a group of individuals is more likely to adopt the *same* set or approach to a problem than are the same number of individuals working independently. The more diverse the approaches to a problem, the greater the expected number of different ideas for the solution of the problem. To the degree that group collaboration reduces the variety of ways of approaching a problem, it inhibits the flow of ideas.

We think may never become as creative as *I think*.

Taylor, D. W., Berry, P. C., and Block, C. H. *Does group participation when using brainstorming facilitate or inhibit creative thinking?* Adm. Sci. Quart., *1958*, *3*, *23–47*.

tives tend to be *selected* from all other members of the business group precisely because they already have certain specified characteristics—characteristics which are assumed to be essential for the successful performance of this role and the occupancy of this position in the group. Persons who lack these characteristics either are not recruited for the position or, if recruited, fail to make the grade. (2) As the business executive continues "to make like an executive," as he *learns* to perform his expected role, his personality characteristics change even more in the direction of the "business executive personality." The well-cast actor begins to live his role off the stage as well as on.

In discussing the ways in which the group behavior of the individual both reflects and shapes his personality, we will first examine the influence of individual characteristics and situational factors upon role behavior, and then turn our attention to the effect upon the individual of the roles he performs as a member of various groups and organizations.

INDIVIDUAL DETERMINANTS OF ROLE BEHAVIOR

Role behavior, like all social behavior, is the product of the interaction between situational factors and the cognitions, wants, attitudes, and interpersonal response traits of the individual. Sarbin [1954] has formulated a role theory which extensively treats both situational and psychological factors governing role enactment.

Role behavior is influenced by the individual's knowledge of the role, his motivation to perform the role, his attitudes toward himself and the other persons in the interpersonal behavior event. Because every individual has acquired a unique set of cognitions, wants, attitudes, and interpersonal response traits, the way in which he performs his various roles will be unique. For example, college students themselves recognize individual variations in the enactment of their role as college student in their use of such terms as "greasy grind," "playboy," "B.M.O.C.," "apple polisher," etc.

ROLE INCOMPATIBILITY. The roles of individuals can be said to vary along a dimension

BOX 14.2: *The inhibited stranger*

Sociologists D. J. Nash and A. W. Wolfe have reported a study of the effect of membership in a strange "laboratory culture" upon the inventiveness of the individual.

In their study, Nash and Wolfe used five pairs of four-person groups. Each pair of groups was treated in the following manner. After a preliminary trial, the subjects in both groups observed the tenth card in the Rorschach Ink-blot Test for 2 minutes, recording their responses in writing. Then each subject in turn pointed out and explained his responses to his fellow group members. After three such trials (period I), one member of each group was shifted to the other group in the pair. For three trials responses to the tenth Rorschach card were again elicited and publicly explained by each person in the paired groups. Thus, during these three trials (period II), the persons who were shifted were "emigrees in a foreign group." At the end of the seventh trial, the strangers were returned to their home group. And again responses to the tenth Rorschach card were elicited and publicly explained for three trials. Thus, during these last three trials (period III), the emigrees were repatriates in their native culture.

Responses to the Rorschach card were classified into three categories:

1. *Invention*—a perception by a subject of a new concept.
2. *Borrowing*—a perception by a subject of a concept reported in an earlier trial by a fellow group member.
3. *Habit*—a perception by a subject of a concept which the subject himself had reported in an earlier trial.

The following table shows the mean number of inventions, borrowings, and habits of the strangers and sedentees in Period II.

	Strangers	Sedentees
Inventions	2.90	5.17
Borrowings	4.60	3.81
Habits	19.00	15.98

The mean number of inventions of the strangers is significantly less than that of the sedentees. When the strangers were repatriated to their home groups in period III, the mean number of their inventions increased significantly over the mean number in period II as compared with those of the sedentary members of their home groups.

This laboratory experiment suggests that a stranger in an alien culture is subject to constraints which inhibit his free inventiveness. But there may also be advantages to be gained from contact with another culture. In this experiment, the repatriate was relatively more inventive than the sedentee upon return to his native culture.

Nash, D. J., and Wolfe, A. W. The stranger in laboratory culture. Amer. soc. Rev., 1957, 22, 400–406.

BOX 14.3: *The titan*

William E. Henry, an industrial psychologist, studied the personality pattern of over 100 successful American business executives by means of projective tests, an unstructured interview, and a number of standard personality tests.

The results suggest the existence of a successful-business-executive-personality pattern. The major features of this pattern were as follows:

Successful executives showed a strong drive to work and a high achievement want. Their relations with their superiors were smooth and constructive. All of them had a high degree of ability to organize unstructured situations, i.e., to see the relations between seemingly unrelated or isolated events or facts. The ability to make decisions was a further trait of this group. They also possessed a firm and well-defined self-identity. "They know what they are and what they want and have well-developed techniques for getting what they want."

The successful executives were typically active, striving, aggressive persons. But ". . . they also harbor a rather pervasive feeling that they may not succeed and be able to do the things they want to do." They are strongly oriented toward practical and immediate realities. They have personal affection for their superiors and tend to identify with them. Their subordinates are viewed in a detached and impersonal way as means for getting work done.

Henry points out that the role of business executive includes these personality characteristics—ways of thinking, feeling, wanting, and acting. And, to some extent, the personality structure of the executive is shaped by these role requirements.

Henry, W. E. The business executive: the psychodynamics of a social role. Amer. J. Sociol., 1949, **54,** *286–291.*

of compatibility-incompatibility. If a person who occupies a given position perceives that most people hold the same or highly similar expectations as to how he should behave in his role, we have an instance of *role compatibility*. If, however, he perceives that the expectations and demands of others are contradictory, we have an instance of *role incompatibility*.

Komarovsky [1946], for example, has reported that many women students attending a college in New York City found the female sex role to be highly incompatible. Because some women college students have an interest in a professional career, they are under pressure from their professors and "intellectual others" in their group to excel academically. On the other hand, the women students' interest in men and marriage, as well as the expectations of family members and "social others" in their group, constrains them to excel in the social graces, and in the pursuit of the male, rather than in the "male pursuits" of the intellect (see Box 14.4).

Approximately 40 per cent of Komarovsky's women students reported that on occasions they tried to resolve the conflict by concealing their intellectual abilities, which threatened their popularity with men. Some of the concealment tactics used are given in the following interview excerpts.

I am engaged to a southern boy who doesn't think too much of the woman's intellect. In spite of myself, I play up to his theories because the less one knows and does, the more he does for you and thinks you "cute" in the bargain. . . . I allow him to explain things to me in great detail and to treat me as a child in financial matters.

One of the nicest techniques is to spell long words incorrectly once in a while. My boy friend seems to get a great kick out of it and

BOX 14.4: *Mind versus marriage*

Mirra Komarovsky, a sociologist at Barnard College, has found that many women college students are caught between the conflicting demands (from parents and others) that they become independent professional women and that they be "feminine" and point toward marriage.

The following excerpts from four different interview protocols illustrate the dilemma faced by some of Komarovsky's students.

How am I to pursue any course singlemindedly when some way along the line a person I respect is sure to say, "You are on the wrong track and are wasting your time"? Uncle John telephones every Sunday morning. His first question is: "Did you go out last night?" He would think me a "grind" if I were to stay home Saturday night to finish a term paper. My father expects me to get an "A" in every subject and is disappointed by a "B." He says I have plenty of time for social life. Mother says, "That 'A' in Philosophy is very nice, dear. But please don't become so deep that no man will be good enough for you." And, finally, Aunt Mary's line is careers for women. "Prepare yourself for some profession. This is the only way to insure yourself independence and an interesting life. You have plenty of time to marry."

I get a letter from my mother at least three times a week. One week her letters will say, "Remember that this is your last year at college. Subordinate everything to your studies. You must have a good record to secure a job." The next week her letters are full of wedding news. This friend of mine got married; that one is engaged; my young cousin's wedding is only a week off. When, my mother wonders, will I make up my mind? Surely I wouldn't want to be the only unmarried one in my group. It is high time, she feels, that I give some thought to it.

All through high school my family urged me to work hard because they wished me to enter a first-rate college. At the same time they were always raving about a girl schoolmate who lived next door to us. How pretty and sweet she was, how popular, and what taste in clothes! Couldn't I also pay more attention to my appearance and to social life? They were overlooking the fact that this carefree friend of mine had little time left for school work and had failed several subjects. It seemed that my family had expected me to become Eve Curie and Hedy Lamarr wrapped up in one.

My mother thinks that it is very nice to be smart in college but only if it doesn't take too much effort. She always tells me not to be too intellectual on dates, to be clever in a light sort of way. My father, on the other hand, wants me to study law. He thinks that if I applied myself I could make an excellent lawyer and keeps telling me that I am better fitted for this profession than my brother.

Komarovsky, Mirra. Cultural contradictions and sex roles. Amer. J. Sociol., 1946, 52, 184–189.

writes back, "Honey, you certainly don't know how to spell."

When my date said that he considers Ravel's "Bolero" the greatest piece of music ever written, I changed the subject because I knew I would talk down to him.

But we should not overgeneralize these findings. Wallin [1950] repeated Komarovsky's study in a private university on the West Coast, which draws its students primarily from the upper middle class. Wallin's subjects— 163 women undergraduates—were, with few exceptions, oriented toward marriage, home, and children rather than toward a professional career. Only 7.5 per cent reported that they had "often" or "very often" played "dumb" on dates. A large majority of the women gave no indication of sex role incompatibility. Apparently sex-role incompatibility is found mainly in women who face strong pressures to seek a career and who are also exposed to a strong tradition of male dominance.

AN EXPERIMENTAL STUDY. Gross, McEachern, and Mason [1958] have developed a theory of role performance that throws light on some of the individual factors which determine the way in which individuals cope with role incompatibility. Because their study is a major, pioneering attempt to study systematically the factors that determine how different individuals perform an important social role, we will report it in some detail.

The subjects were 105 school superintendents, representing a random sample of all school superintendents in Massachusetts in 1952–1953. During the course of an interview, each superintendent was presented with four problems which most superintendents have to face. These problems, assumed to arouse incompatible expectations, concerned (1) the hiring and promotion of teachers, (2) the allocation by the superintendent of his after-office hours, (3) salary increases for teachers, and (4) the priority given by the superintendent to financial or educational needs in preparing the school budget. For each problem three alternative expectations that people might hold were presented. For the problem concerned with salary increases for teachers, for example, these three expectations were given:

A. Expect me to recommend the highest possible salary increases for teachers . . . commensurate with their professional responsibility.
B. Expect me to recommend the lowest possible salary increases for teachers.
C. Have no expectations one way or another.

A list of 18 groups and individuals, with an interest in the problem, was then presented to the superintendent with the request that he indicate which of the three statements most nearly represented what each of these groups or individuals expected him to do about the problem.

If he reported that one or more groups or individuals held expectation A and one or more held expectation B, he presumably perceived incompatible expectations. The situation was then, for him, one of role incompatibility.

In addition, the superintendents were asked whether they felt the expectations were *legitimate* or *illegitimate*. If incompatible expectations were perceived, the interviewer proceeded to determine how the incompatibility was resolved and what *sanctions* the subject thought would be applied if one or the other of the incompatible expectations were chosen.

The teacher-salary issue was a source of role incompatibility for 88 per cent of the superintendents. When these superintendents were asked how they resolved the incompatibility, the following distribution of the codable responses was obtained: 64 per cent said they conformed to the expectation of recommending the highest possible salary increases; 9 per cent recommended the lowest possible salary increases; 27 per cent adopted some kind of compromise solution.

What determined the choices of the superintendents in resolving their role incompatibility? Or, to put the question differently, what determines how an individual will perform the role of school superintendent?

To help answer this question, the authors formulated a "type theory" of role-incompatibility reduction. The theory is based on the individual's perception of the situation. First, the theory assumes that individuals will perceive whether the expectations of others are legitimate or illegitimate. Second, it assumes that they will have knowledge of the sanctions that would be applied if they did not conform to each of the expectations. Finally, it assumes that individuals may be classified into decision types according to whether they pay more attention to legitimacy or to sanctions.

The three decision types were as follows:

1. "Moralists." Moralists, when confronted with a role incompatibility, give most weight to the legitimacy of expectations. They are predisposed to perform their role in such a way as to fulfill expectations perceived as legitimate and to reject expectations perceived as illegitimate. The perception of probable sanctions for noncompliance with expectations is assumed not to influence their choice behavior.

2. "Expedients." Individuals in this type weigh most heavily the sanctions others will apply for noncompliance. In role-incompatibility situations, they try to minimize negative sanctions for nonconformity. The legitimacy of the expectations of others is irrelevant or of secondary importance. If the Expedient individual perceives no sanctions for nonconformity, his perception of the legitimacy of the expectations of others will determine his behavior.

3. "Moral-Expedients." Persons in this type give primacy neither to the legitimacy of expectations nor to sanctions for noncompliance, but take both into account. They are predisposed to behave in such a way that the two factors are balanced.

A paper-and-pencil test was developed which enabled the experimenters to classify the superintendents as "Moralists," "Expedients," or "Moral-Expedients." The results provided striking support for their type theory. In 91 per cent of the role-incompatibility cases, the test scores (as interpreted by the type theory) correctly predicted the actual resolution of the role incompatibilities as reported by the superintendents. Merely to know that a man is a superintendent, these results suggest, is not enough to predict how he will behave in an incompatible role. What is of decisive importance is to know whether he is a moralist, an expedient, or a moral-expedient. Every role played within a group, where there are incompatible expectations with respect to this role, has considerable room for individuality. But this individuality, as we shall next see, is not restricted to performance of incompatible roles.

THE RANGE OF INDIVIDUAL VARIATION IN ROLE PERFORMANCE

Although the norms of most groups allow considerable freedom of movement within the roles assigned to the various group members, there are limits to individual variability. Newcomb [1950] points out that role behavior ranges from those behaviors that are *demanded* of all occupants of the position to those behaviors that are *prohibited* to all occupants of the position. Between these two extremes there are various behaviors that are *permitted* but not demanded. If the occupant of the position performs the prohibited behaviors or fails to perform the demanded behaviors, agents of the group may remove him from the position. A lawyer must respect the confidence of a client; a lawyer must not bribe a witness. If he violates the confidence of a client, if he suborns a witness, he may be disbarred. On the other hand, a lawyer may but is not required to accept labor cases; he may or may not join the American Bar Association, as he chooses.

AN EMPIRICAL STUDY. A follow-up study of the readjustment of British prisoners of war [Curle and Trist, 1947] illustrates the wide variation among individuals in role performance.

Many of these men experienced major difficulties in trying to readjust to the demands of civilian society after their long absence in the army and in prison camps. Transitional communities were organized to facilitate the readjustment process, and the effectiveness of the rehabilitation program was carefully evaluated in a follow-up study. The social readjustment of the men was measured in 15 different role relations, called "criteria of social participation":

Criterion 1. Husband-Wife, Domestic Work.
Criterion 2. Husband-Wife, Leisure Pursuits.
Criterion 3. Father-Child, Play and Encouragement.
Criterion 4. Father-Child, Authority and Discipline.
Criterion 5. Ritual in the Home.
Criterion 6. Quarreling in the Home.
Criterion 7. Staying Home and Going Out.
Criterion 8. Parents and Relatives.
Criterion 9. Neighbours and Neighbourhood.
Criterion 10. Workmates and Unions.
Criterion 11. Employers and Management.
Criterion 12. Wider Personal Contacts.
Criterion 13. Women Outside the Family.
Criterion 14. Organized Group Activities.
Criterion 15. Impersonal Authorities.

The role performances of the men were rated on a four-grade scale for each of the 15 role relationships. Grade 4 is a "supernormal" level of performance; Grade 1 is a complete inability to perform the role with consequent loss of the position. Illustrations of role performance at each of the four grades for "Husband-Wife, Domestic Work" are given in the following quotation from Curle and Trist.

Norm—Grade 3

The husband is prepared to help in some ways about the house, for example, in such things as washing up, though he tacitly makes it clear that this depends on his whim and on the degree of domestic stress, and that his assistance must not be taken for granted. He is responsible for business affairs—and often makes major decisions such as moving house, without any consultation—and for decorating and carpentry jobs, but refuses to do certain jobs, like bed-making, which are unspecialized and with which he could easily help. Some jobs are completely taboo—sewing, for example, however proficient the man may be. Certain times of day are also sacrosanct to the man and at these times violent outbursts of "righteous rage" are often aroused by ill-timed, even if modest, requests for assistance.

Positive Deviation—Grade 4

There is greater co-operation, and a continual interchange of jobs wherever needful or desirable. Habits and taboos about work spheres are not formed, or are broken down. Men are not only prepared to help when asked, but volunteer to do things outside their normal range of activity without the pressure of domestic crisis. (One man would dispatch his wife to the cinema and himself put the children to bed and prepare supper against her return.) Not only the interchange of jobs, but the combining of forces is characteristic of these families; thus the investigator would find a couple together decorating a room.

Minor Negative Deviation—Grade 2

Increased rigidity of role differentiation; practically no common ground between husband and wife. The slightest encroachment, or threatened encroachment, on the man's role, causes domestic upheaval. (One man flew into furious rage if his wife put coals on the fire—a job he had been accustomed to do for her.)

Major Negative Deviation—Grade 1

Collapse of all husband-wife relationships through failure to accept the role of husband, without misconduct on the wife's part. This is through separation, desertion, or in extreme domestic violence.

The four-step rating scale used by Curle and Trist illustrates the wide range in role behavior which individuals exhibit.

ROLES AND MULTIPLE GROUP MEMBERSHIP

We have seen previously (page 397) that an individual living in a complex society is a member of many different groups. In each group, he learns the role behaviors that are appropriate to the position he occupies in the group. In the course of a single day a man may perform the roles of husband, father, clandestine lover, employee, customer, club member (see Box 9.2, page 312). Despite this multiplicity of roles, conflicts as to what is the appropriate role behavior to perform at any one moment in any given situation are not too frequent. This is true for two reasons. First, as Linton [1949] has pointed out, individuals usually occupy positions successively rather than simultaneously. Second, easily discriminable situational cues are usually available which will trigger the appropriate role behavior (see page 311).

In a fair number of situations, however, not one but several different role behaviors are equally appropriate and relevant. A study by Charters and Newcomb [1952] throws some light on the factors that determine which of several available and appropriate roles will become salient. These investigators selected all students from a large class in psychology who had previously identified themselves as members of the Roman Catholic Church. These students were divided into two groups. The subjects in the control group had no knowledge that they had been especially selected for the study. In introducing the study to these students, no mention was made of its religious bearing.

The members of the experimental group were told they had been selected to help construct an attitude scale relevant for members of the Roman Catholic Church. Membership in the Catholic Church was further emphasized by a discussion of the "basic assumptions which underlie the opinions of all Catholics." Both groups were then given a series of attitude statements of which only a small number were relevant to membership in the Catholic Church. These statements were so worded that the students *could* respond to them as members of the Catholic Church, or as members of a class in psychology, or as members of other groups.

The results indicate that subjects in the experimental group for whom saliency of membership in the Catholic Church had been experimentally enhanced responded to the "Catholic" items in a significantly more orthodox Catholic manner than did the control subjects. This experiment suggests that if some feature of a situation emphasizes a particular group membership, that group will become the dominant reference group for the individual and will determine the role he assumes.

ROLE CONFLICT

When an individual simultaneously occupies two positions whose roles are antagonistic, we have to do with role conflict. The individual may experience difficulty and be unable to perform either role adequately. For example, a college student may occupy simultaneously the position of son and fraternity member. The role of son includes temperance in drinking; as a fraternity member he may be expected to drink heavily (see Box 11.6, page 405). The conflict between the roles of housewife and career woman in the American society has been studied extensively. Women who occupy both positions frequently experience trouble because the two roles involve conflicting demands. For the housewife, her home and family are primary; for the career woman, the demands of the job are her first concern. To a greater or lesser degree, we are all Pooh-Bahs (see Box 14.5).

RESPONSES TO ROLE CONFLICT. The modes of resolution of role conflicts are the same as in any other type of conflict between antagonistic, competing responses. Any number of resolutions—good, bad, and indifferent—are available. Two empirical studies may be cited. Burchard [1954] interviewed a number of military chaplains. He found that several forms of defense mechanisms were used to resolve the conflict between the warrior role of *military officer* and the nonviolent role of *minister*. To illustrate:

Rationalization. "Some one has to carry the gospel to these boys."

Compartmentalization. "Render therefore unto Caesar the things which are Caesar's; and unto God the things that are God's."

Repression. "I don't see any conflict."

Withdrawal. "I'd rather not talk about it."

BOX 14.5: *The many hats of Pooh-Bah*

Ko-Ko and Pooh-Bah in *The Mikado* illustrate the role conflicts of the many-faceted person.

KO-KO: Pooh-Bah, it seems that the festivities in connection with my approaching marriage must last a week. I should like to do it handsomely, and I want to consult you as to the amount I ought to spend upon them.

POOH-BAH: Certainly. In which of my capacities? As First Lord of the Treasury, Lord Chamberlain, Attorney-General, Chancellor of the Exchequer, Privy Purse, or Private Secretary?

KO-KO: Suppose we say as Private Secretary.

POOH-BAH: Speaking as your Private Secretary, I should say that, as the city will have to pay for it, don't stint yourself, do it well.

KO-KO: Exactly—as the city will have to pay for it. That is your advice.

POOH-BAH: As Private Secretary. Of course, you will understand that, as Chancellor of the Exchequer, I am bound to see that due economy is observed.

KO-KO: Oh! But you said just now "Don't stint yourself, do it well."

POOH-BAH: As Private Secretary.

KO-KO: And now you say that due economy must be observed.

POOH-BAH: As Chancellor of the Exchequer.

KO-KO: I see. Come over here, where the Chancellor can't hear us. (They cross the stage.) Now, as my Solicitor, how do you advise me to deal with this difficulty?

POOH-BAH: Oh, as your Solicitor, I should have no hesitation in saying, "Chance it—"

KO-KO: Thank you. (Shaking his hand.) I will.

POOH-BAH: If it were not that, as Lord Chief Justice, I am bound to see that the law isn't violated.

KO-KO: I see. Come over here where the Chief Justice can't hear us. (They cross the stage.) Now, then, as First Lord of the Treasury?

POOH-BAH: Of course, as First Lord of the Treasury, I could propose a special vote that would cover all expenses, if it were not that, as Leader of the Opposition, it would be my duty to resist it, tooth and nail. Or, as Paymaster-General, I could so cook the accounts that, as Lord High Auditor, I should never discover the fraud. But then, as Archbishop of Titipu, it would be my duty to denounce my dishonesty and give myself into my own custody as First Commissioner of Police.

KO-KO: That's extremely awkward.

Gilbert, W. S. The Mikado. *New York: Modern Library, Random House.*

Cousins [1951] presented subjects with a role conflict in a contrived situation. The subjects were asked to assume the role of a student monitor pledged to enforce an unpopular curfew rule. They were then asked whether they would report or not report two student violators to the school authorities. The conflict in this situation is between the role of monitor and the role of student. After making their decision, the subjects were asked to select three reasons for their decision from a list of six. Persons who did not choose to perform the prescribed role of monitor selected self-defensive mechanisms as reasons more frequently than did subjects who chose to enact the prescribed role. The specific self-defensive mechanisms chosen were rationalization, displacement, and wish-fulfilling fantasy. Those subjects who chose to enact the prescribed role of monitor accepted their own responsibility for the decision; those who chose the conflicting role of student externalized responsibility for the decision, i.e., attributed responsibility away from the self.

THE MARGINAL MAN. Stonequist [1937] defines the marginal man as "one whom fate has condemned to live in two societies and in two, not merely different, but antagonistic cultures." Marginal men occupy an ambiguous position between two culture groups with contrasting ways. They are motivated to affiliate with both groups; they are fully accepted by neither. Severe conflict often develops because the role behavior appropriate in the two groups is antagonistic.

Examples of marginal persons in the American society include members of various minority ethnic groups; persons of "mixed blood" such as mulattoes; members of criminal groups, social climbers, and immigrants. The children of immigrants, second-generation Americans, are especially likely to suffer severe conflicts because of their marginality (see Box 14.6).

Sutherland [1937] has pointed out that the professional thief is a marginal man and cannot avoid role conflict because the norms of the larger society are at odds with the norms of the society of thieves. Sutherland pictures the plight of the thief as follows:

> The professional thief in America feels that he is a social outcast. This is especially true of the professional thieves who originated in middle-class society, as many of them did. He feels that he is a renegade when he becomes a thief. Chic Conwell [himself a professional thief] states that the thief is looking for arguments to ease his conscience and that he blocks off considerations about the effects of his crimes upon the victims and about the ulti-

mate end of his career. When he is alone in prison, he cannot refrain from thought about such things, and then he shudders at the prospect of returning to his professional activities. Once he is back in his group, he assumes the "bravado" attitudes of the other thieves, his shuddering ceases, and everything seems to be all right. Under the circumstances he cannot develop an integrated personality, but the distress is mitigated, his isolation reduced, and his professional life made possible because he has a group of his own in which he carries on a social existence as a thief, with a culture and values held in common by many thieves.

Child [1943] has studied the responses of second-generation Italian-American males to the conflicts they face. The nature of their dilemma is revealed in the following quotation:

> Due to the widespread prejudice against Italians, those who are considered more nearly "American" find it easier to obtain the more desirable jobs. This is an important influence on the individual, for his job is concerned not only with his basic interests of hunger and self-maintenance, but also with such secondary interests as prestige, amusement, etc. . . . The second-generation Italian cannot escape from being a member of American society and from being constantly shown that he will be punished, or will not be rewarded, by his fellow Americans for behavior like an Italian.
>
> It is not merely Italian behavior, however, that may lead to rejection of the second-generation individual. . . . Non-Italians may fail to reward or may reject an individual simply because he is Italian, even if his behavior is such as would usually lead to acceptance on their part. No matter how thoroughly Americanized he becomes, he may still on occasion, as a member of a nationality of low status, be rejected, partially or entirely, by certain American groups.
>
> The structure of the Italian family denotes a secure and reasonably tranquil family life for the member of the second generation. . . . Membership in the Italian group permits enjoyment of participation in social functions with people who may accept one more

completely as an equal than will any group of mixed nationality. Distinctive Italian patterns of recreation afford special forms of enjoyment for the second-generation Italian which American culture cannot provide. . . . Certain rewards are offered by the Italian group rather than the non-Italian . . . acceptance as a perfect equal in status, freedom from attack, and the security of feeling oneself to be a part of a national and cultural group which has displayed great power and achievement.

Child noted three major types of response. (1) The assimilationist reaction took the form of rejecting the Italian background and emphasizing "American" values and behavior patterns. (2) The in-group reaction took the form of identifying closely with the Italian community and rejecting Americans and American ways. In these two types of reaction, the individuals tried, never with complete success, to choose one of the two possible

BOX 14.6: *Second generation—second class*

In his examination of the assimilation of immigrants and their descendants into the American society, Milton M. Gordon, a sociologist at the University of Massachusetts, has commented upon the plight of the second-generation American of Jewish parentage.

The second generation found a much more complex situation. Many believed they heard the siren call of welcome to the social cliques, clubs, and institutions of white Protestant America. After all, it was simply a matter of learning American ways, was it not? Had they not grown up as Americans, and were they not culturally different from their parents, the "greenhorns"? Or perhaps an especially eager one reasoned (like the Jewish protagonist of Myron Kaufmann's novel *Remember Me to God,* aspiring to membership in the prestigious club system of Harvard undergraduate social life), "If only I can go the last few steps in Ivy League manners and behavior, they will surely recognize that I am one of them and take me in." But, alas, Brooks Brothers suit notwithstanding, the doors of the fraternity house, the city men's club, and the country club were slammed in the face of the immigrant's offspring. That invitation was not really there in the first place; or, to the extent it was, in Joshua Fishman's phrase, it was a " 'look me over but don't touch me' invitation to the American minority group child." And so the rebuffed one returned to the homelier but dependable comfort of the communal institutions of his ancestral group. . . . All could now join in the task that was well within the realm of the sociologically possible—the build-up of social institutions and organizations within the ethnic enclave, manned increasingly by members of the second generation and suitably separated by social class.

Those who had for a time ventured out gingerly or confidently, as the case might be, had been lured by the vision of an "American" social structure that was somehow larger than all subgroups and was ethnically neutral. Were they, too, not Americans? But they found to their dismay that at the primary group level a neutral American social structure was a mirage. What at a distance seemed to be a quasipublic edifice flying only the all-inclusive flag of American nationality turned out on closer inspection to be the clubhouse of a particular ethnic group—the white Anglo-Saxon Protestants, its operation shot through with the premises and expectations of its parental ethnicity. In these terms, the desirability of whatever invitation was grudgingly extended to those of other ethnic backgrounds could only become a considerably attenuated one.

Gordon, M. M. *Assimilation in America: theory and reality.* Daedalus, Spring, *1961,* *263–285.*

group memberships. (3) The apathetic or withdrawal reaction was an attempt to deny the conflict situation. Those persons who used this solution tried to avoid being known either as Italians or as Americans. They withdrew from situations in which their ethnic status aroused anxiety.

Child emphasizes that these three solutions are not pure types. The important point to understand is that marginal persons, such as second-generation Italian-Americans, face a serious conflict situation which they try to cope with in various ways. Affiliation with one membership group or the other—or with neither—becomes a goal which determines such various behaviors as choice of friends, relations with work associates, political interests, attitudes toward international affairs, identification with public figures.

THE EFFECTS OF ROLE PERFORMANCE UPON THE INDIVIDUAL

In the preceding section, we examined the influence of the individual's cognitions, identifications, values, etc., upon his role performances as a member of groups and organizations. We now reverse the coin in order to look at the effect of role performance upon the individual.

SEX ROLES—AN ILLUSTRATION. The influence of role upon personality is nowhere better illustrated than in the sex roles. Through genetic accident, it is determined whether a person be born a male or a female. The massive and far-reaching consequences of this accident can hardly be overstated.

Perhaps the most comprehensive study of sex differences in personality between American men and women is that of Terman and Miles [1936]. Many hundreds of men and women were compared on a variety of instruments and procedures: a word association test, an ink-blot association test, an information test, an emotional and ethical response questionnaire, an interest inventory, an opinion

questionnaire, and an introversion-extroversion inventory.

The investigators concluded:

The males directly or indirectly manifest the greater self-assertion and aggressiveness; they express more hardihood and fearlessness, and more roughness of manner, language, and sentiments. The females express themselves as more compassionate and sympathetic, more timid, more fastidious and esthetically sensitive, more emotional in general (or at least more expressive of the four emotions considered), severer moralists, yet admit in themselves weaknesses in emotional control and (less noticeably) in physique.

Both constitutional and experiential factors undoubtedly interact to determine the sex differences observed by Terman and Miles. The biologically determined differences between the sexes are, to use Margaret Mead's phrase, "culturally elaborated." That is, the personality characteristics a culture demands of the two sexes are superimposed upon biologically determined differences. Mead [1949], in describing the various ways in which different cultures elaborate the sex roles, shows how sex differences are culturally molded during infancy and childhood.

Komarovsky [1950] has studied some of the "cultural elaborations" of the female sex role in the American culture. From biographical materials written by college women, she found that parents "tended to speed up, most often unwittingly, but also deliberately, the emancipation of the boy from the family, while they retarded it in the case of his sister." For example, boys are allowed more personal privacy than girls (see Box 14.7). Girls are under greater pressure to honor filial and kinship obligations than are boys. "When the grandmother needs somebody to do an errand for her, or Aunt Jane who doesn't hear very well needs help, the girl is more likely to be called upon. The pressure to attend and observe birthdays, anniversaries, and other family fes-

BOX 14.7: *The sheltered female*

Mirra Komarovsky, a sociologist at Barnard College, has examined the different treatment received by boys and girls in the American culture.

The following three different interview excerpts illustrate the sheltered, protected life of the American middle-class girl.

My mother is very hurt if I don't let her read the letters I receive. After a telephone call she expects me to tell her who called and what was said. My brother could say "a friend" and she would not feel insulted.

My brother is fifteen, three years younger than I am. When he goes out after supper mother calls out: "Where are you going, Jimmy?" "Oh, out." Could I get away with this? Not on your life. I would have to tell in detail where to, with whom, and if I am half an hour late mother sits on the edge of the living-room sofa watching the door.

I have a brother of twenty-three, and a sister of twenty-two, and a younger brother who is sixteen. My brothers come and go as they please. Even my younger brother feels that his current girl friend is his personal affair. No one knows who she is. But the family wants voluminous files on every boy my sister and I want to date. It is not easy for us to get the complete genealogy of a boy we want to go out with.

Komarovsky, Mirra. Functional analysis of sex roles. Amer. soc. Rev., 1950, 15, 508–516.

tivals is apparently greater upon her than upon the boy."

As a result of these culturally determined differences in treatment, girls are less emancipated from the parental family than are boys. To illustrate: From another set of data on 937 students, Komarovsky found that girls were more often extremely attached to their parents; more often made major life decisions "very much" in accordance with the wishes of their parents; and were more often homesick than were boys. In the American culture, it would appear that the silver cord is more binding upon girls than it is upon boys.

THE EFFECTS OF OCCUPATIONAL ROLES

There has long been much speculation on the influence of a man's occupation upon his personality. Among others, we would mention Herbert Spencer on the military mind, Max Weber on bureaucracy, and Thorstein Veblen who made of this factor a major guiding principle. As MacIver [1937] has put it,

Veblen assumed that "the kind of work by which men live and particularly the kind of technique which that work involves . . . is the influence which shapes men's thoughts, their relations with one another, their culture and their institutions of control."

A number of studies of "professional deformation" have been made. For one vivid illustration from an ancient profession, see Box 14.8. Other studies have looked at the teacher, the bureaucrat, and the industrial worker.

THE TEACHER. Waller [1932] did an early study of "What Teaching Does to Teachers." In this study he made use of personal documents, case studies, and personal observations. His impressions of the "teacher personality," 1932 model, are summarized by him in these words:

There is first that certain inflexibility or unbendingness of personality which is thought to mark the person who has taught. That stiff and formal manner into which the young

From his study of the taxi-dancer, P. G. Cressey concluded that she comes

> . . . to view the patrons, young or old, not so much as *ends,* but rather as *means* toward the achievement of her objectives—the recouping of her personal fortunes. Romantic behavior, along with other less desirable forms of stimulation, becomes merely another acceptable method for the commercial exploitation of the men. . . . "I can take care of myself. I'm not just trying to keep them from putting something over on me; I'm trying to put it over on them. I know what I'm after and I'm out to get it." With the seasoned taxi-dancer this philosophy of exploitation, the zealous practicing of her techniques, the revengeful impulses arising from blasted dreams and romances, and honest though carefree view of her own . . . conduct blend together to make of her a distinct . . . type.

The distinct personality type of the taxi-dancer is reflected in her special language (see page 304):

Buying the groceries. Living in clandestine relationship.
Fish. A man whom the girls can easily exploit for personal gain.
Fruit. An easy mark.
Make, "to make." To secure a date with.
Monkeys. Dancing girls, either chorus girls or taxi-dancers.
Monkey-chaser. A man interested in a taxi-dancer or chorus girl.
Paying the rent. Living in clandestine relationship.
Playing. Successfully exploiting one of the opposite sex.
Playing Africa. Clandestine prostitution in the Black Belt.

Cressey, P. G. The taxi-dance hall. *Chicago: Univer. of Chicago Press, 1932.*

teacher compresses himself every morning when he puts on his collar becomes, they say, a plaster case which at length he cannot loosen. One has noticed, too, that in his personal relationships the teacher is marked by reserve. . . . As if this reserve were not in itself enough to discourage ill-considered advances, it is supplemented, when one has become very much the teacher, by certain outward barriers. . . . Along with this goes dignity . . . that consists of an abnormal concern over a restricted role and the restricted but well-defined status that goes with it. One who has taught long enough may wax unenthusiastic on any subject under the sun. . . . The didactic manner, the authoritative manner, the flat, assured tones of voice that go with them, are bred in the teacher by his dealings in the classroom, . . . and it is said that these traits are carried over by the teacher into his personal relations. It is said, and it would be difficult to deny, that the teacher mind is not creative. . . . If these traits . . . are found among the generality of teachers, it is because these traits have survival value in the schools of today. If one does not have them when he joins the faculty, he must develop them or die the academic death.

THE BUREAUCRAT. Merton [1940] has commented as follows about the impact of performing the bureaucratic role upon the personality of the bureaucrat:

> The bureaucrat's official life is planned for him in terms of a graded career, through the organizational devices of promotion by seniority, pensions, incremental salaries, etc., all of which are designed to provide incentives for disciplined action and conformity to the official regulations. The official is tacitly expected to and largely does adapt his thoughts, feelings, and actions to the prospect of this career.

GROUPS, ORGANIZATIONS, AND THE INDIVIDUAL

But *these very devices* which increase the probability of conformance also lead to an over-concern with strict adherence to regulations which induces timidity, conservatism, and technicism. Displacement of sentiments from goals onto means is fostered by the tremendous symbolic significance of the means (rules).

THE INDUSTRIAL WORKER. McGregor, in the work earlier cited (page 414), has commented that the industrial organization, constructed according to traditional organizational principles, provides little opportunity for the rank-and-file worker to satisfy the "higher-order" wants of belongingness, esteem, and self-actualization. And with the satisfaction of the "lower-order" physiological and safety wants, it is just these "higher-order" wants which become dominant (see page 76). The importance of the higher-order wants of belongingness and esteem to workers is well illustrated in Box 14.9. As McGregor notes, "If the practices of 'scientific management' were deliberately calculated to thwart those needs [the belongingness, esteem, and self-actualization wants]—which, of course, they are not—they could hardly accomplish this purpose better than they do."

The failure of American industrial management to define the job role of the industrial worker so that his social wants are met, McGregor interprets as being due to management's fear that if workers are given greater freedom on the job, they will use their freedom to combine against organizational objectives.

However, as Argyris [1957] has argued, the thwarting of the dominant social wants by traditional managerial practices has brought about among industrial workers widespread hostility, apathy, and rejection of the goals of management. That which management has tried to prevent through rigid control of the jobs of the rank and file has come about because of those very control techniques. In support of his thesis "that the formal organization creates in a healthy individual feelings of failure and frustration, short time perspective, and conflict," Argyris cites an extensive body of studies of the modern industrial worker. In one study by Friedman and Havighurst [1954] of over 600 steel workers, miners, salespersons, skilled workers, and doctors, it was concluded that "workers of the lower skill and socio-economic levels regard their work more frequently as merely a way to earn a living and in general recognize fewer extra-financial meanings in their work than do workers of high skill and socio-economic levels." (See the meaning of "work," page 283.)

A retired worker described the situation of the industrial worker in this way:

Q: Was there anything you liked about the job?
A: No, I can't think of anything. It was hard, hard work and I wouldn't go through it again.
Wife: Come, now, honey, you couldn't have worked there all those years and not found something you liked.
A: There is nothing I can think of—only the money—I couldn't think of anything else.

BUT REMEMBER. As we have stressed earlier in this chapter, the relation between the occupation of an individual and his personality is a reciprocal one. "Professional deformation" occurs as the individual adjusts to the demands of his occupational role in working out his career. But this is not the whole story. An individual tends to *select* an occupation which he believes will meet his requirements and whose requirements he believes that he can meet. The study by Rosenberg, earlier cited (page 130), offers clear evidence of the important part which the cognitions, wants, interpersonal response traits, values, and attitudes of the individual play in his choice of an occupation.

If the job choice of an individual proves, for whatever reason, to be unwise, he will tend to be "selected out" of the occupation.

Social scientists Nicholas Babchuk and William J. Goode report a case study of a work group in which, by a social invention, the members resolved internal conflict which had depressed job satisfaction. The innovation made by the work group indicates the importance of harmonious friendship relations to the workers.

The work group studied by Babchuk and Goode was a selling unit in a large "cash and carry" department store in Detroit. The group was made up of 15 highly skilled, long-service sales-persons and a manager, assistant manager, and a stock boy. The unit was engaged in selling men's clothing.

Job satisfaction and sales productivity had been high. The base pay of the salespersons was one of the highest in the store and their commissions were above average. All in all, the department was a highly desirable work area.

In 1941, the management introduced a new wage plan in an attempt to retain employees who might have been tempted to leave for better-paying defense jobs. Under the old system, the workers received a base wage plus a commission of 1 per cent. Under the new system, the workers had an option of the old system or a straight 6 per cent on all final sales, depending upon which was the higher total for the week.

After the introduction of the new system, the salespeople began to engage in a number of devices for getting a larger sales figure. "Sales grabbing" and "tieing up" customers were commonly practiced. Display and stock work were neglected. "High pressure" selling was frequently practiced. Marked differences in the take-home pay of the sales personnel appeared. Most of the informal

---

Thus the relation between occupational role performance and personality is, in part, due to "self-selection in" and "other-selection out."

TO RECAPITULATE

The manner in which the individual performs his various roles reflects both his personality and the incompatible and conflicting demands and expectations of other persons.

The way in which the individual resolves role incompatibility is influenced by the relative importance which he attaches to the legitimacy of the expectations of others and the punishments for noncompliance.

The fact that every individual must play multiple roles opens the way for role conflict. The modes of resolution of role conflict are the same as in any other type of conflict between antagonistic, competing responses.

The marginal man faces extremely severe role conflict which may make for serious difficulties. Examples of marginal persons in the

American society include members of various minority ethnic groups, persons of "mixed blood," members of criminal gangs, social climbers, and immigrants.

The relation between role behavior and personality is a complex, reciprocal one. The effect of occupational role behavior in "deforming" personality has been extensively studied. The evidence suggests that the personality of the individual is shaped by his work—the occupational role he performs. But his occupational role behavior also is shaped by his personality.

GUIDE 41: *The conformity or independence of the individual under group pressure depends upon the nature of the situation and the characteristics of the individual*

Up to this point we have been considering the long-range ways in which society and the

504

social relations broke down as a result of the competition and individualistic sales practice. Job satisfaction was low.

In the latter part of 1941, two employees informally introduced a new plan called "pooling." Informal pooling began with the equal distribution of stock work among the workers. Soon they agreed to cooperate in all work activities. This forced them to make the volume of sales equal among the members of the group so that each would receive equal pay. This was accomplished by establishing a quota. When one person was low on sales, others would direct customers to him. Any person who fell below the quota was given supplementary credit to equalize sales tallies.

The results of this innovation are summarized by Babchuk and Goode:

> Production has increased since the plan was finally put into effect. High morale did not exist before the inauguration of pooling, but prevailed after that point. In intensive interviews, not one employee believed that the present selling plan should be changed. Such statements as the following were common: "I'm willing to work harder because I feel better." "Ever since we started pooling, I don't have to worry about my job outside the store. When I leave work, I can forget about it." Or, "We don't aggravate ourselves. No one cuts a throat."

> Babchuk, N., and Goode, W. J. Work incentives in a self-determined group. Amer. soc. Rev., 1951, 16, 679–687.

group exert enduring influences on the behavior and personality of the individual through the social roles he performs. There are also more direct and immediate ways in which the group comes to control and shape the behavior of the individual. As the individual acts in interpersonal behavior events, in face-to-face contact with other group members, he is often placed under group pressure to *conform*—to judge, believe, act in agreement with the judgment, belief, and action of the group. It is to this extremely important topic of conformity that we now turn.

MEANING AND NATURE OF CONFORMITY

The problem of conformity has become one of the foremost concerns of the editorial writer, the commencement speaker, the social scientist. Indeed ours has been called the Age of Conformity (to say nothing of the Age of Anxiety, the Age of Togetherness—all of which designations are, in fact, psychologically related). The term "conformity" is used in many different ways, however, and we should first clarify the particular meaning that we shall attach to it in the following discussion—a meaning which, for our purposes, differentiates among "conformity," "uniformity," and "conventionality."

That high degrees of *uniformity* in social beliefs, values, and practices may exist is not alone a sufficient criterion of conformity. As we have already seen (page 404), there are many reasons why common attitudes and actions are widely found in a society. Such uniformity may derive from many sources, quite unrelated to social pressures toward orthodoxy. That most people in our society believe the earth is round is scarcely evidence of conformity.

Nor can demonstrations of sheer *conventionality* be simply equated with conformity. Conventional ways of acting represent established solutions to problems; conventions are well-oiled grooves of social conduct which are provided ready-made and often followed with minimal conflict. For a man to wear trousers in our society does not convict him of conformity. Conventionality and uniformity do, of course, result partly from conformity. As we shall later see, the conformist tends to hold more conventional values. But the converse does not necessarily hold. Highly conventional individuals may often be quite able to resist conformity pressures.

The essence of *conformity*, in distinction to uniformity and conventionality, is *the yielding to group pressures*. For there to be conformity there must be *conflict*—conflict between those forces in the individual which tend to lead him to act, value, and believe in one way and those pressures emanating from the society or group which tend to lead him in another way.

The pressures from the group need not be explicit; that is, the group need not overtly threaten or coerce the individual. The pressures may be implicit; that is, the mere existence of a group judgment or action which the individual perceives to differ from his own may exert pressures on him, pressures arising out of fears of being wrong, of "being out of step" with the group, etc. Thus, when an individual is required to express a judgment in a group on some particular issue, and when his own private conviction on the matter is at noticeable variance with the expressed judgments of all the other group members, he is placed in a conflict situation. There are two main courses of action open to him: he may announce his own deviant judgment, thus remaining *independent* of the group consensus; or he may announce his agreement with the group judgment, thus *conforming*.

The actual conformity response under group pressure may take the form of overt action by the individual. He may, for example, join his fellow villagers in stoning a victim. Or the conformity response may be merely verbal; the individual may *say* something that is in agreement with what the group *says*. Such verbal behavior is, of course, of prime significance

in our complex society where most social "action" is actually indirect and symbolic. The greater part of the conformity behavior manifested by the individual in the course of his everyday social life is of this verbal type.

Conformity pressures also often take the form of an *inhibition* or *prevention* of action— whether direct or indirect. The individual may be led by conformity pressures to refuse to take action on an issue, to refuse to express a stand. Under many social circumstances this may be the more insidious and ultimately more deadly form of conformity behavior, in that the individual eventually comes not only to yield on particular opinions but to yield even his right to *express* an opinion.

"EXPEDIENT" VS. "TRUE" CONFORMING. Not all acts of conforming are identical in psychological meaning. One significant distinction is between "expedient" conforming (discussed by Kelman [1958] as "compliance"), in which the individual *outwardly* agrees with the group but remains in *inward* disagreement, and "true" conforming, in which the individual *both* inwardly and outwardly is brought to agree with the group. We would expect "expedient" conforming—unlike "true" conforming—to be transitory and unstable, with the individual tending to revert to his unaffected private judgment when the immediate group pressure is removed, e.g., after he leaves the group scene. (One is reminded of the politician who, after losing an election, said bitterly, "Well, I shook hands with ten thousand liars!") And as we shall later see, there is good evidence that these two different types of conforming exist, as well as for the point that there are differences in the personality make-up of persons who are typically one or the other type of conformer.

COUNTERFORMITY VS. INDEPENDENCE. Just as we must distinguish among types of conforming behavior, so must we distinguish among types of behavior where the group pressure is resisted. The avoidance of conformity is often talked about under the general rubric of "nonconformity," but unfortunately this term fails to allow for important distinctions. Not all nonconformity is the same. One crucial type to distinguish from others is what we may call *counterformity*. This is the case in which the person is actively *opposing* the group, being negativistic, hostile, compulsively dissenting from it. The counterformist not only resists having his judgments and actions move toward those of the group; his judgments and actions tend to be repelled by the group norms; he seeks to *widen* disagreement between himself and the group. The counterformist may thus be driven at all costs to repudiate the group's beliefs or actions even when he perceives that the group is right! One might argue that the cognitions and actions of the counterformist are just as surely and predictably being determined by the group as are those of the conformist. For the counterformist, the group serves as a *negative* reference group.

Distinct both from conformity and counterformity is *independence* of judgment and action, wherein the individual makes up his own mind, being able to "take the group or . . . leave it," as his own good sense would dictate. The independent person, in short, is neither unduly susceptible to the pressure of the group nor unduly driven by forces of alienation from the group.

Conformity, independence, and counterformity are thus not to be thought of as three points along a single continuum. Rather they represent three vertices of a triangle. A proper understanding of the whole problem of conformity must take full account of the important differences among these three forms of reaction to group pressure.

CONFORMITY AS "TRAIT OF THE SITUATION." Every individual displays a good deal of conformity behavior throughout his social life. He inevitably finds himself in kinds of situations where conforming is the only "reasonable" or possible form of behavior, and in which virtually everyone conforms. Here conformity

might be thought of as a "trait of the situation." There are also marked individual differences in general readiness to conform, over a wide variety of situations. These differences, as we shall later see, reflect conformity as a "trait of the person."

This distinction between conformity as reflecting the conformity-inducing properties of a situation and as reflecting the conforming propensity of a person should be kept well in mind. Much of the controversy and misunderstanding about the facts and theories of conformity stems from a confusion of these two aspects of conformity.

EXPERIMENTAL MEASUREMENT AND STUDY OF CONFORMITY

The power of group pressure to induce conformity of judgment in the individual is dramatically revealed in the widely known experiments of Asch [1951, 1952, 1956]. His technique enables the experimenter to place an individual under group pressure that can be systematically manipulated and controlled, and then measure the individual's readiness or tendency to yield to such pressure.

In one of his basic experiments, groups of seven to nine college students were assembled and given the following instructions:

This is a task which involves the discrimination of length of lines. You see the pair of white cards in front. On the left is a single line; on the right are three lines differing in length. They are numbered 1, 2, and 3 in order. One of the three lines at the right is equal to the standard line at the left—you will decide in each case which is the equal line. You will state your judgment in terms of the corresponding number. There will be twelve such comparisons. As the number of lines is few and the group small, I shall call upon each of you in turn to announce your judgment, which I shall record here on a prepared form. Please be as accurate as possible. Suppose we start at the right and proceed to the left.

Actually, all but one of the students were confederates of the experimenter, who had been instructed beforehand to give, unanimously, incorrect responses on certain of the line-judgment trials. It was so arranged that the one naive subject sat near the end of the row, so that he gave his judgment following most of the group. The naive subject thus found himself in a situation where the correct answers, on certain critical trials, would be in opposition to those given by a unanimous majority.

The line stimuli were chosen by Asch so that the bogus judgments by the group were grossly different from the correct judgments, the discrepancies ranging from one-quarter of an inch to an inch and three quarters (see Figure 14.1).

FINDINGS WITH THE ASCH TECHNIQUE. In Asch's first experiments, 123 naive subjects were tested on twelve critical judgments. Of the total number of judgments given, 37 per cent were in error, that is, were in conformity with those of the unanimous majority. Control subjects, judging alone, made virtually no errors.

Marked individual differences in response to the majority pressure were found, ranging from complete independence of the majority by some individuals to complete yielding on all twelve critical trials by other individuals.

After each session, the naive subject was interviewed. None of the subjects reported that he had wholly disregarded the judgment of the majority. For most of the subjects, the discrepancy between their judgment and that of the majority created a difficulty which they localized in themselves, that is, they tended to question their own judgment, not that of the majority. Most of the subjects reported that they "longed" to agree with the majority.

As Asch notes:

Most subjects miss the feeling of being at one with the group. In addition, there is frequent reference to the concern they feel that they might appear strange and absurd to the majority. One of the strongest [independent, non-yielding] subjects reported: "Despite everything there was a lurking fear that in some way I did not understand I might be wrong; fear of exposing myself as inferior in some way. It is more pleasant if one is really in agreement." Another subject asserted: "I don't deny that at times I had the feeling to heck with it, I'll go along with the rest." Or "I felt awfully funny, everything was going against me." "I felt disturbed, puzzled, separated, like an outcast from the rest. Every time I disagreed I was beginning to wonder if I wasn't beginning to look funny."

The inner conflict experienced by one of Asch's subjects who succeeded in resisting the group pressure is vividly depicted in "candid photos" filmed during an actual experimental session (see Figure 14.2).

THE CRUTCHFIELD TECHNIQUE. In order to avoid the uneconomical use of confederates necessary in the Asch method, Crutchfield

FIGURE 14.1: One of the stimulus presentations used in Asch's group-pressure experiments. The standard line (8 inches) is on the card to the left; the three comparison lines are on the card to the right. The cards are about 40 inches apart. In one of the pressure trials the majority picks line 1 (6¼ inches) as equal to the standard line. [Asch, 1956.]

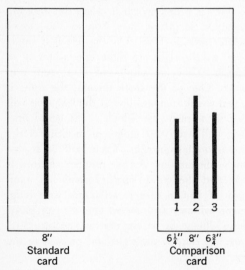

8"
Standard
card

6¼" 8" 6¾"
1 2 3
Comparison
card

[1955] devised a different group-pressure technique, suitable for large-scale research use. Five subjects at a time are seated side by side in individual booths, screened from one another. Each booth has a panel with a row of numbered switches which the person uses to signal his judgments on items presented on slides projected on the wall in front of the group. Also displayed on his panel are signal lights which indicate what judgments the other four members are giving to the item. The booths are designated by letters A, B, C, D, and E, and the subjects are instructed to respond one at a time in that order. They are not permitted to talk during the session.

Although this is the way the subjects are led to understand the situation, they are in fact being grossly deceived by the experimenter. There are really no electrical connections among the five individual panels; the signals are actually delivered by the experimenter from a master control panel in such a way that pre-established sequences of lights appear in the same way on all five individual panels (see Figure 14.3). Moreover, all five booths are really labeled E, so that *each* subject sees the sequence of judgments allegedly emanating from persons A, B, C, and D before he makes his own judgment. On those critical items where the experimenter wishes to impose group pressure, he makes it appear that all four members—A through D—agree on an answer which is clearly at variance with the correct answer. In this way all five subjects are confronted with the same conflict between their own judgment and the bogus consensus. They may resolve the conflict either by giving the same judgment as the group's, thus conforming, or by giving their own answer, thus remaining independent.

In a typical one-hour session as many as fifty pressure items can be given, with neutral items interspersed. The items can vary widely in content—some being matters of objective fact or logic, others of opinion and attitude; some being easy to judge, others difficult.

This standard technique has been used by Crutchfield [1954a, 1954b, 1955, 1958, 1959a, 1959b, 1962] in studies on more than 600 people, all of them clearly above average in intelligence, education, and occupational status. Some of the general findings can be briefly summarized as follows:

1. Substantial amounts of yielding are produced by the group pressure, and this is true despite the fact that the bogus group consensus to which the person conforms may be manifestly wrong. For example, one of the perceptual items asks which of two figures, a circle and a star presented side by side, is the larger in area, the circle actually being about one-third larger. In a sample of 50 military officers, 46 per cent of the men expressed agreement with the bogus group consensus that the star was the larger!

The astonishing extent to which some inveterate conformers can be induced to agree with illogical and nonsensical statements is illustrated in Box 14.10.

2. Many individuals can be pressured into yielding on opinion and attitude items, even those having personal or social relevance to them. For example, among the military officers questioned privately, not a single one expressed agreement with the statement: "I doubt whether I would make a good leader," whereas under unanimous group pressure in the test situation, 37 per cent of the officers expressed agreement with the statement. Among a sample of college students only 19 per cent expressed private agreement with the statement: "Free speech being a privilege rather than a right, it is proper for a society to suspend free speech whenever it feels itself threatened." But in the experimental situation, when confronted with a unanimous group consensus agreeing with the statement, 58 per cent expressed agreement.

3. Yielding is far greater on difficult items than on easy ones. (This fact is confirmed by many investigators; for example, Coleman, Blake, and Mouton [1958] report that among

women there is a correlation of .89 between difficulty of general information items and tendency to conform.) The greater yielding on difficult items presumably reflects differences in the certainty the individual feels about his judgment; where he is initially certain he is much less susceptible to the group pressure. Direct evidence for this fact is given by first asking a person to judge items and rate his judgments on a certainty scale from 0 to 5, and then later determine how much he yields when these items are exposed under group pressure. Table 14.1 shows the results.

4. There are extremely large individual differences in amount of yielding. Some few individuals give way on almost all the items;

some few yield on none. Most individuals yield on some items and not on others.

5. Over an hour-long session with as many as 50 pressure items presented, the *average* amount of yielding remains at about the same level throughout. But some individuals grow increasingly *more* conforming and others grow steadily *less* so. When an identical item is presented a second time later in the series, the average amount of yielding is about the same as the first time. But here again there are individual differences, some individuals being more susceptible the second time, and some being more resistant.

6. When individuals are retested privately and individually on the items some time after the group session, a major part of the original yielding effect disappears, that is, the person tends to revert to his own unchanged, private judgment. However, not all the yielding effect disappears. For example, in a study of applicants to medical school who showed considerable yielding under group pressure on a set of attitude items, it was found that when individuals were retested on the same items several weeks later, approximately one-half of the original group-pressure effect persisted. Moreover, the amount of this persistence varied markedly among the individuals. Some of them retained a very substantial amount;

TABLE 14.1: AMOUNT OF YIELDING ON ITEMS AS A FUNCTION OF INITIAL LEVEL OF CERTAINTY OF JUDGMENT (MEASURED ON 0–5 CERTAINTY SCALE)

Initial level of certainty of individual judgment on item	Per cent of subjects who yield to group pressure on item
High (scale values 4, 5)	15
Medium (scale values 2, 3)	24
Low (scale values 0, 1)	36

others—presumably the wholly "expedient" conformers—retained no effect at all.

COMPARISON OF TECHNIQUES. The Asch and the Crutchfield techniques illustrate the two main types used in the experimental study of conformity. There have been, of course, many variants of these two types, both earlier and more recently (see, for example, Blake and Brehm [1954]).

It should be noted that there are certain major differences in these two main approaches. The Asch procedure engages the subject in an interpersonal behavior event, with face-to-face oral communication among the group members. In the Crutchfield setup the individuals are somewhat removed from one another, communicate only indirectly, and are to some degree anonymous. It would thus seem that the Asch-type situation should, other things being equal, impose more powerful group pressure on the individual, and this is indeed the finding. Deutsch and Gerard [1955] and Levy [1960] have shown that when identical judgment items are used in the two types of situations, the average amount of conformity is appreciably greater in the Asch-type group. In general, however, it appears that the *kind* of yielding that occurs and its psychological significance are the same in the two situations.

In evaluating the research results from use

FIGURE 14.2: The effect of group pressure on an "independent" subject. Shown at top is a group of seven "subjects" seated beside the stimulus display. All of these subjects except Number 6 are confederates of the experimenter. Number 6 is the only bona fide subject in the experiment. In the second picture, Number 6 makes a judgment which disagrees with the unanimous (false) consensus given by the confederates of the experimenter. The same thing occurs in the next picture. In the fourth and fifth pictures, Number 6 shows obvious signs of disturbance, but he continues to give his own independent judgment. As he says (last picture), "he has to call them as he sees them." [Asch, 1955.]

FIGURE 14.3: The Crutchfield technique for subjecting individuals to group pressure. The five persons are seated in individual booths, each one facing a signal board. Unknown to them, the experimenter delivers signals from a control board, thus faking for each person the judgments of the other group members. On the critical pressure trials the experimenter delivers unanimously wrong "group" judgments to each person.

of these laboratory techniques for the measurement of conformity, it should be borne in mind that these "artificial" procedures may differ from "real life" conformity pressures. Perhaps the most important difference is that the individual in the laboratory experiment is precluded by the instructions from engaging in free and prolonged discussion of the issue with the other group members, from going out and searching for facts bearing on the issue, from withholding a judgment altogether if he is not sure. All of these factors might be expected to increase yielding in the laboratory over what it is in "real life" where these limitations need not apply.

However, it is also noteworthy that "real life" situations often do have some of these restrictions. The social circumstances are often such that the person has no real opportunity to discuss the issue with others because he is physically or socially isolated. Or he may fail to use the opportunity to do so, perhaps because of "pluralistic ignorance" (see page 249). As Cantril [1958] has indicated in his *Politics of Despair,* the dissident individual's assumption (even though mistaken) that everyone else holds a certain belief on an issue often weakens his will to find out and to do something about it. Moreover, in "real life" the crucial issues are often so complex that the individual cannot seek for evidence; the "truth" cannot be objectively ascertained. He must then rely solely upon his own judgment and that of the group (see page 404). And yet in these circumstances he may still be *forced* to take a stand, denied the luxury of withholding judgment.

In almost all the experimental approaches to measuring conformity, some form of deception is practiced on the subjects. In Asch's case the experimenter's confederates lie; in Crutchfield's case the communication between group members is deliberately rigged and falsified. In certain other methods the stimulus setup is so constructed that the subjects believe that they are looking at and judging the *same* stimulus, but actually are not. This use of deception also may make the laboratory situation differ psychologically from "real life" in crucial respects. Nevertheless, "real life"—as we all know—sometimes involves deception; the group *is* trying to mislead the individual, or opinion leaders who control the mass media *are* deliberately misrepresenting what the group believes.

SITUATIONAL FACTORS
GOVERNING CONFORMITY

As we have said, the amount and kind of conformity induced by group pressure depend upon the nature of the situation. We have already seen, for one thing, that the specific issue being judged makes a big difference. Another set of crucial determinants has to do with the nature of the group—its size, composition, unanimity, extremeness of judgment, coercive force. And, finally, it is important to consider the nature of the larger social context within which the group is functioning.

GROUP SIZE. It would appear reasonable that group pressure is more intense the larger the

GROUPS, ORGANIZATIONS, AND THE INDIVIDUAL

In a study of the marked effect that a highly distorted bogus majority consensus can have on individual judgments of information and opinion, Read D. Tuddenham, a psychologist at the University of California, Berkeley, administered his adapted form of the Crutchfield technique to a sample of college students. If a person had yielded to all the fictitious judgments of the group which Tuddenham "fed" his college students—and there were a few such extreme yielders—he would in effect have assented to a collection of statements that would depict the United States in the following grotesque way (the item designations "I" and "O" refer to information and opinion items, respectively):

The United States is largely populated by old people, 60 to 70 per cent being over 65 years of age (Item I-1). These oldsters must be almost all women, since male babies have a life expectancy of only 25 years (I-2). Though outlived by women, men tower over them in height, being eight or nine inches taller, on the average (I-4). The society is obviously pre-occupied with eating, averaging six meals per day (I-5), this perhaps accounting for their agreement with the assertion, "I never seem to get hungry" (O-9). Americans waste little time on sleep, averaging only four to five hours a night (I-3), a pattern perhaps not un-related to the statement that the average family includes five or six children (I-9). Never-theless, there is no overpopulation problem, since the USA stretches 6,000 miles from San Francisco to New York (I-6). Although the economy is booming with an average wage of $5.00 per hour (I-7), rather negative and dysphoric attitudes characterize the group, as expressed in their soundly rejecting the proposition, "Any man who is able and willing to work hard has a good chance of succeeding" (O-3), and in agreeing with such statements as, "Most people would be better off if they never went to school at all" (O-5), "There's no use in doing things for people; they don't appreciate it" (O-6), and "I cannot do anything well" (O-10). Such is the weird and wonderful picture of the world and of themselves, allegedly entertained by "the others in the group."

Tuddenham, R. D., and Macbride, P. D. The yielding experiment from the subject's point of view. J. Pers., 1959, 27, 259–271.

majority arrayed against the individual. But it is also likely that beyond a certain range of group size, additional members do not add appreciably to the effective pressure. Asch discovered that when the individual was opposed by a single other person, there was very little yielding; with two opposing him there was some yielding; with three or four opposing him the amount of yielding approached a maximal level and was just about as much for these groups as for groups of fifteen or more.

These results do not mean, of course, that a *single* individual cannot effectively influence the judgment of another person. For example, Sherif [1935], in a by now classic experimental study of social norms, showed

that when pairs of subjects judged a highly ambiguous stimulus (a visual illusion of move-ment of a stationary light in a darkroom—*autokinetic movement*), the judgments of each tended to converge toward the other. But in Asch's case we are dealing with highly structured stimuli, where the degree of discrepancy is very great, and here we find the individual better able to resist a single other person.

In some "real life" situations it is quite pos-sible that larger groups *can* produce additional conformity above and beyond that produced by somewhat smaller groups simply because the threat of reprisal to the deviant individual can be made stronger the larger the group.

The main point, however, is that under many circumstances there exists a kind of crucial "threshold of yielding." If the person can resist the growing opposition up to a certain point, then he will not be easily moved regardless of how big the opposition becomes.

GROUP COMPOSITION. Aside from sheer size of group there is the important matter of *who* the opposing members are. The members may be equal in status to the individual, or they may be seen by him as superior or as inferior in various attributes. If the attributes are relevant to the issue being judged, it is likely that the effective pressure will be greater or smaller depending upon whether the individual views the others as more competent or less competent than himself. For example, a layman is very likely to conform to the consensus of a group of atomic physicists on the dangers of atomic fallout—even if they are wrong. Conversely, an atomic physicist, contradicted by a group of laymen on this issue, may easily resist the group pressure—even if the laymen are right.

When a group is composed entirely of peers, the conflict engendered by the discrepancy between the individual and the group judgment often tends to be particularly acute. A scientist in a group of scientists when judging a relevant scientific issue may feel highly competent. Yet he is confronted by the fact that his scientific peers *whom he must also regard as highly competent* disagree with him. Thus he may conform. For example, in one of Crutchfield's studies, groups of high-level mathematicians were subjected to the standard group-pressure treatment, including some items involving simple arithmetical logic. Some of these mathematicians—though not many, to be sure—conformed to a false group consensus on some of these items, giving wrong answers that they would never have given under normal circumstances. The fact that the items were very easy did not necessarily help them resist the pressure because *they*

had to assume that the items must also be easy for the other mathematicians, all of whom agreed on another answer.

Whether the group is composed of friends or of strangers is also significant for amount of conformity. The relations are complex, however. Among friends an individual may feel emotionally more secure than among strangers and thus feel less threat if he deviates. On the other hand, he may respect the judgments of his friends more highly and thus be more swayed by them; and he may fear the danger of losing their respect if he deviates, whereas among strangers he may not care. However, if he is the single lonely stranger in a group, the rest of whom are friends, and he wishes to be accepted as part of their group, then—being a "marginal man" (page 498)—he is likely to be under even greater pressure to conform. In short, much depends upon what, for the individual in the given situation, constitutes his immediate and functional reference group (page 197). Among the people Crutchfield studied it was regularly observed that persons belonging to ethnic and racial minorities conformed highly when tested in groups where they were the only minority member.

UNANIMITY OF GROUP CONSENSUS. Asch has found strong experimental evidence demonstrating the importance of social support for resistance to group pressure. He did this by comparing the amount of yielding in groups which were unanimously arrayed against the single individual with the amount in those groups in which the single individual had the support of *one other person* in the group, a "partner," who agreed with his judgment. Yielding was markedly lower in the latter kind of group. The social implications of this finding may be very great. It suggests, for example, that a dissident opinion, if expressed loudly and clearly, can have a tremendous effect in strengthening the independence of like-minded people. The expression of a dissident opinion may not *change* the majority's beliefs, but it can *conserve* the minority view.

EXTREMENESS OF GROUP CONSENSUS. How *large* the individual perceives the discrepancy to be between the group consensus and his own judgment affects the resulting conformity behavior. But—as we have also seen with respect to extremeness of "propaganda" in attitude-change experiments (page 239)—the effects are complex; there appears to be no simple relation between amount of yielding and size of discrepancy.

Tuddenham [1961] makes the interesting suggestion that when the distorted group norm lies within the range of judgments acceptable to the individual, its effect is to increase the homogeneity of judgments—a process for which Tuddenham would reserve the term "conformity." In contrast, when the distorted norm lies well outside the range of acceptable judgments, so-called "yielding" occurs in some individuals only, the net effect being a *decrease* in homogeneity among the judgments.

STRENGTH OF COERCION. The extent of conformity elicited will also depend heavily upon the strength of the coercion exerted by the group. Explicit threats of reprisal for resisting or explicit promises of reward for conforming may have powerful influence. Yet we should not underestimate the coercive power of *implicit* group pressure. Silent reproach or silent contempt from the group, whether really present or merely imagined by the individual, can be a crushing force on him.

How much coercive power the group applies depends upon the significance of the issue being judged to the functioning of the group. On many kinds of issues individual dissent will have little or no effect on achievement of the group's goals; hence the group may tolerate or ignore such dissent. But on other issues central to the group welfare, dissent may be regarded as threatening to the group and the deviant member may be punished (see Schachter [1951], cited on page 407; Schachter et al. [1954]).

LARGER SOCIAL CONTEXT. No single group lives a self-contained life; it is always part of a larger social context—a context of the existing political, sociological, and historical conditions. The amount of conformity induced by group pressure to some extent reflects this larger context.

When the general climate is one of attack on deviancy—for instance, in an era of McCarthyism or of Communist or other forms of totalitarian suppression—then conformity tendencies are likely to be heightened. Part of this is due to the fact that the individual's face-to-face groups, mirroring the prevailing social orthodoxy, may demand more conformity of him; part of it may be that he realistically recognizes (or thinks he does) that deviancy at this inauspicious time will have serious personal consequences for himself.

It also happens, all too rarely, that a general climate develops which *favors* independence of thought and expression. Sometimes, too, these climates shift rapidly and the individual may be hard-pressed to accommodate to the prevailing political winds. When Mao Tse-tung, the Chinese Communist leader, briefly encouraged free dissent a few years ago, proclaiming that "A thousand flowers shall bloom," many unwary Chinese intellectuals, eager for the opportunity to express their deviant ideas, took him at his word—much to their subsequent distress. And American college students have had their perplexities, too. It is not so long after the era of McCarthyism, of academic loyalty oaths, and all the other pressures toward safe orthodoxy that students are now being nationally berated for their passivity and overconformity!

PSYCHOLOGICAL PROCESSES INVOLVED IN CONFORMITY BEHAVIOR

Having looked at some of the main findings on amount and conditions of conformity behavior, we now need to examine a little more closely the nature of the cognitive, motivational, and emotional processes that may be inferred to underlie the phenomena.

COGNITIVE DISSONANCE AND CONFORMITY. In the group-pressure situation the person experiences cognitive dissonance (see page 261) arising from the gross discrepancy between his own private judgment and that announced by the group. There are various ways of interpreting and reinterpreting the situation that will aid in reducing this dissonance. The particular way that the person takes is intimately related to whether he will conform or remain independent. He can arrive at interpretations of the cognitive discrepancy that will make it easier for him to resist the group pressure, or interpretations that make it harder for him. He can arrive at interpretations that serve to take the sting out of going along with the group in violation of his own judgment, or at interpretations that increase his feelings of disturbance in so doing. Moreover, there are various *post-mortem* rationalizations and suppressions through which the person defends or denies the conformity he may have displayed. That such rationalizations and self-deceptions do occur is plainly seen in the marked inconsistencies often observed between what the person afterward reports that he did in the pressure situation and what the objective record reveals that he actually did.

Some of the main modes of cognitive resolution that have been observed to occur commonly in the group-pressure experiments are the following:

1. One way is for the individual to *blame himself,* that is, he accounts for the discrepancy in judgments by coming to believe that his own judgment is faulty and that of the group correct. Thus he may say that he "isn't good at mathematics," that he "has a poor memory for facts," that he has not thought much about the issue, that his eyesight is not well suited to making the visual judgments, that he "misread the question." This self-blaming reaction paves the way directly, of course, for the individual to yield to the group position.

2. Another way is for the individual to *blame the group,* to locate the source of the discrepancy in its faulty judgments rather than in his own. The other members "misread the question," gave their answers too hastily, know less than he does about the issue, etc. This form of cognitive resolution obviously paves the way for the individual to resist the group pressure and to remain independent.

3. A third way is to blame neither oneself nor the group but to try to *reconcile the discrepant judgments.* In this attempt to "explain away" the disagreement, the person looks for good reasons that will rationally account for it in such a fashion as to allow him to accommodate *both* his judgment and that of the group. Thus he may come to infer that because of the different angle from which he views the stimulus he gets a different physical image from that seen by the others. Or he may come to see that the question asked could actually be interpreted in quite different ways, leading to different and equally correct answers. This form of cognitive reconciliation obviously makes it far easier for the person to stick to his own judgment. But this is not always the outcome. Some individuals, recognizing that there are two different and equally legitimate frames of reference, will nevertheless choose to change their answer to the group answer, preferring to accept the group's frame of reference in preference to their own. In this way a perfectly "reasonable" man, one who is aware that there "exist many sides to a problem," can end as a conformist.

4. Where it is possible to do so, the individual may account for the discrepancy by simply *accepting the fact of individual differences,* believing that people *can* reasonably have different opinions on the issue, that there is no reason why there should be absolute agreement in the group. This mode is clearly most possible when the items are subjective and personal in nature; it is far less possible when the items are matters of objective fact. Moreover, this form of explanation is pre-

sumably more available to those individuals who are characteristically tolerant in attitude toward others, readier to accept individual differences (see below, page 526). Thus they may say, "That's life," "People are different."

5. All the foregoing are direct ways of trying to cope with the discrepancy in judgments. Quite a different mode of resolution of the conflict is to *avoid evidence of the discrepancy*. Some subjects in Crutchfield's experimental apparatus were observed to shield their eyes so that they could not see the signal lights of their fellow members, thus maintaining their independent judgments by "isolating" themselves from the group. Conversely, some subjects appeared to avoid looking closely at the slides projected before them, concentrating instead on the signal lights; in this way, by "isolating" themselves from the facts, they could more easily go along with the group.

6. Finally, the person may resolve the discrepancy by coming to infer that the experimenter has *deceived* him about the nature of the apparatus and the situation, that in fact he is getting "faked" information about what the others think. This insight sometimes occurs in the experimental situation, but it is fairly infrequent. It tends to occur more often in those who are characteristically independent—it is as though they are more strongly driven to this explanation (which happens to be the truth) just because they *are* so resistant to the group pressure and have no other available way of making cognitive "sense" of the apparent discrepancy.

This "laboratory" reaction of skepticism and suspicion has its counterpart in "real life" social situations, especially those in which the person gets his information about what other people think in a second-hand way—through mass media, through authorities, etc. Exposed to group pressure under these circumstances, he may come to distrust the communication, dismissing it as propaganda, as misrepresenting what other people really think. Sometimes,

indeed, he may overdo this and come to distrust perfectly reliable information (see page 189).

There are actually two quite different sources of cognitive dissonance in the group-pressure situation. One is what we have been talking about—the dissonance arising from discrepancy between own judgment and group judgment. The second is the potential dissonance between what a person inwardly believes and what he outwardly says or does (see, for example, Box 7.15, page 262). This second type of dissonance appears in the case of "expedient" conforming, where the individual publicly announces agreement with the group answer while he privately believes the group to be wrong. This kind of dissonance also tends to undergo reduction through various kinds of cognitive change. Thus the person may rationalize that the issue "is unimportant," that "it is not worth sticking your neck out about," that "it's better to be safe than sorry," that "everybody else in the group went along, so why shouldn't I?" And, occasionally, the person *projects* the blame for his action on the others. He may say that "the other people in the group followed each other like sheep," apparently unaware that he is describing precisely his own behavior!

FEEDBACK AND CONFORMITY. The likelihood of occurrence of any given one of the alternative forms of cognitive resolution can be raised or lowered through changes in the situation. It is possible, for example, for the individual to get "feedback" following upon his judgment in the group-pressure situation. The feedback may consist of additional information that tells him whether his judgment was right or wrong, or tells him how well he has been performing. If he finds that his answers are right and those of the group wrong, he is likely to be reinforced in his tendency to doubt the group judgment on future occasions and thus to remain independent of the group. If he finds that he was wrong and the group right, he is likely to blame himself in future disagreements with the group and thus more readily yield.

In "real life" such feedback is often actively sought after by the person; it is in this way that he tries to check his judgment against reality. Often in "real life" the feedback cannot come directly—particularly in complex kinds of social judgments where the "correct" answer is not readily ascertainable. More often it is indirect—supplied by authorities, e.g., experts, leaders, teachers.

In the group-pressure studies in the laboratory the feedback can be supplied by the experimenter as "authority." Thus it has been possible to study just what effect feedback of various kinds can have on conformity behavior.

"AUTHORITATIVE" CRITICISM OF THE INDIVIDUAL. The feedback can deliberately be manipulated so as generally to heighten the individual's readiness to blame himself for the discrepancies in judgment. For example, in one study, groups of college women were tested in Crutchfield's standard group-pressure procedure on a series of factual and logical items. At the end of the series the experimenter made the following announcement to the group, while they were still seated in their individual booths:

"Most of you have done very well indeed in your judgments up to this point. However, there have been certain cases of serious individual errors. So I shall now repeat some of the slides."

On immediate repetition of the same pressure items after this announcement, the average conformity scores increased by about 15 per cent. And this effect was most pronounced in those persons who—as ascertained by personality tests—were characteristically disposed toward feelings of self-blame. (Similarly, Schroder and Hunt [1958] report evidence that "the self-evaluative judgments of self-devaluators are more susceptible to the effects of disapproval.")

"AUTHORITATIVE" CONFIRMATION OF GROUP. In another study the standard group-pressure technique was modified by informing the subjects that immediately following the group judgments on each slide another slide would be projected that would tell what really was the correct judgment on the previous slide. (This procedure pertained only to the objective-type items for which there was a correct answer.) The experimenter then compounded the basic deception of the technique by naming as the "correct" answer on each slide the one that had been given as the bogus group consensus. In short, he gave authoritative confirmation of the "rightness" of the group.

The effect of this feedback on conformity scores was dramatic. The average amount of yielding on this series of twelve items was approximately 70 per cent, as compared with 45 per cent in a control sample tested without feedback. The effect was found to be cumulative over a series of judgments. As might also be predicted, the reinforcing effect on conformity was greater for difficult judgments than for easy ones. This increased power of the group over the individual's judgments was also found to extend to judgments of different content and type from those on which the feedback had been given, the degree of generalization depending upon the similarity of the new material to the old. In short, authoritative confirmation of the "rightness" of the group in one sphere can produce a somewhat *generalized* readiness to conform to the group in other spheres.

"AUTHORITATIVE" REPUDIATION OF THE GROUP. With other groups of subjects the opposite procedure was employed, that is, the experimenter named as the correct answer what was *actually* the correct answer, that is, he repudiated the group consensus. As might be expected, the effect was markedly to reduce conformity on subsequent items. Here again there was generalization of this negative reinforcement; having been led to doubt group judgments in one sphere, the individual tended to come to doubt the group in other spheres. But again the amount of generalization depends upon how similar the different spheres are.

A study by Jones, Wells, and Torrey [1958] using the above technique found evidence to suggest that authoritative repudiation may be comparatively more powerful in enabling the individual to resist group pressure than is authoritative confirmation in increasing his yielding.

SHIFTS IN CERTAINTY OF JUDGMENT. One thing that may be expected to happen as a result of group pressure, regardless of whether one conforms or resists, is a shift in the *certainty* with which one holds his opinion. The experimental data confirm this expectation but also shed some very unexpected light on what happens.

It turns out that even though an individual may be able to resist the group pressure, there is a noticeable impact of the group on him in weakening his level of certainty about his judgments. He may maintain his own deviant judgment but his confidence in his answers is shaken. This is, of course, not an entirely unreasonable reaction to the group pressure, for the individual must somehow take account of the brute fact that the group judgment is unanimously different from his own. Significantly also, the nonyielder tends to show a somewhat *generalized* loss in certainty about his judgments *even on those "neutral" and relatively easy items where there is no contradiction with the group.* Independence also pays a price!

We have pointed out previously that those items on which there is a high level of initial certainty (i.e., very "easy" items) are much less susceptible to change through group pressure. On such items the weakening of certainty under pressure also tends to be less. But sometimes people *will* yield to the opposing group consensus even on these high-certainty items. What happens to their certainty estimates on these items when they do yield? Here we have an astonishing finding. For it turns out that where there is high initial certainty attaching to a judgment (as measured individually before the group session) and where the group pressure *is* effective in making the person reverse his judgment to fit that of the group, he *still attaches high certainty to this reversed judgment!* Table 14.2 presents some relevant data on this point.

There may be in this experimental finding some support, therefore, for the common observation that it is the recent convert from the extreme opposite camp who is likely to be the most fanatically convinced, that it is the "new believer" who is the "true believer."

MOTIVATION AND CONFORMITY. The level of the individual's motivation in the group situation and the particular character of his aroused wants doubtless play a major role in governing his conformity behavior. It would seem probable that, other things being equal, the individual will more readily conform or remain independent, or counterform, as the case may be, if he perceives that by so doing he will satisfy urgent wants.

Frequently the wants to be served by conformity are the wants for acceptance and prestige, or for avoidance of rejection by the group. Thus Gerard [1954] and Jackson and Saltzstein [1958] found greater conformity when the groups were more attractive to

TABLE 14.2: CERTAINTY OF JUDGMENT ON ITEMS BEFORE AND AFTER YIELDING TO GROUP PRESSURE (CERTAINTY MEASURED ON 0–5 SCALE)

Average initial level of certainty of judgment on items	Average certainty of judgment after yielding on items
0.21	1.24
2.78	3.22
4.25	4.00

the members. And there may be stronger wants for group status in some members than in others: Harvey and Consalvi [1960] discovered that the *second* highest status member in a small group was more conforming to the group than either the leader or those lower in status.

Sometimes conformity serves as the means to ulterior ends. For example, the organizational "yes man" may gain economic security and advancement by slavishly agreeing with the boss. Although he may be aware that he is conforming and may actually despise the judgments of his boss, the immediate gains through expedient conforming outweigh for him the loss of his overt independence.

An individual may choose to be independent because he sees the greater chance for satisfaction of his wants that way; he may seek in this fashion to be autonomous, to be self-reliant and self-expressive. Or he may anticipate an extrinsic reward for showing independence. An employee may surmise that his boss is looking for someone to promote who is not a "yes man"; the student may calculate that the teacher will give him a better grade for appearing to "think for himself" in opposition to the rest of the class; a politician may believe that the electorate will vote for him if he takes an unpopular stand on some controversial issue.

The counterformist may gratify aggressive and exhibitionistic wants by his behavior. He may be motivated by sheer aversion to the group. He may seek certain extrinsic goals. Sometimes his counterformity may mean conformity to another group: the adolescent's rejection of his family's opinions may be an expression of conformity to his teen-age peer group.

THE WANT TO BE RIGHT. All of the above wants and goals of the conformist, the independent, and the counterformist are really extrinsic and irrelevant to what should presumably be the basic intent of the action or judgment that the individual is making on the particular issue—the intent to make the *correct* judgment, to take the *right* action. Very often, of course, it is this intrinsic aim which is at work. What effect does a strong want to be right have on one's conforming tendency?

It might seem obvious that intensified striving to be right should necessarily reduce conformity to a bogus group norm, and this is what some studies have shown. For example, Thibaut and Strickland [1956] found that conformity decreased when members of a group were given the set to do the best job possible—the "task set." Some facts, however, point to an opposite conclusion. In one of Crutchfield's studies, for example, twelve five-man groups tested in his usual conformity procedure were told that they would compete for a $50 prize, to be divided equally among the five members of that group which got the highest number of items correct in the series of judgment items (all matters of fact or logic). Instead of showing reduced conformity, these motivated groups showed *greater* conformity to the false group consensus than did control groups run under the standard instructions. One possible explanation of this paradoxical finding is that each individual, not wishing to reduce his group's chances of winning the prize, decided to go along with the group judgment when there was any discrepancy. And undoubtedly this kind of extra force for conformity to the group, arising out of cooperative motivation, does often function in "real life": the individual does not want to be the fly in the group's ointment; he may be ready to compromise his own position "in the interests of the group welfare."

But this explanation ought not to apply in noncooperative situations where the individual's dissident judgment would *not* interfere with the group welfare. To test this prediction, a further experiment was accordingly done with twelve other five-man groups in which each person was told that he was competing for a $10 prize against just those indi-

520

viduals in the *other* eleven groups who had occupied his booth. Thus he was neither cooperating nor competing with his *own* group members, and had no reason to tailor his judgments in such a way as to serve their interests. Under these circumstances there was found to be *just as much* conformity in the individually motivated subjects as there was in control subjects run in the standard procedure. In short, motivating the person to be right did *not* make him less conforming to the bogus and incorrect group consensus. Why not? We may speculate that though the individual is strongly seeking to get the right answer *he also assumes that each other group member is trying equally hard to get the right answer;* thus he is led to ascribe added validity to the judgments given by the others. We see vividly illustrated here some of the very complex dynamics of the processes underlying conformity behavior.

It should be noted that the above experiment did not involve direct competition for the prize between members of the *same* group. A study by Di Vesta [1958] suggests that where there is such direct competition the amount of yielding is less.

EMOTIONAL AROUSAL AND CONFORMITY. Group pressures on the individual tend to arouse states of emotion in him. Some individuals, confronted with a gross discrepancy between their own judgment and that of the group, are led to doubt seriously the competence of their own thought processes, come to feel dejected, depressed, and isolated—an emotional state wherein susceptibility to conformity is heightened.

If the sharp discrepancy between the individual's judgment and that of the group appears threatening to him—because he envisages punishment for dissent, or because he cannot "make sense" of the discrepancy—he is likely to develop feelings of anxiety. Here, too, the act of conforming may be the easy way out; through conforming the person may allay the anxiety. Indeed, there is recent ex-

perimental evidence on this very point. Bogdonoff et al. [1961], working at the Duke Medical Center, determined conformity scores for 36 normal, fasting males, using a technique similar to that of Crutchfield. While the subjects were working at the perceptual judgment task in their individual booths, sequential physiological measures were taken of the increase in plasma-free fatty acid level, "an index of central nervous system arousal." The general effect of the group-pressure situation was a substantial increase in this fatty acid level. But the effect differed among subjects depending upon their conformity behavior: for those who resisted the group, the fatty acid level remained high; for those who yielded, the level was reduced. The correlation between conformity scores and decrease in fatty acid level was .63. It seems reasonable to infer that the act of conforming resulted in a lowering of the general aroused state. Hoffman [1957] has presented evidence that conformity not only can reduce anxiety but can also avoid it; that is, conformity can serve a defensive function.

The particular avenue by which emotional upset in the person leads to heightened susceptibility to conformity is not clear. Judging from usual psychological data on the effect of emotion, one possibility would seem to be that the emotion is accompanied by a general disorganization of cognitive processes. The individual is thus rendered less capable of making cool, considered, rational judgments and, being unable to cope, is likely to get even farther into a state of panic. In such a disorganized state, his resistance to the group pressure is likely to be low.

Emotional arousal need not always, however, lead to increased conformity. In some circumstances the state of emotion may render the person *more* resistant to the group judgment. His cognitive processes may undergo rigidification and narrowing; he may thus focus only on his own judgment, stubbornly shutting out information from the group. This kind of defense against the group pressure is not, however, synonymous with increased capacity for "true" independence of judgment. The individual becomes insensitive to whatever valid information may inhere in the group judgment, and consequently he may come to cope more poorly in the situation as a whole. "Blind" independence can prove as stupid and as socially and personally deleterious as "blind" conforming.

Individual differences doubtless play a large role in governing the manner in which emotional arousal affects conformity. For example, individuals with high tolerance for stress will be affected quite differently than persons who "panic" easily under stress. Individuals who are anxiety-prone or dejection-prone may also prove conformity-prone. We shall see relevant evidence on this as we turn now to a consideration of individual and personality differences in conformity behavior.

INDIVIDUAL DIFFERENCES IN CONFORMITY-PRONENESS

Common observation over the ages seems to make obvious the point that individuals vary widely in their tendencies to conform. Yet the facts are not so simple as they seem. That some individuals give way to group pressure and others do not *may only mean that their situations are different.* One man yields because he fears reprisals of the group against his family; another man resists the same group pressure because he has no family that can be threatened through him. Clearly it would not do to call the first man more of a conformist than the second.

We need to compare different individuals' reactions to the group pressure when they are in the *same* situation. But situations are never identical for different people, no more than the same situation ever recurs identically for an individual. The best we can do is to find situations that are as objectively similar as possible. And even when we do, the *meanings* of these objectively similar situations may

differ for different people. Any specific situation cannot be artificially isolated from the larger life situation of the person; he brings to the specific situation much of what is involved in the larger situation.

If then we are looking for evidence of a trait of conformity in the individual, we must see him react to group pressure in many different kinds of situations. No single act of conforming alone can be taken as proof of the existence of the trait. What we look for is *consistency* of conforming over many situations. Only if we find such consistency are we properly entitled to speak of a "trait of conformity."

To be able to recognize the consistency, if it is there, we must compare the individual with other individuals over the same set of situations. We can be sure that the given person is properly characterized as "conformist" only if he more or less regularly exceeds most other people in the degree of conformity shown in the various situations, even though the average level of conformity may fluctuate widely from situation to situation.

The experimental methods of eliciting and measuring conformity behavior, which we have described, fall far short of what is ideally required for ascertaining a "trait of conformity." Nevertheless, they do make an effort to compare individuals in a standard group-pressure setting and with respect to a considerable variety of kinds of judgments.

Most of the experimental studies of conformity reported by various investigators agree in showing that there are extremely large and consistent individual differences in amount of conformity behavior displayed. For example, the marked differences in yielding in a group of 50 military officers shown in Figure 14.4. The intercorrelations of yielding scores for different kinds of items and tasks have also been found to be of appreciable size. (See, for example, Blake, Helson, and Mouton [1957]; Tuddenham [1957]; Rosner [1957].) Taken together these many different findings argue for the existence of stable and enduring conformity tendencies in people—in short, for an interpersonal response trait (see page 104) of *conformity-proneness.*

Assuming, then, that there is such a trait, what can be said about its origins? Why are some people high in conformity-proneness and others low? By this time a large body of individual and personality test data has been accumulated, which, together with a great deal of theoretical speculation about the psychology of conformity, gives a fairly clear picture of some of the basic determinants of conformity-proneness. Some of these determinants have to do with the effect of the individual's specific past experiences. Others have to do with his social roles. Others have to do with his basic personality make-up. These three classes of determinants are intimately and intricately interwoven.

PAST EXPERIENCE AND CONFORMITY. Every individual growing up in his society necessarily goes through a great many group-pressure situations, varying from the trivial to the deadly serious. The concrete nature of these events and the particular manner in which the individual has behaved in them play a major role in the shaping of his generalized "habits" of conforming or of resisting. As we have seen in Guide 12 (page 115), the interpersonal response dispositions of the individual are the end products of his characteristic experiences in satisfying his wants.

The nature of the particular culture in which the individual grows up significantly shapes his conformity experiences. As Mead [1939] and many other anthropologists have shown, primitive societies vary widely in the degree of conformity to social norms that they demand of their members. There is some evidence that modern national cultures, too, differ in the extent to which they inculcate conformity-proneness in their members (see Box 14.11). Cultures also differ in the salient wants engendered in their members, and this may differentially affect the way the individ-

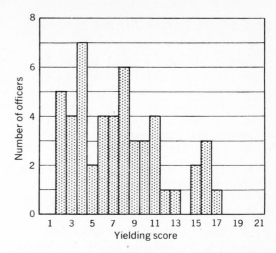

FIGURE 14.4: Distribution of total yielding scores for a sample of 50 military officers tested on a set of 21 items. The scores spread widely, covering most of the maximum possible range (0 to 21). [Crutchfield, 1954b.]

ual learns to conform in satisfying these wants.

As part of this learning process the individual also comes to develop particular beliefs, values, attitudes with respect to the abstract concepts of "conformity" and "independence." And these values help govern in a powerful way just how ready he is to conform or to resist when he is faced with group pressure. He may, for instance, come to accept the idea that conforming is appropriate to a given social role and inappropriate to another.

SEX ROLE AND CONFORMITY. In our culture, and in many others, there would appear to be a pronounced difference in the definition of *sex roles* in regard to the matter of conformity. The typical feminine role tends to be defined as involving promulgation of the conventional values of the culture, dependence upon the group, submissiveness to the male, avoidance of disagreement with others in the interests of group harmony. The typical masculine role tends to lay more stress on the ideals of self-sufficiency, self-assertion, independence of thought, "standing on one's two feet and casting a shadow."

Stanley Milgram, a social psychologist at Yale University, compared conformity-proneness of Norwegians and Frenchmen through the use of a modified form of the group-pressure technique. The subject judged which of two tones, delivered through headphones, was the longer. On prerecorded tape recordings, he would hear five taped judgments before he was asked to give his own. In 16 of the 30 trials (the "critical trials"), the prerecorded judgments were unanimously wrong. Milgram reports that the "synthetic groups" thus created were accepted as real groups by his subjects.

In the first experiment, the conformity-proneness of 20 Norwegian students at the University of Oslo was compared with a matched sample of French university students. The Norwegian students conformed to the group on 62 per cent of the critical trials; the French students, on 50 per cent.

In a second experiment the subjects were told that the results of the study would be used in the design of aircraft safety signals, thus linking their performance to a life-and-death matter. (This same instruction was used in all subsequent experiments.) As expected, the over-all amount of yielding was lower than in the first experiment. But, once again, the level of conformity was higher among the Norwegians (56 per cent) than among the French (48 per cent).

In the first two studies, the subjects made their judgments aloud for all (or so they thought) to hear. In a third study, the subjects recorded their judgments on a secret ballot. As anticipated, the over-all amount of yielding dropped considerably, but once again the Norwegian students yielded more often (50 per cent) than the French students (34 per cent).

A fourth experiment tested the sensitivity of Norwegian and French subjects to various kinds of criticism from the group when they opposed majority opinion. Thus, for example, the Norwegian subject who opposed a majority opinion would hear, *"Skal du stikke deg ut?"* ("Are you trying to show off?"); the French subject, *"Voulez-vous vous faire remarquer?"* ("Trying to be conspicuous?"). Criticism of nonconformity significantly increased conformity, but still again, the Norwegian subjects were less independent (yielding on 75 per cent of the trials) than the French (who yielded on 59 per cent). The Norwegian subjects accepted the criticism impassively. In dramatic contrast, more than half of the French subjects retaliated to the criticism of

Thus the socially dictated *meaning* of the group-pressure situation might be expected to differ in significant aspects for males and for females, and females might be predicted to conform more readily in it. There is considerable evidence to support this prediction (Applezweig and Moeller [1958]; Beloff [1958]; Asch [1956]; Tuddenham [1958]). In Crutchfield's studies females consistently earned higher conformity scores than did males. Moreover, this difference tended to get larger as the testing session continued; on the average the conformity scores for males tended to decline over the duration of the session, whereas the average score for females tended

to rise. Finally, there was evidence that high-conforming females tended to be generally characterized by easier acceptance of the conventional feminine role. On the contrary, many of the females who independently resisted the group pressure tended to be characterized by marked signs of conflict in their feelings about the conventional feminine role, by rejection of a dependent relationship with parents and with others, and by hostile attitudes toward family. On a personality scale intended to measure "socialization" [Gough, 1960], the independent females scored significantly lower than did the conforming females. Among males, it is interesting to

the group. Two of the French students became so enraged that they "directed a stream of abusive language at their taunters."

Many of the Norwegian subjects rationalized their yielding by saying that they doubted their own judgment and that, if they had been given an opportunity to dispel their doubts, they would have been more independent. In a fifth experiment, they were provided with this opportunity. The subjects were told that if they wished to hear a pair of tones again they were to sound a bell. As in the fourth experiment, the subjects were censured for failure to conform, but not for asking to have a pair of tones repeated. Only 5 of the 20 Norwegian subjects asked for a repetition of a tone on any trial, whereas 14 of the French subjects were "bold" enough to do so. And, once again, the French students were more independent.

Milgram's impressions of the Norwegians and French societies throws some light upon his experimental findings.

> I found Norwegian society highly cohesive. Norwegians have a deep feeling of group identification, and they are strongly attuned to the needs and interests of those around them. Their sense of social responsibility finds expression in formidable institutions for the care and protection of Norwegian citizens. The heavy taxation required to support broad programs of social welfare is borne willingly. It would not be surprising to find that social cohesiveness of this sort goes hand in hand with a high degree of conformity.
>
> Compared with the Norwegians, the French show far less consensus in both social and political life. The Norwegians have made do with a single constitution, drafted in 1814, while the French have not been able to achieve political stability within the framework of four republics. Though I hardly propose this as a general rule of social psychology, it seems true that the extreme diversity of opinion found in French national life asserts itself also on a more intimate scale. There is a tradition of dissent and critical argument that seeps down to the local *bistro*.

Milgram, S. *Nationality and conformity*. Sci. Amer., *1961*, **205**, *45–51*.

note, there was little difference in socialization scores between the independents and the conformers.

We have earlier cited similar findings with respect to sex differences in persuasibility and its personality correlates (see page 221).

It should be emphasized that, though females and males do differ on the average in conformity-proneness, there are still very large individual differences in conformity in both groups. In the many samples of persons tested, females, like males, ranged all the way from complete independence to complete conformity in their test performance. Obviously there is much more to individual differences

in conformity than is accounted for by "habits" or social roles. There still remain the basic personality variables.

PERSONALITY AND CONFORMITY

In conjunction with a number of intensive personality-assessment studies of military officers, medical school applicants, engineers, research scientists, creative writers, and architects, Crutchfield has administered his standard conformity-measuring procedure as part of the total assessment battery. Thus for each of these persons whose conformity score has been determined there is available an unusually comprehensive set of measures of personality characteristics. Study of the correlations of these measures with the conformity scores offers compelling evidence that there are numerous basic personality factors associated with tendency to conform, or with tendency to remain independent, under group pressures.

In summarizing the following main findings it should be noted that each finding is based not upon a single measure in a single sample, but upon multiple measures—including objective tests, personality inventories, projective techniques, etc.—and is found to hold generally for all the diverse samples studied (though it is also worthy of note that the relationships are less characteristic of females than of males).

1. *Cognitive functioning.* The conformists prove to be significantly less intelligent than the independent persons. For example, the correlation of conformity with scores on the Concept Mastery Test [Terman, 1956], a high-level test of intelligence, is −.50 or higher. Conformists show greater tendencies toward rigidity of cognitive processes and poverty of ideas, as contrasted with the greater capacity for cognitive restructuring and for novel ideas found in the independent subjects.

2. *Motivational and emotional functioning.* The conformists are clearly lower in "ego-strength" and in ability to cope under stress. For example, a measure based on the readiness of soldiers to fire their guns effectively under battle conditions in the Korean conflict is found to correlate −.38 with conformity score in a sample of military officers. The conformists tend to exhibit emotional constriction, lack of spontaneity, repression of impulse, and indirect expression of hostility to a greater degree than do the independents. They also tend to be more anxious. (Scores on the Manifest Anxiety Scale [Taylor, 1953] correlate in the range from .30 to .40 with conformity scores.)

3. *Self-conception.* Conformists are inclined toward pronounced feelings of personal inferiority and inadequacy. They lack self-confi-

dence. They tend to be less insightful and realistic in their self-perceptions than are the independent subjects. For example, their self-descriptions on an adjective check list (Gough, 1960) tend to differ much more from the composite adjective descriptions of them given by an expert assessment staff than do those of the independent subjects.

4. *Interpersonal relations.* The conformists exhibit intense preoccupation with other people, as contrasted with the more self-contained, autonomous attitudes of the independent persons. The interpersonal behavior of the conformists tends to show far more passivity, suggestibility, and dependence upon others, while at the same time there is considerable evidence of basically disturbed and distrustful attitudes toward other people. Moreover, the conformist proves to be poorer than the independent person in his ability to judge other people's traits accurately (see page 56).

It is of incidental interest to note that while the conformist does tend to be generally suggestible in his relations with others, this type of suggestibility is *not* the same thing as the "primary" kind of suggestibility found, for example, in hypnosis (see Box 14.12).

5. *Personal attitudes and values.* The conformists express attitudes and values of a far more conventional and moralistic nature than do the independent subjects. This is often coupled with a low "tolerance for ambiguity" (see page 46), and a rigid, dogmatic, and authoritarian outlook. Thus, Nadler [1959] reports that F-scale scores (see page 201) correlate .48 with conformity scores as measured in the Asch technique (though this correlation may stem partly from the negative correlation commonly found between F-scale scores and intelligence).

Conforming subjects tend to have occupational interest patterns (as measured by the Strong Vocational Interest Blank) which are similar to those professions generally regarded as placing more stress on conventional social values. Thus they score relatively higher than

BOX 14.12: *A suggestive study*

An extensive experimental analysis of the relation of conformity behavior to other types of suggestibility has been made by Karl-Gustav Stukát, psychologist at the University of Gothenburg in Sweden.

As a first step the investigator administered a large number of tests of suggestibility to two samples of children, 9 and 11 years old, and one of young adults. Included were such diverse tests as body sway; progressive weights; auditory, tactile, olfactory, and visual suggestibility; social suggestion in interpreting Rorschach cards; leading questions; contradictory suggestions from experimenter; co-judge suggestions on perceptual discriminations; majority suggestions on aesthetic judgments; perceptual illusions; etc.

Factor analyses of the scores from these many tests were then carried out. One major factor isolated was a "primary suggestibility" factor, characterized by tendency for the person to make unconscious movements following the experimenter's monotonous verbal suggestions. The automatic, dissociated nature of this behavior is found most pronouncedly in hypnosis, and the investigator stresses the close connection of "primary suggestibility" to hypnotizability. Prominent among the other factors that were isolated was one termed "secondary suggestibility," characterized by a tendency for the person to yield to influence from the experimenter, from a co-judge, and from a group majority, and to be affected by subjective factors in judgment. This factor was found to be related to need for conformity in the individual.

It would appear, therefore, that these two kinds of suggestibility—hypnotizability and conformity-proneness—are different and relatively independent of one another.

Stukát, K.-G. Suggestibility: a factorial and experimental analysis. Acta Psychologica, Gothoburgensia, II. Stockholm: Almquist and Wiksell, 1958.

independent subjects on the scales for policemen, office men, bankers, real estate salesmen, etc. (They also, by the way, score much higher on the mortician scale, quite appropriate in light of the special stabilizing social role of the undertaker in our culture!)

The interest patterns of independent subjects, on the other hand, tend to be similar to those of persons in occupations calling for artistic and scientific originality, e.g., artist, musician, author-journalist, mathematician, physicist, architect.

RATINGS OF CONFORMISTS AND INDEPENDENTS. The above findings on personality characteristics are based on objective personality measures. It is of further interest to see how conformists and independent persons are *rated* by expert psychological observers. In two of Crutchfield's studies, the conformity-testing procedure was administered to 50 military offi-

cers and 68 applicants to medical school, each of whom had been observed and interviewed by a staff of assessors over a three-day assessment period who then rated each subject on a long list of psychological traits. Table 14.3 shows the traits that were found significantly to differentiate persons with high conformity scores from those with low scores. (It is to be emphasized that these ratings were made by the raters in complete ignorance of the performance of the subjects on the conformity task.) It is clear that the same picture of the personality of the conformist and of the independent individual described by objective test data is revealed in these ratings.

GENERAL COMMENT. The above findings offer strong support for the proposition that conformity tendencies are significantly related to enduring personality factors in the individual. Evidence for the validity of this state-

TABLE 14.3: Q-SORT DESCRIPTIONS BY ASSESSMENT STAFF OF HIGHLY INDEPENDENT SUBJECTS VERSUS HIGHLY CONFORMING SUBJECTS IN TWO SAMPLES

Independents tend to be described as	*Conformists tend to be described as*
Military officers	
Is an effective leader.	With respect to authority, is submissive, compliant, and overly accepting.
Takes an ascendant role in his relations with others.	Is conforming; tends to do the things that are prescribed.
Is persuasive; tends to win other people over to his point of view.	Has a narrow range of interests.
Is turned to for advice and reassurance.	Overcontrols his impulses; is inhibited; needlessly delays or denies gratification.
Is efficient, capable, able to mobilize resources easily and effectively.	Is unable to make decisions without vacillation or delay.
Is active and vigorous.	Becomes confused, disorganized, and unadaptive under stress.
Is an expressive, ebullient person.	Lacks insight into his own motives and behavior.
Seeks and enjoys aesthetic and sensuous impressions.	Is suggestible; overly responsive to other people's evaluations rather than his own.
Is natural; free from pretense, unaffected.	
Is self-reliant; independent in judgment; able to think for himself.	
Applicants to medical school	
Values his own independence and autonomy.	Withdraws in the face of adversity.
Is original and imaginative.	Allows others to exploit him.
Thinks and associates to ideas in unusual ways, has unconventional thought processes.	Judges self and others in conventional terms, such as "popularity," the correct thing to do, group opinion, etc.
Is concerned with philosophical problems.	Has readiness to feel guilty.
Appears straightforward, forthright, and candid in relations with others.	Is aware of his impressions on others.
Is masculine in style of behavior.	Is suggestible, overly responsive to other people's evaluations rather than his own.
Expresses his hostilities directly.	
Is self-reliant, independent in judgment, able to think for himself.	

ment comes from many different studies, for example, Barron [1953], Di Vesta [1958], Tuddenham [1958]. And it is noteworthy, too, that the general picture of the conformist found in these studies bears considerable similarity to the picture of the "persuasible person" studied in attitude-change experiments (see page 223).

But there remains the critical question of whether the influence of such personality factors is universal for all kinds of conformity situations. In view of what we have learned earlier about the powerful governing role of situational factors, it would seem prudent to conclude that, although personality factors undoubtedly play a major role in determining conformity behavior, their influence may be substantially modulated by variations in those specific situations in which the conformity behavior is elicited. In short, we cannot properly speak simply of the "conformist" or the "independent" person. Rather, we must speak of the conforming person or the independent person as described *within a specified range of situations.* The personality factors predisposing toward conformity in one type of situation are to some extent different from those relevant to other situations. In some kinds of situations, indeed, personality factors may play a negligible part.

There are, we see, many unresolved psychological questions about the problems and processes of conformity. For a further exposition of some of these questions, see Berg and Bass [1961] and Walker and Heyns [1962].

THE FATE OF THE INDIVIDUAL IN SOCIETY

In our examination of the behavior of the individual in his group, in our attempt to see wherein the individual can retain his individuality and wherein group forces are too overwhelming, we have been opening a wedge to the basic problem facing society today. For the critical problem toward which all the behavioral sciences must be directed is how man can remain an *individual in society.* On the outcome of the solution to this problem rests the possibility of the very existence of a society as a stable group, and the very existence of the individual as an "intact" man of dignity within the society. The problem can of course never be phrased as individual *or* society, individual *versus* society, or even as individual *and* society. The problem can only be phrased as individual *in* society. Whether a man expresses his own basic personality or the pattern imposed upon him by the society, whether he is a conformist or an independent, will inevitably and simultaneously reflect his uniqueness and his collectiveness.

The paradox of modern man is that only as the individual joins with his fellows in groups and organizations can he hope to control the political, economic, and social forces which threaten his individual freedom. This is especially true now that massive social groupings—in nations and combinations of nations—are the order of the day. Only as the individual in society struggles to preserve his individuality in common cause with his fellows can he hope to remain an individual.

CHAPTER GUIDES AND GLOSSARY

GUIDE 40: *The roles which the individual performs in his various groups both reflect and enduringly shape his personality*

GUIDE 41: *The conformity or independence of the individual under group pressure depends upon the nature of the situation and the characteristics of the individual*

autokinetic phenomenon. An illusion of movement of a stationary pinpoint of light in an otherwise dark room. This phenomenon was used by Sherif in his studies of the effect of group norms upon individual judgments.

conforming, "expedient." A form of conformity behavior in which the individual *outwardly* agrees or complies with the group but remains in *inward* disagreement.

conformity. The yielding of the individual's judgment or action to group pressure arising from a conflict between his own opinion and that maintained by the group.

conformity-proneness. An interpersonal response trait characterized by the consistent tendency of the individual to yield in judgment and action to the pressures of the group.

counterformity. A form of nonconformity in which the person's judgment and action are induced, by the group pressure, to deviate even more widely from the group norm. The counterformist individual tends to be one who actively opposes and compulsively dissents from the group.

independence of judgment. A form of behavior in the group-pressure situation in which the individual judges and acts mainly on the basis of his own position and is neither unduly susceptible to the group norms nor unduly driven to deviate from them. Independence of judgment is to be distinguished from both conformity and counterformity.

marginal man. A person who stands on the boundary between two groups, feeling uncertain about his status in both.

role conflict. The situation in which an individual is expected to play two roles that involve responses that are competing or antagonistic.

role incompatibility. The situation in which an individual believes that other persons hold differing and incompatible expectations about how he should perform a particular role.

Ackerman, N. W., and Jahoda, Marie. *Anti-Semitism and emotional disorder: a psychoanalytic interpretation.* New York: Harper, 1950.

Adler, A. *The practice and theory of individual psychology.* New York: Harcourt, Brace, 1925.

Adorno, T. W., Frenkel-Brunswik, Else, Levinson, D. J., and Sanford, R. N. *The authoritarian personality.* New York: Harper, 1950.

Allport, G. W. *Pattern and growth in personality.* New York: Holt, Rinehart & Winston, 1961.

Allport, G. W., and Cantril, H. Judging personality from voice. *J. soc. Psychol.*, 1934, **5**, 37-55.

Allport, G. W., and Kramer, B. M. Some roots of prejudice. *J. Psychol.*, 1946, **22**, 9-39.

Allport, G. W., and Vernon, P. E. *Studies in expressive movement.* New York: Macmillan, 1933.

Andrewes, C. H. The viruses of the common cold. *Sci. Amer.*, 1960, **203**, 88-102.

Ansbacher, H. L. Attitudes of German prisoners of war: a study of the dynamics of national-socialistic followership. *Psychol. Monogr.*, 1948, **62**, no. 1.

Applezweig, M. H., and Moeller, G. Conforming behavior and personality variables. *Tech. Rep.*, No. 8. Contract NONR 996(02). Connecticut College, New London, Conn., 1958.

Arbous, A. G., and Maree, J. Contribution of two group discussion techniques to a validated test battery. *Occup. Psychol.*, 1951, **25**, 73-89.

Argyle, M. Social pressure in public and private situations. *J. abnorm. soc. Psychol.*, 1957, **54**, 172-175.

Argyle, M., Gardner, G., and Cioffi, F. The measurement of supervisory methods. *Hum. Relat.*, 1957, **10**, 295-313.

Argyris, C. *Personality and organization.* New York: Harper, 1957.

Aristotle. *Politics.* Transl. by B. Jowett. Oxford: Clarendon Press, 1885.

Aristotle's Psychology. W. A. Hammond (Ed.). New York: Macmillan, 1902.

Aronson, E., and Mills, J. The effect of severity of initiation on liking for a group. *J. abnorm. soc. Psychol.*, 1959, **59**, 177-181.

Asch, S. E. Personality development of Hopi children. Cited in G. Murphy, L. B. Murphy, and T. M. Newcomb, *Experimental social psychology.* (Rev. ed.) New York: Harper, 1937.

Asch, S. E. Forming impressions of personality.

J. abnorm. soc. Psychol., 1946, **41**, 258-290.

Asch, S. E. Effects of group pressure upon the modification and distortion of judgment. In H. Guetzkow (Ed.), *Groups, leadership, and men.* Pittsburgh: Carnegie Press, 1951.

Asch, S. E. *Social psychology.* Englewood Cliffs, N.J.: Prentice-Hall, 1952.

Asch, S. E. Opinions and social pressure. *Sci. Amer.*, 1955, **193**, 31-35.

Asch, S. E. Studies of independence and conformity. A minority of one against a unanimous majority. *Psychol. Monogr.*, 1956, **70**, no. 9 (whole no. 416).

Axline, V. M. Play therapy and race conflict in young children. *J. abnorm. soc. Psychol.*, 1948, **43**, 300-310.

Babchuk, N., and Goode, W. J. Work incentives in a self-determined group. *Amer. soc. Rev.*, 1951, **16**, 679-687.

Back, K. W. Influence through social communication. *J. abnorm. soc. Psychol.*, 1951, **46**, 9-23.

Bailey, J. C. A classroom evaluation of the case method. In K. R. Andrews (Ed.), *Case method of teaching human relations and administration.* Cambridge, Mass.: Harvard Univer. Press, 1953.

Bakke, E. W. *Bonds of organization: an appraisal of corporate human relations.* New York: Harper, 1950.

Bales, R. F. *Interaction process analysis: a method for the study of small groups.* Cambridge, Mass.: Addison-Wesley, 1950.

Bales, R. F. Some uniformities of behavior in small social systems. In G. E. Swanson, T. M. Newcomb, and E. L. Hartley (Eds.), *Readings in social psychology.* (2nd ed.) New York: Holt, 1952.

Bales, R. F. The equilibrium problem in small groups. In T. Parsons, R. F. Bales, and E. A. Shils, *Working papers in the theory of action.* Glencoe, Ill.: Free Press, 1953.

Bales, R. F., Strodtbeck, F. L., Mills, T. M., and Roseborough, Mary. Channels of communication in small groups. *Amer. sociol. Rev.*, 1951, **16**, 461-468.

Baltzell, E. D. *Philadelphia gentlemen: the making of a national upper class.* Glencoe, Ill.: Free Press, 1958.

Barker, R. G., Dembo, T., and Lewin, K. Frustration and regression: an experiment with young children. *Univer. Ia. Stud. Child. Welf.,* 1941, **18**, no. 1.

Barker, R. G., and Wright, H. F. *One boy's day.* New York: Harper, 1951.

Barker, R. G., and Wright, H. F. *Midwest and its children: the psychological ecology of an American town.* Evanston, Ill.: Row, Peterson, 1954.

Barron, F. Some personality correlates of independence of judgment. *J. Pers.,* 1953, **21**, 287-297.

Bass, B. M. *Leadership, psychology, and organizational behavior.* New York: Harper, 1960.

Bass, B. M., and Coates, C. H. Forecasting officer potential using the leaderless group discussion. *J. abnorm. soc. Psychol.,* 1952, **47**, 321-325.

Bass, B. M., and White, O. L. Situational tests: III. Observers' ratings of leaderless group discussion participants as indicators of external leadership status. *Educ. psychol. Measmt.,* 1951, **11**, 355-361.

Bass, B. M., Wurster, C. R., Doll, P. A., and Clair, D. J. Situational and personality factors in leadership among sorority women. *Psychol. Monogr.,* **67** (10), no. 366.

Baumgartel, H. Leadership, motivation, and attitudes in twenty research laboratories. Paper read at Amer. Sociological Society, 1955. Cited in H. W. Peter, Human factors in research administration. In R. Likert and S. P. Hayes, Jr. (Ed.), *Some applications of behavioural research.* Paris: UNESCO, 1957.

Bechterew, V. M., and de Lange, M. Die Ergebnisse des Experiments auf dem Gebiete der Kollektiven Reflexologie. *Z. angew.Psychol.,* 1924, **24**, 305-344.

Beloff, H. Two forms of social conformity: acquiescence and conventionality. *J. abnorm. soc. Psychol.,* 1958, **56**, 99-104.

Bender, I. E., and Hastorf, A. H. On measuring generalized empathic ability (social sensitivity). *J. abnorm. soc. Psychol.,* 1953, **48**, 503-506.

Benedict, Ruth. Rituals. In *The Encyclopedia of Social Sciences.* New York: Macmillan, 1935.

Bennett, Edith B. Discussion, decision, commitment, and consensus in "group decision." *Hum. Relat.,* 1955, **8**, 251-273.

Benoit-Smullyan, E. Status, status types, and status inter-relations. *Amer. sociol. Rev.,* 1944, **9**, 151-161.

Bentham, J. *An introduction to the principles of morals and legislation.* (First published 1789.) Oxford: Clarendon Press, 1879.

Berelson, B. *Content analysis in communication research.* Glencoe, Ill.: Free Press, 1952.

Berelson, B. Content analysis. In G. Lindzey (Ed.), *Handbook of social psychology,* vol. I. Cambridge, Mass.: Addison-Wesley, 1954.

Berelson, B., Lazarsfeld, P. F., and McPhee, W. N. *Voting.* Chicago: Univer. of Chicago Press, 1954.

Berg, I. A., and Bass, B. M. (Eds.). *Conformity and deviation.* New York: Harper, 1961.

Berger, E. M. The relation between expressed acceptance of self and expressed acceptance of others. *J. abnorm. soc. Psychol.,* 1952, **47**, 778-782.

Berkowitz, L. Group standards, cohesiveness, and productivity. *Hum. Relat.,* 1954, **7**, 509-519.

Berkowitz, L. Personality and group position. *Sociometry,* 1956, **19**, 210-222.

Berkowitz, L., and Howard, R. C. Reactions to opinion deviates as affected by affiliation need (n) and group member interdependence. *Sociometry,* 1959, **22**, 81-91.

Berlyne, D. E. Conflict and information-theory variables as determinants of human perceptual curiosity. *J. exp. Psychol.,* 1957, **53**, 399-404.

Berlyne, D. E. *Conflict, arousal, and curiosity.* New York: McGraw-Hill, 1960.

Bernstein, B. A public language: some sociological implications of a linguistic form. *Brit. J. Sociol.,* 1959, **10**, 311-326.

Berrien, F. K. Homeostasis theory of groups—implications for leadership. In L. Petrulo and B. M. Bass (Eds.), *Leadership and interpersonal behavior.* New York: Holt, Rinehart & Winston, 1961.

Bettelheim, B., and Janowitz, M. *Dynamics of prejudice: a psychological and sociological study of veterans.* New York: Harper, 1950.

Bexton, W. H., Heron, W., and Scott, T. H. Effects of decreased variation in the sensory environment. *Canad. J. Psychol.,* 1954, **8**, 70-76.

Bieri, J., and Blacker, E. The generality of cognitive complexity in the perception of people and ink blots. *J. abnorm. soc. Psychol.,* 1956, **53**, 112-117.

Birch, H. G. The role of motivational factors in insightful problem-solving. *J. comp. Psychol.,* 1945, **38**, 295-317.

Blackwood, Beatrice. *Both sides of Buka passage: an ethnographic study of social, sexual, and economic questions in the north-western Solomon Islands.* Oxford: Clarendon Press, 1935.

Blake, R. R., and Brehm, J. W. The use of tape-recording to simulate a group atmosphere. *J. abnorm. soc. Psychol.,* 1954, **49**, 311-313.

Blake, R. R., Helson, H., and Mouton, J. S. The generality of conformity behavior as a function of factual anchorage, difficulty of task, and amount of social pressure. *J. Pers.,* 1957, **25**, 294-305.

Blau, P. M. *The dynamics of bureaucracy.* Chicago: Univer. of Chicago Press, 1955.

Bleuler, M., and Bleuler, R. Rorschach ink-blot tests and social psychology. *Charact. and Pers.,* 1935, **4**, 99-114.

Blum, G. S. *The Blacky Pictures.* New York: The Psychological Corp., 1950.

Boas, F. (Ed.). *General anthropology.* Boston: Heath, 1938.

Bogardus, E. S. Measuring social distance. *J. appl. Sociol.,* 1925, **9**, 299-308.

Bogardus, E. S. *Immigration and race attitudes.* Boston: Heath, 1928.

Bogart, L. *The age of television.* (2nd ed.) New York: Frederick Ungar Publishing Co., 1958.

Bogdonoff, M. D., Klein, R. F., Estes, E. H., Jr., Shaw, D. M., and Back, K. W. The modifying effect of conforming behavior upon lipid responses accompanying CNS arousal. *Clin. Res.,* 1961, **9,** 135.

Bousfield, W. A., and Cohen, B. H. The occurrence of clustering in the recall of randomly arranged words of different frequencies of usage. *J. gen. Psychol.,* 1955, **52,** 83-95.

Brayfield, A. H., and Crockett, W. H. Employee attitudes and employee performance. *Psychol. Bull.,* 1955, **52,** 396-424.

Bredemeier, H. C., Toby, Marcia L., and Riley, Matilda W. Reputation. In Matilda W. Riley, J. W. Riley, and J. Toby, *Sociological studies in scale analysis.* New Brunswick, N.J.: Rutgers Univer. Press, 1954.

Brim, O. G., Jr. The acceptance of new behavior in child-rearing. *Hum. Relat.,* 1954, **7,** 473-491.

Brodbeck, May. The role of small groups in mediating the effects of propaganda. *J. abnorm. soc. Psychol.,* 1956, **52,** 166-170.

Bronfenbrenner, U. Socialization and social class through time and space. In Eleanor E. Maccoby, T. M. Newcomb, and E. L. Hartley (Eds.), *Readings in social psychology.* New York: Holt, 1958.

Brown, E. J. The self as related to formal participation in three Pennsylvania rural communities. *Rural Sociol.,* 1953, **18,** 313-320.

Brown, J. F. *Psychology and the social order.* New York: McGraw-Hill, 1936.

Brown, R. *Words and things.* Glencoe, Ill.: Free Press, 1958.

Brown, R. W., Black, A. H., and Horowitz, A. E. Phonetic symbolism in natural languages. *J. abnorm. soc. Psychol.,* 1955, **50,** 388-393.

Brown, R. W., and Lenneberg, E. H. A study in language and cognition. *J. abnorm. soc. Psychol.,* 1954, **49,** 454-462.

Bruch, Hilde. Psychological aspects of obesity. *Bull. N.Y. Acad. of Med.,* 1948, **24,** 73-86.

Bruner, J. S., Goodnow, J. J., and Austin, G. A. *A study of thinking.* New York: Wiley, 1956.

Bruner, J. S., and Perlmutter, H. V. Compatriot and foreigner: a study of impression formation in three countries. *J. abnorm. soc. Psychol.,* 1957, **55,** 253-260.

Buchanan, W., and Cantril, H. *How nations see each other.* Urbana: Univer. of Illinois Press, 1954.

Burchard, W. Role conflicts of military chaplains. *Amer. sociol. Rev.,* 1954, **19,** 528-535.

Campa, A. L. Language barriers in intercultural relations. *J. Communication,* 1951, **1,** 41-46.

Campbell, A. A. Factors associated with attitudes toward Jews. In T. M. Newcomb and E. L. Hartley (Eds.), *Readings in social psychology.* New York: Holt, 1947.

Campbell, A., Converse, P. E., Miller, W. E., and Stokes, D. E. *The American voter.* New York: Wiley, 1960.

Campbell, A., Gurin, G., and Miller, W. E. Television and the election. *Sci. Amer.,* 1953, **188,** 46-48.

Campbell, A., Gurin, G., and Miller, W. E. *The voter decides.* Evanston, Ill.: Row, Peterson, 1954.

Campbell, D. T. The generality of a social attitude. Unpublished doctoral dissertation, Univer. of California, Berkeley, 1947.

Cantril, H. *The politics of despair.* New York: Basic Books, 1958.

Cantril, H. *Soviet leaders and mastery over man.* New Brunswick, N.J.: Rutgers Univer. Press, 1960.

Carlson, E. R. Attitude change through modification of attitude structure. *J. abnorm. soc. Psychol.,* 1956, **52,** 256-261.

Carroll, J. B., and Casagrande, J. B. The function of language classifications in behavior. In Eleanor E. Maccoby, T. M. Newcomb, and E. L. Hartley (Eds.), *Readings in social psychology.* (3d ed.) New York: Holt, 1958.

Carter, L. F. Leadership and small group behavior. In M. Sherif and M. O. Wilson, *Group relations at the crossroads.* New York: Harper, 1953.

Carter, L. F., and Haythorn, W. The behavior of authoritarian and equalitarian personalities under various leadership conditions. In W. Haythorn, A. Couch, D. Haefner, P. Longhorn, and L. F. Carter, The behavior of authoritarian and equalitarian personalities in groups. *Hum. Relat.,* 1956, **9,** 57-74.

Carter, L. F., Haythorn, W., Meirowitz, Beatrice, and Lanzetta, J. The relations of categorizations and ratings in the observation of group behavior. *Hum. Relat.,* 1951a, **4,** 239-254.

Carter, L. F., Haythorn, W., Meirowitz, Beatrice, and Lanzetta, J. A note on a new technique of interaction recording. *J. abnorm. soc. Psychol.,* 1951b, **46,** 258-260.

Carter, L. F., Haythorn, W., Shrirer, B., and Lanzetta, J. The behavior of leaders and other group members. *J. abnorm. soc. Psychol.,* 1951, **4,** 589-595.

Carter, L. F., and Nixon, Mary. An investigation of the relationship between four criteria of leadership ability for three different tasks. *J. Psychol.,* 1949, **27,** 245-261.

Cartwright, D. Some principles of mass persuasion: selected findings of research on the sale of United States war bonds. *Hum. Relat.,* 1949, **2,** 253-267.

Cartwright, D., and Harary, F. Structural balance: a generalization of Heider's theory. *Psychol. Rev.,* 1956, **63,** 277-293.

Cattell, J. McK. *American men of science.* (2nd ed.) (App.) Lancaster, Pa.: Science Press, 1910.

Cattell, R. B. The dimensions of culture patterns by factorization of national characters. *J. abnorm. soc. Psychol.,* 1949, **44**, 443-469.

Cattell, R. B. The principal replicated factors discovered in objective personality tests. *J. abnorm. soc. Psychol.,* 1955, **50**, 291-314.

Cattell, R. B. *Personality and motivation structure and measurement.* New York: World, 1957.

Cattell, R. B., Saunders, D. R., and Stice, G. F. The dimensions of syntality in small groups. *Hum. Relat.,* 1953, **6**, 331-356.

Centers, R. *The psychology of social classes.* Princeton, N.J.: Princeton Univer. Press, 1949.

Charters, W. W., Jr., and Newcomb, T. M. Some attitudinal effects of experimentally increased salience of a membership group. In G. E. Swanson, T. M. Newcomb, and E. L. Hartley (Eds.), *Readings in social psychology.* (2nd ed.) New York: Holt, 1952.

Chase, S. *The tyranny of words.* New York: Harcourt, Brace, 1938.

Child, I. L. *Italian or American? The second generation in conflict.* New Haven, Conn.: Yale Univer. Press, 1943.

Child, I. L. Children's preference for goals easy or difficult to obtain. *Psychol. Monogr.,* 1946, **60**, no. 4.

Child, I. L., Potter, E. H., and Levine, Estelle M. Children's textbooks and personality development: an exploration in the social psychology of education. *Psychol. Monogr.,* 1946, **60**, no. 3 (whole no. 279).

Child, I. L., and Whiting, J. W. M. Determinants of level of aspiration: evidence from everyday life. *J. abnorm. soc. Psychol.,* 1949, **44**, 303-314.

Chinoy, E. The tradition of opportunity and the aspiration of automobile workers. *Amer. J. Sociol.,* 1952, **57**, 453-459.

Christiansen, B. *Attitudes towards foreign affairs as a function of personality.* Oslo: Oslo Univer. Press, 1959.

Christie, L. S., Luce, R. D., and Macy, J., Jr. *Communication and learning in task-oriented groups.* Cambridge, Mass.: Research Laboratory of Electronics, 1952.

Church, J. *Language and the discovery of reality.* New York: Random House, 1961.

Cline, V. B., and Richards, J. M., Jr. Accuracy of interpersonal perception—a general trait? *J. abnorm. soc. Psychol.,* 1960, **60**, 1-7.

Coch, L., and French, J. R. P. Overcoming resistance to change. *Hum. Relat.,* 1948, **1**, 512-532.

Cohen, A. R. Need for cognition and order of communication as determinants of opinion change. In C. I. Hovland *et al., The order of presentation in persuasion.* New Haven, Conn.: Yale Univer. Press, 1957.

Coleman, J. F., Blake, R. R., and Mouton, J. S. Task difficulty and conformity pressures. *J. abnorm. soc. Psychol.,* 1958, **57**, 120-122.

Comte, A. *The positive polity.* (Original French ed., vol. 1, 1852; vol. 4, 1854.) Transl., London: Longmans, Green, 1875.

Converse, P. E. The shifting role of class in political attitudes and behavior. In Eleanor E. Maccoby, T. M. Newcomb, and E. L. Hartley (Eds.), *Readings in social psychology.* (3d ed.) New York: Holt, 1958.

Converse, P., and Campbell, A. Political standards in secondary groups. In D. Cartwright and A. Zander (Eds.), *Group dynamics.* (Rev. ed.) Evanston, Ill.: Row, Peterson, 1960.

Cook, T. H. The application of the Rorschach test to a Samoan group. *Rorschach Res. Exch.,* 1942, **6**, 51-60.

Cooley, C. H. *Human nature and the social order.* New York: Scribner, 1902.

Coombs, C. H. Some hypotheses for the analysis of qualitative variables. *Psychol. Rev.,* 1948, **55**, 167-174.

Cooper, J. B. Emotion in prejudice. *Science,* 1959, **130**, 314-318.

Cottrell, L. S., and Eberhart, Sylvia. *American opinion on world affairs in the atomic age.* Princeton, N.J.: Princeton Univer. Press, 1948.

Cousins, A. N. Social equilibrium and the psychodynamic mechanisms. *Soc. Forces,* 1951, **30**, 202-209.

Crespi, L. P. Public opinion toward conscientious objectors: III. Intensity of social rejection in stereotype and attitude. *J. Psychol.,* 1945, **19**, 251-276.

Cressey, P. G. *The taxi-dance hall.* Chicago: Univer. of Chicago Press, 1932.

Crockett, W. H. Emergent leadership in small, decision-making groups. *J. abnorm. soc. Psychol.,* 1955, **51**, 378-383.

Cronbach, L. J. Response sets and test validity. *Educ. psychol. Measm.,* 1946, **6**, 475-494.

Crow, W. J., and Hammond, K. R. The generality of accuracy and response sets in interpersonal perception. *J. abnorm. soc. Psychol.,* 1957, **54**, 384-390.

Crutchfield, R. S. A new technique for measuring individual differences in conformity to group judgment. *Proc. Invitational Conf. on Testing Problems.* Princeton, N.J.: Educational Testing Service, 1954a, 69-74.

Crutchfield, R. S. The measurement of individual conformity to group opinion among officer personnel. Institute of Personality Assessment and Research, Univer. of California, Berkeley, *Res. Bull.,* 1954b.

Crutchfield, R. S. Conformity and character. *Amer. Psychol.,* 1955, **10**, 191-198.

Crutchfield, R. S. Conformity and creative thinking. Paper delivered at Symposium on Creative Thinking, Univer. of Colorado, 1958.

Crutchfield, R. S. Personal and situational factors in conformity to group pressure. *Acta Psychologica*, 1959a, **15**, 386-388.

Crutchfield, R. S. The effect on individual conformity of authoritative confirmation or repudiation of group consensus. Paper delivered at annual meeting of the Eastern Psychological Association, Atlantic City, N.J., 1959b.

Crutchfield, R. S. Detrimental effects of conformity pressures on creative thinking. *Psychol. Beiträge*, 1962, **6**, 463-471.

Culbertson, Frances M. Modification of an emotionally held attitude through role playing. *J. abnorm. soc. Psychol.*, 1957, **54**, 230-233.

Curle, A., and Trist, E. L. Transitional communities and social reconnection, part II. *Hum. Relat.*, 1957, **1**, 240-288.

Davis, A., Gardner, B. B., and Gardner, M. R. *Deep south: a social anthropological study of caste and class.* Chicago: Univer. of Chicago Press, 1941.

Davis, A., and Havighurst, R. J. Social class and colour differences in child-rearing. *Amer. sociol. Rev.*, 1946, **11**, 698-710.

Davis, K. *Human society.* New York: Macmillan, 1949.

Davis, M. Community attitudes toward fluoridation. *Pub. Opin. Quart.*, 1959, **23**, 474-482.

Davitz, J. R. The effects of previous training on post-frustration behavior. *J. abnorm. soc. Psychol.*, 1952, **47**, 309-315.

Dearborn, DeWitt C., and Simon, H. A. Selective perception: a note on the departmental identification of executives. *Sociometry*, 1958, **21**, 140-144.

De Fleur, M. L., and Westie, F. R. Verbal attitudes and overt acts: an experiment on the salience of attitudes. *Amer. sociol. Rev.*, 1958, **23**, 667-673.

Deutsch, M. An experimental study of the effects of co-operation and competition upon group process. *Hum. Relat.*, 1949, **2**, 199-232.

Deutsch, M., and Collins, Mary E. *Interracial housing: a psychological evaluation of a social experiment.* Minneapolis: Univer. of Minnesota Press, 1951.

Deutsch, M., and Gerard, H. A study of normative and informational social influences upon individual judgment. *J. abnorm. soc. Psychol.*, 1955, **51**, 629-636.

De Vries, P. *The Mackeral Plaza.* New York: Little, Brown, 1958.

Dexter, E. S. Personality traits related to conservatism and radicalism. *Charact. and Pers.*, 1939, **7**, 230-237.

Di Vesta, F. J. Susceptibility to pressures toward uniformity of behavior in social situations: a study of task, motivational and personal factors

in conformity behavior. Contract AF 18(603)-20. Syracuse University, 1958.

Douglass, H. P. *1000 city churches.* New York: Doran, 1926.

Douvan, Elizabeth. Social status and success strivings. *J. abnorm. soc. Psychol.*, 1956, **52**, 219-223.

Douvan, Elizabeth, and Adelson, J. The psychodynamics of social mobility in adolescent boys. *J. abnorm. soc. Psychol.*, 1958, **56**, 31-44.

Dubin, S. S., Burke, L. K., Neel, R. G., and Chesler, D. J. Characteristics of hard and easy raters. *USA Persona. Res. Br. Note*, 1954, no. 36.

Dudycha, G. J. An objective study of punctuality in relation to personality and achievement. *Arch. Psychol.*, 1936, no. 204.

Duffus, R. L. Review of "The Jungle" by Upton Sinclair. *New York Times*, Oct. 13, 1946.

Duncker, K. On problem-solving. *Psychol. Monogr.*, 1945, **58**, no. 5.

Edwards, A. L. The relationship between the judged desirability of a trait and the probability that the trait will be endorsed. *J. appl. Psychol.*, 1953, **37**, 90-93.

Edwards, A. L. *Techniques of attitude scale construction.* New York: Appleton-Century-Crofts, 1957.

Edwards, A. L., and Kilpatrick, F. P. A technique for the construction of attitude scales. *J. appl. Psychol.*, 1948, **32**, 374-384.

Elkin, F. The soldier's language. *Amer. J. Sociol.*, 1945-1946, **51**, 414-422.

Estes, S. G. Judging personality from expressive behavior. *J abnorm. soc. Psychol.*, 1938, **33**, 217-236.

Feldman, H. *Problems in labor relations.* New York: Macmillan, 1937.

Ferguson, L. W. The influence of individual attitudes on construction of an attitude scale. *J. soc. Psychol.*, 1935, **6**, 115-117.

Ferguson, L. W. Primary social attitudes. *J. Psychol.*, 1939a, **8**, 217-223.

Ferguson, L. W. The requirements of an adequate attitude scale. *Psychol. Bull.*, 1939b, **36**, 665-673.

Feshbach, S., and Singer, R. D. The effects of fear arousal and suppression of fear upon social perception. *J. abnorm. soc. Psychol.*, 1957, **55**, 283-288.

Festinger, L. Informal social communication. *Psychol. Rev.*, 1950, **57**, 271-282.

Festinger, L. *A theory of cognitive dissonance.* Evanston, Ill.: Row, Peterson, 1957.

Festinger, L., and Carlsmith, J. M. Cognitive consequences of forced compliance. *J. abnorm. soc. Psychol.*, 1959, **58**, 203-210.

Festinger, L., Riecken, H. W., Jr., and Schachter, S. *When prophecy fails.* Minneapolis: Univer. of Minnesota Press, 1956.

Festinger, L., Schachter, S., and Back, K. *Social pressures in informal groups: a study of human factors in housing.* New York: Harper, 1950.

Fiedler, F. *Leader attitudes and group effectiveness.* Urbana: Univer. of Illinois Press, 1958.

Fiedler, F. E. The leader's psychological distance and group effectiveness. In D. Cartwright and A. Zander (Eds.), *Group dynamics.* (2nd ed.) Chicago: Row, Peterson, 1960.

Fleischman, Doris E. Notes of a retiring feminist. *Amer. Mercury,* 1949, **68,** 161-168.

Foley, J. P., Jr., and MacMillan, F. L. Mediated generalization and the interpretation of verbal behaviour: V. Free association as related to differences in professional training. *J. exp. Psychol.,* 1943, **33,** 299-310.

Force, R. W., and Force, Maryanne. Keys to cultural understanding. *Science,* 1961, **133,** 1202-1206.

Fortune, R. Arapesh warfare. *Amer. Anthropologist,* 1939, **41,** 36.

Fouriezos, N. T., Hutt, M. L., and Guetzkow, H. Measurement of self-oriented needs in discussion groups. *J. abnorm. soc. Psychol.,* 1950, **45,** 682-690.

French, J. R. P., Jr., Israel, J., and Ås, D. An experiment on participation in a Norwegian factory: interpersonal dimensions of decision-making. *Hum. Relat.,* 1960, **13,** 3-19.

French, J. R. P., Jr., Ross, I. C., Kirby, S., Nelson, J. R., and Smyth, P. Employee participation in a program of industrial change. *Personnel,* 1958, **35,** 16-29.

French, Vera. V. The structure of sentiments. 1. A. restatement of the theory of sentiments. *J. Pers.,* 1947, **15,** 247-282. II. A preliminary study of sentiments. *Ibid.,* **16,** 78-108. III. A study of philosophico-religious sentiments. *Ibid.,* **16,** 209-244.

Frenkel-Brunswik, Else. Intolerance of ambiguity as an emotional and perceptual variable. *J. Pers.,* 1949, **18,** 108-143.

Frenkel-Brunswik, Else, and Sanford, R. N. Some personality factors in anti-Semitism. *J. Psychol.,* 1945, **20,** 271-291.

Friedman, E., and Havighurst, R. J. *The meaning of work and retirement.* Chicago: Univer. of Chicago Press, 1954.

Fromm, E. *Escape from freedom.* New York: Farrar & Rinehart, 1941.

Gage, N. L., and Cronbach, L. Conceptual and methodological problems in interpersonal perception. *Psychol. Rev.,* 1955, **62,** 411-422.

Gale, H. On the psychology of advertising. In *Psychological studies.* Privately printed, 1900.

Gardner, G. H. The Arab Middle East: some background interpretations. *J. soc. Issues,* 1959, **15,** no. 3.

Gerard, H. B. The effect of different dimensions of disagreement on the communication process

in small groups. *Hum. Relat.,* 1953, **6,** 249-271.

Gerard, H. B. The anchorage of opinions in face-to-face groups. *Hum. Relat.,* 1954, **7,** 313-325.

Ghiselli, E. E., and Brown, C. W. *Personnel and industrial psychology.* (2nd ed.) New York: McGraw-Hill, 1955.

Ghiselli, E. E., and Lodahl, T. M. Patterns of managerial traits and group effectiveness. *J. abnorm. soc. Psychol.,* 1958, **57,** 61-66.

Gibb, C. A. The emergence of leadership in small temporary groups of men. Unpublished doctoral dissertation, Univer. of Illinois, 1949. Cited in C. A. Gibb, Leadership. In G. Lindzey (Ed.), *Handbook of social psychology,* vol. II. Cambridge, Mass.: Addison-Wesley, 1954.

Gibb, C. A. The effects of group size and of threat reduction upon creativity in a problem-solving situation. *Amer. Psychologist,* 1951, **6,** 324 (abstract).

Gibb, J. R., Platts, G. N., and Miller, L. E. *Dynamics of participative groups.* St. Louis: J. S. Swift, 1951.

Gilbert, G. M. Stereotype persistence and change among college students. *J. abnorm. soc. Psychol.,* 1951, **46,** 245-254.

Gilbert, W. S. *The Mikado.* New York: Modern Library, Random House.

Gilchrist, J. C., Shaw, M. E., and Walker, L. C. Some effects of unequal distribution of information in a wheel group structure. *J. abnorm. soc. Psychol.,* 1955, **51,** 119-122.

Goldman, I. The Zuñi Indians of New Mexico. In Margaret Mead (Ed.), *Cooperation and competition among primitive peoples.* New York: McGraw-Hill, 1937.

Goldschmidt, W., and Edgerton, R. B. A picture technique for the study of values. *Amer. Anthropologist,* 1961, **63,** 26-47.

Gollin, E. S. Forming impressions of personality. *J. Pers.,* 1954, **23,** 65-76.

Goodenough, Florence L. The use of free association in the objective measurement of personality. In *Studies in personality contributed in honor of Lewis M. Terman.* New York: McGraw-Hill, 1942.

Gordon, M. M. Assimilation in America: theory and reality. *Daedalus,* Spring, 1961, 263-285.

Gough, H. G. *Manual for the California Psychological Inventory.* Palo Alto, Calif.: Consulting Psychologists Press, 1957.

Gough, H. G. The Adjective Check List as a personality assessment research device. *Psychol. Rep. Monogr. Suppl.,* 1960a, **6,** 107-122.

Gough, H. G. Theory and measurement of socialization. *J. Consult. Psychol.,* 1960b, **24,** 23-30.

Greer, F. L. *Small group effectiveness.* Rep. no. 6. Philadelphia: Institute for Research in Human Relations, 1955.

Gross, N., McEachern, A. W., and Mason, W. S. Role conflict and its resolution. In Eleanor E. Maccoby, T. M. Newcomb, and E. L. Hartley (Eds.), *Readings in social psychology*. (3d ed.) New York: Holt, 1958.

Guetzkow, H. S., and Bowman, P. H. *Men and hunger: a psychological manual for relief workers*. Elgin, Ill.: Brethren Press, 1946.

Guetzkow, H., and Dill, W. R. Factors in the organizational development of task-oriented groups. *Sociometry*, 1957, **20**, 175-204.

Guetzkow, H., and Simon, H. A. The impact of certain communication nets upon organization and performance in task-oriented groups. *Mgmt. Sci.*, 1955, **1**, 233-250.

Guilford, J. P. *Personality*. New York: McGraw-Hill, 1959.

Guilford, J. P., Christensen, P. R., Frick, J. W., and Merrifield, P. R. The relation of creative-thinking aptitudes to non-aptitude personality traits. *Rep. psychol. Lab.*, no. 20. Los Angeles: University of Southern California, 1959.

Gulliksen, H. Intrinsic validity. *Amer. Psychologist*, 1950, **5**, 511-517.

Guthrie, E. R. *The psychology of human conflict*. New York: Harper, 1938.

Guttman, L. *Questions and answers about scale analysis*. Research Branch, Information and Education Division, Army Service Forces, Report D-2, 1945.

Guttman, L. The third component of scalable attitudes. *Int. J. Opin. Attitude Res.*, 1950, **4**, 285-287.

Guttman, L., and Foa, U. G. Social contact and an inter-group attitude. *Publ. Opin. Quart.*, 1951, **15**, 43-53.

Guttman, L., and Suchman, E. A. Intensity and a zero point for attitude analysis. *Amer. sociol. Rev.*, 1947, **12**, 57-67.

Haire, M. Projective techniques in marketing research. *J. Marketing*, 1950, **14**, 649-656.

Haire, M., and Grunes, W. F. Perceptual defenses: processes protecting an original perception of another personality. *Hum. Relat.*, 1950, **3**, 403-412.

Hallowell, A. I. Culture, personality, and society. In A. L. Kroeber (Ed.), *Anthropology today*. Chicago: Univer. of Chicago Press, 1953.

Halpin, A. W., and Winer, B. J. A factorial study of the leader behavior descriptions. In R. M. Stogdill and A. E. Coons (Eds.), *Leader behavior: its description and measurement*. Bur. Bus. Res. Monogr. 88. Columbus: Ohio State Univer., 1957.

Hamblin, R. L. Leadership and crisis. *Sociometry*, 1958, **21**, 322-335.

Hammond, K. R. Measuring attitudes by error-choice: an indirect method. *J. abnorm. soc. Psychol.*, 1948, **43**, 38-48.

Harding, J., and Hogrefe, R. Attitudes of white department store employees toward Negro co-workers. *J. soc. Issues*, 1952, **8**, no. 1, 18-28.

Hare, A. P. A study of interaction and consensus in different sized groups. *Amer. sociol. Rev.*, 1952, **17**, 261-267.

Hartley, E. L. *Problems in prejudice*. New York: King's Crown Press, 1946.

Harvey, O. J. An experimental approach to the study of status relations in informal groups. *Amer. sociol. Rev.*, 1953, **18**, 357-367.

Harvey, O. J., and Consalvi, C. Status and conformity to pressures in informal groups. *J. abnorm. soc. Psychol.*, 1960, **60**, 182-187.

Haveman, E., and West, Patricia S. *They went to college: the college graduate in America today*. New York: Harcourt, Brace, 1952.

Haythorn, W. The influence of individual members on the characteristics of small groups. *J. abnorm. soc. Psychol.*, 1953, **48**, 276-284.

Haythorn, W. The effects of varying combinations of authoritarian and equalitarian leaders and followers. *J. abnorm. soc. Psychol.*, 1956, **52**, 210-219.

Hebb, D. O. Drives and the C.N.S. (conceptual nervous system). *Psychol. Rev.*, 1955, **62**, 243-254.

Heider, F. Social perception and phenomenal causality. *Psychol. Rev.*, 1944, **51**, 358-374.

Heider, F. *The psychology of interpersonal relations*. New York: Wiley, 1958.

Heider, F., and Simmel, M. An experimental study of apparent behaviour. *Amer. J. Psychol.*, 1944, **57**, 243-259.

Heinicke, C., and Bales, R. F. Developmental trends in the structure of small groups. *Sociometry*, 1953, **16**, 7-38.

Helson, H. Adaptation level theory. In S. Koch (Ed.), *Psychology: a study of a science*, vol. I, *Sensory, perceptual, and physiological formulations*. New York: McGraw-Hill, 1959.

Hemphill, J. K. Relations between the size of the group and the behavior of "superior" leaders. *J. soc. Psychol.*, 1950, **32**, 11-22.

Hemphill, J. K. Why people attempt to lead. In L. Petrullo and B. M. Bass (Eds.), *Leadership and inter-personal behavior*. New York: Holt, Rinehart & Winston, 1961.

Henry, W. E. The business executive: the psychodynamics of a social role. *Amer. J. Sociol.*, 1949, **54**, 286-291.

Herskovits, M. J. *Man and his works: the science of cultural anthropology*. New York: Knopf, 1949.

Herskovits, M. J., and Herskovits, Florence S. *Rebel destiny: among the Bush Negroes of Dutch Guiana*. New York: McGraw-Hill, 1934.

Hewitt, D., and Parfit, J. A note on working morale and size of group. *Occup. Psychol.*, London, 1953, **27**, 38-42.

Hiller, E. T. *Principles of sociology*. New York: Harper, 1933.

Himmelstrand, U. *Social pressures, attitudes, and democratic processes*. Stockholm: Almquist and Wiksell, 1960.

Hinckley, E. D. The influence of individual opinion on construction of an attitude scale. *J. soc. Psychol.*, 1932, **3**, 283-296.

Hobbes, T. *Leviathan*. Reprint of 1st (1651) ed. London: Cambridge Univer. Press, 1904.

Hodgen, Margaret T. Change and history. *Viking Fd. Publ. Anthrop.*, 1952, no. 18.

Hoffman, L. R. Homogeneity of member-personality and its effect on group problem solving. *J. abnorm. soc. Psychol.*, 1959, **58**, 27-32.

Hoffman, M. L. Conformity as a defense mechanism and a form of resistance to genuine group influence. *J. Pers.*, 1957, **25**, 412-424.

Hoijer, H. The relation of language to culture. In A. L. Kroeber (Ed.), *Anthropology today*. Chicago: Univer. of Chicago Press, 1953.

Hollander, E. P. Interpersonal exposure time as a determinant of the predictive utility of peer ratings. *Psychol. Rep.*, 1956, **2**, 445-448.

Hollingshead, A. B. *Elmtown's youth: the impact of social classes on adolescents*. New York: Wiley, 1949.

Hollingshead, A. B., and Redlich, F. C. *Social class and mental illness: a community study*. New York: Wiley, 1958.

Hollingworth, H. L. *Judging human character*. New York: Appleton, 1922.

Hollingworth, L. S. *Children above 180 I.Q. Stanford-Binet: origin and development*. Yonkers-on-Hudson, N.Y.: World, 1942.

Holmberg, A. R. *Nomads of the long bow: the Siriono of Eastern Bolivia*. Washington: Smithsonian Inst. of Soc. Anthrop., 1950.

Homans, G. C. *The human group*. New York: Harcourt, Brace, 1950.

Horney, K. *Our inner conflicts*. New York: Norton, 1945.

Horowitz, E. L., and Horowitz, Ruth E. Development of social attitudes in children. *Sociometry*, 1938, **1**, 301-338.

Horsfall, A. B., and Arsenberg, C. M. Teamwork and productivity in a shoe factory. *Hum. Org.*, 1949, **8** (1), 13-25.

Horwitz, M. The recall of interrupted group tasks: an experimental study of individual motivation in relation to group goals. *Hum. Relat.*, 1954, **7**, 3-38.

Houser, J. D. *What the employer thinks*. Cambridge, Mass.: Harvard Univer. Press, 1927.

Hovland, C. I., Campbell, E. H., and Brock, T. The effects of "commitment" on opinion change following communication. In C. I. Hovland et al., *The order of presentation in persuasion*. New Haven, Conn.: Yale Univer. Press, 1957.

Hovland, C. I., Harvey, O. J., and Sherif, M. Assimilation and contrast effects in reactions to communication and attitude change. *J. abnorm. soc. Psychol.*, 1957, **55**, 244-252.

Hovland, C. I., Lumsdaine, A. A., and Sheffield, F. D. *Experiments on mass communication*. Princeton, N.J.: Princeton Univer. Press, 1949.

Hovland, C. I., and Mandell, W. An experimental comparison of conclusion-drawing by the communicator and by the audience. *J. abnorm. soc. Psychol.*, 1955, **47**, 581-588.

Hovland, C. I., and Pritzker, H. A. Extent of opinion change as a function of amount of change advocated. *J. abnorm. soc. Psychol.*, 1957, **54**, 257-261.

Hovland, C. I., and Sears, R. R. Minor studies of aggression. VI. Correlation of lynchings with economic indices. *J. Psychol.*, 1940, **9**, 301-310.

Hovland, C. I., and Sherif, M. Judgmental phenomena and scales of attitude measurement: item displacement in Thurstone scales. *J. abnorm. soc. Psychol.*, 1952, **47**, 822-832.

Hovland, C. I., and Weiss, W. The influence of source credibility on communication effectiveness. *Publ. Opin. Quart.*, 1951, **15**, 635-650.

Hughes, E. C. The knitting of racial groups in industry. *Amer. sociol. Rev.*, 1946, **11**, 512-519.

Hutchins, R. M. The nurture of human life. *Bull. Center for the Study of Democratic Institutions of the Fund for the Republic*, no. 10, March, 1961.

Hyman, H. H. The psychology of status. *Arch. Psychol.*, 1942, no. 269.

Hyman, H. H. *Interviewing in social research*. Chicago: Univer. of Chicago Press, 1954.

Hyman, H. H., and Sheatsley, P. B. Some reasons why information campaigns fail. *Publ. Opin. Quart.*, 1947, **11**, 412-423.

Hyman, H. H., and Sheatsley, P. B. The authoritarian personality: a methodological critique. In R. Christie and Marie Jahoda (Eds.), *Studies in the scope and method of "The Authoritarian Personality."* Glencoe, Ill.: Free Press, 1954.

Inkeles, A. *Public opinion in Soviet Russia*. Cambridge, Mass.: Harvard Univer. Press, 1950.

Isaacs, H. R. *Scratches on our minds*. New York: John Day, 1958.

Jackson, J. M. The effect of changing the leadership of small work groups. *Hum. Relat.*, 1953, **6**, 25-44.

Jackson, J. M., and Saltzstein, H. D. The effect of person-group relationships on conformity processes. *J. abnorm. soc. Psychol.*, 1958, **57**, 17-24.

James, W. *Principles of psychology*. New York: Holt, 1890.

Janis, I. L., and Feshbach, S. Effects of fear-arousing communications. *J. abnorm. soc. Psychol.*, 1953, **48**, 78-92.

Janis, I. L., and Field, P. B. A behavioral assessment of persuasibility: consistency of individual differences. In I. L. Janis et al., *Personality and persuasibility*. New Haven, Conn.; Yale Univer. Press, 1959a.

Janis, I. L., and Field, P. B. Sex differences and personality factors related to persuasibility. In I. L. Janis et al., *Personality and persuasibility*. New Haven, Conn.: Yale Univer. Press, 1959b.

Janis, I. L., Hovland, C. I., Field, P. B., Linton, Harriet, Graham, Elaine, Cohen, A. R., Rife, D., Abelson, R. P., Lesser, G. S., and King, B. T. *Personality and persuasibility*. New Haven, Conn.: Yale Univer. Press, 1959.

Janis, I. L., and King, B. T. The influence of role-playing on opinion-change. *J. abnorm. soc. Psychol.*, 1954, **49**, 211-218.

Jenkins, W. O. A review of leadership studies with particular reference to military problems. *Psychol. Bull.*, 1947, **44**, 54-87.

Jones, E. E., Wells, H. H., and Torrey, R. Some effects of feedback from the experimenter on conformity behavior. *J. abnorm. soc. Psychol.*, 1958, **57**, 207-213.

Kahn, R. L. An analysis of supervisory practices and components of morale. In H. Guetzkow (Ed.), *Groups, leadership and men; research in human relations*. Pittsburgh: Carnegie Press, 1951.

Kahn, R. L., and Katz, D. Leadership practices in relation to productivity and morale. In D. Cartwright and A. Zander (Eds.), *Group dynamics*. Evanston, Ill.: Row, Peterson, 1953.

Katz, D. The functional approach to the study of attitudes. *Publ. Opin. Quart.*, 1960, **24**, 163-204.

Katz, D., and Braly, K. W. Racial stereotypes of 100 college students. *J. abnorm. soc. Psychol.*, 1933, **28**, 280-290.

Katz, D., and Kahn, R. L. Human organization and worker motivation. In L. R. Tripp (Ed.), *Industrial productivity*. Madison, Wis.: Industrial Relations Research Association, 1951.

Katz, D., Maccoby, N., Gurin, G., and Floor, Lucretia G. *Productivity, supervision, and morale among railroad workers*. Ann Arbor: Survey Research Center, Institute for Social Research, Univer. of Michigan, 1951.

Katz, D., Maccoby, N., and Morse, Nancy C. *Productivity, supervision, and morale in an office situation*, part I. Ann Arbor: Survey Research Center, Institute for Social Research, Univer. of Michigan, 1950.

Katz, D., Sarnoff, I., and McClintock, C. Ego-defense and attitude change. *Hum. Relat.*, 1956, **9**, 27-45.

Katz, D., and Stotland, E. A preliminary statement to a theory of attitude structure and change. In S. Koch (Ed.), *Psychology: a study of a science*, vol. 3. *Formulations of the person and the social context*. New York: McGraw-Hill, 1959.

Katz, E., and Lazarsfeld, P. F. *Personal influence: the part played by people in the flow of mass communication*. Glencoe, Ill.: Free Press, 1955.

Katz, I., Goldston, Judith, and Benjamin, L. Behavior and productivity in bi-racial work groups. *Hum. Relat.*, 1958, **11**, 123-141.

Keller, Suzanne. The social origins and career lines of three generations of American business leaders. Unpublished doctoral dissertation, Columbia University, 1953.

Kelley, H. H. The warm-cold variable in first impressions of persons. *J. Pers.*, 1950, **18**, 431-439.

Kelley, H. H. Communication in experimentally created hierarchies. *Hum. Relat.*, 1951, **4**, 39-56.

Kelley, H. H. First impressions in interpersonal relations. Unpublished doctoral dissertation, Mass. Inst. of Technology, 1948. Cited in J. S. Bruner and R. Tagiuri. The perception of people. In G. Lindzey (Ed.), *Handbook of social psychology*, vol. II. Cambridge, Mass.: Addison-Wesley, 1954.

Kelley, H. H., and Thibaut, J. W. Experimental studies of group problem solving and process. In G. Lindzey (Ed.), *Handbook of social psychology*, vol. I. Cambridge, Mass.: Addison-Wesley, 1954.

Kelley, H. H., and Volkart, E. H. The resistance to change of group-anchored attitudes. *Amer. sociol. Rev.*, 1952, **17**, 453-465.

Kelley, H. H., and Woodruff, Christine L. Members' reactions to apparent group approval of a counternorm communication. *J. abnorm. soc. Psychol.*, 1956, **52**, 67-74.

Kelly, E. L. Consistency of the adult personality. *Amer. Psychologist*, 1955, **10**, 659-681.

Kelly, G. A. *The psychology of personal constructs*. New York: Norton, 1955.

Kelman, H. C. Compliance, identification, and internalization. *J. Conflict Resolution*, 1958, **2**, 51-60.

Kelman, H. C. Processes of opinion change. *Publ. Opin. Quart.*, 1961, **25**, 57-78.

Kelman, H. C., and Cohler, J. Reactions to persuasive communications as a function of cognitive needs and styles. Paper read at Eastern Psychological Association, 1959. Cited in H. C. Kelman, Processes of opinion change. *Publ., Opin. Quart.*, 1961, **25**, 57-78.

Keys, A., Brozek, J., Henschel, A., Mickelson, O., and Taylor, H. L. *The biology of human starvation*. Minneapolis: Univer. of Minnesota Press, 1950.

King, B. T., and Janis, I. L. Comparison of the effectiveness of improvised versus non-improvised role playing in producing opinion changes. *Hum. Relat.*, 1956, **9**, 177-186.

Kinsey, A. C., Pomeroy, W. B., and Martin, C. E. *Sexual behavior in the human male*. Philadelphia: Saunders, 1948.

Kluckhohn, C. Patterning as exemplified in Navaho culture. In *Language, culture, and personality: essays in memory of Edward Sapir.* Menasha, Wis.: Sapir Memorial Publ. Fund, 1941.

Kluckhohn, C. A Navaho personal document with a brief Paretian analysis. *Southwestern J. Anthrop.,* 1945, **1**, 260-283.

Kluckhohn, Florence R. Dominant and variant value orientations. In C. Kluckhohn, H. A. Murray, and D. M. Schneider (Eds.), *Personality in nature, society, and culture.* New York: Knopf, 1953.

Köhler, O. Über den Gruppenwirkungsgrad der Menschen Körperarbeit und die Bedingung optimaler Kollectiv Kraftreaktion. *Indus. Psychotechn.,* 1927, **4**, 209-226. Cited by J. F. Dashiell, *Experimental studies of the influence of social situations on the behavior of individual human adults.* In C. Murchison (Ed.), *Handbook of social psychology.* Worcester, Mass.: Clark Univer. Press, 1935.

Komarovsky, Mirra. Cultural contradictions and sex roles. *Amer. J. Sociol.,* 1946, **52**, 184-189.

Komarovsky, Mirra. Functional analysis of sex roles. *Amer. soc. Rev.,* 1950, **15**, 508-516.

Koos, E. L. *Families in trouble.* New York: King's Crown Press, 1946.

Kornhauser, Ruth R. The Warner approach to social stratification. In R. Bendix and S. M. Lipset (Eds.), *Class status and power.* Glencoe, Ill.: Free Press, 1953.

Korzybski, A. *Science and sanity.* (Rev. ed.) Lancaster, Pa.: Science Press, 1941.

Krech, D., and Crutchfield, R. S. *Theory and problems of social psychology.* New York: McGraw-Hill, 1948.

Kremers, J. *Scientific psychology and naive psychology.* Nijmegen: Drukkerij Gebr. Janssen N.V., 1960.

Kroeber, A. L. *Anthropology: race, language, culture, psychology, prehistory.* (Rev. ed.) New York: Harcourt, Brace, 1948.

Kuhn, M. H., and McPartland, T. S. An empirical investigation of self-attitudes. *Amer. sociol. Rev.,* 1954, **19**, 68-76.

Kutner, B., Wilkins, Carol, and Yarrow, Penny R. Verbal attitudes and overt behavior involving racial prejudice. *J. abnorm. soc. Psychol.,* 1952, **47**, 647-652.

Lambert, W. E., Libman, Eva, and Poser, E. G. The effect of increased salience of a membership group on pain tolerance. *J. Pers.,* 1960, **28**, 350-357.

Lanzetta, J. T. Group behavior under stress. *Hum. Relat.,* 1955, **8**, 29-52.

Lazarsfeld, P. F., Berelson, B., and Gaudet, H. *The people's choice.* New York: Duell, Sloan & Pearce, 1944.

Leavitt, H. J. Some effects of certain communication patterns on group performance. *J. abnorm. soc. Psychol.,* 1951, **46**, 38-50.

Le Bon, G. *Psychologie des foules.* Paris: Oleon, 1895. Transl., *The crowd.* London: Unwin, 1896.

Leighton, A. H. *The governing of men: general principles and recommendations based on experience at a Japanese relocation camp.* Princeton, N.J.: Princeton Univer. Press, 1945.

Lenneberg, E. H., and Roberts, J. M. The language of experience: a study in methodology. *Int. J. Amer. Linguistics.* Suppl. to vol. 22, no. 2, 1956.

Levy, L. Studies in conformity behavior: a methodological note. *J. Psychol.,* 1960, **50**, 39-41.

Lewin, K. In D. Cartwright (Ed.), *Field theory in social science,* New York: Harper, 1951.

Lewin, K. Group decision and social change. In G. E. Swanson, T. M. Newcomb, and E. L. Hartley (Eds.), *Readings in social psychology.* (2nd ed.) New York: Holt, 1952.

Lewin, K., and Dembo, T. Untersuchungen zur Handlungs-und Affektpsychologie. X. Der Arger als dynamisches Problem. *Psychol. Forsch.,* 1931, **15**, 1-144.

Lewin, K., and Lippitt, R. An experimental approach to the study of autocracy and democracy: a preliminary note. *Sociometry,* **1**, 292-300.

Lewis, H. B. An experimental study of the role of the ego in work. I. The role of the ego in cooperative work. *J. exp. Psychol.,* 1944, **34**, 113-126.

Lewis, H. B., and Franklin, M. An experimental study of the role of the ego in work. II. The significance of task-orientation in work. *J. exp. Psychol.,* 1944, **34**, 195-215.

Lewis, M. M. *Language in society: the linguistic revolution and social change.* New York: Social Science Publishers, 1948.

Lewis, O. *Life in a Mexican village: Tepoztlan restudied.* Urbana: Univer. of Illinois Press, 1951.

Likert, R. A. technique for the measurement of attitudes. *Arch. Psychol.,* 1932, no. 140.

Likert, R. A. *Organization theory.* New York: McGraw-Hill, 1961.

Likert, R., and Hayes, S. P., Jr. (Eds.). *Some applications of behavioral research.* UNESCO, 1957.

Linton, Harriet, and Graham, Elaine. Personality correlates of persuasibility. In I. L. Janis et al., *Personality and persuasibility.* New Haven, Conn.: Yale Univer. Press, 1959.

Linton, R. *The study of man.* New York: Appleton-Century-Crofts, 1936.

Linton, R. *The cultural background of personality.* New York: Appleton-Century-Crofts, 1945.

Linton, R. Problems of status personality. In S. S. Sargent and M. W. Smith (Eds.), *Culture and Personality.* New York: Viking Fund, 1949.

Linton, R., and Kardiner, A. The change from dry to wet rice cultivation in Tanala-Betsileo. In

G. E. Swanson, T. M. Newcomb, and E. L. Hartley (Eds.), *Readings in social psychology.* (2nd ed.) New York: Holt, 1952.

Lionberger, H. F. Some characteristics of farm operators sought as sources of farm information in a Missouri community. *Rural Sociol.,* 1953, **18**, 327-338.

Lippitt, R., Polansky, N., Redl, F., and Rosen, S. The dynamics of power: a field study of social influence in groups of children. In Eleanor E. Maccoby, T. M. Newcomb, and E. L. Hartley (Eds.), *Readings in social psychology.* (3d ed.) New York: Holt, 1958.

Lippitt, R., and White, R. K. An experimental study of leadership and group life. In Eleanor E. Maccoby, T. M. Newcomb, and E. L. Hartley (Eds.), *Readings in social psychology.* (3d ed.) New York: Holt, 1958.

Lipset, S. M., and Bendix, R. *Social mobility in industrial society.* Berkeley: Univer. of California Press, 1959.

Loomis, C. P. Informal groupings in a Spanish-American village. *Sociometry,* 1941, **4**, 36-51.

Loomis, C. P., and Beegle, J. A. *Rural social systems.* Englewood Cliffs, N.J.: Prentice-Hall, 1950.

Loomis, F. *Consultation room.* New York: Knopf, 1939.

Lorimer, F. *The growth of reason.* New York: Harcourt, Brace, 1929.

Luchins, A. S. Primacy-recency in impression formation. In C. I. Hovland (Ed.), *The order of presentation in persuasion,* vol. I. New Haven, Conn.: Yale Univer. Press, 1957.

Lumsdaine, A. A., and Janis, I. L. Resistance to "counter-propaganda" produced by one-sided and two-sided "propaganda" presentations. *Publ. Opin. Quart.,* 1953, **17**, 311-318.

Lynd, R. S., and Lynd, H. M. *Middletown: a study in contemporary American culture.* New York: Harcourt, Brace, 1929.

McClelland, D. C. *Personality.* New York: Holt, Rinehart & Winston, 1951.

McClelland, D. C., Atkinson, J. W., Clark, R. A., and Lowell, E. L. *The achievement motive.* New York: Appleton-Century-Crofts, 1953.

McClosky, H. Conservatism and personality. *Amer. pol. Sci. Rev.,* 1958, **42**, 27-45.

MacCrone, I. D. *Race attitudes in South Africa.* New York: Oxford Univer. Press, 1937.

McDougall, W. *Introduction to social psychology.* London: Methuen, 1908.

McGarvey, H. R. Anchoring effects in the absolute judgment of verbal materials. *Arch. Psychol.,* 1943, no. 281.

McGranahan, D. V., and Wayne, I. German and American traits reflected in popular drama. *Hum. Relat.,* 1948, **1**, 429-455.

McGregor, D. *The human side of enterprise.* New York: McGraw-Hill, 1960.

McGuire, W. J. Order of presentation as a factor in "conditioning" persuasiveness. In C. I. Hovland et al., *The order of presentation in persuasion.* New Haven, Conn.: Yale Univer. Press, 1957.

McGuire, W. J. Cognitive consistency and attitude change. *J. abnorm. soc. Psychol.,* 1960, **60**, 345-353.

MacIver, R. M. *Society, a textbook of sociology.* New York: Farrar & Rinehart, 1937.

MacKenzie, Barbara K. The importance of contact in determining attitudes toward Negroes. *J. abnorm. soc. Psychol.,* 1948, **43**, 417-441.

Madariaga, S. de *Englishmen, Frenchmen, Spaniards.* New York: Oxford, 1931.

Maier, N. R. F., and Solem, A. R. The contribution of a discussion leader to the quality of group thinking: the effective use of minority opinions. *Hum. Relat.,* 1952, **5**, 277-288.

Malinowski, B. *Argonauts of the Western Pacific.* New York: Dutton, 1922.

Malinowski, B. *Myth in primitive psychology.* New York: Norton, 1926.

Mandell, M. M. Validation of group oral performance test. *Personnel Psychol.,* 1950, **3**, 179-185.

Mann, F., and Baumgartel, H. Absences and employee attitudes in an electric power company. Ann Arbor: Survey Research Center, Institute for Social Research, Univer. of Michigan, 1952.

Mann, R. D. A review of the relationships between personality and performance in small groups. *Psychol. Bull.,* 1959, **56**, 241-270.

Marriott, R. Size of working group and output. *Occup. Psychol.,* London, 1949, **23**, 47-57.

Marsh, C. P., and Coleman, A. L. Farmers practice adoption rates in relation to adoption rates of leaders. *Rural Sociol.,* 1954, **19**, 180-183.

Martin, J. G., and Westie, F. R. The tolerant personality. *Amer. sociol. Rev.,* 1959, **24**, 521-528.

Maslow, A. H. A theory of human motivation. *Psychol. Rev.,* 1943, **50**, 370-396.

Maslow, A. H. *Motivation and personality.* New York: Harper, 1954.

Masserman, J. H. *Principles of dynamic psychiatry.* Philadelphia: Saunders, 1946.

Mead, G. H. *Mind, self, and society: from the standpoint of a social behaviorist.* Chicago: Univer. of Chicago Press, 1934.

Mead, Margaret. *Sex and temperament in three primitive societies.* New York: Morrow, 1935.

Mead, Margaret. *Cooperation and competition among primitive peoples.* New York: McGraw-Hill, 1939.

Mead, Margaret. The application of anthropological techniques to cross-national communication. *Trans. N.Y. Acad. Sc.,* series II, vol. 9, no. 4, February, 1947.

Mead, Margaret. *Male and female: a study of the sexes in a changing world.* New York: Morrow, 1949.

Meerloo, J. A. M. *Conversation and communication.* New York: Int. Universities Press, 1952.

Melikian, L. H. Authoritarianism and its correlates in the Egyptian culture and in the United States. *J. soc. Issues,* 1959, **15**, no. 3.

Mérei, F. Group leadership and institutionalization. *Hum. Relat.,* 1949, **2**, 23-39.

Merton, R. K. Bureaucratic structure and personality. *Social Forces,* 1940, **57**, 560-568.

Merton, R. K., and Kitt, Alice S. Contributions to the theory of reference group behavior. In R. K. Merton and P. F. Lazarsfeld (Eds.), *Continuities in social research: studies in the scope and method of "The American Soldier."* Glencoe, Ill.: Free Press, 1950.

Meyer, Charlene T. The assertive behavior of children as related to parent behavior. *J. Home Econ.,* 1947, **39**, 77-80.

Michotte, A. *La perception de la causalité.* (2nd ed.) Louvain: Publications Universitaires de Louvain, 1954.

Milgram, S. Nationality and conformity. *Sci. Amer.,* 1961, **205**, 45-51.

Miller, D. R., and Swanson, G. E. *The changing American parent: a study in the Detroit area.* New York: Wiley, 1958.

Miller, D. R., and Swanson, G. E. *Inner conflict and defense.* New York: Holt, Rinehart & Winston, 1960.

Miller, G. A. *Language and communication.* New York: McGraw-Hill, 1951.

Miller, N. E. Effects of group size on group process and member satisfaction. Proc. Adm. Conf., Univer. of Michigan, Ann Arbor, 1950 (abstract).

Miller, R. E., Murphy, J. V., and Mirsky, I. A. The modification of social dominance in a group of monkeys by interanimal conditioning. *J. comp. physiol. Psychol.,* 1955, **48**, 392-396.

Milton, O. Presidential choice and performance on a scale of authoritarianism. *Amer. Psychologist,* 1952, **7**, 597-598 (abstract).

Mitnick, L. L., and McGinnies, E. Influencing ethnocentrism in small discussion groups through a film communication. *J. abnorm. soc. Psychol.,* 1958, **56**, 82-90.

Moreno, J. L. *Who shall survive?* Washington: Nervous and Mental Disease Pub. Co., 1934.

Morris, D. P., Soroker, E., and Buruss, G. Follow-up studies of shy, withdrawn children. I. Evaluation of later adjustment. *Amer. J. Orthopsychiat.,* 1954, **24**, 743-754.

Morrissette, J. O. An experimental study of the theory of structural balance. *Hum. Relat.,* 1958, **11**, 239-254.

Morse, Nancy C. *Satisfactions in the white-collar job.* Ann Arbor: Survey Research Center, Institute for Social Research, Univer. of Michigan, 1953.

Mosier, C. I. A psychometric study of meaning. *J. soc. Psychol.,* 1941, **13**, 123-140.

Mowrer, O. H. Self-injury as a "mechanism of defense." Cited in J. Dollard, L. W. Doob, N. E. Miller, O. H. Mowrer, and R. R. Sears, *Frustration and aggression.* New Haven, Conn.: Yale Univer. Press, 1939.

Mulder, M. Communication, structure, decision structure, and group performance. *Sociometry,* 1960, **23**, 1-14.

Murdock, G. P. *Social structure.* New York: Macmillan, 1949.

Murphy, G., and Likert, R. *Public opinion and the individual: a psychological study of student attitudes on public questions, with a retest five years later.* New York: Harper, 1938.

Murphy, G., Murphy, Lois B., and Newcomb, T. M. *Experimental social psychology.* New York: Harper, 1937.

Murphy, Lois B. *Social behavior and child personality.* New York: Columbia Univer. Press, 1937.

Mussen, P. H. Some personality and social factors related to changes in children's attitudes toward Negroes. *J. abnorm. soc. Psychol.,* 1950, **45**, 423-441.

Nadel, S. F. A field experiment in social psychology. *Brit. J. Psychol.,* 1937, **28**, 195-211.

Nadler, E. B. Yielding, authoritarianism, and authoritarian ideology regarding groups. *J. abnorm. soc. Psychol.,* 1959, **58**, 408-410.

Nash, D. J., and Wolfe, A. W. The stranger in laboratory culture. *Amer. sociol. Rev.,* 1957, **22**, 400-406.

Newcomb, T. M. *Personality and social change: attitude formation in a student community.* New York: Dryden, 1943.

Newcomb, T. M. Autistic hostility and social reality. *Hum. Relat.,* 1947, **1**, 69-86.

Newcomb, T. M. *Social psychology.* New York: Dryden, 1950.

Newcomb, T. M. Individual systems of orientation. In S. Koch (Ed.), *Psychology: a study of a science,* vol. 3, *Formulations of the person and the social context.* New York: McGraw-Hill, 1959.

Newcomb, T. M. Varieties of interpersonal attraction. In D. Cartwright and A. Zander (Eds.), *Group dynamics.* (2nd ed.) Evanston, Ill.: Row, Peterson, 1960.

Newcomer, Mabel. *The big business executive.* New York: Columbia Univer. Press, 1955.

Nisbet, R. A. The study of social problems. In R. K. Merton and R. A. Nisbet (Eds.), *Contemporary social problems.* New York: Harcourt, Brace & World, 1961.

Norsworthy, N. The validity of judgments of character. In J. Dewey (Ed.), *Essays philosophical and psychological in honor of William James.* (2nd ed.) New York: Longmans, 1910.

Nunnally, J. C., Jr. *Tests and measurements.* New York: McGraw-Hill, 1959.

Osgood, C. E. An analysis of the cold war mentality. *J. soc. Issues*, 1961, **27**, 12-19.

Osgood, C. E., and Suci, G. J. Factor analysis of meaning *J. exp. Psychol.*, 1955, **50**, 325-338.

Osgood, C. E., Suci, G. J. ,and Tannenbaum, P. H. *The measurement of meaning*. Urbana: Univer. of Illinois, 1957.

Osgood, C. E., and Tannenbaum, P. H. The principle of congruity in the prediction of attitude change. *Psychol. Rev.*, 1955, **62**, 42-55.

Otis, Nancy B., and McCandless, B. Responses to repeated frustrations of young children differentiated according to need area. *J. abnorm. soc. Psychol.*, 1955, **50**, 349-353.

Peak, Helen. Observations on the characteristics and distribution of German Nazis. *Psychol. Monogr.*, 1945, **59**, no. 276.

Peak, Helen. Attitude and motivation. In M. R. Jones (Ed.), *Nebraska symposium on motivation, 1955*. Lincoln: Univer. of Nebraska Press, 1955.

Pelz, D. C. Influence: a key to effective leadership in the first-line supervisor. *Personnel*, 1952, **29**, 209-217.

Pelz, D. C. Some social factors related to performance in a research organization. *Adm. Sci. Quart.*, 1956, **1**, 310-325.

Pennington, D. F., Hararey, F., and Bass, B. M. Some effects of decision and discussion on coalescence, change, and effectiveness. *J. appl. Psychol.*, 1958, **42**, 404-408.

Pepitone, A. Motivational effects in social perception. *Hum. Relat.*, 1950, **3**, 57-76.

Pettigrew, T. F. The measurement and correlates of category width as a cognitive variable. *J. Pers*, 1958a, **26**, 532-544.

Pettigrew, T. F. Personality and sociocultural factors in intergroup attitudes, a cross-national comparison. *J. Conflict Resolution*, 1958b, **2**, 29-42.

Pettigrew, T. F., and Cramer, M. R. The demography of desegregation. *J. soc. Issues*, 1959, **15**, 61-71.

Piaget, J. *The language and thought of the child*. New York: Harcourt, Brace, 1926.

Piaget, J. *The child's conception of the world*. New York: Harcourt, Brace, 1929.

Piaget, J. Principal factors determining intellectual evolution from childhood to adult life. In *Factors determining human behavior*. Cambridge, Mass.: Harvard Univer. Press, 1937.

Pintner, R., and Forlano, G. The influence of attitude upon scaling of attitude items. *J. soc. Psychol.*, 1937, **8**, 39-45.

Plato. *The republic*. Vol. 3 of Dialogues of Plato (5 vols.). Transl. by B. Jowett (2nd ed.). Oxford: Clarendon Press, 1875.

Porter, L. W. Preliminary survey of a study of management job perceptions. Ms., Univer. of California, Berkeley, 1962.

Postman, L., and Brown, D. R. The perceptual consequences of success and failure. *J. abnorm. soc. Psychol.*, 1952, **47**, 213-221.

Powdermaker, Hortense. *Life in Lesu*. New York: Norton, 1933.

Preston, M. G., Peltz, W. L., Mudd, Emily H., and Froscher, H. B. Impressions of personality as a function of marital conflict. *J. abnorm. soc. Psychol.*, 1952, **47**, 326-336.

Proctor, C. H., and Loomis, C. P. Analysis of sociometric data. In Marie Jahoda, M. Deutsch, and S. W. Cook (Eds.), *Research methods in social relations: with especial reference to prejudice*. New York: Dryden, 1951.

Rasmussen, G., and Zander, A. Group membership and self-evaluation. *Hum. Relat.*, 1954, **7**, 239-251.

Raven, B. H., and Rietsema, J. The effects of varied clarity of group goal and group path upon the individual and his relation to his group. *Hum. Relat.*, 1957, **10**, 29-45.

Redfield, R. *Tepoztlan, a Mexican village: a study of folk life*. Chicago: Univer. of Chicago Press, 1946.

Redl, F. The clinical approach. *Intercult. Educ. News*, 1946, **7**, no. 4, 3-5.

Report No. B-157, Information and Education Division, Army Service Forces, U.S. War Department, 1945. Cited in G. E. Swanson, T. M. Newcomb, and E. L. Hartley (Eds.), *Readings in social psychology*. (2nd ed.) New York: Holt, 1952.

Richards, Clara B., and Dobyns, H. F. Topography and culture: the case of the changing cage. *Hum. Org.*, 1957, **16**, 16-20.

Riesman, D. *The lonely crowd*. New Haven, Conn.: Yale Univer. Press, 1950.

Riley, J. W., Jr., and Schramm, W. *The Reds take a city*. New Brunswick, N.J.: Rutgers Univer. Press, 1951.

Riley, Matilda W., and Riley, J. W., Jr. Notes on a conceptual model. In Matilda W. Riley, J. W. Riley, Jr., and J. Toby, *Sociological studies in scale analysis*. New Brunswick, N.J.: Rutgers Univer. Press, 1954.

Roethlisberger, F. J., and Dickson, W. J. *Management and the worker*. Cambridge, Mass.: Harvard Univer. Press, 1939.

Rogers, C. R. A comprehensive theory of personality and behavior. Unpublished paper, 1948. Cited in D. C. McClelland, *Personality*. New York: Sloane, 1951.

Rokeach, M. A method for studying individual differences in "narrow-mindedness." *J. Pers.*, 1951, **20**, 219-233.

Rokeach, M. *The open and closed mind*. New York: Basic Books, 1960.

Rokeach, M., Swanson, T. S., and Denny, M. R. The role of past experience. In M. Rokeach, *The open and closed mind*. New York: Basic Books, 1960.

Rokeach, M., and Vidulich, R. N. The formation

of new belief systems. In M. Rokeach, *The open and closed mind.* New York: Basic Books, 1960.

Rommetveit, R. *Social norms and roles: explorations in the psychology of enduring social pressures.* Minneapolis: Univer. of Minnesota Press, 1955.

Rosander, A. C. An attitude scale based upon behavior situations. *J. soc. Psychol.,* 1937, **8,** 3-15.

Rosen, B. C. The achievement syndrome: a psychocultural dimension of social stratification. *Amer. sociol. Rev.,* 1956, **21,** 203-211.

Rosenberg, M. *Occupations and values.* Glencoe, Ill.: Free Press, 1957.

Rosenberg, M. J. Cognitive structure and attitudinal affect. *J. abnorm. soc. Psychol.,* 1956, **53,** 367-372.

Rosenberg, M. J., and Abelson, R. P. An analysis of cognitive balancing. In M. J. Rosenberg et al., Attitude organization and change. New Haven, Conn.: Yale Univer. Press, 1960.

Rosenthal, D., and Cofer, C. N. The effect on group performance of an indifferent and neglectful attitude shown by one group member. *J. exp. Psychol.,* 1948, **38,** 568-577.

Rosner, S. Consistency of response to group pressures. *J. abnorm. soc. Psychol.,* 1957, **55,** 145-146.

Ross, E. A. *Social psychology: an outline and source book.* New York: Macmillan, 1908.

Rossi, P. H., and Rossi, Alice S. Some effects of parochial-school education in America. *Daedalus,* Spring, 1961, 300-328.

Rosvold, H. E., Mirsky, A. F., and Pribram, K. H. Influence of amygdalectomy on social behavior in monkeys. *J. comp. physiol. Psychol.,* 1954, **47,** 173-178.

Ruesch, J. Social technique, social status, and social change in illness. In C. Kluckhohn, H. A. Murray, and D. M. Schneider (Eds.), *Personality in nature, society, and culture.* New York: Knopf, 1953.

Ruesch, J., Jacobsen, Annemarie, and Loeb, M. B. Acculturation and illness. *Psychol. Monogr.,* 1948, **62** (5), 1-40.

Sanford, F. H. Speech and personality: a comparative case study. *Character and Pers.,* 1942a, **10,** 169-198.

Sanford, F. H. Speech and personality. *Psychol. Bull.,* 1942b, **39,** 811-845.

Sanford, F. H. The follower's role in leadership phenomena. In G. E. Swanson, T. M. Newcomb, and E. L. Hartley (Eds.), *Readings in social psychology.* (2nd ed.) New York: Holt, 1952.

Sapir, E. The status of linguistics as a science. *Language,* 1929, **5,** 207-214.

Sarbin, T. R. Role theory. In G. Lindzey (Ed.), *Handbook of social psychology,* vol. 1, *Theory and method.* Cambridge, Mass.: Addison-Wesley, 1954.

Saunders, L. *Cultural differences and medical care.* New York: Russell Sage Found., 1954.

Schachter, S. Deviation, rejection, and communication. *J. abnorm. soc. Psychol.,* 1951, **46,** 190-207.

Schachter, S. *The psychology of affiliation: experimental studies of the sources of gregariousness.* Stanford, Calif.: Stanford Univer. Press, 1959.

Schachter, S., Ellertson, N., McBride, Dorothy, and Gregory, Doris. An experimental study of cohesiveness and productivity. *Hum. Relat.,* 1951, **4,** 229-238.

Schachter, S., Nuttin, J., De Monchaux, C., Maucorps, P. H., Osmer, D., Duijker, H., Rommetveit, R., and Israel, J. Cross cultural experiments on threat and rejection. *Hum. Relat.,* 1954, **7,** 403-439.

Schanck, R. L. A study of a community and its groups and institutions conceived of as behaviours of individuals. *Psychol. Monogr.,* 1932, **43,** no. 2.

Schatzman, L., and Strauss, A. L. Social class and modes of communication. *Amer. J. Sociol.,* 1955, **60,** 329-338.

Schroder, H. M., and Hunt, D. E. Dispositional effects upon conformity at different levels of discrepancy. *J. Pers.,* 1958, **26,** 243-258.

Schumpeter, J. *Imperialism and social classes.* New York: Meridian Books, 1955.

Schutz, W. C. What makes groups productive? *Hum. Relat.,* 1955, **8,** 429-465.

Schutz, W. C. *FIRO: a three-dimensional theory of interpersonal behavior.* New York: Rinehart, 1958.

Scott, W. A. Attitude change through reward of verbal behavior. *J. abnorm. soc. Psychol.,* 1957, **55,** 72-75.

Scott, W. A. Attitude change by response reinforcement: replication and extension. *Sociometry,* 1959, **22,** 328-335.

Sears, R. R., Maccoby, Eleanor E., and Levin, H. *Patterns of child rearing.* Evanston, Ill.: Row, Peterson, 1957.

Seashore, S. E. *Group cohesiveness in the industrial work group.* Ann Arbor: Survey Research Center, Institute for Social Research, Univer. of Michigan, 1954.

Secord, P. F. Facial features and inference processes in interpersonal perception. In R. Tagiuri and L. Petrullo (Eds.), *Person perception and interpersonal behavior.* Stanford, Calif.: Stanford Univer. Press, 1958.

Seeman, M. Moral judgment: a study in racial frames of reference. *Amer. sociol. Rev.,* 1947, **12,** 404-411.

Seibert, J. *The influence of television on the election of 1952.* Oxford, Ohio: Miami University (no date).

Shaw, M. E. Some effects of problem complexity upon problem solution efficiency in different communication nets. *J. exp. Psychol.*, 1954, **48**, 211-217.

Shaw, M. E., Rothschild, S. H., and Strickland, J. F. Decision processes in communication nets. *J. abnorm. soc. Psychol.*, 1957, **54**, 323-330.

Sherif, M. A study of some social factors in perception. *Arch. Psychol.*, 1935, no. 187.

Sherif, M. A preliminary experimental study of intergroup relations. In J. H. Rohrer and M. Sherif (Eds.), *Social psychology at the crossroads*. New York: Harper, 1951.

Sherif, M., Harvey, O. J., White, B. J., Hood, W. R., and Sherif, C. W. *Experimental study of positive and negative intergroup attitudes between experimentally produced groups*. Robbers Cave Study. Norman: Univer. of Oklahoma, 1954 (multilithed).

Sherif, M., and Hovland, C. I. Judgmental phenomena and scales of attitude measurement: placement of items with individual choice of number of categories. *J. abnorm. soc. Psychol.*, 1953, **48**, 135-141.

Sherif, M., and Sherif, C. W. The standardization of names. A neglected problem in the study of symbolic behavior. Unpublished manuscript, 1949. Summarized in M. Sherif and C. W. Sherif, *An outline of social psychology*. (Rev. ed.) New York: Harper, 1956.

Sherif, M., White, B. J., and Harvey, O. J. Status in experimentally produced groups. *Amer. J. Sociol.*, 1955, **60**, 370-379.

Shouby, E. The influence of the Arabic language on the psychology of the Arabs. *Middle East J.*, 1951, **5**, 284-302.

Siegel, Alberta E., and Siegel, S. Reference groups, membership groups, and attitude change. *J. abnorm. soc. Psychol.*, 1957, **55**, 360-364.

Simon, H. A. *Administrative behavior*. New York: Macmillan, 1947.

Simon, H. A. Recent advances in organization theory. In *Research frontiers in politics and government*. Washington, D.C.: Brookings, 1955.

Simon, H. A., and Stern, F. The effect of television upon voting behavior in Iowa in the 1952 presidential election. *Amer. polit. Sci. Rev.*, 1955, **49**, 470-477.

Sims, V. M. Factors influencing attitude toward the TVA. *J. abnorm. soc. Psychol.*, 1938, **33**, 34-56.

Singer, J. L., and Goldman, G. D. Experimentally contrasted social atmospheres in group psychotherapy with chronic schizophrenics. *J. soc. Psychol.*, 1954, **40**, 23-37.

Slater, P. E. Contrasting correlates of group size. *Sociometry*, 1958, **21**, 129-139.

Smith, A. *An inquiry into the nature and causes of the wealth of nations*. London: Strahan and Caddell, 1776.

Smith, H. P., and Rosen, Ellen W. Some psychological correlates of world mindedness and authoritarianism. *J. Pers.*, 1958, **26**, 170-183.

Smith, M. B. The personal setting of public opinions: a study of attitudes toward Russia. *Publ. Opin. Quart.*, 1947, **11**, 507-523.

Smith, M. B., Bruner, J. S., and White, R. W. *Opinions and personality*. New York: Wiley, 1956.

Smollet, T. *Humphrey Clinker*, 1771.

Social Science Research Council. *Public reaction to the atomic bomb and world affairs*. Ithaca, N.Y.: Cornell Univer., 1947.

Sorokin, P. A. *Altruistic love: a study of American "good neighbors" and Christian saints*. Boston: Beacon Press, 1950.

South, E. B. Some psychological aspects of committee work. *J. appl. Psychol.*, 1927a, **11**, 348-368.

South, E. B. Some psychological aspects of committee work. *J. Appl. Psychol.*, 1927b, **11**, 437-464.

Spector, A. J. Expectations, fulfillment, and morale. *J. abnorm. soc. Psychol.*, 1956, **52**, 51-56.

Spiro, M. E. *Children of the Kibbutz*. Cambridge, Mass.: Harvard Univer. Press, 1958.

Srole, L. Social dysfunction, personality and social distance attitudes. Paper read before Amer. Sociological Society, 1951.

Starbuck, E. D. *The psychology of religion*. London: Scott, 1899.

Stephan, F. F., and Mishler, E. G. The distribution of participation in small groups: an exponential approximation. *Amer. sociol. Rev.*, 1952, **17**, 598-608.

Stonequist, E. V. *The marginal man*. New York: Scribner, 1937.

Stotland, E., Katz, D., and Patchen, M. The reduction of prejudice through the arousal of self-insight. *J. Pers.*, 1959, **27**, 507-531.

Stott, L. H. Persisting effects of early family experiences upon personality development. *Merrill-Palmer School Quart.*, Detroit, Spring, 1957, vol. 3, no. 3.

Stouffer, S. A., Lumsdaine, A. A., Lumsdaine, M. H., Williams, R. M., Jr., Smith, M. B. Janis, I. L., Star, Shirley A., and Cottrell, L. S., Jr. *The American Soldier*, vol. II, *Combat and its aftermath*. Princeton, N.J.: Princeton Univer. Press, 1949.

Stouffer, S. A., Suchman, E. A., DeVinney, L. C., Star, Shirley A., and Williams, R. M., Jr. *The American soldier*. vol. I, *Adjustment during army life*. Princeton, N.J.: Princeton Univer. Press, 1949.

Stukát, K. Suggestibility: a factorial and experimental analysis. *Acta Psychologica*, Gothoburgensia, II. Stockholm: Almquist & Wiksell, 1958.

Suchman, E. A. The intensity component in attitude and opinion research. In S. A. Stouffer et al., *Measurement and prediction*. Princeton, N.J.: Princeton Univer. Press, 1950a.

Suchman, E. A. The utility of scalogram analysis. In S. A. Stouffer et al., *Measurement and prediction*. Princeton, N.J.: Princeton Univer. Press, 1950b.

Sullivan, H. S. *Conceptions of modern psychiatry*. New York: Norton, 1953.

Sullivan, H. S. *The psychiatric interview*. New York: Norton, 1954.

Sumner, W. G. *Folkways*. New York: Ginn, 1906.

Sumner, W. G., and Keller, A. G. *The science of society*. (4 vols.) New Haven, Conn.: Yale Univer. Press, 1927.

Sutherland, E. H. (Ed.). *The professional thief*. Chicago: Univer. of Chicago Press, 1937.

Swanson, C. E. Predicting who learns factual information from the mass media. In H. Guetzkow (Ed.), *Groups, leadership and men: research in human relations*. Pittsburgh: Carnegie Press, 1951.

Symonds, P. M. *Diagnosing personality and conduct*. New York: Century, 1931.

Tagiuri, R., Bruner, J. S., and Blake, R. R. On the relation between feelings and perception of feelings among members of small groups. In Eleanor E. Maccoby, T. M. Newcomb, and E. L. Hartley (Eds.), *Readings in social psychology*. (3d ed.) New York: Holt, 1958.

Tagiuri, R., Kogan, N., and Bruner, J. S. The transparency of interpersonal choice. *Sociometry*, 1955, **18**, 624-635.

Tannenbaum, P. H. Initial attitude toward source and concept as factors in attitude change through communication. *Publ. Opin. Quart.*, 1956, **20**, 413-425.

Tarde, G. *The laws of imitation*. (Original French ed., 1890.) Transl., New York: Holt, 1903.

Taylor, D. W., Berry, P. C., and Block, C. H. Does group participation when using brainstorming facilitate or inhibit creative thinking? *Adm. Sci. Quart.*, 1958, **3**, 23-47.

Taylor, D. W., and Faust, W. L. Twenty questions: efficiency in problem solving as a function of size of group. *J. exp. Psychol.*, 1952, **44**, 360-368.

Taylor, Janet A. A personality scale of manifest anxiety. *J. abnorm. soc. Psychol.*, 1953, **48**, 285-290.

Telber, Ina. They don't do it our way. *Courier* (UNESCO), 1950, **3**, no. 4.

Telford, C. W. An experimental study of some factors influencing the social attitudes of college students. *J. soc. Psychol.*, 1934, **5**, 421-428.

Terman, L. M. *Concept mastery test manual*. New York: Psychological Corp., 1956.

Terman, L. M., Buttenwieser, P., Ferguson, L. W., Johnson, W. B., and Wilson, D. P. *Psychological factors in marital happiness*. New York: McGraw-Hill, 1938.

Terman, L. M., and Miles, Catherine C. *Sex and personality. Studies in masculinity and femininity*. New York: McGraw-Hill, 1936.

Thelen, H. A. Group dynamics in instruction: principles of least group size. *Sch. Rev.*, 1949, **57**, 139-148.

Thibaut, J. An experimental study of the cohesiveness of underprivileged groups. *Hum. Relat.*, 1950, **3**, 251-278.

Thibaut, J. W., and Kelley, H. H. *The social psychology of groups*. New York: Wiley, 1959.

Thibaut, J. W., and Riecken, H. W. Some determinants and consequences of the perception of social causality. *J. Pers.*, 1955, **24**, 113-133.

Thibaut, J. W., and Strickland, L. H. Psychological set and social conformity. *J. Pers.*, 1956, **25**, 115-129.

Thistlethwaite, D. L., de Haan, H., and Kamenetzky, J. The effects of "directive" and "nondirective" communication procedures on attitudes. *J. abnorm. soc. Psychol.*, 1955, **51**, 107-113.

Thomas, E. J. Effects of facilitative role interdependence on group functioning. *Hum. Relat.*, 1957, **10**, 347-366.

Thomas, W. I. *Primitive behaviour: an introduction to the social sciences*. New York: McGraw-Hill, 1937.

Thomas, W. I., and Znaniecki, F. *The Polish peasant in Europe and America*. (5 vols.) Boston: Badger, 1918-1920.

Thorndike, E. L. The psychology of semantics. *Amer. J. Psychol.*, 1946, **59**, 613-632.

Thurstone, L. L. Attitudes can be measured. *Amer. J. Sociol.*, 1927-1928, **33**, 529-554.

Thurstone, L. L. Theory of attitude measurement. *Psychol. Bull.*, 1929, **36**, 222-241.

Thurstone, L. L. The measurement of social attitudes. *J. abnorm. soc. Psychol.*, 1931, **26**, 249-269.

Thurstone, L. L., and Chave, E. J. *The measurement of attitudes*. Chicago: Univer. of Chicago Press, 1929.

Time, Jan. 24, 1955, p. 80.

Titus, H. E., and Hollander, E. P. The California F-scale in psychological research: 1950-55. *Psychol. Bull.*, 1957, **54**, 47-64.

Toki, K. The leader-follower structure in the school-class. *Jap. J. Psychol.*, 1935, **10**, 27.56. English summary in E. L. Hartley and Ruth E. Hartley, *Fundamentals of social psychology*. New York: Knopf, 1952.

Tolman, E. C. *Purposive behavior in animals and men*. New York: Century, 1932.

Tolman, E. C. *Drives toward war*. New York: Appleton-Century, 1942.

Torgerson, W. S. *Theory and methods of scaling*. New York: Wiley, 1958.

Tresselt, M. E., and Volkmann, J. The production

of uniform opinion by non-social stimulation. *J. abnorm. soc. Psychol.*, 1942, **37**, 234-243.

Triplett, N. The dynamogenic factors in pace-making and competition. *Amer. J. Psychol.*, 1897, **9**, 507-533.

Trotter, W. *Instincts of the herd in peace and war.* (Rev. ed.) London: Unwin, 1920.

Tryon, R. C. Identification of social areas by cluster analysis: a general method with an application to the San Francisco Bay Area. *Univer. Calif. Publ. Psychol.*, 1955a, **8** (1).

Tryon, R. C. Biosocial constancy of urban social areas. Paper read before Amer. Psychological Association, 1955b.

Tryon, R. C. The social dimensions of metropolitan man (revised title). Paper read before Amer. Psychological Association, 1959.

Tuddenham, R. D. The influence upon judgment of a grossly distorted norm. *Tech. Rep.*, no. 2. Contract NR 170-159, Univer. of California, Berkeley, 1957.

Tuddenham, R. D. Some correlates of yielding to a distorted group norm. *Tech. Rep.*, no. 8. Contract NR 170-159, Univer. of California, Berkeley, 1958.

Tuddenham, R. D. The influence upon judgment of the apparent discrepancy between self and others. *J. soc. Psychol.*, 1961, **53**, 69-79.

Tuddenham, R. D., and Macbride, P. The yielding experiment from the subject's point of view. *J. Pers.*, 1959, **27**, 259-271.

Turner, R. H. Preoccupation with competitiveness and social acceptance among American and English college students. *Sociometry*, 1960, **23**, 307-325.

Van Zelst, R. H. Validation of a sociometric re-grouping procedure. *J. abnorm. soc. Psychol.*, 1952, **47**, 299-301.

Vernon, P. E. The validation of civil service observation method in the selection of trained executives. *Occup. Psychol.*, 1948, **22**, 587-594.

Vetter, G. B. The measurement of social and political attitudes and the related personality factors. *J. abnorm. soc. Psychol.*, 1930, **25**, 149-189.

Vigotsky, L. S. Thought and speech. *Psychiatry*, 1939, **2**, 29-54.

Voelker, J. D. Preface in F. McNaughton, *Mennen Williams of Michigan, fighter for progress.* New York: Oceana Publications, 1960.

Vroom, V. H. Some personality determinants of the effects of participation. *J. abnorm. soc. Psychol.*, 1959, **59**, 322-327.

Walker, C. R., and Guest, R. H. *The man on the assembly line.* Cambridge, Mass.: Harvard Univer. Press, 1952.

Walker, E. L., and Heyns, R. W. *An anatomy for conformity.* Englewood Cliffs, N. J.: Prentice-Hall, 1962.

Waller, W. *The sociology of teaching.* New York: Wiley, 1932.

Wallin, P. Cultural contradictions and sex roles: a repeat study. *Amer. sociol. Rev.*, 1950, **15**, 288-293.

Warburton, F. E. Malpighii, the newsletter (circulation 18) of the Malpighian Society of Montreal, vol. 2, no. 2, 14 Jan., 1960.

Warner, W. L., and associates. *Democracy in Jonesville.* New York: Harper, 1949.

Warner, W. L., and Lunt, P. S. *The social life of a modern community.* New Haven, Conn.: Yale Univer. Press, 1941.

Warner, W. L., Meeker, M., and Eels, K. *Social class in America.* Chicago: Science Research, 1949.

Watson, Jeanne. Some social and psychological situations related to change in attitude. *Hum. Relat.*, 1950, **3**, 15-56.

Weiss, W. The relationship between judgments of a communicator's position and extent of opinion change. *J. abnorm. soc. Psychol.*, 1958, **56**, 380-384.

Weiss, W., and Fine, B. J. Opinion change as a function of some interpersonal attributes of the communicatees. *J. abnorm. soc. Psychol.*, 1955, **51**, 246-253.

Welker, W. I. Some determinants of play and exploration in chimpanzees. *J. comp. physiol. Psychol.*, 1956, **49**, 84-89.

Weschler, I. R. The investigation of attitudes toward labor and management by means of the error-choice method. *J. soc. Psychol.*, 1950a, **32**, 51-62.

Weschler, I. R. The personal factor in labor mediation. *Personnel Psychol.*, 1950b, **3**, 113-132.

Weschler, I. R., Kahane, M., and Tannenbaum, R. Assessing organizational effectiveness: job satisfaction, productivity, and morale. In R. Tannenbaum, I. R. Weschler, and F. Massarik, *Leadership and organization: a behavioral science approach.* New York: McGraw-Hill, 1961.

Wever, E. G., and Zener, K. E. The method of absolute judgment in psychophysics. *Psychol. Rev.*, 1928, **35**, 466-493.

White, R. W. Motivation reconsidered: the concept of competence. *Psychol. Rev.*, 1959, **66**, 297-333.

Whiting, J. W. M. The cross-cultural method. In G. Lindzey (Ed.), *Handbook of social psychology*, vol. I. Cambridge, Mass.: Addison-Wesley, 1954.

Whiting, J. W. M., and Child, I. L. *Child training and personality: a cross-cultural study.* New Haven, Conn.: Yale Univer. Press, 1953.

Whorf, B. L. In J. B. Carroll (Ed.), *Language, thought, and reality.* New York: Wiley, 1956.

Whyte, W. F. Corner boys: a study of clique behavior. *Amer. J. Sociol.*, 1941, **46**, 647-664.

Whyte, W. F. *Street corner society; the social structure of an Italian slum.* Chicago: Univer. of Chicago Press, 1943.

Whyte, W. F. *Human relations in the restaurant industry.* New York: McGraw-Hill, 1948.

Whyte, W. F. Observational field-work methods. In Marie Jahoda, M. Deutsch, and S. W. Cook (Eds.), *Research methods in social relations,* vol. II. (1st ed.) New York: Dryden, 1951.

Wilkening, E. A. Informal leaders and innovators in farm practices. *Rural Sociol.,* 1952, **17,** 272-275.

Wilkens, L., and Richter, C. P. A great craving for salt by a child with cortico-adrenal insufficiency. *J. Amer. med. Ass.,* 1940, **114,** 866-868.

Williams, R. M. *American society: a sociological interpretation.* New York: Knopf, 1951.

Wishner, J. Reanalysis of "Impressions of Personality." *Psychol. Rev.,* 1960, **67,** 96-112.

Withey, S. B. Consistency of immediate and delayed reports of financial data. Unpublished doctoral thesis, Univer. of Michigan, 1952. Cited in A. A. Campbell and G. Katona, *The sample survey: a technique for social science research.* In L. Festinger and D. Katz (Eds.), *Research methods in the behavioral sciences.* New York: Dryden, 1953.

Wolfenstein, Martha. Trends in infant care. *Amer. J. Orthopsychiat.,* 1953, **23,** 120-130.

Woodworth, R. S. *Experimental psychology.* New York: Holt, 1938.

Worthy, J. C. Organizational structure and employee morale. *Amer. sociol. Rev.,* 1950, **15,** 169-179.

Wright, C. R., and Hyman, H. H. Voluntary association memberships of American adults: evidence from national sample surveys. *Amer. sociol. Rev.,* 1958, **23,** 284-294.

Wright, M. E. The influence of frustration upon the social relations of young children. *Charact. and Pers.,* 1943-1944, **12,** 111-122.

Wundt, W. *Beiträge zur theorie der Sinneswahrehmung.* Leipzig: Winter, 1862.

Wundt, W. *Völkerpsychologie der Entwicklunge setze vor Sprache, Mythus und Sitte.* (10 vols.) Leipzig: Engelmann, 1900-1920. Transl. (vols. 1-3), *Elements of folk psychology.* New York: Macmillan, 1916.

Wurster, C. R., and Bass, B. M. Situational tests, IV. Validity of leaderless group discussions among strangers. *Educ. psychol. Measm,* 1953, **13,** 122-132.

Zeigarnik, B. Das Behalten erledigter und unerledigter Handlungen, III, The memory of completed and uncompleted actions. *Psychol. Forsch.,* 1927, **9,** 1-85.

Zelditch, M. Role differentiation in the nuclear family: a comparative study. In T. Parsons, R. F. Bales, *et al., Family, socialization, and interaction process.* Glencoe, Ill.: Free Press, 1955.

Ziller, R. C. Leader acceptance of responsibility for group action under conditions of uncertainty and risk. *Amer. Psychologist,* 1955, **10,** 475-476 (abstract).

Zillig, M. Einstellung und Aussage. *Z. Psychol.,* 1928, **106,** 58-106.

Coleman, A. L., 438, 541
Coleman, J. F., 509–510, 534
College of the City of New York, 195
Collins, M. E., 256–257, 535
Colorado, University of, 59, 261, 285
Columbia University, 127, 195, 287
Common Cold Research Unit (England), 8
Comte, A., 6, 534
Congress of Industrial Organization, 279
Connecticut, University of, 499
Connolly, C., 75
Consalvi, C., 520, 537
Converse, P., 146, 200, 251, 314–315, 533, 534
Cook, S. W., 543, 548
Cook, T. H., 341, 534
Cooley, C. H., 82, 129, 534
Coombs, C. H., 177, 534
Coons, A. E., 537
Cooper, J. B., 141, 534
Cornell University, 317, 413, 483
Cottrell, L. S., 189, 199, 534, 545
Couch, A., 533
Coughlin, Father, 227
Cousins, A. N., 497, 534
Cox, E. E., 279
Cramer, M. R., 12, 543
Crespi, L. P., 154, 534
Cressey, P. G., 502, 534
Crockett, W. H., 400, 424, 426, 533, 534
Cronbach, L. J., 62, 144, 534, 536
Crosby, B., 377
Crow, W. J., 59, 534
Crutchfield, R. S., 172, 508–528, 534, 535, 540
Culbertson, F. M., 259, 535
Curle, A., 494–495, 535

Dashiell, J. F., 540
Davis, A., 19, 378, 535
Davis, K., 288, 535
Davis, M., 188, 535
Davitz, J. R., 127, 385, 535
Dearborn, D. C., 22, 535
De Fleur, M. L., 164, 535
De Lange, M., 532
De Monchaux, C., 544
Dembo, T., 37, 120, 531, 540
Denny, M. R., 49, 50, 543
Denver, University of, 284
Deutsch, M., 256–257, 479, 511, 535, 543, 548
De Vinney, L. C., 545
De Vries, P., 399, 535
Dewey, J., 542
Dexter, E. S., 199, 535
Dickson, W. J., 289, 407, 543
Dill, W. R., 469, 537
Di Vesta, F. J., 521, 528, 535
Dobyns, H. F., 483, 543
Doll, P. A., 532
Dollard, J., 542
Doob, L. W., 542
Douglass, H. P., 398, 535
Douvan, E., 330, 333, 535
Dubin, S. S., 62, 535
Dudycha, G. J., 113, 535
Duffus, R. L., 23, 535

Duijker, H., 544
Duke University, 521
Duncker, K., 27, 535

Eberhart, S., 189, 534
Edgerton, R. B., 367–368, 536
Edinburgh, University of, 21
Educational Testing Service, 428
Edwards, A. L., 62, 153, 155, 178, 535
Eels, K., 315, 547
Eichmann, A., 487
Eisenhower, D. D., 146, 168, 174–175, 196, 238, 391
Elkin, F., 304, 535
Ellertson, N., 544
Estes, E. H., 533
Estes, S. G., 57, 535

Faust, W. L., 462, 546
Federal Mediation and Conciliation Service, 166
Feldman, H., 476, 535
Ferguson, L. W., 145, 150, 157, 535–546
Feshbach, S., 25, 244, 246, 535, 538
Festinger, L., 42, 190, 218, 261, 262, 269, 395, 404, 410, 535, 536, 548
Fiedler, F. E., 475, 477, 536
Field, P. B., 221, 223, 538, 539
Fine, B. J., 222, 547
Fishman, J., 499
Fleischman, D. E., 417, 536
Floor, L. G., 426, 539
Foa, U. G., 256, 537
Foley, J. P., Jr., 21, 536
Force, M., 294, 536
Force, R. W., 294, 536
Forlano, G., 150, 543
Fortune, R., 360, 536
Fouriezos, N. T., 384, 478, 536
Franco, F., 252
Franklin, M., 399, 540
French, J. R. P., 479–481, 534, 536
French, V. V., 201, 536
Frenkel-Brunswik, E., 46, 67, 185–186, 203, 531, 536
Freud, S., 122, 129
Frick, J. W., 537
Friedman, E., 503, 536
Fromm, E., 430, 536
Froscher, H. B., 543

Gage, N. L., 62, 536
Gale, H., 536
Gallup, G., 7
Gandhi, M. K., 70
Gardner, B. B., 19, 535
Gardner, G., 476, 531
Gardner, G. H., 343, 536
Gardner, M. R., 19, 535
Gaudet, H., 195, 233, 234, 540
Gerard, H. B., 464, 511, 519, 535, 536
Ghiselli, E. E., 419, 466, 536
Gibb, C. A., 446, 460, 536
Gibb, J. R., 396, 536
Gilbert, G. M., 194, 536
Gilbert, W. S., 497, 536
Gilchrist, J. C., 469, 536
Goebbels, P. J., 227
Goldman, G. D. 437, 545
Goldman, I., 96, 536

Goldschmidt, W., 367–368, 536
Goldston, J., 467, 539
Gollin, E. S., 52, 536
Goode, W. J., 504–505, 531
Goodenough, F. L., 282, 536
Goodnow, J. J., 40, 533
Gordon, M. M., 499, 536
Gothenburg, University of, 527
Gough, H. G., 114, 524, 526, 536
Graham, E., 223, 224, 539, 540
Greer, F. L., 400, 536
Gregory, D., 544
Gross, N., 493, 537
Grunes, W. F., 47, 537
Guest, R. H., 484, 547
Guetzkow, H. S., 70, 76, 384, 478, 531, 536, 537, 539, 546
Guilford, J. P., 46, 57, 106, 107, 111, 113, 537
Gulliksen, H., 159, 537
Gurin, G., 174–175, 193, 196, 235, 237, 426, 533, 539
Guthrie, E. R., 128, 537
Guttman, L., 131, 154–157, 178, 256, 369, 537

Haan, H. de, 243, 546
Haefner, D., 533
Haire, M., 47, 165, 537
Hallowell, A. I., 303, 537
Halpin, A. W., 432, 433, 537
Hamblin, R. L., 427, 537
Hamilton, W., 21
Hammond, K. R., 59, 161, 534, 537
Hammond, W. A., 531
Harary, F., 42, 187, 230, 533, 543
Harding, J., 258, 537
Hare, A. P., 459–460, 462, 537
Hartley, E. L., 138, 195, 436, 443, 451, 531, 533, 534, 537, 540, 541, 543, 544, 546
Hartley, R. E., 451, 546
Harvard University, 33, 36, 39, 40, 192, 208, 277, 292, 499
Harvey, O. J., 81, 82, 240, 520, 537, 538, 545
Harwood Manufacturing Company (Virginia), 481
Hastorf, A. H., 61–62, 532
Haveman, E., 195, 537
Haverford College, 443
Havighurst, R. J., 378, 503, 535, 536
Hayes, S. P., Jr., 532, 540
Haythorn, W., 423, 447, 463, 464, 533, 537
Hebb, D. O., 87, 537
Hebrew University, 256
Heider, F., 27, 28, 41, 66, 187, 218, 404, 537
Heinicke, C., 467, 537
Helson, H., 32, 66, 522, 532, 537
Hemphill, J. K., 428, 462, 537
Henry, W. E., 491, 537
Henschel, A., 70, 539
Heron, W., 87, 99, 532
Herskovits, F. S., 359–360, 537
Herskovits, M. J., 356, 359–360, 537
Hewitt, D., 459, 537
Heyns, R. W., 529
Hiller, E. T., 304, 538
Himmelstrand, U., 148, 538

Mead, M., 283, 360, 500, 523, 541
Meeker, M., 315, 547
Meerloo, J. A. M., 287, 542
Meirowitz, B., 533
Melikian, L. H., 343, 542
Mérei, F., 442, 542
Merrifield, P. R., 537
Merton, R. K., 10, 334–335, 409–410, 502, 542
Meyer, C. T., 121, 542
Michigan State University, 49
Michigan, University of, 145, 174, 187, 200, 254, 314–315, 330, 333, 352, 411, 424, 427, 473, 475, 478, 481
Michotte, A., 29–30, 542
Mickelsen, O., 70, 539
Miles, C. C., 500, 546
Milgram, S., 524–525, 542
Miller, D. R., 373–375, 542
Miller, G. A., 274, 542
Miller, L. E., 396, 536
Miller, N. E., 459, 542
Miller, R. E., 110, 542
Miller, W. E., 146, 174–175, 193, 196, 235, 237, 533
Mills, J., 395, 531
Mills, T. M., 531
Milton, O., 439, 542
Minnesota, University of, 52, 70, 282
Mirsky, A. F., 108–109, 544
Mirsky, I. A., 110, 542
Mishler, E. G., 460, 545
Mitnick, L. L., 227–228, 542
Moeller, G., 524, 531
Moreno, J. L., 390, 393, 421, 542
Morris, D. P., 112, 542
Morrissette, J. O., 187, 542
Morse, N. C., 473, 539, 542
Mosier, C. I., 284, 542
Moustache (Navaho Chief), 80, 82
Mouton, J. S., 509–510, 522, 532, 534
Mowrer, O. H., 120, 542
Mudd, E. H., 543
Mulder, M., 470–471, 542
Murchison, C., 540
Murdock, G. P., 309–310, 344, 361, 542
Murphy, G., 149, 157, 160, 531, 542
Murphy, J. V., 110, 542
Murphy, L. B., 97, 160, 531, 542
Murray, H. A., 90, 351, 540, 544
Mussen, P. H., 258, 542
Myrdal, G., 195

Nadel, S. F., 342, 542
Nadler, E. B., 526, 542
Napoleon Bonaparte, 96
Nash, D. J., 490, 542
Nasser, G. A., 391
Natal, University of, 208
National Conference of Christians and Jews, 215
National Opinion Research Center, 92, 175
Neel, R. G., 62, 535
Nehru, J., 391
Nelson, J. R., 481, 536
Nevada, University of, 64
Newcomb, T. M., 42, 123, 138, 160, 251–255, 411–412, 436, 443, 494,

496, 531, 533, 534, 537, 540–544, 546
Newcomer, M., 329, 542
New York City Health Department, 267
New York Edison Company, 159
New York University, 467
Nijmegen, University of, 60
Nisbet, R. A., 10, 542
Nixon, M., 446, 533
Nixon, R. M., 235
Nkrumah, K., 391
Norsworthy, N., 57, 59, 542
Northwestern University, 359
Nunnally, J. C., Jr., 281, 542
Nuttin, J., 544

Office of Strategic Services (OSS), 447
Oklahoma, University of, 82, 306
Osborn, A. F., 488
Osgood, C. E., 42, 167–169, 179, 219, 279–281, 543
Oslo, Military Academy of, 211
  Naval Academy of, 211
Osmer, D., 544
Otis, N. B., 126, 543
Oxford University, 476

Parfit, J., 459, 537
Parsons, T., 531, 548
Patchen, M., 266, 545
Peak, H., 238, 437, 543
Peltz, W. L., 464, 543
Pelz, D. C., 472, 473, 478, 543
Pennington, D. F., 230, 480, 543
Pennsylvania, University of, 25
Pepitone, A., 24, 543
Perlmutter, H. V., 33, 533
Peter, H. W., 532
Petrullo, L., 64, 428, 532, 537, 544
Pettigrew, T. F., 12, 40, 208, 543
Piaget, J., 17, 18, 273–274, 276, 278, 543
Pintner, R., 150, 543
Pittsburgh, University of, 110
Plato, 6, 543
Platts, G. N., 396, 536
Polansky, N., 541
Pomeroy, W. B., 334, 539
Porter, L. W., 461, 543
Poser, E. G., 397, 540
Postman, L. J., 21, 543
Potter, E. H., 362, 534
Powdermaker, H., 94, 543
Preston, M. G., 464, 543
Pribram, K. H., 108–109, 544
Prince, M., 7
Princeton University, 194, 195
Pritzker, H. A., 239, 538
Proctor, C. H., 390–392, 543
Prudential Insurance Company, 473

Radcliffe College, 277
Rasmussen, G., 352, 543
Ravel, M., 492
Raven, B. H., 400, 543
Redfield, R., 358, 360, 543
Redl, F., 184, 541, 543
Redlich, F. C., 332, 333, 538
Reserve Officers Training Corps, 447
Rice University (Texas), 343

Richards, C. B., 483, 543
Richards, J. M., 58, 534
Richter, C. P., 74, 548
Riecken, H. W., 53, 190, 535, 546
Riesman, D., 192, 543
Rietsema, J., 400, 543
Rife, D., 539
Riley, J. W., Jr., 234, 347–348, 441, 533, 543
Riley, M. W., 347–348, 440–441, 533, 543
Roberts, J. M., 297, 298, 540
Rodrigues, J. S., Jr., 40
Roethlisberger, F. J., 289, 407, 543
Rogers, C. R., 96, 543
Rohrer, J. H., 545
Rokeach, M., 40, 46–50, 543, 544
Rommetveit, R., 404, 544
Roosevelt, F. D., 97, 168, 251, 252, 443
Rosander, A. C., 150, 544
Roseborough, M., 531
Rosen, B. C., 330, 331, 544
Rosen, E. W., 207, 545
Rosen, S., 541
Rosenberg, M., 130–133, 503, 544
Rosenberg, M. J., 43, 44, 181, 544
Rosenthal, D., 401, 544
Rosner, S., 522, 544
Ross, E. A., 7, 544
Ross, I. C., 481, 536
Rossi, A. S., 197, 544
Rossi, P. H., 197, 544
Rosvold, H. E., 108–109, 544
Rothschild, S. H., 469, 545
Ruesch, J., 104, 375–378, 544
Rutgers University, 234, 440

Saltzstein, H. D., 519, 538
Salvation Army, 240
Sanford, F. H., 292–293, 443, 544
Sanford, R. N., 185–186, 203, 531, 536
San Jose State College, 141
Sapir, E., 129, 294–295, 354, 544
Sarbin, T. R., 489, 544
Sargent, S. S., 540
Sarnoff, I., 263, 539
Saunders, D. R., 464, 534
Saunders, L., 285, 544
Schachter, S., 88, 91, 93, 190, 401, 407, 410, 515, 535, 536, 544
Schanck, R. L., 249, 544
Schatzman, L., 295, 544
Schneider, D. M., 351, 540, 544
Schramm, W., 234, 543
Schroder, H. M., 518, 544
Schumpeter, J., 328, 544
Schutz, W. C., 464, 465, 544
Schweitzer, A., 68
Scott, T. H., 87, 99, 532
Scott, W. A., 261, 544
Sears, R. R., 20, 317, 378, 538, 542, 544
Sears, Roebuck and Company, 462
Seashore, S. E., 400, 459, 544
Secord, P. F., 63, 64, 544
Seeman, M., 167, 544
Seibert, J., 237–238, 544
Shaw, D. M., 533
Shaw, M. E., 468–469, 536, 545

SUBJECT INDEX

Entries marked by an asterisk are Chapter Glossary terms.

Absenteeism, relation to group cohesiveness, 459
Accepting of others, interpersonal response trait of, 106–107
*Accessory group goal, 420
Acculturation to American core culture, 375–378
Achievement want, measurement of, 90
social class difference in, 330, 331
*Acquisitive want, 100
Acquisitive want, 93–95
in communal societies, 95
Action patterns, relation to behavior settings in "Midwest," 370–372
*Action tendency component of attitude, 177
*Adaptation level, 66
Adaptation level, 32, 34
*Affiliation want, 100
Affiliation want, 89–93
and anxiety, 91, 93
and birth order, 91
and frequency of organizational membership, 92
and group membership, 394
*Aggression, 134
Aggression, defense mechanism of, 120
latent, as factor in internationalist attitudes, 212
and prejudice, 183–184
social class differences in expression of, 374–375
Aggressiveness, interpersonal response trait of, 106–107
Allport-Vernon Study of Values in study of personality and religious attitudes, 201
*Altruistic want, 100
Altruistic want, 97, 99
American society, core culture of, 375–378
occupational subcultures in, 372–374
social class subcultures in, 372–375
American town, culture of, 368–372
Anthropology, use of field method in, 356, 358–360
Anticipatory socialization, 334
Anti-democratic ideology, and education, 204
F scale as measure of, 201–202
Anti-Semitism, consistency of, 143–144
economic and political dissatisfaction in, 183, 184
generality of, 201
measure of, 201
personality factors in, 201–203

Anti-Semitism, repression and projection in, 185–186
(*See also* Ethnocentrism; Prejudice)
Anxiety, and affiliation want, 91, 93
and conformity, 521, 526
and pseudo-communication, 291
Applied social psychologist, role and research of, 10–11
Arabic (people and language), 290, 293, 340, 343
Arapesh (New Guinea tribe), 360
Arkansas, 295
Arousal of wants (*see* Wants, arousal of)
Ascendance, interpersonal response trait of, 106–107, 111
Ashanti (West African tribe), 344
*Assimilation, 66
Assimilation effect in perception, 31
Atomic energy, Acheson-Lilienthal report on, 175
*Attitude, 177
Attitude, authoritarian (*see* Authoritarian attitude)
components of, 140–142
definition of, 139
measurement of, 147–177
attitude scales in, 147–160, 162–164
problems involved in, 174–177
special techniques in, 161, 164–169
survey interview in, 169–175
objects of, 140
of opinion leaders, toward China, 5
toward India, 5
reasons for invalid, 188–190
resistance to change of self-anchored, 239–240
and self-concept, 239–240
similarity in, as factor in group formation, 411–412
in social areas, 324–325
typology, 145
Attitude change, 215–268
and amount of change advocated, 239–240
in self-involved attitudes, 239–240
in superficial attitudes, 239
and attractiveness of communicator, 231–232
and centrality of group norm, 247
and change, in instrumental value of object, 238
in membership groups, 246–248
in reference groups, 248
and college education, 251–255

Attitude change, communication situation in, 226–231
and conclusion drawing by communicator, 242–243
congruent, 216
and credibility of communicator, 231
and effectiveness of group monitoring system, 247–248
and enforced contact with object, 253–259
and enforced role playing, 259–261
and extremeness of attitude, 238–239
and form and content of persuasive communication, 238–246
and group affiliations of communicator, 232–233
group audience in, 227–228
and group characteristics, 247–250
and group cohesiveness, 247
group decision in, 228–231
and group support, 268
incongruent, 215
information in, 226–246
and informational support, 268
and intensity of fear appeal, 244, 246
and medium of persuasive communication, 233–238
multiple factors in, 266–268
one-sided vs. two-sided messages in, 240–242
and order of arguments in persuasive communications, 242–245
and personality change, 263–266
and prestige of communicator, 267
principles of congruent and incongruent, 216
and source of information, 231–238
and theory of cognitive dissonance, 261–262
word-of-mouth communications in, 233–234
*Attitude cluster, 177–178
Attitude cluster, 145–146
consonance of, 146
and attitude modifiability, 219
*Attitude constellation, 178
Attitude constellation, 144
Attitude development, 180–213
group beliefs in, 191, 194–195
group norms in, 193
group values in, 192–193
information in, 186–190
personality in, 199–213
primary groups in, 193, 195–196
reference groups in, 197
wants in, 181–186

*Attitude interconnectedness, 178
Attitude modifiability, 216–225
  and centrality of related values, 220
  and characteristics of existing attitude, 216–220
  and cognitive needs, 223
  and cognitive styles, 223
  and consistency of existing attitude, 217, 218
  and consonance of attitude cluster, 219
  and extremeness of existing attitude, 217
  and general persuasibility, 221, 223
  and group support, 223–225
  and intelligence, 220–221
  and interconnectedness of existing attitude, 217–219
  and multiplexity of existing attitude, 217
  and personality factors, 220–224
  and self-defensiveness, 223
  and strength and number of wants served, 219–220
  and valuation of group membership, 224–225
Attitude scales, criteria for selection of items, 147–148
  cumulative scale, 154–155
  definition of, 147
  disguised techniques, 161, 164–167
  equal-appearing interval scale, 150–153
  in measuring attitudes, 147–160, 162–164
  neutral region of, 155–158
  reliability of, 157, 159
  scale-discrimination technique, 155
  social-distance scale, 153–154
  in study of cultures, 365, 369
  summated ratings scale, 153
  types of items, 149–150
  validity of, 159–160, 162–164
Attitude Sphere for study of social areas, 324
Attitude system, 139–140
  consistency of, 142–145
Australia, 171
Authoritarian attitude, among Arabs of Middle East, 343
  and conformity-proneness, 526
  and decision making in supervisions, 482
*Authoritarian leadership, 452
Authoritarian leadership, 434–438
  emotional insecurity in acceptance of, 437
  stress situations favoring acceptance of, 437–438
  susceptibility to, 437–438
*Authoritarian personality, 213
Authorities as sources of information, 188–189
Authority, reaction to, and enforced contact upon attitude change, 258–259
*Autism, 134
Autism, defense mechanism of, 123
Autokinetic movement, and group effects on social norms, 513
*Autokinetic phenomenon, 529

*Balance theory, 66
Balance theory, 41–44
Bales category system, 385
Bay Area cities (California), 321–326
Behavior settings in "Midwest," 368–372
Beliefs, of cultures and societies, 349–351
  of group, 402–403
    and attitude development, 191, 194–195 resistance to change of, 403 sources of, 402–403
Birmingham (England), 336
Blacky Pictures Test as measure of latent aggression in internationalist attitudes, 212–213
Boomerang effect, 239
Boston, 378, 379, 387
Brainstorming, 488–489
Britain, 171, 283, 328, 342, 391, 494
British New Guinea, 358
Bureaucracy, definition of, 409–410
  leadership style in, 440–441
Bureaucrat role, effect on personality, 502–503
Bush Negroes, use of field method in study of, 359–360
Business leaders, social origins of, 329

California F scale, 201–212
  review of studies using, 205
  in study, of authoritarian attitudes in Middle East, 343
    of conformity, 526 of preferences for political leaders, 440 of validity of semantic differential as attitude measure, 169
*Category-system method, 420
Category-system method for study of groups, 384–388
Catholics, 138, 197, 198, 200, 251, 253, 343, 411, 414, 437, 496
*Causal system, 66
Cause and effect, perception of, complex stimulus determinants of, 28–30
  proximity in, 27
  similarity in, 27–28
  social implications of, 28
Change of attitudes (see Attitude change)
Change of groups (see Group, changes in)
Chicago, 144, 378, 379, 483
Child-training, changes in practices over time, 378–379
  effects of, on cultural beliefs, 363
  occupational-status differences in, 373–374
  social class differences in, 317
Children, in behavior settings of "Midwest," 370–371
  confusion of word and object in, 276, 278
  in cultural milieu of "Midwest," 372
  curiosity arousal in, 100–101
  education of, in England, 336
  effect of group therapy on social attitudes of, 264–265
  effect of language on cognition in, 299–302

Children, effects of training on response to frustration in, 127
  egocentric perception in, 18
  frustration and regression in, 120–121
  parental behavior and aggressiveness in, 121
  preference for easy vs. difficult goals, 71–72
  responses to frustration and strength of wants in, 126
  social class differences in defense mechanisms of, 374–375
  social and egocentric speech in, 273–274
  social episodes in "Midwest," 309
  special language in use of toys by, 306
  status striving in, 330, 331
  sympathetic behavior in, 97
Chimpanzees, arousal of curiosity in, 98
  want strength and problem solving, 35, 37
China, attitudes toward, 5
Chinese, 150, 344
Church, Protestant (see Protestants)
Cincinnati, 237
Classroom, analysis of "culture" of, 362
Closed-mindedness, 46–50
Cluster, attitude (see Attitude cluster)
Cognition, 17–67
  changes in, 34–51
  disorganization of, under conformity pressures, 521–522
  as influenced by language, 294–303
  and occupational choice, 130
  part-whole principle governing, 30–32
  selective organization of, 20–25
    in executives, 22 personal factors in, 21–23 social implications of, 23–24 stimulus factors in, 20–21
  and want arousal, 86–87
Cognitive change, 34–51
  adaptiveness of, and perception of block, 37
    and want strength, 35–37
  and changes in wants, 34–35
    social implications of, 37
  and nature of cognitive system, 42, 44–45
  personality factors in, 46–50
    closed-mindedness, 46–50 intellectual ability, 46 intolerance of ambiguity, 46
  resistance to, 44–45, 47
  and responses to blocking, 50
*Cognitive component of attitude, 178
*Cognitive consonance, 66
*Cognitive dissonance, 269
Cognitive dissonance, and attitude change, 261–262 and conformity pressures, 516 theory of, 261
*Cognitive interconnectedness, 66
*Cognitive multiplexity, 66
Cognitive needs and attitude modifiability, 223

Cognitive resolution of conformity pressures, 516–517
*Cognitive selectivity, 66
Cognitive style, and attitude modifiability, 223
and category width, 40
*Cognitive system, 66
Cognitive systems, 25–34, 38–46
characteristics of, 38–42
consonance, 38, 40–42
interconnectedness, 42
multiplexity, 38–40
development of, 25–30
grouping in, 26–27 learning and cultural influences in, 26–27 stimulus factors in, 26
*Cognitive world, 66
Cognitive world, definition of, 17
determinants of, 17–18
errors in describing, 19–20
*Cohesiveness, 420
Cohesiveness of group (see Group cohesiveness)
College education, effect on political-economic attitudes, 251–255
Commitment, public, as factor in resistance to counterpropaganda, 228–229
Common cold, social psychology of, in chicks, 8
*Communication, 307
Communication, 273–307
accuracy of, and common wants and cognitions, 288–289
and cultural barriers, 283–286 judging, 288
definition of, 275
failures of, in United Nations, 346
and functions of words, 275–278
nature of process of, 287–288
pattern in group, and status hierarchy, 265–467
persuasive, amount of change advocated in, and amount of attitude change, 239–240
form and content of, and attitude change, 238–246 medium of, and attitude change, 233–246 one-sided vs. two-sided, and attitude change, 240–242 order of arguments in, and attitude change, 242–245 situation, in attitude change, 226–231 word-of-mouth, in attitude change, 233–234
and pseudo-communication, 289–291
two-step flow of, 234
(See also Language)
*Communication net, 485
Communication net, efficiency of, in problem-solving, 468–471
Communicator, attractiveness of, and attitude change, 232
conclusion drawing by, and attitude change, 242–243
credibility of, and attitude change, 231–232
group affiliations of, and attitude change, 232–233
prestige of, and attitude change, 267
Communist party (China), 515

Communist party (United States), 181, 251, 252
Communists (North Korea), 234
Communities as units of society, 308–310
Community participation and social status, 375, 376
Compartmentalization in role conflict, 496
Competition and group productivity, 479
Competiveness, among English and American students, 369
interpersonal response trait of, 106–107
Components of attitude (see Attitude, components of)
Concept Mastery Test, correlated with conformity scores, 526
Conflict of roles (see Role conflict)
*Conforming, "expedient," 529
Conforming, "expedient" vs. "true," 506
*Conformity, 529
Conformity, 504–529
anxiety and, 521, 526
authoritative confirmation or repudiation of group and, 518–519
in business executives, 461
and cognitive dissonance, 516
cultural effects on, 523, 524
distinguished from conventionality, 505–506
effect of feedback of information, 517–519
effect of reward for being right, 520–521
emotional factors in, 521–522
experimental findings on, 508–511
experimental measurement of, 507–512
Asch technique in, 507–508, 511–512 Crutchfield technique in, 508–509, 511–512
generalization of effects of group pressure on, 518–519
individual differences in, 510, 522–525
meaning and nature of, 505–507
and military promotion, 334, 335
motivational factors in, 519–521
nationality differences in, 524–525
past experience and susceptibility to, 523
personality factors in, 525–529
psychological processes involved in, 515–522
related to certainty on issue, 509–510
sex differences in, 523–525
and shifts in certainty of judgment, 519
situational factors governing, 512–515
composition of group, 514 extremeness of group consensus, 515 general social context, 515 size of group, 512–514 strength of group coercion, 515 unanimity of group consensus, 514–515

Conformity, and suggestibility, 526, 527
as "trait of person," 507, 522
as "trait of situation," 507
Conformity pressure, modes of cognitive resolution of, 516–517
*Conformity-proneness, 529
Conformity-proneness as interpersonal response trait, 522–523
*Congruent atttiude change, 269
Congruent attitude change, 216
*Connotative meaning, 307
Conservatism, political, personality in development of, 205, 208–210
and political partisanship, 210–211
Consideration dimension of leader behavior, 432–433
*Consideration leadership dimension, 452
*Consistency, trait, 134
*Consistency of attitude system, 178
Consistency of attitude system, 142–145
and attitude modifiability, 217, 218
in multiplexity, 144–145
in valence, 143–144
Consistency of interpersonal response traits, 113
*Consonance of attitude cluster, 178
Consonance of attitude cluster, 146
and attitude modifiability, 219
Consonance of cognitive system, 38, 40–42
Constellation of attitudes, 144
interconnectedness in, 144–146
Contact with Negroes, enforced, effect on racial attitudes, 253–259
*Content analysis, 380
Content analysis, of classroom "culture," 362
of culture, 361
of German and American plays, 363
method of, 360–361
*Contrast, 67
Contrast effect in perception, 31–32
Conventionality, distinguished from conformity, 505–506
Cooperation, and group productivity, 479
Cooperativeness, and conformity, 520–521
*Core culture, 380
*Counterformity, 529
Counterformity, 506–507
Counterpropaganda, resistance to, and one-sided vs. two-sided persuasive communications, 241–242
and public commitment, 228–229
Creative groups, distribution of participation in, 460–461
leadership style in, 472–475
productivity of, 462–463
size and effectiveness of, 459, 460
Creative thinking, brainstorming in, 488–489
Creativity, effect of strange group on, 490
*Cross-cultual method, 380
Cross-cultural method, 361–363
Cuba, 391
*Cultural beliefs, 380

Cultural beliefs, 349–351
Cultural differences and communication failure, 346
Cultural "elaboration" of sex roles 500–501
*Cultural norms, 380
Cultural norms, 351–353
 for sexual behavior, 344
*Cultural premises, 380
Cultural premises, 353–354
*Cultural values, 380
Cultural values, 349–351
 methods of ascertaining, 350–351
 projective test of, among Menomini, 367
*Culture, 380
Culture, 339–380
 borrowed from other cultures, 345
 change, 378–379
 and child-training practices, 363
 complex relations of, to individual, 355
 constituents of, 344, 346–355
 core, of Americans, 375–378
 as determinant of cognitive grouping, 26–27
 determinants of, 341–342, 344
 effects of, on authoritarian attitudes, 343
 on conformity-proneness, 523, 524–525 on memory, 342 on perception, 340–341
 explicit, 346–349
 implicit, 346, 349–353
 and meaning of words, 281–286
 methods for study of, 355–368
  attitude scales, 365, 369 content analysis, 360–363 cross-cultural method, 361–363 factor analysis, 364–365 field method, 356, 358–360 projective techniques, 365, 367–368
 of "Midwest," 368–372
 and occupational subcultures, 372–374
 patterns of, 354–355
 reciprocal relation of to language, 293–303
 and social class subcultures, 372–375
 transmission of, through language, 303–307
Cumulative attitude scale, 154–155
 reliability of, 159
 undimensional property of, 155
*Cumulative scaling method, 178
*Curiosity want, 100–101
Curiosity want, 99–101
 arousal of, in chimpanzees, 98
 stimuli effective in arousing, 100–101

Dayton (Ohio), 237
Decatur (Illinois), 233
Defense mechanisms (see Self-defense mechanisms)
*Democratic leadership, 453
Democratic leadership, 435–437
 (See also Leadership)
Democratic party (United States), 146, 168, 174–175, 195, 196, 235, 237, 238, 251, 252, 324

Demography Sphere for study of social areas, 321
*Denotative meaning, 307
Desegregation of Negroes, locus of resistance to, 12
 (See also Negroes)
Detroit, 373, 379, 504
Disguised techniques of attitude measurement, 161, 164–167
Dissonance, theory of cognitive (see Cognitive dissonance)
Dogmatism Scale, 47–48
Dominance, effect of avoidance training on, 110
 effect of brain lesions on, 108–109
 interpersonal response trait of, 106–107
Doodlebug problem, 48–50

Education, and antidemocratic ideology, 204
 and community participation, 376
 opportunities for, in England, 336
 and response to one-sided vs. two-sided persuasive communications, 241
 stratification of U.S. population by, 314
Effectiveness of groups (see Group effectiveness)
Egocentric perception, 18
Egypt, 391
Elmira (New York), 195
Emotion and cognitive distortion, 23, 25
Emotional factors in conformity, 521–522
England (see Britain)
English (people and language), 143, 283, 285, 290, 293, 294, 296–298, 300–302, 336, 369, 376
*Equal-appearing-interval scaling method, 178
Equal-appearing intervals attitude scale, 150–153
 effect of judges' attitudes on scale values, 150, 152–153
 reliability of, 157
Erie County (Ohio), 195
Error-choice attitude scale, 161, 164, 166
Eskimo (people and language), 293, 296, 297
*Ethnocentrism, 213
Ethnocentrism, personality factors in development of, 201–205
Ethnocentrism scale, 201
 in study of attitude change, 248–249
Eugene (Oregon), 379
Executives, cognitive selectivity in, 22
 personality and role of, 488–489, 491
 power want in, 96
 satisfaction of, and organization size, 461
Exhibitionistic interpersonal response trait, 106–107
*Explicit culture, 380
Explicit culture, 346–349
Expressive dispositions, 106–107

F Scale (see California F Scale)
Factor analysis, of attitudes, 145–146
 of personality tests, 107, 110–111
 in study of cultures, 364–365
Family, leadership in, 434, 450, 452
 and political behavior, 195–196
Fantasy and want arousal, 86–87
Farm leaders, 438
Fascism scale (see California F scale)
Fear, and distortion in perceiving people, 25
 intensity of appeal, and attitude change, 244, 246
*Feeling component of attitude, 178
Female sex role, 500–501
 and conformity, 523–525
Field-interview method for study of groups, 390
*Field method, 380
Field method in study of cultures, 356, 358–360
*Fixed-alternative question, 178
Fixed-alternative survey question, 170–172
*Folkways, 380
Folkways, 351–352
Followers' perception of leader, 438–441
 as exemplar of group values, 438, 440–441
 as having in-group character, 438
 as task specialist and expert, 439
*Formal organization, 420
*Frame of reference, 67
Frame of reference, 32
France, 328
Fraternity norms, 405
French (people), 171, 293, 337, 524–525
Friendliness, interpersonal response trait of, 106–107
*Frustration, 134
Frustration, and biological structure, 119
 caused by status discrepancy, 336–337
 of child and cultural beliefs, 363
 and cognitive change, 35–37, 50
 definition of, 117
 effects of training on responses to, 127
 and formation of interpersonal response traits, 119–125
 of group and aggression, 49
 and morale, 332
 and physical environment, 119
 and psychological complexity, 119
 reactions to, and strength of wants, 126
 and social environment, 119
 sources of, 119
 and want development, 72–74

*General evaluative set, 67
Georgia, 279
Germany and Germans, 171, 194, 241, 292, 328, 337, 363, 431, 437
 (See also Nazi leadership)
Ghana, 391
*Goal, 101

Level of aspiration, effect of success and failure on, 116–117
Likert attitude scale, 153

Manifest Anxiety Scale correlated with conformity scores, 526
*Marginal man, 530
Marginal man, role conflicts in, 498–500
  susceptibility to conformity by, 514
Maryland, 12
Mass media, effectiveness of, as compared with personal influence, 233–234, 236
Massachusetts, 493
Maternal want, effects of frustration of, 124
Mating ways, in Kurtatchi, 353, 356
  in middle-class North Americans, 353, 357
*Meaning, 307
Meaning, connotative, 279
  cultural differences in, 281–286
  definition of, 279
  denotative, 279
  dimensions of, 280–281
  effect of context on, 283–287
  learning of, 281–283
  measurement of, 279–281
  sex differences in, 282
  and sounds of words, 277
Measurement of wants, 87–89
Medical school applicants, conformity and independence in, 527, 528
*Membership group, 213–214
Membership groups, changes in, and attitude change, 246–248
Membership in group, valuation of, and acceptance of group-anchored attitude, 250
  and attitude modifiability, 224–225
Memory, cultural influences on, 342
Menomini Indians, 367–368
Mental illness, social class differences in, 332–333
*Mental set, 67
Mental set, 21–23
Methodist Church, 248
Mexicans, 143, 350–351
Micronesia, 294
"Midwest," study of culture of, 368–372
Military chaplains, role conflict in, 496
Military officers, conformity tendencies in, 522, 523, 527, 528
Minneapolis, 209
Missouri, 12
Mohammedans, 343, 365
Monkeys, avoidance training and dominance in, 110
  brain lesions and dominance in, 108–109
Morale, group (see Group morale)
*Mores, 380
Mores, 351–353
Mormons, 377
Moroccans, perceptual tendencies in, 340–341
Moslems (see Mohammedans)
Motivation, 68–102

Motivation, in classroom, 362
  for conformity, 519–521
  for counterformity, 520
  group-task, effect of, on group productivity, 478–483
  for independence of judgment, 520
  (See also Goal; Want)
Motive (see Want)
*Multiplexity of attitude component, 178
Multiplexity, of attitude components, 142
  consistency in, 144–145
  measurement of, 148
  and modifiability, 217
  of cognitive system, 38–40
Muncie (Indiana), 94
Myth of cultures and societies, 349

Nape (African tribe), 342
National character of Germans and Americans, 363
Nationalism as factor in internationalist attitudes, 212–213
Nationalist party (Union of South Africa), 208
Nationality, conformity-proneness related to, 524–525
Navaho Indians, 80
  witchcraft beliefs among, 354
Navaho language and form discrimination, 301–302
Nazi leaderships, 337, 363, 487
  insecurity of Germans favoring acceptance of, 437
  (See also Hitler in Name Index)
Need (see Want)
*Negative attitude change, 269
Negroes, 143, 144, 150, 152, 153, 157, 162–164, 167, 169, 194, 208, 228, 238, 246, 251, 370, 467
  attitudes toward, effect of enforced contact on, 253–259
  effect of living in integrated housing project on 256–258 effect of reduction in self-defensiveness on, 263–266 effect of role playing on, 259 learning of, 72
  communication patterns of, in groups, 467
  consistency of attitudes toward, 144
  discriminatory treatment of, 162–163
  economic factors in lynching of, 20
  opposition to desegregation of, 12
  personality factors in development of prejudice toward, 201–206
  social norms concerning segregation of, 353
*Net attitude change, 269
*Net connectivity, 485
*Neutral region, 178
Neutral region, and attitude intensity, 156, 158
  of attitude scales, 155–158
New Haven, 331–333, 379
New Jersey, 347
New Mexico, 390
New York (City), 450
New York Times, 23, 391
New Zealand, 376

Norm sending, 404–408
Norms, group, 404
  and attitude development, 193
  centrality of, and attitude change, 247 legitimacy of, and acceptance of group-anchored attitudes, 250–251 relevancy of, and enforcement of, 407
North Korean People's Army, 234
Norway, 171, 524–525
Norwegians, conformity in, 524–525

Obesity, motivational basis of, 75
*Objective method of measuring social class, 338
Objective method of measuring social class, 313
Observation methods for study of groups, 384–390
Occupancy time in behavior settings of "Midwest," 369, 371
Occupation, and child-rearing practice, 373–374
  choice of, and cognitions, 130
  determinants in, 130–133 and interpersonal response traits, 131–133 and values, 130–131 and wants, 130–131
  and community participation, 376
  influence of, on personality, 501–504
  self-selection of, 503
  and social class, 319, 320
  stratification of U.S. population by, 314
  as subculture in American society, 372–374
Oklahoma, 12, 240
*Open-end question, 178
Open-end survey question, 170–172
  advantages of, 171–172
  coding of, 170
Organization, informal organization in, 418–420
  principles of, 414–415
  size of, and executive satisfaction, 461
  social, definition of, 384
Organizational membership, frequency of, in America, 92
Other-directed man, 192

Palau (people), 294
Palestine, Anglo-American Commission on, 175
Palo Alto (California), 379
Panel method, 195, 251
Part-whole principle in cognition, 30–32
  stereotypes as instance of, 31–33
*Participant observation, method of, 421
Participant observation method for study of groups, 387, 390
*Participatory leadership, 485
*Patterning, trait, 134
Patterning of interpersonal response traits, 113
Pennsylvania, 375
Perception, of cause and effect, 27–30
  cultural influences, on Moroccans, 340–341

Perception, cultural influences, on Samoan, 341
  egocentric, 18
  (See also Cognition)
Perception of persons, 51–65
  accuracy of, 56–61
    and ability of judge, 56–59 amount of information in, 57 and attribute judged, 58–59, 61 characteristics of other in, 57 conformity-proneness, 526 interpersonal behavior event and, 56 order of information in, 57–58 psychological training and, 60
  assimilation in, 31
  balance theory in, 41–44
  cognitive multiplexity in, 39
  contrast in, 31–32
  defenses against changes in, 47
  effect of first impressions on, 54–55
  effect of national stereotypes on, 33
  halo effect in, 52
  implicit personality theory in, 52–54
  influence of emotions on, 25
  influence of wants on, 24
  selective organization in, 51–52
  status factors in, 81–83
  stereotypes in, 53–54
  warm-cold effect in, 53
  (See also Public figures, perception of)
Personal factors, in cognitive selectivity, 21–23
  and mental set, 21–23
Personal influence, effectiveness of, as compared with mass media, 233–234, 236
Personality, as affected by role performance, 500–504
  in attitude development, 199–213
  and attitude modifiability, 220–224
  of business executives, 488–489, 491
  changes in, and attitude change, 263–266
  and cognitive change, 46–50
  and conformity, 525–529
  correlates of general persuasibility, 223–224
  as determinant of group effectiveness, 463–466
  in development, of anti-Negro prejudice, 201, 205–206
    of anti-Semitism, 201–203 of ethnocentrism, 201–205 of internationalist attitudes, 207 of political conservatism, 205, 208–210 of religious attitudes, 201
  effects of, on enforced contact with Negroes, 258–259
  effects of occupational role on, 501–504
  effects of, on participation in group-decision, 482–483
  of leaders, 441, 443–444
    shaped by role, 444–445
  pathology and prejudice, 182–183
  reciprocal relation to roles of individual, 488–504
  relationship of, to language, 291–293
  sex differences in, 500

Personality, social factors in, vs. inherent nature of, 487
  and social mobility, 327
  and style of speech, 292–293
*Persuasibility, bound, 269
Persuasibility, bound, definition of, 221
  and susceptibility to propaganda, 221–222
*Persuasibility, general, 269
Persuasibility, general, and attitude modifiability, 221, 223
  definition of, 221 method of measuring, 221 personality correlates of, 223–224 sex differences in, 221, 223
*Pervasiveness, trait, 134
Pervasiveness of interpersonal response traits, 112–113
Philadelphia, 336, 443
Physiology, and emergence of wants, 71
  and want arousal, 85
*Pluralistic ignorance, 269
Pluralistic ignorance, 512
  definition of, 248
  result of ineffectiveness of group monitoring system, 248
Political attitudes, 146
  consonance of, and political behavior, 146
  effect of college training on, 251–255
  and family influences, 195–196
  personality in development of, 205, 208–210
  and political behavior, 174–175
  and primary group influences, 193, 195–196
  and religious leaders as reference individuals, 197–198
  and salience of religious groups, 200
  television in, 235–238
Pooh-Bah, role conflicts of, 497
Portuguese (people and language), 297, 298
*Position, 338
*Position centrality, 485
Positions, definition of, 310
  discrepancy in status of, 335–337
  functions of, 310
  multiple, 312–313
*Positive attitude change, 269
Power, sociometric pattern of, 392
*Power want, 101–102
Power want, 96–97
  and group membership, 394
*Prejudice, 214
Prejudice, and aggression induced by frustration, 183–184
  consistency of, 143
  and cultural norms, 208
  and defense of self, 186
  effect on, of enforced contact with Negroes, 253–259
    on job, 258 of living in integrated housing project, 256–258 of reduction of self-defensiveness, 263–266 of role playing, 259
  and personality pathology, 182–183
  as projection of repressed impulses, 185–186

Prejudice, as rationalization of disapproved behavior, 184–185
*Prestige want, 102
Prestige want, 94, 96
  in Zuñi and Hopi, 96
Primacy in impression formation, 54–55, 58
*Primary group, 214
Primary group, in attitude development, 193, 195–196
  mechanisms of influence, 196–197
  and political behavior, 193, 195–196
Problem solving group, and communication nets, 468–471
Productivity of groups (see Group productivity)
"Professional deformation," 501
*Projection, 134
Projection, of blame for conforming, 517
  defensive reaction of, 123
  in formation of prejudice, 185–186
*Projective technique, 102
Projective techniques, in attitude measurement, 161, 165
  in measurement of wants, 89, 90
  in study of cultures, 365, 367–368
Propaganda, adaptation level and acceptance of, 34
  amount of change advocated in, and amount of attitude change, 239–240
  form and content of, and attitude change, 238–246
  medium of, and attitude change, 233–238
  one-sided vs. two-sided, and attitude change, 240–242
    and resistance to counterpropaganda, 241–242
  order of arguments in, and attitude change, 242–245
  resistance to counterpropaganda and public commitment, 228–229
  selective exposure to, 233–235
  susceptibility to, and bound persuasibility, 221–222
    and general persuasibility, 221, 223
Propagandist, attractiveness of, and attitude change, 232
  conclusion drawing by, and attitude change, 242–243
  credibility of, and attitude change, 231
  group affiliations of, and attitude change, 232–233
  prestige of, and attitude change, 267
Protestants, 197, 198, 208, 253, 343, 364, 376, 397–399, 411, 437, 499
Proximity as factor in group formation, 410–411
*Pseudo-communication, 307
Pseudo-communication, anxiety and, 291
  cultural sources of, 290 idiosyncratic perception and, 289–291
Psycho-logic, 219
Psychological ecology of "Midwest," 372

Sociability, interpersonal response trait of, 106–107, 110–111
*Social area, 338
Social areas, 319–326
  Attitude Sphere for study of, 324
  attitudes found in, 324–325
  Demography Sphere for study of, 321
  method of identifying, 320–323
  in San Francisco Bay Area, 321–323
  stability of, 325–326
  as subcultural areas, 323–325
*Social class, 338
Social class, differences, in achievement want, 330, 331
  in child-rearing practices, 317, 378–379 in defense mechanisms, 374–375 in language and speech, 295–297 in mental illness, 332–333 in status striving, 327, 330, 331
  differing perspectives on structure, 19
  difficulty of entry into upper, 336
  effect on perception of class structure, 19
  and high-school dating, 318
  identifications in U.S., 314–315
  measurement of, 313–316
    objective method in, 313 reputational method in,315–316 subjective method in, 313–315
  mobility in Western societies, 328
  and perception of self-autonomy, 53–54
  as social environment, 316–319
  as status system, 313
  structure in American communities, 315–316
  as subculture in American society, 372–375
  and word meanings, 283
Social cohesiveness and conformity in Norwegians, 525
Social-distance attitude scale, 153–154
  reliability of, 157
*Social-distance scaling method, 179
Social-distance scores, stability of, 195
Social environment and social class, 316–319
Social episodes, frequency of, in children, 309
Social initiative, interpersonal response trait of, 106–107
Social mobility, amount of, 326–327
  in Western societies, 327, 328 in history of American society, 327, 329
  and class loyalty, 337
  psychological costs of, 327, 330–333
  and sexual conduct, 334
  social costs of, 334–335
  and status striving, 327, 330, 331
*Social mobility, vertical, 338
Social mores, 351–353
Social norms, and autokinetic movement and, 513
*Social organization, 421
Social organization, definition of, 384
  informal organization in, 418–420
  principles of, 414
    criticism of, 414–415

Social psychology, as applied science, 9–11
  and common cold, 8
  milestones in history of, 6–7
  need for scientific principles of, 3
  vs. practical knowledge, 2–3
  related to general psychology, 7, 9
  as science of interpersonal behavior events, 5
Social techniques, 104
Socialist party (United States), 251, 252
*Socialization, anticipatory, 338
Socialization and conformity, 524–525
*Society, 338
Society, 308–338
  definition of, 308
  positions and roles in, 310–313
  social-class structure in American, 314–315
*Sociogram, 421
Sociogram, 390–392
  of UN visiting, 391
Sociometric dispositions, 106–107
Sociometric grouping of work teams, 483–484
*Sociometric method, 421
Sociometric method, 390–392
  index analysis in, 392
Soldiers, attitudes, toward Army job, 158
  effect of enforced contact with Negroes, 254–256
  toward WACs, 158
  group influences in attitude toward combat, 198–199
  special language of, 304–305
South Korea, 234
Soviet Russia, 171, 182, 193, 227, 241, 242, 391
  distinctive definition of words in, 283, 286
  use of word-of-mouth propaganda in, 234
*Span of apprehension, 67
Span of apprehension, 21
Spanish (people and language), 284, 285, 293, 350–351
Spanish-Americans, cultural beliefs among, 350–351
*Special language, 307
Speech, egocentric, 273–274
  interpersonal nature of, 273–275
  and personality characteristics, 292–293
  social class differences in, 295
  as tool, 273–275
  (See also Communication; Language)
*Stability, trait, 134
Stability of interpersonal response traits, 111–112
*Standard behavior event, 380
Standard behavior event, definition of, 347
Standard interpersonal behavior event, and behavior setting, 368
  definition of, 347
  experimental illustration of, 347–348
Standard situations and roles, 311–312
Starvation, psychological effects of, 70
*Status, 338

Status, and community participation, 375, 376
  and conformity to group norms, 250
  discrepancies in, 335–337
  hierarchy of, and group effectiveness, 465–468
  and social class, 315
  and social cues, 82–83
  striving for, 327
    in different social classes, 330, 331
  subjective, 81
  systems, 313
    openness to change, 326
    social mobility in, 326–335
  want for, and conformity, 520
*Status discrepancy, 338
Status-equilibration hypothesis, 336
*Status symbol, 421
Status symbols, 415–418
*Stereotype, 67
Stereotypes, resulting from part-whole perception, 31–33, 53–54
  stability of ethnic, 194
Stimulus factors, in cognitive selectivity, 20–21
  in perceptual grouping, 26
Strong Vocational Interest Blank correlated with conformity scores, 526–527
Structure, group (see Group structure)
*Subculture, 380
*Subjective method of measuring social class, 338
Subjective method of measuring social class, 313–315
*Substitute goal, 102
Suggestibility and conformity, 526, 527
*Summated-rating scaling method, 179
Summated ratings attitude scale, 153
  reliability of, 157
Superstition in American culture, 354
Supervision, effects of, on productivity of work groups, 473–478
Survey interview technique, 169–175
  reliability and validity of, 172–175
  types of questions in, 170–172
Sweden, 328
Switzerland, 328
*Symbol, 307
Symbols, status, 415–418
  words as, 275–276
Sympathetic behavior on playground, 97
Sympathetic interpersonal response trait, 106–107

Taxi-dancer, role effect on personality, 502
Teacher, role effect on personality, 501–502
  values held by, 352
Television, and image of political candidates, 237–238
  in political behavior, 235–238
  and selective exposure to propaganda, 234–235
Tepoztlan (Mexico), 359–360
Texas, 12
Thematic Apperception Test, in measurement of achievement want, 90